OTHER A TO Z GUIDES FROM
THE SCARECROW PRESS, INC.

1. *The A to Z of Buddhism* by Charles S. Prebish, 2001. *Out of Print. See No. 124.*
2. *The A to Z of Catholicism* by William J. Collinge, 2001.
3. *The A to Z of Hinduism* by Bruce M. Sullivan, 2001.
4. *The A to Z of Islam* by Ludwig W. Adamec, 2002. *Out of Print. See No. 123.*
5. *The A to Z of Slavery and Abolition* by Martin A. Klein, 2002.
6. *Terrorism: Assassins to Zealots* by Sean Kendall Anderson and Stephen Sloan, 2003.
7. *The A to Z of the Korean War* by Paul M. Edwards, 2005.
8. *The A to Z of the Cold War* by Joseph Smith and Simon Davis, 2005.
9. *The A to Z of the Vietnam War* by Edwin E. Moise, 2005.
10. *The A to Z of Science Fiction Literature* by Brian Stableford, 2005.
11. *The A to Z of the Holocaust* by Jack R. Fischel, 2005.
12. *The A to Z of Washington, D.C.* by Robert Benedetto, Jane Donovan, and Kathleen DuVall, 2005.
13. *The A to Z of Taoism* by Julian F. Pas, 2006.
14. *The A to Z of the Renaissance* by Charles G. Nauert, 2006.
15. *The A to Z of Shinto* by Stuart D. B. Picken, 2006.
16. *The A to Z of Byzantium* by John H. Rosser, 2006.
17. *The A to Z of the Civil War* by Terry L. Jones, 2006.
18. *The A to Z of the Friends (Quakers)* by Margery Post Abbott, Mary Ellen Chijioke, Pink Dandelion, and John William Oliver Jr., 2006.
19. *The A to Z of Feminism* by Janet K. Boles and Diane Long Hoeveler, 2006.
20. *The A to Z of New Religious Movements* by George D. Chryssides, 2006.
21. *The A to Z of Multinational Peacekeeping* by Terry M. Mays, 2006.
22. *The A to Z of Lutheranism* by Günther Gassmann with Duane H. Larson and Mark W. Oldenburg, 2007.
23. *The A to Z of the French Revolution* by Paul R. Hanson, 2007.
24. *The A to Z of the Persian Gulf War 1990–1991* by Clayton R. Newell, 2007.
25. *The A to Z of Revolutionary America* by Terry M. Mays, 2007.
26. *The A to Z of the Olympic Movement* by Bill Mallon with Ian Buchanan, 2007.
27. *The A to Z of the Discovery and Exploration of Australia* by Alan Day, 2009.
28. *The A to Z of the United Nations* by Jacques Fomerand, 2009.
29. *The A to Z of the "Dirty Wars"* by David Kohut, Olga Vilella, and Beatrice Julian, 2009.
30. *The A to Z of the Vikings* by Katherine Holman, 2009.
31. *The A to Z from the Great War to the Great Depression* by Neil A. Wynn, 2009.
32. *The A to Z of the Crusades* by Corliss K. Slack, 2009.
33. *The A to Z of New Age Movements* by Michael York, 2009.
34. *The A to Z of Unitarian Universalism* by Mark W. Harris, 2009.
35. *The A to Z of the Kurds* by Michael M. Gunter, 2009.
36. *The A to Z of Utopianism* by James M. Morris and Andrea L. Kross, 2009.
37. *The A to Z of the Civil War and Reconstruction* by William L. Richter, 2009.

D0109160

38. *The A to Z of Jainism* by Kristi L. Wiley, 2009.
39. *The A to Z of the Inuit* by Pamela K. Stern, 2009.
40. *The A to Z of Early North America* by Cameron B. Wesson, 2009.
41. *The A to Z of the Enlightenment* by Harvey Chisick, 2009.
42. *The A to Z Methodism* by Charles Yrigoyen Jr. and Susan E. Warrick, 2009.
43. *The A to Z of the Seventh-day Adventists* by Gary Land, 2009.
44. *The A to Z of Sufism* by John Renard, 2009.
45. *The A to Z of Sikhism* by William Hewat McLeod, 2009.
46. *The A to Z Fantasy Literature* by Brian Stableford, 2009.
47. *The A to Z of the Discovery and Exploration of the Pacific Islands* by Max Quanchi and John Robson, 2009.
48. *The A to Z of Australian and New Zealand Cinema* by Albert Moran and Errol Vieth, 2009.
49. *The A to Z of African-American Television* by Kathleen Fearn-Banks, 2009.
50. *The A to Z of American Radio Soap Operas* by Jim Cox, 2009.
51. *The A to Z of the Old South* by William L. Richter, 2009.
52. *The A to Z of the Discovery and Exploration of the Northwest Passage* by Alan Day, 2009.
53. *The A to Z of the Druzes* by Samy S. Swayd, 2009.
54. *The A to Z of the Welfare State* by Bent Greve, 2009.
55. *The A to Z of the War of 1812* by Robert Malcomson, 2009.
56. *The A to Z of Feminist Philosophy* by Catherine Villanueva Gardner, 2009.
57. *The A to Z of the Early American Republic* by Richard Buel Jr., 2009.
58. *The A to Z of the Russo-Japanese War* by Rotem Kowner, 2009.
59. *The A to Z of Anglicanism* by Colin Buchanan, 2009.
60. *The A to Z of Scandinavian Literature and Theater* by Jan Sjåvik, 2009.
61. *The A to Z of the Peoples of the Southeast Asian Massif* by Jean Michaud, 2009.
62. *The A to Z of Judaism* by Norman Solomon, 2009.
63. *The A to Z of the Berbers (Imazighen)* by Hsain Ilahiane, 2009.
64. *The A to Z of British Radio* by Seán Street, 2009.
65. *The A to Z of The Salvation Army* by Major John G. Merritt, 2009.
66. *The A to Z of the Arab-Israeli Conflict* by P. R. Kumaraswamy, 2009.
67. *The A to Z of the Jacksonian Era and Manifest Destiny* by Terry Corps, 2009.
68. *The A to Z of Socialism* by Peter Lamb and James C. Docherty, 2009.
69. *The A to Z of Marxism* by David Walker and Daniel Gray, 2009.
70. *The A to Z of the Bahá'í Faith* by Hugh C. Adamson, 2009.
71. *The A to Z of Postmodernist Literature and Theater* by Fran Mason, 2009.
72. *The A to Z of Australian Radio and Television* by Albert Moran and Chris Keating, 2009.
73. *The A to Z of the Lesbian Liberation Movement: Still the Rage* by JoAnne Myers, 2009.
74. *The A to Z of the United States–Mexican War* by Edward R. Moseley and Paul C. Clark, 2009.
75. *The A to Z of World War I* by Ian V. Hogg, 2009.
76. *The A to Z of World War II: The War Against Japan* by Ann Sharp Wells, 2009.
77. *The A to Z of Witchcraft* by Michael D. Bailey, 2009.

78. *The A to Z of British Intelligence* by Nigel West, 2009.
79. *The A to Z of United States Intelligence* by Michael A. Turner, 2009.
80. *The A to Z of the League of Nations* by Anique H. M. van Ginneken, 2009.
81. *The A to Z of Israeli Intelligence* by Ephraim Kahana, 2009.
82. *The A to Z of the European Union* by Joaquín Roy and Aimee Kanner, 2009.
83. *The A to Z of the Chinese Cultural Revolution* by Guo Jian, Yongyi Song, and Yuan Zhou, 2009.
84. *The A to Z of African American Cinema* by S. Torriano Berry and Venise T. Berry, 2009.
85. *The A to Z of Japanese Business* by Stuart D. B. Picken, 2009.
86. *The A to Z of the Reagan–Bush Era* by Richard S. Conley, 2009.
87. *The A to Z of Human Rights and Humanitarian Organizations* by Robert F. Gorman and Edward S. Mihalkanin, 2009.
88. *The A to Z of French Cinema* by Dayna Oscherwitz and MaryEllen Higgins, 2009.
89. *The A to Z of the Puritans* by Charles Pastoor and Galen K. Johnson, 2009.
90. *The A to Z of Nuclear, Biological and Chemical Warfare* by Benjamin C. Garrett and John Hart, 2009.
91. *The A to Z of the Green Movement* by Miranda Schreurs and Elim Papadakis, 2009.
92. *The A to Z of the Kennedy–Johnson Era* by Richard Dean Burns and Joseph M. Siracusa, 2009.
93. *The A to Z of Renaissance Art* by Lilian H. Zirpolo, 2009.
94. *The A to Z of the Broadway Musical* by William A. Everett and Paul R. Laird, 2009.
95. *The A to Z of the Northern Ireland Conflict* by Gordon Gillespie, 2009.
96. *The A to Z of the Fashion Industry* by Francesca Sterlacci and Joanne Arbuckle, 2009.
97. *The A to Z of American Theater: Modernism* by James Fisher and Felicia Hardison Londré, 2009.
98. *The A to Z of Civil Wars in Africa* by Guy Arnold, 2009.
99. *The A to Z of the Nixon–Ford Era* by Mitchell K. Hall, 2009.
100. *The A to Z of Horror Cinema* by Peter Hutchings, 2009.
101. *The A to Z of Westerns in Cinema* by Paul Varner, 2009.
102. *The A to Z of Zionism* by Rafael Medoff and Chaim I. Waxman, 2009.
103. *The A to Z of the Roosevelt–Truman Era* by Neil A. Wynn, 2009.
104. *The A to Z of Jehovah's Witnesses* by George D. Chryssides, 2009.
105. *The A to Z of Native American Movements* by Todd Leahy and Raymond Wilson, 2009.
106. *The A to Z of the Shakers* by Stephen J. Paterwic, 2009.
107. *The A to Z of the Coptic Church* by Gawdat Gabra, 2009.
108. *The A to Z of Architecture* by Allison Lee Palmer, 2009.
109. *The A to Z of Italian Cinema* by Gino Moliterno, 2009.
110. *The A to Z of Mormonism* by Davis Bitton and Thomas G. Alexander, 2009.
111. *The A to Z of African American Theater* by Anthony D. Hill with Douglas Q. Barnett, 2009.

112. *The A to Z of NATO and Other International Security Organizations* by Marco Rimanelli, 2009.
113. *The A to Z of the Eisenhower Era* by Burton I. Kaufman and Diane Kaufman, 2009.
114. *The A to Z of Sexspionage* by Nigel West, 2009.
115. *The A to Z of Environmentalism* by Peter Dauvergne, 2009.
116. *The A to Z of the Petroleum Industry* by M. S. Vassiliou, 2009.
117. *The A to Z of Journalism* by Ross Eaman, 2009.
118. *The A to Z of the Gilded Age* by T. Adams Upchurch, 2009.
119. *The A to Z of the Progressive Era* by Catherine Cocks, Peter C. Holloran, and Alan Lessoff, 2009.
120. *The A to Z of Middle Eastern Intelligence* by Ephraim Kahana and Muhammad Suwaed, 2009.
121. *The A to Z of the Baptists* William H. Brackney, 2009.
122. *The A to Z of Homosexuality* by Brent L. Pickett, 2009.
123. *The A to Z of Islam, Second Edition* by Ludwig W. Adamec, 2009.
124. *The A to Z of Buddhism* by Carl Olson, 2009.
125. *The A to Z of United States–Russian/Soviet Relations* by Norman E. Saul, 2010.
126. *The A to Z of United States–Africa Relations* by Robert Anthony Waters Jr., 2010.
127. *The A to Z of United States–China Relations* by Robert Sutter, 2010.
128. *The A to Z of U.S. Diplomacy since the Cold War* by Tom Lansford, 2010.
129. *The A to Z of United States–Japan Relations* by John Van Sant, Peter Mauch, and Yoneyuki Sugita, 2010.
130. *The A to Z of United States–Latin American Relations* by Joseph Smith, 2010.
131. *The A to Z of United States–Middle East Relations* by Peter L. Hahn, 2010.
132. *The A to Z of United States–Southeast Asia Relations* by Donald E. Weatherbee, 2010.
133. *The A to Z of U.S. Diplomacy from the Civil War to World War I* by Kenneth J. Blume, 2010.
134. *The A to Z of International Law* by Boleslaw A. Boczek, 2010.
135. *The A to Z of the Gypsies (Romanies)* by Donald Kenrick, 2010.
136. *The A to Z of the Tamils* by Vijaya Ramaswamy, 2010.
137. *The A to Z of Women in Sub-Saharan Africa* by Kathleen Sheldon, 2010.
138. *The A to Z of Ancient and Medieval Nubia* by Richard A. Lobban Jr., 2010.
139. *The A to Z of Ancient Israel* by Niels Peter Lemche, 2010.
140. *The A to Z of Ancient Mesoamerica* by Joel W. Palka, 2010.
141. *The A to Z of Ancient Southeast Asia* by John N. Miksic, 2010.
142. *The A to Z of the Hittites* by Charles Burney, 2010.
143. *The A to Z of Medieval Russia* by Lawrence N. Langer, 2010.
144. *The A to Z of the Napoleonic Era* by George F. Nafziger, 2010.
145. *The A to Z of Ancient Egypt* by Morris L. Bierbrier, 2010.
146. *The A to Z of Ancient India* by Kumkum Roy, 2010.
147. *The A to Z of Ancient South America* by Martin Giesso, 2010.

148. *The A to Z of Medieval China* by Victor Cunrui Xiong, 2010.

149. *The A to Z of Medieval India* by Iqtidar Alam Khan, 2010.

150. *The A to Z of Mesopotamia* by Gwendolyn Leick, 2010.

151. *The A to Z of the Mongol World Empire* by Paul D. Buell, 2010.

152. *The A to Z of the Ottoman Empire* by Selcuk Aksin Somel, 2010.

153. *The A to Z of Pre-Colonial Africa* by Robert O. Collins, 2010.

154. *The A to Z of Aesthetics* by Dabney Townsend, 2010.

155. *The A to Z of Descartes and Cartesian Philosophy* by Roger Ariew, Dennis Des Chene, Douglas M. Jesseph, Tad M. Schmaltz, and Theo Verbeek, 2010.

156. *The A to Z of Heidegger's Philosophy* by Alfred Denker, 2010.

157. *The A to Z of Kierkegaard's Philosophy* by Julia Watkin, 2010.

158. *The A to Z of Ancient Greek Philosophy* by Anthony Preus, 2010.

159. *The A to Z of Bertrand Russell's Philosophy* by Rosalind Carey and John Ongley, 2010.

160. *The A to Z of Epistemology* by Ralph Baergen, 2010.

161. *The A to Z of Ethics* by Harry J. Gensler and Earl W. Spurgin, 2010.

162. *The A to Z of Existentialism* by Stephen Michelman, 2010.

163. *The A to Z of Hegelian Philosophy* by John W. Burbidge, 2010.

164. *The A to Z of the Holiness Movement* by William Kostlevy, 2010.

165. *The A to Z of Hume's Philosophy* by Kenneth R. Merrill, 2010.

166. *The A to Z of Husserl's Philosophy* by John J. Drummond, 2010.

167. *The A to Z of Kant and Kantianism* by Helmut Holzhey and Vilem Mudroch, 2010.

168. *The A to Z of Leibniz's Philosophy* by Stuart Brown and N. J. Fox, 2010.

169. *The A to Z of Logic* by Harry J. Gensler, 2010.

170. *The A to Z of Medieval Philosophy and Theology* by Stephen F. Brown and Juan Carlos Flores, 2010.

171. *The A to Z of Nietzscheanism* by Carol Diethe, 2010.

172. *The A to Z of the Non-Aligned Movement and Third World* by Guy Arnold, 2010.

173. *The A to Z of Shamanism* by Graham Harvey and Robert J. Wallis, 2010.

174. *The A to Z of Organized Labor* by James C. Docherty, 2010.

175. *The A to Z of the Orthodox Church* by Michael Prokurat, Michael D. Peterson, and Alexander Golitzin, 2010.

176. *The A to Z of Prophets in Islam and Judaism* by Scott B. Noegel and Brannon M. Wheeler, 2010.

177. *The A to Z of Schopenhauer's Philosophy* by David E. Cartwright, 2010.

178. *The A to Z of Wittgenstein's Philosophy* by Duncan Richter, 2010.

179. *The A to Z of Hong Kong Cinema* by Lisa Odham Stokes, 2010.

180. *The A to Z of Japanese Traditional Theatre* by Samuel L. Leiter, 2010.

181. *The A to Z of Lesbian Literature* by Meredith Miller, 2010.

182. *The A to Z of Chinese Theater* by Tan Ye, 2010.

183. *The A to Z of German Cinema* by Robert C. Reimer and Carol J. Reimer, 2010.

184. *The A to Z of German Theater* by William Grange, 2010.

185. *The A to Z of Irish Cinema* by Roderick Flynn and Patrick Brereton, 2010.
186. *The A to Z of Modern Chinese Literature* by Li-hua Ying, 2010.
187. *The A to Z of Modern Japanese Literature and Theater* by J. Scott Miller, 2010.
188. *The A to Z of Old-Time Radio* by Robert C. Reinehr and Jon D. Swartz, 2010.
189. *The A to Z of Polish Cinema* by Marek Haltof, 2010.
190. *The A to Z of Postwar German Literature* by William Grange, 2010.
191. *The A to Z of Russian and Soviet Cinema* by Peter Rollberg, 2010.
192. *The A to Z of Russian Theater* by Laurence Senelick, 2010.
193. *The A to Z of Sacred Music* by Joseph P. Swain, 2010.
194. *The A to Z of Animation and Cartoons* by Nichola Dobson, 2010.
195. *The A to Z of Afghan Wars, Revolutions, and Insurgencies* by Ludwig W. Adamec, 2010.
196. *The A to Z of Ancient Egyptian Warfare* by Robert G. Morkot, 2010.
197. *The A to Z of the British and Irish Civil Wars 1637–1660* by Martyn Bennett, 2010.
198. *The A to Z of the Chinese Civil War* by Edwin Pak-wah Leung, 2010.
199. *The A to Z of Ancient Greek Warfare* by Iain Spence, 2010.
200. *The A to Z of the Anglo–Boer War* by Fransjohan Pretorius, 2010.
201. *The A to Z of the Crimean War* by Guy Arnold, 2010.
202. *The A to Z of the Zulu Wars* by John Laband, 2010.
203. *The A to Z of the Wars of the French Revolution* by Steven T. Ross, 2010.
204. *The A to Z of the Hong Kong SAR and the Macao SAR* by Ming K. Chan and Shiu-hing Lo, 2010.
205. *The A to Z of Australia* by James C. Docherty, 2010.
206. *The A to Z of Burma (Myanmar)* by Donald M. Seekins, 2010.
207. *The A to Z of the Gulf Arab States* by Malcolm C. Peck, 2010.
208. *The A to Z of India* by Surjit Mansingh, 2010.
209. *The A to Z of Iran* by John H. Lorentz, 2010.
210. *The A to Z of Israel* by Bernard Reich and David H. Goldberg, 2010.
211. *The A to Z of Laos* by Martin Stuart-Fox, 2010.
212. *The A to Z of Malaysia* by Ooi Keat Gin, 2010.
213. *The A to Z of Modern China (1800–1949)* by James Z. Gao, 2010.
214. *The A to Z of the Philippines* by Artemio R. Guillermo and May Kyi Win, 2010.
215. *The A to Z of Taiwan (Republic of China)* by John F. Copper, 2010.
216. *The A to Z of the People's Republic of China* by Lawrence R. Sullivan, 2010.
217. *The A to Z of Vietnam* by Bruce M. Lockhart and William J. Duiker, 2010.
218. *The A to Z of Bosnia and Herzegovina* by Ante Cuvalo, 2010.
219. *The A to Z of Modern Greece* by Dimitris Keridis, 2010.
220. *The A to Z of Austria* by Paula Sutter Fichtner, 2010.
221. *The A to Z of Belarus* by Vitali Silitski and Jan Zaprudnik, 2010.
222. *The A to Z of Belgium* by Robert Stallaerts, 2010.
223. *The A to Z of Bulgaria* by Raymond Detrez, 2010.

224. *The A to Z of Contemporary Germany* by Derek Lewis with Ulrike Zitzlsperger, 2010.
225. *The A to Z of the Contemporary United Kingdom* by Kenneth J. Panton and Keith A. Cowlard, 2010.
226. *The A to Z of Denmark* by Alastair H. Thomas, 2010.
227. *The A to Z of France* by Gino Raymond, 2010.
228. *The A to Z of Georgia* by Alexander Mikaberidze, 2010.
229. *The A to Z of Iceland* by Gudmundur Halfdanarson, 2010.
230. *The A to Z of Latvia* by Andrejs Plakans, 2010.
231. *The A to Z of Modern Italy* by Mark F. Gilbert and K. Robert Nilsson, 2010.
232. *The A to Z of Moldova* by Andrei Brezianu and Vlad Spânu, 2010.
233. *The A to Z of the Netherlands* by Joop W. Koopmans and Arend H. Huussen Jr., 2010.
234. *The A to Z of Norway* by Jan Sjåvik, 2010.
235. *The A to Z of the Republic of Macedonia* by Dimitar Bechev, 2010.
236. *The A to Z of Slovakia* by Stanislav J. Kirschbaum, 2010.
237. *The A to Z of Slovenia* by Leopoldina Plut-Pregelj and Carole Rogel, 2010.
238. *The A to Z of Spain* by Angel Smith, 2010.
239. *The A to Z of Sweden* by Irene Scobbie, 2010.
240. *The A to Z of Turkey* by Metin Heper and Nur Bilge Criss, 2010.
241. *The A to Z of Ukraine* by Zenon E. Kohut, Bohdan Y. Nebesio, and Myroslav Yurkevich, 2010.
242. *The A to Z of Mexico* by Marvin Alisky, 2010.
243. *The A to Z of U.S. Diplomacy from World War I through World War II* by Martin Folly and Niall Palmer, 2010.
244. *The A to Z of Spanish Cinema* by Alberto Mira, 2010.
245. *The A to Z of the Reformation and Counter-Reformation* by Michael Mullett, 2010.

The A to Z of France

Gino Raymond

The A to Z Guide Series, No. 227

The Scarecrow Press, Inc.
Lanham • Toronto • Plymouth, UK
2010

Published by Scarecrow Press, Inc.
A wholly owned subsidiary of
The Rowman & Littlefield Publishing Group, Inc.
4501 Forbes Boulevard, Suite 200, Lanham, Maryland 20706
http://www.scarecrowpress.com

Estover Road, Plymouth PL6 7PY, United Kingdom

British Library Cataloguing in Publication Information Available

Library of Congress Cataloging-in-Publication Data
The hardback version of this book was cataloged by the Library of Congress
as follows:

Raymond, Gino.
  Historical dictionary of France / Gino Raymond. — 2nd ed.
    p. cm. — (Historical dictionaries of Europe ; 64)
  Includes bibliographical references and index.
  1. France—History—Dictionaries. I. Title.
  DC35.R39 2008
  944.003—dc22   2008018160

ISBN 978-0-8108-7206-6 (pbk. : alk. paper)

⊗™ The paper used in this publication meets the minimum requirements of
American National Standard for Information Sciences—Permanence of Paper
for Printed Library Materials, ANSI/NISO Z39.48-1992.
Printed in the United States of America

To my partisan girl, Svetlana

Contents

Editor's Foreword   (*Jon Woronoff*)   xv

Acronyms and Abbreviations   xvii

Map   xx

Chronology   xxi

Introduction   xxxv

The Dictionary   1

Appendix: Monarchs, Presidents, and Prime Ministers   395

Bibliography   397

About the Author   471

Editor's Foreword

France reached a high point in international dominance under Louis XIV and again under Napoléon Bonaparte, achieving an eminent position in Europe when that continent held an unrivaled amount of power. But it has suffered periodic decline, overshadowed by British imperial might, crushed by German power, and shorn of its own empire to become just another European country in a Europe that no longer holds the power it once did. Yet France has stubbornly sought a larger role. While not all its efforts have succeeded, it has influenced much of the world economically, politically, culturally, and intellectually. In a worldwide community of some 200 members, France still matters.

The A to Z of France describes how France has risen and then declined and why it is still holding its own on the world stage. The dictionary includes entries on rulers and leaders, from the first kings to the most recent presidents and premiers; assorted kingdoms, empires, and republics; numerous wars and revolutions; and the transition from absolutism to democracy and an agrarian to an industrial and service-based economy. France's glorious past is examined in detail, but even more attention is paid to the present, with entries on the arts and sciences and significant figures in those sectors, as well as various political institutions and parties. The country's long and involved past is traced in both the chronology and introduction, and a list of acronyms and abbreviations clarifies the players. The select but extensive bibliography lists a substantial number of books dealing more specifically with major subjects.

It is never easy to find a suitable author for a book of this scope, but this volume was written by someone with considerable academic background and personal experience. Born in Mauritius, a former French colony, Gino Raymond studied French and politics at the University of Bristol and Cambridge University. He lectured in English at the Université de Paris X, Nanterre, and the Ecole Normale Supérieure, and in French at the Universities of Bradford and Aston. He is currently professor of modern French studies at the University of Bristol. Professor Raymond has written numerous articles and papers as well as seven books, including works on André Malraux, the French power structure, and the French Communist Party. He is therefore an unusually competent and fluent guide to an amazingly rich and varied country.

Jon Woronoff
Series Editor

Acronyms and Abbreviations

CFDT	Confédération Française Démocratique du Travail (centrist labor union)
CFTC	Confédération Française des Travailleurs Chrétiens (Catholic labor union)
CGT	Confédération Générale du Travail (communist-dominated labor union)
CNPF	Conseil National du Patronat Français (French employers' organization)
DGSE	Direction Générale de la Sécurité Extérieure (bureau for external security)
EADS	European Aeronautic Defense and Space Company
EDF	Electricité de France (national electric company)
EEC	European Economic Community
EMS	Système Monétaire Européen (European Monetary System)
ENA	Ecole Nationale d'Administration (National Business School)
ETA	Euskadi ta Askatasuna (Basque terrorist organization)
EU	European Union
FGDS	Fédération de la Gauche Démocratique et Socialiste (former left-wing coalition)
FIS	Front Islamique du Salut (Islamic Salvation Front)
FLN	Front de Libération National (National Liberation Front)
FN	Front National (National Front, extreme right-wing party)
FO	Force Ouvrière (labor union set up in opposition to communist CGT)
FPF	Fédération Protestante de France
GDF	Gaz de France
GIA	Groupe Islamique Armé (Armed Islamic Group)

INSEE   Institut National de la Statistique et des Etudes Economiques (National Office of Statistics and Economic Surveys)

MoDem   Mouvement Démocrate (independent centrist party)

MRP   Mouvement Républicain Populaire (former Christian democratic movement)

MRG   Mouvement des Radicaux de Gauche (center-left party)

MRP   Mouvement Républicain Populaire

MSF   Médecins sans Frontières (Doctors without Borders)

NATO   North Atlantic Treaty Organization

ORTF   Office de Radiodiffusion-Télévision Française (former French broadcasting service)

PCF   Parti Communiste Français (French Communist Party)

PR   Parti Républicain (centrist party)

PS   Parti Socialiste (Socialist Party)

PSU   Parti Socialiste Unifié (United Socialist Party)

RTF   Radiodiffusion-Télévision Française (former French broadcasting service)

RPF   Rassemblement du Peuple Français (a former name of the Gaullist party)

RPR   Rassemblement pour la République (a former name of the Gaullist party)

SFIO   Section française de l'Internationale Ouvrière (former name of Socialist Party)

SMIC   Salaire minimum interprofessionnel de croissance (minimum wage)

SMIG   Salaire minimum interprofessionnel garanti (former name for minimum wage)

SNCF   Société Nationale des Chemins de fer Français (national railway company)

SOFRES   Société Française d'Etudes par Sondages (French polling organization)

TGV   Train à grande vitesse (high-speed train)

TNP   Théâtre National Populaire

UC   Union Calédonienne (political party seeking independence for New Caledonia)

UDF   Union Pour la Démocratie Française (Union for French Democracy, liberal center party)

UDR	Union des Démocrates pour la République (Union of Democrats for the Republic)
UIMM	Union des Industries et Métiers de la Métallurgie (Union of Industry and Steel Workers)
UMP	Union pour la Majorité Populaire (current vehicle for Gaullist party)
UN	United Nations
UNR	Union pour la Nouvelle République (former name of Gaullist party)
USSR	Union of Soviet Socialist Republics

Chronology

52 BC The people of Gaul come under Roman domination when their leader Vercingétorix is defeated at Alésia.

406 AD Gaul is invaded by the barbarians.

481 Clovis ascends the throne.

732 Charles Martel ends the threat from invading Moors in the battle near Poitiers.

800 The Pope crowns Charlemagne emperor.

843 The Treaty of Verdun divides Charlemagne's empire.

987 Hugues Capet is elected king.

1163 The construction of Notre-Dame de Paris begins.

1180 Philippe II Auguste takes the throne.

1208–1213 Crusade against the Albigensians.

1214 The Battle of Bouvines.

1226 Louis IX takes the throne.

1285 Philippe IV le Bel takes the throne.

1337–1453 The Hundred Years' War.

1348 The plague known as the Black Death begins.

1429 Joan of Arc liberates Orléans from the English and enables Charles VII to be crowned king at Reims.

1461 Louis XI takes the throne.

1470 Approximate date of the introduction of the printing press to France.

1526 Construction of the Château de Chambord begins.

1532 *Pantagruel* by Rabelais is published.

1539 The Decree of Villers-Cotterêts, which makes French the obligatory language in all official documents.

1562–1598 The wars of religion.

1580 The first edition of *Essais* by Montaigne is published.

1589 Henri IV takes the throne.

1598 The Edict of Nantes.

1610 Henri IV is assassinated and the child Louis XIII ascends the throne, followed by the regency of Marie de Médicis.

1636–1637 *Le Cid* by Corneille and *Le discours de la méthode* by Descartes are published.

1643 Louis XIII dies, followed by the regency of Anne d'Autriche.

1648 The beginnings of la Fronde.

1670 *Bérénice* by Racine and *Le bourgeois gentilhomme* by Molière are published, as well as a partial version of Pascal's *Pensées*.

1685 Revocation of the Edict of Nantes.

1715 Louis XV takes the throne, followed by the regency of duc d'Orléans until 1723.

1748 *De l'esprit des lois* by Montesquieu is published.

1751 The first volume of the *Encyclopédie* appears.

1762 *Du contrat social* by Rousseau is published.

1774 Louis XVI ascends to the throne.

1789 **14 July:** The Bastille falls. **4 August:** Feudal privileges are abolished. **26 August:** Declaration of the Rights of Man and the Citizen.

1790 France is divided into 83 départements.

1791 Metric system is established.

1792 Proclamation of the République.

1793 **21 January:** Louis XVI is executed. **September:** The Terror begins.

1794 Robespierre loses power.

1799 Bonaparte stages a coup d'état.

1800 Office of préfet is created.

1801 Concordat is signed.

1802 *Le génie du christianisme* by Chateaubriand.

1804 **21 March:** Civil Code is promulgated.

1808 L'Université Impériale is established. **2 December:** Bonaparte is crowned emperor.

1812 **September–October:** Napoléon Bonaparte's troops occupy Moscow.

1814 Allied invasion of France. **6 April:** Bonaparte is forced to abdicate. **6 June:** Constitutional Charter of Louis XVIII.

1815 **March:** Bonaparte returns for the Hundred Days, culminating in Waterloo. **22 June:** Second abdication of Bonaparte. **8 July:** Second restoration.

1821 Bonaparte dies.

1825 Charles X ascends to the throne.

1830 *La symphonie fantastique* by Hector Berlioz; *Hernani* by Victor Hugo. **27–29 July:** Les Trois Glorieuses, three days of insurrection. **2 August:** Charles X is forced to abdicate in favor of Louis-Philippe.

1831 *La liberté guidant le peuple* by Delacroix.

1834 *Le Père Goriot* by Honoré de Balzac.

1836 Railway line is laid between Paris and Saint-Germain-en-Laye.

1840 Bonaparte's remains are entombed in Les Invalides.

1848 **24 February:** Popular discontent ends the régime of Louis-Philippe. **4 November:** Constitution of Second Republic. **10 December:** Bonaparte's nephew, Louis-Napoléon, is elected president of the Republic.

1850 Falloux law on education.

1851 Coup d'état by Louis-Napoléon.

1852 Empire is restored.

1854 War with Russia.

1855 Paris Exhibition.

1856 Peace congress in Paris.

1857 Port of Dakar is established by Louis Faidherbe; *Madame Bovary* by Gustave Flaubert.

1859 Construction of Suez Canal begins.

1860 Annexation of Savoie and Nice; free trade treaty with Britain.

1861 Military expedition to Mexico.

1862 Annexation of Cochin-China.

1863 *Le déjeuner sur l'herbe* by Edouard Manet.

1864 Right to strike recognized in law.

1866 French troops evacuate Mexico.

1869 Suez Canal is opened.

1870 **19 July:** France declares war on Prussia. **4 September:** Empire collapses and Third Republic is proclaimed.

1871 **18 March:** The Commune begins. **10 May:** Treaty of Frankfurt cedes Alsace-Lorraine to the Germans. **28 May:** Communards defeated.

1873 Death of Louis-Napoléon; foundation stone of Sacré Coeur is laid.

1875 **February:** Amendement Wallon.

1877 **16 May:** President Maurice de MacMahon attempts coup d'état.

1879 Ferry begins educational reforms.

1880 Amnesty for exiled Communards.

1881 Tunisia becomes French protectorate.

1882 Foundation of Ligue des Patriotes.

1884 Trade unions legalized.

1886 Boulanger is appointed minister of war.

1887–1889 Eiffel Tower is built.

1888 Pasteur Institute is founded.

1889 **January:** Georges Boulanger is elected in Paris. **April:** Boulanger's flight.

1892 **November:** Panama Canal scandal.

1894 Lumière brothers make first film. **December:** Alfred Dreyfus is condemned.

1895 Confédération Générale du Travail is established.

1896 Madagascar is annexed.

1898 **January:** Emile Zola's *J'accuse*.

1899 **September:** Second court-martial also finds Dreyfus guilty.

1902 *Pelléas et Mélisande* by Claude Debussy.

1904 Anglo-French Entente; 10-hour-day law.

1905 Section Française de l'Internationale Ouvrière is founded; law of separation of church and state is passed.

1908 *Réflexions sur la violence* by Georges Sorel.

1909 Joan of Arc is beatified.

1912 Morocco becomes a French protectorate.

1913 Military service is extended to three years.

1914   28 June: Archduke Ferdinand is assassinated at Sarajevo. **31 July:** Jean Jaurès is assassinated. **3 August:** Germany declares war on France. **22 August:** French are defeated in the Ardennes. **5–12 September:** Battle of the Marne.

1916   21 February: Battle of Verdun begins. **July–September:** Battle of the Somme. **December:** Robert Nivelle is appointed commander-in-chief.

1917   16 April: Nivelle offensive. **May:** Nivelle is dismissed; mutinies in French army; Foch and Pétain are appointed. **November:** Georges Clemenceau government is formed.

1918   March–July: Ludendorff offensive. **18 July:** Foch's counteroffensive. **11 November:** Armistice.

1919   28 June: Treaty of Versailles is signed.

1920   December: Socialist Congress at Tours.

1923   January: Occupation of Ruhr.

1924   André Breton issues Manifesto of Surrealism; Dawes Plan.

1925   July: Evacuation of Ruhr begins. **October:** Locarno Accords are reached.

1928   Decision to build Maginot Line.

1929   October: Wall Street crash.

1930   June: French evacuate the Rhineland.

1933   Stavisky affair.

1934   6 February: Right-wing *ligues* make halfhearted attempt at coup d'état. **9 February:** Left wing counterdemonstrates.

1935   May: Franco-Soviet pact is negotiated.

1936   March: Rhineland is remilitarized. **April–May:** Popular Front victory in legislative elections; strikes and sit-ins. **June:** Léon Blum becomes premier; Matignon agreements. **October:** Devaluation of franc; Spanish Civil War.

1937   **February:** Blum announces "pause" on road to reform. **June:** Blum government falls. Jean Renoir's film *La grande illusion* is released.

1938   **29 September:** Munich conference.

1939   **February:** France recognizes government of Franco. **March:** Anglo-French guarantee to Poland. **1 September:** Germany invades Poland. **3 September:** Great Britain and France declare war on Germany.

1940   **May:** French front is broken on Meuse; Philippe Pétain enters government. **14 June:** Germans enter Paris. **16 June:** Paul Reynaud is succeeded by Pétain. **18 June:** General de Gaulle calls from London for continued resistance. **22 June:** Armistice with Germany. **1 July:** French government moves to Vichy. **10 July:** National Assembly votes full powers to Pétain. **24 October:** Hitler-Pétain interview at Montoire.

1941   Germany invades Russia; French communists begin resistance.

1942   **8 November:** Allies invade North Africa. **11 November:** Germans move into unoccupied France.

1943   **June:** Committee of National Liberation formed at Algiers under Charles de Gaulle and Giraud.

1944   *Huis Clos* by Jean-Paul Sartre. **6 June:** Allies land in Normandy. **26 August:** De Gaulle enters Paris.

1945   **21 October:** Referendum ends Third Republic.

1946   **January:** De Gaulle resigns.

1947   **April:** Gaullist Rassemblement is formed. **May:** Paul Ramadier dismisses Communist ministers. **November–December:** Communist-led strikes; *La peste* by Camus.

1949   North Atlantic Treaty is signed.

1951   Coal and steel pact is signed by France, Germany, Italy, and Benelux.

1953   Poujadist League forms.

1954 **May:** Dien Bien Phu falls. **November:** Algerian revolt.

1956 **March:** Independence of Morocco and Tunisia is recognized. **November:** Suez crisis. **December:** Saar returns to German sovereignty. Bardot myth is launched in *Et dieu créa la femme*.

1957 Assembly ratifies Common Market treaties; *Mythologies* by Roland Barthes.

1958 **13 May:** Revolt of Europeans and army in Algeria. **1 June:** De Gaulle's government is accepted by the Assembly. **28 September:** Constitution of the Fifth Republic is accepted by referendum. **21 December:** De Gaulle is elected president.

1959 **January 8:** De Gaulle is proclaimed president and Michel Debré his premier.

1960 **January:** "New franc" is introduced. **February:** First French nuclear bomb explodes.

1961 **January:** Referendum on future of Algeria. **April:** Army revolt in Algeria collapses.

1962 **March:** Franco-Algerian agreement. **April:** Georges Pompidou becomes prime minister. **July:** Independence of Algeria is proclaimed. **October:** Referendum approves future presidential election by universal suffrage.

1964 *Ecrits* by Jacques Lacan.

1966 *Les mots et les choses, Une archéologie des sciences humaines* by Michel Foucault.

1967 *L'Ecriture et la différence* by Jacques Derrida.

1968 **22 March:** Student unrest at the University of Nanterre. **10–11 May:** "Night of the barricades" in the Latin Quarter of Paris. **13 May:** Major left-wing demonstration. **30 May:** Gaullist demonstration on Champs-Elysées. **23–30 June:** Gaullists triumph in legislative elections. **July:** Maurice Couve de Murville becomes prime minister.

1969 **27 April:** Referendum on constitutional change. **28 April:** De Gaulle resigns. **15 June:** Georges Pompidou becomes president and Jacques Chaban-Delmas his premier.

1970 **9 November:** De Gaulle dies.

1971 François Mitterrand takes control of the Socialist Party.

1972 Common Program agreed to by Socialists and Communists. **July:** Pierre Messmer becomes prime minister.

1973 First oil crisis.

1974 **2 April:** Pompidou dies. **27 May:** Valéry Giscard d'Estaing becomes president and Jacques Chirac his premier. **October:** Neuwirth law allows sale of contraceptive pill in pharmacies.

1975 Weil law legalizing abortion is passed by Assembly.

1976 **August:** Raymond Barre becomes prime minister.

1977 Common Program ends.

1979 Second oil crisis.

1980 Scandal of undeclared gift of diamonds allegedly received by Giscard d'Estaing.

1981 **10 May:** François Mitterrand becomes president and Pierre Mauroy his premier. **9 October:** Death penalty abolished; devaluation of franc.

1982 **January:** Another devaluation of franc. **February:** Wave of nationalizations. **March:** Defferre law starts process of decentralization.

1983 **March:** Mauroy government announces third devaluation and austerity plan.

1984 **June:** Socialists are defeated in European elections; 1 million take to the streets in protest against proposed changes to private education. **July:** Proposed changes to private education are dropped; Laurent Fabius is the new prime minister.

1985 Rainbow Warrior affair; Socialists opt for proportional representation in legislative elections of the following year.

1986 **March:** Center-right wins majority in legislative elections; Jacques Chirac becomes prime minister and starts period of "cohabitation"; National Front rejoices at winning 35 seats; Chirac launches privatization program.

1987   January: Single European Act comes into force. **October:** Share values crash on Black Monday.

1988   8 May: Mitterrand is reelected president well ahead of Chirac and chooses Michel Rocard as his premier.

1991   January–February: French participation in Gulf War. **May:** France's first female prime minister, Edith Cresson, forms government. **December:** Maastricht Treaty concludes.

1992   April: Pierre Bérégovoy becomes prime minister. **20 September:** Referendum on Maastricht Treaty reveals only 51.04 percent in favor.

1993   March: Landslide victory for center-right in legislative elections and another period of cohabitation for Mitterrand, who is obliged to accept Edouard Balladur as his premier. **May:** Suicide of former prime minister, Pierre Bérégovoy; new wave of privatizations.

1994   April: *Le premier homme* by Albert Camus appears 34 years after his death; Paul Touvier becomes first Frenchman to be found guilty of crimes against humanity. **September:** Pierre Péan's controversial book on Mitterrand appears. **November:** First picture in *Paris-Match* of Mitterrand's illegitimate daughter.

1995   May: Jacques Chirac is elected president, with Alain Juppé as his premier. **June:** International outcry at resumption of French nuclear tests in Pacific. **25 July:** Terrorist bomb, allegedly planted by Islamic fundamentalists, explodes at Saint-Michel Metro station, killing eight and wounding many others. **November:** Massive demonstrations and strikes in protest of austerity measures of Juppé government.

1996   January: François Mitterrand, France's longest-serving president, dies. **November:** Prime Minister Alain Juppé and his government back down on the proposed sale of French company Thomson Multimédia to Korean conglomerate Daewoo.

1997   21 April: President Chirac announces dissolution of Assembly in order to call legislative elections one year ahead of schedule. **25 May:** Second-highest-ever level of abstentions in first round of elections. **1 June:** Stunning defeat for center-right as the left wins majority in new Assembly. **2 June:** Chirac appoints Socialist leader Lionel Jospin his premier, France enters third period of cohabitation.

1998 **10 February:** First Aubry law on 35-hour week.

1999 **13 June:** Left emerge as winners in European elections. **2 July:** Bernard Kouchner becomes civil administrator in Kosovo. **12 August:** McDonald's restaurant in Millau is destroyed by followers of José Bové. **November:** Law is passed creating the Pacte Civil de Solidarité.

2000 **1 January:** *Couverture maladie universelle* comes into force, guaranteeing free health care for those on low incomes. **20 March:** Creation of Euronext, a merger of the stock exchanges in Paris, Brussels, and Amsterdam. **24 September:** Referendum in favor of shortening the presidential mandate from seven to five years.

2001 **11 September:** Security measures known as Vigipirate stepped up after terrorist outrages in the United States. **14 December:** Distribution of euros begins in France.

2002 **1 January:** Euro becomes the official currency of France and the European Union. **17 February:** Franc ceases to be legal tender in France. **31 March:** Synagogue attacked by arsonists in Strasbourg. **21 April:** Shock spreads as Jean-Marie Le Pen comes second behind Jacques Chirac in first round of presidential elections. **5 May:** Chirac is reelected president with 82.21 percent of votes cast and chooses Jean-Pierre Raffarin as his premier. **14 July:** Right-wing extremist fails in attempt to shoot Chirac. **6 October:** Mayor of Paris, Bertrand Delanoë, is victim of non-fatal knife attack; French petrol tanker is attacked by terrorists in waters off Yemen. **8 November:** Former president Valéry Giscard d'Estaing declares his opposition to Turkish membership of the European Union (EU).

2003 **21 January:** President George Bush declares the United States' willingness to intervene in Iraq. **23 January:** German Chancellor Gerhard Schröder and Chirac voice opposition to U.S. intervention in Iraq, and on 7 February Chirac threatens use of French veto in United Nations. **18 February:** Chirac lectures future members of EU for "lack of manners" in supporting United States over Iraq. **2 April:** EU censures France for exceeding its agreed budget deficit. **10 April:** Air France and British Airways announce the end of flights by Concorde supersonic airliner. **13 May:** Major demonstrations against proposed reforms to the pensions system by the government. **25 September:** Summer heat wave (la canicule) is estimated to have killed almost 15,000 people.

2004   5–7 April: Queen Elizabeth II of Britain visits France to mark the centenary of the Entente Cordiale. **23 April:** Last coal mine in France closes at Creutzwald. **27 April:** Airbus 380 plane flies for the first time at Toulouse. **30 April:** Jewish cemetery at Herlisheim desecrated. **5 June:** Mayor of Bègles, Noël Mamère, officiates at first French gay marriage. **17 June:** Mamère suspended from office for officiating in gay marriage. **27 July:** Two French inmates at U.S. prison camp in Guantanamo are returned home. **12 September:** Laurent Fabius announces opposition to EU constitution. **November:** L'Affaire Clearstream hits the headlines, with the revelation that a list of names had been sent anonymously to Judge Renaud van Ruymbeke alleging that a number of leading politicians, including Nicolas Sarkozy, were implicated in a scheme to receive illegal commissions for facilitating the sale of French frigates to Taiwan.

2005   25 February: National Assembly adopts law recognizing "positive role" played by French colonization. **29 May:** Majority of French electorate vote against ratification of EU constitution. **31 May:** Dominique de Villepin replaces Jean-Pierre Raffarin as prime minister. **20 June:** Interior minister Nicolas Sarkozy gains notoriety by suggesting the "cleansing" of undesirable elements from France's violent suburbs. **28 October:** Two adolescents of immigrant origin die accidentally after hiding in an electrical substation from chasing police, sparking off three weeks of rioting in France's poorest working-class suburbs.

2006   31 January: Nicolas Sarkozy initiates legal proceedings to clear his name in l'Affaire Clearstream. **7 February:** Demonstrations against the Contrat Première Embauche, the government's proposed measures for greater flexibility in employment regulations governing young people. **1 April:** Government adopts 10 May as the date for the annual commemoration of the end of slavery. **27 April:** An article in the weekly journal *L'Express* claims that Defense Minister Michèle Alliot-Marie knew l'Affaire Clearstream was a plot to blacken the reputations of certain people. **4 May:** In a press conference Prime Minister Dominique de Villepin admits that Nicolas Sarkozy's name was mentioned in a discussion with one of the actors in l'Affaire Clearstream, General Philippe Rondot, but that no connection was made between Sarkozy and any scandals. **14 May:** In an interview in the *Journal du Dimanche* about l'Affaire Clearstream, General Rondot affirms that Dominique de

Villepin and President Jacques Chirac are not involved in any "machinations," in spite of the widespread awareness of their dislike of Sarkozy. **6 June:** An administrative tribunal formally acknowledges the responsibility of French railways in the deportation of the country's Jews during World War II. **6 December:** The rolling international French language news channel, France 24, is launched. **21 December:** Dominique de Villepin is interviewed for 17 hours as a witness in the judicial investigation into l'Affaire Clearstream.

2007 **6 May:** Nicolas Sarkozy elected President of the Republic, beating the candidate of the left, Ségolène Royal, and chooses François Fillon as his premier. **9 May:** Students at l'Université de Paris I occupy the university in protest of educational reforms aiming to give universities more autonomy, sparking off a series of similar protests nationwide. **17 June:** L'Union pour la Majorité Populaire secures a solid majority for Nicolas Sarkozy in the National Assembly with 46.37 percent of the vote in the second round of the legislative elections giving them 314 seats, followed by the Parti Socialiste with 42.25 percent of the vote and 186 seats, out of a total of 577. **5 July:** Police remove evidence that might be connected to l'Affaire Clearstream from Dominique de Villepin's Parisian residence. **6 July:** Police remove evidence that might be connected to l'Affaire Clearstream from Dominique de Villepin's Parisian office. **24 July:** Bulgarian nurses condemned to death in Libya for allegedly infecting children with AIDS are allowed to leave the country accompanied by Cecilia Sarkozy, the wife of President Nicolas Sarkozy. **27 July:** Dominique de Villepin is placed under investigation for being an accessory to libel, receiving stolen goods, and fraudulent use of documents. **10 August:** Law promulgated reforming universities and giving them, notably, greater autonomy. **5 September:** French railway unions warn the government that attempts at pension reform that target "special arrangements," such as early retirement with full pension rights for certain groups of workers, will be vigorously opposed. **18 October:** A series of strikes is launched, with unions militating against pension reform paralyzing public transport. **25 October:** After consulting with numerous interested parties in the forum called Le Grenelle de l'Environnement, President Nicolas Sarkozy announces measures such as a carbon tax that the government hopes to implement. **2 December:** The centrist party Mouvement Démocrate (MoDem) holds its founding congress in Villepinte, a suburb of Paris, and formally elects François Bayrou its leader. **14 December:** Libyan leader Muammar Gaddafi makes a controversial visit to France. **15 December:** President Nicolas Sarkozy allows himself to be photographed visiting Euro Disney with his new partner, Carla Bruni.

Introduction

France grew sporadically and was subject to major migrations and invasions until it entered the second millennium and embarked on a phase of slow but steady development. By that time the threat to the southern regions from the Muslim armies of North Africa had ceased, the Norsemen had learned to cultivate the land of Normandy rather than raid it, and, as a result of the creation of the Holy Roman Empire in 962, the region of Burgundy to the east was safe from the horsemen of the Hungarian plain. The gradual consolidation that followed secured the position of the crown, established its co-identity with the country's fortunes, and was marked by the emergence of the literary culture that would play such an important part in the global projection of France's image.

In contrast to what some historians have called the slow phase in France's development, the Renaissance brought rapid change. The advantages France enjoyed as a large, centralized, absolutist monarchy enabled it to impose itself on its European neighbors and develop a vocation for greatness that, paradoxically, was enhanced by the Revolution of 1789. For although it overthrew the monarchy, the Revolution had intellectual ambitions that were clearly universal and aimed at making France a model for the rest of the world. However, these ambitions were unsustainable in the real world of great power rivalry. The advent of the Industrial Revolution showed how much France had fallen behind in economic terms, first in relation to Great Britain and then more crucially in regard to Germany.

The Franco-Prussian War of 1870 between a tottering French empire and a confident, united, new Germany showed the measure of the gap between the way the French perceived themselves and the real weight of French power. As Germany eclipsed France and then Britain in the technical prowess of its manufacturers and the capture of world markets for its goods, France entered the 20th century increasingly dependent on

Britain and other allies to contain the new colossus on its eastern flank. While the convulsions caused by the two world wars convinced France's political elite of the wisdom of knitting European nations together in a supranational body like the European Union, France has nonetheless not forsaken the civilizing mission articulated by the authors of the Revolution. This explains the importance all French governments give to great cultural projects and investment in international collaboration, whether through scholarships or subsidized programs for teaching the French language; these maintain its profile as the purveyor of a great culture.

TERRITORY AND GEOGRAPHY

France sits at the western edge of the European mainland, bounded by Belgium and Germany in the northeast, Switzerland and Italy in the east, the Mediterranean in the south, Spain and Andorra in the southwest, and the Atlantic Ocean in the west. Metropolitan France (including Corsica) covers an area of 551,553 square kilometers or 212,960 square miles, but the French Republic also covers a number of territories found outside the Hexagon, as French commentators frequently call it: Guadeloupe, French Guyana, Martinique, Réunion, St. Pierre-et-Miquelon, the Southern and Antarctic territories, New Caledonia, French Polynesia, and Wallis-et-Futuna.

While modern France sits comfortably within what appear to be easily identifiable and natural borders, namely its coastlines and mountain ranges, the territory it now covers resulted from a long process of accumulation that began in the first millennium. The first piece of French territory was outlined by the Treaty of Verdun in 843, which divided Charlemagne's empire between his three grandsons. Francia Occidentalis was the area bounded by the waters of the Rhône, Saône, Meuse, and Escaut, and which was given to Charles the Bald. The restoration of a Holy Roman Empire in 962 isolated France from its Germanic neighbor, and the Meuse started to constitute the linguistic and political frontier that was to play such an important role in the historical relationship between the two peoples.

When Hugues Capet was elected king of the Franks in 987, the domain over which he could exercise his authority directly was modest indeed compared to modern France. It fell to his successors, through negotiation with powerful nobles, matrimonial alliances, and war, to extend that domain. When Philippe II Auguste came to the throne in 1180, the royal domain covered the area around Paris and tapered to a thin strip of territory south of Orléans. Philippe waged a particularly successful campaign to extend the royal domain to make him the undisputed master of what is now northern France, and his famous victory at Bouvines in 1214 against a coalition of his enemies from England and the Holy Roman Empire marked the beginning of a sense of unity among the Frankish people behind their king. The dispute with the Plantagenet dynasty in England over the rightful ownership of much of France persisted for generations, leading to the Hundred Years' War (1337–1453). During that conflict, tracts of territory changed hands until the English were gradually pushed out as Paris was retaken from them in 1436, Normandy was reconquered in 1450, and English hopes were finally extinguished after the battle of Castillon in 1453.

The growth of the kingdom toward the west in the 15th century and toward the north and east in the 17th century meant that the territory we now call France did not become recognizable until the beginning of the 19th century. In 1860, Savoie and Nice in the east and southeast were peacefully integrated into France's frontiers, but barely more than a decade later a violent change was to take place. As a result of losing the war against Prussia in 1871, France had to cede its eastern region of Alsace-Lorraine to Germany. However, this loss was reversed as one of the outcomes of World War I, and the territorial integrity of the Hexagon has suffered no permanent, major alteration since that time.

In terms of its physical geography, France can be broadly divided into five natural regions: an oceanic and temperate zone in the northwest stretching from the Vendée to Champagne and forming a fertile lowland region; the northeast, an area of plateaus and limestone slopes with few fertile areas and given to severe weather conditions; the southwest, a verdant combination of plains, hills, and plateaus; the southeast, a patchwork of contrasts stretching from the Limousin to the plains of Provence and from Rousillon to the plains of the Saône, encompassing infertile limestone plateaus and discontinuous areas of plain and valley enjoying a Mediterranean climate; and the mountain ranges of the Massif Central, the Jura, the Alps, and the Pyrenees, generally resistant to settlement and cultivation because of their poor soils and short growing seasons.

Inevitably, after centuries of vegetation clearance, grazing, fertilizing, and cropping, there are few natural soils left in France. In the majority of cases French soils fall somewhere between the true brown forest and the podsol type. Brown forest soils with plenty of organic matter predominate in France, as most of the country lies in cool to warm, temperate climates with moderate rainfall. In the wetter climates of the west, in some of the colder climates of the north, and especially in the mountainous zones, podsolized soils are characteristically thinner and less fertile than elsewhere. The soil of the Mediterranean region is memorable for its typically red color, and there the agricultural yield of the land is determined by soil-moisture conditions and the availability of irrigation.

Apart from the climate, the other major factor in soil development is the parent material. Throughout northern France the soils successfully cultivated rest on deposits of loess, or *limon*. In about a third of the country the soils developed on limestone, and although on the elevated plateaus of southern France and the mountains in general this produced soils of poor agricultural potential, in the limestone-based soils of lowland areas the yield in agricultural terms could be far greater. In parts of the Paris basin, for example, the limestone-based soil proved light and easy to work and enrich, thus attracting cultivation well before the technology was developed for breaking up the heavier clays.

Many generations of settlement and agriculture resulted in techniques that worked with the advantages of the physical geography of the regions of France or compensated for their deficiencies. Thus in the southern, Mediterranean region, a characteristic form of agriculture called for the construction of innumerable terraces on hill slopes to retain scarce soil and facilitate the cultivation of wheat, olives, and vines. By way of regional contrast, but equally traditional, the preoccupation in the northwest with soil retention shaped the traditional *bocage* landscape of Brittany, with its patchwork of small fields bounded by ditches and hedges.

Techniques for enhancing soil fertility have taken various forms according to the regions where they are employed. An example is the centuries-old practice of using natural fertilizers, including night soil from urban districts, seaweed from the coast, and animal manure in pastoral areas. By the end of the 19th century, the importation of nitrates and potash allowed a more systematic and widespread use of fertilizers on arable land. A new phase began after World War II, when traditional fertilizers began to be replaced by synthetic ones. In general, therefore, the soils of France have proved to possess good depth, texture, and organic material, and throughout the country's history have showed their potential for improvement and their capacity for sustaining intensive farming systems. The universal perception of France as a land of gastronomic plenty rests on a sound empirical basis, and in the present day this is borne out by the fact that France is the largest exporter of agricultural products among the countries of the European Union.

Apart from its effect on the soils of the country, the French climate displays distinct regional variations around two main divides: the primary divide is between the cool north and the warm south, and the secondary divide distinguishes the more continental east from the maritime west. The effect of latitude on temperature variations between north and south is easily illustrated by the mean annual temperature range, from 15 degrees Celsius in the Mediterranean to 9 degrees Celsius at the border with Belgium. However, the effect of the secondary divide is that in the north, while the January temperature in Brest averages 6 degrees Celsius, on the other side of the country in Strasbourg the temperature hovers around the freezing point. This is because the temperature in Brest is moderated by the warm oceanic currents of the North Atlantic, while Strasbourg endures the harsher continental climate of the European land mass. In the higher altitudes of the Alps, Pyrenees, and Massif Central, extremes of temperature are exacerbated, with summer averages below 10 degrees Celsius and winter averages well below freezing.

In addition to more extreme variations in temperature, the mountain regions have an annual precipitation that rises to 2,000 millimeters, while in most of France it is slightly in excess of 500 millimeters. Generally, rainfall totals are higher in the west than in the east, with a seasonal distribution of precipitation that shows a winter maximum along the Atlantic coast and a summer maximum in northeast France. More complicated rainfall patterns occur in parts of southeast France that are situated in a transitional zone between a continental climate and a true Mediterranean one. The maximum precipitation in those areas often occurs around October, when high sea-surface temperatures lead to atmospheric instability.

The leisured classes of English society constituted the first wave of tourists to discover the varied charms of the French landscape and climate, especially in the south, toward the end of the 19th century, and the trails they left are preserved in attractions like the Promenade des Anglais in Nice. Exploitation of the country's geography as a commercial resource has become much more systematic over the last few decades, particularly through efforts to develop expensive tourist facilities. For example, the site of the new Alpine ski resort Isola 2000 was chosen only after close scientific study of the climate to ensure good snow cover for the maximum period during the skiing season. A rich history and natural geographical advantages, along with astute exploitation of both factors, make France the world's top tourist destination, receiving over 76 million visitors in 2005.

Population

Recent archaeological discoveries in places such as the grottoes of Aquitaine suggest that the settlement of the territory we now call France was well under way by 15,000 BC, facilitated by its being spared many of the ravages of the great glaciers of the Ice Age. Anthropological studies show that the inhabitants then, as now, possessed ethnic diversity resulting from successive waves of migration that, by the time of the Roman conquest, meant that ancient France, or Gaul as it was known, boasted a population of approximately 10 million. A dramatic demographic change coincided with the beginning of the Christian era in France, and the population began to decline, reaching a low of five million by the fifth century. France would have to wait until the end of the 11th century before its population crossed the threshold of 10 million again.

In contrast, France in the Middle Ages enjoyed a demographic takeoff, culminating in a population that stabilized at approximately 20 million by the beginning of the 13th century. This was both a cause and a consequence of the economic growth of the period. A balance appeared to have been reached between the population of France and the productive capacity of the economy, enabling the kingdom to survive even the catastrophic ravages of the Black Death. The 17th century brought another rapid rise in population, and by the end of the ancien régime in 1789, the people of France constituted the largest nation in Western Europe, numbering some 29 million.

Thereafter, however, demographic trends in France began to assume some very particular, and ultimately costly, characteristics in terms of France's economic and military weight in Europe. The modern demographic trend that developed in Europe in the 19th century was made up of two phases. In the first phase, elimination of famine and great epidemics allowed already high birthrates to produce substantial population growth. The second phase was one in which birthrates would slowly decline, thereby restoring a new demographic balance. The peculiarity in France was that there seemed to be no time lag between the two phases. With mortality rates and birthrates dropping at the same time, France was unable to enjoy the same demographic explosion as her neighbors. The long-term consequence of this was dramatic. Whereas in the middle of the 18th century the people of France represented one-third of the population of Western Europe, by the beginning of the 20th century they made up barely 10 percent of that population mass.

The enormous number of French soldiers killed in World War I exacerbated the decline in the French population, and in the 1930s the nation's death rate actually exceeded its birthrate. Paradoxically for France, the sole major factor counteracting this decline came from abroad, in the shape of the Italian, Polish, Spanish, and Belgian migrants who, in 1931, constituted 7 percent of the country's population. The end of World War II, however, was marked by a baby boom in France as in the rest of Europe, and the country's population increased in the 30 years following 1945 by as much as it had during the previous century and a half. By 2000 France had a population of almost 60 million, and with a birthrate superior to that of its neighbors like Germany and Italy, it appeared to have overcome the structural demographic deficiency that provided so much concern for its governing elite since the 19th century.

History

Any overview of the emergence of a French identity and the fashioning of a political nation must accommodate the interaction of a number of factors, including the widely accepted view that the evolution of French civilization was marked by the tension between the town and the country. The predominance of rural traditions endured far longer in France than in other comparable European countries like England or Germany. It is unquestionably true that under Roman rule the civilization of Gaul was focused on a number of urban centers. But after the breakup of the empire, France quickly reverted to a country of scattered and small rural communities, the largest of which were grouped either around a seigniorial seat or a place of worship.

It was not until the 11th century that an urban renaissance took place, with towns confirming their importance as nodal points in emerging communication networks and as focal points for the exercise of power. The growth of commerce and the products of skilled artisans confirmed the economic superiority of the town over the countryside and led to the characteristic medieval urban patterns whose remnants can still be found today—city walls, fine merchants' houses, and winding alleys interspersed with workshops. A new social order developed in the towns, determined by craft guilds or corporations and commercial activities that contrasted with the constraints of feudal life in the countryside. This explains why, in spite of their insignificance in population terms, the towns had an autonomy that gave them a decisive role in shaping the economic, cultural, and political changes that marked the evolution of French society. Commerce and the preindustrial products of the town-based artisans provided the dynamic for growth in the 18th century and started the trickle of migration from the countryside to the town that was to become a torrent during the following century. The polarization of economic life in industrial urban centers became evident from the 1850s onward, also confirming the role of the great municipalities as hubs of political activity and cultural innovation.

Yet in tracing this evolution, a paradox remains that may help to explain some of the social and political reflexes of the French as a nation and that has endured to the present. It was not until the 1930s that the urban population overtook the rural population in numerical terms, and it would be unwise in focusing on the crucial role of the city to overlook the legacy of the rural experience of the majority of France's people for most of the country's existence. Some commentators have argued that the peculiarly Gallic mix of distrust toward modern forms of political authority and deference toward established hierarchies may reflect a mentality shaped over generations by solitary labor and traditional ties of deference—in other words, a kind of willful nonconformity that lends itself easily to street protests, allied with a respect for the marks of social distinction that contrasts markedly with social attitudes in Anglo-Saxon societies. Less contentiously, it is certainly the case that the peasant reflex of stuffing savings under the mattress or in some other domestic hiding place, rather than entrusting it to an institution, was a historical hindrance to the emergence of a modern banking system and therefore to French capitalism.

The contradictions of French identity and nationhood owe much, according to respected historians like François Furet, to the notion that France was catapulted too abruptly into the modern age by the Revolution of 1789. Up to that point, the political structures that had shaped France were hierarchies that had evolved very slowly over the centuries, from the pyramid of priests, warlords, and agrarian producers that can be traced back to Gaul to the centralizing monarchy that began to emerge under François I in the 16th century, with the influence of the Catholic Church running through the period like a thread. Alongside this, the notion of "Frenchness" was also characterized by a process of slow, organic growth, conditioned culturally from the Middle Ages onward by texts like the *Chanson de Roland*, which pitted "Frenchmen" against "pagans." This process was conditioned socially by conflicts, most notably the Hundred Years' War, which, with the advent of Joan of Arc, became a crusade to preserve France from the foreign invader. The emergence of a monarch whose power was solidly established helped forge a political and cultural convergence resulting in a distinct identity for the French people as a nation united around a Catholic king in a divinely ordained and immutable relationship.

The violent break with the old order, the ancien régime, in 1789, was indeed a systemic change since the institutions of state, like the courts, were emanations of an absolute monarchical authority that allowed the king to boast that he was the state and the personification of France. By destroying the monarchy the Revolution also destroyed the hierarchy of relations that flowed from it. In contrast to the organic whole that deferred to the divine authority of the king and in which every individual knew his or her station, the Revolution promoted a new sacrosanct notion of the individual, free and equal to all others, who deferred to nothing but the law that defended his or her liberties. The challenge therefore lay in defining a new source of social cohesion to replace the ubiquitous expressions of absolute royal authority that had once provided the means of articulating French society. The answer was to cultivate the loyalty of the people of France, as citizens, to the institutions of the republican state.

For almost a century following the Revolution, however, the idea of a body of free and equal citizens united in loyalty to the democratic institutions of the Republic was to dwell in the realm of political idealism rather than reality. In a sense, the coup d'état of Napoléon Bonaparte in 1799 profited from a desire among many French people for a return to stability, even if it was in the context of a political order that betrayed some of the fundamental principles of the Revolution. It was the start of a tradition of Caesarism in French political life, characterized by the nation's willingness to countenance the sacrifice of ineffectual but nonetheless democratic structures in favor of the dictates of a providential leader capable of rescuing the nation's fortunes.

The monarchical restorations that followed in 1814, 1815, and 1830 were undone because they were both inefficient and regressive in democratic terms, allowing, for example, the return and ascendancy of ultra-Catholic aristocrats who had formerly fled the Revolution. Corruption became endemic under the Restoration monarchs, in a style reminiscent of the ancien régime. Posts in the gift of the king and his ministers were often awarded on a nepotistic basis, at the expense of the meritocrats, in many cases people of modest background who had nothing to commend them except their talent, who were promoted under the Bonapartist system in the army, the administration, and education. But the process of intellectual emancipation begun by the Revolution was to bear fruit in 1848. Whereas the regime of the Bourbon king Charles X was brought down in 1830 by the antidemocratic excesses of the ultra-royalists surrounding him at court, in 1848 the regime of the Orleanist king Louis-Philippe was brought down by the connivance between the crown and the emerging oligarchy of financial interests governing France at the expense of popular democracy.

In both cases the downfall of the monarchs was precipitated by street protests in Paris that turned to violence. And the second instance was marked historically by the participation of students, those beneficiaries of the expansion in access to education that started during the Revolution and that was organized systematically under Bonaparte. But the characteristic tension in French history between the radicalized city, especially Paris, and the conservative countryside was soon to surface. The high hopes of real—and lasting—popular democracy entertained by the leaders of the uprising in Paris against Louis-Philippe in February 1848 were soon to be dashed by the decision of the conservative, rural majority to vote for Napoléon Bonaparte's nephew, Louis-Napoléon, in the presidential election of December 1848. Playing on the suscepti- bility of an electorate fearful of radical change and susceptible to the Caesarist myth of the providential leader, Louis-Napoléon promised a return to stability and national greatness, thus securing the presidential power that he was able to exploit in preparation for his coup d'état in 1851 and the declaration of a Second Empire the following year, in im- itation of his uncle.

It was not until the crushing defeat at the hands of the Prussians 18 years later that the collapse of the Second Empire, followed by five years of political squabbling and drift, finally gave way to the consen- sus that allowed the constitutional laws framing the Third Republic to be passed in 1875. Almost a century had elapsed, therefore, before gov- ernment, elected by universal suffrage, operating through republican in- stitutions governed by an impartial and sovereign legal system, could become a permanent fact of French life. It was during the first two decades of the Third Republic that a modern pattern of party politics de- veloped, legislation was passed enshrining the secular nature of the Re- public by clearly delimiting the influence of the church in education, and, especially after the Dreyfus Affair, a consensus was established for the emerging interest groups in society that the legitimate route for the pursuit of change was through the democratic institutions of the Re- public.

Unfortunately for France, the consensus established regarding its democratic institutions was to last barely more than two generations. The extraordinary flowering of cultural life that took place in France, and especially Paris, from the 1880s onward, making it a magnet for creative talents from all over Europe and abroad, earned the period its renown as a *belle époque*. But it was a *belle époque* in economic and social terms also. While starting somewhat later than its neighbors across the English Channel and across the Rhine, by the end of the 19th century France was beginning to reap the benefits of industrialization on a major scale, particularly with regard to the new industries like chemicals and automobile production. By the second decade of the 20th century the French automobile industry was second only to that of the United States in terms of the volume of cars produced. As a society, the emergence of an industrial working class and the bodies championing their interests, on the one hand the trade unions and on the other the numerous parties of the left, meant that politics in France had to become increasingly pluralist and democratized. But the apparent virtue of the parliamentary system of the Third Republic would also become its fatal flaw. Whereas in Britain, for example, the trade union movement gave birth to the Labour Party as the parliamentary vehicle tasked with promoting working-class interests, in France the unions refused to concede that mission to a parliamentary party, and so a plethora of voices arose, party political and syndicalist, to defend the interests of the workers. This was symptomatic of the broader political culture in which interests were not represented by parties operating as homogenous blocks, but by tendencies, groups, and factions usually grouped together in often-quarrelsome political families. The consequences for the conduct of parliamentary business could often reduce the Assembly, in the eyes of the electorate, to an interminable talking-shop. More significantly, as the life of the Third Republic wore on, the difficulty encountered by governments in securing the backing of a parliamentary majority led to their replacement with ever-increasing frequency. While the people of France could generally afford to ignore the weaknesses of a party-dominated political system during times of plenty, it was much harder to do during times of hardship, such as those ushered in by the catastrophe of 1914.

The tragic irony for France at the end of World War I in 1918 was that, although victorious, it had suffered a greater demographic and economic loss in proportion to its size than its vanquished enemy, Germany. What would also be telling in later decades was the blow to the national psyche represented by what came to be called colloquially "la der des der" ("la dernière des dernières"), or the war to end all wars. The naive assumptions about being in Berlin by the Christmas of 1914 soon evaporated in the terrible reality of mass casualties generated by the static war of attrition that came to characterize the conflict. By 1917 the unity of the nation was under severe strain, with strikes in the munitions industry and incidents of mutiny among the troops. Only the decisive entry of the United States into the war and a change of leadership in France allowed the country to sustain its determination to triumph.

However, during the two decades that followed, France's diminished standing in the international community and the social and economic burdens resulting from the war at home led to increasing disillusionment with the failings of government and the political system as a whole. By the late 1920s groups on the fringes of political life were beginning to be drawn to the radical solutions to the problem of national decline offered by the Fascists in Italy. By the mid-1930s another model, this time from Nazi Germany, was behind the rise of the *ligues*, those extreme right-wing organizations trying to influence government policy through action, frequently violent, on the street rather than from the floor of the National Assembly. This led to a mobilization of democratic forces in France in an alliance aimed at shutting out the far right in the legislative elections of May 1936. The success of this alliance brought the Popular Front government to power in a brief but fervent explosion of hope. However, those expectations could not outweigh the reality that in terms of economic and foreign policy, the Popular Front government was as powerless as its postwar predecessors without the support of its Anglo-American allies. Without support for the franc on the international exchanges, the Popular Front government could not pursue successfully a reflationary economic policy, and without the active cooperation of Great Britain, France could not side openly with the republicans in the war against the fascists in Spain.

By the time the leader of the Popular Front government, Léon Blum, resigned in 1937, the nation had been sucked into a mood of despondency and disillusionment with the institutions of the Third Republic, as the country drifted toward the inevitable conflict with Nazi Germany. When actual hostilities commenced on French territory in 1940, the common aversion in France to enduring once more the kind of carnage inflicted by World War I was a crucial influence in the people's willingness to heed Marshal Philippe Pétain's call to cease fighting. Less than eight weeks after the Germans had launched their offensive, the members of the National Assembly voted the Third Republic out of existence.

For Charles de Gaulle and the Free French leading the struggle for liberation from outside France, and for the resistance to the German occupiers from within, a central plank of their appeal to the people of France was that their legitimacy sprang from the desire to reinstate the Republic, and with it the democratic and egalitarian values that had characterized modern France since 1789. By the same token, de Gaulle and the Resistance constantly emphasized that the collaborationist government based in Vichy and represented by Pétain had no moral or legal standing since it had unconstitutionally replaced the French republic with the French state. In his famous speech in the town hall of Paris after the capital's liberation in August 1944, de Gaulle was unequivocal in expressing his determination to return France to her vocation as a Republic inspired by the ideals of 1789 and to restore her to the top table in the concert of nations. But in spite of his triumphal return in the summer of 1944, by the beginning of 1946 de Gaulle had quit the political scene.

The Fourth Republic that was voted into existence and designed to carry the hopes of the postwar generation was destined, in de Gaulle's opinion, to repeat the mistakes of the Third Republic, particularly in the way executive power was shackled by the legislative. The inability of successive governments to manage the painful process of decolonization justified de Gaulle's misgivings. The year of France's final defeat in Indochina, 1954, marked the beginning of the war in Algeria against French rule. Four years later the conflict had necessitated the dispatch of many thousands of French conscripts, deeply divided civil society at home, and pushed the French military in Algeria to the verge of defying the government in Paris. The politicians' inability to manage the crisis forced them to turn to de Gaulle as the only man with the charisma and credibility necessary to persuade all parties of the need to pull the country back from the precipice.

The price de Gaulle extracted was a new constitution that would rebalance power in favor of the executive and make the presidency the seat of power in a new republic. The constitution of the Fifth Republic was duly approved by referendum in September 1958. In 1962 de Gaulle introduced an amendment to the constitution, also approved by referendum, which allowed for the direct election of the president by the people, rather than by an electoral college. De Gaulle's intention was to elevate the president even more clearly above the party political fray, making France more amenable to strong leadership. Successive presidents, whether originally from the left or the right of the political spectrum, have all adapted to the mold cast by de Gaulle for the exercise of executive power in France. Even the successful project by Jacques Chirac to reduce the presidential mandate from seven to five years, approved by referendum in September 2000, did not fundamentally alter the fact that the French political system remains powerfully presidential.

When de Gaulle made his heroic return to a newly liberated France in 1944, there was an understandable and universal enthusiasm for a reestablishment of the French republican paradigm of nationhood, citizenship, and universal rights. But now a new debate has emerged in France as to whether the legacy of 1789 should be reassessed with a view to making it more relevant to the challenges of the 21st century, particularly in terms of France's identity as a democratic nation. France, like most postindustrial nations, is seeing a creeping disaffection on the part of its citizenry in relation to the political process. The language of politics, as articulated by traditional political parties, has a quantifiably diminishing purchase on the loyalty of voters, who show themselves more inclined to pursue their individual or sectional interests through parallel organizations and campaigns that refuse to be absorbed into traditional political structures.

For France this poses a particular intellectual challenge, since one of the fundamental premises of the Revolution was the co-identity of the individual and the citizen. This meant that any endeavor to change society by the individual citizen or group of individual citizens was inevitably routed through the mechanisms established by the polity—in practice, the institutions of the Republic. The separation of the concept of the individual from the citizen and the redefinition of the relationship of the individual to the nation-state, itself a concept under review in light of the looming European supranational polity, is currently a source of much speculation among political philosophers in France—particularly in light of the social unrest in recent years stemming from the alienation of certain minorities. But as French history illustrates, the democratic instinct of the people of modern France, and the manner in which the nation's political institutions have been shaped, serve to identify France strongly as one of the leading democratic nations of the world community.

France in Europe and the World

In concrete terms, France's weight in Europe and the world makes it a significant economic and political power. In 2003 it had the fifth-largest economy among the group of seven industrialized nations just behind Great Britain, but by 2006 both had been overtaken by China. In common with the rest of the Eurozone, growth in the French economy was sluggish after the inception of the euro, but 2006 marked a significant reversal of that trend with a growth rate of over 2.5 percent and a decline in unemployment to 9 percent from a record high of over 12 percent two years earlier. In contrast with Britain and the United States, in recent decades France has registered a consistent surplus in its balance of trade with the rest of the world, no doubt helped by a strong industrial base and its position as Europe's leading exporter of agricultural products. In spite of strong dirigiste instincts that, since the days of the ancien régime, provided a stronger role for central government in the economic affairs of the country than in its major European neighbors, France pursued an economic policy during the 1980s that showed increasing conformity, partly through the force of circumstance and partly through choice, to the economic orthodoxies that govern the world economy.

Ironically, it was the Socialist governments of the early 1980s that began the process of disengagement by central government from the wealth-generating sectors of the economy. The wave of nationalizations that took place in the first flush of Socialist victory in 1981 was not allowed to become a blank check for the unions in the state sector. Market disciplines were introduced into state-owned enterprises like the vehicle manufacturer Renault to reduce overmanning and reverse the recurrent losses suffered by the company. The government subsequently invested billions of francs with the long-term aim of cutting the company's dependence on the state. The example of Renault is particularly appropriate because, since its nationalization after World War II as the result of its owner's collaboration with the German occupiers of France, the vehicle manufacturer had come to symbolize the immovable nature of unionized vested interests in the state sector. The opening up of the company to private investors in 1996 marked the culmination of a process whose foundation had been laid over a decade before by a left-wing government.

Reconciliation with free-market ideas accelerated under the center-right governments of 1986–1988 and 1993–1995, the so-called periods of "cohabitation," when the governments had to find a *modus vivendi* with the socialist presidency of François Mitterrand. These periods were marked by ambitious privatization programs that placed significant sectors of state-owned industry firmly into the private sector, but more particularly freed the financial markets, allowing the Paris stock exchange, or bourse, to enjoy its own "big bang," following in the footsteps of New York and London. Although the stock market crash on

Black Monday in October 1987 was a painful illustration of the fact that the value of investments can go down as well as up, the liberalization of financial markets in France had locked the country into the world economy and in the process had created seven million more small investors among the country's citizens.

Historically France, since its emergence under Louis XIV as the dominant nation-state on the continent, has had ambitions to shape Europe. However, since 1945 this ambition has been pursued peacefully and through cooperation, especially with Germany, in a partnership aimed at precluding the possibility of these two countries ever again going to war against each other. This explains the underlying motivation for France's leading role in the development of the European Community. It was the plan drafted by the Frenchman Jean Monnet for the elimination of internal tariffs on trade in coal and steel among the states of Europe that led to the formation of the European Coal and Steel Community in 1951, the forerunner of the European Economic Community founded by the Treaty of Rome in 1957.

From that time onward, France has initiated or supported actively all the amendments to the treaty aimed at strengthening the community as a supranational body, at the expense of individual national sovereignty if necessary. In 1978, for example, under the presidency of Valéry Giscard d'Estaing, France joined Germany in pressing for the creation of a European monetary system designed to bring stability to the exchange rates of European currencies. Again, during the 1980s and especially during the term of Jacques Delors's presidency of the European Commission, France argued powerfully for the acceptance of the Single European Act enshrining the right of movement for persons, goods, and capital across the community's member states, thus preparing the ground for the transformation of the European Community into the European Union.

In a testament to French voluntarism, France has provided the technological sinews needed to sustain the European body politic, especially in the face of competition from the United States and Asia. France is by far the biggest single national investor in the space program that now provides Europe with an independent capacity to launch satellites from the French territory of Guyana and compete successfully against the United States and Russia for the business of launching the satellites of non-European nations. French companies have pioneered alliances with other European companies to attack world markets more effectively—for example, Alsthom's alliance with the British company GEC to develop the high-speed train technology that by the 1990s had been exported to North America and Asia. The most ambitious, and successful, of the French plans for a coordinated European attack on world markets has been in the aerospace industry. Together with Germany and Spain, France is the senior partner in the Airbus consortium, and in 2003 Airbus pulled off the remarkable feat of outselling Boeing on world markets. European ties were strengthened in 2000 when Aérospatiale merged with DASA of Germany and CASA of Spain to form the European Aeronautical Defense and Space Company (EADS). As a result of this merger EADS held 80 percent of the shares in Airbus, and the consortium appeared to pull off another coup at the expense of the American competition when the A380 "superjumbo" took to the skies over Toulouse in 2004. However, in 2006 the shine was taken off this achievement by the announcement of serious delays in the delivery times for these aircraft, resulting in a number of cancelled orders that damaged the image of Airbus.

France's attempt to define an identity for itself in Europe has a military, as well as a political and economic, dimension. The tension caused by General de Gaulle's suspicion that the United States was attempting to steer Europe's destiny through the North Atlantic Treaty Organization (NATO), and France's arm's-length relationship with the organization for most of the post-1945 period, now seems to have been resolved as France pushes for a more proactive part in conflict resolution in Europe and elsewhere. As one of only two European nations (together with Britain) with a nuclear arsenal, France tried in the mid-1990s to float the idea that its nuclear capacity could be viewed as a European nuclear umbrella, but this notion failed politically, largely because of a lack of enthusiasm from Germany.

On other fronts, however, France's attempts to bolster Europe's credibility as a peacemaker have brought more tangible results. It contributed 8,500 soldiers to the United Nations Protection Force troops that were sent to keep the warring factions apart in the former Yugoslavia, and followed this up with 11,000 troops for the Implementation Force contingent, under the command of NATO, that was sent to police the agreements concluded in the U.S.-brokered Dayton peace accord in 1995 and that brought an end to the large-scale hostilities in the former Yugoslavia. But France had already signaled its intention to retain a role for itself as a global player at the beginning of the decade, when it contributed an armored division to the U.S.-led coalition against Saddam Hussein of Iraq in the Gulf War.

During the years that followed, France used its position as a permanent member of the United Nations Security Council to try and initiate reforms of UN structures. For example, France has argued that the Security Council should be enlarged through the attribution of permanent seats to Germany and Japan. On the enduringly thorny issue of finance for the organization, France has used its position as the contributor of 6.5 percent of the UN's regular budget to formulate proposals backed by the European Union for the establishment of a better funding formula for the UN. In the prelude to the second U.S. intervention in Iraq in 2003 France tried to use its influence in the UN to dissuade the U.S. and its allies from embarking on this course. The chill that settled on France–U.S. relations subsequently, especially from the American side, did not last very long. France, with American approval, was instrumental in securing a UN-brokered ceasefire in Lebanon after 34 days of fighting between Israeli troops and Hezbollah guerillas in 2006 had displaced a quarter of Lebanon's civilian population.

It would, however, be unwise to assume that the process of European convergence that would subsume the singularity of France's profile as a nation into a wider, continental destiny is somehow ineluctable as conceived in the Maastricht Treaty on European union, signed by the (then) 12 heads of state of the European Community on 7 February 1992. During the campaign preceding the ratification of the treaty by the French people, there was a conspicuous lack of enthusiasm even among the political establishment resulting from concerns about the cost of the treaty in terms of France's capacity for independent decision making and the preservation of the country's generous social security system. Mindful of the misgivings in his own party, Jacques Chirac's support for a yes vote in the referendum was at times notably guarded, and in the final political rally before the referendum was held, Chirac advocated a yes vote "without enthusiasm."

In spite of these lukewarm appeals to ratify the treaty, the narrowness of the victory for the yes camp was still a surprise, with 51.04 percent of votes cast in favor of the treaty, 48.95 percent of votes cast against, with an abstention rate of 30.30 percent among all those registered to vote. The years that followed did little to appease the anxieties of a significant portion of the French electorate. Government policies, particularly under the premiership of Alain Juppé during the mid-1990s, provoked the kind of widespread industrial stoppages and demonstrations not seen since the late 1960s. The nub of the dispute lay in government attempts to relax employment protection measures and reduce social security deficits, in order to bring the nation's economy into line with the strict financial criteria governing admission to the club of EU nations willing and able to sign up for the single currency that was to replace their own in 2002.

Not only was the social cost of remaining in the inner core of the European Union challenged by mass protests, but questions were raised from within the political establishment, as well as from the street, as to the cost of this ambition to France's industrial base. As part of an attempt to identify synergies among leading French industrial groups to help them become stronger global players and make them less dependent on financial lifelines from the French state, the government of Prime Minister Juppé in 1996 sanctioned the sale of the electronics group Thomson to the largely defense industry–based Lagardère group. The national pride of many ordinary French citizens, as well as politicians, was hurt when it was revealed that the terms of the deal included the sale of Thomson Multi Média, the consumer electronics side of Thomson dedicated principally to the manufacture of televisions, for the symbolic sum of one franc. Hurt turned to outrage when it was discovered that Lagardère proposed to sell Thomson Multi Média on to the Korean company Daewoo and focus only on integrating the defense electronics capacity of Thomson.

A heated debate erupted, fanned by Juppé's dry observation that Thomson Multi Média's level of indebtedness made it worthless. For a large section of French public opinion, this smacked of careless indifference to the fate of the employees of the company and abject industrial defeatism, quitting the field of battle for the electronics consumer goods market in the face of the supposed invincibility of the manufacturers from the Pacific Rim. Whether rightly or wrongly in terms of industrial logic, the resistance to the knockdown sale of Thomson Multi Média to the foreigner Daewoo became overwhelming, and within weeks of the matter coming to public attention in November 1996, the government was forced to back down and agree to look for a French white knight, like the company Alcatel, to purchase the business and retain a national player in the field. A decade later, French governments remained wedded to the idea of defending national champions. As a consequence of this, for example, in 2006 Electricité de France could enjoy the freedom of operating very profitably as the main supplier of electricity to the citizens of London after its takeover of British utility companies, while the French energy market, in spite of French assurances to the European Commission, remains essentially closed to foreign suppliers. The anxiety to preserve the national interest, however, is not restricted to the governing elite. The decision of the French electorate to vote against the ratification of a constitution for the EU in 2005 was a huge shock, given the country's historic role in the construction of the European community. But it was in retrospect not such a surprise, given the voice consistently given to the fears regarding the consequences of EU enlargement for France, even from the former president who had been given the responsibility for drafting the EU's constitution, Valéry Giscard d'Estaing.

If the destinies of France and Europe are not as smoothly coterminous as the advocates of European integration would have us believe, France's role in world politics is likely to become more problematic as the country's economic importance, along with that of other European nations, declines in the face of Asian—and particularly Chinese—economic advances. The universal intellectual and ethical ambitions of the French Revolution were rapidly integrated into the political ambitions of the French state and projected into expansionist policies overseas under the banner of France's *mission civilisatrice*—a vocation to spread the benefits of the culture of the French Enlightenment to the rest of the planet. When the captive colonial audience for the propagation of what was regarded, by Paris at least, as the unique value system of French culture found independence after World War II, France invested heavily in diplomatic and pedagogic initiatives to promote the image of France by means other than outright colonialism.

The French language has operated as a major vehicle for the preservation of French influence outside Europe. In cultural terms, the funds poured into the development of *francophonie* have demonstrated the determination of all French governments to use the maintenance of the French language in their former colonies as a way of fostering a privileged relationship with those states. In Africa particularly, France has presumed on those special relationships to intervene and restore the postcolonial order. This was the case most notably in Chad in the 1970s. In the 1990s, France remained the major economic partner of its former colony in Algeria and the chief external prop for the regime there in its increasingly bitter struggle with the Islamic fundamentalists attempting to seize power. During the intervening years, French foreign policy further south has benefited regimes of dubious reputation like that of the erstwhile emperor of Central Africa, Jean Bedel Bokassa, and more recently, President Mobutu of Zaire.

By the mid-1990s, however, French foreign policy in Africa had proved to be a two-edged sword. Although France's role on that continent served its ambition of retaining a place among the great nations on the world stage, the cost was increasingly called into question by France's citizens and the nation's friends abroad. The tacit support given to the regime in Algeria, in spite of its disregard for the verdict of the ballot box and its civil rights abuses, provoked the armed wing of the Islamic fundamentalists into taking their struggle to mainland France through outrages like the bombing campaign on the French underground. The ambiguity of France's involvement in the regional politics leading to the genocide in Rwanda in 1995 heightened skepticism about the wisdom of French foreign policy. And by 1996, the social and economic meltdown in Zaire led to thinly veiled criticisms from the United States of France's role in Africa and particularly its willingness to support undemocratic regimes on the basis that they were preferable to chaos, despite the fact that, as the evidence suggested, this simply deferred the chaos and rendered it ultimately more dramatic.

The importance of the linguistic dimension to France's self-image as a great nation and the increasing clash with commercial values in the new world order that followed the end of the Cold War were illustrated by the conflict with the United States in the early 1990s over the protectionist regime enjoyed by films and television in France. The introduction of measures to protect the French language by the center-right government elected in 1993 included a formal interdiction of Anglo-Americanisms in advertising and the media. So, for example, a "fax" became a *télécopie* and a "Walkman" became a *balladeur*. This was followed by stubborn resistance to U.S. pressure to have cultural products like films and television programs treated in the same way as any other consumer items traded across international frontiers. The ensuing stand-off allowed the French film industry to continue to enjoy the kind of state support that makes it by far the largest and most important of national cinema industries in Europe and allowed limits to remain on the proportion of television schedules on French channels than can be devoted to foreign language programs. But the truth remains that the penetration of French-language cultural products abroad is very modest, and the new age of multichannel satellite broadcasting, with its insatiable appetite for programs, will continue to be dominated by American English.

As the forecasts by bodies like the Organization for Economic Cooperation and Development suggest, the future of France in the 21st century will be one in which an erstwhile great power will have to adapt to the reduced circumstances, particularly in the areas of foreign and economic policy, commensurate with its diminishing weight in the world. On the other hand, no other country enjoys the same prestige as France with regard to those less tangible concerns that nonetheless fix a nation's standing among its neighbors. It is perhaps not surprising for a country producing over 400 different cheeses that, for the foreseeable future, from Chicago to Capetown, the staff, menu, and functioning of any restaurant aiming for elite status will be defined by French standards. On catwalks from Tokyo to Turin, the aesthetic language that transforms tailoring into haute couture will remain French. In spite of the ritual obituaries in France for the French intellectual class, the synonymous relationship between "intellectual" and "French" endures as ubiquitously as the versions of the ideas of French critical theorists sweeping campuses from Maryland to Manila. And now the familiar busloads of Japanese tourists on the Champs Elysées are joined in ever-increasing numbers by what the tourist industry in France has called *les BRICs* (Brazilians, Russians, Indians, and Chinese), citizens from the emerging economic world players pursuing the old mystique of French class and sophistication.

But the irresistible mystique of France is one that also seduces the nation's nearer neighbors, more familiar with the reality of French life. Europe-wide surveys consistently show France to be perceived as the European country offering the best quality of life. In 2006 it was estimated that the British alone had bought 60 percent of the secondary residences on sale in the southwest of the country. One could venture that it is a testament to the intellectual ambition of the authors of the French Revolution that their legacy has made of modern France an ideal, reflected in innumerable ways by the styles and concepts that have inspired the highest levels of achievement in the refinement of the human spirit.

The Dictionary

– A –

ABSURD, THEATER OF THE. A theatrical movement that emerged in France in the 1940s and whose influence spread well beyond Europe. Interestingly, its most famous practitioners in French were of foreign origin, such as Samuel Beckett (Irish) and Eugène Ionesco (Romanian). The seminal text in this genre was Beckett's play *En attendant Godot* (*Waiting for Godot*), written in 1947 but not performed until 1953, under the direction of Roger Blin in **Paris**. *Godot* displayed what became the characteristic features of absurdist theater: serious themes conveyed in a superficially whimsical manner, the portrayal of dislocated minds and disembodied speech, and a highly stylized language full of fugitive allusions and aphorisms in a frequently anachronistic context. In short, it was the kind of drama that aimed to shake audiences out of their traditional complacency about the theatrical experience by making them confront their preconceived ideas.

ACADEMIE FRANCAISE. A learned society founded by Cardinal **Richelieu** in 1634 and initially entrusted with the task of preserving the French language, but it was 1694 before the first edition of the *Dictionnaire de l'Académie* appeared. The "Immortals," as the members of the Académie are known, guard the privilege of membership jealously, even idiosyncratically. Thus, prominent men of letters like Racine, **Victor Hugo**, and **Alexandre Dumas** had to make repeated applications before gaining entry, and modern figures like **Jean-Paul Sartre** and **Albert Camus** were never inducted. In 1980, **Marguerite Yourcenar** was the first woman inductee. *See also* LITERATURE.

1

AEROSPACE. French ambitions were manifested early in the race for manned flight when the Montgolfier brothers launched their first hot-air balloon in 1783. When Wilbur Wright went to France in 1908 to demonstrate his flying machines, the modern age of powered flight took off there. Louis Blériot had already constructed and flown his own plane in France in 1907 and in 1910 became France's first qualified pilot. But it was the exploits of the Wright brothers that caught the imagination and stoked huge public interest in the age of the plane. **World War I** gave much impetus to aircraft production, and in 1915 the first fighter plane factories were built in **Toulouse**.

The experience of two world wars helps explain why the strategic importance of military aircraft shelters certain famous manufacturers, such as Dassault, from international competition even though few foreign air forces buy their fighter planes. However, the competition in the market for civilian aircraft is ferocious. France had some notable success after **World War II**, with the launch of the Caravelle airliner, for example, in 1955. Three famous old French companies, La Sereb, Nord Aviation, and Sud Aviation, had contributed to the program. But their disappearance, swallowed up in the new Aérospatiale company in 1970, signaled the consolidation that had to occur due to the spiraling development costs of new planes. France had already been looking for international collaboration in aircraft development and in 1962 signed an agreement with **Great Britain** to produce the world's first supersonic airliner, Concorde. But even as early as 1969 there were doubts, ultimately justified, as to the commercial viability of the project.

More importantly, 1969 saw the creation of Airbus Industrie, a Franco-German consortium aimed at challenging the domination of the **United States** in the civil aviation market. In the same year, the French engine maker Société Nationale d'Etudes et de Constructions de Moteurs d'Aviation signed an agreement with General Electric of the United States that would allow France to develop the engines to power the civilian aircraft later built by Airbus. By 1988 Aérospatiale, the French partner in Airbus, had invested enough that Airbus's civilian aircraft accounted for 30 percent of its business, up from just a few percentage points in the 1970s. By 2000, the consolidation in the French aerospace industry that had seen Aérospatiale join with Matra, had become international, as those French companies merged with **Germany**'s DASA and Spain's CASA to form the European Aeronautic Defense and Space Company (EADS), of which Airbus is now a wholly owned subsidiary.

Since then Airbus has gone head to head with the American giant, Boeing, for the top slot on world markets. Soon after the creation of EADS the French realized that Airbus needed a more thorough commercial management structure and the French state as a shareholder retreated, allowing for a more unified and streamlined structure at the head of the company. The benefits of this reorganization, however, were soon eclipsed by the technical problems faced in the production of the A380, the world's largest passenger plane. When it finally rolled out of its Toulouse hangar in 2007 for delivery to its first customer, Singapore Airlines, the plane was almost two years late. Moreover, the rapid decline in the value of the dollar, the currency in which the aviation industry trades internationally, pushed up production costs in Europe, and the Power 8 cost-cutting program drawn up by Airbus management heralded some painful restructuring in the company. Thus, although Airbus beat Boeing to the top slot in the world in 2003, Boeing bounced back to take the lion's share again with the success of its 777 large passenger carrier and the advance orders for its 787 Dreamliner. The air shows at Le Bourget and Dubai in 2007 saw a fight back by Airbus, and in Dubai particularly, an order placed for seventy A350s and eleven A380s represented, in value terms, the largest order ever placed with Airbus by an airline.

A sector of the aerospace industry where the French state takes a proudly proactive lead is the Ariane space program. After the failure of the Europa 2 rocket program, in 1972 the French government took the lead in proposing a partnership to Germany and Great Britain that could give Europe its own launch-vehicle technology for putting satellites into space; and in 1973 the Ariane program was born. While initially the program started thanks to a technology transfer agreement with NASA, the clear ambition of the French was ultimately to free Europe from dependence on American space technology. This independence was achieved when the Ariane 1 space rocket was successfully launched in 1979. In 1997 the program moved to the Ariane 5 generation of launch vehicles, and in 2003 a new corporate entity, Arianespace, was created to manage the project. Shareholders from 10 different European countries have stakes in the company, but over

50 percent of the shares are in French hands, and the company head-quarters is a short distance from Paris near the town of Evry. The launch base for Ariane is Kourou, in French Guyana, and Ariane-space's success can be gauged from the fact that in 2007 it controlled over 50 percent of the world market for the launch of satellites into geostationary orbit.

AGRICULTURE. The mainstay of the **economy** for most of France's history. In common with its European neighbors, French agriculture suffered the cyclical ravages of nature, war, and pestilence. But by the 19th century structural problems became apparent that prevented France from taking full advantage of the technological advances that were making farming manifestly more efficient and profitable in England. On a general level, a protectionist regime governing trade in agricultural products acted as a brake on innovation and invest-ment. But there were also cultural specificities that resulted in what economic historians at the time identified as the *parcellisation* of the land. One of the consequences of the legal system reshaped by **Napoléon Bonaparte** was the introduction of inheritance laws that gave an equal share of a parental legacy to each child, as opposed to, for example, a family estate going solely to the firstborn son. In the case of farmland, this led to a proliferation of ever-smaller farms as the generations succeeded each other. This created a rural archetype, which dominated until 1945, of small farms with low investment in machinery or fertilizers that struggled to be self-sufficient.

The accelerating **urbanization** of the postwar years made change inevitable, but there were also specific factors that altered the face of French farming: the creation of farming cooperatives, which pooled resources at the local level; incentives from national government to invest in more modern farming methods; and generous subsidies from the European Economic Community common agricultural pol-icy that, in some cases, encouraged farmers to turn their land to uses other than farming. Therefore, whereas 25 percent of the French la-bor force worked on the land in 1945, in 1989 this was down to 6.5 percent, while productivity levels in French agriculture had risen to match those of **Germany**. The advantage of having the richest land in the **European Union** is now a key factor in securing France's suc-cess as a trading nation. France is by far the most important agricultural producer in Europe, and the export of agricultural goods has been a major contributor to the country's run of balance of payments surpluses since 1993. *See also* WINE.

ALGERIA, RELATIONS WITH. This long association began with France's conquest of the territory in 1830. After 1848, Algeria's three *départements* were considered integral parts of France. For most of the years since that period Algeria has made a unique contribution to the way France has used its overseas territories and colonies in the construction of its image in relation to the rest of the world. For example, after the humiliating defeat of the **Franco-Prussian War**, emigration to Algeria was held up to the French population of the eastern provinces ceded to the Germans as part of the peace as a means of reconstructing not only their lives but also a sense of national greatness. During the **World War II** occupation of France by the Germans, both Marshal **Philippe Pétain** and General **Charles de Gaulle** used the existence of France's overseas territories, notably Algeria, as a means of preserving a semblance of French sovereignty, though the two men had diametrically opposed intentions.

One of the chief casualties of World War II for European colonial powers like France and **Great Britain** was the myth of European supremacy. The emergence of national campaigns for self-determination was irresistible, and the first dramatic manifestation of this in Algeria was the fighting between the Europeans and the native Algerians that followed the demonstration in the market town of Sétif on 8 May 1945. Over 100 Europeans and 1,000 Muslims were left dead as a result. The *pieds-noirs* (as the European population in Algeria was called) accounted for approximately 10 percent of a population of 10 million but owned one-third of the land fit for cultivation and enjoyed preferment when it came to competition with native Algerians for the better jobs. This inequality was underpinned by arrangements for the government of the territory that allowed for two electoral colleges, one European and one Muslim, with equal representation in the National Assembly, in spite of the disparity in the size of the two populations. Attempts at reform foundered on the insistence by the *pieds-noirs* that equal representation could only occur in the context of full integration in France, thereby putting the Muslims in an overall minority vis-à-vis the 50 million Europeans in France.

This insistence on the co-identity of Algeria and France struck at the fundamental purpose of the Muslim nationalists in Algeria, who united as the Front de Libération Nationale (FLN) and launched their war of independence against France on 1 November 1954. The war was expensive in human and material terms, costing the lives of 17,456 French soldiers and, according to French sources, approximately 141,000 FLN fighters. European civilian casualties, including those killed by the terrorist anti-independence Organisation de l'Armée Secrète (Secret Army Organization), exceeded 10,000, and losses among Muslim civilians exceeded 82,000 according to the French, or 1 million according to the Algerian government. Fearing a growing inclination on the part of the government in **Paris** to compromise with the FLN, on 13 May 1958 the *pieds-noirs* and the army seized power in Algiers and formed a Committee of Public Safety. Believing that their salvation lay in de Gaulle, on 28 September 1958 the European (as well as the Muslim) population voted overwhelmingly for the new republic he proposed. However, in what came to be seen by many *pieds-noirs* as a bitter betrayal, de Gaulle, once in power, recognized the inevitable and initiated contacts with the FLN that ultimately resulted in the peace and independence agreed at Evian on 18 March 1962 (*see* BEN BELLA, AHMED).

The destinies of France and Algeria remained closely bound after independence, with France retaining its position as Algeria's principal trading partner in Europe and the chief source of job opportunities for Algerian migrants. However, this relationship became increasingly problematic as the secular FLN establishment in Algeria began to lose credibility in the eyes of the electorate there at the end of the 1980s and lost ground to the fundamentalist Front Islamique du Salut (Islamic Salvation Front), or FIS. In 1992 Liamine Zeroual became president of Algeria after the military canceled elections that would almost certainly have brought the FIS to power. France's diplomatic support for Zeroual's regime and an annual aid package of six billion francs made it a target for terrorist supporters of the extreme fundamentalist Groupe Islamique Armé (Armed Islamic Group), or GIA. To force France to sever its support for Zeroual's regime, the GIA initiated a terrorist campaign in France with a bomb attack at the Paris Métro station of Saint-Michel on 25 July 1995 that resulted in seven deaths and 80 injuries.

Algeria's struggle with the colonial legacy left by the French is ongoing. Its 16 million French speakers represent the largest Francophone community outside France, but since 2002 the government has pursued a policy of Arabization and in 2006 President Abdelaziz Bouteflika ordered 42 private Francophone schools to deliver their curriculum in Arabic. The attempt by some center-right politicians and parties in France to argue that colonialism had offered benefits to the former territories of the French empire was met with hostility in Algeria, preventing the signing of a friendship treaty between the two countries that had been proposed by President **Jacques Chirac** in 2005.

During a state visit to Algeria in December 2007, President **Nicolas Sarkozy** made a major speech condemning the injustice of the colonial system, while maintaining that many of the French men and women who had worked within it nonetheless loved Algeria. The general reaction in the Algerian media was that Sarkozy's words represented progress but still fell short of a full apology for French crimes in that country. For his part, Sarkozy made no mention of reviving the friendship treaty proposed by his predecessor, Chirac. *See also* COLONIALISM; DECOLONIZATION.

ALLIANCE FRANCAISE. An association set up in 1883 to promote the French language abroad. Its board of directors was established in 1884 and included famous figures such as **Jules Verne** and **Ferdinand de Lesseps**. In 1886 the Alliance was accredited by the French state and its activities have been growing ever since. By 2003 the Alliance network numbered 1,072 associations in 130 countries.

ALTHUSSER, LOUIS (1918–1990). Philosopher and Marxist theorist of major importance in postwar France. He was born in **Algeria** and was a devout Catholic until the end of **World War II**, when, under the influence of his wife, Hélène, and other committed communists, he joined the **Parti Communiste Français (PCF)**. Althusser remained a loyal supporter of the PCF during some of its most difficult times, such as the aftermath of the Soviet clampdown on nascent democratic movements behind the iron curtain, in places like Hungary and Czechoslovakia. The height of Althusser's influence in French Marxist circles extended from the mid-1960s to the early

1970s, when his theoretical approach eclipsed the existential Marxism of figures like **Jean-Paul Sartre**. Reflecting the methodological assumptions of the **structuralist** movement, Althusser's major works, such as *Pour Marx* (1966) and *Lire le capital* (1965), express his preoccupation with the return to a critical rereading of key texts to analyze the way they are constructed, and his consequent refinement of the understanding of ideology was one of his most original contributions to Marxist theory.

Althusser's final break with the PCF in 1978 coincided with periods of severe depression and withdrawal into his role as a teacher at the Ecole Normale Supérieure. The French intellectual world was stunned when, in September 1980, Althusser turned himself in to the police after having strangled his wife. This amazement turned to anger in some quarters when he was acquitted of murder on grounds of insanity and committed to Saint Catherine's Hospital in Paris. He died on 22 October 1990 from heart failure.

AMIENS, TREATY OF. This treaty of 27 March 1802 brought peace between France and **Great Britain** for the first time since 1793. The key concessions by France included the promise to respect the integrity and independence of Naples, Portugal, and the Batavian Republic (Holland) in return for a British agreement to return conquered former possessions of France or its allies (except Ceylon and Trinidad) and to evacuate Elba and Malta. The fact that this treaty contained no commercial agreement was a major reason why it lasted barely a year.

ANCIEN REGIME. A term that, literally translated, means "old rule," referring to the monarchical system under which France was governed until 1789.

ANTICLERICALISM. A continuous strand in the political culture of modern France that has its origins in the **Enlightenment** perception of the institution of the Catholic Church as a pillar of reaction, inimical to the emancipation of the individual. After 1789, this antipathy toward the religious establishment became a manifest part of the revolutionary republican creed, according to which the victory of the Republic could not be fully secured until the influence of the church had been removed from the institutions of civil society. While the **Concordat of 1801** signaled a compromise in the conflict between Rome and the Republic over the destinies of France's citizens, tensions between church and state in France continued to flare up, particularly in moments of crisis, for the rest of the century. The triumph of anticlericalism was achieved during the early years of the **Third Republic** when the drive for secularization resulted in a series of laws that left the Catholic Church with little scope to deploy its influence in those areas of public life, notably **education**, where it had once been a major force. The republican government of **Jules Ferry** gained passage of legislation in 1881, 1882, and 1886 that laid the foundation for a universal system of primary education that was free, compulsorily secular, and specifically closed to the influence of religious orders. This fulfilled the republican ambition of turning the school into the primary influence for shaping the allegiance of France's citizens to the Republic through the inculcation of a new secular and civic faith. The irreversible nature of this change was underlined when the government of **Emile Combes** in 1902 closed down more than 3,000 Catholic educational establishments and when the government of **Aristide Briand** passed legislation in December 1905 formally and finally separating church and state in France. *See also* RELIGION.

ARC DE TRIOMPHE. This triumphal arch is situated in the center of the place de l'Etoile, **Paris**. The site had been proposed as a location for a monument since the beginning of the 19th century, but it was **Napoléon Bonaparte**, returning from his victory at Austerlitz, who, on 18 February 1806, ordered that a triumphal arch be built on the site to honor the exploits of the French armies. A design by Jean-François Chagrin was chosen, and construction began on 15 August 1806. However, the basic structure was not finished until 1831, and the main groups of sculpture took several more years to complete. The arch was formally inaugurated on 29 July 1836. Since then it has been the focal point of major ceremonial occasions, especially every year on **Bastille Day**.

ARCHITECTURE. As in so many other areas of civil society until the **French Revolution**, the Catholic Church played the dominant role in defining the styles that characterize French architecture. The Abbey of Cluny, founded in the 10th century but destroyed in the 19th, was a triumph of Romanesque architecture, and under the abbot Hugh of Semur it became the greatest church in Europe. In spite of the technical limitations that forced the architects to build with very thick walls, numerous arches and pillars, and small windows, records show that the abbey church alone was 120 meters long and 35 meters wide—the size of a large cathedral. This achievement, however, paled into insignificance beside the construction that constituted the great leap forward into Gothic architecture: Chartres. The old Romanesque church at Chartres was destroyed by fire in 1194, leaving only the west front and the towers. It was decided to build a new cathedral, larger than before, but following the foundations of the Romanesque original. This posed a major technical problem because of the width of the space the vaulting had to cover. The answer lay in the innovation known as flying buttresses—supports provided by shafts and clusters of columns that passed without interruption into the vault and the pointed arch, creating a sense of weightlessness and freeing space that could be surrounded by glass.

Gothic architecture flourished during the centuries that followed, but secular tastes also exerted an influence. The **Renaissance** in France saw the assimilation of Italian style in the construction of aristocratic residences, and as the **Bourbon dynasty** began to establish France as the greatest nation-state in Europe, the prerogatives of absolute monarchy found expression in the grandeur of the architecture commissioned by the king, as in the magnificent symmetry of the palace at Versailles. The notion of state-funded architecture reflecting the grandeur of the regime, and by extension of France, is well reflected in the neoclassical solidity of the **Empire style**, reflecting the dynastic aspirations of **Napoléon Bonaparte** and his nephew, **Louis-Napoléon Bonaparte**. As the 19th century progressed, the simple neoclassical columns became adorned, even occluded, by ornate confections such as the extraordinary decorative flourishes evident in a building like the Palais Garnier, place de l'Opéra in **Paris**. But by this time, industrial advances in metallurgy and its applications had opened vast possibilities for innovation in architectural design.

In spite of the fact, however, that French engineers were instrumental in developing the great architectural innovation of the 20th century, the skyscraper, the predominance of North America left relatively little room for the emergence of major French figures or achievements in this field. Two major exceptions were Charles Edouard Jeanneret Le Corbusier (1887–1965) and Auguste Perret (1874–1954). Perret was given the task of reconstructing Le Havre in 1947, and his willingness to experiment with reinforced concrete earned him a reputation as one of the most important architects of his generation in France. Le Corbusier's reputation as one of the most influential figures in world architecture in the 20th century is secure, and his work in France is among his most strikingly innovative. His pilgrimage Chapel of Ronchamp (1950–1954) displays the sculptural quality Le Corbusier gave to concrete. The body of the building is of molded white concrete topped with a contrasting dark concrete roof that nonetheless seems to hover over it. Setting a now familiar fashion, the concrete retains all the roughly patterned imperfections left by the timber shuttering in which it was encased. An irregular disposition of windows of different shapes and sizes illuminates the interior with tunnels of light that are peculiarly apt given the spiritual purpose of the building. Another example of the originality Le Corbusier brought to his work with concrete can be found at the monastery of La Tourette at Evreux (1957–1960), where a block of undressed concrete is arranged in a U shape around a central courtyard. Elements of Le Corbusier's earlier ideas concerning urban dwelling in "vertical cities" are also reflected in the complexes of *unité d'habitation* that he designed, like the one in **Marseille** (1947–1952), a self-contained block with restaurants, shops, gymnasium, rooftop nursery, and ingenious apartments with double-height living rooms whose 15-foot windows offer a view of either the mountains or the **Mediterranean**.

For the last third of the 20th century in France, the most famous architectural achievements have been predominantly by foreigners. The cultural aspirations of the 1970s were summed up in the Georges Pompidou Center of Art and Culture (1971–1977), popularly known as Beaubourg because of its location. The transparent glass, plastic, and steel six-level construction designed by the Italian Renzo Piano (1937–) and the Englishman Richard Rogers (1933–) quickly established itself as a much-visited Parisian landmark, especially for the way its functions are color coded and displayed, with pipes, ducts, and corridors fully exposed. However, the 1970s was a quiet period compared to the vast architectural program that characterized the *grands projets* that have become the lasting legacy of the presidency of **François Mitterrand**, whose two terms began in 1981 and ended in 1995.

Following his election, Mitterrand announced projects worth $3 billion, the first of which was the renovation of the Louvre. The Chinese-born American architect I. M. Pei (1917–) presented the winning submission, in what amounted to a daring attempt to combine innovation with tradition. As a result, a 21-meter-high glass pyramid, 32 meters wide at the base and employing 105 tons of glass, now forms the new entrance to the museum, complemented by a new plaza facing the Tuileries gardens. Pei's design also added over 200,000 square meters of exhibition space below ground, under the Cour Napoléon. Other notable architectural projects commissioned by Mitterrand include the conversion of the old railway station on the Left Bank into the Musée d'Orsay, by Gae Aulenti; the new opera house at the **Bastille**, by the Canadian Carlos Ott; the concrete and cube-shaped Grande arche in the business district of La Défense, which stands in perfect alignment with the original **Arc de Triomphe**; and the Institut du Monde Arabe, by arguably the most distinguished living French architect, Jean Nouvel. The last great architectural project of this era, unfinished by the time Mitterrand left office, was the new home for the Bibliothèque Nationale at Tolbiac in Paris, which attracted considerable controversy due to the intention to house the national library's holdings in a series of glass towers, architecturally striking to some but, in the view of others, detrimental to the preservation of books.

ARMED FORCES. For most of their history French armed forces were raised by local lords to serve their monarch and were frequently supplemented by foreign mercenaries paid out of the king's coffers. It was after the **French Revolution** that the armed forces became a citizen army, composed of free men taking up their responsibility to defend the Republic. The defining moment in this transition came at the battle of **Valmy** in 1792, when the populace of **Paris** took up arms and defeated the invading Austrian army to the cries of *"Vive la Nation!"* This attachment to a people's army helps explain why

France was among the last of the significant powers with a global profile to give up national military service (in 2001), four decades after **Great Britain**, and make its armed forces fully professionalized. In 2007 French land forces numbered 138,000; the navy comprised 54,600 service personnel and 146 vessels; and the air force deployed 65,000 personnel across 37 bases in metropolitan France and nine bases overseas. *See also* GRANDE ARMEE.

ART. The practice of art and access to it, as with **literature**, was limited in medieval France and revolved around theological pursuits, such as the decoration of manuscripts and the depiction of sacred themes. The great breakthrough came with the **Renaissance** and the liberating ideas that spread north from the courts of the Italian city-states, notably the belief in the artist as an inspired creator. By the 18th century, **Paris** had established itself as a center for art, in no small measure because of the emergence of the *salon*, those cultural gatherings presided over by gifted hostesses like Madame du Deffand, where painters could hope to find material as well as moral encouragement. It was the age of Watteau and Chardin, and it endured until the **French Revolution**, when, on the one hand, painters like **David** resorted to the familiar constraints of classic conventions to depict his master, **Napoléon Bonaparte**, and the themes he admired, and, on the other hand, nascent talents like **Théodore Géricault** suggested that an irresistible undermining of artistic dogma was already under way at the beginning of the 19th century.

While the restoration of the monarchy under **Louis XVIII** suggested a return to tried and tested values, the decades that followed illustrated the waves of intellectual ferment that swept across all creative disciplines, including the arts and letters. **Romanticism** had its repercussions on painting, and this is seen in the protest and compassion found in the best work of **Eugène Delacroix**. But as the century progressed, the pursuit of the sublime gave way to artistic experiments characterized by the speed of perception and execution shaped by the modern age. And as if to bear witness to the accelerating epoch in which they emerged, increasingly brief artistic movements like **impressionism, symbolism, cubism, fauvism,** and **surrealism,** among others, punctuate the history of art in France.

France was the undisputed center of the artistic world until **World War II**, exercising a major influence on the development of movements elsewhere, such as German expressionism, Russian constructivism, and Italian futurism. This dominance, however, ended after 1945 with the emergence of newer and more vigorous artistic centers in places like the United States, South America, and Japan. Experimental art in particular became international and unfettered by national or cultural traditions. Arguably the most important painter to emerge in France after the war was the prolific Jean Dubuffet (1901–1985), who held his first one-man show in 1944 in Paris at the relatively late age of 43. He experimented with materials such as sand, glass, and tar to create a "pigment" shaped in a manner resembling human forms in works called *Pâtes*. Rejecting traditional notions of perspective, he communicated depth through a process of stratification, with the lowest level nearest the viewer. During the mid-1960s he produced a series of free-flowing abstract shapes covering diverse surfaces, one as long as eight meters. Another gifted artist to emerge in the postwar years but whose life was cut tragically short by suicide was Nicolas de Staël (1914–1955). His most characteristic work expresses an unusual sense of depth and sensitivity to the juxtaposition of color resulting from his use of a palette knife for painting with masses of pigment. Also a product of the Paris school, Yves Klein (1928–1962) experimented with almost every sort of material and with none at all, being the first artist to exhibit the bare walls of an art gallery as the product of his own creativity. He is credited with the invention of body art, from the time he covered his models in blue pigment and asked them to leave imprints of their bodies by rolling on the canvas. His "fire paintings," created by the application of a naked flame to painted asbestos, remain the most familiar part of his legacy.

The development of modern figurative sculpture was continued in France by Germaine Richier (1904–1959), whose more famous works include a large bronze piece called *Don Quixote of the Forest* and the remarkable *Horse with Six Heads* (1953), a bronze casting of almost transparent thinness whose ripped surface looks as if it has been torn at by birds of prey. César Baldaccini (1921–1998) also produced figurative studies in bronze, such as his *Nude*, represented by a lower torso with a pair of legs. In the 1960s he experimented with crushed and compacted automobiles to produce dense blocks of varying colors. The opposite of density can be found in the 1960s experimentation of Daniel Buren with nothing more substantial than pieces of striped cloth, exhibited conventionally indoors, outdoors on billboards, and paraded on boards carried by a sandwich man. French art and sculpture in the last third of the 20th century defy not only the conventions imposed by tradition but also the terms that categorize the modern, displaying instead the fugitive significance and fragmentation associated with **postmodernism**. *See also* EMPIRE STYLE.

ASTERIX THE GAUL. Most famous cartoon character in postwar France, first created for the weekly magazine *Pilote* by René Goscinny and Albert Uderzo in 1951. The tales relate the exploits of Astérix and his friends in their efforts to defeat the imperial ambitions of the invading Romans. They are aided in this endeavor by the superhuman strength gained from the magic potion prepared by their friend, the wise druid Panoramix. Anachronisms and puns provide the obvious humor, such as the fact that all names end in -ix, as in Idéfix and Analgésix. But the creators also make clever use of satire to underline the less heroic aspects of life in contemporary France, such as xenophobia and snobbery. The commercial success of this creation is evident in the building of an Astérix theme park, and the fact that 31 adventures of Astérix have been translated into 80 languages and sold hundreds of millions of copies worldwide. The third of Astérix's adventures to come to the big screen was the most expensive film ever produced in France and topped the box office in France and many countries of Europe when it was released in January 2008.

AURIOL, VINCENT (1884–1966). Veteran socialist parliamentarian of the **Third Republic**, who distinguished himself as the first president of the **Fourth Republic**. He was born into a family of farmers in Revel (Haut-Garonne) and grew up to become a lawyer in **Toulouse**. He joined the socialist party, **Section Française de l'Internationale Ouvrière**, in 1905 after being involved in left-wing politics as a student, and in 1909 he was the founding editor of *Le Midi Socialiste*. His career as a deputy started with his election in 1914 to represent his home district of Muret, which he did until the fall of the Republic in 1940. In the meantime he held a number of ministerial posts, including that of minister of finance in the **Popular Front** cabinet of 1936. Auriol was one of the minority of deputies who voted against the granting of executive power to **Philippe Pétain** under the **Vichy regime**. Briefly imprisoned by the regime and then placed under house arrest, he finally escaped France to join **Charles de Gaulle** in London in October 1943.

Auriol's experience, reputation for competence, and integrity made him an easy winner in the competition to be the first president of the Fourth Republic. Auriol believed that power should reside on the floor of the National Assembly, but at the same time he took more than a ceremonial part in the affairs of state. The widespread respect he enjoyed enabled him to take an active part in the resolution of the 12 ministerial crises he had to deal with during his seven-year term. He was not reluctant to give advice to premiers, believing he was responsible for making parliament accountable to the people. Auriol traveled widely and spoke vigorously against Soviet expansionism and in favor of the **North Atlantic Treaty Organization**. Auriol took pride in his role as president of the **French Union**, and although a supporter of an enlightened attitude to **colonialism** he was nonetheless reluctant to countenance the breakup of France's overseas empire. He did not seek reelection in 1953, and by the end of the decade he expressed serious reservations about the potentially authoritarian nature of the new **Fifth Republic**, under de Gaulle. Auriol was a humanist and a socialist in the tradition established by **Jean Jaurès** and is regarded as having served his country well, especially during the difficult days of the Fourth Republic.

AVIGNON. One of the most attractive towns of France, largely owing to its manifest origins as a walled city in the 14th century. Once the seat of the papacy and the site of the famous Palais des Papes, which figures among its chief tourist attractions, Avignon has remained a city of modest proportions with a population of approximately 88,000. Its annual summer arts festival soon acquired a worldwide reputation after it was launched in 1947 by **Jean Vilar**.

– B –

BABEUF, FRANCOIS-NOEL (LATER GRACCHUS) (1760–1797). Leader of the communist movement for equality during the first decade of the **French Revolution**. Born into an extremely poor family in Saint-Quentin, Picardy, Babeuf managed to educate himself and by the age of 21 had become an expert in feudal law, especially the injustice inflicted on peasants through the survival of feudal dues. However, Babeuf's unceasing agitation for change and his call for the abolition of private property, to be replaced by a board of redistribution that would share out all the products of human labor, made him too radical even for the revolutionary authorities after 1789. He was imprisoned more than once and was tried for the last time in February 1797 for leading a conspiracy to overthrow the **Directory** to pave the way for the establishment of a society of perfect equality. He was found guilty and executed on 28 May 1797.

BALLADUR, EDOUARD (1929–). Technocrat and former prime minister. He was born the son of a French banker in Turkey and followed the classic route to high office in French administration. After studying law at Aix-en-Provence and undergoing the almost obligatory period of study at the Ecole Nationale d'Administration (1952–1957), Balladur progressed to an attachment to the cabinet of **Georges Pompidou** while he was prime minister. Balladur's proven competence in a number of senior administrative positions explains why, after his election as a deputy for **Paris** in 1986, he was given the major ministerial portfolio with responsibility for finance and **privatization**. His accession to the post of prime minister at the head of a center-right majority in parliament, after the collapse of the Socialist vote in the legislative election of 1993, was a predictable one, and his reputation for sound management served him well. But his decision to stand as a candidate in the presidential election of 1995 was regarded by many as ill judged, especially in view of the tacit undertakings he had previously made not to impede the path of the obvious **Gaullist** candidate, **Jacques Chirac**.

Predictably, the qualities that served Balladur as a prime minister were inadequate for the challenges of presidential politics. Competence was no substitute for charisma in the highly personalized game of presidential campaigning. By mid-February 1995 it was clear that the much more engaging and dynamic Chirac was the man most likely to rally the voters of the center-right. This was confirmed in the first round of voting in March. Chirac went on to challenge successfully for the supreme prize in French politics in the second round a fortnight later, while Balladur was forced to quit the stage. He continued his work as a parliamentarian, however, and in 2002 he was elected by his colleagues to head the National Assembly's foreign relations committee.

BALZAC, HONORE DE (1799–1850). A prodigiously productive French novelist who was a key figure in establishing the novel as a major literary genre. He was born in Tours of a mother who was 32 years younger than his father and who showed little affection for her son. In 1819 Balzac announced to his family that he was abandoning his law studies in favor of literature. But a failed publishing venture during the following decade and a tendency for ill-informed financial speculation meant that he had to spend the rest of his life writing at a dizzying rate simply to keep up with the demands of his creditors. Consequently, his nocturnal work routine consisted of 12-to-14-hour writing stretches sustained by black coffee, with predictable consequences for his health.

By 1834 Balzac had decided to give an overall shape to his novels, which eventually came under the title *La comédie humaine*. Most of the novels are studies of the social manners of the time. Some are notable for their melodrama and the use of the grotesque or the mystical, but in his acutely analytical portrayal of issues like the sordid consequences of the pursuit of material gain, Balzac displayed a cogent form of **realism**. Coverage of the broad social canvas Balzac aspired to depict was well served by the introduction of reappearing characters, which occurred first in 1834–1835 in *Le Père Goriot*. While Balzac did not complete the 150 novels he envisaged for *La comédie humaine*, he nonetheless wrote some 90 novels and created over 2,000 characters.

Balzac's ambition to resolve his financial problems by marrying a rich widow was finally achieved in 1850 by the union with Eveline Hanska, the Polish ex-wife of a Russian nobleman. But his lifestyle had exacted a high price physically, and he died just five months later. *See also* LITERATURE.

BANKING. France's transition to a service-based economy is illustrated by the fact that in 2007 the banking sector employed 500,000 salaried staff and was consequently the third largest employer in the private sector. The biggest change to the banking system over the last two decades has been **privatization**. The withdrawal of the French state from this sector of the economy has forced it to modernize, rationalize, and adapt to the global market. Whereas in 1984 there were 1,556 banking businesses in France, by 2007 this was down to 500. The 1990s and the beginning of the following decade were marked by major mergers, such as Crédit du Nord being taken over by Société Générale in 1997, Banque Nationale de Paris merging with Banque Paribas in 1999, and Crédit Lyonnais being bought by Crédit Agricole in 2003. There was also a first in 2000 when the British banking group HSBC was able to take over the French bank CCF with no expression of anxiety from either the industry in France or the French government. The reality now is that 90 percent of the legislation governing the banking sector in France is European, and French banks are increasingly dependent on the European market. Over two-thirds of French banking businesses have set up operations in fellow **European Union** member countries and over two-thirds of the foreign banks in France are European. The pressure to conform to European norms will eventually lead to the disappearance of some typically French practices in retail banking, such as the free processing of checks.

BARDOT, BRIGITTE (1934–). Originally a teenage model, Bardot was cast in a series of forgettable roles until Roger Vadim found the perfect vehicle for her vibrant but childishly innocent sensuality in the film that brought her worldwide stardom and that was released in the United States as *And God Created Woman* (1957). Sun, sea, sand, and the clever projection of Bardot's pouting beauty in Cinemascope and Eastmancolor transformed her into an iconic "sex kitten." Vadim married her and rather cuttingly observed that she could play any part as long as it was herself, but her technical limitations as an actress did not prevent her from becoming the 1960s archetype of liberated feminine sexuality combined with an infantile disregard for the inhibitions of the adult world. For **Simone de Beauvoir**, she was the epitome of the "Lolita syndrome," which, by definition, would deprive her career of the longevity or range of a contemporary like **Catherine Deneuve**. While she worked with some of the most innovative and challenging directors in the industry, such as **Jean-Luc Godard**, in *Le Mépris* (1963) and *Masculin-féminin* (1966), few of Bardot's movies retain the enduring quality of a talent subtle or enigmatic enough to engross generations of film enthusiasts. She ceased making movies in the mid-1970s and in 1986 set up the *Fondation Brigitte Bardot* in Saint-Tropez to care for animals. When she appears in the media it is usually as a result of her campaigns, sometimes exaggerated, in defense of helpless animals. *See also* CINEMA; WOMEN.

BARRE, RAYMOND (1924–2007). Former prime minister of France. He was born on the Indian Ocean island of Réunion but came to metropolitan France to be educated. There he distinguished himself as an extremely able scholar, first at the Lycée Leconte-de-Lisle and then at the Institut d'Études Politiques. He began his career in the academic profession at the University of Caen (1950) and in 1955 established his reputation by writing what came to be a standard reference book on political economy. Barre's ministerial breakthrough came in January 1976 when he was given the portfolio for trade and commerce in the cabinet of **Jacques Chirac**, and he stepped into the role of prime minister in August of the same year, after Chirac was sacked by President **Valéry Giscard d'Estaing**.

Barre's economic rigor, particularly the austerity measures contained in the *Plan Barre*, aimed at restoring France's finances after the ravages of the oil crises of the 1970s, made him an unpopular prime minister. The triumph of **François Mitterrand** in the presidential elections of 1981 prompted Barre's resignation and return to academic life. Barre gathered an influential coterie of centrist supporters around him in the mid-1980s and appeared to be a strong challenger to Mitterrand prior to the presidential election campaign of 1988. But his poor showing confirmed the view of many commentators that although he enjoyed the respect of his peers for his intellect and integrity, Barre's reluctance to tie his fortunes too closely to that of one of the mainstream political formations cost him dearly. However, Barre's enduring appetite for public life and the esteem in which he was held by his colleagues and the electorate were proved by his election to the post of mayor of **Lyon** in October 1995, at the age of 71, in which he served until 2001.

BARTHES, ROLAND (1915–1980). Structuralist, semiologist, and critic, famous for his idiosyncratic and trenchant analyses of French culture. Barthes was born into a Protestant, middle-class family in Cherbourg but moved to **Paris** with his mother at the age of nine after the early death of his father. His education and early career as a teacher were punctuated by bouts of tuberculosis, and he did not obtain a secure teaching post until 1962, at the Ecole Pratique des Hautes Etudes. However, he had begun challenging the traditional assumptions of literary criticism as early as 1947 with articles published in *Combat* based on his reading of **Albert Camus**. These articles developed into *Le degré zéro de l'écriture* (1953), followed by the iconoclastic critique of mass culture in *Mythologies* (1957) and the structuralist science of **literature** found in *Critique et vérité* (1966) and *S/Z* (1970).

Barthes's criticism displaces the author from the central role traditionally ascribed to him and affords an active role to the reader, thereby implying the now familiar "death" of the author. But Barthes's disinclination to allow himself to become a fixed point of reference was evident in the mocking self-deprecation with which he wrote about himself, as in *Roland Barthes par Roland Barthes* (1975). His intellectual consecration came with a chair in literary semiology at the Collège de France in 1976. It was while crossing the road in front of the Collège de France in February 1980 that he was struck by a bus. He died four weeks later. *See also* STRUCTURALISM.

BASQUE COUNTRY. *See* SEPARATISM.

THE BASTILLE. Fortress-prison whose seizure by the crowd in **Paris** on 14 July 1789 marked the beginning of the **French Revolution**. The fortress was built in 1370 to defend one of the entrances to Paris, and in the 18th century it was intended for use in suppressing possible uprisings by the Parisians. Under **Louis XIV**, it acquired the additional role of state prison, a place where the king could incarcerate subjects without trial and for indefinite periods, and thus it became the symbol of royal despotism. The Bastille's seizure was the first great *journée* of the Revolution and epitomized the collapse of absolute monarchy, and in 1790 the anniversary date of 14 July was chosen as the national day. This was abolished under the monarchical restorations, but 14 July became the national day once more in 1880. The fortress no longer exists, but a column marks the spot where it stood, at the place de la Bastille.

BAUDELAIRE, CHARLES (1821–1867). Poet and **art** critic. He was born in **Paris** to a father aged 62 and a mother aged 28. His father died in 1826, and the subsequent remarriage of his mother contributed to the development of a problematical relationship between mother and child. The fact of possessing a fortune of 75,000 francs turned Baudelaire the young adult into a spendthrift and a dandy. But when this fortune was put in trust, he began a long acquaintanceship with debt.

After a brief flirtation with radical republicanism, Baudelaire began his career as an art critic in the mid-1840s and became a staunch defender of the work of a number of artists whose painting was not fully appreciated, notably **Eugène Delacroix**. Baudelaire's ability to recognize unappreciated talent also operated in the literary field and attracted him to the morbid escapism of Edgar Allen Poe (1809–1849). In 1854 and 1855 Baudelaire translated 35 of Poe's stories into French, and some of the resulting versions are regarded by certain critics as superior to the originals. Baudelaire's own poetic output, however, was painfully slow. In 1848 he published *Les limbes*, but his first book of poetry, *Les fleurs du mal*, did not appear until 1857. The poems reflected his loves, most memorably that for the mulatto actress Jeanne Duval, and his exploration of forbidden appetites and subliminal drives that shocked the conservative society of his day. Baudelaire was fined for producing a work that was an offense to public morals.

Baudelaire's brilliant observations on art in the years that followed secured his reputation as a critic, but he was frustrated by the lack of recognition for his poetry. His personal life began to disintegrate when Jeanne Duval left him in 1861. Because of poverty and the ravages of syphilis, his health deteriorated as well. Baudelaire wrote his last serious poems in 1863. Three years later he collapsed and lingered for 18 months in a state of speechless semiparalysis before dying on 31 August 1867. While only a limited number of his contemporaries, such as **Victor Hugo**, appreciated his talent, his reputation was secured posthumously by successive generations who hailed him as a seminal influence on modern poetry and art criticism. *See also* LITERATURE.

BAUDRILLARD, JEAN. *See* POSTMODERNISM.

BAYROU, FRANCOIS (1951–). Centrist political leader. He was born into a farming family in a small town in the southwest of the country. His studies in Greek and Latin had barely begun at Bordeaux University when he married, aged 20, the woman who became his lifelong partner and bore his six children. He entered parliament in 1986 on a centrist **Union pour la Démocratie Française (UDF)** ticket and gained his first ministerial post with the portfolio for **education** in the **Edouard Balladur** government in 1993. It was a painful lesson for Bayrou. When he tried to introduce a reform that would give local authorities the possibility of providing subsidies more easily for church schools, those accusing him of threatening the secular vocation of the French education system mobilized, and he was forced to withdraw the reform. But Bayrou was too big a talent to ignore, and he was offered an expanded portfolio for education in the following government under **Alain Juppé**.

In terms of party politics, Bayrou spent the 1990s trying to fashion the disparate elements that constituted the political center in France into a cohesive political force and in 1998 was elected head of the UDF. He stood as a candidate in the presidential election of 2002 and was placed fourth at the end of the first round with a 6.84 percent share of the vote, which was somewhat higher than the pundits predicted. But it was in the presidential election of 2007 that he made his breakthrough as a potential leader of the country. Seeing the widespread disillusionment with the way politics was practiced in France, Bayrou called for a "civic revolution" that allowed civil society to exert a genuine influence on the conduct of politics. When in March 2007, to coincide with his campaign for the presidency, Bayrou released a book entitled *Projet d'espoir* that outlined his vision for France, it sold 370,000 copies in two months. He impressed socialists like **Michel Rocard** and **Bernard Kouchner** sufficiently for them to call for an alliance between the Socialists, Bayrou's UDF, and the Greens to defeat the center-right candidate **Nicolas Sarkozy**. In the end, the **Parti Socialiste** hierarchy rejected an overt alliance with the UDF, but the strength of Bayrou's campaign was such that he came in a very creditable third at the end of the first round with 18.57 percent of the vote.

Bayrou's ambition for his party was to give it a pivotal role in the center of the political action, making it a force with which the left or right would have to negotiate if they wanted to exercise power. Unfortunately for Bayrou, in the legislative elections of July 2007 he overplayed the card of independence vis-à-vis the vehicle for the **Gaullist party**, the Union pour un Mouvement Populaire (Union for a Popular Movement/UMP) and the majority of UDF deputies decided to maintain their de facto electoral alliance with the UMP. Those UDF deputies who remained loyal to Bayrou's vision rallied to him under the banner of Mouvement Démocrate (MoDem), but they emerged from the elections with only three seats in the new National Assembly. But Bayrou remained undeterred and on 2 December 2007 MoDem held its first and founding congress in the Paris suburb of Villepinte and formally elected Bayrou its leader. *See also* POLITICAL PARTIES.

BEAUVOIR, SIMONE DE (1908–1986). Author and highly influential feminist. She was born into a conservative, Catholic bourgeois family in **Paris**. Her academic brilliance was confirmed when she was placed second behind **Jean-Paul Sartre** in the competition for the *agrégation*. She had met Sartre at the Ecole Normale Supérieure and remained his companion until his death in 1980.

After a series of teaching appointments in secondary education from 1931 to 1943, she decided to devote herself entirely to her writing career and in 1943 produced *L'Invitée*, a novel based on Sartre and his circle. In 1945 she joined Sartre in editing the monthly journal *Les temps modernes* and subsequently published works of a philosophical nature whose optimistic humanism contrasted with Sartre's own, bleaker picture of the human condition. But it was *Le deuxième sexe* (1949) that brought her an international following. In this well-documented and powerfully argued essay she contends that the second-class status of women is sustained by pervasive sexual discrimination that has its roots in social and cultural factors that have operated since the dawn of time and is systematically reinforced in contemporary society and education. The essay rapidly established itself as a seminal text for feminists across the Atlantic as well as in France. De Beauvoir demonstrated the courage of her convictions when she signed the "Manifesto of the 343" in France, a public admission by 343 **women** that they had had illegal abortions and a proclamation of their belief that women should have the right to make that choice legally. De Beauvoir's action made her an inspirational figure to a new generation of French feminists, and in 1974 she became president of the League for Women's Rights.

Her substantial body of work also includes autobiographical texts (*Mémoires d'une jeune fille rangée*, 1958) and novels (*Les Mandarins*, 1954) that illustrate her reaction to her conservative upbringing and her intellectual coming of age. When she died, she was judged by many to be the last of that great generation of French writers that had included **Albert Camus** and Sartre. And even her critics admitted that in *Le deuxième sexe* she had produced one of the most influential works of the 20th century. *See also* LITERATURE.

BELLE EPOQUE. An expression rich in nostalgic overtones that gained currency after **World War I**. It refers to the period, roughly the years 1890 to 1914, that was perceived as a high point of stability, prosperity, and serenity in the lives of the French people, especially the middle class. In intellectual terms it was a time of optimism that science was a source of ever-expanding opportunities for the improvement of the human condition. In social terms, as the art and photography of the time illustrate, it was an era marked by the emergence of leisure pursuits generated by the new prosperity and in particular the beginnings of consumerism, exemplified by the building of the large department stores. In view of the material hardships that followed **World War I** and the mass destruction caused by warfare waged with all the means of modern technology, it is not surprising that the loss of confidence in the future and the nostalgia for the *belle époque* tended to overlook the fact that the benefits of the period were fully available only to a minority of the French people.

BEN BELLA, AHMED (1918–). Leading spirit of the Algerian Revolution and first president of the Algerian Republic. Ben Bella served with distinction in the Free French troops of **World War II** and was decorated for his valor. After the war he was among the group of members of the nationalist Mouvement du Triomphe des Libertés Démocratiques who in 1947 founded the secret Organisation Spéciale, committed to evicting the French from **Algeria**. The group was dismantled by the French police and Ben Bella was arrested, but he escaped in 1952 and made his way to Cairo. In 1954 he became one of the nine founding members of the Front de Libération Nationale (FLN), which began the insurrection against France on 1 November. Ben Bella represented the FLN in Cairo and led the negotiations for support from the government of Gamal Abdel Nasser. In an infamous incident in 1956, a Moroccan plane carrying Ben Bella was hijacked by its French flight crew, as a result of which Ben Bella found himself imprisoned in France. However, when independence was granted to Algeria in 1962, Ben Bella became the republic's first president. He was deposed in a military coup three years later led by his former ally Houari Boumedienne and was not released from detention until 1980, after which he went into exile. While in exile he created the Mouvement pour la Démocratie en Algérie. He returned definitively to Algeria in 1990.

BEREGOVOY, PIERRE (1925–1993). Socialist prime minister of France. Born into a working-class milieu in Déville-les-Rouen (Seine-Maritime), Bérégovoy first started to earn his living at 16 as a machine operator. He became involved in socialist youth organizations at a very young age and initiated his close association with **François Mitterrand** in 1971, when Mitterrand became the new first secretary of the **Parti Socialiste**. Bérégovoy held a number of ministerial portfolios during the years of the Mitterrand presidency and began to shape the public perception of him as a solid and competent minister when he was given the finance and economics portfolio in July 1984. During his tenure he gained the confidence of the financial community and oversaw the launch of a financial futures market, the Marché à Terme International de France.

Following the resignation of France's first woman prime minister, **Edith Cresson**, after an unhappy period in office, President Mitterrand appointed Bérégovoy prime minister on 2 April 1992 in the hope that his reputation for sound common sense and solid virtues would help steady the fortunes of the Socialist administration. These hopes were dashed by the scandal that engulfed Bérégovoy and his party less than a year later. In February 1993 the satirical newspaper *Le Canard Enchaîné* broke a story about the interest-free loan Bérégovoy had accepted from Roger-Patrice Pelat, a businessman of dubious reputation, to buy an apartment in **Paris**. The press as a whole picked up on the story and played heavily on the irony of the fact that Bérégovoy had made the drive against corruption one of the key concerns of his government. In the accounts subsequently published by his colleagues, Bérégovoy interpreted the press reports as part of a campaign to destroy him personally. The collapse of support for the Socialists in the legislative elections of March 1993 deepened his sense of persecution, depression, and guilt at what he saw as his responsibility for the defeat of the Socialists. Impervious to the attempts of family and friends to revive his morale, Bérégovoy shot himself and died on 1 May 1993 after ostensibly setting off for a stroll along a country path close to Nevers. *See also* POLITICAL PARTIES.

BIDAULT, GEORGES (1899–1983). Resistance leader and Christian Democratic politician. He succeeded **Jean Moulin** as head of the Resistance and was there to greet **Charles de Gaulle** on his triumphal return to **Paris** on 25 August 1944. This earned him the foreign affairs portfolio in the provisional government, a post he held for five years under the **Fourth Republic**. Bidault was premier twice (July–December 1946 and October 1949–June 1950) and was one of the leaders of the **Mouvement Républicain Populaire**, France's only real Christian Democratic party. As foreign minister he played a major part in coordinating the European response to the **Marshall Plan** for the reconstruction of Europe. As the 1940s progressed, Bidault became increasingly concerned by what he perceived as the threat of Soviet communism and played a leading role in promoting the defense links that led to the formation of the **North Atlantic Treaty Organization**. It was during Bidault's premiership that Jean Monnet proposed the creation of the Coal and Steel Pool, to which France, **Germany**, Italy, and the Benelux countries agreed on 18 April 1951. This was the precursor of the **European Economic Community**.

Bidault was less farsighted with regard to **decolonization**, fearing that this process would diminish France's standing in the world. He opposed French withdrawal from Indochina until it became inevitable, and his opposition to French withdrawal from **Algeria** went so far as to lead him to support the attempted putsch by the generals there and the resistance of the terrorist Organisation de l'Armée Secrète (Secret Army Organization) to independence for that country. This resulted in the lifting of his parliamentary immunity in 1962 and forced him to seek refuge in Spain. He returned to France following an amnesty given by de Gaulle in the aftermath of the **student rebellion** of May 1968.

BINOCHE, JULIETTE (1964–). Leading French actress of her generation. Born to an actress mother and a sculptor father, Binoche was destined to perform and made her film debut at the age of 22 in *Mauvais sang* (1986), directed by Leo Carax. She found an appreciative and worldwide audience in the following year when she had a major role in the film version of Milan Kundera's famous novel *The Unbearable Lightness of Being*. Her fragile beauty underlined the intensity of her performances and established her reputation as an international star in films like *Damage* (1992), the story of a doomed, adulterous affair that neither protagonist has the courage to quit. Her most famous role came in the multi-award-winning *The English Patient* (1997), for which she won the Oscar as best supporting actress, a distinction that no French actress had enjoyed since Simone Signoret 37 years earlier. Faithful to her artistic instincts, she turned down the offer to star in Steven Spielberg's *Jurassic Park* in favor of a part in the *Three Colors* series of films by the Polish auteur Krysztof Kieslowski. Independent, eclectic in her choice of roles and indifferent to the trappings of stardom, by 2007 she had 49 films to her credit and had worked with some of the best directors in Europe, the **United States**, and Asia. She enjoys the highest international profile of the current crop of France's leading actresses. *See also* CINEMA.

BLACK DEATH. The popular name given to the bubonic plague, a disease carried by rats. It arrived overland via the silk routes from Asia and reached **Marseille** by sea in 1348, through the rats that infested the holds of Italian trading ships. There were recurrent outbreaks of plague in France until around 1420, and their effects were devastating; the population density of France dropped 70 percent between 1315 and 1450.

BLANC, LOUIS (1811–1882). Influential **socialist** theorist, politician, journalist, and historian. He was born into a royalist family, and his mother's connections with the **Bourbons** after the restoration enabled him and his brother to have an excellent classical education. The end of the Bourbon restoration brought hard times for Blanc and made him turn to journalism for a living. Blanc abandoned the royalism of his youth in the 1830s and founded a periodical entitled *Revue du Progrès*, which published his most famous work, *Organisation du travail* (1839). Blanc's socialist theory centered on the creation of a democratic state similar to the **First Republic** of 1793–1794, through the mobilization of the workers in alliance with middle-class sympathizers. This new state would assume the role of financing social workshops (ateliers) owned collectively by the workers, and what Blanc considered the great evil of competition would be eliminated through cooperation within and between workshops. Thus a new era of fraternity would be ushered in that would allow every worker to contribute according to his strengths and consume according to his needs.

The **Revolution of 1848** propelled Blanc into the new provisional government as minister without portfolio, but lack of support undermined his ability to tackle the labor problems he identified, and the reaction to the heady aspirations of February 1848 forced him into exile in England. The 22 years he spent there were devoted to journalism and working on his voluminous *History of the French Revolution*. He returned to France after the fall of the **Second Empire** in 1870 and became one of the founding figures of the **Third Republic**, serving for 12 years as a deputy. Blanc was a model of commitment to democratic socialism and helped shape the ideas of a new generation of left-wing politicians after his return from exile.

BLANQUI, AUGUSTE (1805–1881). Legendary figure of the French left. A brilliant law student, he abandoned his academic pursuits in the mid-1820s to immerse himself in politics. Blanqui's active and open commitment to the republican cause made him a target of the French authorities for most of his adult life, and as a result of numerous prosecutions he spent 43 years in prison. However, the stubbornness with which he held to his convictions merely served to enhance his reputation with the left and made him a hero to the insurrectionists of the **Commune of Paris** and a totemic figure in the subsequent campaign for an amnesty for Communards in the years following the crushing of the insurrection. Blanqui's idealism and courage help to explain the fierce loyalty of his followers in the 19th century. In terms of his intellectual legacy, although he is regarded as having inspired Vladimir Lenin and other 20th-century revolutionaries for whom the role of the revolutionary party was crucial in the radical reconstruction of society, Blanqui's conception of social and political change has its roots in the radical republicanism of the **sans-culottes**.

BLOC NATIONAL (1919–1924). Conservative and nationalist coalition that won a majority in the election to the Chamber of Deputies after **World War I**. As the result of a prewar campaign for proportional representation, a change in the voting procedures allowed a system of departmental-wide voting that favored those parties best able to combine in electoral coalitions. The parties of the right were able to do this, but those of the left were not. The left was further disadvantaged by the fact that it was accused of having failed to prepare France sufficiently for war in 1914 and of sympathizing with communism afterward. The net result was the most conservative National Assembly since 1871—the right outnumbered the left by almost two to one—and, because of the high proportion of deputies who were former army officers, it was nicknamed "sky blue," after the color of army uniforms.

BLUM, LEON (1872–1950). Lawyer, man of letters, **socialist** leader, and prime minister during the **Third Republic**. He was born into a bourgeois family of Alsatian-Jewish origins in **Paris**, where he grew up to study law and engage in theater and literary criticism. Although a member of the Parti Socialiste Français of **Jean Jaurès** from 1902, it was not until **World War I** that Blum took an active part in public life with a post attached to the Ministry of Works. By 1919, Jaurès's death and the war had thrust him into a leading role in the socialist movement. It was he who made the most memorable speech in defense of the Jauresian tradition of democratic socialism at the **Congress of Tours** in 1920, becoming the natural leader of what was left of the **Section Française de l'Internationale Ouvrière (SFIO)** when the communists carried the day. During the decade that followed, Blum articulated the belief that while the socialists had a revolutionary objective, they nonetheless could not shirk the responsibilities of power. Whereas the conquest of power through outright electoral victory would justify a revolutionary break with the status quo, victory in coalition with others would impose responsibility for the exercise of power, allowing for reform and improvement in the condition of the workers, but could not provide a mandate for revolutionary change.

This was the conviction that Blum carried with him in the alliance that resulted in the election of the **Popular Front** in 1936. However, as premier Blum had to reconcile the very high expectations of the workers with the implacable opposition of moneyed interests, the ambitions of a reflationary economic policy in France with the reality of deflationary policies by France's major trading partners, and the desire of the left to help the republicans in the civil war in Spain with the constraints of international diplomacy. He resigned after 13 months in office. Blum was arrested by the **Vichy** authorities after the collapse of the Third Republic, but the intellectual brilliance and commitment to principle he displayed in the defense of his beliefs during the course of his trial at Riom in 1941 turned defeat into moral victory. He was deported to Buchenwald in April 1943 and liberated by U.S. troops two years later. Blum returned very briefly to prime-ministerial office after the war, continued to guide the SFIO away from the ideological rigidities of Marxism, and traveled abroad to promote French interests. He died suddenly at a party meeting on 30 March 1950, admired by many for his exemplary commitment to the defense of democratic socialism.

BONAPARTE, LOUIS-NAPOLEON (1808–1873). Nephew of **Napoléon Bonaparte**, who himself became emperor of France half a century after his uncle. He was born in **Paris**, the third son of Louis Bonaparte and Hortense de Beauharnais. After the separation of his parents in 1815, Louis-Napoléon resided with his mother, mostly in Switzerland, and became a naturalized Swiss citizen in 1832. He embarked on a career as a professional soldier, but Louis-Napoléon's fatalistic belief in his destiny to rule France was soon to spur him to action. The death of Bonaparte's son, the Duke of Reichstadt, in July 1832 made Louis-Napoléon the obvious Bonapartist pretender to the throne of France. Encouraged by his ardent Bonapartist mentor, Victor Fialin Persigny, Louis-Napoléon on 30 October 1836 tried to persuade the garrison at **Strasbourg** to rise up against the regime of **Louis-Philippe**. His failure resulted in transportation to the United States and then exile in England. Undeterred, Louis-Napoléon returned to Boulogne in August 1840 to lead another insurrection. On this occasion, his failure led to a sentence of life imprisonment in the fortress of Ham in Picardy. However, he made a dramatic escape from prison on 25 May 1846 and found refuge once more in England.

Louis-Napoléon's historic opportunity came with the **Revolution of 1848**. The overthrow of Louis-Philippe's regime in February was followed by civil disorder in Paris in June and its brutal repression. But Louis-Napoléon's absence from France meant that his reputation was untainted by this episode. He returned to Paris in September and ran a clever campaign promoting stability and a restoration of national greatness that led to his overwhelming victory in the presidential election in December 1848. True to his Bonapartist inheritance, Louis-Napoléon took his popular mandate as justification for steering a collision course with the deputies in the Legislative Assembly. Conscious of the fact that he was legally prohibited from seeking another mandate as president, Louis-Napoléon staged a coup d'état in December 1851. But he manipulated his image as the savior of France with considerable success, as demonstrated by the plebiscite that confirmed his seizure of power in 1851 and a second plebiscite in 1852, when 7.8 million Frenchmen voted for the replacement of the **Second Republic** by the **Second Empire**. A mere 250,000 voted against Louis-Napoléon.

Once Louis-Napoléon had transformed himself into Napoléon III, his bargain with a predominantly conservative France was clear: a curtailment of civil liberty in return for order and prosperity. Thus a clampdown on the press coincided with a period of sustained growth in the economy and financial inducements from the central government for railway investments that played a major role in launching France into the industrial age. Moreover, Napoléon III found a ready excuse to persecute his republican critics after the failed attempt on his life in 1858 by an Italian patriot named Orsini.

Ordinary citizens reaped the benefit of state funding for projects like urban redevelopment. For example, Paris was transformed under the authority given to Baron **Georges-Eugène Haussmann** to re-create a planned city, with modern amenities like sewers and clean running water. But the bargain began to seem less alluring with the downturn in the economic cycle in the 1860s. Dissatisfaction on the part of the business community and an increasingly numerous and militant industrial working class forced concessions from the emperor, notably in terms of accountability before the previously neglected legislature and a relaxation of the rules on press censorship.

Declining fortunes on the home front prompted Napoléon III to undertake risky military ventures abroad in the hope of restoring his tarnished prestige. Unfortunately, he did not possess the instinct or skill of his uncle. Napoléon III had already endured the humiliation of being told by the United States to withdraw French troops from Mexico in 1865 after his support for the ambitions of Maximilian of Austria to the Mexican throne. Undaunted, and in the face of mounting pressure at home as the decade drew to a close, Napoléon III picked a quarrel with the Prussians over the succession to the vacant throne of Spain. When the concessions he demanded were not forthcoming, he launched his country into the **Franco-Prussian War**. France's declaration of war on Prussia was formulated on 19 July 1870. By 4 September 1870 the Second Empire was pronounced dead and a republic declared in Paris. The collapse of France's slow and old-fashioned military machine was hastened by Napoléon III's attempts to take military command of his army, resulting in his humiliating surrender of 84,000 men, 2,700 officers, and 39 generals to the Prussians at Sedan on 1 September 1870. Weakened by illness and burdened by failure, the former emperor found refuge again in England and died there in 1873.

BONAPARTE, NAPOLEON (1769–1821). Military commander, statesman, and emperor of the French. He was born Napoleone Buonaparte, the second of eight children, in Corsica, which had been acquired by France from Genoa in 1768. He emerged from the Ecole Militaire as a sublieutenant of artillery at the age of 16 in 1785 and began establishing his military reputation during the decade that followed, first in his successful action against the allies of the **counter-revolution** at the important port of Toulon and second when he saved the **Convention** from an insurrectionary mob in 1795. In 1796 he married Josephine de Beauharnais, a widow with two children. During the following 12 months he repeatedly defeated larger Austrian armies as commander of the French army in Italy and forced peace on his continental enemies. To strike at France's one unbeaten rival, Britain, Bonaparte decided to damage its trade by seizing Egypt (1798), but he was left stranded when Admiral Horatio Nelson destroyed his fleet. In order, as he argued, to save France from the new alliance among Britain, Austria, Russia, and lesser European powers, Bonaparte left his army and returned to overthrow the **Directory** in what came to be called the coup d'état of 18 Brumaire.

Bonaparte's skillful populism meant that he had nothing to fear from the Constitution of Year VIII, which gave the vote to all adult males, since they voted for the constitutional amendments that made him consul for life in 1802 (Year X) and emperor in 1804 (Year XII). Bonaparte's assumption of the crown of Italy the following year was perceived by Austria and Russia as a threat, but their alliance against him was defeated at the battle of Austerlitz. In 1806 Bonaparte began to employ various members of his family to head France's client states, making his brother Joseph king of Naples and his brother Louis king of Holland. He made himself protector of the Confederation of the Rhine (most of the German states). When the Prussians and Russians allied in opposition to these measures, they were defeated, and the treaties of Tilsit (July 1807) added the Duchy of Warsaw and the Kingdom of Westphalia to the empire. Bonaparte continued his campaign against British commercial interests through his Continental Blockade, begun in 1806 and later joined by Prussia and Russia, which aimed to exclude British goods from Europe. In 1807 he occupied Britain's ally, Portugal, and in 1808 began his foray into Spain by deposing the Spanish Bourbons and installing Joseph Bonaparte as king (with Naples passing on to Marshal Joaquim Murat and his wife, Caroline Bonaparte). Although Spain appeared subdued, the Peninsular War that ensued, with Britain backing the Spanish, lasted five years and proved costly to the French in men and money.

In spite of Bonaparte's unsubtle attempts to create a dynasty, he was not insensitive to the need to create more genuine and therefore acceptable alliances with the ruling houses of Europe. He divorced Josephine in 1809 and in March 1810 married the 18-year-old daughter of the Austrian emperor, Archduchess Marie-Louise. Bonaparte's hope was that the son born from this union in 1811 would take his natural place among the established monarchs of Europe, but this was not to be.

Bonaparte's costliest mistake came in 1812. He invaded Russia in retaliation for the decision of Czar Alexander I to leave the continental system that Bonaparte had devised to ensure favorable terms of trade for France vis-à-vis her European neighbors. Unprepared for the rigors of the Russian winter, the French retreated from Moscow, costing the lives of 400,000 men. Bonaparte's army was chased and harried all the way back to France as the whole of Europe united against him, and on 6 April 1814 he accepted the inevitable and abdicated. His wife and son became the responsibility of the emperor of Austria, and **Louis XVIII** was placed on the throne of France by the allies. However, when news of divisions among the allies and the unpopularity of Louis XVIII reached Bonaparte in exile on Elba, he was encouraged to make a last bid for power. In March 1815 he escaped from Elba and returned to France. In a remarkable display of charismatic leadership, Bonaparte won over the troops sent to capture him and initiated the period known as the **Hundred Days**, culminating in his final defeat at the battle of Waterloo on 18 June 1815. On this occasion he was exiled to the island of St. Helena in the south Atlantic, where he died on 5 May 1821.

However, the Napoleonic legend did not die with him, and in 1840 his remains were returned to France and entombed with much pomp and ceremony at Les Invalides in **Paris**. Bonaparte's claim to be a historical personage and not just a man is confirmed by the enduring legacy of modernization he left to France and other countries of Europe, especially the reforms of the legal system and public administration and the shaping of state **education**. His achievements in these areas are what enable history to judge him to have been an enlightened monarch as well as a military commander of genius. *See also* CAMPO FORMIO, TREATY OF.

BORDEAUX. France's sixth-largest town and the heart of the Aquitaine region in the southwest of the country. Lasting settlement began in the third century BC, with the realization that the shelter and security afforded by the bend in the **Garonne River** allowed control of the Gironde Estuary and access to the sea. With submission to the Roman empire in 56 BC, Burdigala, as it was known, became a bustling center of commerce with an estimated population of 20,000. Down the centuries that followed the town was much fought over, first by Gauls and Germanic tribes and later by the crowned heads of England and France, until the town was definitively acquired for France in 1453 by Charles VII. It was in the 18th century that Bordeaux enjoyed its greatest economic boom. French colonial expansion had made it the nation's great port for ocean-going trade, bringing in commodities that could be exported to the rest of Europe along with its wine. Furthermore, in 1716 it received the royal authority to engage in the very lucrative slave trade.

These factors turned Bordeaux into Europe's second-biggest port, after London. They are also at the root of much of the wealth invested in the fabric of the city, notably the architecture and public spaces that enabled Bordeaux in 2007 to join the list of world heritage cities designated by the United Nations Educational, Scientific and Cultural Organization. According to the national statistical service INSEE, the town itself had a population of 230,600 in 2005 and was at the heart of an agglomeration of 735,000. The demographic growth of the city from 1990 to 1999 was twice the national average at 6.2 percent a year and approximately a third of the current population is aged less than 25. The town is the center of a region rich in resources, such as the largest cultivated forest in Europe at 1.7 million hectares, and of course the vineyards that make the name Bordeaux synonymous with **wine**, covering 110,000 hectares. *See also* CHABAN-DELMAS, JACQUES.

BORDEAUX, PACT OF (10 MARCH 1871). Compromise engineered between **Adolphe Thiers** and the National Assembly sitting in **Bordeaux**. It enabled Thiers to pursue his objective of rescuing the country from the disastrous consequences of the **Franco-Prussian War** while reassuring the Assembly that the de facto republic in France was not definitive and that he would initiate no constitutional changes without their knowledge or approval.

BOSSUET, JACQUES-BENIGNE (1627–1704). Church leader and writer. He was born in Dijon, into a fiercely royalist family of magistrates. Destined from an early age for the church, he completed his education in **Paris** in 1652. Such was the growth of his renown as a churchman and scholar during the years that followed that in 1662 he was called to preach at the Louvre, before **Louis XIV**, and in 1670 he was made preceptor to the king's son. It was during his years in this capacity that Bossuet wrote some of his most famous pedagogical works, such as his *Discours sur l'histoire universelle* (1681) and *Traité de la connaissance de Dieu et de soi-même* (published posthumously). However, Bossuet's commitments at court did not diminish his profile nationally, especially in the field of religious controversy. In his *Exposition de la doctrine de l'Eglise catholique sur les matières de controverse* (1671), Bossuet showed a much greater inclination than many of his contemporaries to enter into a dialogue with the Protestant church in France, as opposed to simply engaging in a blanket condemnation of what were perceived as its doctrinal errors.

Bossuet's willingness to countenance the idea that the pope's judgments were not always entirely appropriate to France earned him a reputation for **Gallicanism** and the implicit censure of the papacy. In the long period since his death, Bossuet has been criticized by some within the Catholic Church for his Gallicanism and by those outside it for his reactionary views. There is nonetheless agreement that he was an individual of exceptional intellectual breadth and formidable exegetical powers.

BOULANGER, GEORGES (1837–1891). Career army officer, war minister, controversial figure of the **Third Republic** because of his central role in a political crisis that came to be known as the Boulanger affair (1886–1889). Boulanger was born into a middle-class family in Rennes, in western France, and graduated from the military academy of Saint-Cyr. Promoted to general in 1880, Boulanger entered the political fray in January 1886 when he was appointed war minister in the cabinet headed by Charles de Freycinet. A vain and ambitious man, Boulanger attempted to build a political vehicle for his ambitions by endeavoring to be all things to all men: a friend to the workers, a committed patriot, a defender of the Republic against the remnants of a royalist establishment. Boulangism polarized discontent with the **Opportunist** leaders of the time. He exploited the loophole that enabled him to present himself for election simultaneously in multiple constituencies, and his campaign peaked with his electoral triumph in **Paris** in January 1889. But the Boulangist movement rapidly dissolved after the government threatened Boulanger with arrest for a plot to overthrow the state. Boulanger fled to Belgium, and subsequent revelations about funds he had received from royalists, in spite of his professed republicanism, further undermined what was left of his credibility. Distressed over the death of his partner, Marguerite de Bonnemains, Boulanger committed suicide at her graveside at Ixelles, Belgium, on 30 September 1891. A master of slogans and soundbites before the advent of the **broadcast media**, Boulanger was a very modern type of political personality who sought to generate mass appeal on the basis of style rather than substance.

BOULEZ, PIERRE (1925–). Composer, conductor, and musicologist. Boulez was a student from 1942 to 1945 at the Paris Conservatory, where he studied classical theory under Olivier Messiaen. But the critical influence on his musical development came from his private studies with René Leibowitz in counterpoint and the serialism techniques of Schoenberg. In early works such as his cantata *Le soleil des eaux,* Boulez broke new ground in France by being the first to experiment with the forces of serial composition in a way similar to composers like Anton von Webern. During the following two decades, Boulez's serial style evolved in different directions, producing one of his most famous orchestral pieces, *Pli selon pli.* The 1960s and 1970s brought him much international fame, first as the chief conductor of the BBC Symphony Orchestra in London and then as director of the New York Philharmonic Orchestra. However, after 1977 Boulez decided to devote more time to composition and experimentation, and he found a milieu conducive to these ambitions when he assumed the post of director of the Institut de Recherche et Coordination Acoustique/Musique in **Paris**. He relinquished this post in 1992, signed a recording contract with Deutsche Grammophon, and embarked on a worldwide series of engagements culminating in a tour of Europe and the United States in 2000 with the London Symphony Orchestra, with the ambition of providing a grand retrospective of the orchestral repertoire of the 20th century. It was in the same year that he was awarded the Grammy for best contemporary composition. Boulez's preeminent position in the ranks of the musical avant-garde is secure, and he remains a major figure in the development of modern music internationally as well as in France. *See also* MUSIC, CLASSICAL AND CONTEMPORARY.

BOURBON DYNASTY. This was the most famous of the royal dynasties to reign in France. It started its slow progress toward the acquisition of power in France under Robert de Clermont (1256–1317) and succeeded the **Valois dynasty** when it died out in 1589. The Bourbons left their most lasting imprint on French history during the 17th and 18th centuries, when the exercise of absolute monarchy reached its apogee, especially during the reign of **Louis XIV**. This was the epoch when France bestrode Europe as the one great continental nation-state and the king reigned unchallenged and unchallengeable in France since, as the king's official historians argued, his sovereign power was divinely bestowed. The monarchy was abolished as a result of the **French Revolution** of 1789 but was restored in 1814, though without great popular acclaim. The last Bourbon to sit on the throne of France was **Louis-Philippe**, from the junior, Orleanist branch of the family. His reign was brought to an abrupt end by the **Revolution of 1848**.

BOURSE (STOCK EXCHANGE). *See* FINANCE.

BOVE, JOSE (1953–). France's most famous environmental campaigner and critic of globalization. He was born in southwest France to parents who were both scientists and spent his early years in the **United States** where his father was employed by the University of California, Berkeley, as a researcher in agricultural sciences. The fluency Bové acquired in English is one of the reasons for his success in putting his arguments to a world audience. He gained widespread notoriety in 1999 when he and his supporters wrecked a McDonald's restaurant in the town of Millau. It was a highly symbolic gesture aimed at underlining the dangers posed by an unfettered world trade system of rootless and exploitative capital which, in the case of McDonald's, results in what Bové terms *malbouffe*, or junk food being forced on people. Bové was particularly dismayed by the failure of the **European Union** to take a firm line against the importation of hormone-fed American beef into Europe.

Although his action resulted in a short jail sentence, Bové's objections to the amorality of globalization made him a folk hero at home and abroad. The visceral feeling that the use of genetically modified food runs contrary to what nature intended is more powerful in France than many of its European neighbors, and Bové succumbed to the pressure of his supporters to put himself forward as a candidate in the presidential election of 2007. His campaign was not very professionally managed, and when the ballot boxes were emptied he was found to have attracted the support of just under half a million of his fellow citizens. Bové's profile remains high, however, and faithful to the lessons of figures like Gandhi and Martin Luther King, whom he claims among his major philosophical influences, he now promotes his causes by purely peaceful means.

BRETON, ANDRE (1896–1966). Writer, poet, theoretician, and leader of the surrealist movement. Breton trained as a doctor and first encountered Freudian theories about the power of the subconscious when he was assigned to military neuropsychiatric wards in 1915. Breton's first piece of surrealist writing, a collection of "automatic texts" that were the spontaneous expression of personal visions and fantasies, came after the war. His *First Surrealist Manifesto*, published in 1924, laid the foundation for the surrealist movement and proclaimed his rejection of logical and utilitarian thinking in favor of the redeeming power of the subconscious. Breton joined the **Parti Communiste Français** in 1927, and although he tried to reconcile the rigidities of ideology with the belief in freedom that was the essence of his artistic creed (e.g., *Position politique du surréalisme*, 1935), this proved impossible and he was expelled from the party in 1933. Breton then flirted with Trotskyism. He sought refuge in New York during **World War II**, returning to **Paris** in 1946. He remained the leader of the surrealist movement there until his death in 1966. Breton was a powerful personality who elicited powerful reactions. While to some he seemed an authoritarian apostle of his creed, to others he was an inspiring leader of unyielding principle.

BRIAND, ARISTIDE (1862–1932). **Third Republic** politician and statesman. Born in Nantes to a family of small-business owners, Briand trained as a lawyer and also entered political journalism. He stood unsuccessfully for election to the Chamber of Deputies on a number of occasions before finally winning a seat in Saint-Etienne in 1902. He joined the cabinet for the first time in 1906, rising to the post of premier for the first of 11 occasions in July 1909 and for the last time in 1929. A man of astute political instincts, a good negotiator, and a pragmatic conciliator, Briand had been a prominent member of the **socialist** movement before gaining high office. A follower of the kind of pluralistic socialism advocated by **Jean Jaurès**, as opposed to the doctrinaire Marxist variant proposed by **Jules Guesde**, Briand, once in power, soon came to be identified with the middle ground in politics. He was a skillful manager of relations with the Anglo-Saxon allies during **World War I**, and his attitude toward **Germany** after 1918 was characterized by a desire for reconciliation within clear parameters set for the defense of French interests. In terms of his personal career path and with regard to many of his political attitudes, Briand was the archetypal Third Republic politician.

BROADCAST MEDIA. Radio broadcasts began in France in 1921 from the top of the Eiffel Tower, and from the beginning the assumption of the French state has been that it should bring the new technology under government regulation, if not outright ownership. Thus in 1923 radio broadcasting became part of the state monopoly on telegraph communication. When television broadcasting began on a regular basis in 1948, it was brought under the same regulatory regime. Between 1945 and 1964 the media were managed by the Radiodiffusion-Télévision Française (RTF), an agency directly controlled by the Ministry of Communication. Often criticized for its lack of editorial independence, the RTF was used by the government, particularly in the early days of the **Fifth Republic**, to counter the effects of a negative press. The importance of television, especially in molding the perception of the presidency, grew rapidly as the number of sets owned in France increased from 1 million to over 10 million in the 1958 to 1968 period.

In 1964 the RTF was replaced by the Office de Radiodiffusion-Télévision Française (ORTF), but the Gaullist stranglehold on the management of the media was not broken until the reforms of 1974 under the presidency of **Valéry Giscard d'Estaing**. He purged the management structure of Gaullists and broke up ORTF into four autonomous companies: one radio group, Radio-France; and three television channels, Télévision Française 1 (TF1), Antenne 2 (A2), and France-Régions 3 (FR3). The impetus toward greater liberalization, in both programming and ownership, was something that the **Socialist** governments of the 1980s also recognized. In 1984–1985 three private television channels—Canal Plus, TV5, and TV6—were authorized. A new supervisory authority sympathetic to a more neoliberal agenda, the Commission Nationale de la Communication et des Libertés, was established in 1986 with a mandate to allocate frequencies to hundreds of new radio stations, privatize TF1, and sell the broadcasting rights for TV5 and TV6.

Concern about the development of private monopolies in broadcasting led to rules such as the one forbidding any person or group to own more than 25 percent of any television channel. Nonetheless, France entered the 1990s with broadcast media that had changed massively since the early days of the Fifth Republic. Radio France still provides an umbrella that covers a variety of public service functions. But in addition to the old commercial networks of Radio-Télévision Luxembourg, Radio-Monte-Carlo, and Europe 1, by 1993 French listeners could tune in to over 1,500 private radio stations in metropolitan France. Of the television channels created by the reforms of 1974, TF1 was privatized but remains the channel with the biggest national audience. Of the new privately owned entrants, the pay-per-view Canal Plus established itself as a solid success, whereas La Cinq (formerly TV5) had exactly the opposite experience. As for extending the range of programs available, the reliance of the M6 channel (formerly TV6) on old U.S. series like *Mission: Impossible* has demonstrated that the multiplication of channels is no guarantee of genuine choice. But the rapid progression of cable and satellite technology on a Europe-wide basis suggests that the national government will be decreasingly able to control the pace of change in the French broadcast media. The accelerating pace of change was underlined in 2005 with the launch of télévision numérique terrestre, offering, in the initial phase, eight new digital channels to the viewers. *See also* PRESS.

BROGLIE, ALBERT, DUC DE (1821–1901). Politician and defender of the Orleanist cause. Son of Victor de Broglie and **Germaine de Staël**, Albert became a man of great intellectual ability and literary endeavor, a fact acknowledged by his election to the **Académie Française** in 1862. He was elected to the National Assembly in 1871 and became the leader of the center-right faction agitating for the restoration of the monarchy. Appointed prime minister by President **Maurice de MacMahon** during 1873–1874, he defended the cause of the Orleanist pretender, **Philippe d'Orléans, comte de Paris.** The miscalculation that led to his downfall came on 16 May 1877, when he supported MacMahon's attempt to exercise his constitutional right to dissolve the National Assembly in an effort to engineer a monarchist restoration. This was immediately branded an attempted coup by the majority of deputies and brought down both men. Though a brilliant man, de Broglie was a poor performer as a politician and was shackled by the ambiguity typical of the Orleanists, believing monarchy to be superior to republican government but recognizing that a return to purely traditional monarchist values was no longer viable.

– C –

CAMBACERES, JEAN-JACQUES-REGIS DE (1753–1824). Duc de Parme. Born into the nobility in Montpellier, he followed his father into the legal profession and became president of the criminal court of the Hérault during the **French Revolution**. Noted for his diligence, intellectual ability, and shrewd political judgment, he was elected to the **Convention**, served under the **Directory**, and rose to second consul under the **Consulate**. Judged a wise and reliable counsel by **Napoléon Bonaparte**, he was effectively chief of the administration of justice from 1799 to 1814. In his absences from **Paris**, Bonaparte often delegated routine matters of state to Cambacérès, who, next to Bonaparte, was chiefly responsible for overseeing the completion of the **Civil Code**. By the time of his death in 1824, Cambacérès had come to personify the new elite of *notables* who exercised much power over French public life in the 19th century.

CAMISARDS. This was the name given to the Protestant insurgents of the Bas-Languedoc and Cévennes regions in southern France who rose up against the persecution of **Protestantism** by **Louis XIV**. By revoking the Edict of Nantes (*see* RELIGION) in 1685, Louis signaled the end of religious toleration in France and the beginning of a new attempt to impose Roman **Catholicism** on all his subjects. This measure led many Protestants to emigrate, and those who remained were subjected to a severely oppressive regime. The violent reaction this provoked in the Protestant Cévennes began with the murder in 1702 of the abbé du Chayla, considered by the Protestants of the region as their chief tormentor. There followed a concerted effort to drive out the priests and end their power by sacking and burning their churches. The ability of the Camisards to hold royal armies in check stemmed from their highly effective guerrilla tactics, rendered possible by their knowledge of the terrain, extreme mobility, and the support of the local population. Their name itself derived from the white shirts they wore (*camisa* in Languedocian, *chemise* in French) to recognize each other in night attacks on their adversaries. In the endeavor to cut the Camisards off from their sources of support, the government adopted a scorched-earth policy under which hundreds of villages were burned and their inhabitants massacred. The offer of peace terms from the government in 1704, including an amnesty, was rejected by the Protestants because the right to freedom of worship was not included. Although sporadic fighting continued until 1710, the threat from the Camisards had effectively been neutralized by 1705 with the capture and execution of most of their leaders.

CAMPO FORMIO, TREATY OF. This treaty of 17 October 1797 between Austria and France allowed France possession of Belgium and (secretly) the left bank of the **Rhine**, while in return France allowed Austria to have Venice, Dalmatia, and Istria. **Napoléon Bonaparte**'s defeat of Austria and its Italian allies had allowed him to propose terms that were very advantageous to France, and the acquisition of the (Venetian) Ionian Islands in particular presaged Bonaparte's later interest in regions further east.

CAMUS, ALBERT (1913–1960). Novelist, playwright, and journalist. Camus was a *pied-noir*, born in **Algeria** of French and Spanish extraction. His father was killed early in **World War I** and the reduced circumstances of his family forced them to move from the countryside to a poor suburb of Algiers. The poverty of his upbringing helps to explain why in early adulthood he was diagnosed as having tuberculosis and was unable to finish the university studies that would have led to the *agrégation*. Camus came to **Paris** in March 1940 and began his journalistic career there on *Paris-Soir*. He left France for Oran after the German invasion. There he began a novel about the ravages of a plague (*La peste,* 1947), symbolic of the Nazi invasion, and about the courage and fraternity required of those committed to fighting it. He returned to France in 1942, joined the **Resistance**, and edited a clandestine journal called *Combat*. This was a productive period that resulted in the major philosophical and fictional works *Le mythe de Sisyphe* (1942) and *L'Etranger* (1942). In their different ways these works express the absurdity of the human condition and the meaningless nature of an existence governed by habit, convention, and the expectations society imposes on us.

The texts published in the 1950s, such as *L'Homme révolté* (1951) and *La chute* (1956), developed further the two sides of Camus's work: on the one hand, despair at the limitations that the absurd places on our endeavors; on the other hand, the determination to revolt against the absurd through the pursuit of justice, tempered by the clear-sighted moderation that preserves humane and fraternal values. Camus's plays, *Caligula* (1939) and *Les justes* (1949), were less successful than his novels. It was principally as a novelist that he was awarded the Nobel Prize for literature in 1957. Camus quarreled with **Jean-Paul Sartre** over support for the **Soviet Union** and was accused of being more concerned with being a "fine soul" than engaging in action. But this did not undermine Camus's status as the moral voice of his generation, tragically and prematurely silenced by his death in a car crash in January 1960. The continuing interest in Camus's work and ideas was highlighted in 1995, when his daughter allowed his unfinished novel, *Le premier homme* (*The First Man*), to be published and brought before a worldwide reading public.

CANAL DU MIDI. Europe's oldest working canal, which provides a continuous waterway between the Atlantic Ocean and the **Mediterranean Sea** by linking the **Garonne River** to the Mediterranean. It was built between 1666 and 1681 under the reign of **Louis XIV**, originally to facilitate the trade in wheat. Originally called the Canal Royal en Languedoc, it was renamed the Canal du Midi after the **French Revolution**. Some historians consider this 240-kilometer-long construction the greatest feat of European civil engineering of the 17th century, and in 1996 it was classed a World Heritage Site by the United Nations Educational, Scientific and Cultural Organization.

LA CANICULE (HEAT WAVE OF 2003). The record-breaking heat wave that hit Europe in August 2003 had followed spring and early summer months of drought. In France, record peaks in temperature were set, particularly in the south with 42.6°C in Orange and 44°C in **Toulouse**. In **Paris** the temperature peaked at 39°C. Retrospective calculations put the death toll in France at 15,000, second only to Italy, where the toll reached 20,000. The political and social consequences in France, however, were profound. For a country that prides itself on having the best healthcare system in the world, the response to the emergency was slow and clearly inadequate. The fact that the heat wave coincided with the annual holiday exodus from the cities, including healthcare professionals, meant that help was slow in reaching the most vulnerable, especially the elderly. The death toll rose so quickly that mortuaries were forced to hire refrigerated trucks to accommodate the corpses. President **Jacques Chirac**, also on holiday at the time, was criticized for his slowness in taking the moral lead in organizing a response to the crisis. But when he made a public pronouncement on the issue, a fortnight after the peak temperatures had passed, it was not to criticize the health system but to underline the lack of social solidarity in France revealed by the crisis. The difficulties experienced by medical staff in tracking down family members of the victims, especially the offspring of elderly parents, illustrated some uncomfortable truths about the decline of family ties in a society that still purports to cherish ties of kinship and of origin in *la France profonde*. More shocking still was the number of victims whose bodies were never claimed at all. On 3 September 2003 Chirac and the mayor of Paris, **Bertrand Delanoë**, attended a funeral for the 57 Parisian victims of the heat wave who had no friend or family to provide them with a proper burial.

CAPET, HUGUES. *See* CAPETIAN DYNASTY.

CAPETIAN DYNASTY. Sometimes nicknamed the kings of the "third race," after the **Merovingians** and the **Carolingians**, the Capetians reigned in direct succession from 987 to 1328, whereupon monarchical succession in France was ensured in a continuous manner by the Capetian-Valois (1328–1498), the Valois-Orléans (1498–1515), the Valois-Angoulême (1515–1589), and the **Bourbon** (1589–1792) dynasties. Hugues Capet was elected king of France at Senlis in 987 by an assembly of lords, *notables*, and churchmen, following the death of the Carolingian Louis V. The challenge faced by Hugues Capet was twofold: territorially the royal domain comprised a small area spread along a Paris-Orléans axis and from the river **Seine** to the **Loire**; politically Hugues Capet was confronted by lords who reigned over their own fiefdoms and who regarded their own authority to be as legitimate as his. These challenges were most successfully addressed during the great age of the Capetian kings (1180–1314), among them **Philippe Auguste**, who made considerable strides in centralizing power in France under the monarchy; secured the influence of the royal domain in southern France; strengthened monarchical power in economic terms by extending it to the trading coastal regions of the **Mediterranean**, the Atlantic, and the English Channel; and recovered most of the territory that had been under the control of the Plantagenet kings of England. It was during this period that France emerged as Christendom's most powerful, prosperous, and prestigious country.

CAROLINGIAN DYNASTY. Royal dynasty that ruled France and whose most illustrious son was **Charlemagne**. The foundation for the rise of the dynasty was laid by Charles Martel, who stopped the advance of the Muslim army from Spain at a battle that took place between Poitiers and Tours in 732. The rise to power of this dynasty was completed by Martel's son, Pépin le Bref (741–768), when he deposed the last of the **Merovingian** kings and had himself crowned king of the Franks in 751. The dynasty ended in 987 with the death of the last Carolingian monarch, Louis V.

CARTEL DES GAUCHES. A left-of-center political alliance that rose to prominence during the interwar years, composed of radical and moderate republican parties. It constituted the major opposition to the **Bloc National**, the right-of-center coalition that formed most of the ministries during this period. The cartel formed ministries in 1924 and 1932, both under the Radical leader **Edouard Herriot**. In both cases the Herriot ministry had to wrestle with difficult foreign policy and economic issues, such as the thorny problem of the payment of war reparations by **Germany** in 1924 and the painful consequences of the Great Depression on France in 1932. The political line adopted by the Radicals within the cartel signaled their general abandonment of the reformist left-wing ambition that had characterized their attitudes before **World War I**, in favor of centrist compromise. The perceived failure of the Cartel des Gauches to challenge the political status quo in an effective manner fueled the phenomenon of antiparliamentarism and disillusionment that grew noticeably in 1930s France.

CATHOLICISM. *See* CIVIL CONSTITUTION OF THE CLERGY; CONCORDAT OF 1801; EDUCATION; GALLICANISM; RELIGION.

LE CENS. A means for determining the eligibility of a French citizen to participate in national elections, depending on the amount of direct tax paid by the individual. This method of qualification was often used cynically between 1815 and the declaration of universal suffrage in 1848 as a means of limiting the size of the electorate under an ostensibly democratic constitutional monarchy. Thus in 1815, in the aftermath of the **Bourbon** restoration, the cens was fixed at 300 francs in direct taxes payable per year, thereby limiting the electorate to a propertied class of 90,000 individuals.

CHABAN-DELMAS, JACQUES (1915–2000). A key actor in postwar French public life. An active member of the **Resistance**, he played a critical role in persuading the Allies not to bypass **Paris** in August 1944 and subsequently joined General Philippe Leclerc and his troops in their triumphal entry into the city on 24 August. He became minister of information in the provisional government that followed under **Charles de Gaulle**, and in 1946 was elected to the Assembly with support from Gaullists and Radicals as a deputy from the Gironde. It was in the following year that Chaban-Delmas started his long association with **Bordeaux** when he became its mayor. The high point of his career was reached in 1969 when he was named prime minister by President **Georges Pompidou**. His government resigned in 1972 and the following year he was reelected mayor of Bordeaux. Chaban-Delmas made a failed bid for the **presidency** of the Republic in the elections of 1974 but his political power base remained the Aquitaine region of France and he was reelected mayor of Bordeaux for the last time in 1989.

CHAMBORD, HENRI (V), COMTE DE (1820–1883). Duc de Bordeaux and **Legitimist** pretender. Chambord's best chance to present himself as the heir to a restored French throne came in the wake of the collapse of the **Second Empire** and the hostility in conservative rural France to the **Commune**. The situation was complicated by the fact that there were two pretenders to the throne, the Orleanist **Philippe, comte de Paris**, and Chambord himself. A compromise was proposed by certain monarchists, as a result of which the aging and childless Chambord would take the throne and be succeeded on his death by the comte de Paris and his offspring. However, the prospect of any such compromise was destroyed by the intransigence of Chambord, who even made a point of principle of refusing to accept the French tricolor as his emblem, insisting instead on a return to the traditional flag of the **Bourbons** bearing the fleur-de-lis. In spite of the energetic efforts of the more moderate Orleanists, the two rival claims to the throne could not be reconciled and the prospects for a restoration faded. Ironically, by his stubborn adherence to a deeply reactionary interpretation of the role of monarchy, Chambord paved the way for the setting up of the **Third Repubic** and ensured that royalist sentiment persisted until the 1880s, but only according to the Orleanist tradition.

CHARLEMAGNE (742–814). He was born the son of Pépin III and became the most prestigious sovereign of the second dynasty of the Franks, to which he gave his name, **Carolingian**. With the death of his brother Carloman in 771, Charlemagne was able to unite the Franks under his sole authority. His remarkable series of conquests began modestly, with what were essentially reprisals against the Saxons in 772 in response to their raids on Frankish territory. However, by the end of the century, Charlemagne reigned over a domain that stretched from what we would now recognize as the frontier of Spain to the edge of German-speaking Europe, and from the North Sea to Italy. Having conquered territories, Charlemagne ruled by demanding solemn and repeated affirmations of loyalty. Conscious of the weaknesses of administrative structures in the kingdom of the Franks and beyond, Charlemagne used the Catholic Church in the service of the state and devolved onto bishops and other senior churchmen the secular responsibilities associated with local government. In return, the church, and the papacy in particular, found in Charlemagne a protector and the champion of Christendom. Thus it was at the instigation of Pope Leon III that Charlemagne was offered the title of emperor by a mixed assembly of Romans and Franks in Rome on 23 December 800. He accepted and was crowned by Leon III at Saint Peter's on Christmas Day 800.

What details there are of Charlemagne the man come mostly from the biography of him written by Eginhard in about 830. He was tall (1.90 meters) and, contrary to popular images, beardless. He had four wives and many concubines and had many children by them. In spite of a deserved reputation for authoritarianism and some infamous acts of despotic cruelty, Charlemagne was deeply conscious of his vocation as a Christian monarch, responsible for the destiny of his people before God. Mindful of the example set by imperial Rome, he instituted the systematic codification of religious and secular law, protection for the ordinary individual from the arbitrary exactions of the rich and powerful, measures against exorbitant rises in the prices of ordinary commodities, and arbitration as the means of settling civil disputes. However, Charlemagne's ambitions, though admired by succeeding generations of kings, bore little fruit in the long run, and his empire was dismembered within a few decades of his death in January 814.

CHARLES X (1757–1836). He was the comte d'Artois, grandson of Louis XV, and fourth son of the dauphin Louis and Marie-Josephe of Saxony. His reputation as the champion of absolutist ideals made him an obvious target for the revolutionaries of 1789 (*see* FRENCH

REVOLUTION), and he fled France on the advice of his brother, **Louis XVI**. Artois spent the years that followed visiting most of the courts of Europe in the attempt to mobilize opposition to the Revolution in France. He returned to France in the wake of **Napoléon Bonaparte**'s series of military reverses in 1813 and entered **Paris** triumphantly on 12 April 1814, following Bonaparte's abdication. He was recognized as lieutenant general of the kingdom by the Napoleonic Senate and accepted the provisional government it had nominated and whose leadership was entrusted to **Charles-Maurice de Talleyrand-Perigord**. This first restoration was brought to an abrupt end by the return of Bonaparte from Elba for the period that is known as the **Hundred Days**. Artois was thus forced to flee France once more, finally joining his brother **Louis XVIII** in Ghent, until Bonaparte's ultimate defeat at Waterloo made a second restoration of the monarchy in France possible.

The ascension of the moderate Louis XVIII to the throne led to tensions with the ultraroyalist Artois. The brothers were eventually reconciled, and in December 1821 Louis XVIII accepted the formation of a ministry predominantly composed of ultraroyalists devoted to Artois. The death of Louis XVIII on 16 September 1824 therefore paved the way to a smooth succession that enabled Artois, crowned Charles X, to enjoy the services of a ministry in tune with his own more conservative views on the role of the monarchy in France. While Charles X earned a reputation as a friendly and generous monarch, particularly in his attitudes toward charities and the patronage bestowed on the arts and letters, the policies of his ministers reflected his disinclination to follow the British model of constitutional monarchy, and his resistance to the pressure from the base of the social hierarchy for government that was more representative and more accountable led to the **Revolution of 1830**, which forced his abdication. Thereafter he was given asylum in Britain and then taken under the wing of the emperor of Austria after the rapprochement between **Great Britain** and France made his presence in the British Isles too embarrassing. He died in 1836 from an attack of cholera and was buried in the crypt of the church of the Franciscans of Castagnavizza.

CHARTER OF 1814. This was the constitutional basis for the restoration of a monarchy in France under **Louis XVIII**. It was, in essence, a document of some ambiguity that allowed the king to maintain that authority in France resided in the person of the king while accepting the main principles established by the **French Revolution**: equality before the law, taxation in proportion to the ability to pay, freedom of **religion**, and freedom from arbitrary arrest and prosecution. However, these principles were not regarded in the charter as the foundation of absolute rights. The right to express one's opinions, for example, had to conform to the laws restraining the abuse of that freedom. As for the rights of a representative assembly, the new legislature had to share its power with the king, notably by being obliged to petition him to initiate laws. Moreover, the king's prerogative under Article 14 of the charter to pass any ordinances necessary for the security of the state, allowed a potential opening for a return of absolutism. But the charter's ratification of the revolutionary land settlement allowing legal title to those having bought lands formerly confiscated from the church and the émigrés and its broad acceptance of the legal system established under **Napoléon Bonaparte** and known as the **Civil Code** rallied liberals to the charter and thus the legitimacy of the restoration. *See also* CHARTER OF 1830.

CHARTER OF 1830. This was a revised version of the **Charter of 1814**. It formed the constitutional basis for the establishment of a new regime under **Louis-Philippe, duc d'Orléans**, after **Charles X** was forced to quit the throne because of revolutionary violence that broke out in **Paris** in July 1830 in protest against his rule. In a simple ceremony on 9 August 1830, Louis-Philippe appeared before a joint session of both chambers of the French Assembly, the Chamber of Deputies and the Chamber of Peers, to accept the throne formally and proclaim his acceptance of the Charter of 1830. In contrast to the Charter of 1814, the new charter was not a royal gift bestowed upon the nation but manifestly the work of a legislative assembly. And this idea of an elective monarchy as opposed to a hereditary monarchy established by divine right was reinforced by the description of the new king as king of the French, instead of king of France.

Among the new charter's 70 articles, a major change was made to the status of the church, describing **Catholicism** as the **religion** of the majority of Frenchmen instead of the religion of the state. The provisions of the old Article 14, which had allowed the king to issue ordinances in matters of national security, were eliminated. Moreover, the king now had to share the right to initiate laws with both chambers of the Assembly. A series of other changes providing more safeguards for civil liberties, greater transparency and more proper regulation in the election of local and national representatives, a wider franchise, and the elimination of notorious abuses like the double vote afforded to those with the highest incomes helped push France a little further along the road to a more recognizably modern, though clearly still very conservative, constitutional monarchy.

CHATEAUBRIAND, FRANCOIS-RENE, VICOMTE DE (1768–1848). Writer and statesman. He was born and raised for the most part in St. Malo, the youngest son of a shipowner of aristocratic origins. After his studies Chateaubriand gained a commission in the Navarre regiment and wore his second lieutenant's uniform with panache, in spite of his modest height of 1.60 meters. The **French Revolution** presented Chateaubriand with an invidious choice; though open to the ideas of the **Enlightenment** philosophes, he was nonetheless a royalist by upbringing. This was a factor in his decision to leave France in 1791 in pursuit of adventure in America. His sojourn in the New World lasted only five months but had a profound effect on his writing. The arrest of **Louis XVI** brought him back to France and led him to join the émigré army that had formed to oppose the Revolution. He was wounded and subsequently exiled to England, and his seven years there convinced him of the virtues of constitutional monarchy. It was also during this period that he developed the fervent Christian faith that resulted in *Le génie du christianisme* (1802). (He had already acquired public acclaim for *Atala*, his tale of love between "two savages in the desert," which was published during the previous year.) *Le génie* found favor with **Napoléon Bonaparte** and Chateaubriand was appointed to the French embassy in Rome. However, he resigned his post in 1804 and became one of the Napoleonic regime's fiercest critics. The restoration of the monarchy brought Chateaubriand once more to ministerial and ambassadorial office before he quit politics in the mid-1820s. The last 20 years of his life resulted in the posthumously published *Mémoires d'outre-tombe* and sealed his reputation as a writer whose romantically melancholy and evocative prose influenced literary figures as diverse as Lord Byron, **Alphonse de Lamartine**, and **Victor Hugo**. *See also* LITERATURE.

CHEVALIER, MAURICE (1888–1972). The most complete personification of French charm and sophistication for **cinema** audiences worldwide for the better part of the 20th century. An accident forced Chevalier to abandon his initial career as an acrobat in favor of singing. He made several short films in France, starting with *Trop crédules* (1908), and decided to seek his fortune in the United States after **World War I**. He received an Oscar nomination for his Hollywood movie debut, *The Love Parade* (1929), a musical that teamed him with Jeanette MacDonald and that was directed by Ernst Lubitsch. During the first half of the 1930s Paramount Pictures used him in a number of vehicles that exploited his carefree French charm and the license he could bring to the delivery of risqué dialogue. Chevalier returned to Europe in the latter half of the 1930s to make several more films before **World War II** interrupted his career. His Hollywood career was given a new lease of life in the mid-1950s, and he was cleverly cast by Billy Wilder as a charmless private detective in *Love in the Afternoon* (1957). The film *Gigi* (1958) provided Chevalier with the songs that remain most closely associated with him, "I Remember It Well" and "Thank Heaven for Little Girls." The year 1958 was also the year in which he was awarded a special Oscar. Chevalier's extraordinarily long movie career continued into the 1960s, and his unique singing style provided him with the opportunity to perform the title song for *The Aristocats* (1970). *See also* MUSIC, POP AND ROCK.

CHINA, FRANCE'S RELATIONS WITH. As with many European countries, historically China has occupied a special place in French national consciousness as a fabled land of mystery and exoticism. The increase in travel and contact that came with the **Renaissance** whetted French appetites for things Chinese and led to the phenomenon that began at the end of the 17th century called *Chinoiserie*. This passion expanded greatly in France and the rest of Europe in the 18th century. Ceramics, wall coverings, screens, and many other ornamental items bore Chinese rural or fantastic images, as well as the effects of Chinese lacquer work. By the 19th century France had followed **Great Britain**, together with other leading powers, into forcing the weak Chinese government to give it territorial concessions, notably in Shanghai, that allowed France to pursue her commercial interests in the country in a sovereign manner.

These concessions were formally relinquished in 1946 as China retreated behind the bamboo curtain of the communist regime headed by Chairman Mao Tse-tung. Though it was a closed society, or perhaps because of this, some French intellectuals in the 1960s were seduced by the Maoist version of communism and tried to promote it during the **student rebellions** of 1968. During the decades that followed, France, like the rest of the world, looked on in awe at the transformation of the country **Napoléon Bonaparte** had called a "sleeping giant" into a wide-awake industrial colossus. In 1989 France criticized China for its violent repression of the students who demonstrated in Tiananmen Square for greater liberty, and supported the consequent **European Union** embargo on arms sales to China. But the importance of China as the world's workshop and its biggest market means that France has become one of its most assiduous suitors, culturally and commercially. 2003–2004 was "China year" in France with hundreds of cultural activities across the country designed to celebrate China, ancient and modern. In 2006 there was a groundbreaking student exchange with 400 French students going to study in Chinese universities and an equal number of Chinese students coming to France the following year. 2006 was also significant commercially because in the first semester French exports to China rose by 30 percent in relation to the corresponding period the year before. It is perhaps not surprising, therefore, that in 2007 France was one of the most proactive of European nations in its push to lift the embargo on arms sales to China.

CHIRAC, JACQUES (1932–). President of the **Fifth Republic**. He was born in **Paris** on 29 November 1932 and completed his higher education there, first at the Institut d'Etudes Politiques and then at the elite Ecole Nationale d'Administration, graduating from the latter in 1959. After a brief period of military service in **Algeria**, Chirac began his fast-track career in the civil service at the Cours des Comptes in Paris. Ministerial office soon followed his election as deputy for the Corrèze; at the age of 34, he became secretary of state for employment. President **Georges Pompidou** noticed Chirac's drive and ambition, and Chirac's ministerial career flourished; in 1974 he secured the ministerial portfolio for the interior.

The presidential election precipitated by Pompidou's premature death in 1974 led to victory for **Valéry Giscard d'Estaing,** who appointed Chirac his prime minister. It appeared to be a dream team of talented and energetic young men, but in August 1976 Chirac resigned, claiming that he was hindered in his management of the nation's affairs by excessive interference by the president. This led to a long period of rivalry between the two men, as manifested by Chirac's decision to run against Giscard d'Estaing in the 1981 presidential race, thus splitting the right-wing vote and indirectly helping to smooth the path to victory for the Socialist challenger **François Mitterrand**. But the honeymoon period between the Socialists and the French electorate soon evaporated, and they were predictably beaten in the legislative elections of 1986. Forced into a period of **cohabitation** with a center-right majority in the new Assembly, President Mitterrand had to choose a prime minister from among one of the leaders of the majority, and Chirac accepted the invitation to become prime minister. It was the first time such a situation had occurred in the Fifth Republic, but in spite of the inevitable tensions, a Gaullist prime minister was able to work with a Socialist president.

However, it has been argued that the very qualities of combativeness and unflagging energy that had earned Chirac the nickname of "le bulldozer" and equipped him so well for the political fray were precisely the factors that militated against him in his challenge to Mitterrand for the presidency in 1988, since he was unable to persuade the French electorate of his merit as the supreme guardian of the nation's interests and one above partisan politics. Chirac also failed to deprive Mitterrand of a second term because the right was once more split, this time by the challenge of **Raymond Barre** as the candidate of the **Union pour la Démocratie Française** and the candidacy of **Jean-Marie Le Pen** on the far right.

Chirac was an astute political operator, and his career illustrates his appreciation of the need to build an organizational and local power base. In 1976 he took control of the **Gaullist party** and relaunched it as the Rassemblement pour la République (RPR), and in 1977 he began to build himself a formidable municipal power base, gaining election as mayor of Paris. The ultimate proof of his appetite for the campaign trail came in the presidential election of 1995. A landslide victory for the center-right in the legislative election of 1993 had forced Mitterrand into another two years of cohabitation with a hostile majority in the Assembly. He appointed as his prime minister **Edouard Balladur,** a reserved and patrician figure who was the antithesis of Chirac in style and who enjoyed the respect, if not the admiration, of the RPR. Balladur's smooth technocratic style was reassuring to both the French electorate and the markets after the widespread collapse of confidence in the Socialist administration. But the prelude to the presidential campaign of 1995 exposed Balladur's lack of presidential charisma, while Chirac, whose presidential ambitions appeared to have been permanently thwarted, emerged from among the center-right aspirants as the most credible candidate. In a cleverly managed campaign that played on a national desire for social healing and cohesion, Chirac emerged from the first round of voting on 23 April 1995 with 20.84 percent of the vote, in second place behind the surprising winner, the Socialist candidate **Lionel Jospin**, who obtained 23.30 percent. Although Jospin was making an unexpectedly strong showing, he was nonetheless the candidate of a discredited party, and his principal achievement in the second-round runoff against Chirac was to avert a collapse in the left-wing vote by scoring 47.36 percent. Thus Chirac was elected president as the result of the second round on 7 May, with 52.64 percent of the votes cast.

The early phase of Chirac's presidency suggested some difficulty in reconciling his Gaullist convictions with the new challenges to French **defense policy** after the collapse of the Berlin Wall and the end of the Cold War. The most cogent illustration of this occurred within months of his electoral triumph when, in the face of international condemnation, Chirac authorized the French military to press ahead with a series of nuclear tests in the Pacific underneath Mururoa Atoll in French Polynesia. While the tests were not condemned by France's most important partner in Europe, **Germany,** the silence from Bonn was the most eloquent expression of the unease felt by the government of Chancellor Helmut Kohl at what appeared to many to be a nationalistic Gaullist desire by Chirac to maintain France's nuclear deterrent, even though the threat from the former **Soviet Union** had disappeared. But on the wider issue of whether Chirac's Gaullist notion of France's vocation as an independent power could be reconciled with France's other key role at the heart of the process of monetary and political union in Europe, Chirac was careful to strike a balance that allowed France to maintain her privileged relationship with Germany as one of the joint leaders in this transformation of Europe.

On the domestic front, the view held by some commentators that Chirac was a complex and erratic personality gained substantial justification as the result of an unnecessary gamble taken by the president. Contrary to the advice of senior figures in the Gaullist camp, Chirac was determined to remain loyal to his premier, **Alain Juppé,** in spite of the latter's deep unpopularity with the electorate. To give the Juppé government a mandate that would enable it to see through the economic austerity package it was failing to sell to the electorate, Chirac decided to dissolve the Assembly in the spring of 1997 and call the legislative elections a year earlier than necessary, in the hope that the government's massive majority would give it a sufficient margin, even if significantly reduced, to squeeze into power again. However, Chirac had massively misjudged the mood of the voters, and in the second round of the elections on 1 June, the left was elected with an outright majority, forcing Chirac to appoint a new premier, **Lionel Jospin**, and inaugurate a third period of cohabitation in the life of the Fifth Republic.

Chirac's second mandate as president was one of increasing detachment from the electorate and was marked by growing doubts in certain sections of the **media** about his integrity, particularly during his time as mayor of Paris. He was elected to that office in 1977 and found that a municipal budget of 15 billion francs and 40,000 employees provided ample means to construct a political power base. In 2000 the paper *Le Monde* published a posthumous confession by the businessman Jean-Claude Méry alleging that during Chirac's tenure as mayor, his party, the RPR, had secretly boosted its finances by soliciting commissions from businesses bidding for building contracts from the municipality. Chirac's reputation was further tarnished when municipal accounts brought to light in 2002 revealed that Mayor Chirac and his wife had claimed the equivalent of 2.13 million euros in expenses on groceries between 1987 and 1995. While enjoying the immunity attached to his office, Chirac could not stem the loss of confidence among the electorate, and his successful reform of the presidential mandate in 2000, cutting it from seven to five years, did not prevent the damage to his credibility.

Both the discredited Socialists and Chirac felt the full force of the public's dismay when the result of the first round of the presidential election was announced on 21 April 2002. Chirac came first, but with the lowest score of any previous incumbent at 19.8 percent. Worse still for the democratic process, the socialist Jospin found himself pushed into third place by the far right candidate Jean-Marie Le Pen. Chirac's victory in the second round of the election with a record 82.2 percent of the vote could not disguise the fact that the electorate had mobilized against Le Pen, rather than for Chirac, as the popular slogan of the time made clear: *votez escroc, pas facho* ("vote for the crook, not the fascist"). Almost from the outset of his second mandate Chirac's ability to manage his relationships with his allies abroad and his electorate at home was severely tested. His opposition to United States policy toward Iraq in 2003 marked a predictable low in Franco-U.S. relations, but Chirac surprised the new members of the **European Union (EU)**, such as the Baltic states, when he accused them of acting like ill-mannered guests at the European table because of the support they had given to U.S. policy on Iraq.

Chirac's inability to regain the trust of the electorate at home was illustrated in the referendum of 29 May 2005 when, in spite of his active campaign for a yes vote, French voters refused to ratify the treaty that would establish a constitution for the EU. As is the custom in the Fifth Republic, it is the role of the prime minister to deflect blame from the president, and it was Prime Minister **Jean-Pierre Raffarin** who paid for that failure with his resignation, to be replaced by the smooth and aristocratic **Dominique de Villepin**. Chirac had started his presidency with optimistic pronouncements about the need to heal social divisions in France, but by the end of his career, the extent to which France had fallen short of this was underlined by the riots that took hold in the *banlieues* or deprived outer suburbs of its major cities for three weeks during the fall of 2005, led largely by unemployed youths of immigrant origin. As the end of his second mandate loomed into view, Chirac could not avoid the perception of him as a lame-duck president with skeletons in the cupboard and an uncertain legacy to bequeath to the nation.

Chirac's powerlessness was underlined by his inability to influence the outcome of the competition to decide who would be the majority center-right's candidate in the presidential election of 2007. His mistrust of **Nicolas Sarkozy** had grown since the latter's initial reluctance to support him in the presidential race of 2002, and it was an open secret that Chirac would have preferred someone else to gain the nomination. But such was Sarkozy's popularity with the faithful in the latest vehicle for the Gaullists, the Union pour un Mouvement Populaire (Union for a Popular Movement), that Chirac was ultimately forced to endorse him. The humiliation of Chirac continued into retirement, once his presidential immunity expired. On 19 July 2007, two months after having quit the Elysée palace, Chirac was interviewed by a judge in his Paris office over the bogus but salaried jobs that were given to RPR party supporters during his time as mayor of Paris. This was an unprecedented situation in the history of the Fifth Republic, but at the same time it should be remembered that Chirac was interviewed as a witness rather than as a suspect. Given Chirac's age and his status as a former French head of state, the overwhelming likelihood is that his reputation may be further compromised, but not his freedom.

CHOUANS. From the Breton word *chouan* (screech owl). This was the nickname given to Jean Cottereau (1757–1794) and the guerrilla bands that followed him in the pursuit of the **counterrevolution** in the Vendée, Brittany, and Normandy, after the peasant Royal and Catholic Army of the Vendée was defeated by republican forces during October–December 1793. The *Chouans* resented government measures against the clergy and the enforcement of conscription, like their Vendéen neighbors, but they were not as committed to the absolutist **Bourbon** regime. Many *Chouans* were small-time smugglers who dealt in contraband salt and who therefore lost income from their illicit trade when the republican regime abolished the tax on salt called the *gabelle*. The struggle of the *Chouans* rapidly degenerated into banditry following the disastrous failure of the royalist émigré landing at Quiberon in July 1795. The phenomenon of Chouannerie had never threatened the Republic, but it continued sporadically for some years until its leaders were forced to negotiate an end to their activities with **Napoléon Bonaparte** in 1801.

CINEMA. In 1900 Georges Méliès set up a film studio in Montreuil exploiting the cinematographic technology pioneered by the Lumière brothers and thereby laying the first stone in the foundation of the French film industry. It was another three decades before French film gained worldwide recognition as a distinct product, characterized by the kind of meticulous attention to fine detail and elaboration of narrative structures that made it renowned as a *cinéma de qualité*. But by the late 1930s, figures like Marcel Carné and Jean Renoir were universally recognized as masters of the genre.

When the hiatus brought about by the advent of **World War II** was over, Carné resumed his vocation for carefully crafted films and released the classic *Les enfants du paradis* (1945), which had been shot under difficult conditions during the occupation. Other figures like Jean Renoir and Max Ophuls returned from Hollywood and, in Renoir's case, directed films such as *French Cancan* (1954) that once more reflected his distinctive brand of often exuberant humanism. For their part, French governments after 1945 made considerable efforts to revive the national film industry and make it viable in the face of the enormous commercial threat represented by Hollywood. The Institut des Hautes Etudes du Cinéma was created to render the training for work in the industry more professional; a government film office, the Centre National du Cinéma Français, was established; and substantial government money was pumped into the organization of the Cannes Film Festival to facilitate its launch in 1946.

Ironically, when a new wave of innovation came, it was in the shape of a generation of directors heavily influenced by American cinema. A group labeled *nouvelle vague* or "new wave" in the early 1960s decided to forsake the studio-bound traditions of the *cinéma de qualité* in favor of the individualistic experiments made possible by advances in camera and film technology. The leaders of this new generation like **François Truffaut**, Claude Chabrol, **Jean-Luc Godard**, and Eric Rohmer had begun in the early 1950s by writing largely about American cinema in the pages of the journal *Cahiers du Cinéma* and were influenced by American films before moving on to make their own films during the years that followed. Directors like Truffaut in particular admired the artistry and individuality of American directors like John Ford and Howard Hawks. In turn, Truffaut and his contemporaries developed the theory of auteur filmmaking, which views a film as a work of art expressing the creativity of the director, for whom the camera is a pen. But the *nouvelle vague*, always loosely defined anyway, had broken on the shore by the early 1970s as the directors who had constituted the movement followed increasingly divergent paths, from the familiar *intimisme* of Rohmer to the trademark psychological thrillers of Chabrol.

French cinema recovered from the decline in audiences it suffered in the 1970s, and in the 1980s and 1990s bounced back in commercial terms with some notable worldwide hits, both by deploying products that would be perceived as quintessentially French, such as the film versions of *Jean de Florette* and *Manon des sources* starring **Yves Montand**, and by gambling Hollywood-style big budgets on massive productions like *Cyrano de Bergerac*, starring **Gérard Depardieu**. The levy on every movie-theater ticket that is used to subsidize the industry is but one example of the measures that make the French film industry the best state-supported and largest film industry in Europe. But the challenge from Hollywood films, which take the lion's share of the market in France, continues to be perceived by French governments as a threat to the cultural integrity of the nation, and this explains why the desire to retain measures protecting the market for movies in France became such a bone of contention between the French and U.S. governments in the 1990s. In general, the cinema in France is still perceived by many of its foreign admirers as being evocative of a fine tradition that goes back to the essentially music-hall talents of **Maurice Chevalier** and that produced 1930s antiheroes like **Jean Gabin** and his modern counterpart Gérard Depardieu, and the troubling, iconic beauty of female leads like **Brigitte Bardot**, **Jeanne Moreau**, and **Catherine Deneuve**.

However, since the 1980s, French cinema has demonstrated its ability to adapt to a fast-paced style of glossy surfaces rather than substance so typical of Hollywood and redolent of advertising and MTV video clips. This emphasis on *le look* found a worldwide audience for films like *Diva* (1981) by Jean-Jacques Beineix and *Subway* (1985) by Luc Besson. Even that most American of cinematic devices, the car chase, was reworked with great success in *Taxi* (1998), scripted by Besson, and which, in true Hollywood fashion, spawned two sequels and even an American remake in 2004. On the other hand, the unexpected success of the brutally realistic *La Haine*

(1995), shot in black and white with a cast of unknowns and on a shoestring budget by the young actor/director Mathieu Kassovitz, revealed a capacity for reflection on the nature of post-industrial urban society reminiscent of Spike Lee in the United States and Danny Boyle in Great Britain. Luc Besson's *Jeanne d'Arc* (1999) was a further demonstration of the willingness of a new generation of French filmmakers to address the preferences of a global audience due to his decision to film the most recent version of this quintessentially French legend in English. Moreover, French stars such as **Juliette Binoche** and Sophie Marceau have cemented their international reputations by their ability to work almost as comfortably in English as in French.

CITROEN. Famous car manufacturer, now part of a group with PSA Peugeot. It was founded by André Citroën, who produced his first car in 1919. Unlike the other great name in French motor manufacture, **Renault,** Citroën's reputation came from its passion for thoroughbred cars aimed at the more select end of the market. Its sleek black cars of the 1930s with long, raking hoods and running boards became favorites with film stars and gangsters. In the 1960s the engineering and design genius of the company was confirmed once more by the universal acclaim given to the Citroën DS, with its revolutionary gas suspension and futuristic look. In common with changes across the whole automobile industry, Citroën was eventually obliged to safeguard its future by becoming part of a larger group. But its cars retain a reputation in Europe for their individuality and robustness.

CIVIL CODE. This was the result of **Napoléon Bonaparte**'s determination to complete the work started by the **French Revolution** of 1789 in sweeping away the 400 or so codes of law used in France up to that point and to replace them with a modern and uniform system that continues to serve as the foundation on which the law operates in contemporary France. Bonaparte chose a commission of four to prepare the Civil Code, and the extent of his commitment to this reform was demonstrated by the fact that he presided over half of the sessions the Council of State devoted to the evaluation of the commission's draft proposals. The key modernizing and democratizing significance of the Civil Code, promulgated in 1804, lay in the guarantees it afforded to all citizens with regard to their civil rights and the entitlement to equal treatment before the law. The Civil Code was followed by the Code of Civil Procedure (1806), the Commercial Code (1807), the Criminal Code and Code of Criminal Procedure (1808), and the Penal Code (1810).

CIVIL CONSTITUTION OF THE CLERGY. Legislation passed by the National Assembly on 12 July 1790 and destined to reorganize and restructure the Roman Catholic Church in France. Given the close relationship between church and state under the **ancien régime,** reform of the church was regarded as inevitable if the aims of the **French Revolution** were to be realized. The document reforming the church was called a civil constitution because its authors argued that it only affected the temporal status of the clergy and not the church's eternal spiritual mission, which was the responsibility of the pope. The ecclesiastical structure of the church in France was reorganized, with dioceses reduced from 135 to 83 (one for each *département*), and bishops to be elected by taxpaying citizens. In view of the **nationalization** of church property in December 1789, the clergy were to be salaried by the state and therefore to perform their duties free of charge. To those in favor of the reform, it simply eliminated the abuses that existed under the ancien régime. To those against, it marked a usurpation of the pope's authority.

On 27 November 1790 the National Assembly decreed that all clergy in public service should take an oath of support for the Civil Constitution. On 26 December, having received no advice from Rome, **Louis XVI** gave the decree his sanction. The number of clergy willing to take the oath and thus be included in the state church was lower than expected by the Assembly, with only seven bishops coming forward to do so. Pope Pius VI finally declared himself in the spring of 1791, denouncing the Civil Constitution as a heresy and threatening the clergy in the new schismatic church with excommunication. On 21 February 1795 the **Convention** separated church and state, but the **Concordat of 1801** between **Napoléon Bonaparte** and Pope Pius VII enabled most of the schismatic clergy to be reconciled with Rome. However, the historic legacy of this episode was the perception of an enduring conflict between the mission of the church and the aims of a secular republic.

CLEMENCEAU, GEORGES (1841–1929). Politician, journalist, and twice premier of France. Born at Mouilleron-en-Pareds in the Vendée, western France, into a family of physician-landowners, Clemenceau qualified as a doctor in Paris in 1865. After four years spent in New York, he returned to practice medicine in the Vendée before moving to **Paris**, drawn by the tumultuous changes occasioned by the **Franco-Prussian War**. He was elected to the National Assembly in February 1871, the start of a very long and varied political career. This career ran in tandem with a very active life as a man of letters that ultimately resulted in 19 volumes of collected newspaper articles and works of fiction, including one novel and one play.

During his time in the Chamber of Deputies between 1876 and 1893, Clemenceau made a reputation for himself as an outspoken leader of the left-wing radicals (Radical-Socialists), fighting for causes like the recognition of **trade unions**, social insurance, and the **nationalization** of utilities and against policies like colonialist expansion. Originally a supporter of General **Georges Boulanger**, Clemenceau subsequently sought his downfall when the danger represented by Boulanger became manifest. Clemenceau was in turn forced out of the Assembly by Boulangists who orchestrated a campaign against him based on unproven allegations about his involvement in the **Panama scandal**. Turning to full-time journalism in 1893, Clemenceau played a leading role in the campaign to secure a retrial for Captain Alfred Dreyfus (*see* DREYFUS AFFAIR), falsely accused of betraying military secrets to the Germans.

Clemenceau returned to cabinet office in 1906 as interior minister and finally became premier from 25 October 1906 to 20 July 1909. His premiership coincided with a period of considerable anarcho-syndicalist activity in France. His uncompromisingly firm responses to violent strikes and civil disorder and his single-minded style of leadership in general frustrated both the newly unified strands of the French socialist movement and the Radicals. However, Clemenceau's combativeness and determination gained him far more praise when he was called upon by President Raymond Poincaré to form his second cabinet during **World War I**, lasting from 17 November 1917 to 18 January 1920. Loss of faith in the army leadership and a string of mutinies among French troops had served to depress the nation's mood. Clemenceau acted quickly to restore faith in the

Allied victory and was instrumental in having **Ferdinand Foch** placed at the head of the Allied armies. It was his unwavering pursuit of victory that earned him the nickname "tiger."

At the peace conference following the armistice, Clemenceau tried to strike a balance between the United States' desire for greater magnanimity toward the defeated enemy and the desire in France for punitive reparations. However, the problems in France provoked by mass demobilization and the adjustment to difficult economic circumstances undermined his prestige, and he was the surprising loser in the presidential election that took place in January 1920, thus retiring from politics at the remarkable age of 78. Clemenceau's endeavors to maintain Allied cooperation after the war in pursuit of a more stable international order met with only qualified success. But his undoubted achievement in taking the reins and leading his country to victory when it had been sliding into deep war-weariness secured his reputation as the most formidable leader of the **Third Republic**.

COHABITATION. A political term denoting three periods, 1986–1988, 1993–1995, and 1997–2002, when a president of the **Fifth Republic** had to face a majority in the National Assembly constituted by the opposition parties and had to choose his government from among them. In the first two cases it was the Socialist **François Mitterrand**, facing a center-right majority in the Assembly, who was forced to appoint the **Gaullists Jacques Chirac** and **Edouard Balladur** to fill the role of premier. In the third case it was Chirac who was forced to name the Socialist **Lionel Jospin** as his premier.

COLBERT, JEAN-BAPTISTE (1619–1683). As controller general of finance (from 1665) and secretary of state for the navy (from 1668) under **Louis XIV**, Colbert was the chief architect of the economic and administrative reforms that made France the dominant power in Europe. Colbert was born into a family of merchants in Reims and entered into public administration via a number of modest posts. His great opportunity arrived in 1651. Cardinal **Mazarin**, the preeminent political figure in France, had been forced to leave **Paris** for the provinces because of a period of tension between the crown and the *parlement*. He appointed Colbert his agent in Paris to remain in touch with developments there. When Mazarin's influence was restored, he recruited Colbert as his assistant and commended him to **Louis XIV** as his successor.

Colbert's major achievement lay in his reorganization of the state's finances, in particular the chaotic tax system. The revenue that accrued to the crown came mostly from a tax called the *taille,* levied in some districts on individuals and in others on land and businesses. The method of collection by royal appointees and a system of exemptions had, over the years, led to creeping and widespread corruption. By systematically reviewing the system of collection and exemptions, Colbert initiated a form of centralized supervision that reduced the level of abuse and spread the burden of taxation more fairly. The modernization of the state's revenue-raising powers was matched by Colbert's attempts to modernize France's productive and trading capacity. The tradition known as *Colbertisme* and its synonym, *dirigisme,* refer to Colbert's setting up state manufacturing plants to secure a share for France in the market for trade goods in the face of competition from countries like Holland and Britain.

By the same token, as secretary for the navy, Colbert understood the link between economic and colonial expansionism and the indispensable need for the effective deployment of military power to support these objectives. He instituted a rigorous program for the construction of warships in the bid to transform France into a great maritime power capable of projecting its influence in regions like the Indies and North America. In spite of the destabilizing effect on France of the wars engaged in by Louis XIV, the reforms pioneered by Colbert were able to take root, leaving France better equipped, with an orderly and efficient administration.

COLLABORATION. *See* VICHY REGIME.

COLONIALISM. The history of French colonialism goes back many centuries and occurs in waves. Although **William the Conqueror** came from Normandy to subjugate the English, the French nation-state had not yet been formed. It was under **Louis XIV** in the 17th century that the French absolutist state began to assert its dominance in Europe, forcing, for example, the Spanish to allow France to extend her reach into the modern-day Netherlands as one of the conditions of the Treaty of Nijmegen (1678).

Outside the European continent, a French presence was well established in North America and the Caribbean by the beginning of the 18th century, and the French preceded the British in attempting to exploit the commercial potential of India. But the **Seven Years' War** in the middle of the century dealt a severe blow to France's colonial ambitions and marked the eclipse of French power in North America and India by British interests. But the last and greatest wave of colonial expansion came in the 19th century. **Napoléon Bonaparte**'s attempt to create a network of small, French-controlled states in Europe at the beginning of the century lasted barely more than a decade. Much more lasting was the expansion into Africa that began in 1830 with military operations in **Algeria**. France joined with countries like **Great Britain**, **Germany**, Portugal, and Belgium in the scramble for more African possessions at the end of the century, enabling it to acquire the territories that formed French West Africa and French Equatorial Africa. Meanwhile France also imposed its domination over Morocco and Tunisia in North Africa. It was during the same period that military adventurism in the East, tacitly sanctioned under the premiership of **Jules Ferry**, allowed France to gain control over what was called French Indochina (presently Cambodia, Laos, and Vietnam). The early 20th century was a period of consolidation. In 1899 the British and the French had agreed on the division of spoils in Africa, and in the years that followed, the French reached accords with Germany over Morocco (1909) and the Congo (1911).

The years between the world wars were marked by a growing realization, particularly among the left in France, that the colonial enterprise was difficult to justify on moral grounds, but for most French people the existence of an empire was a fact of life. In the colonies, however, there were clear signs that the conquered peoples would not accept the unequal nature of the colonial relationship indefinitely, as the **Rif War** in Morocco illustrated. But it was not until after the collapse of France in **World War II** and the new order that emerged in 1945 that the push for independence in the colonies became irresistible and **decolonization** began. Despite the loss of its former colonies, France has retained a number of smaller overseas territories, namely New Caledonia, French Polynesia, Austral and Antarctic territories, and Wallis and Futuna. There are also two overseas "territorial collectivities": Mayotte and St. Pierre and Miquelon.

COMBES, EMILE (1835–1921). Radical republican politician and premier who became famous for his **anticlericalism**. Combes was educated in Catholic seminaries and originally intended to become a priest, but he abandoned this vocation and opted instead for a career in medicine. Combes entered public life when he was elected mayor of Pons in 1874 and eventually acceded to the post of premier when he was appointed to succeed **René Waldeck-Rousseau** in June 1902. Combes was committed to diminishing the power of religious institutions in French society and set about implementing Waldeck-Rousseau's Association Law of 1901 with the utmost rigor, resulting in the closure of thousands of religious schools by 1903. By 7 July 1904 he had obtained the abrogation of the **Falloux law** and prevented all religious bodies from teaching in France. However, Combes was eventually the victim of his own zeal when his cabinet was toppled in January 1905 because of the adverse reaction to the *Affaire des fiches*: the revelation that army officers had been spied upon to discriminate against those who retained certain loyalties to the Catholic Church.

COMMON PROGRAM. This program was the fruit of an alliance between the **Parti Socialiste** and the **Parti Communiste Français**, and was elaborated in 1972 with the intention of enabling the parties to secure the kind of parliamentary majority that would bring them to power. The program's proposals included the elimination of France's nuclear deterrent (known as the *force de frappe*); a package of **nationalizations** covering the financial and industrial sectors; social reforms, including an overhaul of the **social security** system; and the reform of institutions like the courts and the **police**. While the **Union of the Left** that had spawned the Common Program lost the 1973 elections, the narrow margin of defeat and the fact that it had secured 46 percent of the votes seemed to confirm the program's validity. But in reality it papered over major rifts between the **Socialists** and the **Communists** regarding areas like foreign policy and ignored the fact that the signatories saw it as a way of enhancing their respective positions on the left as well as defeating the right. Finally, and in spite of the left's success in the municipal elections of March 1977, negotiations aimed at updating the Common Program revealed irreconcilable differences between the Socialists and the Communists, and the alliance collapsed in September 1977. This, however, was exploited by the Socialists as proof of their independence vis-à-vis the Communists and, it has been argued, contributed to the success of **François Mitterrand**'s campaign in the presidential elections of 1981.

COMMUNARDS. *See* COMMUNE OF PARIS.

COMMUNE OF PARIS. An insurrection that took control of **Paris** from 18 March to 28 May 1871 in the aftermath of the **Franco-Prussian War**. The immediate cause of the uprising was a deep sense of grievance among Parisians at what they regarded as the punitive measures taken against them by the provisional government in Versailles headed by **Adolphe Thiers**. These measures included the end of the wartime moratorium on mortgages and rents, the end of the daily wage paid to **National Guard** militiamen in Paris, the arrest of popular left-wing leaders because of their opposition to the government's war policy, **press** censorship, and the attempt by the government to seize the cannons from Montmartre that the Parisians had forged for the defense of their city against the Prussians. Underlying these grievances was a sense of impending betrayal, sharpened by the privations endured by Paris during the war as the result of the provisional government's apparent desire to make peace at any price with the victorious Prussians. Though a Communal Assembly was popularly elected and the institutions of a revolutionary government were set up, the Commune did not have the benefit of a unified leadership. Instead, two recognizable factions emerged among the Communards, **Jacobin** and Proudhonist (*see* PIERRE-JOSEPH PROUDHON). The former, patriotic and authoritarian, drew their inspiration from the **French Revolution** of 1789 and identified with the revolutionary ideals of nationalism and fraternity with the community formed through revolutionary struggle, whereas the latter promoted the rights of the workers and preferred local autonomy to the centralizing tendencies of the Jacobins. It was Proudhonist thinking sympathetic to the formation of self-governing municipalities that helped inspire the formation of communes in **Lyon**, **Marseille**, **Bordeaux**, and St. Etienne.

The Commune of Paris was brutally suppressed by government troops during what came to be called Bloody Week (21–28 May 1871). Estimates of the number of Communards killed by government troops vary from 17,000 to 25,000, and over 50,000 were sentenced by military courts. A campaign for an amnesty for convicted Communards, largely animated by the nascent **socialist** movement in France, was soon under way, lasting from 1871 to 1880. The Commune rapidly became part of the mythology of the left in France and is now commonly regarded by academic historians as the last of the Parisian insurrections inspired by the ideals and the perceptions of the French Revolution.

COMMUNES. These constitute the most basic administrative units in France, formed after 1789 and based largely on preexisting parishes. There are 36,494 communes in France, and by the late 1980s approximately 30,000 of them had populations of less than 2,000. Led by an elected mayor, the commune has responsibility for decisions concerning local services, urban planning, and land use. But the inability of small communes to raise enough in local taxes to pay for necessary services helps to explain the development over recent years of collaborative projects, jointly administered by two or more communes. *See also* REGIONS.

COMMUNISTS. *See* PARTI COMMUNISTE FRANCAIS.

COMTE, AUGUSTE. *See* POSITIVISM.

CONCORDAT OF 1801. This agreement, signed by Pope Pius VII after secret negotiations in July of that year, reconciled the Catholic Church with the new regime in France and was the instrument that governed church-state relations for the next century. The concordat recognized **Catholicism** as the religion of the majority of the French people but not as the state **religion**. The pope was guaranteed possession of the reduced Papal States in Italy. The French government would pay the salaries of the clergy and have power of decision over the most senior appointments. The concordat allowed those who had purchased church property to have their titles to it validated. But most important, by reconciling refractory clergy to the government, the agreement neutralized much of the hostility to **Napoléon Bonaparte**'s regime from the members of the majority rural population of France who were still loyal to the church.

CONFEDERATION FRANCAISE DEMOCRATIQUE DU TRA-VAIL (CFDT)/DEMOCRATIC LABOR CONFEDERATION OF FRANCE. The **trade union** federation that emerged from a split within the **Confédération Française des Travailleurs Chrétiens (CFTC)** in 1964 and succeeded in drawing about 80 percent of the CFTC membership to its new secular ethos. Usually supportive of the **Socialists**, the CFDT took the middle ground between the **Communist Confédération Générale du Travail (CGT)** and the anticommunist **Force Ouvrière (FO)**. Though still a long way behind the CGT, the CFDT rapidly established itself as France's second-largest union confederation. It assumed a prominent role in the agitation of May 1968 and established itself as a major forum for new-left ideas.

Rather like the **Parti Socialiste**, which it supported conspicuously during the 1980s and for whom it became a source of many new ideas, the CFDT's bedrock support is found among white-collar salaried workers, especially those in high-technology industries. Rejecting the rhetoric of left-wing statism and the brute logic of free-market capitalism, the intellectual convictions that define the CFDT are essentially social democratic, stressing social justice, equality, and the rights of collectives at the grassroots, whether at the workplace or in society, to manage themselves. François Chérèque became general secretary of the union in 2002, and in 2005 it enjoyed the support of 806,829 members, a third of whom were over 50 years of age.

CONFEDERATION FRANCAISE DES TRAVAILLEURS CHRE-TIENS (CFTC)/FRENCH CONFEDERATION OF CHRISTIAN WORKERS. This is a Catholic union confederation that has its origins in the 19th-century attempt through the Catholic Workers' Circles founded by Albert de Mun in 1873 to offer the working classes an alternative to revolutionary Marxism and anarchosyndicalism. The recognizably modern CFTC had taken shape by 1919 but always harbored contradictory ambitions, notably the desire to draw blue-collar workers into a militant faith while preserving the movement from any ideological orientation. After 1945 and the onset of the Cold War, the CFTC tried to steer a course between the procommunist **Confédération Générale du Travail (CGT)** and the anticommunist **Force Ouvrière**, but its endeavor to remain above party politics prevented it from forming a mutually profitable relationship with France's only Christian Democratic party, the **Mouvement Républicain Populaire**. The irreversible shift to a secular society that developed in France after 1945 meant that the left-wing elements in the CFTC found the confessional basis of the union increasingly redundant. Thus they broke away in 1964 to form the **Confédération Française Démocratique du Travail (CFDT)**, taking the majority of the CFTC's members with them. The CFTC is now a minor player in the **trade union** movement, counting only 150,000 members in its ranks in 2004, and recruits predominantly among moderate white-collar and supervisory personnel.

CONFEDERATION GENERALE DU TRAVAIL (CGT)/GENERAL CONFEDERATION OF LABOR. France's most important **trade union**. After reunification with the communist-dominated Confédération Générale du Travail Unitaire, the CGT was dominated by communists during the period of the **Popular Front**. Tensions between communists and noncommunists within the union resurfaced in the wake of the Nazi-Soviet pact at the outset of **World War II**, and after the war the challenges of the noncommunists to the leadership during 1946 led ultimately to the emergence of a new tendency under the banner of **Force Ouvrière**. One of the consequences of the Cold War in France was the politicization of CGT tactics, notably in the wave of antigovernment strikes in 1947. The defeat of those strikes pushed the CGT into political isolation together with the **Parti Communiste Français (PCF)** and prompted a definitive split with Force Ouvrière.

During the mid-1950s the CGT succeeded in securing a relative degree of autonomy in regard to the PCF and thus gained credibility for its campaigns to improve the lot of the workers, but its broader credibility was undermined by its obedience to the PCF party line, as shown, for example, by its refusal to condemn the crushing of nascent popular democracy in Hungary in 1956 and Czechoslovakia in 1968 by Soviet tanks. The extent to which the CGT had lost touch with the feelings of the grassroots of the union movement was illustrated by its surprise about, and mistrust of, the alliance between students and workers in the **student rebellion** of May 1968. It demonstrated a more constructive attitude toward the other forces of the left by its active part in the negotiation of the **Common Program** in 1972, but when this came to an end in 1978 after the break between the Communists and the **Socialists**, the CGT followed the lead of the PCF.

During the period that followed, the CGT was similarly disinclined to share a common strategy with its fellow unions and showed little enthusiasm for the policy of self-management *(autogestion)* espoused by the **Confédération Française Démocratique du Travail (CFDT)**, even though the closures across heavy industry and the subsequent effects on CGT membership underlined the need for a more modern and effective pursuit of workers' interests. The CGT supported the Auroux laws of 1982, which were promulgated by a Socialist government and sought to reinforce the rights of workers in the workplace. But the union's membership and influence continued to decline. The unpopular attempt of the center-right government of **Alain Juppé** to push through reforms of the **social security** system and the employment conditions of state employees provided the CGT with a good opportunity to regain influence and prestige. It did so through its successful organization of strikes that paralyzed the public sector, especially the transport network, for three weeks from the end of November to the middle of December 1995, ultimately forcing the Juppé government into a more conciliatory negotiating position. Bernard Thibault has been general secretary of the union since 1999, and while its membership increased from 634,000 to 711,000 between 1997 and 2005, this has to be measured against a long-term pattern of decline given that in 1975 it was able to count on the support of 2,377,000 members.

CONSEIL FRANCAIS DU CULTE MUSULMAN. *See* ISLAM.

CONSTANT DE REBECQUE, BENJAMIN (1767–1830). Swiss-born man of letters and political activist and subject of society gossip for his tempestuous affair with **Anne-Louise-Germaine de Staël**, which lasted from 1794 to 1811. A critic of **Napoléon Bonaparte**, he described Napoléon's return to France in March 1815 (*see* HUNDRED DAYS) as that of a modern-day Attila or Genghis Khan. He made a reputation for himself as a novelist during the **Bourbon** restoration with works like *Adolphe* (1816) and also served as a liberal in the Chamber of Deputies (1819–1822, 1824–1830). His journalism and his political essays expressed a conviction that liberty had to be defended against democracy as well as despotism, since the former can be equivalent to the tyranny of the majority.

CONSTITUTION OF THE REPUBLIC. The constitutions of all the French republics have taken as their fundamental template the ambitions spelled out in the Declaration of the Rights of Man and the Citizen, essentially the manifesto of the **French Revolution** of 1789 that established the sovereignty of the people; the inalienable right of each individual citizen to liberty, equality, and fraternity; the independence and impartiality of the law; and the principle of representative government. The differences lay in the institutional interpretation given to those principles. Thus it was not until the **Third Republic** that universal suffrage was applied in the modern sense, irrespective of a property or tax qualification, and then only to men. Women had to wait until October 1944 before the interpretation of that right was extended to them.

The extension of suffrage to women was in recognition of their contribution to the fight against the one regime in 20th-century France that had rejected the template bequeathed in 1789, **Vichy**. The regime established under Marshal **Philippe Pétain** rejected even the very notion of the republic and took as its guiding principle the belief in a national community identified in racial terms and united in a faith in hierarchical values reminiscent of pre-revolutionary France. The moral legitimacy of the **Resistance** derived from its determination to restore the republic and the values that defined it, which was accomplished with the adoption of the constitution of the **Fourth Republic** in 1946. However, the difficulties faced by postwar France led to disagreement as to the constitutional arrangements defining the balance of power between the executive and the legislature. The constitution of the Fourth Republic, like that of its predecessor, made the **presidency** a largely ceremonial office and left the head of government, known as the président du conseil, in a state of perpetual negotiation with the parties in the Assembly in the attempt to secure a majority that would allow him to push through government measures. By the 1950s, as during the 1930s under the Third Republic, the life of a government could more accurately be measured in months rather than years.

Forced to confront their inability to manage the threat of civil war in the colony of **Algeria**, in 1958 the political parties were obliged to call on the providential leader they feared, General **Charles de Gaulle**. The quid pro quo was a new constitution for a **Fifth Republic**, which restored the balance of power in favor of the executive and gave it the power of unilateral decision making that it had previously lacked. The constitution was approved by a massive majority of the French people in a referendum in the fall of 1958, and in the legislative elections of November that year the **Gaullist party** won a majority in the Assembly. The constitution had created a presidential system with a president, now armed with the big stick provided by the power of dissolution, who delegated the everyday management of domestic matters to a prime minister that he could hire and fire, drawn from a compliant majority in the National Assembly, while he kept as his reserve the elaboration of **foreign** and **defense** policy. De Gaulle further reinforced his power by proposing an amendment to the constitution that freed him from the old system of being chosen by a parliamentary college and allowed him to seek a mandate directly from the people, which was adopted by referendum in 1962.

The test of the adaptability of the constitution came in 1981 with, for the first time, the defeat of the Gaullist majority and its allies by the **Parti Socialiste (PS)** in the presidential and legislative elections of that year. In reality, **François Mitterrand**, the PS leader, fitted very comfortably into the presidential mold established by de Gaulle. He played the dominant role in the exercise of executive power with his own brand of aloofness, and even when the Gaullists regained power in the Assembly in the legislative elections of 1986, the unprecedented **cohabitation** of a president with a prime minister who had to be drawn from a hostile majority did not dent Mitterrand's credibility. When Prime Minister **Jacques Chirac** tried to impinge on the president's territory, namely foreign policy, he was rapidly outmaneuvered by Mitterrand and forced to carry the can for the failures of domestic policy, thus contributing to Mitterrand's reelection as president in 1988, backed up by a left-wing majority from the ensuing legislative elections.

The debate that has developed over the constitution of the Republic since the 1990s has not centered on the balance between executive and legislative power, but has been essentially about the philosophical assumptions underlying the constitution, notably regarding the freedoms and obligations of citizens. Talk of a sixth republic with a constitution equipped for 21st-century France has been spurred by events such as the banning of Muslim girls wearing headscarves from the state **education** system. For some commentators, the universalist assumptions made about the citizen were shaped in a different era, and the belief that the abstract principles of liberty, equality, and fraternity are enough to secure the loyalty of the citizen to a secular republic is now naive in a multicultural France where millions of citizens make no distinction between the secular and religious in their daily lives. Conversely, anxiety has arisen among those who espouse the traditional republican ethos of secularism in public life due to some of the pronouncements of President **Nicolas Sarkozy**, such as his address to the Grand Mosque in Paris to mark the end of Ramadan in 2007, when he explicitly committed himself to recognizing the needs of the Muslim community in France and thus, according to his critics, encouraged the prospect of a France divided by differences rather than united by the common values enshrined in the constitution of the secular republic.

THE CONSULATE. The three-man executive body of government set up in 1799, with **Napoléon Bonaparte** as first consul with overriding authority. Bonaparte's consecration as consul for life in 1802 illustrated his irresistible grip on power, preparing the way for the establishment of his empire in 1804 and thereby making the simulacrum of power-sharing represented by the Consulate redundant.

CONVENTION (1792–1795). Representative body elected by universal male suffrage on 10 August 1792, after the overthrow of **Louis XVI**, with the aim of writing a constitution for a French republic. It was the Convention that tried the king and sent him to the **guillotine** on 21 January 1793. Dominated by the radical **Montagnard** deputies, the Convention expelled the more moderate **Girondins** in June 1793. This provoked a revolt in cities such as **Lyon, Bordeaux, Marseille**, and Toulon. In view of the threat to the **French Revolution** from within France and the threat externally from the major European powers (except **Russia**), a war government was formed with a Committee of Public Safety whose work was ultimately presided over by **Maximilien Robespierre**. The ensuing centralization of power and the ruthless persecution of the presumed enemies of the

Revolution that occurred during 1793–1794 came to be known as the **Terror**. When the tide turned against the enemies of the Revolution, the Convention rebelled against the Terror and the dictatorial Robespierre, sending him to the guillotine on 28 July 1794. The Convention then took a conservative turn in the so-called Thermidorian reaction (*see* THERMIDOR), when the populace of **Paris** revolted against the Convention on 5 October 1795 and tried to storm the Tuileries, where it was sitting. The Convention was saved by the artillery deployed by **Napoléon Bonaparte**, but it had effectively run its course and was replaced by the **Directory**.

CORDELIERS CLUB (1790–1795). Parisian political society whose power over the militant revolutionaries of the capital between 1790 and 1794 rivaled that of the **Jacobins**. Formally named the Société des Amis des Droits de l'Homme et du Citoyen (Society of Friends of the Rights of Man and the Citizen), it was founded in April 1790 under the leadership of figures who had taken the lead in democratic agitation in **Paris** during the previous year, such as **Georges Jacques Danton**, **Jean-Paul Marat**, and **Camille Desmoulins**. The name of the club derived from its first meeting place, a former Franciscan, or *Cordelier*, monastery in the rue des Cordeliers on the Left Bank. The club portrayed itself as a watchdog against the abuse of power by the pubic authorities and campaigned vigorously for universal suffrage and measures of direct democracy like the passing of legislation by referendum. It began to challenge the centralization of power by the autumn of 1793 but antagonized **Robespierre** and his Committee of Public Safety. The leaders of the Cordeliers Club were arrested in the spring of 1794 on a charge of conspiring to overthrow the **Convention** and executed, thereby ending the club's influence. *See also* FRENCH REVOLUTION.

CORSICA. *See* SEPARATISM.

COTY, RENE (1882–1962). He was the last president of the **Fourth Republic** and played a crucial role in bringing General **Charles de Gaulle** back to power. He was born into a republican family of schoolteachers in Le Havre and obtained his higher education at the University of Caen, eventually qualifying as a lawyer specializing in maritime law. He was elected for the first time to the Chamber of Deputies in 1923. After having voted to give power to Marshal **Philippe Pétain** in 1940, he kept his distance from the wartime regime in France and returned to parliamentary politics after the **liberation**. Coty's bid for the **presidency** came in 1953, at the end of **Vincent Auriol**'s term in office. By that time a 71-year-old conservative senator, Coty was finally elected on the 12th ballot as the most neutral candidate. In naming a premier, Coty usually opted for the candidate most likely to secure consensus, but he placed himself conspicuously in the line of fire when the Fourth Republic entered the fatal climax to the crisis in **Algeria**. In the immediate aftermath of the mutinous stirrings of the French army in May 1958, Coty decided to push for a Gaullist solution and, citing the prospect of civil war, threatened to resign if the National Assembly did not overcome its reservations and invest de Gaulle as head of the government. Coty's gamble was successful, and when he decided not to seek a renewal of his presidential mandate seven months later, the way was left open for de Gaulle.

COUNTERREVOLUTION. The movement aimed at reversing the **French Revolution** and critical of revolution in general. The counterrevolution was born with the Revolution and driven by those, notably members of the clergy and nobility, who had most to lose with the demise of the **ancien régime**. However, counterrevolutionaries did put forward a philosophical justification for their actions, based on the beliefs articulated by thinkers like the Englishman Edmund Burke, who argued that it was not possible to build a lasting society through a utopian desire to wipe the slate clean and start anew (*Reflections on the Revolution in France*, 1790). Later in the decade the counterrevolutionaries found support in the work of French thinkers like Joseph de Maistre and the comte de Bonald, who argued that man had duties, not rights, and that it was necessary to return to the church and a divinely ordained social order if the moral decadence that had provoked the Revolution was to be repaired.

However, the counterrevolutionaries acted before these theories were disseminated. They had begun to flee France almost immediately after 14 July 1789, and by the end of 1791 there were small émigré armies on the banks of the **Rhine**. They joined the Prussian army when it launched its offensive against France in April 1792, but their hopes were frustrated with the defeat of the Prussian army at **Valmy** (20 September 1792). The great counterrevolutionary threat from within France arose in the Vendée. Although originally in favor of the Revolution, the Vendéens had been alienated by the mass conscription of their young men into the French army and by what they, as devout **Catholics**, regarded as the assault on the church. Thus on 11 March 1793, peasants from Vendée and Anjou rose up against the **Convention** and formed a poorly organized Catholic and Royal Army of over 10,000 men. This insurrectionary army failed to secure the ports from which it might have been successfully supported by the émigrés and their British allies, and was definitively beaten by regular troops nine months later. Resistance in the region moved to Brittany and was continued by the *Chouans*, but these were essentially guerrilla operations.

The other major threat to the Revolution was constituted by the federalist uprising, which also occurred in 1793. Many elected councils and revolutionary clubs in the provinces had been outraged by the way the **Paris Commune** had pressured the Convention into expelling 29 **Girondin** deputies, also known as federalists, in June 1793, in an act that seemed to symbolize the dictatorship of **Paris** over France. The reaction in southeastern France was particularly fierce, with violent revolts against the Convention in **Lyon, Marseille,** Nîmes, and Toulon. However, the opposition in the regional centers was not coordinated, and the rebels fell to the troops of the Convention as the year progressed. This last major counterrevolutionary threat was eliminated with the victory of the Convention's forces in December 1793 at the key port of Toulon (which had appealed to the English and Spanish fleets for help), thanks to the leadership of a young artillery commander named **Napoléon Bonaparte**.

COUVE DE MURVILLE, MAURICE (1907–1999). Civil servant and politician who served most notably as **Charles de Gaulle**'s foreign minister for 10 years. Couve de Murville was born into a highly respected **Protestant** family in Reims and educated in **Paris** before embarking on a career as a civil servant in 1932. The war brought an end to his political impartiality, and he joined the **Resistance** in **Algeria**. With the end of the war and the advent of the **Fourth Repub-**

lic, Couve de Murville's career led him to focus on **Germany** and in particular France's attitude to the creation of the Federal Republic of Germany. His experience in this domain and his personal commitment to de Gaulle's vision of the future for France resulted in the offer of ministerial office when de Gaulle returned to power in 1958. Couve de Murville is recognized as having played a key part, as foreign minister, in guiding his country toward the Franco-German treaty of cooperation in 1963 and in laying the foundation for the Paris-Bonn axis that remains the driving force behind the project to build a united Europe. Couve de Murville was appointed prime minister by de Gaulle in July 1968, but he remained in that post only until April 1969, when the referendum de Gaulle had called to gain approval for his administrative reforms went against him, prompting the general's resignation. Couve de Murville was a **Gaullist** deputy in the National Assembly until he was elected a senator for Paris on 28 September 1986.

CRESSON, EDITH (1934–). Socialist politician and first, though short-lived, woman prime minister of France. She was born in **Paris**, the daughter of a civil servant, and was also educated there, emerging with a business degree from the school of Hautes Etudes Commerciales. Her political career, as well as her alliance with **François Mitterrand**, began in the fall of 1965 when she helped organize Mitterand's presidential campaign. She rose to become national secretary of the new **Parti Socialiste (PS)** shaped by Mitterrand in 1971, but her attempts to become a deputy were frustrated until 1981, when she was elected to the National Assembly as a Socialist representative from Vienne. She soon resigned her seat to become France's first female minister of agriculture (1981–1983), and this was followed by other ministerial portfolios, including industrial restructuring and European affairs. Cresson resigned her ministerial career to join the private sector in 1990 because of differences with Prime Minister **Michel Rocard** over what she perceived to be Rocard's failure to prepare France to face the increasing rigors of international competition, especially in the industrial sphere.

Mitterrand's choice of Cresson as the successor to Rocard in 1991 came as a surprise to many observers, but with hindsight the choice of a supporter of such proven loyalty was not without logic given the increasingly tense relationship that had developed between Mitterrand and his old rival. Rocard's emergence as a presidential aspirant and as the focus of expectation for the "new left" in the PS had made his departure, whether forced or voluntary, inevitable. By the same token, Rocard's standing in the party and, according to the opinion polls, in the country as a whole was destined to make Cresson's tenure as prime minister a difficult one. Her task was rendered more complex by the fact that she was not given the leeway by the president to refashion her cabinet comprehensively to make a new start. Lacking the immense experience of her predecessor, Cresson gave a lackluster prime-ministerial performance in parliament. More important in terms of her relationship with her party, she paid scant regard to what had been achieved by her Socialist forerunners in the post and the overarching ambitions of the PS. These omissions did little to compensate for the absence of a power base in the party, so when Cresson was attacked by her opponents on the right during the forthcoming months, the party did not mobilize in her defense.

When Cresson made awkward statements on prickly issues like **immigration**, such as when she affirmed that the government would charter planes if necessary to repatriate illegal immigrants, she was condemned by members of her own party for adopting the rhetoric of the far right, although her government explicitly strengthened its commitment to the right of asylum in France for political refugees. When Cresson presented plans for government-sponsored incentives to increase the competitiveness of French small and medium-size businesses, she was criticized by the right for measures that would increase the tax burden on the private sector and castigated by sections of the left for giving financial breaks to traditional supporters of the right while the left-wing constituency in the public sector was having to cope with ever tighter budgets. These were individual difficulties occurring against a general background of inexorably rising unemployment and poor economic trends. Furthermore, as her cabinet braced itself for the verdict of the electorate in the regional and local elections scheduled for the spring of 1992, Cresson found her control over ministerial colleagues who were also heavyweights in the PS increasingly challenged, particularly in the case of the man who would succeed her, **Pierre Bérégovoy**. The regional and local elections of March 1992 inflicted a heavy defeat on the PS. In view of Cresson's poor standing in the party and her exceptionally low standing in the country, it was clear that she would have to pay the price after ten months in office. On 2 April 1992 Mitterrand appointed Bérégovoy her successor as prime minister.

Cresson had herself provided the neatest obituary to her prime ministerial career when she confessed that there were only two high points in holding such a post—being formally appointed prime minister and resigning. Between 1994 and 1999 she served as European Commissioner with particular responsibility for science, research, and development. But this was also to be tainted with failure when, in 2006, the European Court of Justice found her to have acted improperly when she had recruited her dentist to work in her cabinet during her time as a commissioner, at the expense of the European taxpayer. *See also* ECONOMY; EUROPEAN UNION.

CUBISM. A major artistic movement of the first half of the 20th century that originated in 1907 with the work of Pablo Picasso and Georges Braque. Cubism has been regarded as the 20th-century antithesis of **impressionism**, and its development fell into two phases. During the first, "analytic," phase beginning in 1907, Picasso and Braque endeavored to challenge fundamentally the representation of three-dimensional forms on the two-dimensional picture plane by replacing the traditional single fixed viewpoint with a number of different viewpoints, thus fusing multiple views of the subject into a single image. At the same time, perspective was transformed into a new shallow space extending both behind and in front of the picture plane, and forms were reduced to simple geometric shapes. The second, "synthetic," phase began in 1913 with the introduction of extraneous elements such as strips of paper, textile, and chair caning into the paintings. This phase continued until 1925, when cubism ceased to be a coherent movement. *See also* ART.

CURIE, MARIE (1867–1934). Polish-born, French Nobel Prize–winning physicist. As Marie Sklodowska she left her native Poland in 1891 to study physical sciences at the Sorbonne, and it was there in 1894 that she met and later married Pierre Curie. Partners in science as well as in marriage, they made discoveries of global significance, most notably the discovery of polonium (so named by Marie in honor of her country of birth) and radium. The Curies shared the 1903 Nobel Prize for the discovery of radioactivity with Henri Becquerel. Pierre's sudden death in 1906 strengthened Marie's determination to finish the work they had started, and her efforts were crowned by a second Nobel Prize in 1911, for the isolation of pure radium. The breakthrough made by Marie Curie lay in her understanding of the need to accumulate intense radioactive sources, vital for the treatment of illness and for research into nuclear physics. Her commitment to her subject exacted a high price; she died from radiation-induced leukemia. But the immensity of her contribution to science is underlined by the institutions named after her in France and elsewhere and the fact that succeeding generations of scientists have acknowledged their debt to her. *See also* WOMEN.

– D –

DALADIER, EDOUARD (1884–1970). Major republican political figure in the 1930s and prime minister when France entered **World War II**. He was born in the town of Carpentras and became a history teacher before being elected to the Chamber of Deputies in 1919. Initially promoted by **Edouard Herriot**, Daladier served in a number of cabinets before becoming premier in January 1933. He returned as premier in January 1934 in the wake of the **Stavisky affair**, seized upon by right-wing groups in their efforts to discredit the republican regime. The affair culminated on 6 February 1934 in a failed attempt to take physical control of the Chamber of Deputies. Daladier resigned his premiership the following day, but the action of the far right mobilized left-wing parties in the defense of the Republic and led to the formation of the **Popular Front**. Daladier returned to the premiership in 1938, but his energies were increasingly devoted to **foreign policy**. He was responsible, together with British Prime Minister Neville Chamberlain, for the policy of appeasement toward Adolf Hitler and eventually led France into the war. He was replaced as premier by **Paul Reynaud** in 1940. Arrested and tried by the **Vichy regime**, he was deported to **Germany** in 1943 and remained there until his liberation in 1945. He served as a deputy after the war from 1946 until his retirement in 1958 and died in **Paris** on 10 October 1970.

DANTON, GEORGES-JACQUES (1759–1794). Famous militant of the **French Revolution** and deputy in the **Convention**. He was born in Arcis-sur-Aube in the Champagne region and left for **Paris** in 1780 to study law. Illness and his indifferent performance as a pupil eventually led him to purchase a diploma from Reims. He first displayed his formidable talents as an orator in Parisian local politics and became a leading light of the **Cordeliers Club**. His most famous speech was given to the Assembly in the late summer of 1792 when France seemed in danger of succumbing to a foreign invasion; he roused his listeners with an injunction to dare and dare again so that France might be saved. Although appointed minister of justice earlier in the summer, Danton took an interest in many other aspects of the government's work and was active in the field of **foreign policy**. He supported the **Terror** and was elected to the Committee of Public Safety.

However, his prestige on the committee waned as **Robespierre**'s grew stronger, and by the end of 1793, Danton was beginning to articulate cautious criticism of the Terror, suggesting that it was casting its net too wide. In the spring of 1794 he was arrested along with others whose pity for the prisoners of the Terror was judged to be endangering the Republic. The charges against him were carefully prepared and the outcome predetermined. Even so, Danton spoke with such engaging passion that at one point the courtroom audience broke into applause in support of him. Consequently, and to avoid further embarrassment, the presiding judge obtained a special decree bringing the trial to a premature close, and Danton was executed on 16 Germinal Year II, according to the revolutionary calendar. Danton's inexplicable wealth suggests that he was a corrupt man, and the twists in his career indicate that his attitudes could be self-serving, but he was also capable of inspiring his fellow citizens through acts of revolutionary heroism.

DARLAN, FRANCOIS (1881–1942). Talented naval officer who rose to become commander in chief of the French navy in 1939, and a leading critic of the **Third Republic** in 1940. Born in Nérac (Lot-et-Garonne) into a republican family, Darlan nonetheless chose a career in the navy, the service known for its royalist sympathies. He graduated from the French naval academy in 1902 and came to prominence during the interwar years for his exceptional contribution in naval affairs. In 1936 he was given the post of navy chief of staff and, through the pursuit of his belief in modernization, helped make the French navy one of the most formidable in the world. As the commander in chief of the French navy at the outbreak of **World War II**, Darlan saw his prestige immeasurably enhanced by the fact that it was the only one of the French services to escape the German onslaught intact. The sinking of the French fleet by the British at Mersel-Kebir in 1940 did not diminish Darlan's standing, and he became a dominant figure in the **Vichy** government, enjoying a privileged relationship with **Philippe Pétain**. However, Darlan countermanded Pétain's orders to Vichy French troops in North Africa to resist the Allies after their landing in November 1942. Instead, he concluded a cease-fire with General Dwight Eisenhower that led to the French troops in North Africa joining the side of the Allies. But this did not prevent him from being assassinated by a young anti-Vichy student on 24 December 1942. *See also* GERMANY.

DATI, RACHIDA (1965–). French justice minister and center-right politician. One of 12 children born in the Burgundy region to a Moroccan worker in the building industry and an Algerian mother, Dati did a variety of jobs to put herself through college, emerging with a master's degree in economics from Dijon University. She then enrolled in the Ecole Nationale de la Magistrature and qualified to be a magistrate in the service of the state in 1999. She joined **Nicolas Sarkozy**, then interior minister, as an adviser in 2002 with a special brief to examine the draft legislation aimed at tackling delinquency. The relationship with Sarkozy went from strength to strength, and when Dati joined the new vehicle for the **Gaullist party**, the Union pour la Majorité Populaire, in 2006, it cleared the way for her to promote his ambitions in the party and ultimately become his chief spokesperson in the presidential campaign of 2007. Dati soon earned a reputation as tough and outspoken, especially on social issues, and used her own racial and social background as evidence for confronting the argument that the alienated youth of the suburbs had no alternative but violence or despair. Her reward came in May 2007 when President Sarkozy appointed her justice minister. It was the first time a young female member of an ethnic minority had been appointed to one of the chief offices of state in France. Since then, Dati has had to deploy her most combative talents vis-à-vis the media, especially when one of her brothers appeared in court in the summer of 2007 on a charge of drug dealing. *See also* IMMIGRATION.

DAVID, JACQUES-LOUIS (1748–1825). First painter to the emperor **Napoléon Bonaparte**. In paintings such as the *Coronation* (1807) and the *Distribution of the Eagles* (1810), David depicted scenes that helped to confirm the legitimacy of the new order under Napoléon and popularize the image of him as the protector of the positive changes brought about by the **French Revolution**. David possessed an independence of mind that sometimes set him at odds with Napoléon and fellow artists, but his work helped determine the style of later historical painting. *See also* EMPIRE STYLE.

DEATH PENALTY. Abolished by the new Socialist government of **Pierre Mauroy** in September 1981 as one of a series of libertarian reforms aimed at asserting France's break with the archaisms of its conservative past.

DEBRAY, REGIS (1940–). One of the most colorful figures of the French intellectual elite. Debray was born into an affluent, conservative milieu in **Paris** whose politics he rejected through his opposition to French policy in **Algeria**. At the age of 18 he gained entrance to the elite Ecole Normale Supérieure, where he came under the influence of figures like **Louis Althusser** and **Jean-Paul Sartre**. In 1961 he began a period of travel and teaching in Latin America, during the course of which he began a much publicized friendship with the revolutionary Che Guevara. He was arrested after traveling to Bolivia in March 1967 to interview Guevara and spent three years in a Bolivian prison. After his release, Debray came to the conclusion that society could be reformed radically through parliamentary means, and in 1974 he gave his allegiance to **François Mitterrand** and the **Parti Socialiste**. Mitterrand's triumph in the presidential election of 1981 resulted in Debray's appointment as a special assistant to the president, with specific responsibility for policy in Latin America and the Middle East. During the course of the following year, he acquired an additional post as adviser to the president on cultural affairs. Yet, in spite of having become a member of the new Socialist establishment, Debray continued to nurture his reputation for controversy through his critique of the pervasive conservatism of French life. The author of numerous books, Debray also contributed to the intellectual debate in France by accepting academic posts, most recently as president of l'Institut Européen en Sciences et Religions, from 2002 to 2004.

DEBRE, MICHEL (1912–1996). The Gaullist politician chiefly responsible for drawing up the constitution of the **Fifth Republic**. Born into an affluent Parisian family where both parents were physicians, Debré received an excellent education that culminated in his receipt of a doctorate in law from the University of Paris in 1934. He escaped France in 1940 and joined the Free French, later returning to France to work with the underground. In 1945 **Charles de Gaulle** appointed him to a new commission entrusted with the task of reforming the civil service. One of its major achievements was the establishment of the Ecole Nationale d'Administration, credited with creating a new generation of technocrats who played a crucial part in the modernization of France.

Debré failed in his bid for a place in the Chamber of Deputies in 1946, but the following year he was elected to the Senate, where he distinguished himself as a Gaullist stalwart and a critic of the weakness of the executive in the **Fourth Republic**, which was caused by the concentration of power in the Chamber of Deputies. It was not surprising, therefore, that when the Algerian crisis brought de Gaulle back to power in May 1958, he named Debré minister of justice and head of the commission appointed to draft the constitution of the new Fifth Republic. This new constitution strengthened the hand of the president considerably, raising him above petty party conflicts while granting him the kinds of prerogatives that enabled him to define the thrust of government policy. Once the constitution was ratified and de Gaulle was elected president, he made Debré the Fifth Republic's first prime minister. Debré made his mark early through the development of a **foreign policy** that was more reconciled to the inevitable, such as the independence of **Algeria** in 1962. After resigning in 1962, he returned within a few years to hold a number of ministerial posts over the next decade, and in 1979 he was elected to the European Parliament. A much respected figure and author of numerous books on a variety of subjects, Debré received many prestigious honors, including the Croix de Guerre and the **Légion d'Honneur**. *See also* CONSTITUTION OF THE REPUBLIC; DECOLONIZATION.

DEBUSSY, CLAUDE (1862–1918). Third Republic composer with the greatest influence on subsequent generations of European and American composers. He was born into a humble family in Saint-Germain-en-Laye (Seine-et-Oise) on 22 August 1862. His education was very focused on **music**, and he studied at the Paris Conservatory from 1872 to 1884. He also studied in Rome as a result of winning the first Prix de Rome for his cantata *L'Enfant prodigue* (1884). He broadened his musical experience by traveling widely in Europe but rejected the influence of Wagner's romanticism on orchestral music and turned instead to the rediscovery of French preromantic musical traditions. His familiarity with the work of **symbolist** poets and **impressionist** painters was a profound source of inspiration for his most important works for orchestra and for piano. In spite of the fame brought by the performance of such orchestral works as *Prélude à l'après-midi d'un faune* (1894) and *La mer* (1905), Debussy had to supplement his income as a composer by teaching piano privately, working as a music critic, and giving concert tours.

Debussy's influence stemmed from the fact that his compositions were unusually unconstrained by traditional norms in form, harmony, and coloring and attempted to evoke an atmosphere in the same way as the symbolists and impressionists. This gave his work a rare degree of psychological penetration through understatement. As well as enlarging the boundaries of European music by turning to medieval and oriental traditions, Debussy challenged the distinctions between dissonance and consonance, paving the way for the many new harmonic developments of the 20th century.

DECENTRALIZATION. A policy trumpeted by groups and parties that were concerned by what they considered the excessive concentration of power in France and that envisaged the transfer of power from the center to the provinces. The historical impulse to centralize had occurred under the **ancien régime** as a means of overcoming strong feudal power bases outside **Paris**, on the road to a unitary sense of nationhood and the creation of a state that could be governed by an absolute monarch. The paradoxical effect of the **French Revolution** of 1789 was to reinforce centralization by focusing legitimacy on nationally elected representatives in Paris, who then legislated for the provinces. After **Napoléon Bonaparte** came to power, an administrative system was completed that meant effectively that any significant decision making at a local level could not occur without referring back to Paris through the figure appointed by the center to govern in local jurisdictions, that is, the prefect.

Under the **Third Republic**, greater autonomy was given to the towns, and the imbalance between Paris and the provinces was attenuated through the greater input offered to local elites in policymaking. However, the pattern remained basically unchallenged until the 1960s. After **Charles de Gaulle**'s plans for decentralization, which included the creation of corporatist regional assemblies, were defeated by referendum in 1969, the next two presidents, **Georges Pompidou** and **Valéry Giscard d'Estaing**, decided to resist the temptation to engage in such reforms. It took the victory of the **Socialists** in 1981 to put the issue on the agenda once more. Decentralization became one of the major policy initiatives of the first term of **François Mitterand**'s **presidency** and resulted in the creation of popularly elected councils in the *départements* and *régions*. Furthermore, these councils were granted new powers over economic initiatives like measures to tackle unemployment, enhanced by new revenue-raising powers. Significant new powers concerning urban and territorial development were also devolved to the regions.

On the one hand, the policy of decentralization was a democratic response to the French electorate's need for more supple, responsive, and closely accountable forms of government. On the other, as exemplified by the numerous local financial and political scandals that had emerged by the mid-1990s, the policy of decentralization sometimes facilitated the emergence of new local elites who answered to no one other than themselves. Between 2002 and 2004 the government of Prime Minister **Jean-Pierre Raffarin**, during the presidency of **Jacques Chirac**, put the issue of decentralization back on the political agenda, but to little effect practically and without eliciting much enthusiasm from the French electorate.

DECOLONIZATION. The process that, during the decade and a half after **World War II**, marked the rapid breakup of the French empire and the end of old-fashioned French **colonialism**. The humiliation of France during the war had done much to tarnish the image of European supremacy among her subject peoples, especially in the Far East. While the Brazzaville Conference of February 1944 had signaled recognition by the French of the need to reform the postwar relationship between **Paris** and the colonies, the conquest of North Vietnam by the nationalists under Ho Chi Minh in September 1944 showed that it was too little, too late. The creation of the **French Union** in 1946 guaranteed equality of individuals among the former members of the empire, but not of the collective entities within it, thus leaving France with a clearly dominant role. The humiliating defeat of the French in the **Indochinese War** set an example for other colonial peoples and brought home the lesson to the politicians in Paris that a certain measure of change was unavoidable. Consequently, the moves were started that resulted in independence for Tunisia and Morocco in 1956.

The return of **Charles de Gaulle** to power in 1958 led to the abandonment of the French Union in favor of the vague but flexible concept of "community." Central African Republic, Chad, Congo, Dahomey, Gabon, Ivory Coast, Madagascar, Mauritania, Niger, Senegal, Sudan, and Upper Volta all contracted into the new community. Although the project lasted little more than a year, it nonetheless paved the way for the independence of all of France's African colonies by the 1960s. It was with **Algeria**, with its million-strong French community, that the parting of the ways was most difficult and painful. Faced with an increasingly costly war of independence waged by the Algerian nationalists, and finally convinced of the impossibility of reconciling the wishes of the French minority there with the wishes of the Algerian majority, de Gaulle concluded that independence was inevitable. The voters in France had also become exhausted by the conflict, and in the referendum of April 1962, 90 percent of them voted for the Evian agreements granting Algeria its independence, thus ending the final chapter in French colonialism. This did not mean, however, that France would abandon attempts to retain a privileged relationship vis-à-vis its former colonies. French influence has been exercised through development aid, trading links, and, especially since the 1980s, through cultural programs that come under the linguistic umbrella of *francophonie*. *See also* NEW CALEDONIA.

DECONSTRUCTION. *See* DERRIDA, JACQUES.

DEFENSE POLICY. The defense posture of successive French governments since 1945, particularly their determination to uphold France's status as a major power and the prickly reaction to any developments that might compromise the independence of French decision makers, needs to be located in a historical context that goes back to the 19th century. The rout of French forces in the **Franco-Prussian War** exposed the chronic complacency of the high command, which was matched only by its failure to appreciate the strengths of the enemy, and created a sense of bitterness that endured into the 20th century. Ironically for France, although it emerged victorious from **World War I**, its dependence on the Anglo-American allies was beyond dispute, and it entered peacetime with an active workforce and an industrial base that had suffered greater losses, in proportional terms, than the beaten enemy, **Germany**. And although France emerged once more on the winning side in 1945, the fact that its army had been routed again by German troops within a matter of weeks at the outset of the war and that its dependence on the Anglo-American allies had this time been complete stoked the French policymakers' determination to preempt the possibility of the recurrence of such national humiliations.

The economic weakness of France in the immediate aftermath of **World War II** reconciled its leaders to the need for alliances against external threats, leading to the Dunkirk Treaty with **Great Britain** in March 1947, which provided for a rapid joint response to any renewal of German aggression. However, with Germany occupied and divided, it soon became clear that the threat to Europe was constituted by the **Soviet Union**, and the two signatories to the Dunkirk Treaty joined with the Benelux countries in March 1948 to establish the Brussels Treaty Organization (BTO), an agreement to act collectively in the defense of any member subject to attack. British Foreign Secretary Ernest Bevin and French Foreign Minister **Georges Bidault** played a major part in promoting the idea of collective security in North America, and eventually, in April 1949, the **United States**, Canada, and 10 European states signed the North Atlantic Treaty, thus establishing the **North Atlantic Treaty Organization (NATO)**, pledged to come to the defense of any member state under attack.

By the mid-1950s U.S. domination of NATO was institutionalized through the permanent deployment of U.S. ground troops on the continent, the important positions of U.S. senior officers in the command structure, and the fact that the member states of the organization came under the American nuclear umbrella, with U.S. nuclear bombers and missiles stationed on their territory. While the French were happy to receive the material benefits of U.S. military assistance, their frustration grew during the 1950s at the reluctance of Washington and London to make France an equal member in a tripartite alliance to oversee the security of Europe. The sharing of nuclear intelligence and technology between the Anglo-American allies that led to Britain's entry into the nuclear club in 1952 exacerbated this sentiment. Frustration turned to bitterness when, in May 1955, after French proposals for an integrated European military force serving a European defense community had been rejected, West Germany was allowed to rearm and join NATO, which was now clearly a coalition of sovereign states under U.S. leadership.

The advent of the **Fifth Republic** under **Charles de Gaulle** marked another failed attempt to revive the notion of a tripartite directorate for conducting European defense policy in which France would enjoy equal status with the United States and Britain. The rebuff was keenly felt by de Gaulle, who had harbored a sense of injured pride since World War II and who felt Washington and London had failed to grant him the consideration due an Allied leader. Thus in 1960 de Gaulle decided to challenge the Anglo-American nuclear weapons monopoly in the West by authorizing the testing of a nuclear device. Within the decade a French nuclear deterrent (*force de frappe*) was established, consisting of long-range bombers and land- and submarine-launched missiles, all under exclusively French national control. To reinforce French independence in military matters, in 1966 de Gaulle expelled the U.S. military presence from France and withdrew French ground and air forces from NATO's integrated military command.

This phase of French defense policy was driven not by petty nationalism but by the conviction that no American president would risk the mass destruction of American cities by retaliating against a Soviet nuclear threat to Europe, particularly since, by the end of the 1950s, Soviet weapons technology had developed sufficiently to allow the Soviets to target the United States directly. French reliance on its modest *force de frappe* was predicated on the belief that it represented an adequate proportional deterrence, that is, that the damage France could inflict on the Soviet Union's population centers would be enough to outweigh any gain the Soviets might contemplate in attacking France. De Gaulle's presidential successors persevered with this rationale, as witnessed by the modernization of the French nuclear deterrent under successive presidents since. However, **François Mitterrand** refined his country's defense policy by, for example, his attempt to promote European defense cooperation through the Western European Union and the intensification of the kind of bilateral security links with Germany that led to the formation of a Franco-German infantry brigade. But the collapse of the Berlin Wall and the demise of the Soviet Union posed fundamental questions about the purpose of the French nuclear deterrent that the French government had still not fully addressed by the mid-1990s. The most notable illustration of this was the determination of Gaullist president **Jacques Chirac,** only months after his election in the spring of 1995, to continue with the modernization of French nuclear weapons by authorizing a series of tests under Muroroa Atoll in French Polynesia, in the face of worldwide condemnation and the embarrassed silence of his European partners, most importantly Germany. However, France confirmed its ability to act in concert with its neighbors and the international community when it contributed to the Kosovo Force troops that were sent to Kosovo in 1999 to guarantee the stability of the region after the civil war in the former Federal Republic of Yugoslavia. Since then, France has demonstrated its willingness to deploy troops under **United Nations** mandate to restore or maintain peace in troubled regions around the world, such as the 4,000 troops it deployed in the Côte d'Ivoire in 2004 and the contingent it sent to southern Lebanon in 2006 to police the cessation of hostilities between Israel and Hezbollah guerillas, after the fierce conflict that had erupted in July of that year. *See also* ARMED FORCES.

DEFFERRE, GASTON (1910–1986). Lawyer and major figure in left-wing politics in postwar France. After school in Nîmes and studies in law at Aix-en-Provence, Defferre began his legal career in **Marseille** in 1931. He served in the **Resistance** during the German occupation of France during **World War II**. He was sent as a deputy to the National Assembly for the first time in 1945 and was reelected again to represent the Bouches-du-Rhône no fewer than six times between 1962 and 1986. Deferre was admired for his efforts in establishing a framework for facilitating the independence of France's African territories as minister for overseas territories in **Guy Mollet**'s government in 1956–1957. He failed in his bid to be the Socialist candidate for the presidency in 1965, owing to the failure of the moderates and the left-wingers to unite behind him. But when he ran as the Socialist candidate for the **presidency** in 1969, he received only 5 percent of the vote.

His contribution to the renaissance of French Socialism lay in the support he gave to **François Mitterrand**'s successful bid to become leader of the **Parti Socialiste** in 1971. He held a number of ministerial portfolios after the Socialist victory in 1981, most notably as minister of state for the interior and decentralization. But it was in his guise as mayor of Marseille, a post he had held for 33 years, that Defferre collapsed and died on 7 May 1986, after having given a speech defending himself against his local critics.

DEGAS, EDGAR (1834–1917). Painter. He was born into a prosperous family and was remarkably at ease with mainstream society, in contrast to so many of his contemporaries. Degas's influence reached its height after 1870, and although often associated with **impressionism**, he did not really belong to that movement. Rather than a preoccupation with subtle brushstrokes, dots, or dabs of color to produce a flowing pictorial composition, Degas's compositions are most notable for their ability to capture a figure in movement, giving many of them an easily recognized snapshot quality. His favorite subjects were found at the racetrack and the ballet. His mature work provides a valuable perspective on Parisian life at the close of the 19th century. *See also* ART.

DE GAULLE, CHARLES (1890–1970). Soldier, leader of the Free French government in exile during **World War II**, and first president of the **Fifth Republic**. He was born in Lille, the son of a teacher at a Jesuit *collège*, and received a traditionalist, Catholic upbringing. De Gaulle graduated from the military academy of Saint-Cyr in 1912 and joined an infantry regiment commanded by **Philippe Pétain**. He served with distinction in **World War I**, but in the years that followed he fell out of favor with the military leaders of France owing to his criticism of the kind of static defensive strategies advocated by Pétain and exemplified by the system of fortifications known as the **Maginot line**, built along the Franco-German border. In books published during the 1930s de Gaulle made the case for creating mechanized divisions whose rapid deployment, in conjunction with air support, could outmaneuver the enemy and inflict considerable damage while suffering moderate losses. Ironically, though ignored by the French military hierarchy, de Gaulle's ideas found ample justification in the German blitzkrieg that routed the French army in 1940.

Belatedly, de Gaulle was appointed undersecretary of state for war in the summer of 1940 but fled to London when the defeat of France became inevitable. On 18 June he broadcast an appeal from the BBC to his compatriots, encouraging them not to give up the fight, and subsequently declared himself the head of the "Free French" government in exile. With diplomatic recognition and material support from the British, de Gaulle consolidated his control of the **Resistance** movement and those parts of France's overseas territories that lay beyond the reach of the collaborationist regime based in **Vichy**. De Gaulle was the obvious candidate to lead the French Republic after the liberation of the country. Thus in the late summer of 1944 his Committee of National Liberation became the provisional government of France, and he was elected president. De Gaulle seized the opportunity to create a new France and embarked on radical changes like the **nationalization** of basic industries and economic planning. But the **political parties** in France preferred a more traditional style of politics in which parliamentary sovereignty prevailed at the expense of the executive. This idea was enshrined in the constitution of the **Fourth Republic**, and when the voters of France approved it in January 1946, de Gaulle resigned.

A **Gaullist party** was formed in 1947, but it failed to attract sufficient support, and de Gaulle abandoned it in 1953. However, a crisis in France's colonial policy prompted his return before the end of the decade. In the mid-1950s, nationalist militancy in the French colony of **Algeria** began to pose a serious military threat and undermine the privileged existence of the 1 million French settlers there. Fearful of concessions by **Paris** to the insurgents, in May 1958 settlers and leaders of the military in Algeria staged mass demonstrations in favor of *Algérie française* that foreshadowed mutiny and even civil war. The party political establishment in Paris, paralyzed by the crisis, turned to de Gaulle, and on 1 June the National Assembly designated him prime minister and granted him the emergency powers he needed to deal with the crisis. His power was consolidated by the new constitution voted that year by the French electorate, which established the dominance of the executive vis-à-vis parliament. In November 1958 the Gaullist party won a majority in the legislative elections, and de Gaulle was elected the first president of the Fifth Republic.

De Gaulle's reputation as a defender of France's interests enabled him to undertake the task of divesting France of her increasingly unviable empire and finally to bring an end to the conflict in Algeria in 1962. It was also in 1962 that he underscored the unique authority of the **presidency** in the French political system when the French voters approved, by referendum, the measure he sponsored that led to the election of the president by direct popular vote instead of through an electoral college, as had previously been the case. It was under the new system that de Gaulle's mandate was renewed three years later. Also, in the field of **foreign policy**, it was under de Gaulle that France became a nuclear power in 1960. His unwavering desire to raise France's standing among the great nations of the world led him into conflict with the Americans, whose leadership of the West in the bipolar world of the Cold War he found difficult to accept. Hence his termination of French participation in the integrated command structure of the **North Atlantic Treaty Organization** and his expulsion of U.S. military personnel from French territory in 1966 (*see* DEFENSE POLICY). De Gaulle was not averse to criticizing U.S. policy in Vietnam and elsewhere, and the "special relationship" between London and Washington made him suspicious of the British, prompting him to block **Great Britain**'s admission to the **European Economic Community**.

The greatest domestic challenge to de Gaulle came in May 1968, when **student rebellions** over the regime in French universities, along with grievances among workers over the lack of democracy in the workplace, led to a nationwide wave of strikes and sit-ins in universities and factories. Though the challenge was short-lived and fear of the left enabled the Gaullists to win a decisive victory in the elections of June 1968, the credibility of the Gaullist regime had been dented, and France had signaled its willingness to move beyond the era of well-meaning paternalism that it represented. De Gaulle staked his reputation for the last time on a referendum on constitutional reform in the following year, and when this was rejected by the electorate, he resigned in April 1969. He died of a heart attack at his country home in Colombey on 9 November 1970, a few days before his 80th birthday. It was the passing of an era and of a man who had seen France through some of the darkest days in its history and who could legitimately claim much credit for its renewal after 1945. *See also* DECOLONIZATION; GAULLISM.

DELACROIX, FERDINAND-VICTOR-EUGENE (1798–1863). An artist of immense influence and a leading exponent of French romantic painting. His art studies began under Pierre-Narcisse Guérin, but his development was most influenced by the Italian Renaissance masters he copied relentlessly in the Louvre. Delacroix first drew public attention with his entry for the Salon of 1822, *Dante and Virgil.* In 1825 he went to England, where he was impressed by the coloring and the subject matter of the English school. His entry for the Salon of 1827, *The Death of Sardanapalus,* inspired by the poem of Lord Byron, gained him his reputation as the leader of the French romantic school. The desire for freedom of expression, whether of the poetic sensibility or from the constraints of having to imitate classical works in art, was symbolized in his famous *Liberty Leading the People* (1830), which captures the sense of liberation following the final collapse of the **Bourbon** restoration in France. Delacroix's insistence on the freedom to experiment often brought him into conflict with the artistic establishment, dominated by neoclassicists. But he persevered, and the paintings inspired by his travels in Spain and North Africa in the early 1830s, such as *Algerian Women* (1834) and *Jewish Wedding* (1841), introduced an exotic and innovative theme to French art. In spite of the snubs from the artistic establishment, Delacroix worked prolifically and received commissions from major institutions like the Palais Bourbon and the Louvre Apollo Gallery. Delacroix's reputation places him at the heart of all the major pictorial innovations of the 19th century, and his stature in the realm of **romanticism in art** is as great as **Victor Hugo**'s in the realm of romanticism in **literature**.

DELANOE, BERTRAND (1950–). Left-wing politician and mayor of **Paris**. He was born in Tunis and returned to France as an adolescent with his family, where he completed his secondary education. He joined the **Parti Socialiste (PS)** in 1971 and two years later became a regional head of the party organization in Aveyron. He entered the National Assembly in 1981 as a PS deputy with a seat representing the 18th district (Montmartre) of Paris and thereafter made his reputation leading the PS campaign to wrest Paris back from the right, particularly in the local election campaign of 1995 against the **Gaullist party**'s anointed successor, former Gaullist mayor of Paris **Jacques Chirac**. It was in that same year that Delanoë acquired another mandate, as a senator representing Paris. His love affair with the city was finally consummated in March 2001 when he was elected mayor with just under 50 percent of the vote, in no small part due to the divisions among his right-wing opponents.

Delanoë committed himself to being a full-time mayor of Paris and broke with the peculiar French tradition called the *cumul des mandats*, which means holding a number of electoral mandates concurrently, by resigning as senator for Paris. During his first term as mayor Delanoë vigorously pursued policies aimed at cutting pollution by discouraging car use, such as the new tram system linking the 13th, 14th, and 15th districts of the city. He secured greater powers for the municipality to compulsorily purchase property with a view to increasing the provision of social housing. On the cultural front, Delanoë's most famous legacy may prove to be *Paris Plage* (Paris Beach), a stretch of the embankment by the **Seine** that, thanks to tons of transported sand and palm trees, is transformed during high summer into an artificial seaside resort for those Parisians unable to join the annual exodus from the city. In the course of a television interview in 1998 Delanoë became the first French politician with an instantly recognizable national profile to profess openly to being homosexual. His honesty earned him considerable respect, and he is generally acknowledged as a conscientious mayor who has attempted to improve the quality of life for his fellow Parisians. In September 2007 he announced that he would be seeking a renewal of his mandate.

DE LESSEPS, FERDINAND (1805–1894). French diplomat and entrepreneur. Born in Versailles and educated in **Paris**, de Lesseps made his career in the French diplomatic service, and it was during his time as a vice consul in Egypt that he was drawn to the plan, originally conceived by **Napoléon Bonaparte**'s engineers, of digging a canal through the isthmus of Suez. An international commission accepted the plan for a canal proposed by de Lesseps in 1856, the technical specifications for which had been drawn up by two French engineers, Bellefond and Mougel. De Lesseps was feted by political and business leaders after his company completed the project in 1869, and a new era appeared to have dawned for the building of canals linking international waters. But de Lesseps's fortunes were destroyed by the **Panama scandal**. In 1882 his company's attempt to build a canal across the isthmus of Panama soon hit unforeseen engineering, climatic, and financial problems, and de Lesseps was fortunate to escape prison when the fraudulent attempt by his company to raise more money for the project was exposed.

DELORS, JACQUES (1925–). Former government minister and president of the European Commission. He was born in **Paris**, the son of a bank employee, and followed in his father's footsteps, but much more illustriously. After graduating with a degree in economic science, he began a long career as a civil servant, with periods in the French central bank and the commissariat responsible for state planning. Delors's expertise was soon recognized after he joined the **Parti Socialiste (PS)**, and he was given responsibility for international economic affairs (1976–1981). After the Socialists swept to power in 1981, he was an obvious choice for the ministerial portfolio covering economics and finance (1981–1983).

But his career in national politics was soon cut short by his accession to a much bigger stage, when he became president of the European Commission in 1985. For the following 10 years, Delors was the most important figure in European affairs, piecing together the policies that cemented the union between the members of what was, initially, the **European Economic Community**, and he was instrumental in persuading the members of the community to adopt those policies. Although he was not universally liked, when he stepped down in 1995, his talent and commitment to the cause of European unity were well respected.

A new career in national politics appeared to beckon when the Socialist succession to **François Mitterrand** had yet to be decided in view of the impending presidential election of spring 1995. In spite of a substantial body of public opinion favorable to him, Delors opted ultimately not to enter the race and bowed out of the spotlight, his reputation intact. His passion for Europe undimmed, in 1996 Delors was the leading light behind the creation of a new think tank, *Notre Europe*, with the mission of developing ideas that would enhance the process of European unity. In 2006 he was still an active member of its governing board.

DENEUVE, CATHERINE (1943–). In contrast to the blatant sensuality of **Brigitte Bardot** or the sultry magnetism of **Jeanne Moreau**, throughout her long film career Catherine Deneuve has retained an impeccable quality of stillness and cool detachment. Her debut came in 1956 with *Les collégiennes*, but critical acclaim followed some years later for her role as a sentimental provincial girl in the musical fantasy *Les parapluies de Cherbourg* (1964). A wide variety of roles ensued, but whether she was playing a psychopath in *Repulsion* (1964), an expensive call girl in her Hollywood movie *Hustle* (1975), or the calculating proprietor of a theater in Nazi-occupied **Paris** in *Le dernier métro* (1980), the abiding quality of Deneuve's acting was the sense she gave of being a woman who moved according to her own inner rhythm, touchable but remote, and in her essence unattainable. It may be argued that this quality was distilled most memorably by the director Luis Buñuel in *Belle de jour* (1967). Deneuve's cool beauty endured well into middle age, and it was notable that she was used in the publicity preceding the **privatization** of some of France's financial institutions in the mid-1980s, no doubt because of her appeal to the French public as pure and incorruptible. Her acting career hit a new high again with the film *Indochine* (1992), which won her a César, the French equivalent of an Oscar, and the best actress award at the Venice film festival. In recent years, Deneuve has distinguished herself in a number of films dealing with the emotional challenges of everyday life, such as *Huit femmes* (2002). *See also* CINEMA.

DEPARDIEU, GERARD (1948–). A rare combination of physical imperfection and emotional vulnerability helped make Depardieu the dominant male figure by far in the French **cinema** during the 1980s and 1990s. Not since the days of **Jean Gabin** has the absence of physical grace been coupled with such a powerful screen presence.

Like Gabin, Depardieu appeals to the French public as a rough diamond with an inner core of complex and tender emotions. His breakthrough movie in France was Bertrand Blier's *Les valseuses* (1974), in which he drew on his own experience as an adolescent runaway to portray with disturbing accuracy an amoral young thug. He has appeared in a very large number of films since then that have displayed his exceptional range: from the peasant in Bernardo Bertolucci's epic *1900* (1977) to the revolutionary intellectual in *Danton* (1983). His most acclaimed performance of recent years was as the tragicomic lead in the worldwide hit *Cyrano de Bergerac* (1990). This was the performance that won him an Oscar nomination and the Best Actor award at Cannes. Depardieu has made a number of English-language films, such as the romantic comedy *Green Card* (1990). But his mastery of the language is not very good, and his handling of the U.S. press in the publicity for *Green Card,* particularly in response to questions about his relationships with women, was not judged to be astute.

However, in the less politically correct climate of France, Depardieu's appetite for love and life has done nothing to damage his popularity. In spite of his frequently professed boredom with the cinema, Depardieu has continued to accept an eclectic range of roles for the small and big screen, ranging from an outrageously comic turn in Disney's *101 Dalmatians* (1996) to a lavish television version of *The Count of Monte Cristo* (1999). The dramas in Depardieu's dysfunctional family have been avidly chronicled in the French **press**, as has his passion in recent years for cultivating his own vineyard. Depardieu's frailties, as well as his talents, have earned him a special place in the affections of the French public.

DEPARTEMENTS. These constitute the main units of administration in France and are situated at an intermediate level between the **commune** and the **région**. Created after the **French Revolution** of 1789 and designed to be of approximately equal size geographically and demographically, each *département* was assigned a prefect (*préfet*) as the local representative of central government. The traditional responsibilities of the *département* covered infrastructure provision such as roads, but after **World War II** these responsibilities grew to include social service provision and the implementation of urban planning schemes. The powers of the *départements* were strengthened in legislation passed in 1972. There are currently 96 such units in continental France and 4 overseas (Guyana, Guadeloupe, Martinique, and Réunion), formed from the remnants of France's colonial empire and referred to as *départements d'outre-mer*. The latter are usually mentioned in the same breath as the two overseas *collectivités territoriales* and the four *territoires d'outre-mer* (territories that enjoy more autonomy than the overseas *départements*), but they are collectively and succinctly categorized in French as **DOM-TOMs**.

DERRIDA, JACQUES (1930–2004). Philosopher and France's most internationally renowned intellectual of the late 20th century. He was born into a Sephardic Jewish family in Algiers. He came to **Paris** as a boarder at the Lycée Louis le Grand before beginning his studies at the elite Ecole Normale Supérieure, where he befriended figures like the communist intellectual **Louis Althusser** and the future structuralist **Michel Foucault**. It was in the 1950s that Derrida initiated his long and fruitful relationship with American academia when he received a scholarship to study at Harvard University.

In contrast to the proponents of **structuralism**, who argued that experience originated from the effect of structures, Derrida turned the focus on the genesis of structures to place the structural phenomenon in the context of a history that is articulated in a broad and complex manner. It is by conceiving of things in an original complexity, instead of an original purity, that Derrida gives his thought a dynamic that destabilizes assumptions. In practice what this means is that his close readings of philosophical and literary texts unpick the apparent structural unity or coherent sense that may have been intended by the author, and through this process of deconstruction uncover their multifaceted complexity. In seminal works such as *Of Grammatology* and *Writing and Difference* (1967), Derrida demonstrated his critical approach through his readings of texts by major authors and philosophers such as Edmund Husserl, Martin Heidegger, Georg Hegel, **Jean-Jacques Rousseau**, and **René Descartes** and engaged in vigorous debates on the implications of his position on both sides of the Atlantic.

By the 1980s Derrida had become an obligatory reference in arts faculties, especially in the **United States**, and in 1986 he returned there to become professor of humanities at the University of California, Irvine. The breadth of his writing is impressive, and in the 1990s he took a more obviously political and ethical slant as a result of his focus on issues of legality, responsibility, and friendship through his readings of the works of figures like Emmanuel Lévinas, Walter Benjamin, and Carl Schmitt. The reactions to his death highlighted the extent to which his work could divide opinion. While some acknowledged the originality of his work, others argued it was flawed by a lack of intellectual rigor, pretentiousness, and obfuscation. What is beyond question is the enormous impact of Derrida's ideas on campuses around the world.

DESCARTES, RENE (1596–1650). Mathematician and thinker often described as the father of modern philosophy. Descartes was born at La Haye in the Touraine. His exceptional intellectual ability manifested itself early, and at the age of eight he was sent to the Royal College at La Flèche, where he received a rigorous training at the hands of the Jesuits and showed a particular talent for mathematics. He graduated with a degree in law from the University of Poitiers and found employment in the service of the Prince of Orange in Holland and then with the Duke of Bavaria. Descartes's itinerant lifestyle continued until 1628, when he returned to Holland, where he spent most of the next 20 years. It was during this period in Holland that Descartes wrote the treatise that established his enduring reputation and influence, *Discours de la méthode* (1637).

Breaking with what he considered the sterile reasoning of the dominant scholastic tradition, Descartes put forward four precepts as the basis for the successful pursuit of knowledge: to accept nothing as true unless it is self-evidently so; to approach problems systematically by analyzing them one part at a time; to proceed incrementally from simple to complex rationalizations; and to review the reasoning process systematically to eliminate the possibility of oversights. It was in the pursuit of self-evident truth that Descartes articulated the principle from which his subsequent propositions flowed, *cogito ergo sum* (I think therefore I am); in other words, he could doubt everything except the fact that he was doubting. Descartes's mathematical training had an obvious influence on the rationalist rigor of his work, which altered fundamentally the nature of philosophical investigations among his successors. Descartes developed his ideas further in other important works, including the *Meditationes de prima philosophia* (1641) and the *Principia philosophiae* (1644). This productive phase in his life was brought to an abrupt end in 1649 when he left Holland to take up a post as instructor to Queen Christina of Sweden, only to fall fatally ill during the following winter.

DESMOULINS, LUCIE-CAMILLE-SIMPLICE (1760–1794). Journalist and politician of the **French Revolution**. He was born into a large middle-class family in Guise and obtained a scholarship to the prestigious Collège Louis le Grand in **Paris**, where his studies brought him to appreciate republican principles, and also where he met and befriended **Maximilien de Robespierre**. He qualified as a lawyer in 1785, but a pronounced stutter brought his law practice to a premature end. Desmoulins took center stage when, for once not suffering from his stutter, he harangued the crowd in front of the Palais Royal on 12 July 1789 and encouraged them to arm themselves to defend the city against possible attack by the royalist troops massing around Paris. The excitement swelled and the momentum grew, eventually leading to the fall of the **Bastille**. Desmoulins emerged a hero, and his reputation was secured by the newspaper he produced, *Les Révolutions de France et de Brabant*, which contained repeated calls for popular sovereignty and direct democracy. This period was the apogee of his revolutionary career. He was given a governmental post by **Georges Danton**, his friend from the **Cordeliers Club**, and was subsequently elected to the **Convention**. But his career there was undistinguished, as were his later attempts at journalism, in the course of which he subtly criticized the **Terror** and suggested a need for clemency. In spite of his friendship with Robespierre, Desmoulins was eventually caught up in the anti-Dantonist purge and executed on 13 April 1794.

DIRECTORY. Created by the Constitution of Year III following the **French Revolution**, it was the government of France between October 1795 and November 1799. The executive comprised five directors who shared the responsibility for the conduct of the nation's affairs and who were elected by the legislature. A system of rotating membership meant that each year one member of the Directory had to retire. Ironically, the constant conflict between the Directory and the legislature, and among the directors themselves, meant that a system designed to prevent dictatorship actually hastened its advent. The credibility of the Directory was fatally undermined by its inability to protect France's interests against the coalition of European powers ranged against it. When **Napoléon Bonaparte** returned from Egypt in October 1799, his prestige as an invincible soldier and peacemaker helped him to destroy an already discredited Directory in his coup d'état of 18–19 Brumaire, Year VIII (9–10 November 1799).

DOM-TOMS (DEPARTEMENTS ET TERRITOIRES D'OUTRE-MER)/OVERSEAS DEPARTMENTS AND TERRITORIES. The four French overseas departments of Guadeloupe, Martinique, Guyana, and Reunion were created by legislation in 1946, and this was an important chapter in the transition of France from a colonial to a postcolonial power. Given that the relationship with France, as in the case of Reunion, went back to the 17th century, the postwar French government realized that the old relationship with these possessions was unjustifiable and that only full equality or full independence were viable options. In contrast with other, larger colonies with majority indigenous populations with their own cultures and religions, such as **Algeria**, offering full integration as overseas départements to these tiny and highly Gallicized possessions was not a problematic option.

Constitutional changes in 2003 meant that the traditional notion of *territoires d'outre-mer* was superseded by the concept of the COM or *collectivités d'outre-mer*, which adapts itself more easily to the subtle differences that govern some of these overseas possessions. Saint-Pierre-et-Miquelon is designated a *collectivité territoriale* with a special status in the French republic, whereas Wallis-et-Futuna is a *collectivité d'outre-mer française*, a status to which Saint-Martin and Saint-Barthélemy acceded in 2007. Mayotte enjoys less decentralized government as a *collectivité départementale d'outre-mer*, while French Polynesia is a *collectivité d'outre-mer* that enjoys more political autonomy, underlined by the fact that the legal and administrative systems operate in the local languages (with translations in French). Constitutional changes in 1999 meant that **New Caledonia** ceased to be a *territoire d'outre-mer* and now enjoys a status all of its own, with its own assembly, and is now referred to in all constitutional documents solely by its name.

DREYFUS AFFAIR (1894–1899). A crisis with enormous social and political repercussions provoked by the arrest of a French officer falsely accused of providing **Germany** with French military secrets. In September 1894 a memorandum (*bordereau*) bearing French military data was discovered by a French agent in the German embassy in **Paris**. Suspicion fell on an officer attached to the general staff, Captain Alfred Dreyfus, a Jew from the Alsace region isolated among a predominantly Catholic and conservatively minded officer corps. Dreyfus's background as the son of an affluent family of textile manufacturers and his exemplary career in the army up to that point made it difficult to envisage a motive for treason. However, he was arrested on the strength of the alleged similarity between his writing and that found on the memorandum. He was rapidly court-martialed and, in a secret session on 22 December from which his lawyers were barred, sentenced to life imprisonment in the penal colony of Devil's Island, off the coast of French Guyana. French public opinion was far more inclined to believe the army, supported by a largely anti-Semitic **press**, than a Jewish officer, and no one petitioned for a retrial except Dreyfus's wife, Lucie, and his brother Mathieu.

The case resurfaced in 1896 when Georges Picquart, the new chief of army intelligence, discovered a suspect German telegram addressed to a French officer named Ferdinand Esterhazy. On comparing Esterhazy's handwriting with that found in the memorandum that had condemned Dreyfus, Picquart came to the conclusion that Esterhazy was the guilty party and not Dreyfus. In 1897 Picquart succeeded in convincing Auguste Scheurer-Kestner, vice president of the Senate, of Dreyfus's innocence, but in an obvious attempt to silence him, the army posted Picquart to North Africa. In the meantime, another front had been opened in the battle to free Dreyfus in the form of a pamphlet by the French Jewish journalist and publicist Bernard Lazare, entitled *A Judicial Error.* The cogency with which Lazare analyzed the inconsistencies in the case against Dreyfus prompted Colonel Hubert Henry of the intelligence service to manufacture further evidence for the file against Dreyfus, in case it should be reopened. As for Esterhazy, so confident was he of the collusion of

Colonel Henry and Commandant Mercier du Paty de Clam (who had originally obtained the "proof" that it was Dreyfus's handwriting on the memorandum) that he offered himself for court-martial to clear his name.

It was Esterhazy's acquittal on 11 January 1898 that so outraged **Emile Zola** and led to his thundering indictment of the general staff in **Georges Clemenceau**'s newspaper *L'Aurore*, under the banner headline "J'Accuse." It was at this point that the case became "L'Affaire" that appeared to divide France into Dreyfusards and anti-Dreyfusards. This view, however, can be exaggerated. It was urban France above all that was gripped by this struggle, and it was not simply one between the forces of **Catholicism** and conservative reaction and the republican and secular forces of progress. Notable nationalist and Catholic figures like Charles Péguy rallied to the Dreyfusard cause, while some leading figures of the socialist establishment, like **Jean Jaurès**, took time to overcome their initial reluctance to join a cause that they at first considered a bourgeois folly.

On 30 August 1898 Colonel Henry was arrested. He committed suicide in his cell the following day. In the summer of 1899 Dreyfus was brought back to France to face a new trial at Rennes, only to be found guilty again, but with "extenuating circumstances." The government of **René Waldeck-Rousseau** pardoned Dreyfus in the wake of this confusing verdict, but it was not until 1906 that the decision at Rennes was overturned and Dreyfus fully exonerated. In the end, justice was done, but the Dreyfus Affair had exposed the morally corrupt underbelly of French society, and many individuals on both sides of the struggle emerged from it dejected and disillusioned. *See also* ARMED FORCES.

DRUMONT, EDOUARD (1844–1917). Anti-Semitic journalist who became infamous for his book *La France juive* (1886), in which he argued that France was ruled by ethnically and culturally alien Jewish interests. Drumont crusaded under a banner of "France for the French," and in 1889 he launched the national anti-Semitic League of France. He also set up the newspaper *La Libre Parole* (1892), which broke the story of the alleged treason and arrest of Captain Alfred Dreyfus (*see* DREYFUS AFFAIR). In 1898 he took his anti-Semitic campaign to the French in **Algeria**, who rewarded him with a seat in the Chamber of Deputies until 1902. However, he was refused membership in the **Académie Française** in 1909.

DUCLOS, JACQUES (1896–1975). Parliamentarian and Communist politician. He was born into a working-class family in the Hautes Pyrénées and was only 12 years old when he was apprenticed to a pastry cook. He served in **World War I**, and the experience helped push him toward the internationalist and proletarian politics of the **Parti Communiste Français (PCF)**. Trained in the party's cadre school, Duclos became a full-time party official in 1924 and in 1926 joined the Central Committee. During the decade and a half that followed he became extremely active in both the politics of the Comintern and the PCF in France. Duclos's position as the second most important person in the PCF was confirmed on the eve of **World War II**, when the party's secretary-general, **Maurice Thorez**, was ordered to Moscow and Duclos was left to head the party in France. Duclos played a similar role after the war, when Thorez was in Moscow from October 1950 until April 1953. However, by the end of that decade Thorez began to maneuver **Waldeck Rochet** into position as his successor, and this succession finally occurred in 1964. For his part, Duclos remained loyal to the party, and above all to its Stalinist orientation, a fact he had proved by his refusal to countenance Nikita Khrushchev's denunciation in 1956 of Stalinist excesses.

In spite of this reputation, he was chosen as the PCF's candidate in the presidential election following **Charles de Gaulle**'s resignation in 1969. Duclos mounted a campaign distinguished by its oratorical verve and ultimately polled 21.36 percent of the vote, considerably more than his rival on the left, **Gaston Defferre**. Until his death in April 1975, Duclos remained unswerving both in his loyalty to the organization in which he had made his career and in the rigid discipline demanded by the principle of democratic centralism.

DUMAS, ALEXANDRE (PÈRE) (1802–1870). Now known mostly for his novels, Dumas first became famous and popular for his plays and was a major dramatist of the romantic period. He was born in Villers-Cotterêts (Aisne), the son of an enthusiastic republican and former general in **Napoléon Bonaparte**'s army, Thomas-Alexandre

Dumas Davy de la Pailleterie. His father's death in 1806 left the family in difficult financial circumstances, and his formal schooling suffered as a result. He was apprenticed to a local notary at the age of 14; but when he was 20, his prospects brightened when General Maximilien-Sébastien Foy found him a post in **Paris** as a copyist with the secretariat of **Louis-Philippe**, duc d'Orléans.

Dumas's first known work, a long poem entitled *La rose rouge et la rose blanche,* was published in 1824, and it was in that year also that his mistress, Marie Labay, gave birth to his son, also named Alexandre. On the literary front, the 1820s brought Dumas into contact with figures like **Alphonse de Lamartine, Honoré de Balzac,** and **Victor Hugo.** In 1828 the success of his play *Henri III et sa cour* lifted Dumas out of obscurity and poverty; the play is now regarded by some critics as the first romantic drama to be performed. In the decade that followed, Dumas made his reputation as a writer of historical drama with popular successes like *Napoléon* and *Antony,* and the formal consecration of his talent came in 1837, when he was made a chevalier of the **Legion d'Honneur.**

While criticized by some for a lack of style or subtlety, Dumas turned his talents as a flamboyant storyteller to the novel form in the 1840s, and novels like *The Three Musketeers, The Queen Margot,* and *The Count of Monte Cristo* ensured his enduring celebrity. A man of wide-ranging appetites, Dumas was also an excellent chef and completed his *Grand dictionnaire de cuisine* in 1869, the year before his death. *See also* LITERATURE.

DURAS, MARGUERITE (1914–1996). Writer. She was born Marguerite Donnadieu in Giadinh, near Saigon in French Indochina. She took her nom de plume from the Gascon village of Duras in France, but she was educated and lived in the Far East until she returned to France at 16 years of age to study mathematics and law at the Sorbonne. After completing her studies, she took up a post in the French Colonial Office and in 1938 married the French left-wing intellectual Robert Antelme, from whom she separated eight years later.

Her first book, *Les impudents,* was published during the war (1943). She became heavily involved in Communist **Resistance** circles, even claiming afterward to have been instrumental in saving the life of the then Resistance fighter **François Mitterrand.** She broke with the **Communists** after the war when they accused her of bourgeois individualism and pursued her belief in a personal notion of revolution based on personal freedom. Her fame in the 1950s became international, as a result of the success of the film *Hiroshima mon amour* (1959), based on a script by Duras and directed by Alain Resnais. Within France, she raised her profile as a controversial figure by opposing the French government's refusal to grant independence to **Algeria**, and she endorsed enthusiastically the **student rebellions** of May 1968. The political positions she adopted were interwoven with her personal convictions, and this relationship was reflected in *Détruire, dit-elle* (1969).

During the 1970s Duras's agitation in favor of **women**'s rights issues like abortion sealed her reputation as a feminist, and she also broadened her creative endeavors, most notably as a film director. Her now characteristic equation of private with public experience was evident in her most successful foray into the genre, *India Song* (1975). She returned to the written word in the early 1980s with a series of opaque fictions that were poorly received. But *L'Amant* was a powerfully controlled evocation of her adolescence and in 1984 won her the Prix Goncourt as well as the admiration of a new and more youthful reading public seduced by her precise, understated prose. She remained remorselessly lucid in the face of her manifestly fading health, and her last literary effort resulted in 1995 in a slim volume, *C'est tout* (That's all), in essence an elegantly argued acceptance of the need to let go. Her death on 3 March 1996 marked the passing of one of France's most gifted and independent creative talents. *See also* LITERATURE.

– E –

ECOLOGISTS. The cause of the ecologists in France, as with so many other reforming causes, was given a considerable impetus by the **student rebellions** of 1968. Part of the intellectual ferment that characterized this era focused concern on the damage being done to the environment and prompted individuals like Alain Hervé, Pierre Radanne, Yves Cochet, and Brice Lalonde to found the French branch of Friends of the Earth in 1970. The first attempt to influence national politics came in 1973, when Antoine Waechter and Solange Fernex founded Ecologie et Survie, with a view to promoting an **environmentalist** candidate in the legislative elections of that year.

Brice Lalonde ran as a pro-ecology candidate for the presidency in 1981 and polled 4 percent of the vote in the first round. The years that followed saw changes in the political organization of the ecologists and gave them the first real taste of electoral success. In 1984 Les Verts (the Greens) was formed, amalgamating a number of ecological pressure groups into something with greater resemblance to a political party. The fear of playing the political game, however, remained an enduring cause of dispute within the movement, and Lalonde left Les Verts in the mid-1980s, allowing Waechter to become the dominant personality in the movement. In spite of these internal tensions, Waechter still managed to poll 4 percent of the first-round vote as the green candidate in the presidential elections of 1988. The significance of the green constituency was signaled by Prime Minister **Michel Rocard** in the same year when he gave the ministerial portfolio for the environment to Lalonde. But the electoral breakthrough came in the European elections of 1989, when Les Verts took 10.5 percent of the vote and returned nine European deputies.

Thereafter, however, the divisions among the ecologists began to exercise a distinctly negative effect. In 1990 Lalonde formed his own green party, Génération Ecologie, and although it formed an alliance with Les Verts in the 1993 legislative elections, they failed to make any impact on the new Assembly. In comparison to Lalonde and Waechter in the two preceding presidential elections, the green candidate in 1995, Dominique Voynet, saw her share of the first-round vote drop by a quarter, to barely more than 3 percent. However, Voynet's belief in a policy of cooperation with the forces of the democratic left in France brought dividends after the strong performance of the left in the legislative elections of 1997. She accepted a post in **Lionel Jospin**'s government as minister for the environment and was joined by another Vert minister in 2000. Voynet left the government in 2001 and in the presidential election of 2002 it was Noël Mamère who carried the Vert standard, taking 5.25 percent of the votes in the first round in the best-ever score by a Vert candidate. Responding to pressures from within the party, Voynet's successor as party leader in 2003, Gilles Lemaire, has steered Les Verts to a position of greater autonomy vis-à-vis the parties of the left. At the beginning of 2008 Les Verts had five senators and four deputies in the national parliament, and five deputies in the European parliament. *See also* ENVIRONMENTALISM.

ECONOMY. The French economy was predominantly **agricultural** until the 19th century, when the switch to **industry** as the principal source of wealth creation began to occur. Global trade had been established well before that time, often driven by **colonialism**. But France was conspicuously slower then her neighbor England in achieving industrial takeoff. The country had to wait until the 1850s before the combination of factors such as better **transportation**, free trade, and greater opportunities for investment could be allied to the technical innovations that allowed the country to espouse wholeheartedly the industrial age. By the 1900s the proportion of national wealth saved and invested and the appetite for innovation had transformed France into a leading industrial nation, with, for example, an automobile industry that was second only to that of the **United States**. **World War I**, however, left a legacy of failure because it exacerbated some of France's key structural weaknesses, demographic, political, and financial. Above all, the period between the two world wars sapped the nation's self-confidence and weakened the belief that the national economy could be managed successfully.

The trauma and national humiliation of the occupation during **World War II** strengthened the nation's resolve to renew itself once victory was achieved. Instrumental in this process was the new and positive form given to state interventionism through the operation of the **Plan**, a system of national planning aimed in the first instance at meeting the shortages caused by the war and then at transforming the French economy so that it could compete on the global stage with the world's leading economies. A French economic miracle took place during the 1950s and 1960s, with growth rates that outstripped those of **Great Britain** and the United States, peaking at almost 8 percent. By the 1980s, France had overtaken Britain and become the world's fourth economic power. The French economy experienced the same difficulties as most of the economies of Europe during the 1990s, namely sluggish growth and rising unemployment, but the fundamental strength of the economy was shown by the consistent trade surplus it registered with the rest of the world.

However, the feeling at home since the 1980s has been one of pessimism, largely due to the failure of successive governments to reduce an unemployment rate that in 2005 still stood at 8.9 percent. Whereas comparable economies like that of Great Britain have undertaken a reform of public sector employment (especially costly benefits such as early retirement), attempts to do this in France have consistently stalled. This is one of the factors that by 2005 led France to slip behind China and Britain into sixth place among the world's leading economies, with a gross domestic product worth $2118 billion. Only 4 percent of French workers are now employed in the primary sector (agriculture and fishing), 24 percent work in the secondary sector (industry), and the remaining 72 percent are accounted for by the tertiary sector (services). *See also* AEROSPACE; BANKING; CITROEN; FINANCE; GANDOIS, JEAN; INDUSTRY; NATIONALIZATION; PRIVATIZATION; RENAULT; TRADE; TRENTE GLORIEUSES.

EDUCATION. The fruits of education and their dissemination were the preserve of the clergy in France until the intellectual ambitions of the **Enlightenment** led to the great process of democratization started by the **French Revolution**. The structures that we recognize today owe much to the system created in the two decades following the Revolution, particularly under **Napoléon Bonaparte**. The importance attached to the systematic recruitment of a meritocratic and technocratic elite characterizes an ethos whose roots were planted by Bonaparte through the expansion of lycées. These secondary schools would educate the able boys, often from modest backgrounds, who would emerge to staff the state apparatus managed by the elite of technocrats trained in the **grandes écoles**, those institutions of higher education established under the Napoleonic regime, which, for those ambitious for high office in the service of the state, came to eclipse old universities like the Sorbonne in prestige. It was also at this time that the foundation was laid for the classic hierarchy of academic qualifications: *baccalauréat* (high school qualification), *licence* (B.A.), *maîtrise* (M.A.), and *doctorat* (Ph.D).

The restoration of a monarchy under **Louis XVIII** in 1815 allowed the Catholic Church to regain its influence in the educational system, and the struggle for a secular school system became a central issue in the campaign of **anticlericalism** waged by republicans for most of the rest of the century. Victory came under **Jules Ferry**, when his law of 28 March 1882 established free and obligatory primary education, removing religious instruction from the curriculum. Further legislation, passed in 1886, laid the foundation for the gradual replacement of clerics in the school system by a body of state-educated lay teachers. Thereafter, the education system in France enjoyed a pattern of incremental expansion comparable to that in other leading industrialized nations, until the extraordinary growth pattern established after **World War II**.

In 1945 the school-leaving age was 14, and only 3 percent of the relevant age cohort took the *baccalauréat*. Within two decades, the baby boom of the postwar era and changing parental expectations transformed the situation radically. In 1959 the Berthoin law raised the school-leaving age to 16, and by the early 1960s, 12 percent of the relevant age cohort were taking the *baccalauréat*.

Successive French governments were also careful not to neglect preschool education. By 1988–1989 over one-third of two-year-olds and 97.5 percent of three-year-olds were enjoying preschool education, in contrast with 50 percent in **Great Britain**. By the same period in the 1980s, 70 percent of older students were staying on at school after 16 to take the *baccalauréat*, in contrast to 36 percent at the end of the 1960s. The rising curve of academic achievement in secondary education inevitably raised expectations with regard to higher education, and since the 1960s French governments have been trying to catch up with the expectations their policies fostered. In spite of the rapid growth of new universities in the 1960s, demand outstripped supply. The resulting mismatch in terms of sufficient numbers of university staff and adequate teaching facilities triggered the **student rebellions** in 1968. The total number of students in higher education grew from half a million in 1960 to 2.2 million in 2003, and the universities, which have borne the brunt of this expansion, have struggled to cope. School students who are successful in negotiating the *baccalauréat* expect to enter university as a right, except in those disciplines that have always relied on selection, like medicine. Attempts in the 1980s to manage the numbers entering university by making entry selective had to be shelved because of massive protests by students.

Currently, higher education in France is fundamentally divided. On the one hand, access to the university system is easy and cheap, making it democratic but at the same time depriving it of prestige. On the other hand, the most talented and ambitious students set their sights on entry to a *grande école,* where the numbers are small, academic criteria for selection are very high—usually involving post-*baccalauréat* examinations set by the receiving institution—but where the prestige of the institution is correspondingly high and its graduates prized by prospective employers. While surveys in 2006 indicated a growing awareness among young French people that a *formation courte* (a course of vocational training or an apprenticeship) might be a better route to employment than a classic university degree, the divide between mass and elite institutions in French higher education is unlikely to change in the short term. The concept of a *grande école* has been broadened to encompass the burgeoning business school sector in France, and the ability of these institutions to cream off the brightest and the best students can only have been enhanced by the *Financial Times* survey of 2006, which placed seven French business schools among Europe's top 10, with Hautes Etudes Commerciales occupying the top slot.

In recent years, however, French governments have become sensitive to the fact that the nation's universities consistently underperform in the yearly ranking of universities worldwide reported by publications such as the *Times Higher Education Supplement*, with not a single French presence in a top 20 dominated by institutions in the **United States** and Great Britain. By the time **Nicolas Sarkozy** was elected to the **presidency** in 2007, the case for reforming universities, particularly with regard to the autonomy that would enable them, for example, to seek research funding from private sources, had become irresistible. When the relevant minister, Valérie Pécresse, proposed the reform at the end of May 2007, it was greeted by the conference of university presidents as an opportunity. But student organizations regarded it as a threat, because what they perceived as the retreat of the state would open the door to the disciplines of the market, reviving the age-old fears of selective entry to university and higher fees. The street protests of the summer had no effect on the legislative program and the reform was voted through parliament in August 2007. The widespread sit-ins that marked the start of the academic year that fall were therefore, strictly speaking, too late. Interestingly, the students who prevented universities from opening their doors were often faced with counterdemonstrations from students simply wishing to resume their studies. By the end of 2007 the sit-ins and protests had all petered out and the Réforme Pécresse had been accepted as a new chapter in the development of tertiary education in France. *See also* FALLOUX LAW.

EIFFEL, GUSTAVE (1832–1923). France's most internationally famous engineer. He was born into a middle-class family in Dijon and completed his studies at the Ecole Centrale, the elite engineering school in Paris, where he graduated as a chemical engineer in 1855. A year later Eiffel met the entrepreneur Charles Neveu, who persuaded him of the remarkable properties of cast iron as a building material. Eiffel's big break came at the tender age of 26, when he was given the task of overseeing the construction of the new railway bridge in the port of **Bordeaux**. Eiffel's work was much appreciated, and by 1866 he had his own company and manufacturing facilities on the outskirts of **Paris**. Major bridges built in Spain, Portugal, and Vietnam secured the reputation of Eiffel's company and highlighted the creativity of his engineering partners, such as Maurice Koechlin, who designed the metal framework that provides the skeleton inside the Statue of Liberty inaugurated in New York in 1886.

But the engineering project that guaranteed Eiffel's posthumous glory was the construction of the tower that would bear his name. The challenge of building a structure over 300 meters tall was one that had frustrated engineers the world over. In 1884 Eiffel bought the plans drawn up by his colleague Koechlin for a cast-iron structure and set about promoting it energetically to the French government as a centerpiece for the great universal exhibition of 1889, marking the centenary of the **French Revolution**. A contract was signed with the government on 8 January 1887, and work began 20 days later. Approval for the project was far from unanimous. Leading figures in France's artistic establishment signed a petition against the project, and some popular newspapers predicted it would collapse, killing thousands of Parisians. But it was completed on time, with the inauguration taking place on 31 March 1889. By the time the great exhibition ended, the tower had received 2 million visitors, and what was once intended to be a temporary structure had become a universally recognized Parisian landmark and a testament to one man's engineering vision.

ELECTORAL SYSTEM. The number and types of elections in France have increased in recent years, owing to changes in France's relationship with Europe and to changes in France itself. At the most modest level, municipal elections determine who will carry out the everyday tasks of local government. After the **Socialists** came to power in the 1980s, they introduced **decentralization** measures aimed at reducing the dependence of the provinces on **Paris**, and one of the consequences of this was the creation of 22 regional councils elected by universal suffrage (*see* REGIONS). On a supranational level, the growing political cohesion of the European Economic Community and later **European Union** led to European elections in all the member states to select deputies to the European Parliament.

The most important elections are, of course, those that determine France's national destiny. The legislative elections to determine the composition of the National Assembly normally occur every five years, and used to overlap with the elections to choose the president, who enjoyed a seven-year mandate until this was reduced to five by referendum in 2000, thus changing the *septennat* to the *quinquennat*. The classic method of voting is the first-past-the-post system, spread over two rounds two weeks apart. This normally allows for numerous parties or presidential candidates to present themselves for election in the first round. If no one party or candidate gains an absolute majority in the first round, normally those sharing roughly the same allegiances agree to promote a compromise party or presidential candidate in the second round. Thus, for example, in the legislative elections, where the **Parti Communiste Français (PCF)** and the **Parti Socialiste (PS)** are contesting the same seat, they would normally agree that the better placed of their two candidates after the first round should go forward into the second round as the unique candidate representing the left, to maximize the voting potential of that constituency. In the case of the PCF and the PS in presidential elections, the choice becomes even more obvious after the first round, given that French voters would never elect a PCF candidate to the presidency.

While the system for electing the president of France has not varied since it was amended by **Charles de Gaulle** in 1962, there is flexibility with regard to the legislative elections, and in 1986 the Socialist government opted for proportional representation to reduce its dependence on the cooperation of the PCF and to preserve as many of its seats as possible in view of the impending inevitable defeat.

EMPIRE, FIRST (1804–1814). Napoléon Bonaparte's short-lived attempt to found his own dynasty to reign over France. Pope Pius VII presided over his coronation as Emperor of the French on 2 December 1804, but barely a decade later, the dream turned to dust. Bonaparte's military machine was broken by the implacable Russian winter in the campaign of 1813–1814, and thereafter his troops were harried all the way back to France by the coalition of European powers ranged against him, ultimately forcing his abdication in 1814. The hope of imperial glory was revived when he returned from exile to France for the **Hundred Days**, but Bonaparte's ambition was definitively crushed at the battle of Waterloo on 18 June 1815.

EMPIRE, SECOND (1852–1870). Proclaimed by Napoléon III (*see* BONAPARTE, LOUIS-NAPOLEON) on 2 December 1852, following the coup d'état that he had instigated on the same day of the previous year. The years up to 1859 were characterized by an authoritarianism that curtailed freedom of expression, notably on the part of the press, and ruthlessly centralized power in the hands of the emperor and his subordinates. However, the majority of French citizens tolerated these actions because of the benefits accruing to the nation's **economy** as the result of France's belated but rapid development as an industrial nation.

Tolerance of the regime began to wane after 1860, largely owing to the inevitable downturn in the economy and the diminishing return to the people in the trade-off between freedom and prosperity. The reaction of the regime was to attempt to appease public opinion by conceding more freedom to the press and introducing a measure of accountability with regard to government policy. However, this simply allowed the people the chance to give greater vent to their grievances. Napoléon III responded by playing the patriotic card by committing France to a series of foreign policy adventures. The last and most catastrophic of these was the **Franco-Prussian War**. The ensuing defeat brought down the Second Empire and led to the proclamation of a republic on 4 September 1870. However, the laws that provided a proper constitutional framework for the **Third Republic** were not passed until 1875, although France had become a de facto republic.

EMPIRE STYLE. The empire created by **Napoléon Bonaparte** was, on the face of it, not one propitious to an unfettered expansion of cultural life and artistic expression, in view of the strict censorship of the written word and the means of cultural production in general. However, the **French Revolution** had generated new myths and symbols that were represented, typically, in the themes depicted in the neoclassicism of the empire's official painter, **David**. Bonaparte's empire also invested itself architecturally with neoclassical solidity, respectability, and symmetry: the pillared glory of the church of La Madeleine harking back to antique times, the Tuileries gardens with their small *arc de triomphe* aligned with its massively imposing counterpart, all bearing testimony to the enduring nature of the emperor's legacy. And this concern with simple but solidly imposing lines is also characteristic of the interior decor and furniture of the time. *See also* ART.

THE ENLIGHTENMENT. An intellectual movement that had its origins in the scientific revolution of the 17th century but that flowered in the 18th century, notable for a humanist credo based on a belief in progress through the application of critical reason, as opposed to reliance on received wisdom. It was led by a group of writers, journalists, scientists, and reformers in France known as the philosophes and among whom the most famous figures were Charles-Louis Montesquieu, François-Marie Voltaire, Jean-Jacques Rousseau, and Denis Diderot. The works of the philosophes spanned different genres: philosophical tales (Voltaire's *Candide,* 1759), epistolary accounts of life in foreign parts (Montesquieu's *Persian Letters,* 1721), essays on society and politics (Rousseau's *Discourse on the Origins of Inequality,* 1750), and novels with a pronounced moral intent (Rousseau's *Emile: or, On Education,* 1762). The work that embodied the intellectual optimism and ambition of the Enlightenment philosophes was the great collaborative venture under the direction of Diderot, the *Encyclopédie* (1751–1772), a digest of the latest advances in philosophy, science, and technology, aimed at changing the mind-set of society.

While the Enlightenment did not possess a coherent ideology and doctrine and was not limited to one intellectual generation, it played a crucial role in the emergence of a set of principles and values centered on the rights and obligations of the individual, which had become widespread in progressive circles on the eve of the **French Revolution**. Much influenced by the tradition of liberal individualism established by John Locke in England, Enlightenment thinking was characterized by the belief in the individual's right to express himself freely, even if this conflicted with the prevailing dogmas (including those of the church); the right to pursue the legitimate avenues to prosperity and to enjoy that prosperity without fearing the arbitrary power of the state or superior social classes to tax it; and the belief that the enjoyment of these rights should be guaranteed for all citizens and in equal manner through the operation of the law. The perception of productive labor as not only a right but also a social duty for every individual would inevitably conflict with a status quo where the aristocracy and the clergy were largely exempted from such an obligation. Furthermore, the ramifications for a social hierarchy based on tradition, and notably inherited privilege, of an intellectual belief in social change through the application of critical reason to reduce the human misery brought about by ignorance could not fail to be explosive.

The extent to which the work of the philosophes provided a blueprint for the Revolution is a matter of debate and not entirely to the point. It is certainly the case that the Declaration of the Rights of Man, framed by the deputies who overthrew the old order, approximates closely to the Enlightenment position on the rights of the individual. On the other hand, Rousseau's radical proposals for popular, democratic government advanced in the *Social Contract* would have been much less familiar to the deputies concerned than the far more moderate proposals in Montesquieu's *Spirit of Laws*. However, more pertinent than the intentions of the philosophes were the intentions of those revolutionary ambitions on which their ideas were grafted after 1789. And although some of the measures promoted by the **Jacobins** that purported to draw inspiration from the philosophes were in fact antithetical to the spirit of the Enlightenment, it is safe to say that the Enlightenment had fostered a revolution in people's heads before the revolution in the streets of **Paris**, and that it was an intellectual revolution of long-lasting significance.

ENVIRONMENTALISM. A widespread consciousness of the threat to the environment was slow to develop in a traditionally conservative country like France in contrast, for example, with the **United States**. The cause was promoted by a small group of politically committed **ecologists**, many of whom had originally been involved in the **student rebellions** of 1968. Over the last two decades, however, the attention of the public has been captured by a certain number of high-profile individuals who have sensed the growing concern about the environment. In France the vigorous protests of people like **José Bové** over what he called *malbouffe*, or the poor-quality food resulting from the excesses of intensive farming, especially genetically modified crops, turned him into a folk hero.

Responding to the irresistible change in the public mood, the government drew up a *Charte de l'Environnement* (Environmental Charter), which came into legal existence in February 2005 and which declares, as the first of its 10 articles, that every individual has the right to live in a balanced environment that respects his or her health. This charter was partly inspired by the journalist and writer Nicolas Hulot, who provoked a wave of public concern over the environment with his television series *Ushuaïa Nature* and even contemplated riding that wave by standing in the presidential elections of 2007. But he decided not to run after persuading the leading candidates in the race, including **Nicolas Sarkozy, Ségolène Royal**, and **François Bayrou**, to sign his *Pacte écologique* (Ecological pact), agreeing to put the environment at the forefront of their concerns. The eventual victor, Sarkozy, kept to his bargain and in October 2007 he announced the recommendations, such as a carbon tax, that his government hopes to implement resulting from the forum on the environment that it had launched, involving numerous interested parties from civil society, called Le Grenelle de l'Environnement.

ESTATES GENERAL (ETATS GENERAUX). Representative body of the **ancien régime**, whose final convocation precipitated the

French Revolution. The Estates General was elected to represent the three orders: the clergy, the nobility, and the Third Estate. It was convoked by the king in exceptional circumstances, and its meeting in May 1789 was the first since 1614. The representatives in 1789 had been elected between February and April of that year and numbered 1,139: 291 representing the clergy, 270 representing the nobility, and 578 representing the Third Estate, over one-third of whom were members of the legal profession, with the others coming from the business class and those of independent means. They met to resolve the state's severe financial problems, and it was the Third Estate's refusal to countenance any contribution to a solution without the concession of corresponding rights that set in motion the events leading to the French Revolution.

EURO. The fruit of European Monetary Union that came into existence on 1 January 1999 and was adopted by 11 members of the **European Union (EU)**, including France, as their currency. Euro notes and coins entered circulation on 1 January 2002 and by 2008 had become the national currency of 15 EU states. The euro is managed by a European Central Bank, established in 1998 and since November 2003 directed by Jean-Claude Trichet, former head of the Banque de France. *See also* BANKING; NOUVEAU FRANC.

EURONEXT. *See* FINANCE.

EUROPEAN COAL AND STEEL COMMUNITY. *See* EUROPEAN UNION (EU); SCHUMAN, ROBERT.

EUROPEAN ECONOMIC COMMUNITY (EEC). *See* EUROPEAN UNION (EU).

EUROPEAN UNION (EU). The foundations for the eventual construction of the EU were laid in 1951, when Jean Monnet's brave plan for eliminating internal tariffs on trade in coal and steel among the states of Europe led to the creation of the European Coal and Steel Community. Postwar prosperity and the desire to bind France and **Germany** together drove this process, and the momentum released eventually resulted in the Treaty of Rome in 1957, formally establishing the European Economic Community (EEC), whose founding member states were France, Italy, the Federal Republic of Germany, Belgium, Luxembourg, and the Netherlands. The notable absentee was **Great Britain**, whose traditional suspicion of Europe, allied to the preference for links across the Atlantic, gave her attitude to the project of a united Europe an enduring ambivalence. However, although France was usually seen as an enthusiastic champion of European integration, her attitude toward the EEC was not itself without ambivalence. There was, on the one hand, the supranationalist vision of Jean Monnet, and on the other there was the kind of vision espoused by **Charles de Gaulle** of a Europe of sovereign nation-states.

The Gaullist vision was expressed most negatively in July 1965, when de Gaulle withdrew France's representative to the EEC as a result of disagreements over agricultural policy, the budgetary independence of the European Commission, and the prospective adoption of majority voting in the Council of Ministers in 1966. The compromise reached in 1966 that defused the crisis over France's famous "empty-chair" policy nonetheless contained an expression of the French government's determination to obstruct the functioning of the EEC were its national interests to be threatened by majority voting. This was the lowest point in France's relationship with the EEC. In 1978, France, under **Valéry Giscard d'Estaing** took the lead, together with West Germany, in setting up the European Monetary System (EMS). The EMS was designed to bring stability to exchange rates by enjoining member states of the EEC (with the exception of Britain) to support the currencies of their neighbors when the floors and ceilings agreed for the value of those currencies were threatened by market movements.

France's commitment to European integration received a major boost when French Socialist **Jacques Delors** took on the role of president of the European Commission. It was with the advocacy of Delors that the Single European Act was adopted, providing for the movement of persons, capital, goods, and services within the Community from 1 January 1986 onward. Delors also headed the committee that in early 1989 proposed the monetary union aimed at making individual national currencies redundant. This ambition was translated into a specific objective by the European Council summit of December 1991 at Maastricht, which resulted in the treaty of that name. It was the Maastricht Treaty that transformed the European Community into the EU and set a timetable and criteria for the convergence in economic performance among the members of the Union that would make monetary union a reality.

France's attitude to her role in Europe was not, however, untroubled by doubts, even under the enthusiastic advocacy of Delors. The prospect of an emergent, reunited German superpower following the collapse of the Berlin Wall led to insecurities in France as to Germany's leadership of the EU. While reassurances from the German leader, Chancellor Helmut Kohl, allayed these fears and closer Franco-German cooperation on issues like **defense** seemed to confirm Germany's commitment to a shared European destiny, faith waned in France as to the real promise of the Union, in economic and social terms. The referendum on the Maastricht Treaty in France in September 1992, ratifying the creation of the EU, suggested that the French people had lost a good measure of their enthusiasm, with 51 percent of votes cast in favor of the treaty and 49 percent against. The election of Gaullist president **Jacques Chirac** in 1995 spread further anxiety in some quarters as to whether France would return to the classically Gaullist attachment to the primacy of the nation-state, to the detriment of the further development of the European Union. When, in June 2000, Chirac responded to the historic invitation to address the German parliament newly reinstalled in Berlin, he made the usual call for the EU to exercise greater economic and political influence on the world stage. However, in contrast with the enthusiasm of his hosts for a supranational European state, Chirac underlined his faith in the sovereignty of the nation-state by arguing that the work of enhancing the Union's power and prestige should be confided to an inner core of pioneer states.

The expansion of the EU to 25 member states in 2004 (with the accession of Cyprus, the Czech Republic, Estonia, Hungary, Latvia, Lithuania, Malta, Poland, Slovakia, and Slovenia), made the acceptance of an inner core by the remaining members even less likely. The uneasy feeling grew in France, among the electorate as well as governing circles, that the expansion of the EU was making it less manageable and its future less clear. This was expressed by the refusal of the French to ratify a constitution for the EU in the referendum of

May 2005, even though its principal architect was the former French president **Valéry Giscard d'Estaing**. It is also Giscard d'Estaing, among Europe's leading mainstream political figures, who had been most open about his misgivings concerning the eventual accession of Turkey to the EU.

The accession of Bulgaria and Romania to the EU in 2007 brought the issue of how to manage the EU into even sharper focus. France's scheduled takeover of the rotating presidency of the EU in July 2008 was seized on by President **Nicolas Sarkozy** as an opportunity for advancing his vision of the EU, but one that was not always appreciated by the other members. During 2007 he had outlined his idea for a Mediterranean Union modeled on the EU and suggested, somewhat unconvincingly, that even though France's principal partner in Europe, Germany, had no border with the **Mediterranean** basin, its border with France would make it a de facto member. Further concern was raised regarding Sarkozy's potentially self-interested interpretation of what France's presidency of the EU could achieve, when he suggested at the beginning of 2008 that it might be an opportunity to change the EU-imposed fishing quotas that the French feel have been detrimental to their fishing **industry**. *See also* ECONOMY; FOREIGN POLICY; SCHUMAN, ROBERT.

EXISTENTIALISM. Major intellectual current in postwar France, most influential in the 1940s and 1950s, whose chief exponent was **Jean-Paul Sartre**. His most famous existential formula asserts that existence precedes essence; that is, that there is no God and no immutable human nature to give us a predetermined sense of who we are in any authentic way and therefore protect us from having to face up to our solitude and human contingency. Sartre rejected not only the kind of religious conceptualization that defines us but also the philosophical rationalizations that remove us from our real situation. The individual cannot fit into an all-embracing set of necessary truths, because existence defies the terms of such abstractions; it is absurd. The experience of this absurdity gives rise to a sense of sickening dread: nausea. One can employ strategies of bad faith to avoid facing the challenge posed by the absurd, or one can choose to confront it positively, through action. Hence the centrality of choice in Sartre's thought. The absence of an essence provides the individual with freedom as a fact, the potential for fashioning a meaning and an identity for his existence, freedom as a goal. Thus choice and action are inseparably linked in determining who we are, because we are defined by the choices we make.

– F –

FABIUS, LAURENT (1946–). Politician and former Socialist prime minister. His academic brilliance led to studies at both the Ecole Normale Supérieure and the Ecole Nationale d'Administration. His talent was spotted early when he joined the **Parti Socialiste (PS)** in 1974, and the positive impression he made on the leader, **François Mitterrand**, led to a safe seat for him in an industrial suburb of Rouen, which returned him as its deputy to the National Assembly in 1978. Fabius rose to the post of PS national secretary in 1979 and demonstrated his loyalty to Mitterrand at the PS party congress of that year, when he mounted a vigorous defense of his mentor against the challenge posed by **Michel Rocard** and **Pierre Mauroy**. Fabius's fidelity was rewarded in 1984, when Mitterrand chose him to replace Pierre Mauroy, thus making him the youngest French prime minister since 1819. The political significance of Fabius's appointment was that it marked a shift away from some of the naive ideological assumptions of the first two years of Socialist government and toward a more open acceptance of the disciplines of the market, with particular regard to the need for industrial restructuring and the unfortunate but inevitable consequences for employment. The emphasis placed by the Fabius government on investment and industrial modernization was also matched by his reputation as a modernizer in the party, although his rapid rise and privileged background elicited more than a little suspicion among other party heavyweights about the authenticity of his Socialist credentials.

The defeat of the left in the legislative elections of 1986 forced Fabius out of prime ministerial office and he became president of the National Assembly in 1988, before being elected to the European Parliament in 1989. During the 1990s Fabius failed to establish a power base in the PS due to his close identification with his former mentor Mitterrand. After the victory of the left in the legislative elections of 1997 he became once more the president of the National Assembly and enjoyed ministerial office from 2000–2002 as **Lionel Jospin**'s finance minister. But the best days of Fabius's political career were far behind him, and his ability to endear himself to the PS was further diminished by his open opposition to a constitution for the **European Union**, which the PS had decided to support. In spite of his undoubted talent and prime ministerial experience, Fabius was never a realistic contender for nomination as the PS candidate in the presidential elections of 2007. When the party was consulted in November 2006, the 18 percent of the votes he received from the members, as opposed to the 64 percent that went to the winner, **Ségolène Royal**, illustrated his failure to create a power base in the party.

FALLOUX LAW. Named after Vicomte Alfred-Frédéric de Falloux, the liberal Catholic minister of education who presided over the commission that drafted the law. The law of 15 March 1850 followed a long campaign by the Catholic establishment for "liberty of education," meaning a legitimate place for church influence in **education**. The result was to establish a new balance between church and state in this domain, largely at the expense of the teaching establishment. Among the law's principal provisions, teacher training colleges (*écoles normales*) were brought under stricter regulation, but teachers were provided with a guaranteed minimum wage; any town could transfer its public *collège* to the clergy if it so wished; government officials had the right to inspect all schools, and the state alone had the right to award the *baccalauréat*. As a consequence of the law, the rate of growth in Catholic schools between the years 1854 and 1867 was 75 percent, as opposed to 34 percent for the secondary school system as a whole during the same period. However, by the early years of the **Third Republic**, cooperation between church and state in the field of education had given way to antagonism as they competed for the same social groups, and most of the libertarian provisions of the Falloux law were abrogated between the years 1880 and 1886 as the state sought to establish the primacy of secular education. Nonetheless, the Falloux law enabled the church to establish an influence in secondary education in France that remains significant to this day.

FASHION. France's role as a center for fashion and a provider of styles to emulate has existed for centuries. Even at the height of France's political isolation from the other great powers in Europe, such as during the years of the **French Revolution**, disapproval of the regime there did not quench the desire among the leisured classes elsewhere to copy the styles pioneered by the French. Thus in the *Ladies Magazine* that appeared in London in February 1801, there were reproductions of the "Paris dress" with its notably simpler and relatively figure-hugging lines, but with a less low-cut bodice than the original in order not to offend English modesty.

By the end of the 19th century, **Paris** fashion was being worn and emulated as far afield as Japan, but the reasons for this were sociological as well as aesthetic. The rebuilding of Paris under **Baron Georges-Eugène Haussmann**, the technological means for the reproduction of images, and a nascent culture of leisure and consumerism all contributed to establishing Paris as the capital par excellence for the deployment of the libido of looking, for seeing and being seen. The role of Paris as a magnet for artists and writers at the turn of the century made its status as a disseminator of ideas indisputable and confirmed its preeminence as an arbiter of taste. Although the international criteria for elegance were set by designers like Coco Chanel in the interwar years, the financial fortunes of the industry had in fact declined in the 1920s and 1930s, and it was the post-1945 generation of figures like Fath, Dior, Balmain, de Givenchy, Cardin, and Saint-Laurent who gave French haute couture a renewed period of ascendancy and worldwide acclaim.

The advent of the 1960s brought new challenges to the "dictatorship" of Paris fashion, as some called it. Greater social equality and the democratization of taste challenged the assumptions behind haute couture. Youth culture in particular was predicated on a rejection of established hierarchies of taste. Furthermore, Paris found itself threatened by new fashion centers like London, Milan, and New York, setting trends with bolder or more practical designs. But while in the 1980s and 1990s Paris had to share the limelight with other capitals in determining the evolution of taste in fashion, it also showed its adaptability in reviving the old tradition of attracting new foreign talent. Designers like Jen Kelly and Yohji Yamamoto, among many others, brought an injection of international flair to Parisian styles. The destiny of the fashion house established by Coco Chanel was placed in the hands of the German designer Karl Lagerfeld. And a younger generation of native talent has shown much openness to other, distinctly non-French influences, such as the assimilation of English eccentricities in the designs of Jean-Paul Gaultier. By the end of the 20th century, the top French fashion houses were recruiting British designers themselves, such as the Londoner Alexander McQueen, who became head of design at Givenchy in 1996, replacing his compatriot John Galliano, who moved on to become the creative force at Christian Dior.

FAURE, FELIX (1841–1899). Sixth president of the **Third Republic** from 1895 to 1899. Born in **Paris**, Faure cut his teeth in local politics in Le Havre, where he became a leading republican. He was elected to the Chamber of Deputies in 1881. He won the election to the **presidency** in 1895 with conservative support. An urbane and elegant figure, Faure was most interested in the stage provided by **foreign policy** and worked skillfully to maintain the Franco-Russian alliance, especially through his contact with Czar Nicholas II. In domestic affairs, he ensured a place for himself in posterity as the president who appeared most impervious to requests to reopen the case at the heart of the **Dreyfus Affair**.

FAUVISM. An artistic movement of short duration that originated in France in 1905. The leading figures of the original group were artists like André Derain, Henri Matisse, and Maurice de Vlaminck; the group later attracted individuals like Georges Braque and Raoul Dufy. A critic applied the term *fauves* (wild beasts) in reaction to their first exhibition in 1905. The fauvists believed in giving free rein to their natural impulses, convinced that the means provided by color, line, and brushwork served a subjective conception of art in which fidelity to the artist's sensations was more important than fidelity to reality. Therefore the greatest value is attached to the reflection of an artistic temperament, whether it be gracious, as in the work of Derain, or aggressive, as in the work of de Vlaminck. The movement began to break up by 1907, but some of its ideas were carried on in the work of Matisse and Dufy, and it had some impact on the German expressionist movement. *See also* ART.

FEDERATION DE LA GAUCHE DEMOCRATIQUE ET SOCIALISTE (FGDS)/FEDERATION OF THE SOCIALIST AND DEMOCRATIC LEFT. A coalition formed by the supporters of

François Mitterrand, socialists from the **Section Française de l'Internationale Ouvrière (SFIO)/French Section of the Workers' International**, and radical politicians, all of whom had become convinced that only a strategy of cooperation among the various factions on the left could bring it to power. The breakthrough took the form of an agreement between the partners that at elections only a single, noncommunist left-wing candidate would stand in each constituency. Furthermore, the FGDS reached agreement with the **Parti Communiste Français** and the **Parti Socialiste Unifié** that only a single left-wing candidate would stand at the second ballot. The results in the 1967 legislative elections were positive, giving the FGDS 19 percent of the vote and, more important, leaving the left as a whole with 192 seats after the second ballot, thus cutting the **Gaullist** majority to six. However, the FGDS felt the backlash that followed the unrest occasioned by the **student rebellions** of May 1968, and its share of the vote fell to 17 percent in the legislative elections of June 1968. By the presidential election of the following year the FGDS had effectively lost its raison d'être, as several candidates from different sections of the left were launched into the race for the **presidency** of the Republic. But its brief existence had indicated what might be achieved by a united left, and it was a milestone on the road to the Socialist victories in the presidential and legislative elections of 1981.

FEMINISM. A sometimes contested term used to describe the movement for change in the condition of **women** that received a major impetus in the 1970s. Women had received the right to vote in France in October 1944, and the first major legislation on equal pay for men and women was passed in July 1946. But it was the **student rebellions** of May 1968 that catapulted a whole range of issues, like the fundamental reappraisal of the role of women in French society, onto the political agenda. The post-1968 climate was highly conducive to meetings and demonstrations by women who wanted to challenge the traditional roles assigned to them in the workplace, the home, and every other sphere of social activity. The term Mouvement de Libération des Femmes was popularized by the press after a demonstration under the **Arc de Triomphe** in 1970 by a small group of women who attempted to place a wreath on the tomb of the unknown soldier, but in honor of the soldier's wife.

In the 1970s the French feminist movement was firmly focused on the issues about the women's right to control their own bodies: sexuality, birth control, and abortion. Women from all kinds of backgrounds rallied to the cause, and in April 1971 the pressure to legalize abortion was exemplified by the publication of a manifesto containing the names of 343 women who admitted having had illegal abortions. In 1974 President **Valéry Giscard d'Estaing** asked his minister of health, **Simone Veil**, to propose legislation liberalizing contraception. When this was passed by the National Assembly, a bill quickly followed allowing abortion under certain circumstances. Conservative opposition to the bill was defeated, and its provisions became law for an experimental period of five years; the bill was permanently adopted in 1979. Another innovation by Giscard d'Estaing in 1974 was to set up a secretariat with a specific brief to handle women's affairs (*see* GIROUD, FRANCOISE). The resourcing of this secretariat and the priority given to it varied during the years that followed, but the work it was engaged in received a substantial financial and political boost after the victory of the **Socialists** in 1981. Yvette Roudy was appointed minister for women's rights and during her five years in office became an advocate of affirmative action and the need to inform women of their new opportunities.

In 1981 the group called Psychanalyse et Politique legally acquired the name Mouvement de Libération des Femmes, and by the 1990s feminism was struggling against the practice of sexism in its most common manifestations. In 1999, the association Chiennes de Garde (The Watchdogs) was created and gained much media attention for the way it mobilized public opinion against sexist insults, in verbal or written forms, whether in contexts such as public discourse or in advertising. The reality in contemporary France is that since the 1970s, issues that were once sharply defined as feminist have permeated the media, written and **broadcast**, so that the concerns that were once clearly visible only in the campaigning press, such as sexual harassment in the workplace and fairer division of domestic labor, are now discussed in the pages of magazines for homemakers and debated in journals for intellectuals. This development attests to the current diversity of the groups that constitute the contemporary French feminist movement, and also some of its divisions.

FERRY, JULES (1832–1893). Opportunist politician and twice premier (23 September 1880–14 November 1881, 22 February 1883–6 April 1885). He is best remembered for his reform of **education** in France and the renewed impetus he gave to French **colonialism**. Born the son of an affluent lawyer in St.-Die (Vosges), Ferry himself became a lawyer-journalist with a nose for a good story. He entered electoral politics as a radical Republican and was much involved in the events in **Paris** following the downfall of the **Second Empire**. He was mayor of Paris during the dreadful winter of 1870–1871, and his experiences of the siege by the Prussians (*see* FRANCO-PRUSSIAN WAR) and the events of the **Commune** made him deeply distrustful of disorder and dangerous populism, turning him instead toward a moderate brand of republicanism. He held a variety of ministerial portfolios, but both in his own cabinets and in those of other premiers he was a prime mover of the educational reforms known as the Ferry laws. Though born a Catholic, Ferry preferred the intellectual influences of **positivism** and freemasonry (he joined in 1875). The educational reforms he pushed through, such as free and universal primary education (16 July 1881), state certification for teachers in the public sector (16 June 1881), and the removal of religious instruction from the curriculum (28 March 1882), reduced the influence of the Catholic Church in education and reflected his belief in the scientific progress of a democratic and secular France.

The impetus Ferry gave to French imperialism was a feature of his second term as premier. In spite of some of his famous speeches about France's civilizing mission, Ferry was driven fundamentally by the desire to restore France's prestige as a great power. He promoted the expansion of the empire into places like Tunisia (1881), numerous territories in West and Equatorial Africa, Madagascar, and Indochina (1883). However, Ferry pursued this policy in the face of considerable hostility, not least from his fellow parliamentarians, who were outraged by his disinclination to inform them of the true scale of the funds and troops needed for these colonial campaigns. Regarded by some as opinionated and arrogant, Ferry was unquestionably a man of broad intellect, and he had the courage of his convictions. On his death on 18 March 1893 he was given a national burial, as befits a founding figure of the **Third Republic** and an individual who exerted a decisive influence in shaping modern France.

FILLON, FRANCOIS (1954–). Center-right politician and prime minister of France. Brought up in the small town of Cérans-Folletourte, Fillon studied law at the provincial Université de Maine before moving on to the Ecole des Sciences Politiques in **Paris**. From 1977 onward Fillon worked on the staff of a series of ministerial cabinets and in 1981 obtained the first of numerous mandates as a local representative when he became a councilor in Sablé-sur-Sarthe. His career took off nationally in 1997, when he became national secretary of the **Gaullist party**, then known as the Rassemblement pour la République (RPR). When the issue of who would succeed **Jacques Chirac** to the presidency came to the fore, Fillon astutely threw his weight behind **Nicolas Sarkozy**. This was partly motivated by the snub Fillon felt he had endured at the hands of Chirac's protégé, **Dominique de Villepin**, who had failed to offer a ministerial post to Fillon when he took over from **Jean-Pierre Raffarin** as prime minister in 2005. Fillon's reward came in May 2007 when the newly elected President Nicolas Sarkozy appointed him prime minister. In contrast to Sarkozy, Fillon was perceived as a smoother, more managerial type of politician. So it came as a surprise when within months of his appointment he confessed to the media of feeling a certain annoyance at Sarkozy's tendency to encroach on the prime minister's remit of managing the administration of the country.

Fillon's suggestion, back in 2000, that France might move to a purely presidential executive and that the post of the prime minister could be abolished, had come back to haunt him. In August 2007 the French **press** questioned what Fillon's role was, given Sarkozy's inclination to articulate policy on issues like managing relations with the **European Union** and the problems being encountered by the French **aerospace industry**. In a joint meeting with the press, Fillon bristled visibly when referred to by Sarkozy as his *collaborateur* or associate. At other times during that summer, Fillon was contradicted by the president's spokesmen, such as when he announced the plan to guarantee a minimum service to the public in the provision of all state services and not just transport. Conversely, Fillon preempted the Elysée when he declared that the key policy of reforming pension regimes in the public sector was ready to be implemented. In the event, Fillon successfully rode out the wave of protests provoked by that policy, just as he did with the protests that greeted his policy of giving greater autonomy to the universities, and by the end of 2007 the presidential team at the Elysée palace and the prime ministerial one at Matignon had achieved a higher level of coordination. But Sarkozy's determination to be a hands-on president would always leave a potential for friction with anyone assuming the post of prime minister.

FINANCE. As in so many other areas of life in France, the **French Revolution** transformed the state's finances. Paradoxically, the Revolution also showed that the centralizing tradition had left an enduring mark on the means by which the ambitions at the center, whether monarchical or republican, were pursued through intervention in the operation of the financial system. Under the **ancien régime**, the task of financing the personal needs and public policies of the monarchy was a perpetual challenge that made individual financiers extremely wealthy and small and unscrupulous banking consortia extremely powerful. These individuals and interests had made themselves indispensable to the smooth functioning of the state's financial mechanisms by providing the money for the crown's ambitions to expand French influence overseas, prosecute wars against its enemies, and invest in the state's infrastructure. The lucrative nature of this relationship reached a peak under **Louis XIV**, when figures like Samuel Bernard and the Paris brothers obtained immense influence over French finances as a result of the fortunes they built as arms suppliers to the crown. Others, like the financier Antoine Crozat, were rewarded for their services to the crown with royal concessions in the colonies—in his case, the monopoly of trade with Louisiana. Even the collection of the state's taxes was effectively contracted out. Thus every six years a group of 40 financiers, called the Farmers General (Fermiers Généraux), purchased the right to collect the indirect taxes owed to the crown.

On his death in September 1715, Louis XIV was succeeded by his great-grandson, owing to the death of his only son and his grandsons. However, because Louis XV was only five years old, a regency was instituted under **Philippe d'Orléans** to manage the crown's affairs during the king's infancy. Mindful of the power of the financiers and bankers over the royal finances, the regent was seduced by the argument that a major hindrance to the liberty of the crown and the prosperity of the country was the absence of a royal bank to issue paper money, guaranteed on the king's credit, which could therefore relieve the chronic deficits suffered by the royal finances. Proof of the efficacy of this enterprise could be found, he believed, in the examples set by England and the Dutch Republic, two tiny states that nonetheless found the money to pursue military campaigns against France and develop their commercial interests overseas. The regent believed that he had found the man to bring his financial reforms to fruition in the shape of the Scottish banker John Law.

In essence, what John Law did in 1720 was to set up a state bank on the promise of overseas trading profits and pay the king's debts in banknotes. Initially, the scheme proved a roaring success, but it soon collapsed, along with the faith in the much vaunted overseas profits, leaving thousands of families with assets amounting to no more than worthless paper. This experience left subsequent generations in France deeply suspicious of the attempt to liquidate debt through the issuance of paper money by a national bank. Thus proposals by **Jacques Necker** to do just this in the immediate aftermath of the events of 1789, in order to refloat the nation's finances, were met with considerable hostility. The compromise that was reached took the form of *assignats,* bonds secured on the value of the nation's lands. In December 1789 the National Assembly authorized the sale of 400 million livres' worth of national lands and the issuance of *assignats* of the same total value, in the form of 1,000-livre notes, bearing 5 percent interest. The intention was that the state would pay its creditors in *assignats*, which the creditors would in turn use to purchase national lands. It was therefore not intended that the *assignats* should become synonymous with paper money, but this is precisely what happened. In April 1790 it was decided that the *assignats* should become legal tender, and during the six months that followed, six supplementary issues of *assignats* were authorized to cover the state's burgeoning deficits. The inevitable and escalating financial chaos following from mounting deficits and increasingly devalued *assignats* was finally tackled by **Napoléon Bonaparte**, who in February 1800 pushed through the establishment of a central bank, the Bank of France.

Thanks to his reforms of revenue-raising and tax collection in France, this put the state's finances on a sound footing and enabled Bonaparte, as First Consul in 1802, to declare a balanced budget.

The defeat of the Napoleonic empire and the restoration of monarchy in France also restored the influence of individual bankers and financiers. But developments in the second half of the 19th century harked back to the days of the Republic and the Empire, when the power at the center used the financial system to lay the foundations for a new society, and presaged the way French governments after 1945 used the system in an interventionist manner to plan a modern and prosperous postwar French society. The seizure of power by Napoléon III (*see* BONAPARTE, LOUIS-NAPOLEON) in the coup d'état of 1851 marked a new chapter in the relationship between the state and capital in France. A new generation of dynamic French industrialists found a sympathetic hearing among the bureaucratic technocrats of the new regime, who were prepared to play an active part in undertakings like organizing industrial exhibitions and steering increased state orders to industrial sectors suffering cyclical downturns, as in the shipyards in 1857. Furthermore, through financial aid and guarantees, the state fostered the development of new technologies like the railways, encouraging vital alliances between heavy industries, sources of finance, railway firms, and utility providers, which transformed deposit banks like Société Générale, and especially Crédit Lyonnais, into industrial banks with an integral role in the modernization of France.

While it is true that the economic slump that marked the end of Napoléon III's regime led to retrenchment in the **banking** and financial services sector and resulted in some famous collapses, such as that of the Crédit Mobilier, whose fortunes evaporated with the end of the boom in railways and utilities, France entered the final two decades of the 19th century with a mature financial system that served extremely well the needs of the increasing cohorts of small savers, as well as the needs of industry. This was the period of rapid growth and general prosperity termed the *belle époque*, to which the French looked with nostalgia after the devastation, material and economic, caused by **World War I**.

But whereas the management of France's finances during the interwar years was characterized by the uncertainties caused by a fragile franc and the consequent reliance of successive French governments on American and British banks to support the national currency, French governments after 1945 showed an unequivocal determination to intervene in the financial system as part of a wide-ranging policy to engineer the renewal of the nation's **economy**. Hence the **nationalization** of the key institutions in the banking sector in 1945 and 1946, including the Bank of France, Crédit Lyonnais, and Société Générale. This nationalization of credit was extended after the **Socialists** took power in 1981, when the state took control of 36 smaller banks and two important providers of financial services, Paribas and Suez.

With the benefit of hindsight, however, it can be seen that the Socialists were swimming against the tide generated by changes in the world economy, notably the liberalization of financial markets. Within five years a newly elected center-right government began to reverse the nationalizations that had followed the end of **World War II** and the additional measures taken by the Socialists in the early 1980s, indicating the end of a long tradition of direct state intervention in the operation of the French financial system. The point was conceded by the Socialists themselves in 1984 when they began removing price controls and freeing markets. This development reached a high point two years later when the Bourse, or Paris stock exchange, followed London by having its own "big bang," thereby opening up its financial markets in a manner comparable to London and New York so that it too could have its own futures market, the Marché à Terme International de France, and offer a similar array of financial products and services. Two major landmarks testifying to the integration of France's financial system into supranational structures came, in the first case, in 1998, with the setting up of the European Central Bank, tasked with determining monetary policy for the (by 2008) 15 **European Union** countries, including France, that had adopted the **euro** as their currency. In the second case, the landmark was reached when the Paris stock exchange, already part of a pan-European alliance with exchanges in Brussels and Amsterdam called Euronext, agreed to be taken over by the New York Stock Exchange in an operation that was completed in March 2007, thereby making **Paris** part of a truly global trading platform.

FLAUBERT, GUSTAVE (1821–1880). Novelist. Born into a bourgeois family of doctors in Rouen, Flaubert chose to study law but gave up the idea of a legal career because of a nervous illness and thereafter spent his life as a man of letters under no financial obligation to earn a living. His method of writing was painfully slow, owing to the extreme importance he attached to an almost scientific objectivity and precision of language. His most famous work, *Madame Bovary*, is notable for the way it penetrates the comforting certainties of bourgeois life to reveal the cruel hypocrisies and moral bankruptcy underlying it. Yet in spite of the legal attack on him for producing a book that was supposed to be an affront to public morals, Flaubert was no revolutionary. His social attitudes were innately conservative, and his distaste for the material greed of his own class and the pretensions this generated did not preclude a marked distrust of the masses. Rather than seeking to improve society through radical politics, Flaubert sought a formal perfection in his literary craft. In life, as in his literature, he showed a characteristically lucid self-awareness and signaled his appreciation of the delusion inherent in his position as a critic of bourgeois hypocrisy while being a member of the same leisured class, when he commented, "Madame Bovary, c'est moi" ("I am Madame Bovary"). *See also* LITERATURE.

FOCH, FERDINAND (1851–1929). Marshal appointed commander in chief of Allied Armies in 1918. A Catholic, born into a modest family with a military tradition, he was commissioned in the artillery in 1874. His intellectual promise was noticed when he held the post of professor of strategy and tactics at the Ecole Supérieure de Guerre (1895–1901). He made his reputation early in **World War I**, foiling a German move on the French center at the Marne (6–9 September 1914) and organizing the defense of Ypres (October–December 1914). His good relations with **Georges Clemenceau** and a consensus among the Allies smoothed the way for his promotion to the post of commander in chief of Allied Armies. But his relations with Clemenceau were soured by his criticisms of Clemenceau's compromises over France's territorial claims after the armistice with **Germany**. Foch was not a military leader with a capacity for inspirational tactics or a genius for strategy; rather, his talents were proved in his planning and coordination of the Allied effort. His ferocious will and unyielding commitment to victory served his country well, and he was entombed near **Napoléon Bonaparte** at the Invalides after his death on 20 March 1929.

FORCE OUVRIERE (FO)/LABOR FORCE. A major **trade union** organization in France since **World War II**. The movement grew out of the **Confédération Générale du Travail (CGT)** owing to the tension within the CGT between the dominant communist majority and noncommunist minorities. Prior to 1939 these tensions had given rise to a noncommunist group called Syndicats, many of whose leaders were subsequently compromised during the war because of alleged contact with the **Vichy regime**. Tensions reemerged soon after the Allied victory, and in 1946 socialists, anarchosyndicalists, Trotskyists, and independents found a new collective identity as the FO. A source of future embarrassment was the money channeled by the U.S. Central Intelligence Agency (CIA) to the organization via the American Federation of Labor's representative in Europe, Irving Brown. However, the FO was not a CIA puppet, and its decision to split from the CGT in December 1947 arose from genuine and deep disagreements over labor tactics in the industrial unrest that broke out during that winter. This split was rendered definitive by the founding congress of the FO in April 1948. It was led initially by the prewar head of the CGT, Léon Jouhaux. He was followed by Robert Bothereau, André Bergeron, Marc Blondel, and the current leader, Jean-Claude Mailly. In contrast to the CGT, the FO cooperated actively in implementing the **Marshall Plan** and soon began to establish a membership base among government employees.

The FO's commitment to a nonideological stance, together with its pursuit of economic gains for workers through collective bargaining within a liberal democratic framework, has sometimes made it appear slow to catch up with the desire for change, among its members and in society as a whole. This was one of the reasons that it appeared to be bypassed by the events of May 1968. Although many of its leaders and most active members sympathize with the **Parti Socialiste (PS)**, it retained an arm's-length relationship with the Socialist administrations appointed after the presidential triumph of **François Mitterrand** in 1981. As the fortunes of the PS declined, this policy proved beneficial to the credibility of the union and its subsequent growth in membership. Mindful of its membership base in the public sector, the FO played a leading and aggressive part in the campaign of industrial stoppages that paralyzed France in November and December 1995, causing the center-right government of **Alain Juppé** to attenuate some of the more brutal aspects of his administration's plans for fundamental reform of the welfare state in France.

FO took to the streets in 2003 to defend its constituency of salaried civil servants against proposals to reform the country's generous pensions system and did so again in 2007. But in 2006 the union portrayed itself as the defender of the young in the battle against the Contrat Première Embauche (First Employment Contract), a reform intended by the government to give employers more flexibility and therefore encourage them to recruit more young people, but one commonly perceived by young people as giving the employers the latitude to hire and fire new young employees, which employment legislation would not allow them to enjoy in relation to established employees.

FOREIGN LEGION. Military corps famous as a magnet for fugitive foreigners willing to serve under the French flag abroad. It was formed in 1831 following the abolition of mercenary units during the previous year and was used to defend reaches of the French empire in places like **Algeria** (1831), Indochina (1883), Morocco (1903), and Syria (1925). French governments were traditionally reluctant to divulge information about the legion, and it did not appear on the published army list until 1931. This contributed to the mystique that grew up surrounding the corps, as did its policy of asking few questions of its recruits, although after **World War I**, recruits had to be fingerprinted and cleared by the police. French citizens were forbidden entry (but some pretended to be Swiss or Belgian to get in), and to avoid citizenship complications with the other recruits, legionnaires were made to take an oath to the legion and not to France. Hence the intense loyalty to the corps, its doctrine of *Legion Patria Nostra* ("The legion is our country"), and its motto of *Honneur et fidélité*. The legion proved its professionalism and fighting ability in numerous conflicts and is still deployed by French governments in the most difficult spheres of operation, such as Bosnia. By the end of

2005 the legion was engaged in 11 deployments, ranging from participation in the **Vigipirate** operation on mainland France to United Nations–mandated interventions in the Côte d'Ivoire and Afghanistan.

FOREIGN POLICY. The pursuit of French foreign policy in historical terms has been guided by three considerations: France's position in the world; the pursuit of her economic interests; and the construction of Europe. In the days when Europe was effectively the global horizon, French foreign policy was aimed essentially at securing the country's borders from foreign powers and extending them where possible. The final expulsion of the English in 1453 marked the ultimate chapter in the **Hundred Years' War** and the opening of a new one as the royal domain grew to encompass first Aquitaine and then Burgundy to give France its recognizably modern borders.

The centralization of power under the **ancien régime** and France's demographic strength, compared to its neighbors, allowed it to adopt a foreign policy of territorial and political self-aggrandizement. The 16th and 17th centuries were characterized by shifting alliances and conflicts with European neighbors aimed at extending the reach of the French crown. France under the rule of **Louis XIV**, the Sun King, was particularly successful in pressurizing its neighbors to the east and by his death in 1715 France's borders had been extended to include the prized German-speaking city of **Strasbourg**. This period also coincided with the exploration of new worlds across the Atlantic and inaugurated the first phase of **colonialism**, as France competed with its eternal rival, **Great Britain**, in India and especially North America, to become the European, and therefore the global, superpower. Ironically, the fate of these French interests abroad was determined by a conflict in Europe, the **Seven Years' War**, at the conclusion of which France's defeat meant that she was eclipsed by Britain in those foreign territories.

The profound transformation effected by the **French Revolution** did not alter the guiding principles of the country's foreign policy, which is indicative of how constant and nonpartisan, in ideological terms, those principles are. The island of Corsica had been ceded to France by Genoa in 1768, and one of the first pronouncements of the new revolutionary Assembly was to declare the island part of the

French empire, subsequently authorizing French troops to put down nationalist unrest there. Whatever hopes the slaves in France's colonies might have had of the Declaration of the Rights of Man were soon dashed as slavery was reinstated and France under **Napoléon Bonaparte** engaged in business as usual in foreign policy terms, deploying French military power in support of French territorial and commercial interests wherever possible. Napoléon's "continental system" locked up as much of Europe as possible, notably through the satellite states created in the Low Countries, northern Italy, and what is now France's eastern border, subjecting them to terms of trade that were clearly beneficial to France and detrimental to them.

The monarchical restorations that followed the defeat of Napoléon at Waterloo in 1815 reduced France's ability to project its power on the world stage but did not destroy its ambition to do so, as was illustrated by the French acquisition of **Algeria** in 1830. When **Louis-Napoléon Bonaparte**, Napoléon's nephew, was elected president of the **Second Republic** in December 1848, his campaign had played on an appeal to the country's thirst for greatness on the world stage, which his uncle had given France, albeit briefly. Once his coup d'état had been put into effect and the Second Republic became the **Second Empire** in 1852, Napoléon III, as Louis-Napoléon now called himself, persisted in the illusion that he could conduct foreign policy in the same manner as his uncle, while possessing none of the same military genius or talent for inspirational leadership. His first piece of foreign policy adventurism was to ally France with Britain in an attempt to stem the growth of Russian influence south of the Black Sea, resulting in the Crimean War (1853–1856). Less costly and more obviously successful during the 1860s was the expansion of France's overseas possessions, notably the acquisition of **New Caledonia**, Djibouti, and Senegal. It was also under Napoléon III that the final piece of the jigsaw puzzle was added that completed the contours of metropolitan France. He supported the Italian nationalists against Austrian domination in their bid to unite the country, but the price that was paid was the annexation of Nice and Savoy by France. French foreign policy under the Second Empire was conducted more by luck than by careful design, and an indication that the luck would run out came with the expedition to Mexico (1861–1867), when Napoléon III allowed himself to be persuaded to place a Catholic conservative on the throne of Mexico, in the shape of a member of the Hapsburg dynasty, the Archduke Maximilian. This doomed attempt to play the kingmaker did not deter Napoléon III from trying to determine who should accede to the vacant throne of Spain, instead of allowing a Prussian-backed candidate to go forward. The attempt by Napoléon III to force the Prussians into what they perceived as a public and humiliating climb down is what led to the **Franco-Prussian War** and the catastrophic defeat endured by the French. The collapse of the Second Empire caused by this defeat was also the last time a monarchical or dynastic regime came to power in France.

But the defeat by Bismarck's new **Germany**, and the loss of Alsace and much of Lorraine to the Germans as part of the terms of the peace, rendered even more acute the need to restore France's standing in the world, even though power had now passed to the republican majority of the **Third Republic**. Left-wing ideology, and especially socialism, had taken root in France in the 1880s, with its emphasis on equality and internationalism. It is at this point that we see more sophisticated attempts to justify the projection of French interests abroad, and in particular the colonial enterprise. A seminal influence was a study by the economist Paul Leroy-Beaulieu, *De la colonisation chez les peuples modernes* (1874), in which he harnessed the pursuit of colonial possessions with the project of modernity. It was morally acceptable for industrial societies like France to take the benefits of their progress to foreign lands, even if accompanied by the establishment of empire, as it allowed those benefits to be shared with populations who would otherwise never enjoy them. Empire was in fact a virtuous circle, taking raw materials from countries unable to exploit them and returning the finished goods, whether machines or medicine, in a way that enriched both the sender and the receiver.

The political reality was that France's crushing defeat by the Prussians had left all the mainstream parties desperately looking for ways to return France to the top table in the concert of leading nations. Even a socialist like **Jean Jaurès**, who later distinguished himself as a pacifist and internationalist, in the 1880s supported a foreign policy whose centerpiece was colonial expansionism. In a famous speech to the **Alliance Française**, Jaurès argued that France could not be reduced to the same destiny as other European states such as Belgium or Switzerland. The heart of Jaurès's plea to support colonialism was what he believed to be a moral one. The legacy of the French Revolution, especially its emphasis on freedom, equality, and human rights was not just national, but universal, and France would be failing in her vocation, or civilizing mission, if she did not take those values to the ends of the earth to share them with the oppressed and unenlightened, even under the flag of empire. Thus it was that **Jules Ferry**'s administration sanctioned the establishment of a French presence in Indochina, and with the scramble by European powers for African possessions well under way as the 19th century drew to a close, France expanded its North African possessions with tacit German and British approval.

For the Germans, it was a way of distracting France from the loss of Alsace-Lorraine and the bitter resentment that generated among the French people, and for the British, a rapprochement with France was already under way that would result in the signing of the Entente Cordiale. The emergence of a confident and powerfully militaristic Germany would drive the French into a policy of alliances, with their obvious partners in the west like Britain and Belgium, and in the east with partners like Serbia and Russia. It was just such a network of alliances that drew France inexorably into **World War I**. Although France emerged victorious, the painful truth was that in the field of foreign relations, France was crucially dependent on its Anglo-American allies. It was an American plan, for example, that resolved the long-running conflict with Germany over reparations. A major factor in pushing France toward accepting a compromise was its dependence on Anglo-American banks to prop up the fragile national currency, the franc, on international markets.

The mismatch between France's ambitions and its economic and military power did not diminish its belief in a global vocation. It still had the world's second largest empire, after Britain, and the justifications for it were becoming more subtle. In Albert Sarraut's *Grandeur et servitude coloniales* (1931), Sarraut admits that empire is based on an act of expropriation but that this is eclipsed by the moral obligation, even the sacred duty, placed on a country like France to help the underdeveloped peoples of its empire to fulfill their enormous potential and become, in effect, the equal of the people of metropolitan France. In terms of the *realpolitik* of 1930s Europe, however, French impotence was manifest. The Spanish Civil

War in 1936 and the crucial contribution of Italian and German fascists to the eventual victory of their counterparts in Spain was a warning of what was to come and was understood as such by many of the supporters of the **Popular Front** government under **Léon Blum**.

But Blum's foreign policy options were limited by the fact that France was not strong enough to act without the British, and the British government was determined to maintain the pretense that the four great powers of Europe (France, Britain, Germany, and Italy) were respecting the agreement not to intervene in Spain. In fact, the sense of defeatism and impotence that infected the management of French foreign policy meant that by 1938 the British were effectively negotiating with Adolf Hitler on behalf of the French as well as themselves. As ever, in the history of modern France, the empire came to the rescue of French national self-esteem. After the collapse of France in 1940, following the declaration of war with Germany in 1939, one of the principal planks of **Charles de Gaulle**'s appeal to the French was that another France, in the form of its overseas possessions, was determined to fight and save the country's honor. While France was one of the victors at the end of **World War II** in 1945, the inescapable truth was that it had been almost entirely dependent on other nations for its freedom.

This may explain the desperation with which it tried to hang on to its doomed empire in its endeavor to retain great nation status. There was first the bitter **Indochinese War**, which ended in defeat for France in 1954, the year that the first shots were fired in the even more painful war of independence in Algeria. These conflicts were punctuated by another foreign policy misadventure, this time in partnership with that other declining postimperial power, Britain, and in connivance with the state of Israel. When Colonel Gamal Abdel Nasser, in the summer of 1956, nationalized the Suez Canal, British Prime Minister Anthony Eden reacted hysterically by calling him another Hitler and set in train Franco-British-Israeli plans to take back the canal by military force, thus sparking the **Suez Crisis**. Although the vital waterway was taken back by Franco-British paratroopers and Israeli ground forces, they were forced to abandon the operation when the **United States** threatened to stop propping up Britain and France financially. Whereas Britain became resigned to the fact that it could no longer take a major foreign policy initiative without at least tacit U.S. approval, it reinforced the suspicion that came to characterize French–U.S. relations.

While the 1950s could be described as the twilight of empire, it was also the dawn of a new era that saw the construction of Europe, first as the European Community, then as the **European Union**, which would allow French foreign policy to project France as a great nation on the international stage. An analysis of **Robert Schuman**'s landmark speech in 1950, outlining his vision for a European Coal and Steel Community, shows France's determination to be at the heart of the new postwar Europe, its principal architect and its intellectual leader. Yet while the logic inherent in the building of a common European home is that the peoples within it should ultimately shelter under the same roof, institutionally and constitutionally, French foreign policy has often found itself in the position of advocating a supranational future for Europe while ferociously protecting the prerogatives characteristic of a conviction that nothing is superior to national sovereignty. Charles de Gaulle returned to power in 1958, the same year that the Treaty of Rome came into effect, creating the **European Economic Community (EEC)**, and inaugurated a series of close relationships between French presidents and German chancellors that made the *couple Franco-Allemand*, or Franco-German relationship, the keystone in the growing European edifice. But de Gaulle did not hesitate to break with his chief ally whenever he perceived France's national sovereignty to be threatened by European federalism. This explains his policy of the "empty chair," effectively boycotting EEC meetings when proposed changes to agricultural subsidies and the system of voting appeared to threaten French interests.

It was clear that for de Gaulle the EEC was a positive development as long as it respected the French blueprint for it and did not succumb to alternative influences, especially Anglo-Saxon ones. He repeatedly turned down Britain's application to join the club, ostensibly because of a lack of economic and political convergence between Britain and the other members of the EEC, but in reality due to his fear that Britain would be a Trojan horse for American influence. The determination not to be a U.S. satellite is also why, unlike all the other EEC states and Britain, who sheltered under the U.S. nuclear umbrella, de Gaulle was determined to give France an independent nuclear deterrent as the centerpiece of its **defense policy**. While for many commentators outside France the French nuclear deterrent was an act of political machismo, since it was inconceivable that France could have squared up to the **Soviet Union** alone, for French diplomacy it was a vital element in the attempt to convey to the international community that the world was not inevitably divided into two opposing camps, presided over by Washington and Moscow. De Gaulle traveled the world, particularly those parts of it that harbored suspicions toward U.S. foreign policy such as Latin America, putting France forward as a privileged interlocutor among the great liberal democracies. When he visited Canada he played on anti–Anglo Saxon sentiment by famously greeting a delirious Francophone crowd in Quebec with the cry, "*Vive le Québec libre!*" ("Long live free Quebec!").

While his successors have been less strident in projecting France globally, the fundamentals of the foreign policy agenda set by de Gaulle have not changed, whether successive French presidents have been of the center-right or the left. Socialist president **François Mitterrand** was sufficiently convinced of the sacrosanct need to modernize France's nuclear deterrent that he faced down worldwide condemnation in the **Greenpeace Affair**, after the *Rainbow Warrior* ship protesting against French nuclear testing in the Pacific was blown up by French secret service agents. There was outrage then in France's closest partner in the European Community, Germany, and there was outrage again when Mitterrand's successor, **Jacques Chirac**, authorized further nuclear testing in 1995. On this occasion, the collapse of the Berlin Wall and the disappearance of the Soviet threat that had preceded the new test program made the French decision even more incomprehensible to opinion in Europe, especially Germany. In 2000, when Chirac went to address the German parliament, his speech underlined the assumptions that continue to move French foreign policymakers. Chirac praised the progress that has been made in the development of the European Union and evoked the progress that could still be made. But the means to this, he suggested, might be through the work of a group of "pioneer nations" rather than, by implication, the kind of supranational initiatives dependent on a broad consensus.

The Gaullist legacy is evident and harks back to the symbiotic relationship between progress and nation-building established by the French Revolution. The state that serves the nation and its sovereign people has a vocation that no supranational body can fulfill. As the Gaullist politician **Philippe Séguin** put it, there cannot be a European state because there is no European people. Furthermore, if the French nation-state declines, civil society declines, because after 1789 the republican state became a guarantor and active promoter of the values that define French society. Senior French political figures like **Bernard Kouchner** have, in the past, promoted the idea of *le droit d'ingérence*, the right to interfere in a sovereign state's affairs in exceptional circumstances, such as the need to avert a humanitarian crisis. But as the former foreign minister Hubert Védrine has pointed out, this should only occur with the approval of the international community, articulated by a body like the **United Nations**. Since the collapse of the Soviet Union and the end of the superpower stand-off between the United States and the USSR, French diplomacy has advanced the cause of a multipolar world as the best guarantee of stability and security, as opposed to a world where one superpower makes or unmakes the rules of the international game in an arbitrary fashion. This was the essential reason why France criticized the United States for its decision to launch the second Iraq war. The guiding assumption at the Quai d'Orsay, the home of French diplomacy, is that the promotion of France as a sovereign nation-state and an interlocutor in its own right in the concert of nations enhances the global community of nation-states and allows France to make a positive contribution to the construction of the EU and the development of the wider world.

Since his election in May 2007, President **Nicolas Sarkozy** has given a vivid profile to French foreign policy due to his relentlessly hectic activity around the globe. One of his pledges on the presidential campaign trail was that France would stand up for women, and this motivated his (and his second wife, Cecilia's) widely publicized involvement in the July 2007 liberation of a group of Bulgarian nurses who had been condemned to death in Libya for allegedly infecting children with AIDS. But in spite of his unique hunger for the limelight, the thrust of Sarkozy's foreign policy is classically Gaullist. Thus, whether it is visiting Libya in July 2007 or attempting to launch an initiative to aid refugees in the Darfur region of Somalia in the following month, the aim is to position France as a leader on the world stage, speaking with a sovereign voice as a powerfully independent nation-state.

FOUCAULT, MICHEL (1926–1984). Social scientist, philosopher, intellectual historian, and arguably the most influential thinker in postwar France since **Jean-Paul Sartre**. Born the son of a surgeon in a comfortable middle-class family in Poitiers, Foucault displayed his prodigious intellectual talents from an early age. From the Lycée Henri IV in **Paris** he went on to the Ecole Normale Supérieure; there and at the Sorbonne, he was taught by some of the finest minds of the French intellectual establishment. He passed the *agrégation* in 1951 and published his first book, *Maladie mentale et psychologie,* in 1954. Following a number of years as a *lecteur* in French in various institutions in Europe, Foucault returned to France in 1960 to take up a post in the department of philosophy at the University of Clermont-Ferrand. Foucault's doctoral thesis was published the following year under the title *L'Histoire de la folie à l'âge classique,* in which he traces the evolution of the notion of madness over hundreds of years and uses it as a means for analyzing the way cultures define their limits and the political motivations for this. In the following book, *Naissance de la clinique: Une archéologie du regard médical* (1963), Foucault preferred a **structuralist** to a classically linear historical method, piecing together the knowledge in an "archeological" manner. It was *Les mots et les choses* (1966) that sealed Foucault's reputation and brought him back to Paris and ultimately to his chair at the Collège de France. In this work Foucault tries to determine the paradigms that constituted the conceptual matrix that in the 19th century had fed the emergence of human sciences, a theme taken up again in *L'Archéologie du savoir* (1969).

Foucault died on 25 June 1984, having half completed what had been intended as a six-volume history of sexuality. It was only some time later that the cause of his death was revealed as AIDS. Foucault's pluridisciplinary approach to knowledge helps explain his extraordinary influence across diverse fields of research, sometimes far removed from his own starting point in history and philosophy, and confirms his reputation as a preeminent figure in the French intellectual establishment of the 20th century.

FOUCHE, JOSEPH (1759–1820). Duc d'Otrante. Born near Nantes and originally destined for the teaching profession, he took the first major step in his political career with his election to the **Convention**

in 1792, where he associated initially with the moderate **Girondins**. Ever the opportunist, he voted for the execution of the king but eventually failed to anticipate the **Thermidorian** reaction and dropped out of sight only to reemerge under the **Directory**. Fouché was appointed minister of general **police** on 20 July 1799, an office that suited his talents very well, and was retained by **Napoléon Bonaparte**. He was dismissed in September 1802 and reappointed from July 1804 until May 1810, when he was dismissed again for negotiating with the English. Fouché collaborated with the allies after Bonaparte's defeat at Waterloo in 1815 and retained his post at the police ministry, which Bonaparte had restored to him during the **Hundred Days**. But he was dismissed in September 1815, accused of regicide, and summarily sent into exile; he died at Trieste on 26 December 1820. Fouché was a formidably efficient policeman and created the first modern political police. But the opportunism that had advanced his career ultimately proved to be his downfall.

FRANCOIS I. *See* RENAISSANCE.

LA FRANCOPHONIE. Description applied to the international French-speaking community. The nations that make up this community were gathered under the banner of their common language for their first summit in **Paris**, 17–19 February 1986, under the leadership of President **François Mitterrand**. The aim of the first summit was to reinforce the sense of shared identity among French-speaking nations and to lay the foundation for cooperation on projects to enhance this identity. Summits have occurred at regular intervals since the first one. The developing nations that participate gain in terms of economic and technical aid, while France enjoys the opportunity to enhance its profile as a nation of high international standing. By 2005 the Organisation Internationale de la Francophonie had a new Charter for its 55 member states (with 13 others enjoying observer status), serving 175 million Francophones across five continents. It is an organization that promotes its mission enthusiastically, as in the agreement signed with Greece and Cyprus on 7 March 2007 that committed those countries' diplomats and civil servants to develop greater competence in French as a medium of communication in their work. The organization declared 20 March 2007 as the international day of

Francophonie and publicized the event with the slogan "Vivre ensemble, différents" (Living together and different). *See also* FRENCH UNION.

FRANCO-PRUSSIAN WAR. War from 19 July 1870–28 January 1871 between France and **Germany** sparked by a dispute over the succession to the vacant throne of Spain. When the French protested against the candidacy of Prince Leopold of Hohenzollern-Simaringen for the throne, put forward to represent the dynasty headed by William I of Prussia, Leopold was withdrawn (12 July 1870). However, when on the following day at Bad Ems the French sought, through ambassador Count Vincent Benedetti, categorical undertakings from William to renounce any further ambitions regarding the Spanish throne, the request was refused. A telegram relating the incident was sent to the Prussian minister president, Otto von Bismarck, which he then released in an edited form (the Ems dispatch), creating the impression that Benedetti had impertinently conveyed unreasonable demands. Public opinion was inflamed in both France and Germany, and in a climate of war fever, Napoléon III (*see* BONAPARTE, LOUIS-NAPOLEON) made a declaration of war (15 July), officially received by Prussia on 19 July.

In contrast to the modernized, well-trained, and well-led Prussian army, the French troops were too often deprived of such advantages, and a catastrophic sequence of failures soon ensued, not helped by Napoléon III's attempts to take a hand in the military campaign. This culminated in the capitulation of the 83,000 French troops surrounded by the Prussians at Sedan and the surrender of Napoléon III on 2 September. The Prussians soon moved on to lay siege to **Paris** (19–20 September), where an uprising on 4 September had proclaimed a republic in place of the empire (*see* EMPIRE, SECOND). Further military disasters followed with the mass surrender of French troops at **Strasbourg** (28 September) and Metz (29 October). On 5 January 1871 the Prussians began the bombardment of Paris, which was now protected largely by untrained reservists (115,000 Gardes Mobiles) and 200,000 or so volunteers and older reservists in the **National Guard**. In spite of the famine and cold endured by Parisians during that harsh winter under siege, many felt a sense of bitter betrayal when the government, based in **Bordeaux**, began to sue for

peace, and this deeply aggrieved sense of republic
a major factor in the formation of the **Commun**
The peace conditions were finally framed in the
furt (20 May). In purely financial terms, the war cost France a.
demnity of 5 billion francs. But the greatest blow to French self-
esteem was the territorial loss of Alsace and approximately one-third
of Lorraine (including Metz). The outcome of the war fundamentally
altered the balance of power in mainland Europe. France, for two
centuries the dominant nation-state in Europe, had now been overtaken by a new, modern, and industrialized German state united behind Prussian leadership. The sense of loss and frustration created by
this change marked French society for generations to come. *See also*
GAMBETTA, LEON.

FRENCH REVOLUTION. In contrast to the **Revolutions of 1830** and
1848, which were undoubtedly popular uprisings but which failed to
alter fundamentally French society, the French Revolution—the cat-
aclysmic events of 1789—took the country down a path that transformed irreversibly its perception of itself and left an indelible mark
on world history.

The act that set in train the sequence of events leading to the Revolution was the meeting at Versailles in 1789 of the **Estates General,**
the representative body of the **ancien régime,** with a view to finding
ways of resolving France's—or, more accurately, the crown's—
severe financial problems (*see* FINANCE). An economic downturn,
added to the drain on the king's purse due to military adventurism in
North America, had made the need for more revenue-raising imperative. By convoking the Estates General, the government of King
Louis XVI took a calculated risk that backfired. Instead of securing
consensus for a rescue plan for the nation's finances, the convocation
of the Estates General, the first since 1614, provided a focus for the
people's grievances against a corrupt regime.

The king's attempt to manipulate the process of decision making
through voting by estates would have secured an automatic majority
for his government, since the clergy and aristocracy of the first two
estates outweighed the bloc representing the rest of society, the Third
Estate. But the representatives of the Third Estate, many of whom
were lawyers of radical persuasion, refused to accept this arrangement.

Six weeks after the estates assembled at Versailles in May, these representatives broke away to constitute themselves as a National Assembly, pledged to engage in the work of national reconstruction. When the king had the assembly locked out of its meeting place, the members adjourned to a nearby tennis court and swore not to disband until they had drawn up a new constitution that would respond to the need of the French people for just and accountable government, particularly in view of the widespread unrest that occurred in France throughout that year because of the high price of food.

The point of no return was reached when the king reacted to the continuing defiance of the assembly by sacking the reforming ministers in his government and strengthening the army around Versailles and **Paris**. This intimidatory tactic merely inflamed the people of Paris, always in the vanguard of radical change, who began an uprising on 12 July. Royal troops were forced to retreat as gunsmiths were looted and customs posts were burned down. The rioting peaked on 14 July when the Paris mob invaded the **Bastille** fortress in the hope of securing the means with which to arm itself. In the initial assault on the Bastille the rioters suffered many casualties, but when two detachments of guards defected to the revolutionary crowd, the Bastille became indefensible and the governor was forced to surrender. Though insignificant in military terms, the storming of the Bastille rapidly assumed a massive symbolic value and came to be viewed as the founding act of the Revolution.

Revolutionary fervor during the ensuing decade ebbed and flowed as the Revolution went through various phases. The famous Declaration of the Rights of Man and the Citizen, in August 1789, expressed the optimism of those bourgeois liberals of France's first National Assembly who had hoped to usher in a property-owning democracy. The second declaration in 1793, in the way it enshrined the right of the people to insurrection, showed the radical turn taken by the Revolution. The climate of intolerance that developed among the revolutionaries could be attributed to the threat to France's borders from the monarchies in Europe and the threat posed by the forces of **counter-revolution** within France. The resulting determination among the **Jacobins** to defend the Revolution at all costs culminated in the **Terror**. But contrary to popular representations of the Revolution, the Terror lasted barely a year and ended with the execution of its leading advocate, **Robespierre**, in 1794.

Success on the battlefield for the military forces of the Revolution lessened the paranoia that had prompted the draconian measures of the Terror against the civilian population of France, and the advent of the Revolution's greatest soldier, **Napoléon Bonaparte**, coincided with a growing desire on the part of the people for order and stability, even at the expense of a certain degree of revolutionary idealism. Historians are divided as to when to situate the end of the Revolution. For some, it comes in 1799 with the formation of the **Consulate**, the three-man executive that succeeded the five-man **Directory** and that provided Bonaparte with a platform for establishing his autocratic power. For others, it comes in 1804, when Bonaparte established his empire (*see* EMPIRE, FIRST). What is beyond question is the way the French Revolution dominated the politics of the 19th century, in a manner comparable to the way the Russian Revolution dominated the 20th century, and provided the world with an enduring example of the transforming power of ideas. *See also* CIVIL CONSTITUTION OF THE CLERGY; CONVENTION; CORDELIERS CLUB; COUNTERREVOLUTION; DANTON, GEORGES-JACQUES; DESMOULINS, LUCIE-CAMILLE-SIMPLICE; GIRONDINS; PARIS COMMUNE; SAINT-JUST, LOUIS-ANTOINE-LEON-FLORELLE DE; SANS-CULOTTES; SUPREME BEING, CULT OF THE; THERMIDOR; VALMY, BATTLE OF; VARENNES, FLIGHT TO.

FRENCH UNION. Association created in 1946 under the constitution of the **Fourth Republic** that endeavored to redefine in a more liberal sense the relationship between France and her colonies. Black African representatives in the French Constitutional Assembly accepted the union because it pointed the way to real equality before the law and the recognition of indigenous cultures, thus breaking with the ambition of the **Third Republic** to assimilate into French culture the peoples colonized by France. The first significant change in the status of the colonies came in 1956 with the drafting of the administrative framework that paved the way for the decentralization of powers. This step toward independence helped soften the blow to France's self-image of the rapid changes that followed the collapse of the Fourth Republic in 1958 and the return to power of **Charles de Gaulle**. By the start of the next decade, 12 former French colonies had become independent African states and entered the **United Nations**. In retrospect, therefore, the French Union marked a transitional phase that allowed the majority of France's African colonies to take a more or less peaceful path to independence, without facing the kind of ferocious opposition from the colonizers and their supporters in France that characterized the situation in **Algeria**. *See also* COLONIALISM; DECOLONIZATION.

LA FRONDE. This refers to the period 1648–1653, when there was a series of bitterly destructive military challenges emanating from within France to royal absolutism. The origins of this resistance lay in the effects of the policies pursued by Cardinal **Richelieu, Louis XIII**'s chief minister from 1624 to 1642; these policies had succeeded in reducing the influence of the nobles and cutting back the power of the *parlements*. When power effectively passed to the queen regent, Anne of Austria, **Louis XIV**'s mother, and her chief minister, Cardinal **Mazarin**, the resistance of the *parlement* of **Paris** stiffened. In 1648 it refused to approve the government's revenue-raising measures, proposing instead its own measures for putting constitutional limits on the prerogatives of the monarchy. Armed conflict between the crown and the *parlement* of Paris broke out in January 1649, resulting in the blockade of the city. The *parlement,* however, refused to surrender, and a compromise peace was agreed on in April of that year.

This phase of opposition to the crown by the *parlements* was followed by a new phase of armed opposition by a number of leading aristocrats, notably the prince de Condé, the king's cousin and a great military leader, who felt that their ambition for power and hope of preferment had been frustrated by the scheming Mazarin. Two rebellions against the government followed, led by Condé and his friends, in 1650 and from 1651 to 1653. Although they managed to force Mazarin's dismissal in 1651, their success was short lived. Condé lost the support of the Parisian bourgeoisie in 1652 and had never been able to secure the support of the *parlement* of Paris. Condé's flight to the Netherlands on 13 October 1652 marked the inevitable and impending failure of the opposition to Mazarin and the monarch. Louis XIV was, however, to emancipate himself from the tutelage of Mazarin and establish himself unquestionably as the stellar center around which everything revolved, the Sun King. The significance of the Fronde's failure lay in the fact that, until 1789, absolute monarchy remained unchallenged in France.

FRONT NATIONAL (FN). The largest and most enduring of the far-right parties in Western Europe. It was founded in 1972 and is presided over by **Jean-Marie Le Pen.** The FN has thrived on the disenchantment with mainstream politics caused by the inexorable rise of unemployment in France and the insecurity the party attributes to the increase in the immigrant population. Its electoral power base is in the south of France among voters, many of whose families had to leave **Algeria** after independence in 1962, who are hostile to immigrants from North Africa. It is not surprising, therefore, that the FN has been strongly represented at the municipal level in the towns of Toulon and Orange. In 1998, Le Pen's chief lieutenant, Bruno Mégret, challenged the former's abrasive leadership and thought he could offer a more emollient style that would be more appealing to mainstream voters. He therefore formed a breakaway party called the Mouvement National Républicain (National Republican Movement), but it failed to dent Le Pen's leadership of the far right in France or draw members in significant numbers away from the FN.

Le Pen's position as the dominant figure on the far right was dramatically underlined when he beat the Socialist candidate, **Lionel Jospin,** to the second spot behind **Jacques Chirac,** with almost 17 percent of the vote, in the first round of the presidential elections in April 2002. But the historic landslide in favor of Chirac in the second round of the elections in May, giving him over 80 percent of the vote against Le Pen, confirmed the view of many commentators that the FN candidate had benefited from a *vote sanction* in the first round, namely the voters' determination to punish the outgoing administration. Le Pen stood again as the FN candidate in the presidential elections of 2007 but with much less success, garnering just under 11 percent of the vote in the first round.

The distinctive and enduring features of FN policy are hostility to **immigration,** greater independence from the **European Union,** economic protectionism in defense of French workers and businesses, and a restoration of the death penalty. The FN's lasting acquisition of a grassroots constituency is a source of concern for the political establishment in France as a whole. Its voters are not only the disaffected former supporters of the center-right, as one might expect, but also working-class people whose traditional allegiance lay with the parties of the left.

The extent to which, however, the party has depended on the charisma of Le Pen for its success has become clearer as old age brings forward the prospect of his retirement as head of the FN. In the aftermath of the presidential elections of 2007 it was evident that certain figures from the party's political bureau were positioning themselves or being positioned as possible successors, such as Le Pen's daughter Marine and another party vice president, Bruno Gollnisch. But what preoccupied the party hierarchy above all was the drop in subscriptions and the ensuing collapse in its finances that even made it contemplate selling its headquarters building.

– G –

GABIN, JEAN (1904–1976). One of the greats of the French **cinema**, whose success spanned four decades from the 1930s to the 1960s. He was born Jean-Alexis Moncorgé in **Paris**, to a music-hall comedian whose stage name was also Jean Gabin. He started his career in the Folies-Bergère in 1923 and got his first break in films in *Chacun sa chance* (1931). Short, stocky, and with a face whose features were not conspicuously refined, Gabin did not look the part of the archetypal leading man. But he had a commanding screen presence and used it to greatest effect in films that portrayed him as an obdurate individualist living on the margins of society, such as *Le quai des brumes* (1938) and *Le jour se lève* (1939), both directed by Marcel Carné. Gabin left behind him an extensive body of work of significant range, from the intellectually challenging antiwar movie *La grande illusion,* directed by Jean Renoir in 1937, to the purely entertaining incarnation of the popular fictional detective Inspector Maigret.

GAINSBOURG, SERGE (1928–1991). Singer, songwriter, and self-styled embodiment of the "poète maudit" or doomed poet. He was born Lucien Ginsburg to Russian Jewish parents in **Paris**, who had settled there as refugees from Bolshevism. **World War II** was hard on the family, and they survived by fleeing to the south of the country and leading a clandestine existence there until the **liberation**. On their return to Paris, Serge began to show the traits that would mark him out as a rebel and misfit. He was frequently in trouble at school, and during his military service in 1948 often found himself confined to barracks for insubordination, which left him plenty of time to develop his tendency toward alcohol abuse. Realizing that his ambition to be a painter was not warranted by his artistic talent, Gainsbourg exploited the musical gifts inherited from his parents. While providing the guitar accompaniment to the cabaret singer Michèle Arnaud in 1957, he revealed his talent as a songwriter. When his first album came out in 1959, some critics called him a French Cole Porter due to the originality and wit of his songs, but it was not a commercial success. His reputation as a writer for others, including singers like Juliette Greco, Petula Clark, Françoise Hardy, and France Gall, was established in the 1960s. In 1968 he sealed his reputation as an artist with a talent for provocation when he enjoyed worldwide success with the breathless eroticism of *Je t'aime . . . moi non plus*, a song originally penned for his former lover, **Brigitte Bardot**, but re-recorded and released with his new lover and future wife, Jane Birkin.

In the 1970s Gainsbourg released four albums regarded as seminal because of their original use of lyrics and subject matter, but the sales remained very modest. By this time Gainsbourg had found new opportunities to offend public morality. During the following years he made a number of films that attempted to deal with taboo subjects, such as sexual exhibitionism in *Stan the Flasher* (1980) and incest in *Charlotte Forever* (1986). Gainsbourg also wrote many film scores, but as a musical performer he pulled off the rare feat of reinventing himself for a new generation. In 1979 he joined the rock group Bijou on stage, to a rapturous ovation from the young fans. It was the same year in which he released the album *Aux armes et caetera*. Conservative opinion in France was deeply offended by his reggae version of the national anthem **La Marseillaise**, but the young loved it and the album went platinum within months. Faithful to his image, Gainsbourg refused to be seen without a cigarette hanging from his lips or to relinquish alcohol and died from a fifth heart attack in 1991. By this time Gainsbourg the rebel had become a national institution. France's biggest stars and government ministers attended his funeral and his grave receives as many visitors as those of **Jean-Paul Sartre** and **Simone de Beauvoir**. *See also* MUSIC, POP AND ROCK.

GALLICANISM. A set of religious doctrines and political convictions that led to conflict with the authority of the seat of **Catholicism** in Rome at various periods during France's history. Gallicanism essentially comprised three beliefs: that the French king should be independent in temporal matters, that the authority of an ecumenical council was superior to that of the pope, and that the union of the king and the clergy in France should act as a check on papal interventionism in the kingdom. The term Gallicanism was coined in France in the 19th century to designate the opposition to Ultramontanism (the position of those whose loyalties lay literally "over the mountain" with Rome), but the ambitions behind it surfaced as early as **Charlemagne**'s reign and led to recurrent conflicts between France and the papacy. The most notable example was the struggle between Philip IV and Pope Boniface VIII (1294–1303), leading to a century and a half of challenges to the pope's authority that reached a high point when a rival pope was established at **Avignon**.

GAMBETTA, LEON (1838–1882). Republican politician who helped found the **Third Republic**. Born the son of an Italian grocer in Cahors (Lot), Gambetta studied law in **Paris** before becoming an outspoken republican critic of the regime of the **Second Empire**. He was elected to the legislative assembly in 1869. When the Second Empire collapsed as a result of the **Franco-Prussian War** and a republic was proclaimed in Paris (4 September 1870), Gambetta was appointed minister of the interior in the provisional government, with special responsibility for continuing the war against Prussia. Gambetta escaped Paris in a hot air balloon when the Prussians besieged the city, but in spite of his resistance to a humiliating capitulation by France, he was forced to accept the peace concluded by the head of the government, **Adolphe Thiers**. He was returned to the National Assembly in the elections of February 1871 and, through his rhetorical talents and passionate convictions, came to lead the republican opposition to royalist and Bonapartist attempts to revive the monarchy during the period 1871–1877.

By 1875 Gambetta had come to the conclusion that the best way of ensuring the future of the republic in France was by securing the middle ground electorally; he therefore abandoned radical republican demands like a unicameral legislature and social legislation favoring the workers. This change earned him and his followers the accusation of being **opportunists**, but it marked the crucial transition of republicanism from a revolutionary to a conservative ideology tailored to respond to the demands of the new aspiring classes in France. The heroic reputation Gambetta had acquired during the Franco-Prussian War and his capacity for inspirational leadership made some of his fellow republicans suspicious of his ambitions, and President **Jules Grévy** did not call on Gambetta to become premier until the overwhelming republican victory in the elections of 1881 made it unavoidable. In the event, Gambetta's ministry lasted barely three months. However, his republican opponents were reconciled to him on his death in 1882, when they voted to have his heart buried alongside the remains of France's other heroes in the Pantheon.

GANDOIS, JEAN (1930–). Born into a comfortable bourgeois milieu in Nieul (Haute-Vienne), Gandois was educated in Limoges and **Paris**, graduating from the Ecole Polytechnique and beginning his professional life as an engineer in the public sector in 1954. He worked in development programs funded by the French state in countries like Brazil and Peru before entering the steel industry in the 1970s. He was chief executive of the French drugs and chemicals multinational Rhône-Poulenc from 1979 to 1982 and moved on to head another international company, Péchiney, from 1986 to 1994. The holder of numerous directorships, in 1994 he became the president of the French employers' organization, the Conseil National du Patronat Français (CNPF). This position made him a key player in all major attempts by the French government to establish a dialogue with French business, with a view to elaborating possible future lines of national economic policy. However, he abandoned his role at the head of the CNPF in 1997 after a noisy disagreement with the then Socialist-led government over its determination to bring in legislation to establish the 35-hour working week in France. *See also* ECONOMY.

THE GARONNE. A river linking Spain and France. It originates in the Spanish Pyrenees and flows northward toward **Toulouse**, thereafter turning west through **Bordeaux** before reaching the end of its 647-kilometer journey when it meets the Atlantic in the Gironde Estuary.

Now no longer navigable by larger vessels for most of its length, the section between the Pyrenees and Toulouse has been harnessed for hydroelectric power generation, while much of the rest is exploited for tourist and sporting purposes.

GAUGUIN, PAUL (1848–1903). Leading figure in symbolist painting. Gauguin was born in **Paris** but spent part of his childhood in Peru (1849–1855), where his mother's family lived. He worked in the merchant marine and then as a stockbroker, beginning to paint and sculpt on a part-time basis in 1873. He befriended the impressionists in the late 1870s and exhibited with them in the last five impressionist exhibitions (1879–1886). In the latter half of the 1880s he developed an artistic approach that combined symbolic themes with a simple, flattened treatment of figures and space, an approach known as synthetism. He left Europe in 1891 in pursuit of intuitive, primitive sources of inspiration, first in Tahiti and finally in the Marquesas Islands, where he died. *See also* ART; IMPRESSIONISM; SYMBOLISM.

GAUL. Known as Gaule in French or Gallia in Latin, this area covered modern France, parts of Belgium, western **Germany**, and northern Italy and was inhabited by the Celtic tribe of Gauls who had migrated south to the **Mediterranean** coast from the **Rhine** River valley by the end of the fifth century BC. During the following century Gallic tribes continued their push south and came to occupy an area stretching from Milan to the Adriatic coast, known as Cisalpine Gaul. However, the plundering of Rome by the Gauls in 390 BC sowed the determination in the minds of the Romans to conquer and colonize Cisalpine Gaul, and this was accomplished by 181 BC.

The second century BC marked the beginning of Roman incursions into southern France, adding military weight to their already established commercial presence in the region. Julius Caesar accomplished the conquest of the rest of Gaul from 58 to 50 BC. After the defeat of the revolt led by Vercingétorix from 53 to 50, Caesar managed his defeated enemies astutely, securing their loyalty by granting them a significant degree of autonomy. Lugdunum (**Lyon**) became the capital of Roman Gaul, and the country as a whole was divided into four provinces: Narbonensis in the south, with Narbonne as its center; Aquitania to the west and south of the **Loire**; Celtica in central France between the Loire and the **Seine**; and Belgica in the north and east. In characteristic fashion, the Romans built a formidable infrastructure of roads and urban centers and promoted the development of a commercial middle class by introducing a taxation system that also required contributions from the great Gallic landowners.

During the next two centuries there were occasional rebellions against Rome and external threats to Gaul, mostly from marauding Germanic tribes. Gaul, Spain, and **Great Britain** even formed an independent Gallic empire, proclaimed in 260 AD. But it was defeated, and Gaul was reclaimed for Rome in 273 by the emperor Aurelian. The slow fragmentation of Rome's power over Gaul was nonetheless under way, and by the fifth century recurrent rebellions and invasions had left the Visigoths in control of Aquitania, the Franks in control of Belgica, and the Burgundians the masters of the Rhine. The establishment of the kingdom of the Frankish **Merovingians** marked the end of Roman power in Gaul early in the 6th century. However, the cultural legacy of Roman Gaul was preserved in, for example, the literary traditions that developed, and the material benefits of the Roman influence can still be appreciated in viaducts like the Pont du Gard and amphitheaters in towns like Orange in the south of France.

GAULLISM. An eclectic set of beliefs rather than a systematic political doctrine or ideology, the Gaullist approach to politics was shaped by the views of General **Charles de Gaulle**, whose perceptions of how to address the needs of postwar France were crucially conditioned by what he and his country had endured during **World War II**. Gaullism cannot be categorized simply as a center-right phenomenon, since it articulates what de Gaulle called "a certain idea of France" that incorporates notions of national grandeur and historical continuity that predate the **French Revolution** and reconciles them with notions of social responsibility, equity, and unity that reflect the aspirations voiced in 1789. The executive power given to the **presidency** to lead and direct change by the **constitution** of the **Fifth Republic** reflects de Gaulle's determination to avoid the divisive party politics that had paralyzed France before the war and the continuing value attached by Gaullism to the idea of governing on behalf of the entire French nation.

The preoccupation with national stability, security, independence, and grandeur was also evident in the realm of **foreign policy**, where the preservation of France's greatness and sovereignty as a nation-state led de Gaulle to oppose the United States' influence in Europe, hence French withdrawal from the **North Atlantic Treaty Organization (NATO)**. This stubborn abstentionism in the face of anything that appeared to compromise French sovereignty also extended, on occasion, to de Gaulle's dealings with the **European Economic Community**. However, Gaullism evolved considerably on the issue of national sovereignty following the general's death, particularly after the collapse of the communist threat represented by the former **Soviet Union**. And this was seen in the attitude of the last Gaullist president, **Jacques Chirac**, who promoted a rapprochement with NATO on military matters and who led France into monetary union in Europe and the adoption of the **euro**, even though this effectively meant France's abandonment of its sovereign right to determine its economic policies in an independent manner. *See also* GAULLIST PARTY; POLITICAL PARTIES.

GAULLIST PARTY. The current incarnation of **Gaullism** in party terms results from a process of frequent mutation and occasional restructuring. The origins of the party go back to the Gaullist Union founded in July 1946 by René Capitant, with the purpose of enabling General **Charles de Gaulle** to continue to lead France in peace, as he had done in war as leader of the Free French. Within half a year the Gaullist Union was superseded by a much more ambitious organization formed by the general himself, the Rassemblement du Peuple Français (Rally of the French People), or RPF. The RPF was not intended to be a party in the traditional mold but a movement that would raise the country above partisan political squabbling and pave the way for fundamental reform of the French state. But the RPF's showing in the polls, such as the 16.5 percent share of the vote in the legislative elections of 1951, did not give it enough presence in parliamentary terms to hasten the pace of change. Furthermore, the inclination of RPF deputies to play old-style party politics was a profound disillusionment to de Gaulle, who severed links with the movement in July 1955 and retired from public life.

The crisis in **Algeria** in 1958 led to calls for de Gaulle to take the reins once more, and the remnants of the RPF were subsumed in a new Gaullist vehicle, Union pour la Nouvelle République (Union for the New Republic), or UNR. Dedicated to the service of the general and his ideas, the UNR campaigned for the constitution establishing the **Fifth Republic** and the election of de Gaulle as its first president, and did so with spectacular success. In response to the crisis provoked by the **student rebellions** of May 1968, the Gaullist party proved its mettle once more, changing its name to Union des Démocrates pour la République (Union of Democrats for the Republic), or UDR, and successfully backed de Gaulle and his prime minister, **Georges Pompidou**, in their resolution of the crisis and the victorious electoral campaign that followed it.

However, the election of a non-Gaullist centrist liberal, **Valéry Giscard d'Estaing**, to the presidency in 1974 provoked another fundamental reform in the Gaullist party. The UDR leader, **Jacques Chirac**, had played a significant part in Giscard d'Estaing's victory and was rewarded with the post of prime minister. But Chirac soon began to feel so marginalized by the new president and so circumscribed in his prime-ministerial role that he resigned in 1976. He swiftly took charge of the UDR again and pushed through a set of reforms that helped turn the current Gaullist party into one of the best-organized political parties in Europe. Part of the revamping was to endow the Gaullist party with a new name, Rassemblement pour la République (Rally for the Republic), or RPR. The high point in the RPR's fortunes was reached in the legislative elections of 1993, when, together with its allies on the center-right, it swept the **Socialists** out of office and took 80 percent of the seats in the new National Assembly. When in 1995 Chirac obtained the ultimate prize in French politics, the **presidency** of the Republic, he began to articulate a discourse aimed at broadening his appeal and that of the party behind him by addressing the problem of *la fracture sociale*, those stubborn social divisions in France that undermined national cohesion. In the months following his reelection to the presidency in 2002 the decision was taken to redefine the RPR's mission and to establish a broader basis for the presidential party in the National Assembly. Thus, at a congress at Le Bourget in November 2002, the Union pour un Mouvement Populaire (Union for a Popular Movement/UMP) was born. With the aim of transcending the old party lines and appealing to a disenchanted electorate, the UMP rallied the Gaullists of the defunct RPR together with a number of Christian democrats, liberals, radicals, and independents.

GERICAULT, JEAN-LOUIS-ANDRE-THEODORE (1791–1824). Influential French artist. The uncontroversial aspect of his work gained him a reputation for his depiction of subjects like horses in *The Derby at Epsom*. But there was also a subversive undercurrent to his work in the ability he displayed for using themes to convey what could be interpreted as political implications, such as the *Raft of the Medusa* (1816), illustrating an incident in which a group of shipwrecked sailors were deliberately set adrift. Géricault's willingness to test the limits of the aesthetic conventions of his time has led some critics to regard him as one of the forerunners of **romanticism**. Géricault counted horseback riding as one of his passions, and it was a fatal accident while riding that cut short his life in 1824. *See also* ART.

GERMANY, RELATIONS WITH. Historically France, as Europe's premier unified and centralized state, related with political and military superiority to the German-speaking territories east of its border, whether under **Louis IV**, when French expansionism allowed it to take control of German-speaking **Strasbourg**, or after the **French Revolution** under **Napoléon Bonaparte**, when his armies seemed able to roll across the patchwork of German-speaking principalities and territories of central Europe at will. The fundamental shift in the balance of power between the two states occurred when Otto von Bismarck took the lead in unifying the German states around Prussia, as was dramatically illustrated by the humiliating defeat inflicted on the French in the **Franco-Prussian War**. The declaration of a second German empire, with Bismarck as its first Chancellor in 1871, symbolized the birth of the modern German state that cast an intimidating shadow over its French neighbor for generations to come. The punitive terms of the peace that ended the Franco-Prussian War had left the Germans in control of Alsace, with Strasbourg at its heart, and much of Lorraine. French resentment seethed for years and engendered an enduring desire for *la revanche*, or revenge. This led to the naive optimism that greeted **World War I** in 1914 and the opening of hostilities once more with Germany.

When peace returned in 1918, although France was victorious, the fact that the Western Front had been predominantly on French soil meant that in terms of the country's productive capacity and even its military casualties, France had lost proportionately more than its defeated German neighbor. The reality of Franco-German relations after 1918 was that France was not strong enough to bring pressure on Germany without the support of its American and British allies. When France sent troops to occupy the Ruhr in 1923 to force the German government to pay the reparations to which the French felt entitled under the **Treaty of Versailles**, it was the **United States** that ultimately brokered a deal put together by General Dawes. Adolf Hitler's rise to power in the 1930s saw a France increasingly reliant on **Great Britain** to define a common foreign policy that might contain the ambitions of the Nazis. By the time **World War II** was declared, a sense of defeatism had already gripped the French nation as many of its citizens decided that living under German rule was preferable to the losses the country had had to endure from World War I, or what was supposed to have been the war to end all wars. In spite of General **Charles de Gaulle**'s organization of the Free French outside occupied France and the work of the **Resistance** within the country, the fact remains that France owed its **liberation** in 1944 principally to its American and British allies.

In contrast to the aftermath of World War I, however, the years following World War II were marked by determination to avoid the repetition of past mistakes, especially the vengefulness that had locked France and Germany into a cycle of military conflict. In 1950 it was the French diplomat **Robert Schuman** who launched the idea of pooling French and German coal and steel production, thus depriving either country of control of the heavy industries vital to the waging of war. It was the first step in creating what would become the **European Union**, with the explicit aim of making war between the two great states at the heart of Europe impossible. Since Schuman's day, the *couple Franco-Allemand*, or Franco-German couple, has been the relationship that France has tried most consistently to nurture. It is the tradition for every newly elected president to make the German chancellor the object of his first overseas visit, as was the case with

Nicolas Sarkozy and Angela Merkel in 2007. Moreover, the French state has invested considerably in enhancing cultural understanding between the two countries, as in the creation of the Franco-German television station, Arte. It also subsidizes educational exchanges that allow over a million French schoolchildren to visit Germany every year.

GIRAUD, HENRI-HONORE (1879–1949). Soldier and politician. He was born and educated in **Paris** and graduated from the military academy of Saint-Cyr in 1900. He was captured by the Germans in **World War I** and suffered the same experience in **World War II**, before escaping to join the Allies in North Africa after the landings there in 1942, where he became the commander in chief of the French forces that had rallied to the defense of France against the Axis powers. From June to October 1943 he served as copresident with **Charles de Gaulle** of the French Committee of National Liberation, but differences between the two men led to Giraud's retirement in April 1944. His postwar public life was limited to membership in the Constituent Assembly and the vice presidency of the Supreme War Council.

GIRONDINS. Political faction during the **French Revolution**. It comprised two subgroups whose roots went back to pre-Revolutionary days. The first group was composed of gifted deputies from the Gironde in southwestern France; the second comprised journalists and intellectuals like Jacques-Pierre Brissot and the Marquis de Condorcet. The Girondins had their greatest success in the days of the Legislative Assembly established by the Constitution of 1791 and in the early period of the **Convention** that followed it in 1792. They won the argument in favor of war against Austria and by March 1792 proved they could mobilize the majority of votes in the Assembly, with Brissot emerging as the most powerful deputy in the legislature. However, their downfall was their disunity and lack of common policy, particularly in contrast to their rivals, the **Montagnards**. This became apparent in the debate over the future of the king. Whereas the Montagnards called for the king's conviction and immediate execution, some of the Girondins agreed with them while others wanted him to be exiled. The conclusion of the king's trial marked the end of

Girondin control of the Convention. Radical disenchantment in **Paris** with the Girondins reached a crisis point between 31 May and 2 June 1793, when 20,000 armed **sans-culottes** surrounded the Convention and demanded a purge of the Girondin deputies. As a result, 29 Girondins were expelled from the Convention, and the general repression that ensued destroyed the Girondins as a political force. Though they were united in their belief in a pluralist, democratic republic and in laissez-faire economic policies, the very individualism that lies at the heart of such convictions put them at a disadvantage vis-à-vis their more disciplined **Jacobin** rivals. *See also* MARAT, JEAN-PAUL.

GIROUD, FRANCOISE (1916–2003). Journalist, essayist, film critic, and politician. She was born in Geneva on 21 September 1916 and was educated in **Paris** before starting her career as a script girl in the film industry. She began to make her name in journalism in 1945 when she was appointed editorial director of *Elle* magazine, a post she held until she cofounded the weekly *L'Express* in 1953 with Jean-Jacques Servan-Schreiber. She assumed a high profile in national politics when in 1974 President **Valéry Giscard d'Estaing** appointed her secretary of state with responsibility for the newly created Secretariat for **Women**. She remained in that post until 1976, when she was made secretary of state for culture in **Raymond Barre**'s cabinet, a position that she held until 1977. Giroud wrote a number of essays, biographies, and movie adaptations. Some of her more familiar and recent works included *La comédie du pouvoir* (1977), *Marie Curie* (1981), and *Alma Mahler* (1988). She wrote a column on French television for the weekly periodical *Le Nouvel Observateur* well beyond retirement and died at age 86 at the American hospital in Paris. *See also* CINEMA.

GISCARD D'ESTAING, VALERY (1926–). Fifth Republic politician and former president (1974–1981). He was born into a wealthy family with aristocratic ties and followed the classic route to academic success, ultimately graduating from two *grandes écoles*, the Polytechnique and the Ecole Nationale d'Administration. He subsequently began his career in one of the most prestigious branches of the civil service, the Inspectorate of Finance. During the 1950s he progressed through a series of important posts in the Ministry of Finance before being elected to the National Assembly in 1956 as an "independent republican" who voted with the Gaullist majority. However, his career stalled when he was dismissed as minister of finance in 1965, because of the unpopularity of the austerity program he had devised. But his years of loyal opposition to **Gaullism** enabled him to develop the kind of intelligently progressive, flexible, and media-friendly image that contrasted with the old-fashioned authoritarianism of General **Charles de Gaulle**. When **Georges Pompidou** became president, Giscard d'Estaing was restored to his position as minister of finance (1969–1974).

He emerged as the front-runner from the center-right in the presidential campaign of 1974 and just managed to fend off the left-wing challenge of **François Mitterrand**, winning with 50.7 percent of the votes cast against Mitterrand's 49.3 percent. Giscard d'Estaing had campaigned on a platform of turning France into an advanced liberal society. Under his presidency this was translated into a number of progressive political and social reforms, notably extending the franchise to 18-year-olds, liberalizing divorce laws, legalizing abortion, modernizing **education**, and loosening state control on the **broadcast media**. In the area of **foreign policy** he worked to improve the cohesion of the **European Economic Community** and was successful in strengthening the ties between France and **Germany**. However, he followed the Gaullist line of preserving France's position in the world by refusing to take his cue from the **United States**, as was shown by his refusal to follow the U.S. boycott of the Olympic Games in Moscow (1980) after the **Soviet** invasion of Afghanistan. He was also resolutely Gaullist in maintaining French influence in Francophone Africa, even if that meant supporting less-than-creditable regimes.

Giscard d'Estaing's **presidency** was undermined for two main reasons: his program of liberal reforms had to give way to one of economic austerity owing to the effect of the oil crises in 1973 and 1979 and his presidency lacked the support of a strong political party. As his presidential term progressed, the broad-based centrist coalition that Giscard d'Estaing had hoped would cohere proved insufficient. Furthermore, those on the Gaullist right were alienated by what they regarded as the president's left-leaning social policies and high-handed manner. Their support was rendered more problematic by the tensions between the president and the leader of the Gaullist right serving as his premier, **Jacques Chirac**. These tensions resulted in Chirac's resignation in 1976. In the country at large, disaffection grew because of the austerity measures of Giscard d'Estaing's new premier, **Raymond Barre**, and rumors of corruption centering on the president's alleged receipt of an undeclared gift of diamonds from the self-styled emperor of the Central African Republic, Jean-Bedel Bokassa.

In spite of the undoubted mastery of economic affairs he displayed in television interviews and his attempt to show a common touch through much publicized visits to the homes of ordinary French citizens, Giscard d'Estaing was unable to restore his political credibility and lost the battle for reelection in 1981 to François Mitterrand.

Urbane, eloquent, and formidably intellectually gifted, Giscard d'Estaing remained a high-profile figure whose opinions were frequently solicited by the media, but it may be argued that the vision of an advanced liberal society that he had articulated in the 1970s, though attractive, was not sufficiently underpinned by ideas of enduring substance. However, his place at the heart of the French establishment was confirmed in 2003 when he was elected to the **Académie Française**. On the international stage, recognition of his standing as one of Europe's elder statesmen came in 2001 when the Council of Europe appointed him to lead the effort to draft a constitution for the **European Union**. Ironically, however, it was his own countrymen who undid his work and dealt a major blow to the constitutional project when they refused to ratify it by referendum in 2005, with a clear majority voting against it.

GODARD, JEAN-LUC (1930–). Highly influential and controversial film director. He made several short films in the 1950s before producing the movie that challenged the universally accepted orthodoxies of filmmaking, *A bout de souffle* (*Breathless*) (1960). The handheld camera work and jump shots delighted some critics and dismayed others, but it sealed Godard's reputation as a leading and subversive talent. The films that followed were exceptionally varied, but as the 1960s wore on, they became increasingly political. *La Chinoise* (1967) is a dialogue among Parisian students on revolution, and

Week End (1968) is remembered for its brilliant attack on the culture of consumerism. The **student rebellions** of May 1968 in **Paris** focused Godard's attempt to create a new kind of **cinema** from the bottom up, with films like *Le gai savoir* (1968) and *Pravda* (1969). While Godard's name comes frequently to the lips of film critics, he has never enjoyed the esteem of the public that his contemporary **François Truffaut** has, nor his commercial success. In fact, the two directors differed bitterly for many years as to the true nature of their *métier*. Godard courted controversy again in 1985 with his iconoclastic portrayal of a modern nativity story in *Hail Mary*, which prompted an extremist group of outraged **Catholics** to burn down a cinema in Paris. In the 1990s his work took on an autobiographical and valedictory quality with films like the semiautobiographical *JLG* (1995) and *For Ever Mozart* (1996). During the same decade his multipart series *Histoire(s) du cinéma* summed up many of the passions and innovations that characterized the commitments in his work, artistic and political.

GONCOURT, EDMOND HUOT DE (1822–1896), AND GONCOURT, JULES HUOT DE (1830–1870). These two brothers represented a unique collaboration in the history of French **literature**. An inheritance from their mother in 1848 gave them the freedom to pursue their literary passions and apply an exceptional form of psychic intimacy to the realm of writing. United by a singular vision of the world, they wrote together and produced a substantial body of works. Although their writing was soon eclipsed by that of **Emile Zola**, they gave an impetus to the development of **naturalism** through their intimate and meticulous observation of daily existence in novels like *Germinie Lacerteux* (1865). Their names were preserved for posterity through the prize they endowed, which aimed to reward bold, innovative novels. It was first awarded in 1903 and remains one of France's most coveted literary prizes.

LA GRANDE ARMEE. Name given to the French army under **Napoléon Bonaparte**. The name reflected the reorganization of the military and the use of tactics under their supreme commander. Bonaparte built on what he had inherited from the **ancien régime** and the **French Revolution**, but where he judged necessary, he broke new ground. His greatest innovation was the creation of the standard corps: 20,000 to 30,000 strong, comprising infantry, cavalry, artillery, engineers, headquarters, train, medical, and service units, all usually commanded by a marshal and capable of doing battle alone if necessary. The efficient mobilization of large bodies of troops was essential to Bonaparte's tactics, as studies of his campaigns have shown. His preference was to engage the enemy, encourage him to expose his weaknesses by reacting, and then respond by launching a devastating strike with a large force that up to that point had been held in reserve. Bonaparte exploited the resource provided by conscription (first introduced in 1793) and between 1800 and 1810 drafted an average of 73,000 young men a year to supplement the regular troops. Furthermore, Bonaparte relied considerably on foreign contingents, illustrated by the fact that two-thirds of the 611,000 troops in the *grande armée* that marched into **Russia** in 1812 were non-French. The Imperial Guard that also marched into Russia was not a bodyguard for the emperor, but a small, elite army that Bonaparte used as an ultimate reserve; it contained significant numbers of Egyptian Mamluks, Italians, Poles, Germans, and Swiss, as well as French.

GRANDES ECOLES. The elite branch of postsecondary **education** in France. Approximately 300 establishments claim to fall into this category, but only a few dozen enjoy the prestige brought by the title. The most famous are the Ecole Polytechnique, the Ecole Nationale d'Administration (ENA), the Ecole Normale Supérieure (ENS), and the Ecole des Hautes Etudes Commerciales. The *grandes écoles* are independent of the university system, enjoying greater autonomy with regard to student programs and selection while reaping the benefit of higher per capita state funding. From their origins under the **ancien régime**, these establishments were intended to be training grounds for the elite who would provide the state with specialized military and technical skills. The development of the *grandes écoles* was given further impetus by **Napoléon Bonaparte**, who established the Ecole Polytechnique to train military engineers and the ENS to train schoolteachers. As the 19th century progressed, specialized schools were established to meet the needs of agriculture and industry, and in 1881 the dictates of commerce were recognized when the Paris Chamber of Commerce founded the Ecole des Hautes Etudes

Commerciales. The most prestigious *grande école* founded in this century is the ENA, established in 1945 to provide France with a technocratic elite to oversee the rebuilding of the country after **World War II**.

The institutions themselves are usually small, averaging 400 students, and select the applicants they will admit through extremely tough competitive examinations. Once they have graduated, however, the former students are almost guaranteed a fast-track career and entrance into an elite whose members are found in every corner of public and corporate life in France. The ENS used to provide many distinguished members of the political establishment, including former *normaliens* such as **Jean Jaurès**, **Léon Blum**, and **Georges Pompidou**. In recent decades graduates of ENA, known as *énarques*, have tended to figure most prominently among the political elite and represent both the left and the right in French politics, through figures such as **Valéry Giscard d'Estaing**, **Jacques Chirac**, and **Michel Rocard**, while the graduates of the Polytechnique gravitate toward top management positions in industry and the civil service. In spite of criticism of the predominantly upper-middle-class intake of the *grandes écoles* and the fact that their special status undermines the position of the universities in France, they are generally perceived by French public opinion as producing specialists of very high caliber who serve their country well.

GREAT BRITAIN, RELATIONS WITH. The destinies of the two countries have been intimately linked since the invasion of England by **William the Conqueror** in 1066. William's English heirs coexisted in a relationship of mutual respect with the French crown until the absence of a male heir to the French throne encouraged England's Edward III, also bearing the title Duc de Guyenne, to make a bid for it, thus sparking the **Hundred Years' War**. Though the English were finally expelled from France in 1453 they did not give up their last claim (to the port of Calais) until 1558. By this time France and England were competing for power and influence not only in Europe, but increasingly across the globe. The Act of Union in 1707, which united the English and Scottish crowns and laid the foundation for the modern British state, also heralded an age of ferocious expansionism overseas by Britain, largely driven by the unparalleled appetite for profit of its commercial classes. British and French geopolitical and commercial interests were therefore bound to clash repeatedly during the generations that followed.

By the middle of the 18th century Britain had clearly gained the upper hand. The **Seven Years' War** in Europe had disastrous consequences for French interests across the globe. By the time the peace was signed in 1763 the British general Wolfe had beaten the French in the battle for Quebec and the French had also been forced to relinquish the conquest of India to the British. While the French exacted some measure of revenge in their support for American independence, notably through their crucial role in the defeat of the British in the battle of Yorktown in 1781, Britain continued to frustrate France's ambition to be a superpower. Under **Napoléon Bonaparte** after the **French Revolution**, France enjoyed a decade and a half when it dominated Europe while the British fleet ruled the oceans. But when the opportunity came, with Bonaparte's retreat from Moscow caused by the merciless Russian winter, Britain played a key role in orchestrating his, and France's, ultimate defeat in the battle of Waterloo in 1815. Thereafter the gap between the two nations as world powers began to widen as Britain reaped the benefits of leading the Industrial Revolution while France stumbled from one fragile political regime to another.

The decline in France's power was illustrated most dramatically by the way it was routed in the **Franco-Prussian War. Germany**'s emergence as a unified and powerful state in the heart of Europe, rapidly clawing back Britain's lead as an industrial economy, was a significant background factor in the reconciliation between Britain and France, culminating in the Entente Cordiale signed in 1904. The immediate aim was to put an end to disputes between the two powers regarding their overseas interests in Morocco, Egypt, and the Far East. But it laid the foundation stone for an alliance that sustained both countries during **World War I** and **World War II**, as they fought the ambitions of German militarism in the first case and German fascism in the second.

After World War II in particular, both countries had to adjust to the harsh realities of becoming post-imperial powers and the loss of influence on the world stage that entailed. It explains their doomed and misguided attempt to reimpose Franco-British influence in Egypt, which resulted in the **Suez Crisis**. After the humiliating conclusion to the Suez Crisis, under **Charles de Gaulle** France became increasingly suspicious of Britain's dependence on the **United States**; this explains his constant refusal to support Britain's bid to join what became the **European Union (EU)**. De Gaulle's presidential successors, however, were convinced that the EU could not be built without Britain, and in spite of occasional disagreements between the two countries about the future direction of the EU, especially between British prime minister Margaret Thatcher and French president **François Mitterrand**, the partnership between France and Britain has endured.

During the years of Conservative government in Britain, first under Margaret Thatcher and then under John Major, there were sporadic moments of tension between the two countries. One common cause of friction was the rebate Britain enjoyed on its contribution to the EU budget, which Thatcher had negotiated in 1984. The strong farming lobby in France was another source of friction. France was always among the first wave of European countries to take measures against Britain when doubts were raised about the safety of its food exports, as with the ban on the import of British beef, traditionally regarded as a premium product by many French restaurants, when the impact on humans of bovine spongiform encephalopathy (BSE or mad cow disease) was reported in Britain in 1996. France adopted the same policy with the outbreak of foot and mouth disease in Britain in 2001.

The end of Conservative government and the election of a Labour administration under Tony Blair in 1997 was greeted positively, not only in France but also in many other parts of Europe. Blair's pro-European declarations inspired the belief that Britain would commit itself to a genuine path of convergence with its European allies. However, Blair's decision to engage British forces alongside those of the United States in the second invasion of Iraq in 2003 damaged his credibility vis-à-vis the French government and led to a tense relationship with President **Jacques Chirac**. The election of **Nicolas Sarkozy** to the **presidency** in 2007 marked a rapprochement, given Sarkozy's open admiration for Blair's attempts to modernize the state sector in Britain. Blair resigned in the same year that Sarkozy was elected, and Sarkozy went so far as to promote Blair as a possible future president of the Council of Europe. That ambition, however, had little hope of being fulfilled in the face of German opposition. But while Germany is unquestionably France's privileged partner in the elaboration of policy for the future of Europe, Britain remains France's privileged partner in matters of **defense policy**, to the extent that the two countries have decided to produce their new generation of aircraft carriers jointly.

GREENPEACE AFFAIR. A scandal resulting from the French secret service operation against a vessel belonging to the environmental organization Greenpeace. On 10 July 1985 the vessel, the *Rainbow Warrior*, was moored in Waitemata Harbor, Auckland, New Zealand, prior to its departure for the waters around the Muroroa Atoll to protest against French nuclear testing there. However, late that evening, two bombs exploded, ripping the hull of the ship and sinking it, and in the process killing a Portuguese photographer, Fernando Pereira. New Zealand police arrested two French secret service agents, a man and a woman posing as Swiss tourists, within a week of the attack. The French government vigorously denied any involvement in the affair, but on 7 August 1985 two French magazines reported that the couple arrested were in reality agents of the Direction Générale de la Sécurité Extérieure (DGSE). The official inquiry that the French government was then forced to launch found that there were two teams of French agents in New Zealand but that they had simply been asked to monitor Greenpeace activities, not to engage in acts of sabotage. This convenient finding was undermined by an investigation in the newspaper *Le Monde* that revealed, on 17 September, the existence of a third team of agents trained in sabotage techniques at a special base in Corsica.

Polls showed that over 50 percent of the French public believed President **François Mitterrand** and Prime Minister Laurent Fabius to be involved in the scandal. Clearly, someone in the chain of command would have to pay the price for this fiasco, and this led to the sacking of the defense minister, Charles Hernu, and the head of the DGSE, Admiral Pierre Lacoste. In November 1985 the agents arrested in New Zealand received 10-year prison sentences, but bargaining between Paris and Wellington reduced this to three years' "exile" on a French Pacific atoll. However, even this sentence was cut short when Prime Minister **Jacques Chirac** repatriated the agents early in an obvious attempt to curry favor with the French electorate prior to the 1988 presidential election.

GREVY, JULES (1807–1891). Lawyer and politician whose career spanned almost the entire second half of the 19th century. Grévy was a prominent republican in the National Assembly between 1848 and 1851. Briefly imprisoned after **Louis-Napoléon Bonaparte**'s coup in 1851, he did not reenter politics until 1869 and was returned to the National Assembly by his constituency in the Jura in 1871. Grévy was elected president of the Republic in 1879 after **Maurice de MacMahon**'s resignation. He was reelected in December 1885 but was forced to resign two years later because he refused to condemn his son-in-law, Daniel Wilson, for his part in a scandal involving influence peddling from an apartment in the Elysée. In his exercise of presidential power, Grévy set the style for many of his successors, pulling strings behind the scenes and attempting to sideline forceful personalities like **Léon Gambetta** from the premiership. He was a man of gravity who inspired respect but who became excessively prudent in his latter years and famous for the parsimony that characterized his personal life.

GUESDE, JULES (1845–1922). Founder of the Parti Ouvrier (Workers' Party) and person chiefly responsible for introducing the Marxist brand of **socialism** to the French socialist movement. He was born Jules Bazile in **Paris** on 11 November 1845 but took his mother's maiden name when he entered opposition politics and journalism during the final years of the **Second Empire**. The articles he wrote in defense of the **Commune of Paris** forced him into exile. He returned to France in 1876 and soon distinguished himself as an advocate of creating a working-class party organized along Marxist lines. Guesde helped lay the foundation for France's first modern socialist party, but a schism occurred in 1882 over the issue of party organization, and Guesde and his followers set up the Parti Ouvrier armed with a Marxist program. The party initially enjoyed limited success, but its fortunes changed in the 1890s, and Guesde was elected to the Chamber of Deputies by a working-class constituency in the Nord *département* in 1893. When a unified socialist party named the **Section**

Française de l'Internationale Ouvrière (SFIO) was created in 1905, Guesde successfully defended his line of orthodox socialism against the reformist tendencies represented by figures like **Jean Jaurès**. Guesde's patriotism led to his support for the government of national unity during **World War I** and the acceptance of a largely symbolic cabinet portfolio from 1914 to 1916. Ill health prevented him from taking too active a role in left-wing politics after 1914. When the socialist movement in France split in two at the **Congress of Tours** in 1920, Guesde sided with the socialist minority against the communist majority, but with regret and disappointment at what had happened. He died on 28 July 1922.

GUILLOTINE. Mechanical system for execution designed by Dr. Antoine Louis during the early days of the **French Revolution** but named after Dr. Joseph Guillotin, who proposed it to the National Assembly as the best method of execution by the state. In spite of the notoriety attached to the use of the guillotine during the **Terror**, it remained the French state's chosen method of execution until the abolition of the **death penalty** in France in 1981.

GUIZOT, FRANCOIS (1787–1874). An academic and a leading statesman after the monarchy was restored in France. He was born the son of a wealthy Protestant lawyer in Nîmes, but his father was executed during the **Terror**, and in 1799 Mme. Guizot moved the family to Geneva. Guizot came to **Paris** in 1805. In 1812 his undoubted intellectual talents and carefully cultivated friendships earned him the post of professor of modern history at the University of Paris. His entry into public life was facilitated by his faith in the restoration of the **Bourbon dynasty** to the throne of France. As a consequence of this he was given a post in the Ministry of the Interior, and his loyalty in accompanying **Louis XVIII** to Belgium after **Napoléon Bonaparte**'s return during the **Hundred Days** was ultimately rewarded by his appointment as secretary-general of the Ministry of Justice.

But Guizot's moderate liberalism was a thorn in the flesh of the ultraroyalists, and he eventually returned to academic life after they engineered his dismissal from government in 1816. It was during the years that followed that Guizot established his reputation as an eminent historian, with works like *Histoire de la révolution d'Angleterre* (1826–1827), *Histoire de la civilisation en Europe* (1828), and *Histoire de la civilisation en France* (1830–1832). But his political ambitions remained undimmed, and in 1827 he became one of the founders of the liberal electoral organization Aide-Toi, le Ciel t'Aidera ("Heaven helps those who help themselves"). After his election to the Chamber of Deputies in 1830 he became a leading light in the opposition to **Charles X**. Once the **Revolution of 1830** gained momentum, Guizot was among the small band of deputies who were instrumental in bringing **Louis-Philippe**, duc d'Orléans, to the throne.

Guizot was in office for 13 of the next 18 years. One of his most lasting achievements was to draft the law of 28 June 1833 that required every **commune** to support a public primary school, thus laying the foundation for universal access to **education** in France. From 1840 to 1848 he also managed France's **foreign policy**, steering a conservative and pacific course. But his conservatism at home was his undoing, owing to the popular perception of him as a leading opponent of the extension of suffrage to ordinary citizens and his preference for government by the affluent for the affluent. Thus when the **Revolution of 1848** occurred, his downfall was inevitable. He fled to England, returning to France in 1849, when the revolutionary impetus had died down, but his attempts to gain reelection to the Legislative Assembly were unsuccessful. Thereafter he devoted himself to his writing and died on 12 September 1874 at his home in Normandy.

– H –

HALLYDAY, JOHNNY (1943–). The most popular singer in France after **World War II** and in later years an accomplished actor. He was born Jean-Philippe Smet and was not yet in his teens when he started in show business, with a bit part in Henri-Georges Clouzot's famous film *Les diaboliques* (1955). Hallyday's big break came when French youth were seduced by American rock and roll and his recordings in the 1960s reflect this, with French cover versions of songs by artists like Chubby Checker, Eddie Floyd, and the Crystals. Hallyday's talent lay in packaging the latest trend in popular music and making it sound authentically French to a Francophone audience. So as the 1960s wore on he changed tack and adopted the style of what in the **United States** was called the British Invasion, producing covers of songs by the Animals and the American guitarist who found fame in England, Jimi Hendrix, and adopting the rebellious cool patented by the Rolling Stones. His ability to sell records and fill concert venues continued unabated through the ensuing decades, and by the beginning of the 21st century he was calculated to have sold over 100 million records and performed to over 17 million fans.

This was partly due to his talents as a showman, which enabled him to turn his concerts into theatrical events. In the 1980s, for example, he seized on the success of Arnold Schwarzenegger's *Conan* movies and incorporated the heroic warrior myth into the costumes and special effects of his stage shows. But Hallyday's talent for imitation is also his Achilles' heel artistically. While his ability to Gallicize American culture may appeal to the Francophone public of France, Belgium, and Switzerland, elsewhere in the world the public prefers to enjoy the original. Hallyday has made forlorn attempts to break into the consciousness of the American public, such as his concert in Las Vegas in 1996. But the reality is that for the non-Francophone public, he remains the most famous rock star no one has heard of. An unquestionably original talent that he does possess, however, is as an actor. Films like *Détective* (1984) by **Jean-Luc Godard** and *L'Homme du train* (2002) by Patrice Leconte, show Hallyday's ability to leave an indelible mark on the screen due to his brooding and quietly menacing presence. *See also* CINEMA.

HAUSSMANN, GEORGES-EUGENE, BARON (1809–1891). Administrator who was the driving force behind the transformation of **Paris** during the middle of the 19th century. He was born in Paris into a Protestant family originally from Alsace. He joined the high ranks of the administration under the regime of **Louis-Philippe** in the early 1830s, after graduating in law. But his great opportunity came after the accession to power of **Louis-Napoléon Bonaparte**, whose autocratic style suited Haussmann's driving ambition. After appointments to prefectures in the provinces, in 1853 Haussmann was given the prized prefecture of Paris. For the next 16 years Haussmann, a skilled administrator with an iron will, worked closely with Louis-Napoléon to transform Paris. Although he has been accused of destroying much of medieval Paris and being obsessed with geometric lines in the rebuilding of the city center, he was nonetheless responsible for major improvements in the living conditions of Parisians, introducing an underground sewage system and a clean water supply. But the downturn in the economy in the 1860s and the declining fortunes of his political master made Haussmann's plans unviable, and he was forced to quit his post in January 1870. Thereafter he retired to his villa in Nice, but the mark he left on Paris was indelible.

HENRI IV. *See* RELIGION.

HERRIOT, EDOUARD (1872–1957). Radical-Socialist politician and statesman. Born in Troyes (Aube), Herriot was an academic highflier and studied at the Ecole Normale Supérieure before embarking on a teaching career. He joined the Radical-Socialist party when it was founded in 1901. His success in local politics was crowned by his election as mayor of **Lyon** in 1905. He entered national politics first as a senator in 1912, becoming a deputy in 1919; he soon became president of the Radical Party until resigning in 1935. He organized the opposition to the postwar **Bloc National** and led the **Cartel des Gauches** to victory in 1924. However, his government was short lived (June 1924–April 1925), undermined by France's severe financial problems and the vexed issue of the war reparations owed by **Germany**. He returned to power in 1932, but his government was unable to cope with the effects of the economic depression in France and was distracted by a complex international situation. Herriot was elected president of the Chamber of Deputies in 1936 and served with distinction until its last session under the **Third Republic** in July 1940. The **Vichy regime** placed him under house arrest between 1942 and 1944 and eventually deported him to Germany.

At the end of the war Herriot attempted to revive the Third Republic but met with little support. However, the institutions of the **Fourth Republic** came to resemble those of its predecessor, particularly in terms of the weakness of the executive vis-à-vis the legislature. Herriot secured his position in the Radical party when he was elected its leader in 1945, holding the post until his death, and in January 1947 he was elected to the presidency of the National Assembly. But some of Herriot's key positions were detrimental to the long-term prospects of his party. The Radicals relied, for example, on alliances with the right to be electorally viable. Yet in 1951 Herriot advocated that the Radicals should distance themselves from **Gaullism**, thus provoking division in the ranks of his party. Damaging splits occurred again in 1957 when Herriot threw his support behind the left wing of the party led by **Pierre Mendès-France**. In a wider sphere, Herriot's stubborn opposition to German rearmament and to **decolonization** in **Algeria** illustrated his failure to understand the changes that were taking place, and by the time he died, both his party and the Fourth Republic were on the verge of collapse. *See also* POLITICAL PARTIES.

HERSANT, ROBERT (1920–1996). Controversial and most powerful press baron in France since 1945. He was the son of a captain in the merchant navy and showed a precocious talent for journalism when he produced his first newspaper layout as a schoolboy of 13 in Rouen. Hersant was unequivocal in his support for **Pétain** during the war and wrote articles for the collaborationist paper *Au Pilori*. But personal friendships with notable Socialist leaders such as **Guy Mollet** and **François Mitterrand** during the 1950s enabled him to overcome impediments created by his past and allowed him to be elected as a deputy in 1956. His fortune was made through the ownership of *Auto Journal,* which he created in 1950. He went on to acquire a string of newspapers, national and provincial, that included some of the most well known in France, such as *France-Soir, Le Dauphiné,* and *Le Progrès.* The editorial independence his editors claimed to enjoy may be explained by the fact that, although an energetic and aggressive proprietor, Hersant liked to consider himself first and foremost a journalist. He nonetheless persevered with his ambitions in public life and in the 1980s was a deputy belonging to the centrist **Union pour la Démocratie Française (UDF)**, serving also as a member of the European Parliament from 1984 until his death.

By the time of his death, Hersant's empire included 40 titles and employed 8,000 people. But his foray into television station ownership in the 1980s had ended in failure, and by 1995 the empire's burgeoning debts had forced the sale of *Auto Journal,* suggesting that its corporate existence would not long survive its founder. *See also* PRESS.

HUGO, VICTOR (1802–1885). A prolific man of letters and an inspirational figure in the French romantic movement. Hugo was born in Besançon in the *département* of Doubs on 26 February 1802, the son of a Bonapartist military officer. Within a year of Victor's birth, his parents' marriage was troubled with all the uncertainties resulting from infidelity by both parties. It was one of these crises that led his mother, Sophie Hugo, to move the children to **Paris** in 1814, enabling Hugo to acquire the benefits of a sound training in the classics at the Lycée Louis le Grand. His burgeoning talent was matched by his limitless ambition. While barely out of his teens, he collected a series of prizes for his odes and essays, culminating in 1820 with a stipend from the king for his *Ode sur la mort du duc de Berry.* Hugo also benefited from the patronage of **Louis XVIII**'s successor, **Charles X**, who made him a chevalier of the **Légion d'Honneur**.

It was during this period in the mid-1820s that Hugo decided to turn his attention to drama, in the form of the work entitled *Cromwell.* His preface to this play made it a kind of manifesto for **romanticism**, and his apartment on the rue Notre Dame des Champs became a focal point for young writers and artists like **Honoré de Balzac**, **Alexandre Dumas**, and **Eugène Delacroix**, to name but a few, thus constituting a center for the propagation of the romantic creed, its emphasis on literary or artistic sensibility, and its rejection of the constraints imposed by the disciplines of classical form. Further notoriety followed with his play *Hernani,* premiering in 1830; and in March 1831, his great novel *Notre-Dame de Paris* (*The Hunchback of Notre Dame*) was published. Domestic unhappiness due to the infidelity of his wife, Adèle, with the critic Sainte-Beuve appeared to sharpen Hugo's appetite for work, and there followed a succession of books of verse and historical drama, most notably *Les feuilles d'automne* (1831), *Le roi s'amuse* (1839), *Lucrèce Borgia* (1833), *Marie Tudor* (1833), and *Claude Gueux* (1834). Hugo received the ultimate accolade that the literary establishment in France can bestow when he was elected to the **Académie Française** in 1841.

Thereafter, Hugo switched his energies increasingly to politics, and his convictions gradually evolved from liberal monarchist to republican. In 1845 **Louis-Philippe** made Hugo a Peer of France, and Hugo spoke on the liberal monarchist side in the upper chamber. But when the regime collapsed in 1848, he threw his weight behind **Louis-Napoléon Bonaparte**'s campaign for the **presidency**. However, Louis-Napoléon's dictatorial ambitions soon provoked scathing attacks from Hugo and led to the decree from President Bonaparte in January 1852 that condemned him to exile on the island of Guernsey. This period of exile lasted almost 20 years, ending with Louis-Napoléon's fall in 1870. During these years the clandestine circulation of Hugo's criticisms of the regime in France made him a leader of the republican opposition. But Hugo's literary output did not cease, and it was also while in exile that Hugo produced his masterpiece of satirical verse, *Les châtiments*, and his most universally popular novel, *Les misérables*. Hugo's return to France was soon marked by a return to public life, and he was elected first as a deputy and then as a senator in the 1870s. When he died of pneumonia on 15 May 1885, it provoked a state of national mourning for a man whose career had spanned most of the 19th century, whose pen had been turned successfully to every major form of literary endeavor, and whose writing had touched the hearts and minds of generations of ordinary French men and women. *See also* LITERATURE.

THE HUNDRED DAYS. The term describing the period from 20 March to 22 June 1815 during which **Napoléon Bonaparte** attempted to reestablish his empire. It was first coined by G. J. Gaspard de Chabrol, prefect of the Seine, in the immediate aftermath of Bonaparte's failure. Spurred by his knowledge of popular discontent with the **Bourbon** restoration, Napoléon escaped from exile on Elba and returned to **Paris**, where he formed what was effectively a government of national defense on March 20. Ranged against him was an alliance including Austria, **Great Britain**, Prussia, and **Russia**, which issued a decree declaring Bonaparte an outlaw. With characteristic energy, Bonaparte set about revitalizing an army much neglected under the Bourbon restoration and by May had raised its numbers from 50,000 to 300,000. Nonetheless, Napoléon's prestige was not enough to allow him to restore the authoritarian regime of old. Many of Bonaparte's supporters had become liberal constitutionalists, and to secure their support, he agreed to moderate his prerogatives as emperor by accepting the measures that led to the establishment of a parliamentary regime on 23 April.

The inevitable confrontation with Bonaparte's military adversaries took place in June in Belgium. His army of 122,000 was faced by an Anglo-Dutch force of 110,000 led by the Duke of Wellington and a Prussian army of 117,000 under Gebhard Leberecht, Prince von Blücher. The French gave the Prussians a mauling at the Battle of Ligny (16 June), but the poor leadership of Bonaparte's senior commanders allowed the Prussians to retreat in good order. On the morning of 18 June, Bonaparte launched his force against Wellington's, which was established in a strong defensive position south of Waterloo. But the French troops had been committed while their commander was unaware that the Prussians had moved up to threaten his right wing, and when three Prussian corps of 70,000 men entered the battlefield in the afternoon, the balance swung irretrievably against the French. When the defeated Bonaparte returned to Paris on 21 June, the hostile Assembly, largely convinced by the arguments of **Joseph Fouché** and **Gilbert du Motier de Lafayette** that it was in the national interest to do so, forced him to abdicate on 22 June. Bonaparte fled on 29 June and was eventually sent into exile on St. Helena. The second Bourbon restoration was inaugurated by the return of **Louis XVIII** to Paris on 8 July 1815.

HUNDRED YEARS' WAR. A state of conflict between France and England punctuated by intermittent military campaigns that spanned the 14th to the 15th century, centered on disputes over land and the succession to the French throne. English claims to France stemmed from the rights conferred on his English heirs by **William the Conqueror**, who as Duke of Normandy had conquered England in 1066. Wars and alliances through marriage had tied the two thrones in a mutual respect for the status quo until the death in 1328 of the French king Charles IV. As the son of Charles IV's sister and given that Charles IV had no sons, King Edward III of England, who also had the title Duke of Guyenne (an area in southwestern France), decided to press his claim to the throne. However, a French assembly chosen to settle the question preferred the claim of the French count of Valois, making him Philippe VI. Fearing the influence of another sovereign in his kingdom, Philippe VI attempted to confiscate Guyenne in 1331, provoking Edward III to land an army in Flanders and thus precipitating the long conflict.

The war ebbed and flowed over generations, marked by some famous battles, such as the crushing English victories at Crécy (1346) and Agincourt (1415). The high point of English influence was reached in 1422 when, in alliance with the Duke of Burgundy, who ruled his fiefdom in the east independently of the French king, the English controlled Aquitaine and all of France north of the **Loire River**, including **Paris**. But the turning point in French fortunes came in 1429, when an army raised by **Joan of Arc** forced the English to abandon the siege of Orléans. Though they sold Joan of Arc into captivity and eventual execution by the English, the Burgundian leaders came to the conclusion that the English throne would not be able to subjugate France and switched sides in 1435. Thus began the gradual reconquest of French territory. Charles VII regained Normandy and by 1453 had regained all of Aquitaine by exploiting the opportunities created by the divisions that had opened up in England owing to the War of the Roses. The English were finally obliged to relinquish their last claim to France in 1558, when they gave up Calais. By the end of the conflict, not only had France regained its territorial integrity, but also the monarchy had established a dominant hold on France by eliminating the challenge posed by powerful, independent princes who might be tempted to challenge the crown through alliances with its external enemies. *See also* GREAT BRITAIN.

– I –

IMMIGRATION. The image of France as a *terre d'accueil*, a new home for foreigners, was a familiar and, until the last two decades, uncontentious notion for the majority of French people. Waves of Spanish and Italian workers came during the days of the **Third Republic**, providing labor, compensating for the deficiencies of the demographic trends in France, and helping to establish France's presence in its overseas territories.

Substantial numbers of "White," or anti-Communist, Russians came to France after the Bolshevik revolution in 1917 and made a particularly vibrant contribution to the cultural life of **Paris**. They were joined in the 1920s and 1930s by many East Europeans. But these numbers were small compared to the waves of immigrants from

Portugal, Greece, and especially North Africa who came after 1945 and who, by the beginning of the 1970s, provided 15 percent of France's manual labor.

The new **presidency** of **Valéry Giscard d'Estaing** marked a shift in policy by the French government. The previous laissez-faire policy, which gave priority to the need of the French **economy** for cheap labor, was stopped in 1974. Primary immigration to France ended, except for those allowed in under the right to family reunification recognized by the government in 1976. Thus between 1976 and 1979, over 95 percent of non-European immigrants admitted to France were family members. In the years since, immigration has become much more of a political than an economic issue, as governments have attempted to articulate policies aimed at assimilating immigrant communities into the broader structure of French society.

The immigration issue has been most politicized by the far right **Front National** party, which has played on the anxieties of the French population regarding employment, law and order, and the survival of French identity, prompted by the rise of the nonwhite, non-Christian immigrant population from North Africa. In 1946 this predominantly Muslim community accounted for only 2.3 percent of the foreign population of France, with 88.7 percent of the rest coming from the other countries of Europe. But by 1982 the proportion of Europeans had fallen to 47.6 percent, while that of North Africans had risen to 38.5 percent. From that point onward governments of left and right introduced progressively tougher policies, such as the legislation passed in 1986 enabling them to expel illegal immigrants peremptorily as the result of an administrative rather than a judicial procedure. And in the 1990s the linkage between immigration, race, and nationality became more obvious as moves developed to change the nationality code so that the children born in France of immigrant parents would have to apply for citizenship instead of being granted it automatically. Under then–interior minister **Nicolas Sarkozy**, in July 2006 a new immigration and integration law was passed, aimed at giving the government new powers to encourage the arrival of highly skilled migrants in France, discourage illegal immigration, and exercise stricter control over immigration for the purposes of family reunification. In the debate surrounding the measures proposed it became clear that this last factor was regarded by Sarkozy as the principal reason why French governments since the early 1970s had failed to manage immigration. By 2007, 10 percent of France's 61 million residents were foreign born, with 64 percent of them having arrived through family reunification.

IMPRESSIONISM. Artistic movement that emerged in the 1870s in **Paris**. In 1874, 30 or so artists, including **Edgar Degas, Claude Monet, Camille Pissarro**, and **Auguste Renoir**, displayed works at Nadar's photography studio that were remarkable for their use of pure colors and their rejection of the typical historical, religious, and allegorical themes that characterized the academic Salon paintings of the era. The use of vibrant colors, rapid brushstrokes, and the dissolving forms resulting in new treatment of light led one critic to condemn these works as "impressionistic." In spite of his refusal to participate in the first exhibition, **Edouard Manet** had shown the way in the late 1850s and 1860s by opting for modern life instead of traditional themes in his depictions of drinkers and picnickers. Rejection of conventions and traditional methods in pursuit of spontaneity and the attempt to capture ephemeral movements of light enabled the impressionists to depict the rapid, shifting nature of modern urban life, as seen in typical subjects like railroads, street scenes, and popular entertainment. Criticism of impressionism as superficial and too concerned with the visual and the decorative began to mount by the late 1880s, and some of its leading figures, like Pissarro, began to go their own way. The final impressionist exhibition took place in 1886. *See also* ART.

INDOCHINESE WAR. The result of French attempts to reimpose colonial rule in the region after **World War II**. A nationalist movement existed in Indochina before the war, and the communist leader Ho Chi Minh had already established himself as the most prominent leader. After the war the nationalist Vietminh agreed to accept independence within the **French Union**, and a protocol to this effect was signed in March 1946. However, during the following summer the French separated Laos and Cambodia from Vietnam and sponsored a Cochin Chinese regime in the south that was independent of the north. The flashpoint occurred when the French high commissioner in Vietnam decided to assert French control over customs enforcement.

Resistance from Vietnamese irregulars resulted in the bombardment of the port of Haiphong by French warships, leading to thousands of civilian deaths.

Vietnamese general Giap's initiation of hostile action against the French after the interim premier **Léon Blum** had been delayed in answering a conciliatory telegram from Ho Chi Minh was interpreted in **Paris** as sufficient cause to launch a full-scale military attempt to reconquer the territory. Although the French persisted in the attempt to create an independent Vietnam within the French Union by sponsoring a noncommunist regime under the leadership of Bao Dai, the conflict with the Vietminh escalated inexorably, with the French controlling the cities while the Vietminh controlled the countryside. The complexion of the conflict changed when the **Soviet Union** decided to recognize the legitimacy of the government of Ho Chi Minh. This event caused the **United States**, which up to that point had regarded the war in Indochina as one of colonial reconquest by the French, to back the noncommunist alternative to the Vietminh represented by Bao Dai. The outbreak of the Korean War in June 1950 gave the French the opportunity to secure more U.S. support by convincing Washington that the conflicts in Korea and Indochina were in fact two related "hot" fronts in the cold war that pitted the free world against communism.

By 1953 the United States had committed almost $800 million in direct and indirect aid to support the French in the conflict, and the French had committed approximately 200,000 troops—but not conscripts, for fear of the consequences at home. As pressure for a negotiated settlement grew in Paris, the French government decided to authorize what was intended to be a decisive push by the French military in Vietnam through the reinforcement of their fortified but isolated outpost at Dien Bien Phu. The misconceived plan only led to greater numbers of French troops being stranded there and left at the mercy of the Vietminh when they succeeded in bringing artillery to bear on the French positions. When the situation became desperate, the French pressed Washington to launch B-29 air strikes against Vietminh positions, but this request was refused and Dien Bien Phu fell on 7 May 1954. The settlement brought about by this defeat was concluded by **Pierre Mendès-France** on the French side and allowed the Vietminh to take power in north Vietnam; Laos and Cambodia to be independent under noncommunist regimes; and the French to regroup in South Vietnam pending elections in 1956. However, French hopes of maintaining a presence in the south faded as the United States became the key player in the region, and the French were forced to quit the territory in 1955 as a much bigger colonial commitment was beginning to unravel in **Algeria**. *See also* COLONIALISM; DECOLONIZATION.

INDUSTRY. While there were instances of large-scale manufacture in France during the 18th century, it was under the control of, if not in fact at the behest of, the absolutist state, as in the case of glass manufacture. In general, industrial enterprise in France was part of a national **economy** constrained by a centralizing state and rendered uncompetitive by protectionist regimes. As a consequence France lived in the shadow of its more successful industrial neighbors, **Great Britain** and **Germany**, until the middle of the 20th century. **Finance** for industry developed, partly through private and partly through public initiatives, during the 19th century. And while France scored some notable industrial successes, such as coming second only to the United States in the production of automobiles until **World War I**, for the first half of the 20th century the feeling persisted in governing circles that France had failed to adapt to the challenges of the Industrial Revolution as well as its two major European competitors.

The period following 1945 marked a dramatic change. The period known as *les trente glorieuses* was marked by purposive state intervention through a process known as the **Plan**, which allowed French industry to profit from the massive increase in demand for basic consumer goods, particularly in the 1950s and 1960s. The hand of the state was strengthened through a process of **nationalization**, which gave it the means to target the investment in industry. By the 1960s this strategy was refined to enable French companies to establish a major presence in high-technology industries such as **aerospace**, telecommunications, and computing. Although France has failed to produce a major player in the global computer industry, its success in aerospace is evident in its leadership of the European space program through the manufacture of the Ariane space rocket, and its role in the Airbus consortium puts it at the leading edge of European competition against the **United States** for dominance in aircraft manufacture for the world market.

In the 1980s and 1990s, however, the French state was forced to recognize the limitations on what it could do directly for industry. Some major sectors of France's manufacturing industry were forced to adapt to market forces through a policy of **privatization**, which even involved the sale of manufacturing capacity to foreign companies. Nonetheless, the close relationship between the state and industry, especially in those companies in which the state retains a share, have given French enterprises a considerable advantage as markets have opened up, especially in Europe. Thus, for example, the utility company Electricité de France has been able to snap up power companies elsewhere, especially in Britain, safe in the knowledge that its home market was protected, irrespective of the European Commission's pleas for national markets to be opened up to Europe-wide competition. The effects of global competition, however, have been harder for the French state to mitigate. This became painfully obvious in 2007 when the industry of which France is proudest, aerospace, could not avoid laying off workers because production problems with Airbus Industrie's A380 large passenger aircraft led to loss of orders. *See also* EUROPEAN UNION.

ISLAM. The French encounter with Islam has a long history that has helped to shape the nation's self-consciousness. Charles Martel's defeat of the invading Moors near Poitiers in 732 AD helped lay the foundation for the emergence of the French people as a European and Christian nation. The arrival of Muslim residents in modern times has altered national self-consciousness and enabled France, sometimes painfully, to see itself as a racially, religiously, and culturally diverse society. In 1922, the Great Mosque of Paris was built in recognition of the sacrifices made by the soldiers from France's North African colonies during **World War I**, notably at the battle of Verdun. But a large Muslim population in France did not begin to develop until after **World War II**, with the arrival in the 1960s and 1970s of much-needed labor from the former North African colonies to work in key sections of the **economy**, such as the automobile industry.

Due to a republican ideology that refuses to distinguish between citizens, the French government is not legally allowed to ask about race or religion in its population censuses. But in 2000 the Haut Conseil à l'Intégration calculated the Muslim population of France to be just over 4 million; most are of Algerian, Moroccan, and Tunisian origin. The relationship between Islam and the secular French state has not always been comfortable, as was evident from the reaction to the French government's determination to preserve the secular nature of its **education** system by banning the wearing of the Islamic headscarf in its schools. The first Muslim school, inevitably funded by private means and catering to 11- to 15-year-olds, opened in the outer Parisian suburb of Aubervilliers in 2003, but such establishments remain very few and far between. Although the secular French state cannot be seen officially to endorse a religious faith, it recognized the importance of Islam to the lives of a growing number of its citizens when in 2002 then–interior minister **Nicolas Sarkozy** initiated the creation of a Conseil Français du Culte Musulman (French Council of the Muslim Faith). In spite of the sometimes dramatic tensions between Islam and the secular state in France, surveys repeatedly show that the Muslim community there considers itself more happily integrated that in most other countries in Europe. *See also* IMMIGRATION; RELIGION.

– J –

JACOBINS. The term Jacobin was coined in early 1790 after a Jacobin (Dominican) convent became the headquarters of the pro-revolutionary Society of Friends of the **Constitution**. The essential ambition of the Jacobins was to establish a more democratic society, although some were prepared to accept undemocratic measures to achieve this. **Gilbert du Motier de Lafayette** was one of the first members, and **Napoléon Bonaparte**, as a young officer, helped organize Jacobin clubs in Corsica. The archetypal Jacobins are often identified with those revolutionaries of 1793–1794, most notably **Maximilien de Robespierre**, who were responsible for the **Terror**. Bonaparte used the threat of a "Jacobin conspiracy" as a pretext for his coup d'état (1799) and crushed this left-wing opposition by having 130 "Jacobins" arrested after a bomb outrage in the rue St. Niçaise on 24 December 1800. *See also* FRENCH REVOLUTION; GIRONDINS; MONTAGNARDS.

JAURES, JEAN (1859–1914). Philosopher, teacher, journalist, and one of the great socialist leaders and theoreticians of the **Third Republic**. He was born in Castres (Tarn) on 3 September 1859 into a family of rural smallholders and traders. His exceptional intellectual ability enabled him to win a place at the Ecole Normale Supérieure, where in 1881 his third place in the agrégation de philosophie launched his teaching career at Toulouse University. Jaurès was elected the youngest republican deputy in the Chamber in 1885, but he soon became disillusioned with **Jules Ferry**'s opportunist politics, and he returned to academic life after his defeat in 1889. His election as a municipal councilor for **Toulouse** in July 1890 brought him into greater contact with the urban working classes, and the Carmaux mining strike of 1892 confirmed his socialist beliefs after he witnessed the suffering caused by the conflict between capital and labor. He was elected as deputy for Carmaux in 1892 and rapidly established himself as a leader of the socialist caucus in the Assembly through his fine grasp of theory and skill as an orator. Jaurès's growing awareness of the complexities of government and the power of the state moderated his perception of what could be achieved by the struggle for socialism. His narrow electoral defeat in 1898 enabled him to invest his energies in journalism, and after some initial reluctance he joined the campaign in defense of Dreyfus (*see* DREYFUS AFFAIR). Jaurès became an energetic proponent of reformist ministerial socialism and subsequently broke with the less compromising **Jules Guesde** to form the Parti Socialiste Français in 1902.

But he abandoned his ministerial approach in 1904 in favor of the more traditional revolutionary line as a prelude to the achievement of socialist unity in the shape of the **Section Française de l'Internationale Ouvrière (SFIO)** in 1905. Jaurès took the lead in formulating policy on almost every subject of concern to the SFIO. He became increasingly preoccupied by the need for greater unity between the **Confédération Générale du Travail** union and the SFIO and by the need for international socialist action to prevent war. Jaurès wrote, traveled, and spoke widely between 1912 and 1914 in his impassioned pursuit of peace. His convictions made him few friends among the nationalist extreme right, and his assassination by one of these fanatics on 31 July 1914 was seen by many as an ominous portent. His standing as one of the giants of French socialism was confirmed on 23 November 1924 when his ashes were transferred to the Pantheon. *See also* POLITICAL PARTIES.

JOAN OF ARC (JEANNE D'ARC) (1412–1431). Known also as Saint Joan and the Maid of Orléans, she became a national heroine in France through her actions during the **Hundred Years' War**. She was the daughter of a tenant farmer, and in response to the voices of the saints, as she claimed, she led French troops against the English in 1429 and forced them to lift the siege of Orléans. She was captured in 1430, condemned for heresy by a predominantly English church court in 1431, and burned at the stake. However, her action had paved the way for a reconciliation in 1435 between the Duke of Burgundy, up to that point allied with the English, and King Charles VII of France, thereby providing France with the means to combat the English on more equal terms. And her heroic example fostered in the French army a belief in ultimate victory. The story of Joan of Arc is the stuff of myth, which helps to explain her lasting fascination for playwrights and filmmakers and her significance to France as a symbol of national resistance. She was declared a saint by Pope Benedict XV in 1920. *See also* WOMEN.

JOSPIN, LIONEL (1937–). Politician and leader of the **Parti Socialiste (PS)**. Like many leaders of the political establishment in France, Jospin completed his education at the training ground for higher civil servants, the Ecole Nationale d'Administration (1963–1965), before beginning his career in the Ministry for Foreign Affairs. Disillusioned with life in the higher reaches of the civil service, Jospin left in 1970 to take up a post teaching economics at the University of Paris XI until 1981.

Jospin first joined a left-wing party when he became a member of the **Parti Socialiste Unifié (PSU)** in 1960. He joined the PS in 1971 and worked his way up the party structure before being elected first secretary in 1981, the same year that he was elected to the National Assembly as a deputy representing a constituency in **Paris**. His period as first secretary of the PS lasted until 1988 and reflected his skill at negotiating compromises between the various factions in the party and the closeness of his relationship with President **François Mitterrand**. However, Jospin began to distance himself from his mentor after 1988. He resigned from the leadership of the party in 1988 and began to construct a separate identity as a prospective political leader in his own right, taking ministerial portfolios in the cabinets formed by **Michel Rocard** and later **Edith Cresson**.

The landslide victory for the center-right in France in the legislative elections of 1993 heralded a period of intense maneuvering in the PS, as leading figures began to jostle for position to see who would succeed Mitterrand as the party's presidential contender. Although he had previously been considered a lightweight compared to figures like Rocard and **Laurent Fabius**, Jospin proved astute at mobilizing the support not only of those PS members who were faithful to the Mitterrand legacy but also of those who were attracted to Rocard's beliefs in the need for more ethics in politics and the modernization of the political system. The proof of Jospin's success came when he emerged as the PS candidate in the presidential elections of 1995. He used all his talents as a conciliator and educator to run an intelligent campaign. Although he lost, his score of 47 percent in the final round of the elections on 7 May was regarded as a moral victory for the PS, which not long before had plumbed the depths of unpopularity in France. Jospin's dominant position in the party was confirmed by his reelection as its first secretary in October 1995 with over 94 percent of the vote and a mandate to renew the party in preparation for governing once more.

President **Jacques Chirac**'s decision to dissolve the Assembly and call legislative elections early, in the spring of 1997, played into Jospin's hands. The image he had succeeded in tailoring for himself as a left-wing realist in touch with the concerns of ordinary people worked very much to his advantage and that of his party. The massive center-right majority was overturned, and the ensuing left-wing majority forced Chirac to nominate the PS leader as his premier on 3 June 1997. Jospin's government was nicknamed *la gauche plurielle* (Plural Left) due to the coalition he headed, which included **Communists**, Greens, and radical left-wing and republican elements. His government was notable for introducing the 35-hour working week, the Pacte Civil de Solidarité (a civil partnership between two people, irrespective of gender), additional health insurance for the poorest, and greater representation for **women** in politics. However, these achievements did not prevent the huge shock that occurred in the first round of the presidential elections of 2002, when Jospin was beaten to the second place behind Chirac by the **Front National** leader, **Jean-Marie Le Pen**. This dealt a fatal blow to Jospin's political career, and although he toyed with the prospect of putting himself forward as the Socialist candidate in the presidential elections of 2007, it was without much conviction and was short lived.

JUDAISM. Historically, the fate of the Jewish community in France was essentially the same as it was in most parts of Europe, characterized by intolerance and persecution. Between 1306 and 1322 the Jews were expelled three times from France, on the pretext that they had brought famine to the country and even been responsible for the madness of King Charles VI. It wasn't until the 16th century that a significant Jewish community appeared once more in France. The **Enlightenment** played a major part in undoing the superstition and ignorance that led to the systematic discrimination suffered by the Jews. But it was the **French Revolution** that finally liberated them legally when in 1791 they were granted the rights of citizenship on exactly the same footing as everyone else in post-revolutionary France. The pogroms toward the end of the 19th century, especially in Russia, swelled the numbers of Jews migrating across Europe to France. Within a very short space of time they established themselves as very successful members of the bourgeoisie, conspicuously distinguished in academia, commerce, and finance.

However, partly due to France's Catholic heritage and the jealousy generated by the success of this community, anti-Semitic instincts came to the surface in French society as a whole. The most blatant example of this during the period in question was the **Dreyfus Affair**, when a young Jewish army officer was found guilty of treason in spite of manifestly trumped-up charges. The economic difficulties that followed **World War I** strengthened the hand of extremist right-wing organizations, and they used anti-Semitic tactics to manipulate the anxieties of a significant section of the population. The determination to find a scapegoat for the country's ills came to the fore after the fall of France in **World War II**. The **Vichy regime**, largely due to German pressure but also due to its own anti-Semitic instincts, connived with Nazi plans for a final solution to the Jewish question and deported over 70,000 Jews to their deaths in Nazi concentration camps.

After half a century the French state finally took steps to recognize unequivocally its complicity in this genocide, and this was articulated by President **Jacques Chirac**. Conversely, French society has shown signs of resurgence in anti-Semitism. The first warning signs came in 1990 when the Jewish cemetery in the French town of Carpentras was vandalized. The growth of a large Muslim population in France has been accompanied by a developing reservoir of hatred for the policies of the Jewish state in Palestine, and this now manifests itself in regular attacks on Jewish cemeteries in particular. For the first time since World War II, there is an undercurrent of unease in the 620,000-strong Jewish community in France regarding their safety and security. *See also* ISLAM; RELIGION.

JUPPE, ALAIN (1945–). Premier of France from 1995 to 1997. He was born in Mont-de-Marsan (Landes), the son of a landowner. He finished his education at Lycée Louis le Grand in **Paris** before taking the classic route in higher education for an ambitious would-be servant of the French state: Ecole Normale Supérieure, Institut d'Etudes Politiques, and Ecole Nationale d'Administration. Juppé was offered a major opportunity to advance his career when he was attached to the office of Prime Minister **Jacques Chirac** in 1976. He was elected to represent a Paris constituency in the National Assembly for the first time in March 1986. In 1993 Juppé was given the prestigious ministerial portfolio for **foreign affairs**, where the sharp intellect and efficiency he displayed influenced his selection by President Chirac in 1995 as the first prime minister under his new **presidency**.

The misfortune for Juppé was that he assumed the post of premier during a period of low economic growth, rising unemployment, and inevitable cutbacks in state spending, particularly if France was to meet the strict budgetary criteria for membership in the single European currency envisaged for 1999. Proposed cutbacks in health, **education**, and unemployment insurance proved especially provocative to the **trade unions** and employees in general, who took to the streets in a wave of protests in the fall of 1995 in numbers that had not been seen since the **student rebellions** of 1968. Juppé's problems were compounded by the image he developed as a coldly cerebral politician, unable to express his economic liberalism in terms that could persuade the French electorate of their painful but ultimately positive necessity. In 1996 Juppé began to expand the scope of economic reforms he wished to introduce to call into question the employment protection laws in France, among the most rigorous in Europe, by criticizing the resulting lack of U.S.-style flexibility in the employment market. Even though French unemployment levels in 1996 were twice as high as those in the **United States**, Juppé's economic argument made little impact on a disenchanted electorate or leading figures of his center-right majority like **François Léotard** and **Philippe Séguin**, whose support he had failed to cultivate. It was these same men who, by the fall of 1996, were making off-the-record suggestions to the press that President Chirac needed to change his prime minister.

Chirac, however, persevered. This tactical mistake was compounded by the decision to call one year early the legislative elections scheduled for the spring of 1998. The rationale was that a government with such a massive majority in the Assembly could afford to lose seats if that meant renewing its mandate for a full term, thereby giving itself time to push through its package of liberal economic reforms. But Chirac had totally miscalculated the mood of the electorate, and Juppé's administration was swept out of office in a dramatic reversal of fortune for the center-right in the elections of May–June 1997. As early as 1995 rumors had begun to circulate that Juppé had abused his position to secure favors for his family and his party. In 1998 a judicial enquiry was launched into allegations that Juppé, during his time as deputy mayor of Paris, had used the funds of the municipality to finance the activities of his party, the Rassemblement pour la République, by giving some of its members fictional jobs that were paid for out of the city's budget. He was found guilty in 2004 and, after appeal, his sentence was reduced to a 14-month suspended prison term and one year's ineligibility for public office. However, in 2006 Juppé reemerged with a regional power base when he was elected mayor of **Bordeaux**.

JUQUIN, PIERRE (1930–). Communist dissident and candidate in the race for the presidency of the Republic in 1988. He joined the **Parti Communiste Français (PCF)** in 1953 and rose steadily through the ranks, becoming a Central Committee member in 1967 and a Political Bureau member in 1979. Juquin's public disaffection with the party hierarchy became manifest in the wake of the PCF's 24th congress in 1982. His critique of party dogmatism and its unresponsive leadership cost him most of his responsibilities within the organization. But Juquin was undeterred and emerged clearly as the leader of the dissident "renovators" in the party. At the party's 25th congress in 1985, Juquin went on the offensive and unequivocally criticized the leadership. But his reaction to the nomination of the safe party man, **André Lajoinie**, as the PCF's candidate in the presidential election in 1988 was still a surprise and something unheard of in the history of the party. Lajoinie's nomination prompted Juquin to declare himself an independent communist candidate for the **presidency**, and as an inevitable consequence he was excluded from the PCF on 14 October 1987. In contrast to what may be seen as this heroic high point in his political career, Juquin's actual showing in the first round of the election was dismal—a mere 1.9 percent of the vote. Juquin joined the Greens in 1989 but was soon relegated to the margins of political life, returning to his original vocation of teaching.

– K –

KOUCHNER, BERNARD (1939–). Doctor, left-wing politician, and cofounder of Médecins sans Frontières (MSF), or Doctors without Borders. He was part of the generation who cut their teeth politically in the ferment of the **student rebellions** of 1968. In his case, it was as a leading figure on the strike committee of the Faculty of Medicine in **Paris**. He then became involved in the humanitarian relief for Biafra necessitated by the civil war in Nigeria. Kouchner's presence there was as a member of the Secours Médical Français, which he helped transform into MSF. However, after falling out with the leadership of MSF he founded Médecins du Monde. This was symptomatic of Kouchner's independence of mind and the reluctance he later displayed to defer to received wisdom, even if it came from the political camp with which he sympathized, the left. His first major ministerial post was in a socialist administration where he served as minister for health and humanitarian aid from 1992 to 1993. By the end of the decade his international profile had grown considerably and he administered Kosovo, in the former Republic of Yugoslavia, from 1999 to 2001 as the United Nations' high representative. Kouchner was most prominent in articulating the principle of *droit d'ingérence*, that is, the right of the international community to interfere in the affairs of a sovereign state in pursuit of a humanitarian imperative.

In 2007 Kouchner joined **Ségolène Royal**'s campaign team as she bid for the **presidency** of the Republic, and he upset quite a few socialist diehards when he argued for an alliance with the centrist **Union pour la Démocratie Française (UDF)** led by **François Bayrou**. His disregard for political loyalties was crowned by his acceptance of the ministerial portfolio for foreign and European affairs in the government headed by **François Fillon**, after the center-right secured a majority in parliament in the legislative elections of July 2007. Dynamic and outspoken as ever, as foreign minister one of his first trips abroad was to Iraq in August 2007, signaling France's willingness to play a part in resolving the conflict. Rather undiplomatically, in September 2007 he warned that the crisis created by Iran's desire to produce nuclear weapons could lead to war.

– L –

LACAN, JACQUES (1901–1981). Psychoanalyst, psychiatrist, and leading figure in the development of **structuralism** in France in the 1960s. He was born and educated in **Paris** and entered medical school in 1920. He chose to specialize in psychiatry six years later, receiving his *doctorat d'état* after four further years. By 1936 he was established in his private psychiatric practice as well as working in the psychiatric hospitals of Paris; it was at this time that he began developing the ideas that would be most closely associated with him.

Lacan readily acknowledged his debt to Sigmund Freud. In 1964 he founded the Ecole Freudienne de Paris, which was succeeded in 1980 by the Ecole de la Cause Freudienne. But the idea that is most distinctly associated with Lacan goes back to the concept of the "mirror phase," which he first began developing in 1936. Lacan argued that this phase occurs in the infant when it first conceives of itself as an independent and coherent entity sometime between the ages of six and 18 months as a result of perceiving its reflection in the mirror. This key moment of self-identification, according to Lacan, explains the individual's later need to pursue the illusion of wholeness that beckons in the mirror image to occlude the many aspects of *manque* (loss or absence) that are intrinsic in life.

In *Ecrits* (1966), the collection of his most important essays, articles like "La lettre volée" and "Fonction et champ de la parole et du langage en psychanalyse" illustrate the structuralist methodology developed by Ferdinand de Saussure. Having envisaged the self as a comprehensive whole comprising, on the one hand, an ideal and unchanging ego created by the individual and, on the other, a constantly changing subject that can be apprehended only in relation to external stimuli, Lacan assimilated the innovations of modern linguists like Saussure by arguing that the unconscious bears the structure of language and that consequently the actions of the decentered subject are crucially determined by the signifier.

Lacan's ideas attracted both admiration and severe criticism, and consensus on the value of his contribution to psychoanalysis and psychiatry remained elusive after his death on 9 September 1981.

LAFAYETTE, MARIE-JOSEPH-PAUL-YVES-ROCH-GILBERT DU MOTIER (1757–1834). Notable figure in both the American Revolution and the **French Revolution**. After service in America (1777–1781) Lafayette became an advocate of constitutional monarchy in France and was a leader of the liberal nobles in the **Estates General**. He was appointed commander of the **Paris** National Guard after the fall of the **Bastille**. In 1790 he irrevocably renounced his title. However, his defense of law and order lessened his popularity, and he retired from politics when the constitution of 1791 was approved. He fled to the Austrian Netherlands (Belgium) after the overthrow of the king in August 1792, where he was captured by the Austrians and held until the **Treaty of Campo Formio** in 1797 secured his release. Lafayette was allowed to return to France in 1800, after **Napoléon Bonaparte** came to power, but declined to support him. He was elected to the Chamber of Deputies during the **Hundred Days** and led the call in the Chamber for Bonaparte's abdication after his final defeat on the battlefield at Waterloo. Subsequently Lafayette became an opponent of the policies of the **Bourbon**

restoration and supported democratic revolutions in the rest of Europe.

LAJOINIE, ANDRE (1929–). Archetypal Communist Party man and official candidate in the French presidential election of 1988. The son of a peasant family in the Corrèze, he joined the **Parti Communiste Français (PCF)** at the age of 19 and became a career functionary who owed much of his success to his closeness to the general secretary, **Georges Marchais**. Lajoinie's specialist field of knowledge was agricultural matters, and in 1977 he became editor of the PCF's farmers' weekly paper, *La Terre*. He became a deputy in 1978, a member of the party's Political Bureau in 1979, the leader of the Communist group in the National Assembly in 1981, and a member of the party secretariat in 1982.

The choice of Lajoinie to represent the PCF in the presidential election of 1988 was regarded by some within the party, notably **Pierre Juquin** and his sympathizers, as a cynical move reflecting Georges Marchais's hold on the party and his determination to find someone who would not constitute a pole of attraction alternative to his own. Though earnest and well-meaning, Lajoinie was singularly lacking in presidential charisma during the campaign and showed great difficulty in operating confidently at events not stage-managed by the Communists; he was sometimes caricatured in the non-party **press** as the dummy to Marchais's ventriloquist. His share of the vote in the first round of the election marked a new low in the fortunes of the PCF, at 6.7 percent. But he persevered as president of the group of Communist deputies in the National Assembly until 1993, and retained his own seat until 2002.

LAMARTINE, ALPHONSE DE (1790–1869). Poet, politician, and diplomat. Lamartine was born into a minor aristocratic family and raised in a devoutly monarchist and Catholic environment. His penchant for a dissolute lifestyle meant that he spent most of his adult life in debt, in spite of the relatively early success he experienced following the publication of his *Méditations poétiques* (1820), which earned him his place in the vanguard of the romantic movement (*see* ROMANTICISM) in France. This literary notoriety coincided with success in public life, notably in the form of his appointment as attaché to France's embassy in Naples.

Lamartine's political ideas matured during the following decade. In the essay *La politique rationnelle* (1830), he expressed his belief in reformist policies like free and universal access to **education**, a free **press**, and a more liberal form of suffrage. Elevated to the intellectual establishment by his membership in the **Académie Française** in 1829, in 1833–1834 Lamartine began his career at the heart of the political establishment, in the Chamber of Deputies. During the 14 years that followed, Lamartine's advocacy of political and social reform in the Chamber ran parallel to a literary career resulting in monumental works like the highly popular *Histoire des Girondins* (1847). His mastery of the French language proved an invaluable gift in the political arena when the regime of **Louis-Philippe** was overthrown in 1848. When the Chamber of Deputies at the Palais Bourbon seemed in imminent danger of invasion by the mob, Lamartine walked there alone and delivered a persuasive speech in favor of a transitional government to pave the way for the advent of a republic, rather than a sudden, brutal, and chaotic change of regime.

Although named the foreign minister in the provisional government that followed, Lamartine was effectively its head and piloted the decrees that established the **Second Republic** and some of the basic welfare measures that he had been arguing for during his parliamentary career. However, the reforming fervor of February 1848 had given way to conservative misgivings by the time a new constituent assembly was convened in May. Lamartine's opportunity to exercise a more lasting influence on the government of France had passed, and he came last in a field of five in the presidential election of December 1848. The victory of **Louis-Napoléon Bonaparte** laid the foundations for the coup d'état he engineered on 2 December 1851, thus ending Lamartine's political career and forcing him to make a living by his pen alone, until some belated recognition for his contribution to French public life came his way in 1867 in the form of a modest stipend from the state. *See also* LITERATURE.

LANG, JACK (1939–). University professor and high-profile minister of culture for the Socialist governments of the 1980s and early 1990s. The son of an industrialist, he was born into a prosperous family in the Vosges. Acting and the law were Lang's twin passions. His talent for the former was crowned by prizes for elocution and comic acting at the Nancy Conservatory for Dramatic Arts. His long years of study in law earned him the *agrégation* in 1970 and culminated in his election as dean of the Nancy Law School in 1977.

Like many of his contemporaries, Lang came to the **Parti Socialiste (PS)** via the **Parti Socialiste Unifié (PSU)** and began his political career with his election to the **Paris** city council in 1977. His talents for organization and publicity were soon noticed, and a year later he became a special adviser to PS leader **François Mitterrand**. Lang was rewarded with the portfolio for culture after Mitterrand's success in the presidential elections of 1981, a post he held until a center-right majority was elected to the National Assembly in the legislative elections of 1986. He resumed his old post in 1988 when fortune favored the left in the legislative elections, before being swept out of the Assembly in the landslide for the center-right in 1993.

Lang's love of the stage served him well during his ministerial career. His good looks, modern fashion sense, and ease in front of the camera kept him in the public eye. He encouraged measures aimed at democratizing culture through mass participation, such as the music festivals that encouraged people to come onto the streets with their instruments, however cacophonous the results. More traditionally, Lang maintained the defense of French culture against negative foreign influences, notably the rampant commercialism of American **cinema** and television, but with little success. However, Lang's unquestionable intellectual talent and his skill as a communicator made him far more useful to the PS than simply as a showman. He ran unsuccessfully for the post of mayor of Paris in 2000 but enjoyed governmental office again between 2000 and 2002 when he was minister of **education** in the Socialist-led government. But Lang's relationship with the PS turned sour in 2007 when, following the failure of the Socialists in both the presidential and the legislative elections, he responded positively to the invitation of the new center-right president, **Nicolas Sarkozy**, to join a commission tasked with reviewing the **constitution** of the republic.

LANGUE D'OC. The old language of southern France. Once widely spoken across the territory stretching below a line from **Bordeaux** to Briançon, it was a language formed by the merging of Latin with the local dialect.

LANGUE D'OIL. In a royal ordinance of 1539 it was stipulated that all official records should be kept in the *langue d'oïl*, as the form of French spoken in **Paris** and the region of the Val-de-Loire was known. This ultimately successful drive toward linguistic uniformity was part of a general attempt by the crown to consolidate its power over the entire kingdom.

LAVOISIER, ANTOINE-LAURENT (1743–1794). The founder of modern chemistry. He was born the son of a lawyer in **Paris** and received an excellent classical **education** as well as a grounding in science. Originally destined for the law, he was ultimately won over by the attractions of science. The first public recognition of his talent in that field came in 1766, when he was awarded the gold medal by the Academy of Sciences for his essay on the best means of illuminating a large town. His reputation was made in 1770 when he demonstrated the inaccuracy of the belief prevailing at the time that the repeated distillation of water converted it into earth. After developing his new theory of combustion, he engaged in fundamental studies on the nature of oxidation, demonstrating the role of oxygen in chemical processes. He formulated the principle of the conservation of matter in chemical reactions, and his work in distinguishing between elements and compounds paved the way for the elaboration of the modern system of chemical nomenclature. Lavoisier was one of the first scientists to introduce quantitative procedures into chemical investigations, and the methodical application of his experimental genius revolutionized chemistry.

While much ahead of his time scientifically, Lavoisier was very much a man of his time politically. In spite of his active support for the **French Revolution** and his service to it, he fell victim to the **Terror**, which closed down the Academy of Sciences and other learned societies. He was arrested on 8 May 1794, summarily tried, and guillotined that afternoon.

LAW, JOHN. *See* FINANCE.

LEDRU-ROLLIN, ALEXANDRE-AUGUSTE (1807–1874). Leading radical republican in mid-19th-century France, famous for his advocacy of universal male suffrage. Born the son of a physician in

Paris, Ledru-Rollin chose to study law and was called to the bar in 1830. He gained his seat in the Chamber of Deputies in 1841 and thereafter earned a reputation as the most radical of the small band of republican deputies in the Chamber. His activities outside parliament led to the founding of the radical daily, *La Réforme*, in 1843 and, most important, his participation in the Banquet Campaign—political meetings billed as dinner receptions to circumvent the legal restrictions put on agitation against the regime of **Louis-Philippe**. When the regime fell in February 1848, Ledru-Rollin's reputation as a radical served him well, and he became minister for the interior in the provisional government. But the conservative reaction that followed in June marked the start of the decline of his political fortunes. He led a new formation of radicals called the Montagne, ran as their candidate in the presidential election in December, and finished third in a field of five. When the government arrested the leaders of the Montagne after a bloody demonstration in June 1849, Ledru-Rollin found exile in England until an amnesty allowed him to return to France in 1870. He was elected to the National Assembly once more in 1871 and spoke effectively in defense of his great cause, universal male suffrage. But the frailty of age and ill health had taken its toll, and he died in 1874. *See also* REVOLUTION OF 1848.

LEGION D'HONNEUR/LEGION OF HONOR. The Légion d'Honneur is an award conferred by the French state. It was originally created by **Napoléon Bonaparte** in May 1812 as a means of securing the support of the great and the good and is bestowed on individuals of eminent merit.

LEGITIMISM (1830–1883). Originally a political movement with the ambition of putting the elder branch of the **Bourbon dynasty** on the throne, it eventually became the expression of a desire among a certain section of the bourgeoisie as well as the aristocracy for the return to a golden age of certainties governed by paternalistic and communitarian values. When the **Revolution of 1830** forced **Charles X** to abdicate, the younger Orleanist line of the Bourbon dynasty ascended the throne in the person of **Louis-Philippe**. While Charles and his family went into exile, hundreds of his supporters in public office refused to swear allegiance to an Orleanist king and registered their protest by effectively retiring from public life. These legitimists reemerged during the **Second Republic**, which lasted from 1848 to 1852, and constituted themselves into the Party of Order, whose aim was to counter the danger posed by **socialism** and popular democracy. They scored a notable victory in the legislative elections of May 1849, but attempts to reach an accommodation with the Orleanists with a view to reestablishing a monarchy in France failed because of the essentially counterrevolutionary mentality of the legitimists. The legitimists withdrew once more from the political arena with the advent of the **Second Empire** but reemerged when the political vacuum that preceded the establishment of the **Third Republic** seemed to offer the faint prospect of another restoration. But the rival branches of the Bourbon dynasty were once more unable to reach the kind of compromise that would enable them to lead a united campaign. The legitimist cause lost its raison d'être with the end of the line, when its pretender to the throne, the childless **Chambord**, died in 1883.

LEOTARD, FRANCOIS (1942–). A leading figure on the center ground of French politics during the 1980s and 1990s. His educational and professional profile is a classic one; a law degree was followed by training for high public office at the elite Ecole Nationale d'Administration, which led initially to the Ministry for Foreign Affairs. He came into politics under the wing of **Valéry Giscard d'Estaing**'s Parti Républicain (PR), a distinct but constituent member of the **Union pour la Démocratie Française (UDF)**, under whose banner he was first elected in 1978. Léotard's relative youth and media-friendly manner meant that after the left came to power in 1981, expectations focused on him as a possible means for renewing the appeal of the center-right parties in French politics. This, allied to his election to the general secretaryship of the PR in 1982, elicited some suspicion among some of the more established leaders of the non-Gaullist right. When the **Socialists** lost the legislative elections of 1986, Léotard in fact supported the Gaullist leader, **Jacques Chirac**, in his successful bid to become prime minister. This resulted in Léotard's appointment as minister for culture and communication from 1986 to 1988. It was under his guidance that the ministry launched the **privatization** of the television channel TF1.

The reelection of **François Mitterrand** in 1988 and the ensuing majority support in parliament for a Socialist administration consigned Léotard once more to the opposition, but his reputation as an economically liberal, modernizing, and moderate center-right politician was established. He was elected a UDF deputy for the Var in the legislative elections that swept the Socialists out of office in 1993 and served in the **Edouard Balladur** government as minister for **defense** during the following two years. Léotard became president of the UDF in 1996, but the prospects for the man once regarded as a future presidential hopeful rapidly dwindled as the decade drew to a close. He resigned the presidency of the UDF in 1998 and relinquished his seat in the National Assembly in 2001, following a scandal concerning irregularities in the funding of the Parti Républicain. *See also* POLITICAL PARTIES.

LE PEN, JEAN-MARIE (1928–). Strident leader of the far-right **Front National (FN)** party. Born in the Breton port of Trinité-sur-Mer, Le Pen was orphaned as a teenager, when his father was lost at sea. While studying law in **Paris**, he began to immerse himself in right-wing politics. He interrupted his law studies to enroll as a paratrooper to fight in the **Indochinese War**. His military activities were interrupted when the attractions of **Poujadism** led him to run successfully for election to the National Assembly in 1956, a seat that he held until 1962. While still a deputy, Le Pen returned to his paratroop unit when it was needed in **Algeria**. His activities there led to accusations that he had participated in the torture inflicted by French troops on captured Algerian fighters against French rule.

A substantial inheritance in the 1970s allowed Le Pen to become a man of independent means, and his rise to the presidency of the FN in 1972 gave him the vehicle he needed to pursue his material ambitions. His campaign to be taken seriously as a presidential candidate in 1981 failed to such an extent that he did not even get on the presidential ballot, but in 1988 he captured slightly more than 14 percent of the vote in the first round of the presidential election. He was elected to the European Parliament in 1984 and 1999, and in the presidential election of 1995 he polled 15 percent of the vote in the first round. Le Pen challenges vigorously, and in the courts if necessary,

anyone who accuses him of racism and purports to espouse very traditional notions of French patriotism. Nonetheless, he has caused outrage
on numerous occasions due to statements that are perceived as nega-
tionist and xenophobic. He was successfully prosecuted for suggesting
in 1987 that the gas chambers in which Jews perished were just a detail
in the history of **World War II**. In 1997 he accused President **Jacques
Chirac** of being in the pay of Jewish organizations and in 2005 he argued that the Nazi occupation of France had not been so inhumane compared to what had happened elsewhere in occupied Europe.

It cannot be denied that Le Pen is a charismatic politician, and his
message of "France for the French" finds a particularly willing audience in the south of the country and in those economically disadvantaged urban areas where insecure communities perceive a direct link
between unemployment, crime, and **immigration**. These were
among the factors behind the shocking result in the first round of the
presidential election of 2002, when Le Pen took almost 17 percent of
the votes cast and beat the incumbent Socialist prime minister, **Lionel
Jospin**, to the second spot behind Chirac. Despite his advancing
years, Le Pen stood again for the presidency in 2007, but there was
little prospect of him repeating the upset caused in 2002. His score of
just under 11 percent in the first round left him well behind the mainstream center-right, Socialist, and centrist candidates. More significantly it underlined the extent to which the eventual winner, the center-right candidate **Nicolas Sarkozy**, has succeeded in stealing Le
Pen's clothes, figuratively speaking, over issues such as immigration
and law and order.

LE ROY LADURIE, EMMANUEL (1929–). Arguably France's most
influential historian since 1945. He was born into a rural, Catholic
milieu in Normandy but left to complete his studies in **Paris**, where
in 1949 he joined the **Parti Communiste Français (PCF)**. The intellectual constraints of Marxism disenchanted Le Roy Ladurie, however, and he resigned from the party in 1956. Fresh inspiration was
provided by the *Annales* school of historians, who believed that the
discipline should take into account material, biological, cultural, and
psychological factors in tracing the evolution of a society so as to
produce a "total history." Appointed to a chair at the University of
Paris in 1970 and also to the chair of modern civilization at the Col-

lège de France in 1973, Le Roy Ladurie continued to build his reputation for his work on the agrarian and rural history of southern France during the medieval and early modern periods and produced in 1975 his most famous book, *Montaillou: Village occitan de 1294 à 1324*. Employing methods influenced by the disciplines of anthropology and semiology, Le Roy Ladurie used the testimonies of villagers as preserved in inquisitorial registers to reconstruct their social attitudes, belief systems, and living conditions. Later works such as *L'Argent, l'amour, et la mort en pays d'Oc* (1980) and *La sorcière de Jasmin* (1983) illustrated the effectiveness of Le Roy Ladurie's methodology in unraveling the symbolic codes and penetrating the subconscious fears that kept those societies together, further justifying his reputation as a historian with an unparalleled gift for understanding communities and changes either ignored or only partially understood by his predecessors. Though showered with academic and state honors, Le Roy Ladurie's appetite for work remained unsatisfied and in 2004 he published a book on the regions of France.

LEVI-STRAUSS, CLAUDE (1908–). Ethnologist, cultural commentator, and famous practitioner of **structuralism**. He was born in Brussels but grew up in **Paris** in a family of Alsatian-Jewish origin. After studying law and philosophy, Lévi-Strauss chose to specialize in ethnology and accepted a position at the University of São Paulo in 1935, taking advantage of the opportunity to conduct fieldwork on the native Indians of the Brazilian interior during the long university vacations.

Lévi-Strauss was fortunate to be able to spend the duration of **World War II** teaching in the United States and thus avoided Nazi persecution. It was at the end of the 1940s that the first of Lévi-Strauss's major theoretical works appeared, the *Elementary Structures of Kinship* (1949). The other seminal works were *Tristes tropiques* (1955), *The Savage Mind* (1962), *Structural Anthropology* (1958, 1973), and *Mythologiques* (1964–1971). Lévi-Strauss's ethnological research was distinguished by the way he worked from a structural linguistic model derived from Ferdinand de Saussure, which allowed him to argue that underlying the vast array of discernible cultural phenomena there exists a much more limited set of patterns, like grammars, that enable us to understand the former.

After returning from the United States, Lévi-Strauss was elected to the prestigious *Collège de France* in 1959, where he was director of the laboratory of social anthropology until he retired in 1982. The importance of his contribution to the intellectual life of France was confirmed in 1973 by his election to the **Académie Française.**

LEVY, BERNARD-HENRI (1948–). Philosopher, novelist, and France's most media-conscious intellectual. He was born in **Algeria** into an affluent family of entrepreneurs who moved to **Paris** in 1954. Lévy's academic brilliance led him to the elite Ecole Normale Supérieure, where he was taught philosophy by figures like **Louis Althusser** and **Jacques Derrida.** Success came early for him, and he was not yet 30 when he published *La barbarie au visage humain* (1977), a denunciation of totalitarianism in all its forms that gained him a wide readership. He was soon bracketed alongside a new wave of intellectuals called the *nouveaux philosophes* or **new philosophers** who brought a mercilessly critical gaze on the assumptions that had shaped the ideologies of both left and right. In *L'Idéologie française* (1981) Lévy took an uncomfortable look at some of the attitudes that define French culture and identified in them the roots of European fascism. Inevitably, the book divided critical opinion in France, but the debate undoubtedly established Lévy as the intellectual most likely to grab the headlines, helped also by his marriage to the beautiful French actress Arielle Dombasle. In addition to philosophical essays, Lévy also wrote prize-winning novels such as *Le diable en tête* (1984) and *Les derniers jours de Beaudelaire* (1988). Ever youthful in appearance and energetic, Lévy has never been reticent in espousing political causes, either through his journalism or on the campaign trail, and in 1994 he led a list of candidates in the elections to the European Parliament to draw attention to the ethnic cleansing in Yugoslavia. In recent years Lévy has been promoting himself on the international stage, and in 2006 he toured the **United States** to discuss his book analyzing American society, *American Vertigo* (2006).

LIBERATION. The liberation of France refers to the process by which the occupying forces of **Germany** were forced to retreat from France at the close of **World War II.** The process began with the Allied landings on the beaches in Normandy in northern France on 6 June 1944, followed by further landings in Provence, in the south, on 15 August 1944. Although the last pockets of German resistance were not cleaned out until the spring of 1945, the key point in the liberation came with the recapture of **Paris**. This task was left to the forces of the Free French army and the **Resistance**. On 19 August 1944 the communist Resistance leader, Rol-Tanguy, organized an uprising against the German occupiers in anticipation of the arrival of the second armored division of the Free French forces, led by General Leclerc. The German commander in Paris, General von Choltitz, surrendered to Rol-Tanguy and Leclerc on 25 August, thereby preparing the way for the return on 26 August of **Charles de Gaulle**, whose triumphal march down the Champs Elysées culminated in his famous speech at the Hôtel de Ville in which he declared Paris a free city.

LIGUES. In the history of modern France, the *ligues* are extraparliamentary political movements aimed at advancing a certain set of right-wing ideas. Classic, or 19th-century, *ligues* like Action Française advocated a return to a hierarchical form of society based on archetypal conservative attachments to family, country, and race. The *ligues* of the 1920s and 1930s, like Solidarité Française, Le Francisme, and Les Croix-de-Feu, were qualitatively different. The first two in particular were heavily influenced by fascist ideas and preached a populist message particularly appealing to the working class and the disaffected lower middle class since it proposed a form of equality that extended only to those of the same race in the bosom of one nation.

LITERATURE. The oldest texts in the French literary tradition date back to medieval times and reflect the way the Catholic Church and religious themes permeated the real and imaginary lives of the people. The oldest literary text in Old French to survive was the *Cantilène de Sainte Eulalie* (c. 880), relating the martyrdom of an obscure Spanish saint. In the 12th century, lyric and romance writing blossomed, notably in the works of Chrétien de Troyes, who modernized themes taken from Latin or Latinized Greek sources to produce works that were the forerunners of the modern novel. The origins of the theater date from slightly later; the first play in Old French on record, *Adam*, dates from the middle of the 12th century and was based on the biblical account of the Fall.

The **Renaissance** was a great incitement to experiment in language. In Rabelais's *Gargantua* (1534), for example, we see on the one hand an uproarious farce about giants but on the other a profound meditation on the quest for truth. The Renaissance was also the period when poetry came into its own, with figures like Du Bellay and Ronsard. In contrast to the early years of the Renaissance, however, the bitter divisions over **religion** that characterized the late Renaissance in France were reflected in the introspective meditations of Montaigne in his *Essais* (1580–1595).

The 17th century was later dubbed by critics the classical age, referring to the attempt, particularly in the theater of Racine and Corneille, to apply the disciplines of time, place, and action that shaped Greek drama. In general, it was a time when the accent was placed on clarity of thought, elegantly and economically expressed. However, as the theater of Molière illustrates, the prevailing perception of good style did not preclude the creation of hilarious social satires or the deftly delivered ironies in La Rochefoucauld's *Maximes* (1665). The temptations of passion, in prose form, were well represented in what was perhaps the first short novel to elicit a debate among the reading public in France, Madame de Lafayette's *La princesse de Clèves* (1678).

The term *age of prose* is often applied to the 18th century, and the term seems apt when one bears in mind the great literary talents and works that characterize that time: Antoine Prévost's *Manon Lescaut*, Voltaire's *Contes*, Jean-Jacques Rousseau's *La nouvelle Héloïse*, Denis Diderot's *La religieuse*, and Chloderos de Laclos's *Les liaisons dangereuses*. But the rise of the novel was not the only literary phenomenon to mark the period. As the work of **Enlightenment** thinkers showed, it was a time of unparalleled reflection on the human condition and of theories speculating on the way to rebuild society. And toward the end of the century, a new dramatic talent emerged that proved wittier and more sparkling than anything since Molière. Pierre-Augustin Caron de Beaumarchais's play *Le mariage de Figaro* (1784) rapidly established itself as the box-office success of the century, not least for its mocking portrayal of the nobility.

In the 19th century, because of the progress of mass literacy and cheaper unit costs due to better technology, the enjoyment of literature became a pursuit of the majority of French people. Newspapers in the 1830s began to boost their circulation by serializing novels, stoking an even greater demand for fiction, which led to the prodigious novel cycles of writers like **Honoré de Balzac**. As the consumption of literature increased massively, debate grew in literary circles about the quality of what was being produced and the aesthetic criteria guiding that production. It was the age when literary movements began to compete with and succeed each other, the most important ones being **romanticism, realism, naturalism**, and **symbolism**.

As France entered the 20th century, its worldwide reputation as a proving ground for literary experiments was confirmed by the talents who came, principally to **Paris**, from all over the world to share in the sense of intellectual adventure. This cosmopolitanism was shown in movements like **surrealism**, the **theater of the absurd**, and **existentialism**, which constitute the literary landmarks of the first half of the 20th century and illustrate the way literary aesthetics were influenced by ideas from disciplines like psychoanalysis and philosophy. Efforts were made in the 1950s and 1960s to rethink the form of the novel in attempts at a **nouveau roman**, but the dominance of literary schools had already given way to more individualistic experiments in the attempt to express personal visions. In recent years young writers like Marie Darrieussecq have gained notoriety for their reworking of Kafkaesque visions while others like Nathalie Nothomb are notable for their prolific output and commercial success. But perhaps the French writer who commands the most attention at home and abroad is Michel Houellebecq, for the nihilistic vision he deploys in novels like *Les particules élémentaires* (1998) and *Plateforme* (2001).

LOCARNO ACCORDS. The agreements reached at the conference that took place in the Swiss town of Locarno from 5–16 October 1925 and negotiated by Gustav Streseman of **Germany, Aristide Briand** of France, and Austen Chamberlain of **Great Britain**. The accords included a Treaty of Mutual Guarantee (Rhineland Pact) that secured the status of the German frontiers of France and Belgium as set by the **Versailles Treaty**, the demilitarization of the Rhineland, and an undertaking not to engage in hostilities. Four nonaggression pacts between Germany and its neighbors were signed, as were two treaties of mutual assistance (between France and Poland and France and Czechoslovakia). In all, seven countries signed the accords. The psychological effect was to renew faith in the belief that the countries of Europe had renounced the option of war in favor of peace and co-operation. This era of hope lasted from 1925 to 1929, but economic depression and the nonpayment of German reparations after 1931 brought it to an end. The Locarno Accords became a dead letter in 1936 when Adolf Hitler ignored the treaties by remilitarizing the Rhineland.

LOIRE RIVER. At just over 1,000 kilometers it is France's longest river and drains an area covering over a fifth of the nation's territory. Originating in the southern highlands of the Cévennes, the river runs north and then turns west to Nantes, where it meets the Atlantic. The westward turn the river takes is the most famous section of its course, much visited by tourists for the idyllic countryside it crosses and the beautiful collection of castles that line the Loire Valley. In 2000 the United Nations Educational, Scientific and Cultural Organization added the central section of the Loire Valley to the list of World Heritage Sites.

LOUIS XIII (1601–1643). Because Louis was only nine when Henri IV died, power was exercised by Louis's mother, Marie de Médicis, in her capacity as regent. However, Louis was finally forced to engage in a trial of wills with his mother that resulted in her condemnation to internal exile and her confinement in the castle of Blois. But his mother's appointment of Cardinal **Richelieu** as chief minister to the crown proved beneficial to Louis. It was Richelieu's policies, aimed at extending the power of the crown in the provinces and against the independent nobility, that paved the way for the triumph of absolute monarchy. When Richelieu died in 1642, Louis appointed a man of very much the same sort, **Jules Mazarin**, who served the king in the manner of his predecessor during the final year of his reign.

LOUIS XIV (1638–1715). Also called the Sun King for the opulent manner in which life revolved around him because of the way his regime carried the practice of absolute monarchy to its apogee. When he acceded to the throne in 1643, Louis XIV inherited a country that was prosperous and powerful. While the period of fierce opposition to the crown on the part of the nobles who constituted the **Fronde** had a deep effect on the king, once his reign was established, with the brilliant **Jean-Baptiste Colbert** at his side, Louis came to preside over a supremely centralized system that left him in control of the key levers of the **economy** and the administration. This helps to explain the confidence with which he built up, at Versailles, a court of grandeur unequaled elsewhere in Europe.

On the domestic front, **Jacques Bénigne Bossuet** elaborated the intellectual justification that underpinned the absolute monarchy, namely, the idea that the king was God's lieutenant on earth. The impression of divine brilliance was reinforced by the sumptuous nature of court life, the glittering entertainments orchestrated by the composer Lulli, and the productions of plays by Racine, Corneille, and Molière, which added to the impression that the heart of European cultural life lay in Versailles.

On the foreign front, the expansionist policies of the French crown were characteristic of a power that would not countenance any opposition and led to a long series of military engagements. France's attempts to profit from the death of Phillip IV of Spain in 1665 resulted in a war with Spain and Holland that was not resolved until 1679. War erupted again in 1688 owing to France's policy of annexation and this time prompted the formation of a coalition comprising the German princes, Spain, Sweden, Holland, and England in an effort to contain the French. The peace that came in 1697 was short lived, as in 1702 France launched itself once more into war over the succession to the Spanish throne. The outcome of this policy by the time of Louis XIV's death in 1715 was that although France had expanded to the east and was now in firm possession of **Strasbourg**, the deficit in the crown's finances amounted to the enormous sum of 2 billion livres. *See also* FOREIGN POLICY.

LOUIS XVI (1754–1793). The last king before the **French Revolution**. While not lacking in intelligence, Louis XVI was a timid and irresolute person, unable to bridle the excesses of his queen, **Marie Antoinette**, and her acolytes. The collapse of his regime was marked by a series of miscalculations that illustrated the extent to which the king was out of touch with his subjects and failed to appreciate the financial constraints faced by the royal exchequer. The cost of France's participation in the American war of independence rendered the crown's finances even more parlous. However, convening the **Estates General** to secure approval for further demands on the taxpayers was a high-risk strategy. Having let the genie of open debate out of the bottle, the king only made it more animated by his clumsy attempts to force it back. Within six weeks of their convocation on 5 May 1789, the Estates General had given way to a revolutionary parliament, and the king found himself caught in a fatal chain of events. Moreover, the king helped neither himself nor those arguing for a constitutional monarchy when he tried to escape from France with his family in June 1791, resulting in their arrest at **Varennes**. This act confirmed the suspicion in the minds of many that the king was in league with France's enemies. Although there were still influential moderates in the **Convention**, they could not prevent the death sentence passed on Louis XVI, and he was executed on 21 January 1793.

LOUIS XVIII (1755–1824). King of France. He was born in Versailles on 17 November 1755, Louis-Stanislas-Xavier, the third of four sons resulting from the marriage between Louis XV and Marie-Josephe of Saxony. As the 16-year-old comte de Provence, he was married in 1771 to Marie-Joséphine, daughter of the king of Sardinia and Savoy. This was an unhappy union that ended with her death in 1810.

As a young man Louis was unable to engage in royal sporting pursuits because of a malformation of the hips. As a result he turned to the cultivation of the arts and an appetite for fine food. These sedentary pleasures explain his problems with obesity. Unlike his older brother King **Louis XVI**, Louis managed to escape the **French Revolution**, fleeing to Belgium on the night of 20–21 June 1791. Louis and his younger brother, Charles, comte d'Artois, joined the forces of the **counterrevolution**, which had rallied to their cousin the prince de Condé and allied with the Austro-Prussian army that entered France in 1792. The defeat of the invading army at **Valmy** resulted in years of exile in many different parts of Europe. Louis had to wait until the invasion of France by forces of the alliance against **Napoléon Bonaparte** in 1814 before the white flag of the old monarchy could be raised again, this time under the protection of Wellington's army in **Bordeaux** (12 March).

Given that the leaders of the coalition against Bonaparte were themselves not unanimously convinced that a **Bourbon** restoration would secure lasting peace, Louis handled the relationship vis-à-vis his foreign allies and his domestic audience astutely, issuing a declaration in which he maintained his historic right to the throne (his nephew, Louis XVII, had died in June 1795) while confirming his acceptance of the basic institutions of the previous regimes. The Treaty of Paris that followed established peace between France and her neighbors and the Constitutional Charter established a new relationship between the French and a more moderate monarch. However, discontent soon resurfaced and encouraged Bonaparte to make a comeback from exile in the last desperate gamble known as the **Hundred Days**. Louis XVIII escaped **Paris** by night on 20 March 1815, his flight prompted by army defections to Bonaparte, but returned on 8 July, after Bonaparte's defeat at Waterloo and the machinations of figures like **Joseph Fouché** in France had paved the way for a second, bloodless restoration. On this occasion the victorious allies were more demanding, and the terms of the second Treaty of Paris (20 November 1815) were more exacting than those of the first.

The political climate was now more embittered, with hard-line royalists (ultras) pressing for retribution against those who had sided with Bonaparte; the monarchist reaction was called the White Terror. The ultras, who rallied to the king's less moderate younger brother, brought pressure to bear on the conciliatory figures chosen by Louis to head the administration, the duc de Richelieu and Elie Decazes. Ultraroyalist pressure forced Louis XVIII to dismiss Decazes and approve a new system under Richelieu of double voting, which strengthened even further the position of the most privileged and conservative members of society at election time. Richelieu was compelled to resign in December 1821, and the ultras finally got their man, comte Joseph de Villèle, in the driving seat as the **finance** minister in the new administration. Illness forced Louis XVIII to take a more remote interest in government, and he was the last French monarch to die peacefully in his palace, on 16 September 1824. Not a dashing or inspiring figure, Louis XVIII was nonetheless politically aware and much more conscious than many royalists of the need to adapt the monarchy to the irreversible political and social changes that had been brought about by the French Revolution and the Napoleonic era. *See also* CHARTER OF 1814.

LOUIS-NAPOLEON. See BONAPARTE, LOUIS-NAPOLEON.

LOUIS-PHILIPPE (1773–1850). Duc d'Orléans and king of the French. He was born in **Paris**, the first son of Louis-Philippe-Joseph, duc d'Orléans and head of the younger branch of the **Bourbon** family. Like previous ducs d'Orléans, Louis-Philippe's father had aspirations to the throne, and he turned his Parisian home, the Palais-Royal, into a meeting place for opponents of **Louis XVI**'s government. Louis-Philippe's enlistment in the republican armies after the **French Revolution** was perhaps not surprising given that his education had been entrusted to his father's former mistress, comtesse de Genlis, who had trained him in the ideas of the **Enlightenment**. However, Louis-Philippe became involved in Charles-François Dumouriez's plot against the Republic and had to flee in April 1793. His father, who had changed his name to Philippe Egalité and been elected to the **Convention**, was found guilty of complicity in the conspiracy and executed.

After 1793 Louis-Philippe spent 21 years in exile, largely in England, and gave his allegiance to the exiled Bourbon pretender to the throne, Louis, comte de Provence. In 1808 he married Marie-Amélie, daughter of the Bourbon king of the Two Sicilies, and brought his family back to France in 1814. But **Napoléon Bonaparte**'s return from exile forced them to flee to England until 1817. Louis XVIII was suspicious of Louis-Philippe's ambitions, but the latter's chance was not to come until 1830, when Louis XVIII's far less flexible brother and successor, **Charles X**, lost control of the political situation in Paris and prompted the deputies in parliament to invite Louis-Philippe to occupy the throne. Thus on 9 August 1830 he took an oath to obey the revised Charter (*see* CHARTER OF 1830) and became Louis-Philippe I, king of the French. He never openly defied his ministers or parliament but was not averse to using manipulation to get his way. Together with his first minister, **François Guizot**, Louis-Philippe made his reign coincide with a period of economic growth and stability in France. But their unwillingness to countenance genuine democratic reform was out of step with the changes occurring in French society, and when a Parisian street demonstration turned into an insurrection in February 1848, Louis-Philippe was forced to abdicate. He and his family took refuge once more in England, where he died on 26 August 1850. *See also* NOTABLES.

LUNEVILLE, TREATY OF. Peace treaty with the Austrians signed in 1801 and followed by the **Treaty of Amiens** in 1802. It brought to an end almost a decade of uninterrupted military hostility between France and her neighbors and allowed **Napoléon Bonaparte** to make unassailable his position as the master of France.

LYON. Originally founded as a Roman colony in 43 BC, it developed just north of where the **Rhône** and Saône Rivers converge, with the historic city center sitting on a kind of *presqu'île* or peninsula. Though France's third city behind **Paris** and **Marseille**, the 1999 census revealed that Lyon, together with its suburbs and satellite towns, is France's largest metropolitan area after Paris with almost 1.7 million inhabitants. Its status was confirmed as the hub of traffic and commerce for the south when the high-speed train link, the TGV, reached Lyon in 1983, making the rail connection with central Paris more convenient than the plane. Lyon is an elegant and prosperous city whose wealth was built on the silk trade. Until new technology made it largely redundant, Lyon also had its own stock exchange and has developed considerably as a financial center since the 1980s. Its international profile is underlined by the fact that it is the headquarters of Interpol and Euronews. A modern metro system, its own opera company, and its situation at the heart of a region famous for its gastronomy have made Lyon a magnet for tourists as well as for businesses.

LYOTARD, JEAN-FRANCOIS. *See* POSTMODERNISM.

– M –

MACMAHON, MAURICE DE (1808–1893). Second president of the **Third Republic** and famous for his attempt to stem the rise of republicanism by dissolving the Chamber of Deputies. A distinguished career soldier who received his marshal's baton in the Austro-Sardinian War of 1859, MacMahon was wounded and captured in the **Franco-Prussian War**. He was released after peace negotiations began and had overall command of the troops that suppressed the **Commune**. Perceived by the monarchist and conservative National Assembly as a means of preventing the permanent establishment of a republic, he was named as the presidential replacement to **Adolphe Thiers**, and with the **duc de Broglie** as his prime minister, a clerical and conservative government was established. Although resolutely conservative, MacMahon refused any appeals to support under-handed attempts to restore a monarchy in France and saw himself as the guardian of the existing constitutional arrangements. By 1876 the increasing representation won by the republicans in the Chamber of Deputies meant that MacMahon had to ask the republican, **Jules Simon**, to form a government.

As a result of the liberal legislation proposed by the Simon government, MacMahon persuaded himself that the government was succumbing to undue influence from the left and forced Simon's resignation in a letter dated 16 May 1877. The 363 republican deputies in the Chamber rejected the new government proposed by Broglie, and although MacMahon acted within the constitutional law when he announced the dissolution of the Chamber on 25 May, the widespread opposition to his action meant that he was perceived as having abused his presidential power. The republicans won the elections that followed and a little over a year later MacMahon was forced to resign over his refusal to replace some royalist generals. The coup of 16 May, as it was called, marked the only attempt by a president of the Third Republic to exercise his prerogative to dissolve the lower chamber. Thereafter the Chamber of Deputies became supreme, with all that this implied for the weakened executive of the Third Republic.

MAGINOT LINE. Technically formidable system of fortifications in northeastern France named after the minister of war in the 1920s who was instrumental in its construction, André Maginot. The chief military adviser in its design was Marshal **Philippe Pétain**, and it typified his belief in the superiority of defensive military strategies. Conceived as a means of compensating for France's demographic and industrial inferiority in relation to **Germany** and of defending the most vulnerable part of its frontier, the Maginot line fostered a false sense of security and, remarkably with hindsight, did not extend to cover the Franco-Belgian border. However, the German blitzkrieg in May 1940 rapidly exposed the inadequacies of the static defensive strategy behind the Maginot line and rendered the line itself redundant. *See also* ARMED FORCES; WORLD WAR II.

MALLARME, STEPHANE (1842–1898). French **symbolist** poet of great influence. A lycée teacher all his life, in spite of his poetic vocation, Mallarmé moved to the post of English teacher at the Lycée Condorcet in **Paris** in 1871. It was shortly afterward that he began holding afternoon gatherings for young Parisian writers. This group quickly turned into a band of disciples with the same love of poetry and commitment to perfection. Mallarmé's output was slim but dense with significance, taking the reader, in works like *Igitur ou la folie d'Elbehnon* (1869), and *Hérodiade* (1871), on a mystery tour of sounds and symbols deliberately charged with fugitive meanings. Mallarmé's legacy provided a fertile field of study in poetry and linguistics, and his attempt to fuse the arts bore fruit when **Debussy** set "*L'Après-midi d'un faune*" to **music**. Mallarmé remained in his post at the Lycée Condorcet until his sudden death in 1898. *See also* LITERATURE.

MALRAUX, ANDRE (1901–1976). Writer, soldier, art critic, and minister of culture under **Charles de Gaulle**. He was born into a modest family that had been established in Dunkirk for generations. By his teenage years Malraux already exhibited a ferociously inquisitive intelligence that would not be channeled in conventional terms. He abandoned his studies at age 17 and soon persuaded a seller of rare books to recruit him. The young man's self-confidence and ability as an autodidact soon brought him into contact with figures working at the leading edge of **art**, and when his first publication appeared, it contained illustrations by Georges Braque and Fernand Léger.

Malraux's greatest works appeared within a decade: *Les conquérants* (1928), *La condition humaine* (1933), and *L'Espoir* (1937). The theme running through all three novels—the first two set in Asia, the third in Spain—is the struggle against oppression. Malraux's reputation as a left-wing defender of the people was immeasurably enhanced by his participation in the Spanish Civil War as a fighter pilot on the side of the republicans. His fight against fascism continued during **World War II**, when he served with distinction in the Free French forces. But many of his left-wing friends turned against him after 1945 owing to his conversion to the center-right politics of **Gaullism**. In his defense, Malraux argued that the ideals of the left had been betrayed by Stalinism, but the shift in allegiance left a legacy of bitterness. However, Malraux proved an energetic minister of culture under de Gaulle, and he played a leading role in the democratization of culture during the 1960s by initiating the creation of a regional network of *Maisons de la culture*.

After 1945 Malraux's publications came to reflect his preoccupation with art as a kind of secular salvation for man, and this sensibility is reflected in his last major work before his death, *Le miroir des limbes* (1976). After diminishing for some years, his reputation as an inspirational defender of the liberty of the human spirit was restored in the 1990s, and in 1996 his remains were moved to the Pantheon, placing him alongside the other great figures of French letters. *See also* LITERATURE.

MANET, EDOUARD (1832–1883). Leading painter of the **Second Empire** and of the **Third Republic**. Manet was born in **Paris**, the son of a magistrate. He first gained notoriety at the *Salon des refusés* in 1863 with his painting *Déjeuner sur l'herbe*, and toward the end of that decade he assumed leadership of a young group of realist artists including **Edgar Degas**, **Claude Monet**, and **Auguste Renoir**. During the 1870s he moved in style and technique in the same direction as the impressionists and concentrated on contemporary urban themes in his painting, but he did not agree to participate in impressionist exhibitions. He was made a chevalier of the **Legion of Honor** by the French government in 1881. *See also* ART.

MARAT, JEAN-PAUL (1743–1793). One of the most famous of the **Montagnards** in the **French Revolution**. His dramatic death has been the subject of paintings and plays. He was born in Boudry, Switzerland, but made his reputation as a physician in London before coming to France to be the personal physician of the comte d'Artois, the future **Charles X**. The events of 1789 led Marat into journalism and in September of that year he became editor of *L'Ami du Peuple* (The friend of the people), through the pages of which he became a potent advocate of the most radical democratic reforms then under consideration. His popularity among the revolutionary mass outside the **Convention** made him a target for the conservative **Girondins**, whose failure to convict him after attempting to have him arraigned before a revolutionary tribunal marked their failing grip on the Revolution. The popular perception of Marat as a martyr for the Revolution was powerfully reinforced by his fatal stabbing in his bath at the hands of Charlotte Corday, a young Girondin supporter from Normandy who had gained entry to his chambers by claiming his protection.

MARCHAIS, GEORGES (1920–1997). Secretary-general of the **Parti Communiste Français (PCF)** from 1972 to 1994. He was born the son of a miner in La Hoguette (Calvados) and trained as a metalworker. He took an active part in **trade union** activity in **Paris** at the end of **World War II** before joining the PCF in 1946. Marchais progressed rapidly upward through the echelons of the party, joining the Central Committee in 1956 and the Politburo in 1959. His promotion to the post of assistant secretary-general in 1970 effectively put him in charge of the party because of the declining health of the leader, **Waldeck Rochet**, and he acceded formally to the post of secretary-general in 1972.

From an outsider's point of view, the choice of Marchais to lead the PCF was not an obvious one; he was neither an intellectual nor was he one of those Communists distinguished by a record of heroism in the **Resistance**. But Marchais's strength lay in his knowledge as a party man. He had known how to profit from the goodwill of his mentors on the way up in the party, and he used the party machinery to make his position unassailable for over two decades. While his forthright manner might have appealed to the party faithful, its appeal to the wider electorate in France was limited. Marchais was sufficiently astute to realize the need for an alliance with the **Socialists** to defeat the right, and this was embodied in the accord on a **Common Program** for government that was struck in 1972. However, the resurgent Socialists proved more adept at expanding their influence among left-wing voters than the PCF, and when the accord broke down five years later, it was the PCF that had been pushed further to the margins of political life in France.

Thereafter, Marchais articulated a PCF relationship with the Socialists that veered from recrimination to unenthusiastic cooperation, as was illustrated by his rival candidacy to **François Mitterrand**, the Socialist leader, in the 1981 presidential election. During this time frustrations also emerged within the party, particularly with what some critics saw as Marchais's failure to mark the PCF's ideological independence in relation to Moscow and steer the party toward a more pluralist vision of its mission and a more openly democratic way of operating. Marchais's reaction was to take one step forward and two steps back, on the one hand initiating discussion in the party and on the other using the party machinery to force his critics into silence or out of the party. The Marchais years were marked by a steady exodus of intellectuals from the PCF and growing discontent among the grassroots. The collapse of the Berlin Wall and the subsequent end to the Cold War undermined many of the rationalizations that Marchais had put forward for maintaining centralized control of the party and not fundamentally reforming the ideological mission of the PCF. When Marchais produced a report in 1993 calling for the abandonment of "democratic centralism" in favor of "democracy," it was too little too late and in the eyes of many of his critics inside and outside the party, failed to salvage his reputation after he declined to seek a renewal of his mandate as party leader at the PCF congress in 1994. The low esteem in which he was held by his comrades was illustrated by the ridicule heaped on his legacy by the communist newspaper *L'Humanité*, shortly before his death of heart failure.

MARIANNE. The name given to the female figurehead who came to symbolize the spirit of the Republic after 1789. Her head adorns French stamps and innumerable busts of her likeness sit ceremonially in, and on, French public buildings.

MARIE-ANTOINETTE (MARIE-ANTOINETTE-JOSEPHE-JEANNE D'AUTRICHE-LORRAINE) (1755–1793). Queen of France at the time of the **French Revolution**. She was born in Vienna, the 11th daughter of Francis I, Holy Roman Emperor, and his wife, Maria Theresa. She married the future **Louis XVI** in 1770, but by the time he ascended the throne in 1774, his inadequacies as a husband had encouraged her to find solace in the extravagance and frivolity for which she became infamous. The costly follies and corruption of her circle contributed to the debts that burdened the French state in the 1770s and 1780s. Furthermore, her insensitivity to the needs of her subjects, most famously when she replied "let them eat cake" on being told that they were hungry, fostered a deep popular animosity toward her. Unlike her indecisive husband after the events of 1789, Marie-Antoinette showed a considerable capacity for intrigue in the endeavor to rescue the fortunes of the royal family, first through secret negotiations with pro-monarchist deputies in the National Assembly and then through the encouragement she gave her brother in Austria, Leopold II, to mount military action against the revolutionary regime in France. These activities enraged the French and fueled the determination to abolish the monarchy in France that came to fruition on 10 August 1792. Marie-Antoinette found little pity when she was brought before a revolutionary tribunal on 14 October 1793, and two days later her sentence of death by **guillotine** was carried out.

LA MARSEILLAISE. National anthem of France. Originally entitled "Chant de guerre de l'armée du Rhin," it was written on 24 April 1792 by captain of engineers and amateur musician Claude-Joseph Rouget de Lisle, in response to the plea from the mayor of **Strasbourg** for a marching song to lift the spirit of the French troops in the face of impending action against the Austrians. It was the popularity of the anthem with volunteer army units from **Marseille** that earned it the name "Marseillaise." A decree passed by the **Convention** on 14 July 1794 made it the national anthem, but it was banned at various times, not least by **Napoléon Bonaparte** during the life of his empire, before being permanently reinstated in 1879. *See also* FRENCH REVOLUTION.

MARSEILLE. The heart of a metropolitan area of over 1.5 million inhabitants according to the census of 1999, and also the capital of the Provence-Alpes Côte d'Azur region. Its origins can be traced back to 600 BC and the arrival of Greeks from Phoceae, and it is often popularly referred to as *la ville phocéenne*. Its famous boulevard, la Canebière, is the main central thoroughfare, and the town itself has long been a cultural crossroads. For much of the 20th century it suffered from its reputation as the favorite city in France for the implantation of gangster activities from Italy and elsewhere in the **Mediterranean**. Since the 1950s it has also housed an influx of immigrants from North Africa, and this has exacerbated the rise of **Front National** elements in the area. Marseille is a place of powerful allegiances, whether to the parties of the left, the famous soccer club Olympique de Marseille, or the **trade unions** that paralyzed the port for weeks in 2007. To combat the decline that became marked after the oil crises of the 1970s, Marseille benefited considerably from the infrastructure funding provided by the **European Union**, and since the late 1990s the city has been dynamic in expanding the service sector of its economy. But it is still true to say that it suffers from a greater concentration of socioeconomic problems than the other great conurbations of France. Marseille is nonetheless a great historical center whose beauty has been revived in recent years with the renovation of its ancient port, dating back to the 8th century, and the investment in social housing and transport aimed at improving its profile as the great urban center of the southern French coast.

MARSHALL PLAN. Proposal for large-scale economic aid to Europe put forward by United States secretary of state George Marshall on 5 June 1947. Its primary purpose was to set the economy of Europe back on its feet and thereby bind **Germany** to the West and protect countries like France and Italy from the political instability caused by economic hardship, especially in view of the strong communist movements in those countries and their loyalty to the **Soviet Union**. The Franco-American agreement that allowed France to become a recipient of aid was signed on 28 June and was the object of a forceful denunciation by the **Parti Communiste Français**. In the four years that followed, France received $2.6 billion (out of a total of $13 billion) largely in the form of grants that played a vital role in restoring much-needed investment in transport systems, electricity generation, and basic industries such as cement, coal, and steel. The program of aid envisaged by the Marshall Plan came to an end in 1952.

MATIGNON AGREEMENTS. Result of negotiations that put an end to the wave of largely spontaneous strikes and factory occupations expressing the hopes of ordinary people following the electoral victory of the **Popular Front**. The agreements, adopted on 7 June 1936, enshrined the right of free collective bargaining and the right of workers to join unions, provided average wage rises of 12 percent for all workers, and instituted an amnesty for strikers. The agreements were signed by the employers' organization, the **Confédération Générale du Travail (CGT)**, and the government. There were concessions and gains on all sides, but the agreements ultimately allowed the employers to get back to business, the CGT to restore its organizational control over the workers, and the government to start managing the economy. The agreements marked the attempt at a new style of government through discussion and consensus and were rapidly followed by a series of legislative measures that ushered in the 40-hour week and paid holidays for workers.

MAUPASSANT, GUY DE (1850–1893). Naturalist novelist and supreme exponent of the art of the short story. Despite the aristocratic particle in his name, Maupassant was of Norman bourgeois origin and grew up in an unhappy broken home, stifled by his neurotic and sickly mother. He began writing in the late 1860s and was taken under **Gustave Flaubert**'s wing until Flaubert died in 1880. It was also the year that Maupassant tasted literary success with the publication of *Boule de suif.* Up to that point Maupassant had supported himself through his work as a civil servant, and in his social life he had developed a liking for the pleasures to be found in the boating taverns along the **Seine**, the most likely source of the syphilis he contracted in 1876. During the decade of 1880 to 1890 Maupassant's output was in 27 published volumes, but it is chiefly for his short stories and their usually powerful and pessimistic evocation of human foibles and obsessions that he is remembered. The symptoms of madness caused by tertiary syphilis meant that Maupassant had to be institutionalized in early 1892. He died of cerebral neurosyphilis in the following year at the age of 43. *See also* LITERATURE; NATURALISM.

MAUROY, PIERRE (1928–). Socialist politician and former prime minister. He was born the son of a primary schoolteacher in Cartignies (Nord) and had a modest technical education before himself entering the teaching profession as a provider of technical training. He entered politics early, initially as national secretary of the Socialist youth movement in 1950, and by 1966 had risen to become deputy secretary-general of the party, then called the **Section Française de l'Internationale Ouvrière (SFIO)**. When the SFIO was reborn as the **Parti Socialiste (PS)** in 1969, Mauroy became the deputy to **François Mitterrand**, the PS first secretary. In 1973 Mauroy became the mayor of Lille, and in 1978 he was elected for the first time to the National Assembly.

Mauroy was a well-established and senior figure in the PS when Mitterrand was elected to the **presidency** of France in 1981. Mauroy's reputation as solid, reliable, and tough made him an obvious candidate for the post of prime minister. But his tenure was a difficult one. He led a government that attempted to pursue reflationary economic policies in France, while its major trading partners had opted for austerity measures. When the inevitable crisis occurred in 1993, leading to three devaluations of the franc, Mauroy was forced into a completely different course that involved a painful program of cost cutting. He was never comfortable with the conservative economic policies forced on his government, and in 1984, in the face of growing voter resentment and a sharp decline in his personal standing in the opinion polls, he resigned.

As mayor of Lille between 1973 and 2001, Mauroy promoted his town energetically as the hub of the railway and commercial network linking France with the Low Countries and beyond, especially since the connection of Lille to the Eurostar rail service connecting **Great Britain** to Europe via the Channel tunnel. After 2001 Mauroy's service to Lille was recognized when he was given the title of honorary mayor.

MAY 1968. *See* STUDENT REBELLIONS.

MAZARIN, JULES (1602–1661). Diplomat, cardinal, and a major influence on European as well as French politics during the 1640s and 1650s. He was born Giulio Raimondo Mazzarino, a papal subject in the kingdom of Naples. Service in the papal army led to service in papal diplomacy, which in 1630 brought Mazarin in contact with **Richelieu** as the result of his mission to France in the papacy's effort to bring about an end to the war between Spain and France over the succession to the crown of Mantua. Mazarin was enormously impressed by Richelieu and was able to renew the acquaintance when he was sent as ambassador to the French court in 1634. On his recall to Rome in 1636 Mazarin became one of the leaders of the French faction there, and his reward came when he was put forward by **Louis XIII** for the post of cardinal in 1638. Granted French naturalization in 1639, Mazarin returned to **Paris** in 1640 and finally forsook papal service for the service of France.

The dominant influence of Richelieu on French politics ended with his death in 1642. But this was soon supplanted by the dominant influence of Mazarin, especially in his role as chief minister after the death of Louis XIII in 1643, when he and the regent, Anne of Austria, governed the destiny of France on behalf of the young **Louis XIV**. Mazarin's skills were instrumental in putting down the challenge to the absolute power of the monarchy represented by the **Fronde**, and he reinforced the mechanisms, especially financial, by which the provinces could be controlled from Paris. Mazarin's attitude to government was undoubtedly nepotistic, and he used his influence to amass a vast personal fortune, which on occasion he placed at the service of France. In the sphere of European politics, Mazarin never renounced the ambition in which he had been steeped as a papal diplomat, and by the early 1660s he had played a crucial role in securing peace among the major powers of Christendom. Athough he considered it on a number of occasions, Cardinal Mazarin died never having been fully ordained a priest.

MEDIA. *See* BROADCAST MEDIA.

MEDITERRANEAN SEA. The sea linking Europe, Africa, and Asia that has played a crucial role in the economic, political, and cultural development of the countries bordering it. The name by which it is now commonly known derives from the seventh-century Latin term *mare medi terra*, meaning "sea between the lands" and is an apt expression of the sea's position as a meeting point between continents. It covers 2.5 million square kilometers and is almost entirely landlocked except for the 14-kilometer-wide opening to the Atlantic at its westernmost point, known as the Straits of Gibraltar. The towns along France's Mediterranean coast bear witness to France's evolution, from antiquity to modern times. Thus Narbonne and **Marseille** in the west prospered as administrative and commercial centers during the days of the Roman Empire, while towns like Nice in the east grew considerably in the 19th century due to the cultural and economic reality of **tourism** invading modern France, led originally by the English. In high summer the Mediterranean coast road is usually congested as tourists attempt to visit fabled destinations such as the village of St. Tropez or small towns like Cannes.

While the thrust of French **foreign policy** since **World War II** has been to secure good relations with its neighbors in the north through the building of the **European Union (EU)**, France's former colonial relationships with North Africa have made it particularly sensitive to the way it is perceived in those countries. President **Nicolas Sarkozy** in particular has tried to breathe new life into the concept of a transnational Mediterranean entity, such as in a campaign speech in February 2007 when he evoked the possibility of a Mediterranean Union modeled on the EU.

MENDES-FRANCE, PIERRE (1907–1982). Radical politician and a major influence on the democratic left during the **Fourth** and early **Fifth Republics**. He was born into a family of Jewish origin in **Paris**, where he received his secondary and university education. He made an early name for himself through his book *La banque internationale* (1930), in which he argued that problems faced by modern economies were international and required international solutions. He was elected a Radical deputy for Louviers in 1932 and was re-elected in 1936 as an ardent supporter of the **Popular Front** strategy. He joined the air force when war broke out in 1939 but was eventually arrested and imprisoned by the **Vichy regime**. Mendès-France managed to escape from prison in June 1941 and found secret passage to England in March 1942, where he joined **Charles de Gaulle**.

He was appointed economics minister in de Gaulle's first government after the **liberation** but resigned in April 1945 after de Gaulle ignored his proposal for a policy of economic austerity. He was subsequently elected to the constituent assembly in 1946 and then to the National Assembly in 1951. It was during the following period that Mendès-France became a rallying figure for the more progressive and technocratic members of the center-left, particularly for his attitude to **decolonization**. He advocated negotiations with the anticolonialists in Indochina as early as 1950, and after the start of his premiership on 18 June 1954, he moved quickly to open direct negotiations to bring the **Indochinese War** to an end. Mendès-France also loosened the constraints on self-determination in Tunisia and strengthened **Great Britain**'s commitment to the security of continental Europe. But his focus on **foreign policy** left him unguarded against his domestic enemies, and they brought down his government on 2 February 1955.

Mendès-France's moral vision and his openness to progressive alliances were the qualities that, to many minds, made him the conscience of the left. He was instrumental in bringing the different strands of the noncommunist left together behind the Republican Front coalition that won the elections of 1956. But his opposition to the hard-line policy of **Guy Mollet**'s government over **Algeria** led him to resign from the coalition in May 1957. As a spokesperson for the democratic left opposition, he opposed the terms of the treaty leading to the formation of the **European Economic Community** and resisted the return of de Gaulle to power. The latter move cost him his parliamentary seat in the elections of November 1958. Mendès-France subsequently left the Radical party and joined a splinter group of the **Section Française de l'Internationale Ouvrière**, the Parti Socialiste Autonome, which disagreed with the policies of Mollet. He was returned as deputy for Grenoble in 1967 and came to public attention again, this time for the high-profile support he gave to the workers and young people involved in the **student rebellions** of May 1968. But the Gaullist landslide in the election that followed swept him out of his seat, and he quit active politics soon thereafter. Mendès-France's moral and intellectual influence on the democratic left was not forgotten, and **François Mitterrand** was conspicuously generous in the attention he paid to Mendès-France when he assumed his presidential functions in 1981.

MEROVINGIAN DYNASTY. The establishment of this dynasty symbolized the triumph of the Francs Saliens, or Franks, and the emergence of **Gaul** as a cohesive territorial entity under one king. The Franks were a Germanic people who, under their king, Clovis (481–511), began to spread into northern France toward the end of the fifth century. Around 486 Clovis defeated the Gallo-Roman army at Soissons and was soon recognized by Rome as the legitimate power in Gaul. A decade later he converted to Christianity, thus becoming a figurehead for the campaign to drive out the pagan and the heretic from Gaul. At a battle near Poitiers in 507, he defeated the Visigoths who had come up from the south and went on to install his court in **Paris** and secure his place in history as the first king of France. His sons completed the process of unifying Gaul under the Franks with the conquest of the kingdom of Burgundy in 534 and the acquisition of Provence from the Visigoths in 536, firmly establishing the Merovingian dynasty, whose name was derived from Clovis's grandfather, Mérovée.

In some respects the Gallo-Roman cultural legacy continued to subsist alongside the Germanic culture of the Franks. But a gradual process of osmosis meant that by the seventh century the foundations were being laid for the emergence of what became a distinctly French medieval culture. In socioeconomic terms the seventh century was marked by the appearance of the vast estates that underpinned the power of the king, the aristocracy, and the clergy. The church and the monarchy increased enormously in power, and the evangelization of the country served to erode the old cultural and ethnic distinctions, binding the people into a common Christian identity.

In political terms, however, the Franks remained a warrior race, and their aspiration to power could only be satisfied militarily. Clovis's successors found themselves in a perpetual struggle to maintain their authority in the face of persistent plots and assassinations. By the reign of Dagobert (629–639), the challenge to the center was so strong that regions like Aquitaine and Provence were already in the process of acquiring a considerable degree of autonomy in their dealings with the monarch. The shrinkage in the effective deployment of Merovingian power led to a reorganization and consolidation of the territory under Merovingian control at the beginning of the eighth century. The threat of destruction at the hands of the invading Muslims from Spain was neutralized by Charles Martel in 732 when he stopped their advance between Poitiers and Tours, and after his death his son (741–768) began his reign as Pépin le Bref by deposing the Merovingian king and crowning himself king of the Franks in 751. Thus the foundation was laid for the ascension of the **Carolingian dynasty**, and a new chapter was opened in the history of Gaul.

MESSMER, PIERRE (1916–2007). Center-right politician and former prime minister of France. A career civil servant in the foreign ministry, Messmer worked in Indochina after **World War II** before taking a succession of posts in Africa during the 1950s. Crucially, he supported the return of **Charles de Gaulle** during the political crisis of 1958 that convulsed the **Fourth Republic**. Messmer became the Gaullist defense minister in 1960 and followed de Gaulle out of office when the general resigned in 1969. Unexpectedly, the presidency of **Georges Pompidou** again brought the opportunity of high office when Messmer was asked to succeed **Jacques Chaban-Delmas** as prime minister in July 1972. Messmer headed three governments but proved unable to provide the kind of leadership that inspired confidence, and it was precisely the issue of confidence, or the lack of it in terms of the public perception of his governmental team, that forced his resignation in 1974. Thereafter he held his seat in the National Assembly from 1974 to 1988 and was also mayor of Sarrebourg from 1971 to 1989. Messmer served his country faithfully for many years but made a modest mark on the course of public life in France. He was elected to the **Académie Française** in 1999.

METRIC SYSTEM. The decimal system of weights and measures introduced throughout France in 1791. It was part of a series of reforms introduced after the **French Revolution** of 1789 with the purpose of creating a new society within the borders of a unified nation-state.

MICHELET, JULES (1798–1874). A historian famous for his work on the **French Revolution**. Born in **Paris**, Michelet, the son of a struggling printer, used his intellectual gifts to become a prize-winning scholar. After acquiring his doctorate and passing the *agrégation* examination in 1819, Michelet followed the classic path of French intellectuals and began his career as a schoolteacher specializing in history before being appointed as a lecturer in philosophy and history at the Ecole Normale Supérieure in 1827. It was at this time that Michelet played an important role in introducing France to the writings of Neapolitan philosopher Giovanni Batista Vico by translating Vico's *Scienza Nuova*. Michelet was particularly attracted by Vico's idea that Promethean man had an active role to play in the shaping of history and that history was in essence a perpetual conflict between human freedom and fatality.

The first two volumes of Michelet's *Histoire de France* were published in 1833, with the sixth volume finally appearing in 1844. In a sometimes lyrical evocation of the path traveled by his country, Michelet takes as his abiding theme the triumph of unity over racial and geographical distinctions and the ineluctable emergence of an indivisible French nation. Michelet envisaged his role as more than a chronicler of France's progress. His elevation to the chair of history at the Collège de France gave Michelet further opportunity to engage in his vocation as a moral educator of his nation. When the Catholic Church attacked Michelet and other professors at the Collège de France in the early 1840s for their hostility to church influence in **education**, he responded vigorously with a series of best-selling lectures and publications attacking the influence of the Jesuits in particular as divisive, inimical to the unity of the nation, and therefore something to be resolutely opposed in the sphere of education. Michelet's writings made clear that for him the true religion was France and the greatest imperative was to bind the people of France together in a love of their country.

While Michelet took no active role in the **Revolution of 1848**, his lack of enthusiasm for the regime that followed cost him his chair at the Collège de France in 1852. But it was between the years 1847 and 1853 that Michelet produced his most famous work, the seven-volume *Histoire de la Révolution française*. In passionate and vivid prose, Michelet re-created the history of the Revolution between 1789 and the fall of **Maximilien Robespierre**. Although he found much to condemn in the turn taken by the Revolution after 1789, Michelet nonetheless saw in its essence a triumph for law, justice, and the force of ideas. His work as a whole constituted an exhortation to the French to follow the vocation for greatness given to them by the Revolution. Michelet published a further 26 volumes of work in the last 20 years of his life, but his reputation was already secure. However, when Michelet died on 9 February 1874, he was a man much troubled by what he had seen his country endure during the **Franco-Prussian War** and its aftermath.

MILLERAND, ALEXANDRE (1859–1943). Lawyer, journalist, and politician of the **Third Republic**. Born the son of a small shopkeeper in **Paris** on 10 February 1859, he studied law at the university there and gained a reputation for defending strikers and socialists involved in major disputes, such as the miners at Decazeville (1886) and Carmaux (1892). He was elected to local office in Paris in 1884 and a year later entered the Chamber of Deputies as a radical, but his interest in social reform had, by 1891, made him turn to **socialism**. Millerand allied his desire for social reform with a strong patriotic streak and differed fundamentally from the Marxists in his opposition to revolution. His entry in **René Waldeck-Rousseau**'s cabinet as commerce minister (1899–1902) was a watershed marking the inescapable presence of socialism as a parliamentary force. However, Millerand's reformist ministerial socialism alienated him from the more revolutionary section of the movement, and he was expelled from the Seine Federation of Socialists in 1904.

Millerand's ministerial career was varied. He instituted such reforms as old age, accident, and unemployment benefits (1909–1910), and as war minister (1912–1913, 1914–1915) he did much to reorganize the army along more modern lines. He led the victorious **Bloc National** after **World War I** and became premier and foreign minister. In those capacities he pushed hard for the application of those provisions of the **Treaty of Versailles** concerning reparations and disarmament, despite German resistance and British equivocation. Millerand became president in September 1920 but was forced to step down in the summer of 1924 after the electoral triumph of the **Cartel des Gauches** because he had compromised his presidential impartiality by clearly involving himself in the campaign. His 55-year parliamentary career ended in the Senate in 1940, and he died in Versailles on 6 April 1943.

MITTERRAND, FRANCOIS (1916–1996). The politician who, after **Charles de Gaulle**, had the greatest impact on public life in postwar France. Mitterrand was born into a Catholic, middle-class family in Jarnac, southwestern France, and was educated in Angoulême before pursuing his higher education at the Sorbonne and the Ecole des Sciences Politiques in **Paris**, graduating with degrees in law and political science. **World War II**, however, transformed Mitterrand's destiny, turning him from a shy student into a **Resistance** organizer, sharpening his talents for leadership, and honing the survival skills that proved invaluable for his postwar political career. Mitterrand met de Gaulle in Algiers in 1943 and accepted the general's leadership of the Resistance from abroad, though not without reservations. It was during this wartime period that Mitterrand met Danielle Gouze, his future wife.

Mitterrand's immediate postwar political career was a glittering one, and by 1958 he had served in 11 different governments under the **Fourth Republic**. But the collapse of the Fourth Republic and the return to power of de Gaulle put an end to this. Mitterrand lost his seat in the National Assembly in the legislative elections that established the new Gaullist Republic in 1958, and he had to wait until 1962 before he was reelected. In the meantime, Mitterrand did not fail to articulate his criticism of the constitution of the **Fifth Republic** and in particular what he regarded as the excessive power vested in the **presidency**. It was an indictment of the regime encapsulated in the title of his book *Le coup d'état permanent* (1964). Mitterrand established himself over the next 20 years as a political author and essayist of some note, publishing more than 10 major works. This activity also had the advantage of keeping him in the public eye in spite of the political reversals he endured. He was an unsuccessful candidate in the presidential elections of 1965 and 1974 and in the meantime had failed to capitalize on the widespread disaffection with the Gaullist regime expressed by the **student rebellions** of 1968.

The 1970s nonetheless constituted the crucial period in Mitterrand's long road to power. The choice of Mitterrand to lead the newly formed **Parti Socialiste (PS)** in 1971 provided him with a broad party base from which to launch his assault on the presidency. The signature of a **Common Program** with the **Parti Communiste Français (PCF)** strengthened the legitimacy of Mitterrand's claim to lead the left in France, and although he lost the race for the presidency to **Valéry Giscard d'Estaing** in 1974, the fact that he captured over 49 percent of the votes cast made it a very creditable performance. He finally captured the ultimate prize in French politics in 1981 when factors like unemployment, inflation, and what was perceived by many as the growing arrogance of Giscard d'Estaing swung the popular vote in Mitterrand's direction. But although Mitterrand had campaigned on a platform of Socialist policies, he was soon to relinquish an overt allegiance to Socialist ideology. The failure of the Socialist government's attempt to reflate the economy along Keynesian lines became apparent within 24 months, as the rest of the world's leading economies adopted deflationary policies. The U-turn forced on **Pierre Mauroy**'s cabinet and the ensuing belt-tightening measures were accompanied by a change of rhetoric by Mitterrand as he projected himself as the defender of the Republic rather than the defender of socialist France.

By 1986 the electorate had become disillusioned with the Socialist government, which was associated in the public mind with economic austerity and somewhat discredited by political scandals like the *Rainbow Warrior* affair, when the Greenpeace ship (*see* GREENPEACE AFFAIR) monitoring French nuclear testing in the Pacific was sunk in New Zealand by French secret service agents. The loss of a left-wing majority in the National Assembly as a result of the legislative elections was not unexpected, but it created a constitutional anomaly that had not been seen before in the Fifth Republic: a Socialist president having to choose a prime minister from a hostile center-right majority in the National Assembly.

This first period of **cohabitation** was one that, paradoxically, strengthened Mitterrand's presidential credibility. Rather than competing with his prime minister, **Jacques Chirac**, Mitterrand retreated into his presidential role as the defender of France's eternal interests, particularly in the realm of defense and foreign policy, and as the embodiment of France's highest aspirations who, by definition, was above petty political squabbling. It was Mitterrand at his most imperious and, ironically, his most Gaullist. Like the founder of the Republic whom he had criticized, Mitterrand distinguished himself as the defender of France's independent nuclear vocation, her freedom to dialogue in her own right with the **Soviet Union**, and her mission to check excessive **United States** influence in Europe. As the first Gulf War illustrated, France under Mitterrand could be relied on to play her part in the western alliance of liberal democracies, but like de Gaulle, Mitterrand was careful not to allow this to be taken for granted. However, unlike de Gaulle, Mitterrand had a commitment to closer ties between the countries of the **European Economic Community** that was unwavering, and he forged a particularly strong relationship with Chancellor Helmut Kohl of **Germany**.

The 1988 presidential election proved the extent of Mitterrand's success in cultivating his credibility and charisma as a *présidentiable*. He swept to victory with a 54 percent share of the vote, in contrast to Jacques Chirac's 46 percent. But the president's party did not enjoy the same credibility as their candidate, and on this occasion there was no honeymoon period between the Socialist government and the electorate. The downturn in the **economy**; the growing malaise in society due to the related problems of unemployment, crime, and racism; and the discrediting of the political establishment because of allegations of the illegal funding of **political parties** created an undercurrent of crisis in government. Mitterrand's reaction was to replace Prime Minister **Michel Rocard** in 1991 with the first and only woman in France to hold that office, **Edith Cresson**. Cresson's previous position as a devotee of Mitterrand did not make her job easier in regard to other senior members of the PS, particularly those preparing for the post-Mitterrand succession. The government fell even lower in the opinion polls, and less than one year after her appointment Cresson was replaced by **Pierre Bérégovoy**.

Defeat for the left in the legislative elections of 1993 was fully expected, and when it came it was catastrophic, with 80 percent of the seats in the new Assembly going to the center-right. Mitterrand was forced once more to cohabit with a prime minister from a hostile majority, in this case **Edouard Balladur**. But unlike the period following 1986, Mitterrand after 1993 was clearly a tired leader waiting to depart office. Mitterrand's obvious physical frailty was finally explained by the fact that he was terminally ill with cancer. Futhermore, unflattering obituaries for his political career began to appear because of the kinds of revisionist exercises exemplified, most sensationally, by Pierre Péan's book on Mitterrand's youth, *Une jeunesse française: François Mitterrand 1934–1947* (1994). Péan's book questioned the authenticity of Mitterrand's commitment to democratic republican values by providing evidence of the decoration he received as an employee of the **Vichy regime** before he joined the Resistance and documenting Mitterrand's friendship with René Bousquet, a man who had played a major part in the persecution of Jews in wartime France. In spite of his illness, Mitterrand chose to address the media speculation by giving lengthy television interviews to two of France's most respected journalists that, according to the opinion polls following the **broadcasts**, elicited a compassionate reaction from many of his compatriots.

When Mitterrand's death was announced on 8 January 1996, the reaction illustrated the unique generosity of the French nation toward someone who is deemed to have assumed the mythified and paternal mantle of leadership. In contrast to what would happen in Anglo-Saxon countries, even the revelation at his private interment that Mitterrand had fathered a daughter by a mistress he had kept in a state apartment for many years did not undermine the solemnity of the homage that the nation paid to him at Notre Dame Cathedral, in the presence of the world's leaders. Mitterrand was unquestionably a complex and contradictory man, but for many French people this did not prevent him from being a worthy embodiment of French intellectual genius and the committed defender of his country's prestige on the world stage.

MOLLET, GUY (1905–1975). Leading Socialist and premier of the **Fourth Republic**. He was born into a modest family in Flers (Orne) and became an English teacher after graduating from the University of Lille. He served in the French army from the beginning of **World War II**, was wounded, interned, and eventually released; he subsequently joined the **Resistance**. Mollet rose quickly in the **Section Française de l'Internationale Ouvrière (SFIO)** after the war and was elected to the post of secretary-general in 1946. His parliamentary career began with his election to the constituent assembly in 1945, and his first ministerial appointment came in 1950. He formed his own government in 1956 and was successful in promoting social reform at home, better relations with West **Germany** on the foreign front, and the advancement of the European project through the formation of a **European Economic Community.** However, Mollet faced severe difficulties outside the European sphere. His commitment of French troops to the Franco-British operation in Egypt during the **Suez Crisis** provoked hostility within his own party ranks, and it was the reluctance of parliament to sanction tax rises to pay for military operations in another troubled region, **Algeria**, that led to his resignation from office in May 1957.

As the Algerian situation turned into a crisis, Mollet figured among the band of left-wing politicians who turned to General **Charles de Gaulle** for salvation in 1958. Mollet served in the de Gaulle cabinet in the transitional period between regimes but ended this alliance in 1962 when he opted to work with Socialist colleagues in building a credible left-wing opposition to **Gaullism**. In one respect, Mollet proved his flexibility in his approach to the pursuit of socialist ideals and was prepared to put country before ideology, as during the Cold War. But in another respect his singular understanding of the organizational needs and political purposes of the SFIO meant that he was out of step with the thinking of a younger generation in pursuit of a more broadly based left genuinely capable of taking power, such as through the formation of the **Fédération de la Gauche Démocrate et Socialiste**, which prompted Mollet's departure from the political scene in 1969.

MONET, CLAUDE (1840–1926). Landscape painter and leading figure in **impressionism**. He was born the son of a wholesale grocer in **Paris**, raised in Le Havre, and trained as a painter largely through informal tutelage. His debut offering of two landscapes at the Salon of 1865 met with approval. During the years that followed he became a recognized practitioner of *plein-air* painting. In 1874, together with **Edgar Degas**, **Camille Pissarro**, and **Auguste Renoir**, he organized the exhibition that brought notoriety to his painting *Impression, soleil levant* and that is regarded as having launched the impressionist movement. However, by the late 1870s Monet began to distance himself from this artistic circle, and in 1883 he withdrew to Giverny, where he lived for the rest of his life and where he created the water lily garden that features in so many of his works after 1900. The most celebrated works of his later career, from about 1890, are the series paintings of subjects like poplars, haystacks, and Rouen Cathedral. *See also* ART.

MONNET, JEAN. *See* EUROPEAN ECONOMIC COMMUNITY.

MONTAGNARDS. Left-wing deputies, generally at one time or other members of the **Jacobin** Club of Paris, who sat with the Montagne or "Mountain," the nickname given to the group that congregated in the seats high on the left of the chamber where the **Convention** met during the **French Revolution**. The actions of the Montagnards are often evoked in terms of their opposition to the **Girondins** over issues like the fate of Louis **XVI** and the institution of the **Terror**. The Montagnards held sway in the Convention after the demise of Girondin influence in the summer of 1793, but military victories by the French army like the one at Fleurus (June 1794), which undermined the justification for the Terror and the position of **Robespierre**, led to a crumbling of the Mountain by July 1794.

MONTAND, YVES (1921–1991). French actor and singer who enjoyed enormous popularity and respect, both for his talent and for his admission of his frailties. He was born Ivo Livi in Florence and came to France as a young boy with his family when they fled Fascist Italy. Show business attracted him at an early age and he was discovered singing in a nightclub by **Edith Piaf**, who gave him a part in her 1946 movie *Star without Light*. He went on, several movies later, to achieve international recognition as one of the desperate truck drivers carrying nitroglycerin in Henri-Georges Clouzot's classic thriller *The Wages of Fear* (1952). His introduction to an American mass audience came in 1960 when he costarred with Marilyn Monroe in *Let's Make Love* (1960). This led to a number of English-language successes, including the musical *On a Clear Day You Can See Forever* (1970).

Together with his wife, the French actress Simone Signoret, Montand was often in the headlines, partly for show business reasons and partly for his very public espousal of left-wing politics. However, Montand's frank but dignified admission in later years that he had been mistaken about the true nature of Soviet politics merely endeared him further to the French public. Some of his most powerful films are precisely those that convey his political commitments, especially those made in collaboration with the radical director Costa Gavras, such as *The Confession* (1970) and *State of Siege* (1973). Montand's appearances as a singer on the concert stage continued to attract sellout audiences of faithful fans, and he came to incarnate the finest traditions of French song, both live and in the recording studio, with his musical renditions of poems by Jacques Prévert. In his later years, Montand's sureness of touch as a character actor was acclaimed worldwide owing to his remarkable portrayal of greed as the Provençal farmer in Claude Berri's two-part adaptation of *Jean de Florette* and *Manon des sources* (1986). Active to the last, he died during the filming of his last movie, *IP5* (1992). *See also* CINEMA; MUSIC, POP AND ROCK.

MONT BLANC. The highest mountain in the French Alps and in Western Europe. The official measurement taken in December 2005 recorded its peak at 4,808.75 meters. It is the focal point for **tourism**

in the regions and is surrounded by many summer and ski resorts. Underneath the mountain runs the famous 11.6-kilometer-long tunnel that links Haute-Savoie in France to the Valle d'Aosta in Italy. The actual tunneling began in 1959 after the signing of an intergovernmental agreement, and the tunnel was inaugurated in 1965. The attraction of the tunnel to ordinary and commercial traffic was obvious since it cut 50 kilometers from the previous route from France to Turin and 100 kilometers from the previous route to Milan. But disaster struck in 1999 when a Belgian truck carrying margarine caught fire inside the tunnel and blocked it. The inferno that rapidly ensued cost 39 lives. The tunnel reopened in 2002 after repair work and a major modernization of its safety features.

MOREAU, JEANNE (1928–). A powerfully enigmatic French actress who, in the 1950s and 1960s, worked with a variety of directors and came to embody the essence of the European sensibility. She began her career on the stage and interspersed this with a number of forgettable film roles until she appeared in Louis Malle's *Ascenseur pour l'échafaud* and *Les amants* (1958). These movies provided the public with its first chance to appreciate Moreau's charismatic style as well as the undercurrent of libidinal chaos in her personality, especially in the frank portrayal of sexual frustration in the second film. In contrast to that other icon of 1960s French **cinema, Brigitte Bardot**, with whom she costarred in *Viva Maria* (1965), Moreau was an unconventional beauty whose magnetism emanated from a complex personality and seductive intelligence, capable of combining self-assurance with disarming vulnerability. Arguably her best role was as Catherine, the center of a tragic love triangle in François Truffaut's *Jules et Jim* (1962). The range of her talent was exploited by some of the most intellectually demanding directors in international cinema, such as Joseph Losey, Luis Bunuel, and Orson Welles. Moreau made her debut as a director in 1976 with *Lumière*, and she has also recorded a number of songs. She received the best actress award at Cannes for her part in *Moderato cantabile* (1960), and the high esteem in which she is still held by the industry, nationally and internationally, is highlighted by her ubiquitous presence on film juries. With over 100 films to her name, she is also the subject of frequent retrospectives in cinemas and on television.

MOULIN, JEAN (1899–1943). Hero of the French **Resistance**. He was born in Béziers, southwest France, and from an early age was influenced by the socialist humanism of his schoolteacher father. He was called up in April 1918, less than a year after having started his law studies at Montpellier University. Fortunately for Moulin, **World War I** ended before he saw serious action on the front line. After returning to his studies he graduated in 1921 and then began his climb up the professional ladder of French regional administration. When **World War II** began in 1939 Moulin was the prefect of the Eure-et-Loir department. He soon fell afoul of the **Vichy regime** when he refused to approve the prosecution of French African troops accused of atrocities against civilians that had in fact been committed by the invading Germans. Thrown into jail for his refusal to collaborate, Moulin almost died when he slashed his own throat with a piece of glass. Relieved of his prefectoral duties by the new regime, Moulin took the opportunity to escape from France following General **Charles de Gaulle**'s radio appeal from London in June 1940, calling French citizens with a love of liberty to join him in the resistance to the German invader.

Moulin arrived in London in September 1940 and impressed the General sufficiently to be tasked with returning to France with the mission of unifying the disparate elements of the Resistance that had emerged there, and establishing de Gaulle's ultimate military and political leadership of the free French, at home and abroad. It was a daunting prospect, given the strong personalities that had emerged to lead the different Resistance groups and the climate of mutual suspicion that existed. After numerous trips to and from France, at great personal risk, by May 1943 Moulin had succeeded in pulling the different Resistance groups together into the Conseil National de la Résistance. This was the crucial step in preparing the ground for the liberation of France and the subsequent reestablishment of the republic. Tragically, Moulin did not live to see the triumph of his labors. He was betrayed, and arrested on 21 June 1943 while meeting with Resistance leaders in **Lyon**. He was transferred to Gestapo headquarters in **Paris** and tortured, but revealed nothing. He died of the effects of this brutal treatment on the train that was taking him to Berlin on 8 July 1943. When Moulin's remains were transferred to the Pantheon in 1964, to rest alongside France's other national heroes, the writer

André Malraux delivered one of the most moving orations of modern times, projecting Moulin as the face immemorial of France's resistance to tyranny and oppression.

MOUVEMENT DES RADICAUX DE GAUCHE (MRG)/MOVEMENT OF LEFT-WING RADICALS. Left-wing radicals who first made their mark in the 1970s. They emerged from a split in the centrist Radical Party, which had been in existence in France since 1901. In keeping with one of the defining characteristics of **political parties** in France, tiny entities like the Radical party and the MRG ally themselves with, and exist in, larger formations. When, at the beginning of the 1970s, the leadership of the Radical Party proposed a shift away from its alliance with the Socialists and a turn toward the center-right, a majority of its deputies disagreed. These dissidents, identifying themselves as the MRG, decided to negotiate a new alliance with the Socialists in preparation for the 1973 legislative elections. As a result of the elections, the 12 MRG deputies joined the Socialist group in parliament, and in December of that year the MRG was formally constituted as a party.

From that point on, the fortunes of the MRG were closely bound up with the fortunes of the **Parti Socialiste (PS)**, and for some commentators it was difficult to see why the MRG had to maintain an identity that was distinct from that of its partner on the left, particularly in view of the fact that the number of deputies elected under the MRG banner did not enter into double digits after 1981. But the MRG continued to promote the need for a humanist left committed to civil liberties and social reform and willing to defend the interests of the individual and small groups against large corporate interests, whether emanating from private capital or state bureaucracies. Collapse in the support for the PS in the legislative elections of 1993 depressed the fortunes of the left as a whole, and in November 1994 the MRG underwent a metamorphosis at its congress in Bourget, when it decided to change its name to "Radical" and appointed Jean-François Hory as its president. It assumed its current incarnation in 1998 as the Parti Radical de Gauche and in 2007 was able to muster eight deputies in the National Assembly, led by Jean-Michel Baylet.

MOUVEMENT REPUBLICAIN POPULAIRE (MRP)/POPULAR REPUBLICAN MOVEMENT. A Christian democratic movement that played an important role during the life of the **Fourth Republic**. It was a movement that was born out of the Catholic **Resistance** and founded at a convention in **Paris** in November 1944. The broad aspirations of the movement harked back to a long and respectable tradition of attempting to reconcile **Catholics** with republicanism in France. In party political terms, the MRP saw itself as offering a middle way between the materialistic assumptions of liberalism and communism. The MRP was certainly well perceived by the French electorate in 1945, no doubt because of its Gaullist persuasions, and in the elections of that October it was second only to the **Communists** in its share of the vote. However, the formation of an explicitly **Gaullist party** in 1947 and the end of **tripartism** led the MRP into cooperation with a series of **third force** governments that were united by little except the desire to prevent the Communists or the Gaullists from taking power. Electoral support for the MRP rapidly evaporated in the early 1950s, and although the party supported **Charles de Gaulle**'s return to power in 1958, this turned to opposition again in 1962 in view of his presidentialization of the regime. Sidelined by the transformation in party politics under the **Fifth Republic**, by 1963 the MRP had lost its significance as a distinct and independent force. *See also* POLITICAL PARTIES.

MUNICH ACCORD. Symbol of the policy of appeasement and the sacrifice of Czechoslovakia to Nazi expansionism by France and **Great Britain**. France was bound to Czechoslovakia by the defense agreement of 1924, and the nationalist agitation (fomented by Nazi agents) among the 3 million Sudeten Germans who found themselves part of Czechoslovakia after the **Treaty of Versailles** reached such a pitch by September 1938 that war seemed imminent in light of Adolf Hitler's demand for the cession and German occupation of the Sudetenland. The government of **Edouard Daladier** was weak and divided, fearful of alienating its chief ally, Great Britain, which had no defense treaty with the Czechs. Faced with the prospect of war or humiliating surrender, Daladier welcomed the proposal from the Italian leader Benito Mussolini for a conference in Munich of the parties concerned to resolve the crisis. Daladier and Neville Chamberlain, the British prime minister, bowed to most of Hitler's demands and on 29 September accepted the transfer of the Sudetenland to **Germany**. The Czechs, under intense Franco-British pressure, also accepted this loss of sovereignty. On his return to **Paris**, Daladier was met by crowds cheering with joyous relief that war had been averted, but subsequent events were soon to demonstrate to what extent the Munich Accord had been a symbol of France's and Britain's weakness in the new German-dominated Europe.

MUSIC, CLASSICAL AND CONTEMPORARY. While the French led developments in European music with the Notre Dame school in the 12th century, there was, until the 19th century, an underlying sense in French cultural circles that the nation's musical achievements were somewhat overshadowed by those of some of its European neighbors. The French determination to resist the influence of Italian opera in the early 18th century flowed from the policy decision of **Louis XIV** to foster the growth of national artistic traditions that would reflect the glory of his monarchy. In musical terms, this projection of French superiority was embodied in the work of Lulli, who between 1673 and his death in 1687 wrote approximately one opera a year, leaving a body of work that dominated the French repertory for nearly a century. The fact that Lulli was an Italian who had come to France as a child of 10 was conveniently overlooked in the desire to build up a French tradition. Other great figures of French music, like Rameau, also proved largely impervious to Italian influences, and in the generations that followed there was a perceptible insularity in the French disinclination to respond to the innovations of German orchestral music.

However, the irresistible attractions of **Paris** as a cultural center from the middle of the 19th century onward brought many foreign influences that added to the renown that accrued to French music through the efforts of Hector Berlioz and **Maurice Ravel**. It was an intellectual climate that stimulated experimentation, sometimes crossing the boundaries between art and music, as reflected in the compositions of **Claude Debussy**. The passion for experimentation grew in the 20th century, with the work of the composers known as **Les Six**, who helped open up French music to African, North American, and Latin American influences. France, and Paris in particular, is now an established center for experimentation in contemporary music, with the work pursued under the directorship of **Pierre Boulez** at the research institute IRCAM attracting musical talent from around the world. *See also* SATIE, ERIK.

MUSIC, POP AND ROCK. Pop and rock music in France, as in the rest of Europe (apart from **Great Britain**), has always suffered from the fact that the genre originated in an English-speaking country, the United States. Attempts in France to produce music that would appeal to the emerging youth culture of the 1950s relied heavily on imitations of the American originals. It was no coincidence that the stars of that generation adopted what seemed American-sounding names, like **Johnny Halliday** and Eddie Mitchell, as well as American musical styles. The longevity of Halliday's career, in particular, results from his uncanny ability to read the changes in pop music, from whichever quarter the wind blows. Thus in the 1960s he was among the first to spot the wave of British bands that would change the face of pop music and relinquished American rock and roll in favor of the new, sultry, strutting narcissism of figures like Mick Jagger of the Rolling Stones. The fact remained, however, that for a worldwide audience, pop and rock music was sung in English, and Halliday, Françoise Hardy, Michel Sardou, and many others had to be content with relatively small audiences restricted to the French-speaking world.

The 1980s was a period of greater confidence among European producers of pop and rock music as a whole and a growing conviction in France that home-grown artists could find an authentic voice in their own language. An artist like Renaud proved that he could harness the energy of British punk rock to his uniquely cutting use of the French language. In the 1990s, artists like MC Solaar demonstrated that French rap songs could convey the realities of urban life to the youth of France more pertinently than transatlantic rap imports. Proof of French confidence in native talent emerged in the 1990s through the organization of pop festivals large enough to rival American or British counterparts. In 1996 the festival at La Rochelle attracted approximately 70,000 spectators while relying solely on French artists. In France, as elsewhere in Europe, promoters have tapped the growing enthusiasm among young people for big outdoor events. For example, the Festival des Eurockéennes de Belfort in 2006 attracted over 90,000 fans. But it is still the case that the export of French pop and rock music on the world market remains modest and that the bands drawing the biggest audiences in France are predominantly the American and British stars with a worldwide following. *See also* GAINSBOURG, SERGE.

– N –

NANTES, EDICT OF. *See* RELIGION.

NAPOLEON. *See* BONAPARTE, NAPOLEON.

NAPOLEON II (1811–1832). François-Charles-Joseph Bonaparte, originally titled king of Rome, the son of **Napoléon Bonaparte** and his second empress, Marie-Louise of Austria. In 1814, at the age of three, he was taken to Vienna by his grandfather, the Austrian emperor, where he was reared as the duke von Reichstadt. After his father's death (1821) he was often portrayed in Bonapartist propaganda as the "eaglet," held captive in Vienna. Napoléon II grew into a handsome and intelligent young man with a keen awareness of his inheritance, but he died prematurely of tuberculosis at the age of 21 after exhausting himself on maneuvers with the Austrian army.

NAPOLEON III. *See* BONAPARTE, LOUIS-NAPOLEON.

NATIONAL GUARD. A national citizen militia that had its origins in the **French Revolution** and that played a part in the major revolutionary convulsions that shook France during the 19th century. The organization of the guard was formalized in 1790 and 1791; its tasks were to maintain order, protect private property, and defend the Revolution against any threat that might arise from an aristocratic conspiracy. It is not surprising, therefore, that throughout most of its history the guard was identified with bourgeois revolutionary aims. It was treated with suspicion and kept largely inactive after the restoration of the monarchy in France under **Louis XVIII**, but it played an important role in the **Revolution of 1830** by enabling the new regime to become established. The abolition of taxpaying requirements to qualify for membership in the guard, which resulted from the **Revolution of 1848**, swelled its numbers but also led to class antagonisms within its ranks.

The prestige and activity of the guard declined significantly during the **Second Empire**, but it came to prominence again in a dramatic manner as a consequence of the **Franco-Prussian War** in 1870. The guard in **Paris** became a focus of patriotic resistance to the inevitable capitulation while the rest of France was preoccupied with suing for peace, and this led to the sense in its ranks that Paris had been betrayed. Thus the attempt by the national government in Versailles to disarm the guard after the armistice provoked a violent reaction and prompted establishment of the **Commune** of 1871. Poor organization, military inefficiency, and indiscipline made the outcome of the ultimate confrontation with government troops inevitable, but few could have foreseen the savagery with which the guard was destroyed in the "bloody week" in May 1871 when the national government reimposed its authority on Paris. Having been suppressed militarily, the National Guard was eliminated as an institution by legislation passed in August 1870.

NATIONALIZATION. A major issue in postwar politics in France and a series of measures that occurred in two waves, 1945–1948 and 1981–1982. Although the tradition of a centralized state in France had resulted in examples of state-directed industry as far back as glassmaking in the 18th century, in modern times **World War II** gave a particular impetus to the debate. From the spring of 1944 calls emanated from within the **Resistance** for the nationalization of some of the nation's key economic assets. Three major reasons were advanced for such a course of action: only the deployment of the nation's resources by the state would enable France to undertake the mammoth task of reconstruction after the war; national sovereignty should not be jeopardized by allowing the ownership of basic industries to be concentrated in a few hands; and those major owners of capital who had collaborated with the enemy should be penalized through expropriation.

Irresistible economic and political pressures led to some nationalizations even before the elections of October 1945. Thus in December 1944 coal was nationalized and became the Houillères Nationales du Nord et du Pas-de-Calais. In January 1945 the automobile manufacturer **Renault** was taken into public ownership and became the Régie Nationale des Usines Renault, and the state acquired its own airplane engine manufacturer in May 1945 when the Société Anonyme des Moteurs Gnome-Rhône was transformed into the Société Nationale d'Etudes et de Constructions de Moteurs d'Aviation. The elections in the fall of that year were followed within six months by the nationalization of the Bank of France and the four largest deposit banks and the creation of the state-owned utilities Electricité de France and Gaz de France. The nationalizations followed a process of market valuation that compensated the proprietors for the loss of their enterprises. Furthermore, as in the case of Air France and the maritime transport industry, there were situations when the state chose to be the major shareholder, as opposed to the outright owner, of an enterprise.

The second wave of nationalizations in postwar France followed the election of **François Mitterrand** to the **presidency** in May 1981 and the victory of the **Socialists** in the ensuing legislative elections. The economic justifications given for the policy were the threat from foreign multinationals, the timid short-termism of French investors, and the prospects for revitalizing the **economy** and creating jobs through state-led investment. Politically, the policy offered the prospect of diminishing inequality in French society. The nationalization law of 13 February 1982 brought almost all of what remained of the **banking** industry into the state sector and brought in a large cross-section of major enterprises in manufacturing and communications, notably Usinor-Sacilor, CGE, Thomson-Brandt, Saint-Gobain, Péchiney, and Rhône-Poulenc. However, the Socialists were swimming against the tide as their major trading partners opted to cut direct state investment in industry and privatize existing state enterprises. Five years later, during the first period of **cohabitation**, the process of reversing these nationalizations through **privatization** began.

NATURALISM. An influential literary theory during the second half of the 19th century. Innovation in printing technology, the improvement of paper manufacture, and the spread of **education** were among the key factors in generating a huge audience for the printed word in France in the second half of the 19th century. The fact that novels were often serialized in newspapers before appearing in a complete version gave them a huge readership and made them the dominant literary form. The writer with the supreme gift for exploiting these changes was **Emile Zola**. Beginning in the 1860s, Zola advanced naturalism as an approach to the novel that had evolved from precursors like **romanticism** but that now offered a perspective accommodating the scientific realities of a modern world.

The defining characteristic of naturalism was to be the application of scientific observation to the novel in the endeavor to reflect the world accurately and in detail. Zola's attempt to document his times was not unique, and some of his assumptions had already shaped the journals and novels of the **Goncourt** brothers. But Zola was unique in his determination to apply the findings of contemporary scientific research to depict characters and groups in society whose paths in life were shaped by social conditioning and the biological laws of heredity. In some works, such as *Germinal* (1885), the result could be a powerful evocation of the depredations a community suffers through poverty, but in others, like *Thérèse Raquin* (1867), Zola's biological determinism could make his characters seem like guinea pigs chosen to prove his theories. While the naturalism Zola propounded was influential, it did not make any true disciples, and even writers like **Guy de Maupassant**, who had come under Zola's influence, were soon to distance themselves from the coarser aspects of his approach. *See also* LITERATURE.

NECKER, JACQUES (1732–1804). Genevan-born banker and minister of finance for Louis **XVI**, who made his reputation as a genius in financial administration during his first ministry (1776–1781). Necker was reappointed the director general of finances on 25 August 1788 to cope with the desperate financial circumstances that would force the king to convoke the **Estates General**. However, Necker was no supporter of despotism and recognized the need for a genuinely representative assembly, favoring a British-style constitutional monarchy. It was his dismissal by the king on 11 July that fueled the discontent leading to the July uprising in **Paris**, forcing the king to recall him for a third ministry (29 July–8 September 1790). However, Necker returned to Paris to find that an increasingly radicalized National Assembly was growing impatient with liberals like himself, who wanted more representation but not popular democracy. The hostility forced him to resign and return to Switzerland, fearing for his safety.

NEUWIRTH LAW. Legislation passed in 1967 that liberalized access to the means of contraception in France.

NEW CALEDONIA. South Pacific island colonized by the French in 1853. It became an overseas territory in 1946 and was given political representation in the National Assembly; it now enjoys a special status of its own as an overseas collectivity. The postwar reforms enfranchising the Melanesian population of the island, known as Kanaks, prepared the way for the formation of the multiethnic Union Calédonienne (UC) (Caledonian Union), a party to represent the Kanak people (about one-half of the population) and also the expatriate small farmers and shopkeepers in their opposition to wealthy commercial interests. In 1953 the UC gained majority control in the Territorial Assembly and held it until 1968. However, the **student rebellions** of 1968 ruptured the UC, with the whites moving toward the island's pro-French **Gaullist party** and the younger and more assertive Kanaks being wooed by a proliferation of other parties because of what they perceived as the UC's excessive caution on the issue of independence. Tensions were exacerbated by the flow of French immigrants to the island, which by 1974 meant that the percentage of Kanaks in the population fell below 50. The election of a Socialist government in France in 1981 coincided with the formation of an Independence Front by Kanaks and a belated commitment to self-determination by the UC to secure its position in the Territorial Assembly.

In 1983 the government in France offered the Kanaks changes in the voting system that would enhance their standing, but the preponderant weight of the votes cast in the region around the capital Noumea, largely inhabited by the European community, would not allow the campaign for independence to succeed. Violence flared prior to the new elections in 1984, when Kanak independence leaders urged their people to boycott the polls. Tit-for-tat killings between Kanaks and European settlers ensued, and in early 1985 the police shot Elio Machoro, one of the Kanak leaders of the boycott. The leaders of the independence movement called for boycotts of further offers of electoral reform, as well as a boycott of the September 1987 referendum on independence itself. The abstention rate was 40 percent and the vote against independence was 58 percent. On the eve of the 1988 presidential election violence flared once more and resulted in hostage taking by pro-independence elements, which provoked a police operation leading to the death of several Kanaks. However, the offer by the government in Paris of a 10-year cooling-off period before the status of the territory was reassessed restored relative calm to the island. In 1998, L'Accord de Nouméa was signed under **Lionel Jospin**'s government, effectively sharing sovereignty with New Caledonia, with metropolitan France prevailing in the areas of defense, security, justice, and monetary policy. *See also* DOMS-TOMS.

NEW PHILOSOPHERS. This was the term applied to a generation of thinkers, many of whom were disillusioned Marxists, who came to prominence in the mid-1970s and acquired a high public profile through their exploitation of the media, especially television. They did not represent a coherent school of thought, but in their different ways they tapped a public mood that was increasingly inclined to reject totalizing systems of thought. Notable works like André Glucksmann's *Les maîtres penseurs* (1977) and **Bernard-Henri Lévy**'s *La barbarie à visage humain* (1977) condemned the brutal logic of the pursuit of power in all its forms, since the dominant ideologies of the 20th century, whether of right or left, had simply crushed the individual. But the skepticism they expressed was not counterbalanced by a clear or coherent response to the crisis they identified. While some, like Jean-Marie Benoist, drifted toward rather well-worn arguments that identified totalitarianism with the left, others, like Bernard-Henri Lévy, seemed inclined to synthesize the oldest kind of response with a very modern sensibility, like the kind of individualized spirituality Lévy appears to advocate in *Le testament de Dieu* (1979) as a form of resistance to totalitarianism. The prominence of the new philosophers had largely diminished by the early 1980s, but Bernard-Henri Lévy in particular retains a striking ability to maintain his profile on the small screen by projecting himself as the defender of just causes in the face of an indifferent establishment, illustrated in the mid-1990s by his campaign to ease the plight of the Muslims in the civil war in the former Yugoslavia.

NORTH ATLANTIC TREATY ORGANIZATION (NATO). *See* DEFENSE POLICY.

NOTABLES. Historically, the term used to describe the upper-class elite that came to prominence under the July 1830 monarchy of

Louis-Philippe. French historians have frequently referred to this chapter in the 19th century as the *régime des notables* because of the way a small elite, with figures like the banker J. Lafitte and the industrialist Casimir Perier, came to exercise a disproportionate amount of influence and grow even richer because of the failure of the regime to separate pursuit of the public interest from acquisition of private gain. The economic, political, and administrative elites were often the same people, illustrated by the fact that figures like Lafitte and Perier were allowed to hold ministerial office while pursuing their private activities as businessmen.

NOUVEAU FRANC (NEW FRANC). This was introduced in 1960 as part of a package of measures to combat inflation and was the currency used until France adopted the **euro**. It was called nouveau franc, in contrast to the ancien—old—franc it replaced. One new franc was equivalent to 100 old ones. For many years after the switch to the new franc, it was not uncommon to find older people referring to *anciens francs*, whereas the switch to the euro appears to have left less of a lingering nostalgia.

NOUVEAU ROMAN (NEW NOVEL). Not a coherent project or school but a term signaling the emergence of work by half a dozen writers in France who, by 1960, had been identified as sharing certain ambitions with regard to novel-writing that revolutionized the genre. The four most important new novelists were Alain Robbe-Grillet, Nathalie Sarraute, Michel Butor, and Claude Simon. By undermining the techniques used in the traditional novel, these writers hoped to bring about a new kind of writing, one that transformed the role of the reader by turning him or her from a passive recipient of information into an active participant in the creative process. In *Les fruits d'or* (1963), for instance, Sarraute departs from conventional novel-writing by destabilizing the presentation of character and plot, making them so vague that the ultimate achievement of the text is to reflect on itself and the artificiality of its creation. The deliberate switching or duplicity of narrative perspective makes characters intentionally incomplete or fugitive, as in Claude Simon's *La route des Flandres* (1960), while in *La modification* (1957) by Michel Butor, the author uses the second person plural (*vous*) to draw the reader into the action as well as to address the principal character in the plot. The traditional perceptions of time and movement become redundant, and in a novel like *La jalousie* (1957) by Alain Robbe-Grillet, we experience the obsessive and recurrent nature of jealousy through events narrated in the present tense, underlining the notion that life can only be lived in the present, and we sense the timeless fixations of jealousy through Robbe-Grillet's minutely detailed descriptions of material objects. *See also* LITERATURE.

NOUVELLE CUISINE. Term coined in 1972 by the restaurant critics Henri Gault and Christian Millau to describe the challenge posed to haute cuisine by a new generation of younger chefs animated by a culinary aesthetic that accented the use of the freshest products in beautifully presented meals that were light on the digestive system. The media attention paid to the fashion made stars of some of the new chefs and converted many famous chefs established in the tradition of haute cuisine. However, the fashion had died by the mid-1980s because of public weariness with innovation for its own sake, high prices, and sometimes absurdly small portions.

NUCLEAR POWER. As in all developed economies, the government in France was forced to reevaluate its national energy strategy in the light of the crisis caused by the quadrupling of oil prices in 1973. In 1975 this resulted in a national energy plan committed to reducing the dependence on foreign fuels, mainly through a massive investment program in nuclear power. Unlike the experience of other countries such as **Great Britain**, the development of nuclear power for civil purposes in France has not been a major battleground between the **political parties**, nor has it provoked sustained antinuclear campaigns from citizens' groups. A continuous construction program meant that by 2007 58 pressurized water reactors were being operated on 19 sites across France, but with concentrations on the **Loire** and **Rhône** rivers. With the national utility giant Electricité de France supplying over four-fifths of the country's electricity through nuclear power, France is more dependent on this source of energy than is any other developed **economy**. In spite of its lack of flexibility and the misgivings that sprang up worldwide after the 1986 explosion of the nuclear reactor at Chernobyl in Ukraine (then a republic of the **Soviet**

Union), nuclear power remains an indispensable part of French governments' efforts to balance the books. The expertise that French companies have developed in the civil uses of nuclear energy has made them world leaders in export markets for this technology, especially fast-expanding ones like China.

– O –

OLLIVIER, EMILE (1825–1913). Lawyer and republican leader. He was born into a family of committed republicans on his father's side and was in his early 20s when, following the **Revolution of 1848**, he was appointed commissioner-general for **Marseille**. While gifted with a remarkable capacity for moving his listeners through his eloquence, Ollivier had a naive belief in the goodness of the people that did not equip him to cope with the demands of more radical republicans to his left or to survive the right-wing reaction when it arrived. His period in public office ended with the election of Louis-Napoléon (*see* BONAPARTE, LOUIS-NAPOLEON) as president, and the ensuing change of regime ended his republican political ambitions in the early 1850s. However, after proclaiming himself Emperor Napoléon III, Louis-Napoléon's political fortunes during the following decade declined, forcing him to introduce liberal reforms to placate his opposition, and Ollivier was able to make a comeback as an opposition deputy. His personal triumph came in January 1870, when he was asked to form a government that would pilot the reforms paving the way for much greater power sharing between Louis-Napoléon and parliament. But, as **Léon Gambetta** presciently observed, Ollivier's administration merely provided the bridge to the republic of the future. And the transition from empire to republic prophesied by Gambetta was soon suddenly and violently thrown into focus by the **Franco-Prussian War**.

OPPORTUNISTS. Term pejoratively applied, in the singular, to the republican politician **Léon Gambetta** by certain radical republicans in response to his abandonment of some of their principal demands in favor of policies aimed at securing the support of the middle ground, increasingly represented by the aspiring classes of late-19th-century

France. The term entered common usage to describe Gambetta's followers, who dominated the republican majority in the legislature in the 1880s and 1890s.

– P –

PANAMA SCANDAL (1892–1893). Political scandal in which it was alleged that officials of the Panama Canal Company had bribed members of the Chamber of Deputies. Famous for masterminding the successful construction of the Suez Canal, **Ferdinand de Lesseps** formed the Panama Canal Company in 1880 with the purpose of driving a sea-level canal through the isthmus of Panama. The digging began in 1882, but major problems caused by a difficult topography, the decimation of the workforce through malaria, mismanagement, and undercapitalization placed the project in serious jeopardy. To secure more capital, the company bribed politicians and journalists across the political spectrum to procure approval by the Chamber of Deputies for a lottery loan in 1888. But the loan failed, and the company slid into bankruptcy in 1889. The affair was covered over until an exposé appeared in **Edouard Drumont**'s anti-Semitic newspaper, *La Libre Parole*, in 1892, feeding prejudices about the corruption of France by Jewish interests. On 21 November 1892 in the Chamber of Deputies, an ex-supporter of General **Georges Boulanger**, Albert de Gauthier Clagny, asserted that over 100 deputies had received checks from Panama Canal Company representatives Baron Jacques de Reinach and Cornelius Herz. The press carried the claims and counterclaims into the spring of 1893, when an inquiry commissioned by the Chamber exonerated all the accused deputies except one, temporarily halting **Georges Clemenceau**'s political career. Reinach committed suicide and Herz fled France. The effect on the general election of the same year was to shift the Chamber of Deputies to the left.

PARIS. Capital of France, located at the confluence of the **Seine** and Marne rivers. It was originally the capital of a tribe of **Gaul**, the Parisii. Its name was changed to Lutetia following the Roman conquest of the city by Julius Caesar in 53 BC. Although it became the seat of the **Merovingian dynasty** around 508, it only assumed major significance during the rule of the **Capetian dynasty** (987–1328). The city was occupied by the English from 1420 to 1436 and besieged by Henri IV from 1590 to 1594. But the modern city is essentially a 19th-century creation. The process of restoration and beautification was given a new impetus by the **Bourbon dynasty**, and a major transformation was achieved by the Bonapartes, especially Louis-Napoléon (*see* BONAPARTE, LOUIS-NAPOLEON), who recruited Baron **Georges-Eugène Haussmann** to give the city the geometrically planned look, punctuated by grand, **empire-style** architecture, that is responsible for its unique elegance today. But this did not eclipse Paris's role as a hotbed of radical debate and occasional insurrection, dating back to the **French Revolution**, the **revolutions of 1830 and 1848**, the Commune, the **student rebellions** of 1968, as well as more recent riots in the city's deprived outer suburbs. A survey carried out in 2005 put the number of inhabitants at 2,153,600 spread across the city's 20 *arrondissements* or districts, with the 18th and 20th being the most populous as they host large migrant populations attracted by dense low-cost housing.

In addition to its physical emergence as the great European capital in the 19th century, Paris also became a magnet for intellectuals wishing to experiment in modern ideas across all the creative disciplines. As the center for the main currents of **art** and **music**, it was the natural home for major concert halls, the opera, and museums old and new, like the Louvre and the Pompidou Center. The centralization of political and cultural life inevitably led to the concentration of the national **press** in Paris, also providing it with a disproportionately large share of institutes of higher **education**, including the *grandes écoles*, the Sorbonne, and several other universities. Many of the great intellectual schools of the 19th and 20th centuries originated there and spread their influence across the world. This trend accelerated particularly in the 20th century, and after 1945 Paris was the home of intellectual trends that universally shaped critical discourse: **existentialism**, **structuralism**, **poststructuralism**, and **postmodernism**.

Becoming mayor of Paris has provided a major power base and a springboard for national office for figures like **Jacques Chirac** and **Bertrand Delanoë**. This, among other factors, has made governments of whatever political persuasion determined to invest in Paris as a showcase for French culture and creativity. Hence the continuing tradition of substantial state investment in the infrastructure of the city and in the kind of public buildings that keep it in the forefront of the quest for modernity, as exemplified by the *grands projets* such as the Louvre Pyramid undertaken during the **presidency** of **François Mitterrand**. The same factors underwrite its position as the capital city that attracts more foreign visitors than any other in the world. The most recent innovation has been the 2006 introduction of a tram system linking the 13th, 14th, and 15th *arrondissements* and carrying 100,000 passengers a day.

However, in government circles awareness has also been growing of the need to undo the damage to the relationship between Paris and the **regions** that was summed up in the old adage "after Paris, the desert." Hence the decision to move the elite Ecole Nationale d'Administration (ENA) to **Strasbourg** in 1992, and which saw ENA finally cease its activities in Paris in 2007. Within Paris itself, it was realized that there had to be a move to the periphery to relieve the pressure on the center. So in 1973, the famous market symbolic of old Paris, Les Halles, was moved to Rungis in the Val de Marne, 14 kilometers from the city. And in spite of the reluctance of some senior civil servants, in 1989 the finance ministry completed its move from the palatial offices it traditionally occupied in the Louvre to a purpose-built building at Bercy in the 12th *arrondissement. See also* PARIS COMMUNE; PARIS REGION; SACRE-COEUR; TOURISM.

PARIS COMMUNE (1789–1795). Revolutionary and radical government of **Paris** that at its height embodied the principles and prerogatives of popular sovereignty. The municipal law of 14 December 1789 provided a legal basis for the communes that had been formed spontaneously after 14 July. A further law passed in June 1790 defined the organizational basis for the municipal government of Paris. The social origin of the elected representatives of the Commune changed as the right to elect them widened. When suffrage was limited to active citizens, as in September 1790, 75 percent of those elected were merchants and members of the legal profession. With the introduction of universal suffrage, this changed, as a far greater number of representatives were drawn from the working class. This fact, allied with the independent prerogatives enjoyed by the Paris Commune, such as the control of the **armed forces** of the interior, caused tension between the representatives of the Paris Commune and the representatives of the nation, particularly at moments of crisis. Thus, after the fall of **Louis XVI**, the insurrectionary Commune behaved as if it were the real authority in France by sanctioning the mass arrest of suspects, the requisitioning of food, and the fixing of prices for necessities. It effectively imposed its will on the **Convention** during the crisis of 31 May–2 June 1793. Its independence, however, was severely cut back in legislation passed in December, and its power as a source of radical expression disappeared with the fall of **Robespierre**. *See also* FRENCH REVOLUTION.

PARISOT, LAURENCE (1959–). Head of the French employers' organization Mouvement des Entreprises de France (MEDEF). She graduated in law from the university of Nancy and in political science from the Institut d'Etudes Politiques in **Paris** before beginning her career working for the Louis Harris polling organization. Her birth, into a family that had made a fortune in the furniture business, destined her for a role in the life of corporate France. She was elected onto the MEDEF executive in 2002 and ultimately elected head of the organization in 2005. From the outset, Parisot made it clear that one of her principal aims was to reconcile market disciplines with a social conscience. It was this ambition that led her to speak out courageously against the golden good-bye of 1.5 million euros that was paid to a departing senior figure in the Union des Industries et Métiers de la Métallurgie (UIMM), an employers' organization in the metallurgical **industry**. Parisot criticized the lack of transparency that characterized this much reported payment and distanced the MEDEF in unequivocal terms from the UIMM.

PARIS REGION. Known as the région Ile de France, it grew out of the royal domain of the **Capetian dynasty** in the 10th century. It is now an area covering 12,072 square kilometers and eight departments (Essonne, Hauts-de-Seine, **Paris**, Seine-Saint-Denis, Seine-et-Marne, Val-de-Marne, Val d'Oise, Yvelines), housing 11 million people known as Franciliens; at its heart rests the city of Paris. Managing the growth of the region became a priority identified in 1960, resulting most significantly in the Plan d'Aménagement et d'Organisation Générale de la Région Parisienne. This initiated a series of planning measures aimed at coping with the growth of the Parisian agglomeration by laying down the transport and housing infrastructure to accommodate this expansion. The biggest commitment in material terms came with the creation of the five new towns designated to be built within 35 kilometers of the city center: Cergy-Pontoise, Evry, Marne-la-Vallée, Melun-Sénart, and St. Quentin-en-Yvelines. While initially not very well served by the public transport system, these towns were eventually connected to the high-speed section of the Métro, the Réseau Express Régional, making them much more accessible. By the early 1990s they provided over 100,000 homes for predominantly young working families—homes of a standard that they would not have been able to afford in Paris proper.

Improvement of communications in and out of the region remains a priority, and this goal received a considerable boost when **Charles de Gaulle** Airport was opened at Roissy, thus taking the pressure off the old airports at Orly and Le Bourget. The national exhibition center, the Parc des Expositions, was built on a site adjacent to the airport, and this part of the Paris region, with its good road and rail connections to the city and the rest of the country, was identified by the government in 1990 as a future growth center for the agglomeration. The Fédération Internationale de Football Association's designation of Paris to host the **soccer World Cup** in 1998 further boosted the infrastructure of the region, which built the first new world-class stadium since the one constructed for the Olympic Games in 1924. Underwritten by the central government, the 80,000-seat Stade de France was built at Saint-Denis and was accompanied by a major upgrade in the road and rail links with central Paris.

PARLEMENTS. The 13 sovereign courts of appeal in **Paris** and the provinces that existed under the **ancien régime** and that had their origins in the supreme courts of the great feudal rulers of medieval times. By the 18th century the *parlements* had come to enjoy extensive administrative powers as well as being the final courts of appeal for their regions. But most important, they played a crucial part in the legislative process, since all laws had to be registered in their records to become valid, and *parlements* had the right to send the king remonstrances if they judged the proposed legislation to be defective. The final decades of the life of the ancien régime were marked by increasing tension between the *parlements* and the crown's ministers, as opposition hardened to what they saw as unacceptable measures to plug the holes in the crown's finances caused notably by expensive military adventures abroad.

PARTI COMMUNISTE FRANCAIS (PCF)/FRENCH COMMUNIST PARTY. The first socialist party in France to place obedience to the doctrinal line emanating from Moscow above fidelity to the pluralist principles of France's own socialist traditions. Its origins lay in the split that occurred at the congress of French socialists at Tours in December 1920. Under pressure from Moscow to adopt a certain number of conditions before they could be allowed to join the Communist International, such as the name "communist" and a correspondingly centralized organization, the French socialist movement divided between those who refused to sacrifice their more democratic traditions and those willing to accept the ideological rigors of Moscow. It was the latter group that went on to form the French Communist Party and thus initiate a long tradition of rivalry with the **Socialists**. The two parties did unite electorally in the mid-1930s under the banner of the **Popular Front** to fight the threat posed by the extreme right, but it was indicative of the French Communists' loyalty to Moscow that they did not throw themselves into the resistance to the Nazi occupiers of France during **World War II** until the pact between **Germany** and the **Soviet Union** had collapsed. With the Western Allies and the Soviets finally on the same side, the French Communists distinguished themselves in the **Resistance** because of their courage, determination, and efficient organization.

The credit accruing to the PCF as the result of some of its members' action during the occupation helps explain the party's solid base of electoral support after 1945, when it regularly polled in the region of 20 percent of the votes cast, more than any other single party—this in spite of its allegiance to the Soviet Union during the Cold War. However, the less rigid kind of Eurocommunism that emerged in countries like Italy during the 1970s and 1980s made the more Moscow-oriented PCF, under the leadership of **Georges Marchais**, appear unnecessarily doctrinaire and out of touch with sister movements in Europe, its own members, and the changing sensibilities of its host society. Furthermore, the PCF was outmaneuvered by the **Parti Socialiste (PS)** during the years of their **Common Program** in the 1970s and saw its electoral credibility decline as the PS's increased. The party's apparently inexorable decline seemed confirmed after the collapse of communism in the Soviet Union and the loss of its ideological raison d'être.

But the replacement of Georges Marchais in 1994 by Robert Hue at the head of the party allowed the PCF to refresh its image, due to the genial and media-friendly manner of its new leader. However, Hue's plans for the "mutation" or transformation of the party into a more pluralist and transparent organization were deemed to be too little too late by significant figures inside the party. As for the wider electorate, it was clear from Hue's 3.37 percent share of the vote in the first round of the 2002 presidential elections that they had not been convinced either. In 2003 Hue gave way to the first female leader of the party, Marie-Georges Buffet. She had risen through the party ranks since joining at the age of 20 in 1969, and made a reputation for herself based on quiet efficiency and consensus building. She stood as the party's presidential candidate in 2007, but her score of 1.9 percent in the first round underlined the fact that the future of the PCF would lie in its ability to federate those nonsocialist forces of the left. *See also* ROCHET, WALDECK; THOREZ, MAURICE.

PARTI SOCIALISTE (PS)/SOCIALIST PARTY. A left-wing coalition born from the ashes of the old **Section Française de l'Internationale Ouvrière** in 1969 but which embarked on its mission to become the premier party of the left at the PS congress of June 1971 in Epinay, when **François Mitterrand** became its leader. Mitterrand's tactical genius was manifested in the electoral alliance he shaped with the PS's more powerful rival for the left-wing vote, the **Parti Communiste Français (PCF)**, which resulted in the **Common Program** for government in June 1972. It was clear that the PS gained more from the alliance than the PCF, and when the alliance ended in acrimony six years later, it had given the PS the time and opportunity to establish its credibility vis-à-vis the PCF's working-class voters, as well as preserving its own more middle-class electorate. Proof of this was given in the 1978 legislative elections, when the PS share of the vote showed that it could now boast of having eclipsed the PCF as the premier party of the left.

The high point of the PS's fortunes came in 1981, when Mitterrand was elected president of the Republic. Under his leadership, the party had proved itself acceptable to the French electorate, in no small measure because of its diminishing attachment to left-wing ideology. As early as 1982–1983 the party began to shift toward more market-orientated policies, introducing the rigor of market forces to the public sector. With Mitterrand, the PS had a candidate with an unparalleled mastery of French presidential politics, and this explains his success as the party's candidate in two consecutive presidential elections (1981 and 1988), even though the party no longer enjoyed the enthusiastic support of the electorate. Mitterrand's inability to stand again in 1995 following the catastrophic performance of the PS's candidates in the legislative elections of 1993 led to a vacuum of leadership at the top of the party, as its leading figures declined the PS candidacy in the presidential elections of 1995 in view of what many perceived as an inevitable drubbing.

The surprisingly good performance of **Lionel Jospin** as the eventual PS candidate (coming second to **Jacques Chirac** but with over 47 percent of the vote) and his confirmation as PS leader underlined that there was still a left-wing constituency in France willing to be wooed by the party. The legislative elections of 1997 confirmed the upturn in the PS's fortunes, when it led a left-wing majority into the National Assembly. This inaugurated a period of **cohabitation** with a novel twist, because this time it was a center-right president facing a socialist-led government. Jospin's government was nicknamed *la gauche plurielle* (plural left) since it included ministers from five different parties of various socialist and **ecologist** persuasions. In spite of major reforms such as the introduction of the 35-hour working week and a civil solidarity pact that recognized the rights of same-sex partners in law, enduring problems such as unemployment led to disenchantment among the electorate. This was signaled dramatically in the first round of the presidential elections of 2002 when Jospin as the PS candidate was edged out of the second place behind Chirac by the far-right candidate **Jean-Marie Le Pen**.

The shock of this result severely dented the self-confidence of the party, but it went into the 2007 presidential elections with a new look and a new style. Headed for the first time by a husband and wife team, with François Hollande as the party leader and **Ségolène Royal** as the PS candidate, the Socialists hoped that they could offer a new vision to the French people. The campaign played on Royal's appeal as a mother of four children and her willingness to heal divisions and defend the rights of workers and citizens against the excesses of global capitalism, in contrast to what was portrayed as the socially abrasive and pro–free market policies of her main rival, the Gaullist **Nicolas Sarkozy**. However, the Socialists' decision to base much of their campaign on a scare tactic of "tout sauf Sarkozy" ("anything but Sarkozy") backfired, and he was elected with 53.06 percent of the vote in the head–to-head contest against Royal in the second round of the presidential election in May 2007. A degree of panic broke out in the ranks of the PS following this result, in the light of the legislative elections scheduled for the following month. Some feared that the party might not even muster a group of deputies running into three figures in the new National Assembly. Those fears proved unfounded, and by the end of June 2007 the PS found itself at the head of a parliamentary group comprising 204 deputies, out of a total of 577 in the Assembly.

This surprisingly positive result did not put an end to the tensions in the party, especially among its major figures, who criticized the management of the party and especially its failure to renew its appeal to the French electorate. Flushed with victory, President Sarkozy was quick to exploit the unhappiness among PS personalities by inviting figures like **Bernard Kouchner** and **Jack Lang** to participate in the business of government. When justifying his decision to join the commission charged with reviewing the **constitution** of the **Fifth Republic**, Lang invited the leadership of the PS to resign and allow the party grassroots to voice its opinion on the direction the party should take in pursuing its renewal.

During the weeks following Royal's defeat in the presidential elections, the announcement that she was parting ways with her partner, Hollande, was a very personal reflection of a very public failure by the PS leadership. However, opinion polls in early 2008 showed Royal to be clearly ahead of her rivals, such as Dominique Strauss-Kahn and **Bertrand Delanoë**, in the popularity stakes vis-à-vis PS members and also the wider electorate. In January 2008 Royal publicly stated that she was confident of her ability to unite the party and gave every indication of challenging for the leadership at the PS congress scheduled for November. *See also* PARTI SOCIALISTE UNIFIE.

PARTI SOCIALISTE UNIFIE (PSU)/UNITED SOCIALIST PARTY. A small but influential party on the French left. It was formed when three splinter groups came together in 1958 to oppose French policy in **Algeria**. One of its most famous early leaders was **Pierre Mendès-France**. After the Algerian war, the PSU turned its attention to the need to draw the socialists and the **communists** in France into a broad alliance as the only way of defeating **Gaullism**. Intellectually, the PSU's awareness of the need to redefine the agenda of the left to account for the changing aspirations of white-collar workers and a widespread desire for greater self-management, or *autogestion*, was crucial in distinguishing the PSU from other components of the left. An example was the speed and intelligence of its reaction to the **student rebellions** of 1968. But by the early 1970s it was clear that the aims of the party could best be served by an alliance with the resurgent **Socialists** led by **François Mitterrand**, although **Michel Rocard**'s decision in 1974 to lead the PSU into the **Parti Socialiste** fold commanded the support of only 40 percent of its members. The fortunes of what remained of the PSU declined to the point of making it insignificant in electoral terms. Nonetheless, it was a political nursery for individuals who were later counted among the most high-profile figures in the Socialist establishment during the 1980s, including Michel Rocard, **Jack Lang**, and **Jacques Delors**.

PASTEUR, LOUIS (1822–1895). Arguably the greatest figure in 19th-century French science. He laid the foundation for the development of modern microbiology, especially immunology, through his discovery that fermentation was caused by microorganisms. Pasteur's development of methods for preventing microbial contamination brought the term *pasteurization* into universal use in regard to, for example, the treatment of milk. Pasteur brought his experimental prowess to a wide variety of challenges, such as the study of anthrax, and his memory is revered by **Lyon**'s silk industry because of the breakthrough he made in counteracting silkworm disease. His posterity was assured in his lifetime when the Institut Pasteur was founded in **Paris** in 1888 as the result of his work in developing an antirabies vaccine. The Institut Pasteur remains a recognized center of excellence for research in science and currently enjoys a worldwide reputation for its work in mapping the human genome.

PETAIN, PHILIPPE (1856–1951). Marshal and leader of occupied France during **World War II**. He was born into a peasant Catholic family on 24 April 1856 in the village of Cauchy-à-la-Tour (Pas-de-Calais). He graduated from the military academy of St.-Cyr in 1878 and by the outbreak of **World War I** had risen to the rank of colonel without distinguishing himself in any particular way, although the war made his reputation. His contribution to the battle on the Marne (1914) and his command at Verdun confirmed the perception that he was a gifted defensive strategist, in contrast to other military leaders who were profligate with their soldiers' lives. At the end of the war Pétain was promoted to the rank of *maréchal de France*. He accepted the portfolio of defense minister in 1934 and in 1939 was sent by the **Edouard Daladier** government as ambassador to Spain.

With his reputation as a great general and his image of benevolent paternalism, Pétain was perceived by many as the providential leader France needed after the collapse in the face of the German advance in May 1940. Thus on 10 July 1940 the National Assembly effectively rendered itself redundant by voting to give Pétain the power to draw up a new **constitution** for the French state. The new **Vichy regime** attempted to persuade the French that although the country was defeated, it still retained a measure of sovereignty. It did this through a policy of collaboration with the German occupiers, and the prestige of Pétain as paternalist head of the regime was used to push through a series of measures that fostered the view that France had been defeated because of the moral failures encouraged by the **Popular Front** and that these measures were justified in terms of a new *révolution nationale*. After the **liberation** Pétain was tried and convicted of treason. His death sentence in 1945 was commuted to life imprisonment because of his advanced age (89). He died on 23 July 1951 on the Ile d'Yeu, where he had been exiled.

PHILIPPE IV, LE BEL (1268–1314). King who laid the foundation for the legal and ethical justification of the absolute sovereignty of the monarch in France. Instead of relying on the manipulation of feudal allegiances to maintain his power, Philippe le Bel recruited legal minds like Guillaume de Nogaret to define a constitutional context in which the king could legitimately claim to be the supreme authority in his kingdom. To secure the widest possible consensus for this legal foundation to the king's power, opportunities were developed for the ritual exaltation of royal authority. Hence the first convocation of barons, clerics, and bourgeois that took place in 1302 and that was a precursor to the **Estates General**.

PHILIPPE AUGUSTE (1165–1223). Distinguished among the kings of the **Capetian dynasty** for the role he played in helping to turn France into the greatest kingdom in Christendom. He is remembered for the successful struggle he led against the territorial claims of Henry II of England over France. By the time of his death Philippe Auguste had secured most of the north of the country for the French crown.

PHILIPPE D'ORLEANS, COMTE DE PARIS (1838–1894). Grandson of **Louis-Philippe**, the last king to succeed to the throne of France, and himself pretender to the throne. He returned to France from exile in 1871, in the wake of the **Franco-Prussian War**, when the prospect of a restoration was revived among royalists. He submitted to his older rival pretender to the throne, the **comte de Chambord**, and when the latter died in 1883, he headed a reunited royalist party, taking the title Philippe VII. Philippe d'Orléans was much more pragmatic than his predecessor and was prepared to cooperate or collude with any interests that might help to restore the monarchy. In 1886 he was expelled from France by the government for his royalist activities. During his exile in **Great Britain**, his agents conspired with General **Georges Boulanger** to overthrow the Republic. Boulanger's failure and the elections that followed in 1889 confirmed the terminal decline of royalist hopes. This, combined with the effects of ill health, led to Philippe d'Orléans's withdrawal from politics.

PHILIPPE, GERARD (1922–1959). Stage and screen actor who enjoyed immense popularity after 1945 but whose career tragically ended with his premature death. He made his stage debut in his hometown of Cannes and in the 1950s successfully took on some of the most demanding roles in French theater, such as *Le Cid* and *Lorenzaccio*. But exposure to a mass public came through films, and Philippe started his career in light romantic comedies like *La boîte aux rêves* (1944). His exceptional good looks and fine voice made him an obvious candidate for swashbuckling roles in films like *Fanfan-la-tulipe* (1952). But he could also use his screen presence with great subtlety to express a sense of insecurity and self-obsession, as in the film version of *Le rouge et le noir* (1954). Philippe resisted the lure of Hollywood and continued to extend his range with films in the European tradition through powerful roles like the portrayal of the doomed alcoholic artist Modigliani in *Montparnasse 19* (1957) and the callously calculating Valmont in the French film version of *Les liaisons dangereuses* (1960). His premature death ensured the survival of his reputation as a legendary talent of French stage and screen. *See also* CINEMA.

PIAF, EDITH (1915–1963). A very popular French singer from the 1930s to the 1950s whose tragic private life was mirrored in some of her most famous songs. She was born Edith Gassion in **Paris**, the daughter of an itinerant acrobat, and had to learn to fend for herself by singing from an early age. She was discovered in 1935 by cabaret owner Louis Leplée, who employed her and gave her the stage name Piaf (meaning "sparrow" in Parisian slang). Within a few years Piaf was cutting records and singing in films. The success of her New York debut in 1947 confirmed her international status, enhanced thereafter by her ability to perform in English. However, her emotionally and materially precarious early life seemed to make her destined to suffer tragic insecurities in her adult life. Piaf married twice, but her most high-profile relationship was the affair with French middleweight boxing champion Marcel Cerdan. His death in 1949 in a plane crash, when he was flying to see her in New York, plunged her into the first of a series of deep depressions. The painful consequences of a car accident in 1951 increased her susceptibility to drugs and alcohol. She was hospitalized on a number of occasions during the years that followed and died on 10 October 1963 as the result of a massive internal hemorrhage.

Piaf was a performer who invested her singing with the power of raw emotion, and she captivated her public through the spirit she displayed, especially in the face of bitter adversity. Her two most enduringly popular songs, "La vie en rose" and "Non, je ne regrette rien," also served as evocative, personal anthems. The poignancy of her life story, reflected in her music, has continued to move the public even generations after her death. This was underlined by the success of the biopic *La vie en rose* (2007), which had the public queuing for tickets in New York as well as Paris and earned the actress playing Piaf, Marion Cotillard, the Oscar for best actress in 2008. *See also* MUSIC.

PISSARRO, CAMILLE (1830–1903). Painter and founding member of the **impressionist** movement. Born the son of a merchant in the Virgin Islands, Pissarro was sent to boarding school in **Paris** in 1842. In spite of success in exhibiting a landscape at the official Salon in 1859, Pissarro soon rejected convention in favor of experimentation and exhibited with other avant-garde artists at the independent Salon des Refusés in 1863. The **Franco-Prussian War** caused Pissarro to seek refuge in London. He returned to France after the fall of the **Commune** in 1871 and settled in the village of Pontoise, where he worked closely with **Paul Gauguin**, among others, for the rest of the decade. Pissarro's **impressionism** emerges mostly through his landscapes, conveying his empathy with nature. But he also produced still lifes and portraits that combined a traditional severity of outline with a notable depth and richness of color. He was liked by his peers for his kindness and respected for his wisdom. He died on 13 November 1903. *See also* ART.

PLAN. Term used to describe the series of four- to five-year plans that have guided France's economic development since 1947. The plans occurred as follows: first 1947–1953, second 1954–1957, third 1958–1961, fourth 1962–1965, fifth 1966–1970, sixth 1971–1975, and seventh 1976–1980. An eighth plan was prepared for 1981–1985 but was never submitted to parliament. An interim plan covered 1982–1983, a ninth plan covered 1984–1988, and a 10th covered 1989–1992. The changing focus of the plans reflects the evolution of the French **economy** and changes in government thinking. The plans of the 1940s and early 1950s reflected the need to boost production through the fixing of growth targets to make up for wartime deficits. By the 1960s the plans had begun to address broad growth strategies and the need for France to position itself in certain key industries, like information technology. By the 1980s even the most ardent advocates of these plans accepted the limitations placed on their accuracy by the increasing integration of France into a global economy; the return of the center-right to government in the late 1980s reinforced this shift in ideological terms. In 2005 Sophie Boissard was named head of the Commissariat Général du Plan and oversaw its transformation during the following year into Le Centre d'Analyse Stratégique, thus underlining the fundamental shift in its purpose.

POHER, ALAIN (1909–1996). Long-serving Christian Democratic senator of the **Fifth Republic**, twice responsible for ensuring the smooth transition between presidencies. He began his career in national politics under the **Fourth Republic** and led the Christian Democratic group in the Senate for several periods during the 1950s and 1960s. It was as president of the Senate in 1968 that he was successful in leading the opposition to the reforms proposed in **Charles de Gaulle**'s referendum, which would have reduced the role of the Senate and strengthened administrative structures in the **regions**. Poher assumed the duties of the **presidency** after de Gaulle's resignation (28 April–19 June 1969) and stood as a candidate in the ensuing elections. But he lost to **Georges Pompidou**, who had characterized a Poher presidency as a throwback to the impotence of the Fourth Republic. Ever the bridesmaid, Poher assumed temporary presidential powers once more after the death of Pompidou until new elections could take place (2 April–27 May 1974).

POINCARE, RAYMOND (1860–1934). Prime minister and president of France. He was born into a bourgeois republican family in Bar-le-Duc (Meuse) with a strong streak of patriotism and **anticlericalism**. A brilliant student, Poincaré became a lawyer at 20 and began his parliamentary career seven years later, representing the *département* of his birth. He was elected first to the Chamber of Deputies (1887–1903) and then to the Senate (1903–1910, 1920–1934). He formed governments in 1912–1913, 1922–1924, and 1926–1928 and served as president of the Republic from 1913 to 1920. Poincaré's republicanism, economic liberalism, and anticlericalism allowed him successfully to occupy the middle ground, even though he was not formally a member of any party.

He began to build his reputation as a sound manager of the nation's budget as finance minister in 1895. He rallied to the **Dreyfus** camp, and although disinclined to support **Emile Combes** for fear of promoting sectarianism, he remained anticlerical and thus distanced from the right. As head of the government in 1912, he reacted to Franco-German tensions by striving to strengthen the alliance with **Russia** and military cooperation with **Great Britain**. In spite of his election to the **presidency** in 1913, Poincaré continued to involve himself actively in French **foreign policy**, for example visiting St. Petersburg in 1914 to encourage preparedness in case of war. He successfully appealed for a coalition government after the outbreak of war (*l'union sacrée*) but became increasingly frustrated by the political impotence imposed by the constitutional limitations on the presidency.

As premier again in 1922 and a believer in the firm application of the terms of the **Treaty of Versailles**, Poincaré sent French troops to occupy the German industrial heartland of the Ruhr (11 January 1923) after he lost patience with German equivocations over the payment of war reparations. The German government gave in after nine months, and the issue was settled by the international conference resulting in the Dawes plan (1924). The defeat of the **Bloc National** in 1924 prompted Poincaré's resignation, but he was called to form another cabinet in July 1926 in the midst of a financial crisis caused by the rapidly falling value of the franc. Through astute deployment of the exceptional powers granted to him and the return to financial orthodoxies, Poincaré halted the slide in the value of the franc and was hailed as the savior of the nation's currency. Poincaré's majority was returned in the legislative elections of 1928, but because of illness, he withdrew from government in 1929 with his reputation as the supreme manager of the nation's finances intact. *See also* GERMANY.

POLICE. In feudal France the powers of policing were part and parcel of the prerogatives of the local lord, who delegated the power to arrest, try, and punish individuals as he saw fit. Separation of powers, an independent system of justice, and impartial enforcement of the law were not established until the **ancien regime** was overthrown. The police force in France and its public service remit were defined in article 12 of the Declaration of the Rights of Man and the Citizen in 1789. The police force as it currently exists comprises three types. The *police municipale*, as the title suggests, comes under the direct control of the local mayor and its main function is to maintain the local peace, provide assistance to the local population in case of civil emergency, and enforce the local bylaws. The *police nationale* is controlled by the Ministry of the Interior and its officers are employees of the state. It takes responsibility for fighting organized crime, **terrorism**, urban violence, and illegal **immigration** and enforcing the highway code. The *gendarmerie nationale* is a police force with a military status and comes under the control of the Ministry of Defense. It replicates some of the *police nationale*'s traffic control and public order functions but outside the urban areas where the *police nationale* operates. The gendarmerie is sometimes called in to reinforce the police in restoring public order when it breaks down in urban areas. The task that the gendarmerie alone can assume, however, is deployment overseas to exercise policing functions for the military. *See also* ARMED FORCES.

POLITICAL PARTIES. The **French Revolution** gave rise to competing groups in the country's first national assembly, divided between the radical **Jacobins** pressing for a republic and the **Girondins** in favor of a constitutional monarchy. But the emergence of what may be recognized as a modern party political system can be traced back to the parliament constituted under the restoration monarchy of **Louis XVIII** during the 1816–1820 period. The popular press of the time portrayed the left as a group of liberal deputies shaped by the ideals of the **Enlightenment** and the right as ultras essentially concerned with the restoration of a system based on privilege. The center was depicted as being composed of opportunistic deputies availing themselves of every opportunity for self-advancement.

In contrast to the long periods of continuity in the service of enduringly stable societies that have characterized Anglo-Saxon political systems, the comparatively rapid sequence of violent changes in

France during the 19th century and the rich variety of intellectual traditions that have competed to shape the political allegiances of the French are crucial factors militating against the development of large and homogeneous parties. The fault line during the second half of the 19th century along which political tendencies allied and opposed each other was the transformation of France into a secular society, led initially by the Radicals and opposed by various strands of the Catholic royalist and Bonapartist right. As the century progressed, however, the pursuit of an **anticlerical** agenda was broadened into a wider desire for social emancipation that was woven into the ambitions of the various manifestations of the left, notably but not exclusively among the socialists and communists. During the life of the **Third Republic** in particular, numerous party political tendencies coexisted in the play of shifting alliances required to constitute a governing majority and conditioned a parliamentary culture where French parties can coalesce around priorities that do not fall within an archetypal left- or right-wing ideology but are instead enunciated by an inspirational leader. The numerous reinventions of **Gaullism** as a party from the end of **World War II** onward are an example. Ideologies that are well established but perceived as stale can also be given a new lease on life in party terms by a charismatic leader who fashions the organization, if not in his image, then to suit his leadership style, as was the case with **François Mitterrand** and the Socialists in the early 1970s.

Party politics in France is not, therefore, about the conflict between two or three big blocs in parliament but rather about the interplay of formations, which themselves can contain small but very distinct tendencies. The left in French politics for most of the twentieth century comprised two major parties, the **Parti Socialiste (PS)**, which united behind **François Mitterrand** in 1971 as the latest incarnation of the gradualist and pluralist tradition in French socialism, and the **Parti Communiste Français (PCF)**, which has been in continuous existence since the split with the previous tradition of French socialism at the **Congress of Tours** in 1920. The parties competed with each other for the votes of the left-wing constituency but also cooperated when faced with the challenge of governmental office or the prospect of defeat by center-right formations. The tactic known as the **Union of the Left** showed the ambiguity of this relationship in the 1970s and 1980s. The relationship between the two parties was further complicated by the fact that the traditionally senior partner in the relationship in terms of organizational strength and support, the PCF, had to endure relegation to a much inferior position because of its eclipse by the Socialist party after its rebirth under François Mitterrand. By the beginning of the 21st century the PCF was reduced to a shadow of what it had been a generation earlier as an electoral force and, at consistently less than 5 percent of the votes cast, was scoring barely a few percentage points higher than far-left parties such as Lutte Ouvrière and the Ligue Communiste Révolutionnaire. This structural change in the architecture of the left-wing vote in France isolated the PS as the last great party of the left and made its mission of successfully competing with the center-right for office even more difficult.

The attempt to create the kind of mass Christian democratic center party that could reconcile moderate Catholic opinion with republican reformism has not found enduring success in France, in spite of the popularity of the **Mouvement Républicain Populaire (MRP)**, which grew out of the Catholic **Resistance** during the **Fourth Republic**. So for most of the life of the **Fifth Republic** the left competed against a center-right represented by two parties, the liberal **Union pour la Démocratie Française (UDF)** and its more right-wing and more powerful partner, the Gaullist Rassemblement pour la République or RPR (*see* GAULLIST PARTY). The UDF in particular reflected the heterogeneous nature of French political allegiances and coalesced as a party of non-Gaullist center-right tendencies behind **Valéry Giscard d'Estaing** in 1978. This idea of a formation containing distinct tendencies explained the apparent confusion that arose when figures in the UDF also claimed loyalty to groups within it, such as the conservatively inclined Parti Républicain or the Christian Democratic Centre des Démocrates Sociaux. Like the left, the parties of the center-right in the National Assembly competed against each other for adherents, but these differences were subsumed by the greater conflicts between the "political families" of left and right that arose when the **electoral system** of the Fifth Republic forced deputies ultimately to unite behind the best-placed candidate of the left or right, even if this was not the candidate of one's preferred party, in order to beat the opposition.

By the beginning of the 21st century, however, the political class as a whole in France was forced to accept that the old ideological divisions that had characterized party politics, such as left and right, were failing to mirror the wishes of an increasing number of voters. So in 2002 the RPR decided to reinvent itself to broaden its appeal by allying with a number of Christian democrats, liberals, radicals, and independents in a new party vehicle called the Union pour un Mouvement Populaire (Union for a Popular Movement/UMP). Old traditions die hard, however, as in the squeeze the left and right put on the center when it comes to elections. In the 2007 legislative elections the leading light of the UDF, **François Bayrou**, attempted to build on his creditable performance in the preceding presidential election by launching a new vehicle, Mouvement Démocrate (MoDem), for the ambitions of centrists like himself to offer the electorate a genuine alternative to the left or right in power. Unfortunately for him, most of the UDF deputies decided to play safe and continue their parliamentary alliance with the UMP, and in the new assembly constituted in June 2007 MoDem saw only three deputies take their seats.

The unique balance and functioning of the French party political system was partly undermined by the emergence in the 1980s of a far-right party, the **Front National (FN)**. Initially, some commentators saw the party as little more than the kind of passing right-wing populism that had sprung up around General **Georges Boulanger** in the 19th century or the lower-middle-class militancy characterized by **Poujadism** in the 1950s. More alarmed members of the left saw in the FN's anti-immigrant discourse a reminder of the proto-fascist *ligues* of the interwar years and even the shadow of the fascist parties under the **Vichy regime** such as the Parti Populaire Français. But in spite of some of its far-right policies, the FN played by the rules of the **constitution** and proved itself capable of taking up to 15 percent of the vote in national elections. The party reached its high point in the first round of the presidential elections of 2002 when its charismatic leader, **Jean-Marie Le Pen**, beat the Socialist candidate, **Lionel Jospin**, to the second place behind the eventual winner **Jacques Chirac**. But the results of the presidential elections of 2007 showed the fortunes of the FN to be in steep decline as the eventual winner, **Nicolas Sarkozy**, wrested issues such as combating crime and curtailment of illegal immigration from the far right and made them legitimate campaigning issues for the center-right. *See also* COMMON PROGRAM; ECOLOGISTS; FEDERATION DE LA GAUCHE DEMOCRATIQUE ET SOCIALISTE; FORCE OUVRIERE (FO)/LABOR FORCE; MOUVEMENT DES RADICAUX DE GAUCHE (MRG)/MOVEMENT OF LEFT-WING RADICALS; MOUVEMENT REPUBLICAIN POPULAIRE (MRP)/POPULAR REPUBLICAN MOVEMENT; PARTI SOCIALISTE UNIFIE (PSU)/UNITED SOCIALIST PARTY; POPULAR FRONT; SOCIALISM; THIRD FORCE; TRIPARTISM; UNION OF THE LEFT.

POMPIDOU, GEORGES (1911–1974). Premier and second president of the **Fifth Republic**. He was born on 5 July 1911 in the community of Montboudif in the Auvergne region of France. A brilliant scholar of classical languages and philosophy, Pompidou studied at both the prestigious Ecole Normale Supérieure and the Ecole Libre des Sciences Politiques. He abandoned his teaching career at the outbreak of war in 1939 and in 1944 joined **Charles de Gaulle**'s staff. He became a member of the **Gaullist** Rassemblement du Peuple Français but distanced himself from **Fourth Republic** politics, opting for a career in banking in 1955. He returned to politics in 1958 and accepted de Gaulle's invitation to form a government in 1962. Pompidou was an adept politician who showed far greater astuteness in his reaction to the **student rebellions** in 1968 than his president. It was Pompidou who opened talks with the **trade unions** in the effort to prevent the country from grinding to a halt, and he proved an effective campaigner prior to the legislative elections in June 1968 that brought the Gaullists victory. In spite of this, de Gaulle replaced him as head of the government during the month that followed the victory. De Gaulle's failed gamble on a national referendum to approve his proposals for the restructuring of the Senate and greater **decentralization** forced him to resign and opened the way for Pompidou as the Gaullist candidate in the ensuing election. Pompidou ran a good campaign on a ticket of "continuity in change," and his victory on 15 June 1969 proved that the Fifth Republic could survive without the general.

Pompidou's presidential style was less regal and more relaxed than de Gaulle's, and he broadened his power base by appealing more to the center and thus reducing his reliance on the Gaullists, but his actions confirmed the presidential nature of the regime of the Fifth Republic in a manner wholly consistent with that of his predecessor. This was exemplified by the summary dismissal of Pompidou's prime minister, **Jacques Chaban-Delmas**, in January 1972 and his replacement with someone more pliable, **Pierre Messmer**, reinforcing the idea that the prime minister of the Fifth Republic draws his authority from the president and not from the **constitution** or the Assembly. Like de Gaulle, Pompidou saw **foreign policy** as a presidential preserve and continued his predecessor's policy of developing France's independent **nuclear** deterrent, or *force de frappe*, maintaining an arm's-length relationship with the **North Atlantic Treaty Organization**, and continuing resistance to political integration in Europe. However, unlike de Gaulle, he approved **Great Britain**'s entry into the **European Economic Community** and announced this change of policy without going through his ministers. On the domestic front, Pompidou made it clear that his main ambition was to speed the modernization of France, particularly the achievement by French enterprises of the kind of critical mass in key industrial sectors that would enable them to compete with foreign multinationals in the global marketplace.

When necessary, Pompidou was prepared to put aside the *hauteur* of his office and engage in party politics, as in the legislative elections of 1973. Faced with the prospect of a victory by the left, Pompidou predicted openly that such an event would damage the institutions of the Fifth Republic. When he died in office from cancer on 2 April 1974, Pompidou enjoyed a popularity rating of over 50 percent among the French public, and his campaign theme of "continuity in change" may be fairly regarded as a fitting epitaph for his career as the second president of the Fifth Republic.

POPULAR CULTURE. For the major part of France's history, the enjoyment of popular culture was orally and aurally based, delivered to a largely illiterate people through traditions of storytelling passed on from one generation to another, or through musical entertainments like those delivered by the medieval troubadours and the performances put on by traveling players. A great change occurred from the middle of the 19th century onward owing to the socioeconomic factors that drove the mass migration from the land to the urban centers and the national **education** policies that, within a matter of decades, had successfully achieved the goal of mass literacy. By the time of the *belle époque*, France's great urban centers possessed increasing numbers of ordinary people with a sufficient measure of disposable income to enjoy cheap entertainments like cabarets, music halls, and variety shows as well as an increasing array of popular newspapers and periodicals.

The advances in recorded **music** and cinematography between the world wars meant that in France, as elsewhere, national audiences were created for popular performers, and the tastes of those audiences could be gratified as soon as a record or film was released. French **cinema** in the interwar years was particularly successful in bringing to mass audiences themes related to the experiences of the common man, making stars of antiheroes like **Jean Gabin** as well as bringing to the screen the kind of popular fiction written by authors like Marcel Pagnol. Furthermore, the **Popular Front** government of the mid-1930s invested significantly in arts and leisure programs, particularly sports, aimed at developing the creativity and dynamism of working people and reflecting a French cultural identity that emanated from the base of society rather than filtering down from the top.

The great period of dedicated investment in popular culture by both the private and the public sectors came after 1945. Attempts by the central government to break down the perceived elitism surrounding enjoyment of the arts resulted in the concept at the end of the 1950s of a regional network of *Maisons de la culture*, envisaged by then–minister for culture **André Malraux** as cultural "cathedrals" dedicated to taking the arts to the people. More obviously successful at the time was the implantation of a pop culture of singers and entertainers in almost every home via television. Expansion of popular culture in all its forms was driven by the increase in leisure time available to the French, resulting, among other things, from the right to a fourth week of annual paid vacation given to workers in 1965. Increasing levels of prosperity for the vast majority of people meant that from 1960 to 1979 the average share of household expenses devoted to culture and leisure rose from 5.5 percent to 7.6 percent.

A changing intellectual climate also contributed to the undermining of the established hierarchy of cultural values in France, and this was dramatically illustrated by the **student rebellions** in 1968. Apart from their specific grievances relating to higher education in France, the students demanded a shift in cultural values away from the classically highbrow expressions of France's cultural identity to a new identity determined by the liberation of the popular imagination. Many on the left who had cut their political teeth in May 1968 saw the advent of a Socialist government in 1981 as the realization of their most cherished cultural ambitions. The ministerial portfolio for culture handed to **Jack Lang** was extremely well funded and prestigious, designed to allow him to pursue a funding policy that recognized the diversity and value of popular forms of cultural production in France. During his tenure, the French state created a comic strip museum at Angoulême, founded a circus school at Chalons, and constructed the Zénith, a 2,000-seat venue in **Paris** designed primarily for rock concerts. The ultimate event in cultural mass participation initiated by Lang remains the festival of music, when once a year French citizens are encouraged to play their instruments in public, whether in the street, on the train, or elsewhere, usually as an act of faith rather than an exercise in genuine musicianship.

Legislation passed in the 1980s and 1990s allowing the creation of hundreds of local radio stations and the ever-burgeoning choice of cable and satellite television tended, paradoxically, to lead to greater homogenization of content, since the programs were bought off the shelf from the greatest manufacturer of these products, the **United States**. What Lang had failed to understand was that the culture of the consumer society had become so democratized as to be enjoyed by people internationally. This is what led to the paradox of a minister of culture defending the fulfillment of popular tastes while at the same time trying to stem the tide of audiovisual products from the United States, for which the French seem to have an insatiable appetite. The attempt by Lang and his successors to restrict the flow of these foreign cultural products into France remains a bone of contention in trade talks between Paris and Washington and suggests that, however great the acceptability of popular culture in France, the perception of France's cultural identity and mission by the governing elite remains distinctly highbrow.

In spite of the ostensibly more free-market persuasion of the center-right administrations that succeeded the Socialists after 1997, the role of the state in determining cultural policy and influencing public taste remained unquestioned. Thus the budget for the Ministry of Culture and Communication announced in 2007 contained a 7.8 percent increase on the previous one and announced a full slate of capital investment programs, notably the *grands projets* or major works that will result in an extension of the Louvre in Lens, a museum of European and **Mediterranean** cultures in **Marseille**, and a Georges Pompidou Center in Metz. *See also* ART; BROADCAST MEDIA; LITERATURE; PRESS.

POPULAR FRONT (1936–1938). Broad coalition against the rise of the extreme right and attempt to lift France out of economic depression through reflationary measures. The antiparliamentary rioting of the right-wing *ligues* in **Paris** on 6 February 1934 that killed 17 people and injured many others roused the left to action and demonstrations on 12 February 1934, resulting in the spontaneous merging of marchers representing **Socialists**, **Communists**, and trade unionists in a call for unity of the left. Socialist and Communist officials, led respectively by **Léon Blum** and **Maurice Thorez**, met in early June to settle their differences, and in October, Thorez proposed that the understanding between the two parties of the left be opened up to include the middle-class Radicals, in pursuit of what the Communist newspaper *L'Humanité* called a "Popular Front against fascism." This alliance was formally initiated as the Rassemblement Populaire on 14 July 1935, and its immediate priority was to secure victory in the legislative elections scheduled for the spring of 1936.

The first round of the elections on 26 April 1936 indicated modest progress for the left, but in the second round on 3 May the Popular Front coalition secured a clear majority, with the **Parti Communiste Français** making the biggest gains. In spite of this, the new Popular Front government headed by Blum would be able to rely only on Communist support, not participation. The victory of the Popular Front was greeted by a wave of frequently spontaneous strikes and factory occupations in May and June by workers who expected the new government to be sympathetic to their demands. The strikes were ended by the **Matignon Agreements**, signed on 7–8 June, which attempted to reconcile the demands of the workers with the need to end the economic paralysis. The social legislation that followed, such as paid vacations and the 40-hour workweek, gave a great impetus to the notion of leisure as a right, even for workers, and started the tradition of the mass summer exodus to cheap holiday resorts.

However, the honeymoon period was short lived, brought to an end by two major crises: the civil war in Spain and the **economy**. Fearful of alienating its ally, **Great Britain**, which was opposed to intervention, or of creating tension with **Germany**, Blum's government resisted calls to help Spanish republicans, much to the dismay of many Socialists and Communists. On the economic front, the French government had attempted to employ Keynesian measures to reflate the economy, whereas the governments of the other major economic powers had cut spending in the face of the international recession. The inevitable run on the franc followed. To stabilize the situation, in February 1937 Blum announced a pause in the reforms of the Popular Front, which alienated the extreme left in the coalition. Although not obliged to resign, Blum did so in June when the Senate refused him the special powers he needed to deal with the country's precarious financial situation. It has been argued that he stepped down to preserve the coalition.

The Popular Front did in fact continue until a definitive split between the Radicals and the other partners took place in the fall of 1938. A second Blum cabinet formed in March 1938, but his first resignation marked the end of the period of high expectation, especially among the workers, generated by the front's electoral victory.

POPULATION TRENDS. In medieval France, sometimes called *la France lente*, change, including demographic growth, occurred exceedingly slowly. Apart from the hazards to life posed by internal strife and economic uncertainty, the population was devastated for generations by the **Black Death**. By the 16th century, steady, long-term growth had begun to transform France, and at the outbreak of the **French Revolution** in 1789, France's 28 million inhabitants made it the most populous country in Western Europe. Thereafter, however, population growth declined continuously. While the French population numbered 30.5 million in 1821, it had only increased to 39.6 million in 1911. French governments of the *belle époque* were particularly alarmed by the low birthrate in France compared to its major European competitors. In the period immediately preceding **World War I**, the French population was growing at 0.1 percent per year, compared to growth rates of 0.9 percent in **Great Britain** and 1.1 percent in **Germany**.

The economic depression and political uncertainty of the interwar years merely confirmed these downward trends, and the aging of France's population was exacerbated by the gains in medical science made during the century that lengthened life expectancy. It is against this historical background that the pro-natalist policies of the French **social security** system after 1945 need to be understood. In common with its neighbors, France experienced a baby boom after 1945 in which the average number of children per couple rose from its prewar figure of 1.9 to 2.4 in 1960. Aided also by the 50,000 or so immigrants per year that came to settle in France after 1945, the population rose from 40.5 million in 1946 to 46.5 million in 1962. But the population trends after 1945 are characterized by periods of sudden decline as well as sudden spurts in growth. The baby boom was followed by a rapid decline in the birthrate between 1964 and 1976, after which the average number of children per couple leveled off at 1.8 before taking off again in the 1980s. According to the French statistical office INSEE, by 1 January 2007 the population of France had risen to 63.4 million, with an average of two children per adult female making it one of the most fertile populations in Europe. Life expectancy has also risen to an average of 77.1 years for men and 84 years for women. *See also* IMMIGRATION.

POSITIVISM. Term invented by Auguste Comte (1798–1857) that came to denote one of the most important intellectual movements in the life of the **Third Republic**. Comte developed his ideas systematically in his six-volume *Cours de philosophie positive*, published between 1830 and 1842. He endeavored to trace the evolution of human thought from the myth-inspired speculations of antiquity through the abstractions of feudal times to the positive understanding of the modern era—a time, Comte argued, when human beings could finally interpret the phenomenal world without resorting to myths or metaphysics. Comte believed that an order was inherent in observable phenomena and that once this was understood, human relations as well as natural processes could be explained. Comte's positivism was attractive to a generation that had become disillusioned with **romanticism** and enamored of the new possibilities science and technology offered.

Although by 1878 a certain disenchantment had set in as the result of what was perceived by some as Comte's desire to turn positivism into a kind of quasi-religious cult, the range of intellectuals willing to accept Comte's analogies between the social and the natural sciences meant that some of his key assumptions had taken root. A representative range of such intellectuals would include Ernest Renan (literary criticism), **Emile Zola** (literature), Hippolyte Taine (history), Claude Bernard (physiology), and Emile Durkheim (sociology). Working in their different fields, these figures rejected the romantic belief in the uniqueness of the individual personality and sought to evaluate human thought and action in terms of the larger forces that shape us: history, heredity, physiological sources of behavior, collective mentalities, and environment. Although this perspective was regarded by its advocates as a means of promoting intellectual liberation, as the Third Republic entered the 20th century, it provoked a backlash from a new generation that began to question the virtues of a standardizing materialism and to engage in self-discovery through the subjective pursuit of fantasy, intuition, and myth.

POSTMODERNISM. A term whose use was first noted in the late 1950s and early 1960s, and that since then has been used in a remarkable range of attributions and meanings. It loosely describes a sensibility that self-consciously and often paradoxically rejects certainty in personal, intellectual, and political life. The debate on the cultural ramifications of postmodernism was given a powerful focus by Jean-François Lyotard's *The Postmodern Condition* (1979), in which Lyotard argued that the grand, totalizing, modernizing claims of reason, which had their origins in the **Enlightenment**, had in fact produced the nightmares of the postmodern world, from high-technology warfare to ecological disaster, and that the Enlightenment narrative of liberation and equality had turned into its opposite. The criteria governing the "truth claims" of knowledge, according to Lyotard, did not derive from absolute rules or standards but rather from discrete, context-dependent "language games," and therefore their grand claims to legitimacy were fundamentally undermined. The projects of universalizing history and the classical paradigms of science are therefore rejected by Lyotard in favor of the decentered, the heterogeneous, the local, the provisional, the pragmatic, the intentional destabilization of the closures of modernity, and the refusal to make political and ethical judgments in advance.

While Lyotard was questioning the end states posited by the grand narrative of history, another influential figure, Jean Baudrillard, was refuting the accepted hierarchies of meaning and reality. In his book *Simulations* (1983), Baudrillard argued that the new communications technologies have created an environment of self-generating, multiplying, depthless images that convey the implosion of image and reality. There is no longer a "real" external world to which signs can refer, but rather the real is now defined by the medium in which it moves. This "dehierarchization" of meaning and reality, together with the rejection of grand narratives of progress, has exercised a considerable influence on the way a range of intellectual disciplines, from philosophy to cultural studies, have been practiced and can be perceived in many forms of cultural production, from architecture to video clips.

POSTSTRUCTURALISM. An intellectual movement that developed toward the late 1960s and that, as the term implies, began with a reappraisal of some of the guiding assumptions of structuralism. Whereas what lay at the heart of structuralism was a grand ambition to comprehend the world of signs in an almost scientific manner, poststructuralism was more self-deprecating and ironic in the treatment of its ambitions. The key structuralist notion it challenged was the assumption that in practice, words (signifiers) and concepts (signifieds) operate in a fixed relationship, like two sides of the same coin, to preserve a certain identity of meaning. For the poststructuralists, this perception of the process of signification was too limiting. The relationship between the signifier and the signified constituting the sign was not that of a stable unit with two sides but, on the contrary, an unstable and transient fit or fix between two moving layers.

The sense in which the poststructuralists prized apart the two sides of the sign could be illustrated, for example, by the way a dictionary continually defers meaning rather than confirming it in a unitary and fixed manner. When looking for a meaning (signified) of a word (signifier), what we find in the dictionary is that every signifier has several signifieds and that each of the signifieds becomes yet another signifier that can be followed in the dictionary with its own set of signifieds in a process that continues indefinitely. The signifier thus changes with each new context and is constantly active as it forms chains and crosscurrents of meaning with other signifiers, perpetually challenging the orderly requirements of the signified. It is this activity that has been the focus of much poststructuralist thought, as its implications have been traced in the fields of historical research by figures like **Michel Foucault**, in cultural studies by **Roland Barthes**, and in the psychoanalytical challenge to the notion of the unified "subject" in the work of **Jacques Lacan**.

POUJADISM. Short-lived populist movement led by Pierre Poujade, a shopkeeper born in Saint-Céré (Lot) in 1920. In 1953 Poujade founded the Union de Défense des Commerçants et Artisans in an appeal to small shopkeepers and artisans to protest against a tax regime that he believed disadvantaged them. Poujadism profited from anxiety among its constituency about the consequences of the rapid economic and social change occurring in France, and its right-wing nationalism tapped the discontent of its supporters with the creeping acceptance of processes like **decolonization**, which appeared to reduce France's standing on the world stage. The rhetoric of Poujadism ranged the small individual against large moneyed interests and the provinces against an authoritarian center. In the parliamentary elections of 1956 the Poujadists gained 11 percent of the vote and sent 52 deputies to the National Assembly, where they formed a group called Union et Fraternité Françaises. However, the movement began to decline as early as the following year as the stock of **Charles de Gaulle** began to rise again, and de Gaulle benefited from the support of Poujadist deputies and voters when he returned to power in 1958. But Poujade himself would not rally to the **Fifth Republic** until 1966 because of de Gaulle's policy on **Algeria**. Discontent with this policy had driven some of Poujade's supporters into the arms of the right-wing terrorist group Organisation de l'Armée Secrète (Secret Army Organization). A famous former Poujadist deputy, **Jean-Marie Le Pen**, is the leader of the extreme right-wing **Front National**.

PRESIDENCY OF THE REPUBLIC. The post was first established in 1848 under the **Second Republic**. It was rapidly exploited by President **Louis-Napoléon Bonaparte** after his election in December of that year as a platform for launching his own dynastic ambitions, resulting in the coup d'état of 1851 that led to the creation of the **Second Empire** in 1852. The collapse of the Second Empire in 1870 paved the way for the **Third Republic** and the restoration of a president as head of state. With the transition to a republic not yet regarded as irreversible, President **Maurice de MacMahon** was encouraged by some of his conservative and royalist friends to dissolve the National Assembly by presidential decree in May 1877, to preempt the rise of the left and usher in a new right-wing majority. Although acting within his constitutional powers, MacMahon was perceived as usurping the will of the people. The successful mobilization of the republican camp prior to the ensuing legislative elections led to a majority in the new assembly that clipped the president's wings, notably depriving him of the power of dissolution and reinforcing the power of the legislature. This shift in the balance of power made for a weak presidency and a political system dominated by the parties.

The events of the 1930s and the collapse of France so soon after the outbreak of hostilities in **World War II** convinced some leaders, such as General **Charles de Gaulle**, that a weak executive and an overpowerful legislature left France incapable of coping decisively with crisis situations. The return to a system dominated by the **political parties** after **liberation** is the reason de Gaulle abandoned politics in 1946, and the failure of that system to manage the crisis in **Algeria** is the reason de Gaulle returned to power in 1958. He was determined to turn France into a presidential system, and the **constitution** of the **Fifth Republic** reflects this, reestablishing the president's power of dissolution, to hire and fire prime ministers tasked with managing domestic policy, while the president retains a direct and decisive say in **foreign policy** and **defense**: the famous *domaine réservé*. An amendment to the constitution in 1962, which allowed the people to elect the president directly instead of by a parliamentary electoral college, showed de Gaulle's determination to raise the presidency above party political considerations and give it a democratic legitimacy that could not be challenged.

Within a short space of time, however, the power and aloofness de Gaulle gave his office led some critics to call him a "republican monarch." His successor, **Georges Pompidou**, adopted a more conciliatory style and was followed by a modernizer, **Valéry Giscard d'Estaing**, but one who grew to love the quasi-monarchical trappings of the presidency. Thereafter, **François Mitterrand** and **Jacques Chirac** reverted to the lofty detachment patented by de Gaulle, but for different reasons. Whereas Mitterrand, often nicknamed "the sphinx," was skilled in using his detachment to belittle his enemies, Chirac was often perceived as not knowing what to do with the ultimate prize in French politics, after having spent half a lifetime striving for it. In an attempt to reconnect with the electorate and secure his place in history, Chirac took the initiative of bringing the presidential mandate down from seven to five years, and this was approved by referendum in 2000. His successor, **Nicolas Sarkozy**, has continued the attempt to bridge the gap between the president and the people through direct discourse, involvement in the day-to-day affairs of the government, and the media profile he has given to his personal life, such as his relationship with former top model Carla Bruni. But for some commentators his populism is hard to reconcile with his function as head of state, as is his interference in the business of government that should fall to his prime minister. The sharing of his personal life with the media is also perceived by some as incompatible with his role of representing France in a dignified manner before the world community.

PRESS. The first recognizable, regular press publication in France appeared weekly, under the editorship of Théophraste Renaudot, in 1631 and was entitled the *Gazette*. In contrast to the situation in **Great Britain** in the 18th century, the development of the press in France was slow and heavily regulated by the absolute monarchy until the advent of the **French Revolution**. The Revolution established freedom of the press as a right, and although that right was attacked in one way or another by all the regimes that followed, its crucial importance was highlighted as it focused opposition to the establishment in France—especially in the way the rally to the defense of a free press sparked the events that led to the **Revolutions of 1830** and **1848**.

Changes during the 19th century had made the ascension of the press irresistible. In 1835, Charles-Auguste Havas set up his press agency, initially gathering news by translating foreign newspapers and then exploiting technological advances like international telegraph links to provide copy for newspapers all over France. The increasing flow of news, added to lower unit costs resulting from mass printing techniques and the appetite of an increasingly literate population, meant that between 1814 and 1870 the circulation of newspapers in France multiplied 30 times. The triumph of republicanism in France at the end of the 19th century marked the triumph of the battle for a free press, and the period from 1871 to 1914 is often recalled as a kind of golden age. Apart from the liberty of journalists to practice their profession, the industry now possessed the means to portray the extraordinary range of interests brought about by the modernization of French society. The number of pages in newspapers grew, the numbers of papers themselves increased, and specialized weekly periodicals flourished, catering to the interest in automobiles, new sports like cycling, new audiovisual **art** forms, and the apparently limitless array of opportunities to gratify the tastes of a nascent consumer society.

A profound challenge to the supremacy of the press as the disseminator of news came with the increasing popularity of radio in the 1930s. But the credibility of the press had already begun to weaken before then because of the inevitably propagandist line the press had been obliged to take during **World War I**. The press of the interwar years in France was marked by a period of concentration, with less successful publications disappearing and national dailies trying to preserve a mass readership by catering to a wider range of interests, reducing the dominance previously enjoyed by political news. The relative stagnation of the press in France between the world wars can be appreciated if one considers that the circulation of French daily newspapers went from 10 to 12 million between 1920 and 1929, whereas the circulation of the dailies printed in London alone went from 5.4 million to 11.5 million during the same period.

The darkest chapter in the history of the French press was written in **World War II**. Freedom of the press was compromised even before the declaration of war on 3 September, with the banning of the communist press in August 1939. The creation of an Office Français d'Information under the **Vichy regime** spelled the end of press freedom, leading respected papers like *Le Figaro* and *Paris-Soir* to wind up their operations for the duration of the war. The only independent alternative to the legal but collaborationist newspapers like *Le Matin*, *L'Oeuvre*, and *Le Petit Parisien*, was the underground press. The Communist daily, *L'Humanité*, made a clandestine comeback as early as October 1939, and this was followed by an increasing number of **Resistance** newspapers like *La Voix du Nord* and *Combat*. This experience shaped the legal framework established after the **liberation**, which closed down the collaborationist newspapers and established very clear rules ensuring the transparency of ownership and management of the press in France.

The war had resulted in an enormous pent-up demand for press publications, and during 1946 alone, in spite of paper rationing, the circulation of daily newspapers increased from 12 million to 15 million. During the same period, 28 dailies were established in **Paris** and 175 in the provinces. Inevitably, many of them failed in an overcrowded marketplace. The weekly press, however, made a steady comeback with the appearance of *Paris-Match* in 1949, replacing the old *Match* of prewar years, and the emergence of serious political weeklies like *L'Observateur*. A period of consolidation followed during the 1950s, and the legal measures taken to prevent the concentration of ownership in too few hands did not prevent the acquisitive rise of postwar France's great press baron, **Robert Hersant**.

The problems the press faced in France during the ensuing decades were experienced universally, particularly the assault of the **broadcast media** on the role of print publications as news gatherers and distributors and the resulting disinclination, especially among younger generations, to look for traditionally written sources of information. However, the press in France does retain some distinctly national characteristics. A vigorous provincial press, on the one hand, and a very profitable market for weekly news magazines like *Le Nouvel Observateur*, *L'Express*, and *Le Point*, on the other, make life difficult for the national dailies, especially in comparison with a market of comparable size as in **Great Britain**. Thus a left-wing newspaper like *Libération* wages a constant struggle to survive financially and is fortunate to sell 200,000 copies, whereas a comparable English paper like the *Guardian* sells four times that number. Similarly, a respectable conservative paper like *Le Figaro* would do well to reach the half-million mark, in comparison to its English equivalent, the *Daily Telegraph*, which sells over a million. Even France's most prestigious newspaper, *Le Monde*, has sales in the region of 300,000 to 350,000. The lower sales also occur across a smaller number of national titles. It is indicative of the severity of the problems caused by a stagnant or shrinking readership that by 2006 *Libération* had been forced to forgo its political persuasions and accept a private financier, Edouard de Rothschild, as its principal shareholder in order to survive. By the end of the same year *Le Monde* was struggling under a debt burden of 100 million euros and obliged to negotiate with media groups such as Lagardère and Groupe Hersant Média to find a way of safeguarding its future financial viability.

In spite of these difficulties, the French press has endeavored to keep up with the age of the Internet, and all major titles offer online versions of their hard copy. *Le Monde* in particular offers a formidable electronic archive of the articles it publishes. Furthermore, it may be argued that one of the virtues of the French national press is the absence of an equivalent to the stable of English tabloid newspapers.

PRIVATIZATION. Policy adopted during the 1980s and 1990s under the premierships of **Jacques Chirac** and **Edouard Balladur** to turn state-owned enterprises over to the private sector. The **nationalization** program of the Socialist government elected in 1981 had assumed that the extension of the state sector would be a way of guaranteeing the continuity of investment needed for the modernization of French **industry** and services. The reality soon dawned that state subsidies, rather than securing the investment for future expansion, in too many cases merely served to mop up considerable losses, as was the case with large enterprises such as Usinor-Sacilor and Thomson. Well before their defeat at the polls in 1986 and the formation of a center-right government under Jacques Chirac, there was a tacit acceptance on the part of the **Socialists** of the need to turn to the market for the capitalization of nationalized enterprises. The new government set in train a vast privatization program covering 65 companies, including some that had come into the public sector before the nationalization program of 1981. The most famous companies destined for the private sector were the major banks like Société

Générale, Paribas, and Suez; TF1, France's largest TV channel; and large industrial groups like CGE, Matra, and Saint-Gobain.

By the time **François Mitterrand** had been reelected president in 1988 and the Socialists had regained a working majority in the legislative elections that followed, the privatization program had widened small-share ownership in France from 2 million to 7 million individuals. Over 500,000 employees bought shares in the newly privatized companies, and the government netted about 71 billion francs from the selloffs. Nonetheless, the shine had been wiped off the privatization program. The program was only 25 percent complete by the time Chirac left office, partly owing to the incapacity of the French capital market to absorb such a huge number of flotations and partly because the crash in share values on stock markets around the world that took place on 19 October 1987, "Black Monday," wiped out the savings of many small investors and taught them the painful lesson that shares, even in undervalued privatized companies, can go down as well as up in value.

The hiatus in privatizations ended with the return of the center-right to power with a massive majority in the legislative elections of 1993 under the premiership of Edouard Balladur. The intervention by the European Commission in the meantime had brought home to the Socialist government that it was no longer possible for the state to subsidize troubled enterprises in contravention of regulations governing European competition. This resulted, for example, in **Renault** being forced to reimburse government subsidies that the commission had judged to be anticompetitive. Thus the new Balladur government's proposal to privatize the erstwhile jewel in the crown of state-owned financial institutions, the Banque Nationale de Paris, was viewed with a certain inevitability. By the time a socialist-led government returned to power under the premiership of **Lionel Jospin** in 1997, privatization was well established as a bipartisan policy. Jospin's government was responsible for returning the major bank Crédit Lyonnais to the private sector and opened up Air France and France Télécom to injections of private capital. The policy was continued under the premierships of **Jean-Pierre Raffarin** and **Dominique de Villepin**, not least because of the French state's need to raise cash in the light of its serious budget deficit. Thus in 2005, the two giant utilities recognized as the bastions of state capitalism, Electricité de France (EDF) and Gaz de France (GDF), were opened up to private investors.

However, it must also be recognized that governments in France, whether of the right or left, do not pursue privatization policies with the same ideological rigor as their counterparts in Anglo-Saxon countries. In early 1995, when the Balladur government wanted to recapitalize the nation's flagship carrier, Air France, with a much-needed cash injection, it made it clear that it would not accept any finding by the European Commission against this subsidy on the grounds of anticompetitiveness. No such finding was forthcoming, and the subsidy was provided on the grounds that it was an interim measure to enable the company ultimately to secure its financial independence from the French state. While **Nicolas Sarkozy** was elected to the presidency of the republic in 2007 on a platform of economic reform, soon after coming to power he articulated a familiar belief in the need to defend those companies that were "national champions." So, for example, while utility companies in the rest of Europe may face the onslaught of EDF and GDF as ferocious private-sector rivals in their markets, the French state will ensure that the energy market at home is protected from foreign private-sector predators. *See also* BANKING; ECONOMY.

PROTESTANTISM. The protestant interpretation of Christian doctrine began to spread in France toward the end of the 12th century through the work of Pierre Valdès (or Valdo) and his followers, the *vaudois*, spreading out from the town of **Lyon** and preaching the gospel in the local language. The word continued to spread, and by the beginning of the 16th century the theological foundations being laid by individuals like Lefèvre d'Etaples in his commentary on the epistles of St. Paul, preaching justification by faith, set the Protestants on a path of sustained conflict with the Catholic establishment. In 1523, for example, the Augustinian monk Jean Vallière was burned at the same stake for his Protestant leanings, and it was in that same year that the young Jean Calvin, whose influence came to dominate the reformation in France, arrived to study in **Paris**. In 1533, Calvin's friend, Nicolas Cop, also rector of the University of Paris, was forced to flee because of a speech he published (rumored to be Calvin's in reality) promoting the ideas of the reformation, and Calvin was soon forced also to take evasive action. The following decade was marked by the persecution of the *vaudois* and the appearance, in 1541, of the first of Calvin's major works on reformation theology in French.

The rising tensions between Protestants and **Catholics** led to the first of a series of wars of **religion** in 1562 that did not come to an end until the Edict of Nantes in 1598 that guaranteed the Protestants freedom of worship. However, in 1685, **Louis XIV**, judging the protestant kingdoms of Holland and England to be too weak to support their co-religionists in France, decided to revoke the Edict and permanently destroy any future prospect of the reformation taking root in France as it had done elsewhere in Europe. The political fortunes of those Protestants in France who had not joined the exodus to countries like England, Holland, and **Germany** did not improve significantly until the **French Revolution** of 1789. The declaration of the rights of man and the citizen guaranteed equal rights to everyone, including Protestants, and in 1790 a law was passed giving an automatic right to French nationality to the descendants of those Protestants who had fled France to escape religious persecution.

Thereafter the Protestant presence in France quietly built a reputation for itself as a small but dynamic community that made a distinguished contribution to the life of the country. In the same year that the separation of church and state in France was formalized constitutionally, 1905, the Fédération Protestante de France (FPF) was formed and acts to this day as an umbrella organization representing a variety of Protestant communities vis-à-vis the public authorities. In 2005 the total number of Protestants in France was estimated to be 1.1 million. In 2007 the FPF comprised 500 Protestant institutions and movements, covered 1,268 parishes, and included 1,065 pastors, of whom 196 were **women**. In recent times, distinguished figures who were either brought up in **Protestant** families or still declared their attachment to the faith have included intellectuals like the Nobel Prize winner Jacques Monod, the philosophers **Jean-Paul Sartre** and **Roland Barthes**, and the prime ministers **Michel Rocard** and **Lionel Jospin**.

PROUDHON, PIERRE-JOSEPH (1809–1865). Political theorist, parliamentarian, and a major influence on revolutionary movements in Europe until **World War I**. He was born of peasant stock in Besançon and was largely self-taught. His early work explored ways of arguing that social equality was the logical outcome of history. The text *Qu'est-ce que la propriété* (1840), in which he argued that property is the greatest obstacle to freedom and equality, established his reputation as an ideologist of the left and is the source of the quotation that made him infamous in conservative circles, "property is theft." The **Revolution of 1848** saw him elected to the National Assembly, and he gained a wide readership for his newspaper articles courageously defending the uprising by Paris workers in June 1848. But his uncompromising opposition to the growing tide of conservative reaction and the emergence of **Louis-Napoléon Bonaparte** led to his arrest and imprisonment until 1852. His cooperative and mutualist ideas remained very influential for the rest of the century, but his antistatist orientation, his emphasis on the free individual conscience, and his rejection of class war brought his ideas into conflict with the emerging ideology of communism. The Russian Revolution in 1917 marked the eclipse of Proudhon's interpretation of **socialism** by Marxism among the revolutionary left in Europe.

PROUST, MARCEL (1871–1922). Novelist, critic, and one of the most important literary influences of the 20th century. He was born in **Paris**, and although his mother was Jewish, he was raised in the **Catholic** religion of his father. Proust was a sickly child, prone to the consequences of asthma. As a young man he resisted his parents' wishes to see him settle into a respectable career and made a reputation for himself in the high society of the faubourg Saint-Germain as a witty if eccentric socialite. However, he was not unconcerned by the major political causes of his day and was part of the mobilization of intellectuals aimed at securing a review of the trial of Alfred Dreyfus (*see* DREYFUS AFFAIR). His early literary forays resulted in *Les plaisirs et les jours* (1896) and some articles and translations. But it is for his remarkable magnum opus, *A la recherche du temps perdu* (1913–1927), that he is remembered. The first of the seven-volume cycle, *Du côté de chez Swann*, marks the beginning of the narrator's quest for a way of redeeming his life from the inevitable decay imposed by his material existence. By the last volume, *Le temps retrouvé*, he perceives that through art there is a way of creating truth and beauty that endures immutably. Along this journey the narrator rediscovers himself in unexpected ways. Stimuli like eating one of his favorite childhood cakes suddenly unlock treasure chests full of memories and restore vital pieces as he endeavors to reassemble his life. Around this, Proust weaves a rich and complex evocation of a social milieu where characters appear and reappear, their movements and development choreographed with great skill, and where psychological states are analyzed with what is now regarded as uniquely Proustian intensity and intricacy. *See also* LITERATURE.

– R –

RAFFARIN, JEAN-PIERRE (1948–). Center-right politician and former prime minister. He was born into a comfortable upper-middle-class family in Poitiers with a keen interest in politics, since his father at one point held a ministerial portfolio in the government of **Pierre Mendès-France.** After studying law at the University of Paris, he turned to business and graduated from the Ecole Supérieure de Commerce de Paris in 1972. In 1977 he joined the young supporters of President **Valéry Giscard d'Estaing,** which was the same year that he acquired his first mandate in local politics, as a councilor in his hometown of Poitiers. On the national stage, he first made a reputation for himself as a figure in the centrist **Union pour la Démocratie Française** and was a leading personality in the creation of a tendency called Démocratie Libérale, serving as its vice president until its merger with the new vehicle for the **Gaullist party,** the Union pour un Mouvement Populaire (Union for a Popular Movement) in 2002. His first ministerial post came in 1995 as minister for small and medium-size enterprises in the government led by **Alain Juppé.**

Never considered a charismatic politician, he was chosen as a safe option to lead the government by President **Jacques Chirac** after his reelection in May 2002, rather than the other main candidate for the job, **Nicolas Sarkozy,** due to the latter's reputation as a more hardline right-winger. Raffarin launched a neoliberal program of reforms, notably aimed at pensions and health insurance. However, he was not as adept at managing the media as his interior minister,

Nicolas Sarkozy, and endured a degree of ridicule for his sometimes idiosyncratic way of expressing his ideas, termed by the satirical press *raffarinades*. His credibility was fatally undermined on 29 May 2005, when in spite of his campaign for a yes vote, the French electorate voted negatively in the referendum that was supposed to approve a draft constitution for the **European Union**, leaving Raffarin no option but to tender his resignation to President Chirac on the following day.

RAINBOW WARRIOR. *See* GREENPEACE AFFAIR.

RAMADIER, PAUL (1888–1961). A leading Socialist politician in the **Fourth Republic**. Born in La Rochelle and educated as a lawyer in **Paris**, he got his first taste of government in the Armaments Ministry under Albert Thomas, his active service having been cut short by a serious injury at the beginning of **World War I**. During the interwar years, Ramadier stood on the right of the Socialist **Section Française de l'Internationale Ouvrière (SFIO)**, and his career in the National Assembly spanned 1928 to 1940, when he was one of the minority of deputies who stood against the attribution of full powers to Marshal **Philippe Pétain**. Ramadier's **socialism** was of the pragmatic variety, and his belief in the ultimate goal of social justice did not deter him from taking unpopular measures in the short term. Thus, as minister for food supply in the autumn following France's liberation in 1944, he earned himself the nickname Ramadan.

His appointment as the first prime minister of the Fourth Republic in January 1947 came in a period of crisis. His government was an uneasy coalition of **Communists**, Socialists, and Christian Democrats of the **Mouvement Républicain Populaire**. On the domestic front, the government had to contend with budget deficits, supply bottlenecks, wage inflation, and a poor wheat crop. On the international front, violence had erupted in the French colony of Indochina in December 1946. Furthermore, the chill leading to the Cold War had set in, making the government fearful of extreme reactions from both right and left. In May 1947 Ramadier expelled the Communist ministers from his cabinet after they failed to endorse his economic policies. However, it was the prospect of aid through the **Marshall Plan**, announced in June, that lifted some of the gloom. Following the October 1947 municipal elections, Ramadier attempted to bolster support for his government from the moderate right by sacking some of the more doctrinaire Socialists in his cabinet, but this failed and his government was replaced within a month. Ramadier held ministerial office in the 1950s, but he opposed the return of **Charles de Gaulle** to power and retired from politics in 1958. Ramadier's determination and integrity were recognized by his contemporaries, but it was his misfortune that his premiership coincided with such a crisis-ridden period in the history of postwar France.

RASPAIL, FRANCOIS-VINCENT (1794–1878). A pioneering man of science, he is usually more remembered for being also a radical politician whose career spanned the major part of the 19th century. The son of a lower-middle-class family in Carpentras, he distinguished himself as a brilliant student of theology before embarking on scientific investigations that led to the publication of approximately 50 articles between 1825 and 1830 and additional research that made his reputation as a founder of microchemistry and a leading advocate of antisepsis. Raspail's commitment to improving the lot of ordinary people through public health measures took a more political and generally militant form in his opposition to the undemocratic regime in France. He took to the barricades in the **Revolution of 1830** and was instrumental in forcing the proclamation of the Republic in the **Revolution of 1848**. Imprisoned for his actions on both occasions, he nonetheless reemerged to found campaigning newspapers that were a thorn in the side of the government. Raspail's unswerving commitment to his beliefs earned him a final spell in jail at the age of 80, but he lived to see the establishment of the **Third Republic** and was elected a deputy for **Marseille** in 1876, two years before his death.

RASSEMBLEMENT POUR LA REPUBLIQUE. *See* GAULLIST PARTY.

RAVEL, MAURICE (1875–1937). Composer. He was born in Ciboure (Basses-Pyrénées) and brought to **Paris** as a small child. He entered the Conservatoire at the age of 14, where a scandal grew up around him owing to the repeated refusal to award him the Prix de

Rome until he had reached the minimum age of eligibility. Ravel's elegant style of composition expresses a sophisticated approach to existing musical forms, a predilection for things both fantastic and natural, and notable sensitivity to the subtleties of harmony. His output for voice, dance, piano, and orchestra was considerable and varied. Famous works include *Rhapsodie Espagnole* (1907–1908), *Daphnis and Chloe Suites* (1911–1913), *La Valse* (1919–1920), and *Bolero* (1928). Years of worsening illness necessitated a brain operation from which he failed to recover, and he died in 1937. *See also* MUSIC.

REALISM. A major literary movement in 19th-century France. A debate began in the 1830s concerning the relationship between the aims expressed in **art** and the real world. In the realm of painting, the term *réaliste* had been used pejoratively to describe the work of Gustave Courbet, but in the world of letters the essential realist idea of representing the truth through close observation of contemporary reality was gaining ground. The novelist Stendhal (pseudonym for Henri-Marie Beyle, 1783–1842) found an apt metaphor for the realist method in his preface to *Le rouge et le noir* (1831). The writer, he argued, was like a man walking down a bumpy road with a mirror on his back; inevitably, that mirror would sometimes reflect the clear blue sky above and sometimes reflect the rough and dirty road below. Accusations of amorality would therefore be inappropriate, since the writer merely reflected the ugliness of life and did not generate it. It was a method that allowed writers like Stendhal to depict more accurately the changes they saw around them, but it also allowed for considerable diversity in literary style. Whereas Stendhal often depended on the skillful selection of a telling detail to encapsulate the truth of a character or scene, **Honoré de Balzac** relied on the accumulation of minutely recorded details as the revealing backdrop to his novels. Significantly, although resistance to authorial interventions in his narratives designated **Gustave Flaubert** as the leader of the realist movement, his manipulation of narrative techniques and his sensitivity to the ironies of language and human behavior made him a supreme stylist with an individual perspective on the world. *See also* LITERATURE.

REGIONS. The emergence of the *région* as a unit of administration with significance other than as a collection of *départements* is relatively recent. Legislation passed in 1972 gave the *régions* a clearer consultative role on planning and development issues, but the breakthrough came in 1982 with the **decentralization** measures of the **Socialists**. Consequently, *régions* were given the financial means as well as the status to operate planning, economic, and cultural activities. Planning contracts were drawn up between central government and the *régions* so that resources could respond more efficiently to local initiatives and needs. Legislation passed facilitating the creation of regional representative bodies paved the way for the first elections of this kind in 1986. France's 22 mainland and four overseas regions now have assemblies where the representatives are elected by direct universal suffrage using a proportional list system for a period of six years. The idealistic ambition of the Socialists was to revitalize the notion of citizenship in France by creating a framework that allowed for effective grassroots participation in decision making on social and economic issues. However, assessments of the results have been mixed, and some commentators have suggested that the new layer of management represented by the *régions* has in fact served to insulate central government from criticism as the implementation of centrally determined, painful policies has been delegated downward. *See also* COMMUNES.

RELIGION. The tribes that roamed the territory we now call France were pagan until the establishment of Roman **Catholicism** as the religion of the monarch in the fifth century. It was the result of a compromise between the Catholic clergy and the pagan king, Clovis. For the clergy, Clovis appeared the most amenable of the barbarian leaders to the Catholic Church exercising its influence in civil society, and to Clovis, acceptance by the church also meant the reinforcement of his authority among the faithful of the Gallo-Roman population. The turning point came when Clovis accepted the advice of the bishops and married Princess Clotilde, an ardent Catholic and niece of the king of the Burgundians. Within three years Clotilde, enthusiastically supported by St. Remi, bishop of Rheims, had persuaded Clovis to accept the faith, and in 496 he was baptized at Rheims, together with 3,000 of his warriors. It was this consecration of the first Christian monarch of Europe, perceived as the protector of the faithful by the Catholic Church in light of the chaos engendered by the decline of Roman power, that gave France its claim to be the eldest daughter of Rome.

Once the crown assumed the role of defender of the faith, a long history of conflict with the dissident interpretations of the Christian faith that emerged in France began. The Albigenses, a sect of the Cathars in the south of France who pursued their Manichean belief in absolute purity, were the victims of a crusade in the 13th century. But the most sustained and damaging conflict took place during the wars of religion that spanned the 16th and 17th centuries. The complicity that characterized the relationship between the Catholic Church and the institutions of political and economic power made it inevitable that there would be conflict with the rising tide of **Protestantism**, a religion that was based on the authority of the Bible alone and that offered deliverance from the oppression of the institutions of the Catholic clergy.

Religious differences were grafted onto political rivalries, and the implantation of Protestantism in the regions often reflected the challenge posed by local magnates to the seat of royal authority, as was the case with the Montmorency-Châtillon and Bourbon families. Initially, most Protestant churches were found in the south and west of France, and at its height the new faith appealed to 20 to 25 percent of the population, mostly in literate urban communities of professionals and artisans. But continuing persecution and military defeats pushed the Protestants, or Huguenots, as the French Calvinists were pejoratively named by the Catholic majority, into a small number of strongholds, such as the region around Montauban, Nîmes, and La Rochelle.

Protestantism in France could not count on a dynamic **press** and university system to propagate its ideas as it could in **Germany**, nor could Calvinism appeal to the religious sensibilities of the French people at large. By the 1560s it was clear that the Protestant Reformation was too weak to triumph in France, but the Protestants were too strong to be eliminated. The violent chaos and bitterness of the conflict was symbolized by the St. Bartholomew's Day massacre in **Paris** on 27 August 1572, when between 5,000 and 6,000 Protestants were slaughtered. Catholic nobles were particularly fearful for their rights and privileges when a Protestant acceded to the throne in 1589, becoming Henri IV. The king was, however, a realist and sought to restore order by, on the one hand, reassuring the **Catholics** by converting to their faith in 1593, and on the other hand by enshrining in the Edict of Nantes the security of the Protestants in the towns they controlled. The assassination of Henri IV in 1610 removed a strong ruler and an effective conciliator. During the decades that followed, Cardinals **Richelieu** and **Mazarin** were leading lights in the campaign to crush Protestantism by military means, to remove what was perceived as an armed state within a state. After 1622 only La Rochelle and Montauban remained under Protestant control, and their cause had been weakened by the desertion of leading aristocrats who were fearful of losing access to royal patronage.

Guided by the principle of "one faith, one king, one law," when Louis XIV decided to revoke the Edict of Nantes in 1685, he was able to do so without encountering serious resistance. The economic consequences were substantial but not immediately evident, as very considerable numbers of Huguenots reacted to the formal loss of guarantees that had already become threadbare by emigrating to nearby countries like the Netherlands, Germany, and **Great Britain**, and even distant destinations like South Africa, taking their talents and enterprising attitudes with them.

The **French Revolution** marked the start of a process that removed definitively any legitimate claim by the Catholic Church to exercise power over civil society. The secular thinking set in train by the **Enlightenment** reached its apogee in the ideals of the Revolution, which aimed to liberate the individual both spiritually and materially. However, the restoration of the **Bourbon dynasty** marked a revival of the influence of the Catholic Church, particularly in the sphere of **education**. Most of the remainder of the 19th century was marked politically by the struggle for genuinely democratic representation, an inherent component of which was **anticlericalism**, given the symbiotic relationship between the Catholic Church and the monarchical state. The triumph of anticlericalism at the end of the century made it easier for non-Christian faiths, like **Judaism**, to be accepted in civil society. Since loyalty to France meant loyalty to the secular values enshrined in the Republic, it was therefore a commitment to which all could aspire, irrespective of race or religion. This was proved by the eventual outcome of the **Dreyfus Affair**, which was seen as the triumph of the secular Republic over the reactionary instincts of the old Catholic order.

At the close of the 20th century, France found itself facing a new religious challenge that would not have been conceivable to **Jules Ferry** and the other founders of the secular republic. Largely because of the **immigration** from North Africa prompted by **decolonization** and labor shortages in France in the 1960s, the faith with the second-largest number of adherents in France is now **Islam**. The potential for conflict between a secular state and a faith that does not recognize the subordination of the spiritual to the secular in the sphere of civil society hit the headlines for the first time in 1989, when three Muslim girls in Creil were excluded from school for wearing Islamic headscarves judged by the school authorities to be in contravention of the law stipulating that the ostentatious wearing of religious apparel had no place in the secular education system. *See also* CIVIL CONSTITUTION OF THE CLERGY; CONCORDAT OF 1801; GALLICANISM; POLITICAL PARTIES.

THE RENAISSANCE. The end of the 15th century was a period of growing confidence and self-assertiveness for France. The scars from the seemingly endless conflict with England had largely healed, and the victory of François I over the Swiss and their Milanese allies in 1515 appeared to have laid a foundation for the expansion of French influence over the northern Italian peninsula. However, the contact with Italy was much more profound in cultural terms and opened the way for the great awakening that characterized the Renaissance in 16th-century France.

François I was instrumental in attracting the legion of Roman and Florentine artists to France who propagated the ideas of the Italian Renaissance. As a consequence, French Gothic **architecture** began to assimilate the rediscovery of antique pillars and plinths and the charm of arabesque flourishes. The ultimate triumph of Italianate style was to be seen in the chateaux of the **Loire**, particularly Chenonceau and Chambord. By the middle of the 16th century, a synthesis had occurred between Italian influences and more indigenous traditions, as exemplified by such recognizably "French" monuments to the Renaissance as the Louvre, by Pierre Lescot, and the Tuileries, by Philippe Delorme.

Technical advances like the invention of the printing press, which made its appearance in **Paris** in 1470, proved invaluable in disseminating the humanist ideas that flourished at this time. **Literature** was at the forefront of the expression of new sensibilities, and its vigor was matched by its diversity, from the delicacy of sentiment conveyed in Ronsard and du Bellay to the optimistic lust for life of Rabelais, not to mention the stoic, humanist tolerance promoted in Montaigne's essays. Moreover, du Bellay played a significant part in promoting the notion of a "national" literature when he published his *Défense et illustration de la langue française* (1549). More generally, the bases for the development of France's intellectual traditions were being laid by the monarchy when François I in 1530 established the forerunner of the Collège de France, with a mission to teach Greek, Hebrew, and mathematics. The process of centralization and standardization was deemed indispensable for the efficient implementation of the monarch's wishes, but it also created a universal medium for the shaping of a national culture. Thus one of the key measures envisaged by the royal ordinance of Villers-Cotterêts in 1539 was the stipulation that all official statutes should be written in the *langue d'oïl*, making it the official language of all France, just as Florentine had become the language of all Italy.

The critical spirit released by the Renaissance was not, however, devoid of a potential for conflict. Between 1510 and 1520 a movement developed around Guillaume Briçonnet and Jacques Lefèvre d'Etaples that prompted a return to the sources of the Scriptures to examine anew the foundations of the Christian faith. This new theological sensibility was given encouragement in 1519 when the writings of Martin Luther first began to appear in Paris. With the tacit approval of certain teachers at the Sorbonne, by the 1530s writings critical of the papacy emerged. And when Jean Calvin systematically adapted Luther's theses in his *Institutio religionis christianae* (1536), the ground was prepared for the conflict over **religion** in France that cast a dark shadow over the humanist ideals of the Renaissance.

RENAULT. Famous car manufacturer founded by Louis Renault, who built his first car in the garden shed in 1898. A man of exceptional drive and energy, Renault rapidly built up to the mass manufacture of vehicles, centered at a plant in Billancourt, on the outskirts of **Paris**.

Renault's unassailable position as the manufacturer of vehicles for the French mass market earned him the nickname "emperor of Billancourt." His downfall, however, came as a result of his alleged collaboration with the German occupiers of France during **World War II**. On 16 January 1945, **Charles de Gaulle** signed the decree **nationalizing** the Renault company without indemnity. Sick and imprisoned, Louis Renault died within the year.

While Renault prospered during the boom years of the *trente glorieuses*, the 1970s revealed the classic structural problems of nationalized industries: overmanning, rigid decision-making processes, and inability to respond quickly to changing markets. It was the Socialist governments of the 1980s that initiated the introduction of strict market discipline to the company while at the same time retaining a key role for the state in determining its destiny. It was the abiding role of the French state that undermined the corporate marriage between Renault and Volvo proposed in the early 1990s. But in 1994 the progress toward effective *société anonyme* or private sector status was confirmed with an influx of private shareholders that brought the ownership of the state down from 80 percent to 53 percent. This was a factor in allowing Renault to spread its wings as a global player, culminating at the end of the decade in an alliance with then–heavily indebted Japanese manufacturer Nissan, which left Renault as the senior partner. Since 2000 Renault has bought the Romanian manufacturer Dacia and entered into an alliance with Samsung Motors of South Korea, with a view to expanding into the giant Chinese market. Renault abandoned its traditional home at Billancourt some years ago and has largely shed its reputation as a hotbed of **trade union** activism. In 2006 it sold almost 2.5 million vehicles worldwide and is expected by industry analysts to be one of the few European manufacturers for the mass market to survive in a sector characterized by overcapacity.

RENOIR, PIERRE-AUGUSTE (1841–1919). Painter and father of film director Jean Renoir, he was born in Limoges (Haute-Vienne). As a child he moved with his family to **Paris**, where he spent the rest of his life. Renoir established himself during the 1860s as a traditionalist painter of promise. But from 1870 to 1874 Renoir discovered a new passion for experimenting with individualistic and impressionistic forms concerned with the depiction of light and color. His subjects were usually selected from the leisure activities of the urban *petite bourgeoisie*, and many of his color combinations appeared to reflect the influence of fellow artist and close friend **Camille Pissarro**. Typical examples of Renoir's work include the famous paintings entitled *Dance in the Country* and *Dance in the City* (1883). The last two decades of his life were marked by increasing infirmity, and he died in 1919.

REPUBLIC, FIFTH (1958–). The constitutional foundation for the Fifth Republic marked a radical departure from the previous constitution and illustrated the determination of its authors to avoid repeating the mistakes of the **Fourth Republic**. Drafted under the guidance of **Michel Debré**, the new **constitution** sidelined the parties and gave the **presidency** both more power and more legitimacy. In addition to the usual term of seven years and the prerogative of appointing a prime minister, the president would now be able to solicit directly the approval of the French people by submitting legislative changes to them by referendum, as well as being able to determine the life expectancy of the Assembly through his right to dissolve it and precipitate an election. Furthermore, Article 16 of the new constitution envisaged giving the president extraordinary powers to act unilaterally in a time of national crisis.

Some critics, notably on the left, mindful of the potentially massive increase in executive power at the expense of the legislature, criticized the proposed constitution as heralding the return of a new kind of absolutism. But the French electorate, frustrated by the ceaseless maneuverings of party politics, thought differently. When the new constitution was put to them by referendum on 28 September 1958, 80 percent of the French voters approved it. The last stage in the transformation of the political system of the Fifth Republic into the most powerfully presidential regime among Western liberal democracies came in 1962, when **Charles de Gaulle** introduced changes that enabled the president to be elected directly by the people, as opposed to an electoral college, further reinforcing the authority of the presidential mandate.

By the end of the 20th century, however, it had become clear that the powerful presidentialism embedded in the constitution, which had been so appealing to the French people in 1958, had become a growing source of alienation. Arguably the most enduring legacy of the presidency of **Jacques Chirac** was his decision to offer the French people the opportunity, by referendum, to bring the presidential mandate down from seven years to five years, which a majority of them voted for in 2000. One of the first initiatives taken by **Nicolas Sarkozy** after his election to the presidency in 2007 was to set up a commission tasked with examining the constitution of the Fifth Republic and how it could be modernized in line with the expectations of the French people.

REPUBLIC, FIRST (1792–1799). The abolition of the monarchy by the **Convention** on 21 September 1792 reflected the radicalization of the **French Revolution**, which had taken place in the face of external threats from monarchist states like Austria and the perceived threats from aristocratic plotters within France's borders. The **Terror** had begun to manifest itself in early September when the **Paris Commune** instigated the first massacres of those individuals judged to be enemies of the Revolution. The increasing momentum toward a republic reached its goal when the Convention declared 22 September 1792 the first day of year I of the Republic. Ironically, the Republic's defender during some of its most troubled times, **Napoléon Bonaparte**, was also the one who effectively brought its democratic raison d'être to an end with his coup d'état of 18 Brumaire 1799.

REPUBLIC, FOURTH (1946–1958). The Fourth Republic was brought into being by a referendum on 13 October 1946 and approved by 53 percent of the French electorate. It was, in constitutional terms, essentially a copy of its predecessor on the crucial issue of where power lay. As before, the president had a seven-year term and designated the leader of the government, but the government's continuous need to answer to the National Assembly and solicit its approval meant that power lay with the Assembly and the **political parties** that comprised it rather than with the executive. This was precisely the source of ineffectual government identified by **Charles de Gaulle** and helps explain the Fourth Republic's short duration.

Frequent changes of government did not impede the reconstruction that was undertaken after 1945, facilitated by the **Marshall Plan**, booming demand, and rapid growth in the world **economy**. But the feats accomplished by France's formidable civil service technocrats during this period were not dependent on strong leadership, since the challenges they faced were material and organizational. It was a political crisis that exposed the failure of the Fourth Republic's political system, notably its inability to accommodate a strong and decisive executive power. While France boomed economically, party politics became increasingly fevered and fractious. It was against this background that the war to maintain France's presence in **Algeria** developed, and in May 1958, facing a political vacuum in France and fearing the prospect of a civil war sparked by those French colonists in Algeria opposed to the country's independence, President **René Coty** turned to de Gaulle in the hope that this strong, unifying figure could pull the country back from the brink of chaos. When, on 3 June 1958, the French parliament voted to give de Gaulle the powers to revise the **constitution**, this signaled the end of the Fourth Republic. *See also* REPUBLIC, FIFTH.

REPUBLIC, SECOND (1848–1852). Established constitutionally on 4 November, in the same year as the **Revolution of 1848**, which ended the regime of King **Louis-Philippe**. The **constitution** reflected the concern of moderate opinion in France that the need for democracy should be reconciled with the need for order, and that the National Assembly should not be allowed to attain the kind of power that would allow it to dictate to the nation, as the **Convention** had done after the **French Revolution**. This concern led to the passing of an amendment providing for the concentration of executive power in the hands of a president, directly elected by the people. Ironically, this provision shifted the balance of power too far in the direction of the executive after the election of Louis-Napoléon (*see* BONAPARTE, LOUIS-NAPOLEON) to the **presidency** in December 1848. He used the prestige attached to his family name ultimately to undermine the Republic, replacing it with the Empire (*see* EMPIRE, SECOND) in 1852.

REPUBLIC, THIRD (1875–1940). The longest-lasting of France's republics to date, it was also the one with the least propitious start. Defeat in the **Franco-Prussian War** had left France bitterly at odds with itself. Although the people of France had elected a predominantly conservative Assembly in February 1871, the fact that it chose the republican **Jules Grévy** as its first president was indicative of the divisions that split the majority. While there existed a strong camp in favor of the restoration of the monarchy, it was split between the supporters of the legitimist heir, the **comte de Chambord**, and the supporters of the Orleanist heir, the comte de Paris. Attempts at a compromise between the two candidates to the throne were lengthy and exhaustive but foundered principally on the unrelentingly reactionary attitudes of the comte de Chambord. In the meantime, **Adolphe Thiers** pursued the task of securing the peace for France, while fear of an accommodation with moderate republicanism began to recede in the Assembly and in the country as a whole. After four years of working through provisional arrangements to pursue the governance of France, the stalemate was broken by the Wallon amendment, passed by 353 votes to 352. The amendment asked the Assembly, if it could not restore a monarchy, not to obstruct the establishment of the institutions that would lay the foundations for a republic.

In an important sense, therefore, the Third Republic was established *faute de mieux*. In terms of its political system, it soon became clear that power rested with the legislature rather than with the executive, a fact that did not impede the rapid race to prosperity and the triumph of **anticlericalism** during the period often referred to as the *belle époque*. However, the social and economic difficulties that came in the aftermath of **World War I** exposed the weakness of a system that made the survival of governments conditional on interpellations and motions of censure put down by deputies who had no need to fear for their seats, since the fall of a government did not automatically entail a general election. By 1936, the 100th government of the Third Republic had come and gone and the long-established self-serving attitudes of the political class that had been bearable when prosperity for all beckoned during the *belle époque* became intolerable to many French citizens during the 1930s. With the defeat of the **Popular Front**, which had represented an attempt at national renewal in the eyes of many ordinary people, a lack of political will and a general sense of resignation marked France's drift toward war with **Germany**. After the rapid military collapse in the face of the German onslaught at the beginning of **World War II**, the National

Assembly voted for its own demise and that of the Third Republic when on 10 July 1940 it vested power, by 666 votes to 80, in Marshal **Philippe Pétain** to lay the basis of what became the **Vichy regime**.

THE RESISTANCE. Movement that sprang up among the French people who refused to accept the occupation of their country by the Nazis during **World War II**. The Resistance consisted of two strands whose efforts combined ultimately in the physical liberation of France: resistance from outside the country led by General **Charles de Gaulle**, and resistance from within the country led by various clandestine groups. The day after his arrival in London following the collapse of France, de Gaulle broadcast to his country over the BBC, effectively setting himself up as the true representative of Free France and inviting others to join him in working for the overthrow of the puppet government of **Vichy**. Supported by the French colonies that had not gone over to Vichy and by the Allies, de Gaulle gradually accumulated the means of establishing a government in exile that projected his authority over the resistance movements that had emerged in France.

The Resistance that sprang up in the autumn of 1940 in France took many forms, including the spontaneous demonstration of Parisian high school students on 11 November 1940 to mark France's victory at the end of **World War I**, and the clandestine presses, secular and spiritual, that operated with the purpose of disseminating ideas that challenged the values of the Vichy regime. But the big increase in armed resistance to Vichy and its German masters came after the German invasion of the **Soviet Union** in June 1941, which put an end to the German-Soviet pact and therefore freed **Communists** in France to obey their consciences as well as their party and pour their energies and formidable organizational talents into the Resistance. By 1942 the Resistance had become a veritable army of the shadows, and its numbers were swelled further in 1943 by individuals fleeing conscription into forced labor in **Germany**. The disparate groups were given a coherent command structure by **Jean Moulin**, dispatched to France by de Gaulle, and the strength of the organization created by Moulin, especially the National Council for the Resistance, was proved by its ability to survive Moulin's arrest and eventual execution in 1943.

The Resistance in France grew to encompass representatives of civil and political groups, including **trade unions** and **political parties**, and by 1944 the movement was looking beyond the end of the war toward the challenge of rebuilding France. Outside France, the Resistance already had a government-in-waiting in Algiers, from June 1943 onward, in the shape of the French Committee of National Liberation. In military terms, de Gaulle's ambitions and national self-esteem could now be carried by the Free French Forces commanded by Generals Philippe Leclerc, Alphonse Juin, and Jean de Lattre, who fought with the Allies in the Italian campaign and participated in the invasion of their home soil. The two branches of the Resistance finally met in the joint operation that forced the German surrender of **Paris** on 25 August 1944, in what amounted to the high point of the **liberation**. De Gaulle then installed commissioners of the Republic in the liberated *départements* to assume the administrative functions of state, and in spite of initial American reticence, this provisional government established by the Resistance was recognized by the Allies as the official and legal government of France.

RESTORATION. *See* CHARTER OF 1814; LOUIS XVIII.

REVOLUTION OF 1789. *See* FRENCH REVOLUTION.

REVOLUTION OF 1830. The uprising in **Paris** that ended the reign of **Charles X** brought **Louis-Philippe**, duc d'Orléans, to the throne and ushered in the liberalization of French political life. Disaffection with the rule of Charles X and the performance of the government under Prince Jules de Polignac had been sharpened by the economic depression that began in 1827 and led to an even larger majority hostile to the regime being voted into the Chamber of Deputies in June and July 1830. Rather than opting for conciliation, Charles X pushed through four ordinances that had an inflammatory effect. The first two ordinances were strictly within his legal prerogatives and were aimed at dissolving the Chamber of Deputies and ordering new elections. The remaining two ordinances, perceived by the opposition as illegal, aimed to institute severe censorship of the **press** and change the electoral laws. The ordinances appeared on 26 July, and on the afternoon of the same day, a group of journalists issued a proclamation declaring their intention to defy the new censorship laws.

By the evening of 26 July the defiance had spread to the streets and was manifested by the attacks on government buildings by Parisian mobs. The defiance on the streets grew, and on the morning of 28 July it had taken the shape of barricades at key intersections. The attempt of government troops under Marshal Auguste de Marmont to restore order was bungled and fatally undermined by the defection of key regiments, and by 29 July it was clear that they could not succeed. The reign of Charles X was effectively over. To fill the void and prevent chaos, a group of liberal deputies made the Marquis de **Lafayette** commander of the revived **National Guard** in Paris. A period of rivalry ensued among the republicans, the supporters of the Bourbons, the supporters of the head of the younger branch of the **Bourbon dynasty** represented by Louis-Philippe, and Bonapartists whose slim hopes were kept alive by the fact that the great man's son was resident in Vienna. However, it was an unequal contest and, with the critical support of Lafayette and at the behest of parliament, on 9 August the duc d'Orléans swore allegiance to the **Charter of 1830**, which reinforced the powers of the elected legislature, and thereby became Louis-Philippe I, king of the French. But the democratic expectations raised by the events of 1830 were soon to be frustrated. As one historian put it, the net effect of the changes was to transfer power from the royal court to the stock exchange, leaving the mass of French people with the conviction that the country was still being run for the benefit of a rich and privileged elite.

REVOLUTION OF 1848. Insurrection that brought down the regime of **Louis-Philippe**. Growing popular resentment over the conservatism of the political regime in France spilled over into violence when the government banned a political banquet, the last of 70 organized by the parliamentary opposition. The social composition of the crowds that took to the streets of **Paris** on 22 February 1848 illustrated the social evolution of France during the years that had elapsed since the **Revolution of 1830**. It included students and *petits bourgeois* as well as artisans. Barricades were erected around the city on 23 February, and when it became clear that the **National Guard** would not restore the status quo, the regime was manifestly finished. However, oblivious to Louis-Philippe's abdication, crowds invaded the parliament building and nominated a republican provisional government.

The members of this government were those who had led the opposition to the old regime and fell roughly into two categories. There were moderate republicans like **Alphonse de Lamartine**, whose views were reflected in the newspaper *Le National*, and radical republicans like **Alexandre Ledru-Rollin**, whose ideas were echoed in *La Réforme*. This initial phase in the life of the Republic was marked by fundamental advances in the field of civil rights through legislation that enshrined the freedom of the **press**, universal suffrage, and the abolition of slavery and capital punishment for political crimes.

The events in Paris led to a wave of less extreme forms of insurrectionary activity in the rest of the country, such as attacks on government offices and the property of large landowners. In the aftermath, hundreds of newspapers and political clubs sprang up in Paris. For its part, the provisional government found itself having to perform a balancing act to meet the expectations that had developed while reassuring employers and the owners of capital in general. The fate of the Republic was determined by the elections of 23 April 1848. While the 851 deputies who were duly elected professed their allegiance to the Republic, recent research suggests that two-thirds of them were former monarchists, most of whom had held office under the previous regime. This was a significant factor in the conservative turn taken by the new regime, as opposition mounted among the middle and upper classes to the expenses involved in government measures like the creation of national workshops (*ateliers*) to tackle unemployment, and revenue-raising through a 45 percent property surtax. However, in Paris, always at the forefront of radical populism, the presence of an unsympathetic Assembly in its midst was interpreted as a provocation, and the government reacted with the introduction of severe sanctions against any activity that might constitute a threat to civil order.

The 21 June vote by the Assembly to cut back the program of national workshops sparked a bloody insurrection that in many respects was a class war, pitting large sections of the pro-government, middle-class National Guard, plus the army, against workers whose existence had been made even more precarious. Ultimately, approximately 800 government troops and 3,000 insurgents were killed. The executive powers voted to the republican general Eugène Cavaignac by the Assembly on 24 June to deal with the emergency were extended, and

Paris was in a virtual state of siege for four months after the insurrection. During this period Cavaignac and his administration found themselves under pressure from an increasingly powerful coalition of provincial landowners and businessmen on the one hand and a vociferous minority of radical republicans critical of his measures on the other. In spite of this, in November Cavaignac succeeded in promulgating the constitution of the **Second Republic**, which included liberal democratic provisions such as the recognition of the state's social obligations. More immediately significant in terms of the future of the new Republic was the measure allowing the president to be elected directly by the nation rather than by the Assembly.

The presidential elections that took place on 10 December 1848 were conducted against a background of universal frustration resulting from unfulfilled hopes on the urban, rural, royalist, and republican sides. In spite of the fact that most of the press was behind him, Cavaignac failed in his bid for election, and the radicals like Ledru-Rollin fared even worse. Instead, the electorate gave a landslide victory to **Louis-Napoléon Bonaparte**. Although Louis-Napoléon had used the legend attached to his family name astutely, his victory stemmed largely from the desire of the electorate for stability and prosperity rather than the costly pitfalls encountered on the rocky road to a fully democratic republic. It was a lesson the new president would not forget in the establishment of his future regime, which replaced the Second Republic with the **Second Empire** in 1852.

REYNAUD, PAUL (1878–1966). Lawyer, conservative politician, and premier of France at the time of her defeat in 1940. Born into a bourgeois family in Barcelonnettes (Basses-Alpes), he was raised and educated in **Paris**, where he received his doctorate in law before launching a successful practice in civil and commercial law. He was elected to the Chamber of Deputies in 1919 and took a particularly active interest in economic issues, supporting the French invasion of the Ruhr (1923) as a reprisal for German stalling over the payment of reparations. Reynaud lost his seat in 1924 but returned as a representative from the Seine in 1928 and continued to represent that constituency until the demise of the Republic in 1940. He held several ministerial portfolios between 1930 and 1932, but his failure to make political friendships kept him out of office for most of the 1930s.

During that decade he advocated the competitive devaluation of the franc, the adoption of **Charles de Gaulle**'s theories on the creation of a mobile armored army corps, and resistance to the policy of appeasement toward **Germany**. He was made minister of justice in the government of **Edouard Daladier** in April 1938 and took over from him as premier in March 1940. Constrained by having the discredited Daladier as his defense minister and a fragile majority in the Chamber, Reynaud nonetheless planned a vigorous defense of France, but this was undone by the lightning success of the German offensive in May 1940. Reynaud resigned on 16 June in favor of Marshal **Philippe Pétain**, who rapidly negotiated an armistice. Reynaud was arrested by pro-**Vichy** elements in 1945 and subsequently deported to Germany, but he was soon liberated and returned to his political career in France. He was a proponent of reconciliation with Germany and of European unity. Although a supporter of de Gaulle when he returned to power in 1958, in the years preceding his death Reynaud became critical of the regime for its negative attitudes toward Europe, the Atlantic alliance, and even the Republic.

THE RHINE. Originating in the Swiss Alps, it is one of Europe's most important rivers and, at 1,320 kilometers long, it constitutes a vital navigable waterway linking several European countries. It forms the southern part of the border between France and **Germany**, where it occupies a wide valley.

THE RHONE. A major European river running 812 kilometers through Switzerland and France. It was an indispensable trade and transportation route before the advent of the railway age since it connected the cities of Arles, **Avignon**, Valence, Vienne, and **Lyon** to the ports on the **Mediterranean** coast, notably **Marseille**.

RICHELIEU, ARMAND-JEAN DU PLESSIS DE (1585–1642). French cardinal and politician. He was born into a noble family in **Paris** and made his career in the church, becoming bishop of Luçon in 1606 and finally a cardinal in 1622. Richelieu became the power behind **Louis XIII**'s throne when, under the patronage of Marie de Médicis, he became the king's chief minister in 1624. It was a position Richelieu monopolized until his death. During that period,

Richelieu worked tirelessly to secure the absolute power of the monarchy at home and abroad. To that end, he endeavored to prevent the differences over **religion** in France from undermining the monarchy by destroying the political power of the Huguenots. In foreign policy he supported Gustavus Adolphus of Sweden and the German Protestant princes against Austria in order to weaken the Hapsburgs vis-à-vis the power of the French crown, thereby bringing France in 1635 into the Thirty Years' War. Richelieu was admired and feared for his ruthlessly astute style of politics. The term *éminence grise* (grey eminence) was originally coined to refer to Richelieu's secretary, Père Joseph.

RIF WAR (1925–1926). Rebellion in Morocco that began as armed resistance to the Spanish army by the Berber mountain tribes in the northeast of the country. Spain had obtained a part of Morocco as a result of the regime established in 1912 by the French and the sultan of Morocco. The Spanish had great difficulty pacifying the area under their control and suffered a stunning defeat at Anual in 1921 at the hands of an army of Rif tribes led by Muhammad Abd el-Krim (1882–1963). The ultimate goal of the Rif leaders was to create an independent Rif republic, and the fact that their tribes straddled the Franco-Spanish territories meant that French interests were threatened. French offers of autonomy within the sultan's domain were refused, and when the French zone was attacked in April 1925, the French responded with an offensive to crush the Riffians in September 1925. Abd el-Krim was forced to surrender in May 1926, but the opposition the French forces faced had been the most ferocious encountered in North Africa for a century, and the struggle of the Rif tribes entered the imagination of Muslim subjects of the European colonial powers in the region.

RIMBAUD, ARTHUR (1854–1891). Poet of the late 19th century. Born near the Ardennes Forest in Charleville, Rimbaud grew up in an austere religious environment. He showed a precocious talent for French and Latin verse, and his later contacts with poets like Paul Verlaine encouraged him to develop a powerful and original poetic language of his own. Rimbaud's poems express a forceful rejection of war and castigate the conventions of bourgeois society. Works like

"Le bateau ivre" and "Les voyelles" project the poet as prophet and visionary. For Rimbaud, the poet was engaged in a promethean quest to enlighten humanity. But this vocation was inextricably entwined with a dark and tortured self-consciousness, as in *Une saison en enfer* (1873). The *Illuminations*, probably written between 1873 and 1875, convey Rimbaud's admission of defeat. Rimbaud's short-lived but provocative genius and his innovative use of form and language inspired succeeding generations rebelling against the conventions of society in pursuit of a poetic absolute. *See also* LITERATURE; SYMBOLISM.

ROBESPIERRE, MAXIMILIEN-FRANCOIS-MARIE-ISIDORE DE (1758–1794). A famous leader of the **French Revolution**. Trained as a lawyer, he was elected to the National Assembly of 1789–1791. He was originally very popular in **Paris**, where his scrupulous defense of democratic principles earned him the nickname "the Incorruptible." He led the **Jacobins** in the **Convention** and voted for the execution of **Louis XVI**. Robespierre made his mark on history when he was elected to the Committee of Public Safety (Comité de Salut Public), where he earned a reputation for his willingness to apply extraordinary measures and exercise summary justice in defense of the Revolution during the period that became known as the **Terror**. An austere man, Robespierre interpreted the revolutionary project in extremely moral terms, as something aimed at producing responsible citizens endowed with a secular faith in the virtues of the Republic. But the concentration of power in his hands and his autocratic manner engendered fear in the Convention and encouraged its members to act preemptively against him. Robespierre attempted to avoid arrest by shooting himself, but he succeeded only in blowing away part of his jaw and survived in agony until his execution at the **guillotine**.

ROCARD, MICHEL (1930–). A leading Socialist politician of his generation and prime minister of France from 1988 to 1991. He was born into a family of Parisian professionals, and as an adolescent during the occupation of France in **World War II** he adopted the ideals of the **Resistance**, which his father, a conservative professor of physics, had joined. This experience had an important influence on the subsequent development of his political philosophy, notably the belief that the pursuit of justice was not the prerogative of **socialists** and **communists** alone. He entered the Institut d'Etudes Politiques, and his heavy involvement in socialist student politics while he was there may help to explain why he twice failed the entrance exams for the Ecole Nationale d'Administration before finally being admitted in 1955.

The failure, as Rocard saw it, of the Socialists to campaign vigorously for an end to the war in **Algeria** led to his joining the new left-wing formation called the **Parti Socialiste Unifié** (PSU) in 1959. During the years that followed, Rocard developed the attractive new ideas of libertarian socialism based on self-management, **decentralization**, and a more pluralist society that enabled him to win the leadership of the PSU in 1967. When the **student rebellions** reached a climax in May 1968, Rocard was one of the few left-wing leaders to gain a positive national profile for his energy and commitment to the push for change. He even stood as a presidential candidate in 1969. The failure represented by his 3.7 percent share of the vote was compensated for when he was elected to a parliamentary seat in the Yvelines almost immediately afterward. During the four years that followed, Rocard realized that the future of the left would be best served through a merger of the PSU with the new **Parti Socialiste (PS)** that had formed around **François Mitterrand**. Thus in 1974 he resigned the leadership of the PSU and threw himself behind Mitterrand's presidential bid.

Rocard was too powerful an intellect and too adept a politician not to rise in the PS, but he was also a thorn in the flesh of many within the party, including Mitterrand. Rocard continued to push his brand of liberal democratic socialism, and although this was popular with the French electorate at large, the reaction within the party was not unmixed. Moreover, his bid to be the Socialist candidate for the presidential race in 1981 alienated Mitterrand and helped to explain the tense relationship that persisted between the two men. When the Socialist government was forced to accept the discipline of the market in 1984, Rocard received little thanks for having been right. Rocard resigned his ministerial post in April 1985, disillusioned by what he saw as an exercise in opportunism when the government opted for proportional representation in the legislative elections that followed.

But Rocard's ideas continued to appeal to the French electorate, and his personal standing in the polls made his appointment as prime minister, when it finally came in May 1988, unsurprising. Although Mitterrand had just been reelected to a second term as president, the Socialist government did not on this occasion benefit from a state of grace, as it had done in 1981. Financial scandal, rising unemployment, and the difficulties endured by the economy focused public dissatisfaction on the governing Socialist elite, and when Mitterrand in 1991 opted for France's first female prime minister, **Edith Cresson**, as a replacement for Rocard, it was an attempt to revitalize the general perception of the Socialists. As the opinion polls showed, Rocard emerged from the experience with his standing largely undiminished. Rocard continued to preach his message of renewal for the PS and the left in general, and appeared to have found a good platform for doing this when he succeeded **Laurent Fabius** as the party's first secretary. But the party's poor showing in the European elections of 1994 provided Rocard's opponents in the PS with the means of forcing his resignation, thereby killing his chances of succeeding Mitterrand as the Socialist candidate in the presidential race of 1995. Rocard was elected to a seat in the Senate in 1995 but resigned it in 1997 to concentrate on his work in the European Parliament, where he had been elected in 1994. He headed a number of European Parliamentary commissions and in 2005 led the delegation of European observers sent to monitor the presidential elections in Palestine.

ROCHET, WALDECK (1905–1983). Secretary-general of the **Parti Communiste Français (PCF)**, 1964–1972. He was born the son of a shoemaker in Sainte-Croix (Saône-et-Loire) and joined the Communist party as a youth of 19. He rose through the party during the 1930s and entered the Central Committee in 1936, the year he was elected a Communist deputy to the Chamber. He was arrested following the outlawing of the PCF in 1939 but resumed his parliamentary career after the war. He was promoted up the party hierarchy by **Maurice Thorez** and in May 1964 acceded to the post of secretary-general. Rochet found himself under criticism by the Stalinists in his party and the Soviets for such actions as the PCF's support of **François Mitterrand**'s candidacy in the presidential campaign of 1965 and the PCF's equivocations over the Soviet invasion of

Czechoslovakia in 1968. Rochet was reelected to the post of secretary-general in 1970, even though his health had been severely affected by Parkinson's disease. He was finally replaced at the head of the party by **Georges Marchais** in 1972. Rochet died in February 1983. The hopes he had entertained as secretary-general of steering the PCF away from its doctrinaire pro-Soviet orientation had been undermined by the opposition he had encountered as well as his own reluctance to pursue too vigorously a course that might split the party. *See also* SOVIET UNION.

ROMANTICISM. A European aesthetic movement that had a profound influence on **literature**, **art**, and **music** and that was most pronounced in France between 1815 and 1848. It was not the first time there had been a reaction against the classical disciplines and the rationalism of the 18th century in the arts. Isolated instances of this can be found, for example, in Jean-Jacques Rousseau's *La nouvelle Héloïse* (1761). But a more systematic breakthrough came after the restoration of the **Bourbon dynasty** with the manifestation of a widespread desire in the arts to celebrate the primacy of emotion over reason, the individual over the general, the mystical over the secular, and the medieval over the classical. The staging of **Victor Hugo**'s play *Hernani* in 1830 caused an uproar, but it also signified an irresistible move away from the unities of time, place, and action that had, up to that point, been the conventions of drama and that exemplified the rigidities of classicism.

After 1830, however, romanticism embraced a growing diversity of interests. The anticlassicism that had been its initial point of departure gave way to a more eclectic approach, and the politics of its proponents inclined more toward the emerging ideas of **socialism**. By the time of the **Revolution of 1848**, the lyrical emotion of **Alphonse de Lamartine**'s *Les méditations poétiques* (1820) seemed to belong to a distant past as its author immersed himself in republican politics. As the second half of the 19th century beckoned, the sentimental idealism and aesthetic diversity that had come to characterize romanticism began to lose ground to the more hard-edged approach of **naturalism**.

ROME, TREATY OF. *See* SCHUMAN, ROBERT.

ROUSSEAU, JEAN-JACQUES. *See* ENLIGHTENMENT; ROMAN-TICISM.

ROYAL, SEGOLENE (1953–). She was born Marie-Ségolène in Dakar, the daughter of a regular army colonel of artillery who was stationed in Senegal. After the family's return to France, she studied economics at the University of Nancy and distinguished herself sufficiently to gain entry to the Ecole des Sciences Politiques in Paris. After graduating from there she followed the well-beaten path of many aspiring members of the French governing elite to the Ecole Nationale d'Administration, where she graduated in 1980. She had joined the **Parti Socialiste (PS)** in 1978 and quickly caught the eye of the party's leaders. In 1982 she became a junior minister for youth and sports in the early days of the **Francois Mitterrand** presidency. Promotion soon followed in 1984 when she became minister for the environment and social affairs. She then held a succession of ministerial portfolios each time a Socialist-led majority was elected to parliament until her final post as minister for family affairs under the government of **Lionel Jospin** from 2000–2002.

Royal's photogenic qualities, her apparent ability to combine being a mother of four children with the enormous demands of a successful political career, and her very modern civil partnership with the father of her children, another Socialist politician, François Hollande, generated much media interest. When Royal won the Socialist candidature to run for the **presidency** of the republic in 2007, she and her husband, given his role as general secretary of the PS, seemed to challenge President **Jacques Chirac** and his wife as France's first couple. But the focus on Royal did not win universal approval, especially among other leading figures in the PS. After her failure to win the presidency their criticism became more overt, variously accusing her of a lack of political ideas, intellectual shallowness, and too great a willingness to compromise with the center led by **François Bayrou**.

Shortly after the elections the media spotlight on Royal became even more intense, but for the wrong reasons, as she announced that her relationship with Hollande had come to an end. In a veiled allusion to the infidelity that had caused the break-up, Royal declared, with considerable dignity, that she wished her ex-partner every happiness in his emotional life. She demonstrated similar composure in the face of criticism from other leading PS figures, following the party's failure in the legislative elections of July 2007. Whatever her critics in the party might say, however, she emerged from the electoral ruins of 2007 with a higher profile in the country than any other PS leader and a greater ability than any other to mobilize the support of grassroots members. This was underlined in the polls at the beginning of 2008, which put her well ahead of socialist rivals like **Bertrand Delanoë** in terms of popularity vis-à-vis the party and the wider electorate. The ensuing public declarations by Royal that she felt capable of uniting the party were a clear signal of her intention to stand for the leadership of the PS.

RUHR, OCCUPATION OF. *See* POINCARE, RAYMOND.

RUSSIA/SOVIET UNION, RELATIONS WITH. It was under Tsar Peter the Great at the beginning of the 18th century that Russia turned toward its more developed neighbors in Europe, not only to acquire the technical knowledge that would enable it to modernize, but also for the cultural enlightenment that would raise its standing in the world. One of the major cultural influences was French, and particularly the French language. By the beginning of the 19th century it was common for educated Russian families as well as the aristocracy to speak to each other in French, and one of the Russian characters in Tolstoy's *War and Peace* is even described as "thinking in French." European power politics, however, were not so amicable, and the pursuit of expanding spheres of interest led to war between France and Russia in the Crimea (1853–1856), where a Franco-British force attempted to stop the extension of Russian influence in the Ottoman Empire.

By the end of the century, however, especially after defeat in the **Franco-Prussian War** had highlighted the weakness of France vis-à-vis the new German state, France began to develop a series of treaty obligations involving Russia, aimed at containing the German threat. It was precisely such a treaty obligation that drew France into **World War I**. The outbreak of revolution in Russia in 1917 and the triumph of the communists created a climate of mutual suspicion between the two countries, especially as many "White" Russians or counterrevolutionaries found refuge in France after 1917. But the ideas behind the creation of the new Union of Soviet Socialist Republics (USSR) that replaced the monarchist Russian state were also an inspiration to a section of the left in France, which led to the split in French socialist ranks at the **Congress of Tours** in 1920 and resulted in the birth of the **Parti Communiste Français**. France tried to engage with the Soviet Union as a potential ally as the prospect of another inevitable conflict loomed with **Germany** but was outmaneuvered by Adolf Hitler, and the signing of the German-Soviet pact in August 1939 sparked an anticommunist witch hunt in France.

The course of **World War II** in Europe took a dramatic turn when Hitler invaded the USSR, which freed members of the PCF to throw themselves wholeheartedly into the **Resistance**, where they made a heroic contribution. It was precisely the role of French communists in the Resistance that allowed the PCF to enjoy great popularity with voters in the postwar years, even though the ideological orientation of the party was determined by Moscow. By the end of the 1970s, however, the French electorate had lost any illusions about the human cost of Soviet communism, as the works of writers like Alexander Solzhenitsyn were read widely in the West, exposing the systematic abuse of human rights that occurred under the pretext of communist equality. The PCF began its sharp decline in the polls, hastened by its refusal (unlike communist parties in Italy and Spain) to acknowledge the abuse in the USSR, and what was once a formidable communist intelligentsia in France rapidly disappeared.

Nonetheless, the collapse of the rotten system that was the Soviet Union was sudden and unexpected. The reaction of the French state was to initiate a series of bilateral agreements with the new Russian state to secure a positive relationship with it, notable among these agreements being the agreement on defense cooperation (1994); the agreement on energy and the environment (1996); the agreement on customs duties (1997); the creation of a Franco-Russian Council for the study of strategic issues (2002); the agreement to cooperate on internal security matters and the fight against criminality (2003); the agreement on freedom of movement for their respective nationals in the two countries (2004); and agreement on the protection of intellectual property rights in the context of military cooperation (2006). There is now also an annual Franco-Russian governmental seminar, presided by the prime ministers of the two countries.

– S –

SACRE-COEUR, BASILICA OF. The church situated on the heights of Montmartre that offers a panoramic view of **Paris**. In social and political terms, the significance of the foundation stone that was laid for its construction in 1873 was that it marked the culmination of a campaign to win people back to **religion** by the order of Assumptionists, a new order formed in 1845 that promoted a massive cult of the Sacred Heart. Montmartre was a profoundly symbolic site because that was where Loyola and his first followers had met, effectively to set in train the Counter Reformation. Politicians also used the church as an emblem of the nation's penitence in the aftermath of the disaster that had befallen France in the form of the **Franco-Prussian War**.

SAINT-JUST, LOUIS-ANTOINE-LEON-FLORELLE DE (1767–1794). Major intellectual figure of the **French Revolution**. Saint-Just was 24 when he wrote *L'Esprit de la Révolution* (1791), followed two years later by *Les institutions républicaines*, and in these texts he described the ethical basis for the Revolution and its universal significance. It was the zealous young Saint-Just who argued in 1793 that a revolutionary situation necessitated revolutionary measures and that, given the cumbersome procedural methods of the **Convention**, the direction of the entire state apparatus should be assumed centrally by the Committee of Public Safety. Saint-Just's intention was that such an extraordinary measure should apply provisionally until the threat to the Revolution was over. But he paid the price for the excesses of the Committee of Public Safety during the **Terror** and was executed along with the figure most closely associated with the Terror, **Robespierre**.

SALAIRE MINIMUM INTERPROFESSIONNEL DE CROIS-SANCE. The minimum wage, popularly known by its acronym, SMIC. This was originally established as the *salaire minimum interprofessionnel garanti* (SMIG) in 1950 under a law on collective bargaining that intended to provide low-paid workers with a basic minimum as wage controls were superseded by free collective bargaining. The level of the minimum wage was fixed after consultation among government, union, employer, and consumer representatives, but in the years that followed it began to lag substantially behind average wage levels, leading to frustrated hopes and the concomitant social inequalities and political tensions. The strike that was prompted by the **student rebellions** in May 1968 brought this issue to the fore. The gap that had opened up between the SMIG and average wages was acknowledged by the government, which rechristened the SMIG the SMIC, raised it by 35 percent, and opted to calculate it on a new basis that took account of national growth and average wage levels. Governments of both right and left maintained their commitment to the SMIC during the 1970s and 1980s. The long cycle of low growth and rising unemployment that began in France in the late 1980s diminished the power of collective bargaining, so that by the middle of the 1990s, approximately 10 percent of workers were reliant on the SMIC to guarantee their incomes. By 2006 dependence on the SMIC had risen to include 2.5 million workers, sometimes referred to as *smicards*, or 12 percent of the active population. As is the case every year, the level of the SMIC is revised on 1 July, and in 2007 it went up by 2.1 percent to 8.44 euros per hour before tax.

SALIC LAW. The code of law established under the **Merovingian dynasty**. Its key significance, in terms of the fate of the monarchy in France, lay in the interpretation of one of its provisions that served to exclude females from dynastic succession.

SAND, GEORGES (1804–1876). A figure in the 19th-century world of letters and politics known as much for her extraordinary lifestyle as for her 60 novels, 25 plays, and numerous essays and political tracts. She was born Amantine Aurore Lucile Dupin, the daughter of a working-class woman who had been married to the aristocratic Maurice Dupin de Francuel without his family's consent. The inevitable tension that ensued, particularly between Aurore's mother and her grandmother, marked Aurore's emotional development and has been used by some critics to explain her constant search for a perfect love.

Aurore married Casimir Dudevant in 1822 precisely to escape her domineering mother. She reached an arrangement with him that allowed her to engage in relationships with other men; she spent half the year with him and their children on the family estate and the rest of the year in **Paris**, where she rapidly accumulated a formidable coterie of friends, including figures like **Honoré de Balzac**. A republican by sentiment and determined to pursue her own inclinations, Aurore dressed as a man to enjoy more freedom of movement and adopted the name Georges Sand for her first novel, *Indiana* (1832), which was greeted with great critical acclaim. She wrote in the **romantic** tradition of high emotion and heroic individualism, but her work was groundbreaking in its frank treatment of feminine sexuality, as in *Lélia* (1833), and also reflected her radical politics through proletarian novels like *Le compagnon de la Tour de France* (1840). Her politics, in fact, eventually placed an intolerable strain on her most famous liaison, with the composer Frédéric Chopin. She supported the radical republicans in the **Revolution of 1848** and greeted with enthusiasm the proclamation of a republic in Paris after the collapse of the regime of Louis-Napoléon (*see* BONAPARTE, LOUIS-NAPOLEON). But in the débâcle that followed, Sand advocated a moderate republic and saw the **Third Republic** established shortly before her death on 8 June 1876. *See also* LITERATURE.

SANS-CULOTTES. A heterogeneous social group made up of master craftsmen, small shopkeepers, and laborers in **Paris** and other cities, united behind the ideals of popular sovereignty and direct democracy. The term *sans-culottes* was originally used to deride the Parisian revolutionaries because they did not wear knee breeches like the aristocrats but were typically attired in trousers with suspenders, a short jacket (*carmagnole*), a Phrygian cap (symbol of the liberated slave in antiquity), a tricolor cockade, and wooden shoes. The name was turned into a source of pride by the revolutionaries. Always at the forefront of the battle for cheap bread and material equality, the sans-culottes wielded the sword and the pike, the latter symbolizing popular sovereignty and the sacred right of insurrection when the interests of the people were threatened. *See also* FRENCH REVOLUTION.

SARKOZY (DE NAGY-BOCSA), NICOLAS PAUL STEPHANE (1955–). Elected president of the French Republic in 2007. He was born in **Paris** to a French mother and a naturalized French father descended from the minor aristocracy of Hungary. His father left the family home in 1959, and the dominant influence on young Nicolas's life was his mother. After obtaining a master's degree in law from the University of Paris in 1978, Sarkozy went on to study at the Ecole des Sciences Politiques with modest results due to his weakness in English. He qualified to practice law in 1981 and followed his mother into the profession. His first contact with the **Gaullist party**, the Rassemblement pour la République (RPR), came in 1974, and in 1976 he took up a representative function for the local RPR in his Parisian home district of Neuilly. By 1980 Sarkozy had become a leading figure in the RPR youth wing, organizing support for **Jacques Chirac**'s campaign for the **presidency** in 1981. Sarkozy himself was elected to parliament for the first time in 1988. He first came to public attention as a minister with special responsibility for the budget in **Edouard Balladur**'s government in 1993. But he backed the wrong horse in the presidential election of 1995, and his support for Balladur instead of the eventual winner, Chirac, led to a period when he was frozen out of government.

The victory of the left in the legislative elections of 1997 forced the RPR to use his undoubted talents once more, and by 1999 he had become head of the party. In the presidential election of 2002 Sarkozy backed the right candidate, Chirac, and was rewarded with the Ministry of the Interior. It was in this post that he first hit the headlines for his dynamic determination to be a hands-on minister, particularly when it came to the fight against crime. After a period as finance minister in **Jean-Pierre Raffarin**'s second cabinet, he returned to the Interior Ministry in the cabinet of Raffarin's successor, **Dominique de Villepin**. It was during this period, in June 2005, that Sarkozy made his famous speech in the deprived suburb of La Courneuve about the need to cleanse the area of thugs with a power spray ("nettoyer au Kärcher"). A section of the political class and anti-racist organizations seized on Sarkozy's words as evidence of his intolerance. On the other hand, a significant proportion of the French public approved of his vigorous stand, given that he had visited La Courneuve after an 11-year-old child had been killed by stray bullets fired by local thugs. In October 2005 Sarkozy created a media storm again when, visiting the deprived suburb of Argenteuil, his ministerial motorcade was stoned and he pledged to rid the area of the "racaille" or scum responsible for such acts of vandalism. This ability to divide opinion was symptomatic of Sarkozy's political career, as was his ability to appeal to the grassroots, in his party and in the country.

Notwithstanding their unspoken but well-known dislike for him, de Villepin and Chirac could not prevent Sarkozy's receiving their party's overwhelming endorsement as its candidate in the presidential election of 2007. The campaign, particularly on the left, soon degenerated into an attempt to frighten the electorate at the prospect of an era of right-wing intolerance should Sarkozy be elected. It was summed up by the slogan "tout sauf Sarkozy" (anything but Sarkozy). For his part, Sarkozy ran a campaign in which he refused to rise to the bait offered by his adversaries and promoted a program of reforms, especially of the labor laws whose inflexibility he believed prevented the rate of unemployment from coming down. In spite of the obvious appeal of his chief opponent, the socialist **Ségolène Royal**, and the feminine virtues of consensus and conciliation she strove to portray, Sarkozy emerged the victor from the second round of the election on 6 May 2007 with a solid majority of the votes cast at 53.06 percent.

Sarkozy's ability to wrong-foot his critics continued after his election when the government he appointed under premier **François Fillon** contained seven female cabinet ministers out of 15, a degree of parity never achieved before and only dreamed of by the left. Moreover, in **Rachida Dati**, France had its first-ever female justice minister, and one from an ethnic minority on top of that. Unlike previous presidents, Sarkozy's style appeared to be one of hyperactivity, as he involved himself in details of policy that were the proper preserve of his premier. His mandate promised to be a tumultuous one, and within months of his election the public sector, especially the transport system, was hit by strikes as unions reacted against Sarkozy's determination to cut back on their employment and retirement privileges. In the sphere of education also there was a mass mobilization of students against his government's plan to give greater autonomy to universities; the plan was nonetheless voted through in the fall of 2007 in spite of the widespread paralysis of universities by student sit-ins.

Sarkozy's inability to resist taking center stage was manifest within weeks of his election. Whereas previous presidents like **François Mitterrand** and Jacques Chirac underlined their connection with the roots of their national culture by frequently retreating to the French countryside to recharge their batteries, Sarkozy chose to recover from the presidential election campaign by taking a high-profile vacation in the **United States**. It was further evidence of his personal enthusiasm for American culture and the expression of his political desire for a rapprochement between the United States and France. Closer to home, he made much of his visit to Libya in July 2007. The visit followed his intervention and that of the first lady, Cécilia, in securing the release of a group of Bulgarian nurses imprisoned there. Sarkozy also enhanced the image of France as facilitating Libya's readmission to the international community when he hosted the visit of the Libyan leader, Muammar Gaddafi, to Paris in December of that year.

By the start of 2008, however, Sarkozy was beginning to pay the price for spending too much time in the media glare. His marital misfortunes mirrored those of his erstwhile presidential rival, Royal, and by the end of 2007 he had effectively split from his second wife, Cécilia. Whatever sympathy this might have provoked was soon dissipated by Sarkozy's determination to pursue the courtship of the woman who would be his third wife, the ex-model Carla Bruni, in front of the camera lenses. Sarkozy responded to suggestions that such a public display of private concerns was undignified for a president by arguing that he wanted to break with the hypocrisies of the past. The low-key wedding of Sarkozy to Bruni in February 2008 did not put an end to the criticism. The entry he had given the **press** to his private life emboldened them to circulate allegations that a text message to Cécilia existed in which he had made a last-minute offer to call off the wedding to Bruni if Cécilia would have him back. The unseemly publicity he had given to his private life, added to a growing feeling in the country that his promises of change were hollow, meant that by March 2008 Sarkozy's approval rating in the polls had dropped to below 40 percent, almost 20 percent behind his prime minister, François Fillon.

SARTRE, JEAN-PAUL (1905–1980). Man of letters, political activist, and most famous figure in French **existentialism**. Sartre was born into a bourgeois milieu and received an excellent education that culminated in his years at the Ecole Normale Supérieure (1924–1928) and his passing of the *agrégation* in 1929. His early writings, such as the novel *Nausée* (1938), chart the emptiness and meaninglessness of modern life. The nausea experienced by the protagonist, Roquentin, expresses the absurdity that confronts him and the arbitrary nature of the meaning that convention imposes on our existence. The only way to combat the sense of alienation from self and the world that flows from the contingency of our existence is through choice. Only by consciously choosing, through action, can the individual define his or her existence in a meaningful manner. The advent of war led Sartre to apply his ideas to politics and history. Wartime plays such as *Les mouches* (1943) and *Huis clos* (1944) and philosophical works like *L'Etre et le néant* (1943) denounce bad faith and underline the importance of authenticity and responsibility.

Crucial to the position Sartre adopts is the distinction he makes between *en-soi*, being deprived of consciousness and thus representative of unfreedom, and *pour-soi*, being that affirms its freedom through a conscious act of will that at the same time makes sense of existence. Sartre became clearly identified with existentialism from 1945 onward, the year he published a lecture entitled "L'Existentialisme est un humanisme" and founded the highly influential review *Les Temps Modernes*, which counted luminaries like his partner **Simone de Beauvoir**, Raymond Aron, and Jean Paulhan among its editorial staff. Sartre's dominance was rapidly asserted, and relations between the editors deteriorated. Differences were accentuated by the onset of the Cold War and Sartre's increasing support for Soviet communism. His praise for the regime of the **Soviet Union** following a trip there in 1954 alienated figures like **Albert Camus** and Aron. However, this did not mean that his relations with the **Parti Communiste Français** were smooth, and they parted company after the Soviet suppression of the nascent democracy in Hungary in 1956. Nonetheless, Sartre continued to situate himself on the left and to consider himself a Marxist. He supported the movement for the independence of **Algeria** and also the students in May 1968 (*see* STUDENT REBELLIONS).

Sartre's autobiography, *Les mots*, appeared in 1963, the same year he turned down the Nobel Prize for **literature** because of his refusal to accept official recognition. His chief work thereafter was the voluminous study of Flaubert *L'Idiot de la famille*, the first part of which appeared in 1971 but which was unfinished because of Sartre's blindness. He died in **Paris** on 15 April 1980 and was mourned as a great mind and a man of conviction, even if sometimes misguided.

SATIE, ERIK (1866–1925). Composer with a major influence on 20th-century music. He was born in Honfleur (Calvados) on 17 May 1866 to a French father and Scottish mother. He studied at the Paris Conservatory (1879–1886), and his early compositions such as *Sarabandes* and *Gymnopédies* (1887) revealed a novel sense of harmony, achieved through unusual progressions presented with a rare simplicity. But Satie had to live in extremely modest circumstances for over two decades before the performance of his compositions by **Maurice Ravel** and **Claude Debussy** between 1911 and 1913 began to bring him success. Satie's music marked a break with the **romanticism** and **impressionism** of the 19th century, and his works sometimes contained ironic allusions to those musical traditions as he strove for a style devoid of grandiose pretensions or transcendental meanings. Satie's approach and innovations exerted a major influence at the beginning of the 20th century, and notably in France on the group of composers known as **Les Six**. *See also* MUSIC, CLASSICAL AND CONTEMPORARY.

SAUSSURE, FERDINAND DE. *See* STRUCTURALISM.

SCHUMAN, ROBERT (1886–1963). Lawyer, politician, and, as author of the Schuman Plan, a founding influence in the cause of European integration. Born in Luxembourg, raised in German-occupied Metz, and educated in **Germany**, Schuman was perfectly at ease in both French and German culture. He represented Metz in the National Assembly after 1918. In spite of his conservative tendencies he avoided involvement with the **Vichy regime** after 1940 and resumed a successful ministerial career after the **liberation**. In June 1946 he became minister of finance and then premier from November 1947 to July 1948. After his term as premier he held the foreign affairs portfolio until 1953, and it was during this time that he had the greatest impact on European affairs.

The Schuman plan was a courageous scheme to bind the economies of France and Germany together in such a way that future military conflict between the two countries would become practically impossible. In his historic speech of 9 May 1950 Schuman proposed that the basic industrial resources of coal and steel in France and Germany should be integrated into a single, common market through the elimination of tariff and transportation barriers governing the flow of these commodities between the two countries. The technical preparation of this plan was assigned to Jean Monnet and resulted in the treaty signed on 18 April 1951 establishing the European Coal and Steel Community, which had been expanded to include Italy and the Benelux countries. The successful cooperation on this front among the six countries set a precedent for the elimination of barriers in other areas and paved the way for the agreements that led to the creation of a **European Economic Community**, established by the Treaty of Rome on 25 March 1957. Although a supporter of good relations with the **United States**, Schuman undoubtedly made the relationship with Germany the key partnership in Europe and focused French **foreign policy** on the Paris-Bonn axis. Schuman became justice minister in 1955, but his career in French domestic politics was largely behind him by the time **Charles de Gaulle** returned to power in 1958. His last major post was, appropriately, as chairman of the European Parliament in **Strasbourg**.

SECTION FRANCAISE DE L'INTERNATIONALE OUVRIERE (SFIO). This was the first unified, properly constituted, socialist party in France with a modern organization that pulled together the various strands in France's long-standing, pluralist socialist tradition. The founding congress, held in **Paris** in April 1905, resulted in the Socialist Unity Pact, which established lines of accountability that went up to a central party machine and, more important, committed the movement ideologically to the pursuit of socializing the means of production and exchange by parliamentary means. *See also* PARTI SOCIALISTE; SOCIALISM.

SEGUIN, PHILIPPE (1943–). A powerful voice on the Gaullist center-right. Born in Tunis, Séguin studied at the University of Aix-Marseille before gaining admittance to the elite Ecole Nationale d'Administration, which smoothed his path to a fast-track career in the civil service that began in 1970. He worked in **Raymond Barre**'s office when the latter was prime minister before gaining election as the deputy for Epinal in 1978. His taste of ministerial office came in the first **cohabitation** government of **Jacques Chirac** in 1986–1988, when he held the portfolio for social affairs and employment. Although responsible for two major and controversial pieces of liberal economic reform, the partial deregulation of working hours and the removal of the requirement for prior administrative authorization for layoffs, Séguin has made clear his belief in the need to promote social cohesion through economic fairness to counterbalance the inequalities that flow from unmitigated economic liberalism.

In 1996 and 1997, Séguin used his position as president of the National Assembly to speak out independently on major social and economic issues, and it was an open secret that he had little faith in the ability of Premier **Alain Juppé** to convince the French electorate of the wisdom of the government's austerity measures. Séguin's misgivings were proved right by the extraordinary reversal of fortune suffered by the government in the legislative elections of spring 1997. As a result of Juppé's defeat, Séguin found himself at the head of a **Gaullist party** shell-shocked by its defeat at the polls and riven with recriminations. He served in this capacity until 1999 but retired from parliamentary life in 2001 after his defeat in the municipal elections of that year.

SEINE RIVER. A major river of northwest France. Broad and slow-moving, especially in the **Paris region**, the river was a great asset for commercial transport and remains a perfect vehicle for tourists wishing to enjoy the beauty of France's showcase capital at a leisurely pace. **Paris** has, however, been threatened by it on a number of occasions, and in 1910 the river burst its banks to produce extensive flooding across the city. The water level is now strictly controlled by a series of reservoirs upstream. Life along the banks of the Seine has been an inspiration for generations of painters, especially in the 19th and 20th centuries, such as **Claude Monet** and **Camille Pissarro**.

SEPARATISM. Strong regional identities existed in France before it was united into one indivisible French Republic, and continued afterward in attenuated form. But in some regions, notably Brittany, the Basque country, and the island of Corsica, these regional identities have been assimilated by small groups into fierce and sometimes violent campaigns for independence from the rest of France. Breton separatism was at its peak in the 1960s and 1970s. Originally prompted by the desire to protect the language, it then developed into a campaign for more economic justice in view of what was perceived as the exploitation of the region by the rest of metropolitan France. This movement subsided in the 1980s due to the leveling up in economic terms with the rest of France and the **decentralization** that occurred under the Socialist governments of the era.

The Basque country straddles northern Spain and southwest France, and there the problem has been principally a Spanish one. The people who consider themselves Basque in France descend originally from the region of Aquitaine, in contrast to the ethnic roots of those with whom they claim coidentity in Spain. The factor that cements Basque identity is linguistic and, whereas in the Spanish Basque country 99 percent of children are taught Basque at school, this proportion falls to 20 percent in the French Basque country. However, the permeability of the border and the passivity displayed by some Basques in France in the face of the violence engaged in by their Spanish cousins have at times necessitated vigorous antiterrorist measures by the French authorities. For example, in 2002 a Franco-Spanish police operation led to the arrest of nine members of the Basque terrorist organization Euskadi ta Askatasuna (ETA) in several towns in southwest France, and in 2003 a cell of three ETA terrorists was discovered in the town of Dax. But in general ETA has been careful to use France as a place of refuge from the Spanish authorities and has not made the French state or civil society a target for terrorist atrocities, in contrast to its activities south of the border.

By far the biggest internal threat to public order and security has come from the separatists in Corsica. The island was only ceded to France by Genoa in 1768, and a yearning for independence has existed ever since. Resentment against metropolitan France was fueled by the lack of real economic development and the resulting outflow of Corsicans, exacerbated in recent years by an inflow of French tourists that is perceived by some as exploitative. A series of violent outrages led to the banning of the Front de Libération Nationale de la

Corse by the government in 1983. But the separatists continued with their campaign, including spectacular attacks on the symbols of French authority like the bombing of the tax office in Bastia in 1987. The economic justifications advanced by the separatists bear little scrutiny in view of the massive per capita funding granted to the island by **Paris**. However, the decline in the relatively scant support given to the separatists was not the result of economic or legal arguments but rather the conviction by many islanders by the mid-1990s that because of a succession of murders with Corsican as well as French victims, the movement had degenerated into an internecine conflict between gangsters. A series of reforms initiated by central government, most recently in 2002, have sought to recognize the specificity of the island and make it the most notable beneficiary of the process of decentralization. The Corsican assembly and the nine-member executive council it elects have at their disposal considerable powers over fiscal and planning policy that exceed those enjoyed by the **regions** of metropolitan France.

SEVEN YEARS' WAR (1756–1763). The origin of this war lay in the Austrian Habsburgs' attempt to retrieve the rich province of Silesia from the grip of Frederick II of Prussia, who had taken it from them during the War of the Austrian Succession. France allied herself with Austria, Saxony, Sweden, and **Russia**, against Prussia, Hanover, and **Great Britain**. By 1758, the British prime minister, William Pitt the Elder, realizing the potential offered by the war for weakening France's ability to compete with Britain in the race for overseas territories, signed a new treaty with Prussia that provided her with robust financial support. But the crucial blow to France and her allies came with the accession of Peter III to the throne of Russia in 1761. When he made peace with Prussia, it became clear that the struggle of his former allies against Prussia and the British could not succeed. A series of victories by Frederick II meant that by late 1762 the sound of battle had been stilled in Europe. However, most crucially for France, the most bitter French defeats had come at the hands of the British overseas. The Franco-British Treaty of Paris, which brought an end to hostilities between the two countries and which was signed in 1763, formalized the fact that the British had won the contest for India and North America, eclipsing France's ambitions in the race for empire. *See also* GERMANY.

SIMON, JULES (1814–1896). Philosopher and republican politician. He was born in Lorient (Morbihan) and began his academic teaching career in 1836. He lost his post at the Sorbonne due to his opposition to the coup of Louis-Napoléon (*see* BONAPARTE, LOUIS-NAPOLEON). In spite of having renounced his **Catholicism**, during the 1860s Simon worked for a reconciliation between free-thinkers and liberal Catholics in pursuit of a moderate republic committed to civil and economic liberty. His secular social conservatism was evident in the measures he proposed during his various ministerial posts in the 1870s. But he is chiefly remembered as the figure given the awesome task of forming a government in December 1876, when the struggle between monarchists and republicans was at its height, and whose cabinet then fell victim to the constitutional crisis prompted by President **Maurice de MacMahon**'s peremptory dissolution of parliament in May 1877. Simon held his final governmental post in 1890 and died six years later in **Paris**.

LES SIX. A loose association of avant-garde composers who came together toward the end of **World War I** through a common admiration for the musical ambitions of **Erik Satie**. The composers were Georges Auric (1899–1983), Louis Durey (1888–1979), Arthur Honegger (1892–1955), Darius Milhaud (1892–1974), Francis Poulenc (1899–1963), and Germaine Tailleferre (1892–1983). Les Six pursued the development of a style that was free from the influence of Richard Wagner's German **romanticism** and **Claude Debussy**'s **impressionism**. They found inspiration in a variety of influences, including Afro-American jazz rhythms and modern polytonal discords and reaching back to the simplicity of 18th-century classicism. An example of the fresh economy of sound they pursued can be found in the piano pieces they wrote for the *Album des six* (1920). The group began to break up in the early 1920s as some members went in search of a more distinctly individual musical voice. Les Six had an enduring impact on France by opening it to the influence of modern **music**.

SOCCER WORLD CUP (1998). Not only was the World Cup staged in France, but for the first time in its history the French team made it to the final against the most famous soccer team in the world, Brazil. While the performance of the Brazilians was uncharacteristically muted, the superiority of the French team was comprehensive. The margin of victory was 3–0 with France's sporting superstar, **Zinedine Zidane**, scoring two goals followed by another by Emmanuel Petit. The country erupted into a remarkable period of national rejoicing, and a new society seemed to emerge, at ease with itself and above all reconciled to France's future as a multiracial society. Given the racially mixed composition of the team, its nickname of *l'équipe Black-Blanc-Beur* (Black, White, and Arab) seemed the perfect metaphor for a rejuvenated and harmonious society in France. That hope in a new beginning, however, did not last as the inequalities created by mass **immigration** and **urbanization**, particularly in **education** and housing, continued to fall disproportionately on France's ethnic minorities.

SOCIAL SECURITY. The foundations of the social security system in France were laid incrementally over many years until the end of **World War II**. Tentative steps were taken in 1910 to provide a legislative framework that would give peasants and workers access to pensions, but it took until 1928 before workers were given a right to some kind of protection against illness. The prospect of wholesale change that appeared, tantalizingly, to be offered by the **Popular Front** did not materialize, and ambitiously generous plans, particularly in the field of retirement pensions, had to be withdrawn.

Rapid and massive strides were taken after 1945 to endow France with one of the most comprehensive social security systems in the world as part of the program of national renewal. Legislation passed in 1945 and 1946 provided France with its famously generous system of family allowances, and in 1947 a minimum wage was fixed that in 1950 took on the guise of the *salaire minimum interprofessionnel garanti*. In line with that of most other developed nations, France's spending on social security continued to rise during the decades that followed, but at a higher rate than in most comparable nations. Thus in 1981, 26 percent of the French gross national product was devoted to social security spending; this had risen to 28 percent in 1990. This increase was due to a significant extent to the egalitarian convictions of the left-wing administrations of the 1980s and early 1990s, which were also guided by the practical desire to find ways of attenuating the consequences of the inexorable rise in unemployment.

It is noteworthy, however, that the center-right administrations that governed during the two periods of **cohabitation** that punctuated this period did not try automatically to reverse the extension of the social security provision envisaged by the left. Left-wing measures to help those living below the poverty line continued to develop under the premiership of the Gaullist **Jacques Chirac** and resulted in, for example, the *revenu minimum d'insertion*, passed into law in November 1988—essentially a minimum income for the long-term unemployed no longer in receipt of benefits, provided through a partnership between central and local governments. Another significant measure implemented at the beginning of the following decade and aimed at providing more finance for social security protection for those on the lowest incomes was the *contribution sociale généralisée*, a levy of 1.1 percent on all sources of income (including unearned income), and collected at the source.

However, after 1993 it became clear to the new center-right government that social security funding, particularly in the fields of health and pensions, distorted the entire structure of public sector financing in such a way that the assumptions conditioning the scope of the French state's commitment to social security would have to be rethought. It was the ensuing program of reform under the premiership of **Alain Juppé**—most notably the cutbacks in the financing of the social security system—that prompted the wave of nationwide strikes in France during the mid-1990s and the eventual return of a Socialist government in 1997. In 1999 the Socialist administration enacted a measure called the *couverture maladie universelle*, guaranteeing medical coverage to anyone having lived in France for over three months. In 2007 the election of a center-right president, **Nicolas Sarkozy**, supported by a substantial majority in the National Assembly, raised the heat once more under the debate concerning France's ability to afford such a generous social security system. Sarkozy vowed to reform the *régimes spéciaux* or special retirement packages in the public sector that allow, for example, workers in the nationalized railway system to retire in their mid-50s with full pension entitlements. However, the attachment to the idea of the state as guarantor of individual well-being remains very strong in France and the Sarkozy **presidency** has also committed itself to extending state provision for the care of the elderly and handicapped.

SOCIALISM. The contribution of French thinkers to the development of socialist ideology was the dominant one in Europe until it was supplanted by the influence of the German intellectual Karl Marx (1818–1883) from the mid-19th century onward. Marx's economic theory, predicated on the notion of progress through class conflict, provided socialism with the kind of analytical tools that it had lacked up to that point. However, the seminal works of the 18th century were written by figures like the mysterious Etienne-Gabriel Morelly, whose biography remains unknown, and more familiar figures like Jean-Jacques Rousseau (1712–1778) (*see* ENLIGHTENMENT) and **Gracchus Babeuf.** As the title of Morelly's famous work *Code de la nature* (1755) implies, the concern all these thinkers shared was the way human society has been corrupted by the obsession with personal ownership of property. Breaking the nexus binding property to private ownership was perceived as the means of reshaping society in a way that would put individuals once more in touch with themselves and with each other, within the context of a new and just society.

This intellectual tradition was continued in the early part of the 19th century by thinkers like Claude-Henri de Rouvroy, Duc de Saint-Simon (1760–1825), Charles Fourier (1772–1837), and **Pierre-Joseph Proudhon.** Proudhon in particular was a major influence on European socialism until the advent of Marx, whose ideas were disseminated in France by **Jules Guesde.** As Marx's ideas took root, a conflict developed in socialist circles between those who advocated the French pluralist tradition, for which socialism was a shared commitment to the ultimate establishment of a just society, and those who were convinced that only by adopting a belief in the means to that end identified by Marx could the objective be realized. Thus tensions developed in left-wing politics in France as the 19th century drew to a close, and although socialists united behind the creation of the **Section Française de l'Internationale Socialiste (SFIO)** in 1905, the left was split fundamentally between Socialists and Communists as a result of the **Congress of Tours** in 1920.

While the Socialists were the dominant force on the left prior to **World War II,** leading the **Popular Front** alliance of the 1930s, the situation was reversed after 1945, with the Communists, whose reputations had been enhanced as a result of their work in the **Resistance,** enjoying the luxury of belonging to the largest political party in France, the **Parti Communiste Français (PCF)**. This situation lasted for over two decades, until a succession of failures forced the SFIO to reinvent itself as the **Parti Socialiste (PS)** in 1969. But the real transformation of its fortunes began in 1971 as a consequence of the Congress of Epinay, when the party placed its destiny in the hands of **François Mitterrand**. Potential rivals like **Michel Rocard** were rapidly neutralized by Mitterrand, who then went on to exploit the advantages offered by an alliance with the traditional rival, the PCF, through a **Union of the Left**, until the PS was strong enough to challenge for power on its own. This ambition was fulfilled in 1981, when Mitterrand was elected president, supported by a PS majority in the National Assembly in the ensuing legislative elections.

Mitterrand went on to become France's longest-serving president, with two consecutive seven-year terms. But socialism lost its appeal as the French electorate came to appreciate that the realities of government left little scope for the pursuit of socialist ideals and that there was ultimately little to choose between the policies of the PS and the center-right. It came as no surprise, therefore, when the Socialists were swept out of office in the legislative elections of 1993 and saw the number of their deputies in the National Assembly cut to less than a quarter of what it had been. The return of a Socialist majority to the National Assembly after the legislative elections of 1997 owed far less to the electorate's positive identification with left-wing ideology than to its bitter disenchantment with the center-right government of **Alain Juppé**. The endeavor of the Socialist prime minister, **Lionel Jospin**, to constitute a *gauche plurielle* or plural left administration, essentially an attempt to give all major factions of the left a seat at the table, failed to save the Socialist cause in the presidential elections of 2002. In fact, Jospin had to endure the humiliation of being beaten by the far-right candidate, **Jean-Marie Le Pen**, to the second-place slot behind the eventual winner, **Jacques Chirac**. Further defeats for the Socialists in the 2007 presidential and legislative elections underlined the failure of their ideology to inspire the electorate, and this failure exacerbated the divisions in the ranks of the leadership regarding the ideas that might modernize and revive their appeal. Moreover, in terms of winning electoral alliances, the Socialist cause has been fatally weakened by the virtual disappearance of what was once the solid and substantial block of votes that could be mobilized by the Socialists' historic partner in the pursuit of a governing majority, the PCF. *See also* BLANC, LOUIS; FEDERA-TION DE LA GAUCHE DEMOCRATIQUE ET SOCIALISTE (FGDS); RUSSIA/SOVIET UNION; TRADE UNIONS.

STAEL-HOLSTEIN, ANNE-LOUISE-GERMAINE NECKER, BARONNE DE (1766–1817). Novelist, critic, hostess of a famous opposition salon during the time of the **Consulate**, lover of **Benjamin Constant**. She sympathized with the coup by which **Napoléon Bonaparte** took power, but her defense of civil and political liberties and her links to the opposition to Bonaparte resulted in her harassment by the imperial authorities and periods of exile from **Paris** and sometimes from France. *De l'Allemagne* (1810), which describes the enthusiasm she developed for German life and letters during her stay in Weimar (1803–1804), played an important part in introducing the French to German literary **romanticism** and the philosophy of Immanuel Kant. However, Bonaparte's police destroyed the French edition, and the first successful edition appeared in London (1813). After an initial period of hesitation in 1814, de Staël rallied to the **Bourbon** restoration that replaced Bonaparte's empire. *See also* LITERATURE.

STAVISKY AFFAIR (1933–1934). Major financial and political scandal of the **Third Republic**. Stavisky was a financier of Ukrainian Jewish origins with a reputation for dubious dealings and for having influential friends. This perception of him was sustained by the fact that although his activities were investigated by the police 45 times between 1927 and 1933, he was never arrested. In 1933 he was the leading player behind the fraudulent sale of municipal bonds in Bayonne. In December of that year the mayor and other figures involved confessed their part in the fraud to the authorities, but there seemed little eagerness to bring the case to trial. In 1934 the **press** sensed a major scandal, especially as the attorney general was the brother-in-law of Premier Camille Chautemps. Under pressure to act, the police located the fugitive Stavisky hiding in a cabin in Chamonix. However, he died from a self-inflicted wound before they were able to arrest him. Public opinion sensed a cover-up, and the ensuing outrage forced Chautemps's resignation and helped provide a pretext for the right-wing *ligues* to riot in **Paris** on 6 February 1934.

STENDHAL. *See* REALISM.

STRASBOURG. Situated on the left bank of the **Rhine** and the heart of the Alsace region in Eastern France, Strasbourg is France's seventh largest urban center, but its demographic importance is far outweighed by its symbolic significance in the history of modern France. As its name suggests, Strateburgum was a community that flourished as a German city in the Middle Ages, selling the wines of its surrounding vineyards to markets as far away as England and Scandinavia, and also growing rich by exporting textiles and cereals. The most conspicuous symbol of this prosperity was its cathedral, finally completed in 1493. In the treaty that brought an end to the Thirty Years' War in 1648, although Alsace was ceded to France, Strasbourg was allowed to remain an independent German city. But weakened by isolation from its beaten German neighbors to the east, in 1681 Strasbourg capitulated to the inevitable and accepted French sovereignty.

In modern times Strasbourg came to symbolize the recurring conflicts between France and **Germany**. When France lost the **Franco-Prussian War** in 1870 the city returned to German hands and in 1918, after the defeat of Germany in **World War I**, it was returned to French hands. So after **World War II**, when it came to finding a home for the International Court of Human Rights, in 1949 British foreign minister Ernest Bevin suggested Strasbourg, as a symbol of unity for Europe and the futility of war as a means of resolving differences. From being initially emblematic of Franco-German reconciliation, during the decades that followed Strasbourg became symbolic of a new and peaceful future for Europe as the home of the Council of Europe and the European Parliament. In spite of its history at the center of so many conflicts, Strasbourg's architectural history has been wonderfully preserved and where necessary restored, leading United Nations Educational, Scientific and Cultural Organization to award it world heritage city status in 1988.

STRUCTURALISM. The dominant school of thought in the 1960s that was concerned with investigating the systems that underlie individual acts across a wide range of contexts — language, rites, rituals, cultural preferences — rather than analyzing the acts themselves. The key contribution to the development of this approach was made by the Swiss linguist Ferdinand de Saussure (1857–1913) in *Cours de linguistique générale* (1915). Rejecting the focus on individual words, Saussure underlined the fundamental distinction between *langue* and *parole*, that is, between the language system that predates examples of language and the individual utterance. Saussure opposed the notion that language is some kind of cumulative resource and that its primary function is to refer to things in the world. Rather than symbols that refer to things, words for Saussure are "signs" made up of two parts: a written or spoken mark called a "signifier" and a "signified" (what is "thought" when the mark is made). By positing an arbitrary relationship between the signifier and the signified, Saussure argues that the sign only acquires meaning as part of a system of relations, the *langue* or language system that we share and draw on as speakers. Applied more broadly, this approach means that if we examine a social myth or economic practice, it is to discover the system of rules, or the grammar, it actualizes in that particular instance.

By the early 1960s the most famous exponent of structuralism was the ethnologist and social thinker **Claude Lévi-Strauss**, who in his four-volume *Mythologiques* (1964–1971) analyzed social myths in the context of structures that govern human thinking and behavior. The effect of structuralism on literary disciplines was revolutionary in the challenge it posed to traditional assumptions about the nature of **literature** and the act of reading. Instead of supposing that the literary work in some way expresses the author's essential self and relates some truth about life, the most committed structuralists argued that, in a sense, the author was dead because literary discourse had no truth function. As the critic **Roland Barthes** argued, the power of writers was limited to reassembling or redeploying already existing works; they could not use writing to express themselves because they had to draw on a dictionary of language and culture that had already been written. The entrenchment of structuralism in the university culture blunted its fashionable appeal by the end of the 1960s and prepared the way for the more skeptical and relativist approach of **poststructuralism**.

STUDENT REBELLIONS. A feature of French political life since students as a recognizable body first involved themselves in a threat to topple the regime, in the **Revolution of 1848**. In modern times mass student mobilization appeared to pose a serious threat to the government on two occasions, in 1968 and 1986.

In a sense the events of May–June 1968 were an ironic testament to the success of postwar France. The entry of unprecedented numbers of the baby-boom generation into higher **education** proved to what extent it had been democratized but at the same time showed the inadequacy of the infrastructure to cope with the surge in numbers. Staff-student ratios were at a record high, classes and lectures were grossly overcrowded, university bureaucracies were overstretched, and rules such as the segregation of sexes in student residences were no longer appropriate to the new generation of students. These grievances were grafted onto a wider sense of disillusionment with the failures of consumer society and a sense of outrage among students around the world at what they perceived as the manifest injustice of United States policy in Vietnam. On 21 March police arrested some students from the faculty at Nanterre for smashing the windows of the American Express building in the rue Scribe in protest against the Vietnam War. News of the arrests was spread at Nanterre the following day by the student leader Daniel Cohn-Bendit, and about 200 students occupied the administration building in protest. Thus was born the 22 March Movement.

Confrontations between police and students multiplied and quickly turned into a general social and political crisis. When students from Nanterre and elsewhere converged on the Sorbonne on 3 May, the dean and rector turned to the police to evict them. On 5 May, the conviction of 13 of the students arrested at the Sorbonne prompted the Union Nationale des Etudiants de France to call for a demonstration on 6 May. The "night of the barricades" began with the street fights that broke out at dusk and that ultimately left over 300 people injured and almost 200 vehicles damaged. At this point the student uprising took on an altogether greater significance as the **trade unions** began to come out on strike. By 24 May, 9 million workers were on strike and not only the government but the republic itself seemed threatened. Public opinion drew back from the prospect of ungovernable change, in spite of the widespread discontent with **Gaullism**, and the authority of the regime was finally reaffirmed in the June legislative elections.

The reforms that followed the events of May 1968 attempted to reduce the overcrowding in higher education and grant a measure of autonomy to universities. However, this could not keep up with the rate of increase in the numbers of young people entering postsecondary education, fueled by a system in which entry to study most disciplines (especially in the humanities) was guaranteed by passing the *baccalauréat*, irrespective of the grade obtained. By the 1980s this means of admission had become firmly fixed as a right in the perceptions of generations of students. Therefore when the minister for research and education, Alain Devaquet, brought legislation before the Senate in October 1986 aimed at reforming the universities by giving them more autonomy, including more freedom to select students, students and prospective students sprang to the defense of their rights, as did their teachers.

On 22 November the teachers' union Fédération de l'Education Nationale called for a strike by students throughout the country to coincide with the arrival of Devaquet's proposals before the National Assembly on 27 November. On that day approximately 200,000 university and lycée students marched from the Sorbonne to the seat of government at the Palais Bourbon and around 400,000 others demonstrated in 50 provincial centers nationwide. The wave of protests did not subside but reached a peak in December. On 5 December thousands of students occupied the courtyard of the Sorbonne, and in a confrontation that night with police, a young demonstrator, Malik Oussekine, was killed. As in 1968, the reaction of organized labor to this tragedy and its causes gave the student rebellion a much broader political and social significance as the **Confédération Générale du Travail (CGT)** supported the call of the student organizations for a general strike on 10 December. Faced with this prospect and the unexpected level of hostility to his proposals, Devaquet resigned on 8 December and the legislation was withdrawn by Prime Minister **Jacques Chirac**.

There was another major mobilization of students forcing a government climb-down a decade later, but it was a sign of the times that on this occasion the issue was not the right to education but the right to work. When the government of Prime Minister **Dominique de Villepin** proposed the Contrat Première Embauche in early 2006, a measure aimed at encouraging the recruitment of young people into the workforce by giving employers more freedom to hire and fire workers under the age of 26, students in particular saw this as an attempt to give young people second-class status as employees. Supported by the parties of the left and the unions in general, hundreds of thousands of students mobilized between February and April, picketing universities and forcing their closure, and ultimately obliging the government to withdraw the measure. But the movement did not provoke the passion or the violence of previous student rebellions, and it was clear that by May 2006 the majority of students wanted to get back to the classroom to prepare for impending exams and avoid having to repeat the year.

The transformation of the student body in France from a source of potential rebellion threatening regime change to just another interest group was underlined in 2007. Soon after its creation, the administration of newly elected President **Nicolas Sarkozy** proposed a reform of the universities that would, notably, give them greater access to nonstate funding for areas like research. As usual, the student unions mobilized to defend their interests, and in particular against the much-feared introduction of Anglo-Saxon–style selection criteria governing admission to university. Although many faculties across the country were paralyzed by sit-ins that delayed the start of the academic year, there were also a significant number of counterdemonstrations by students simply wishing to resume their studies. The student demonstrations had no impact on the government's legislative timetable, and the reform was voted through the National Assembly in the fall of 2007.

SUEZ CRISIS. Result of a military expedition by **Great Britain** and France, with the collaboration of the Israelis, to retake control of the Suez Canal after it had been nationalized by Egypt's President Gamal Abdel Nasser on 26 July 1956. Whereas the attitude of the Israelis was explained by their perennial concern with security, the British and the French purported to see far more than their economic interests compromised by any capitulation to Nasser. In both countries, the media portrayed Nasser's action as dictatorial and therefore a threat to peace and international security. Moreover, the French were motivated by the desire to eliminate a major source of support for the rebels opposing French rule in **Algeria**. Plans for the military expedition were finalized by the three countries concerned on 22 October, and Israeli troops, supported by French air power, invaded Egypt on 29 October. Franco-British forces bombarded Egyptian positions on 31 October and sent in their paratroopers on 5 November, in spite of a U.S.-sponsored **United Nations** resolution calling for a cease-fire that had been passed four days earlier.

However, the British prime minister, Anthony Eden, was forced to accept a cease-fire on 6 November, as Franco-British forces were marching toward Cairo, because of strong opposition at home and intense opposition from abroad, including threats from the **Soviet Union** and powerful economic pressure from the **United States**. Given the attitude of its principal ally in the expedition, France had to accept a withdrawal, and the last of its troops left on 22 December. The immediate consequence of the Suez Crisis was economic hardship in the form of oil shortages. But in the longer term, the abortive attempt to impose Franco-British policies outside Europe illustrated the extent to which the international balance of power had shifted toward Washington, thus deepening French distrust of U.S. **foreign policy**.

SUPREME BEING, CULT OF THE. This was launched with a speech by **Maximilien de Robespierre** to the **Convention** on 7 May 1794. The leaders of the **French Revolution** had come to the conclusion that the policy of de-Christianization that they had promoted in France had been a moral disaster and that the nation's spiritual life needed to be revived, but encouraged to grow in a more patriotic manner. Thus it was that Robespierre proclaimed the existence of a Supreme Being, to be celebrated ritually on rest days, and the existence of a soul. These two articles of a new republican faith, Robespierre believed, would encourage the individual citizen to walk a more virtuous path and promote the cause of social justice. *See also* RELIGION.

SURREALISM. *See* BRETON, ANDRE.

SYMBOLISM. Movement formally announced in Jean Moréas's manifesto published in the newspaper *Le Figaro* (18 September 1886) and that was at its height during the years 1885 to 1895. Its influence was international and felt in the realms of **literature**, visual arts, theater, and **music**, but its center was located in **Paris**. The reaction to the standardization and materialism of the industrial age that was a defining characteristic of the movement had already found its way into the poetry of **Stéphane Mallarmé** during the two decades preceding the publication of the manifesto. Symbolism was by definition a perspective on the world that shunned conformity to the formal features of a movement, rejecting convention and breaking down barriers to experience. Thus typical symbolist techniques evoked commingled sounds, sights, smells, and feeling (drawing on the poet **Charles Baudelaire**'s theory of *correspondances*), in allusions that were highly personal adaptations from an eclectic range of sources enabling the artist to explore his or her own personality.

The artistic vocation of the symbolists was marked by a self-conscious desire to create art as a means of protecting the uniquely personal against the patterns of existence imposed by an indifferent society. The self-consciousness of the artist was justified by the idea that the concern with the exploration of the artist's own identity that is reflected in the work of **art** would be a source of inspiration for the exploration of individual identity by others. In addition to Mallarmé, major literary figures involved in the movement or influenced by it were Paul Verlaine, **Paul Valéry**, and **Arthur Rimbaud**. The movement began to splinter in the late 1890s, and some of its aesthetic concerns were embodied in the cult of the dandy. The effect of symbolism on the 20th century was to create a niche for the artist in the host industrial society he or she vilified, creating a subculture that both sustained the artist and created the possibility of access to the cultural mainstream that would be exploited by later movements like dadaism and **surrealism**.

– T –

TALLEYRAND-PERIGORD, CHARLES-MAURICE, PRINCE DE (1754–1838). **Napoléon Bonaparte**'s foreign minister and a central figure in his downfall. Born in **Paris** to one of the most illustrious families of France, Talleyrand had to forgo a military career in favor of the church because a childhood accident had left him with a deformed left foot. He rose to become bishop of Autun in January 1789 and in April was elected by his diocesan clergy to represent them in the **Estates General**. However, sensing the irreversible tide of change, he switched sides and in October proposed to the Constituent Assembly that the nation repossess ecclesiastical properties. He renounced his vocation after consecrating the new bishops who swore allegiance to the **Civil Constitution of the Clergy** on 24 February 1791. Talleyrand took refuge in the **United States** during the **Terror** but returned in 1797 to serve as minister for **foreign affairs** under the **Directory** and then under Bonaparte (1799–1807). Bonaparte had great faith in Talleyrand's ability and continued to use him even after he left his ministry. But having come to the conclusion that the emperor's career was doomed, Talleyrand betrayed him to the point of taking Austrian money in return for acting as an informer. Talleyrand's instinct for joining the winning side was shown after the occupation of Paris in March 1814 by the troops of Bonaparte's adversaries, when on 1 April he persuaded the Senate to vote for a provisional government with himself as president and to approve the deposition of Bonaparte on the following day.

THE TERROR (JUNE 1793–JULY 1794). Infamous and most brutal period of the **French Revolution**. The coercive security measures passed by the **Convention** and the regulation of the **economy** that prepared the ground for the Terror sprang from the need to respond to a series of crises that came to a head in the spring of 1793: a peasant insurrection, a conservative rebellion in the provinces, defeat on the battlefield against the foreign powers ranged against France, economic crisis, and popular agitation in **Paris**. The Terror was aimed at eliminating the threat to France from within, enabling her armies to fight against her enemies from without. By the fall of 1793 the Terror had become the policy of the national government, and its work was centralized in the Comité du Salut Public (Committee of Public Safety) under **Maximilien Robespierre**.

Essential measures facilitating the prosecution of the Terror included the Law of Suspects, which permitted the arrest and execution of anyone whose words or actions were judged detrimental to the survival of the Republic or anyone thought likely to engage in treason, such as members of the nobility and clergy. Armed with an ethos of moral regeneration, the Terror punished economic crimes and sometimes redistributed the property of those it had executed, deeming great wealth to have a corrupting influence. The requisitioning of food and other necessities for the army was systematically organized, and through the Law of the Maximum an attempt was made to manage the economy by fixing prices for almost all commodities. On the ground, the Terror was usually implemented by **Jacobins** of more modest social origin and **education** than the previous local officials, and they enforced the sanctions decreed by the government through the Revolutionary Committees.

The arbitrary system of denunciation and arrest meant that the victims of the Terror came from all social classes. Figures vary, but at least 16,600 people were executed and 100,000 may have been arrested and imprisoned. In addition to many nobles and clergy, the Terror claimed the lives of more moderate or suspect revolutionaries, including such leading lights as **Georges Danton** and **Louis-Antoine Saint-Just**. By 1794 the success of France's armies against her enemies had weakened the justification for the Terror, and it came to an end in July when concern in the Convention about Robespierre's dictatorial inclinations brought about his downfall and execution.

TERRORISM. Acts of terrorism in France have stemmed from three main causes: the **separatism** pursued by radical groups in places like Corsica and **New Caledonia** who were convinced that their region or island did not belong to France but had been deprived of its independence by illegitimate means; groups ideologically committed to the destruction of the French state; and individuals or groups pursuing a grievance that has its origins outside France altogether but to which France may be directly or indirectly connected. The most dramatic example of an ideologically motivated attack on the French state came with the assassination of its supreme representative, the president, in the shape of Sadi Carnot. The articulation of an anarchist ideology in late 19th-century Europe challenged the authority of the state to organize its citizens' lives and found its converts in France — dramatically so when Auguste Vaillant threw a bomb into the Chamber of Deputies of the French parliament. He was tried and sentenced to death, even though his action had not resulted in any fatalities. Anarchists and others militated for a presidential pardon, but Sadi

Carnot refused and Vaillant was executed in February 1894. This prompted Italian anarchist Sante Caserio to stab Carnot fatally while the president was touring an exhibition in **Lyon** on 24 June 1894.

The misguided and deadly idealism of France's homegrown anarchists surfaced again in the 1970s, ultimately leading several groups to unite under the name Action Directe in 1979. They committed themselves to a guerrilla war against international capitalism, the symbols of state power, and the business elite, all in defense of the proletariat. In 1984 the **Paris** section of Action Directe established a formal alliance with the German Red Army Faction, who for their part were terrorists of an unequivocally Marxist-Leninist persuasion, and the aim was to achieve revolutionary unity among those waging the war in Western Europe. Action Directe was responsible for numerous hold-ups and robberies to fund its activities, but it also scored some notable hits against the French establishment: it assassinated two policemen in Paris in 1983; murdered Général René Audran (responsible for French arms sales) in 1985; and murdered also Georges Besse, chief executive of state-owned **Renault** automobiles, in 1986. The ringleaders were arrested during the year following Besse's murder.

Within less than a decade France was facing a new terrorist threat of foreign inspiration. The Islamic Salvation Front emerged in **Algeria** as an organization to lead the campaign for the founding of an Islamic state in that country. When it was banned there in 1992 some of its leaders took refuge abroad, including Imam Sahraoui. His assassination in Paris put a network led by Khaled Kelkal on the offensive, and although Kelkal himself was shot dead by French police in September 1995, his associates were able to sustain a campaign of terror that continued until October 1995. Between 25 July 1995 and 17 October 1995 Kelkal's network was responsible for eight terrorist attacks that resulted in 10 dead and 200 injured. The attack with the highest profile launched the campaign on 25 July, when a bomb was set off in the metro station at Saint-Michel in the heart of the Latin quarter of Paris, killing eight people.

1995 also marked the year in which the series of measures constituting a heightened security alert, called **Vigipirate**, was revived. It was originally conceived by President **Valéry Giscard d'Estaing** in 1978, then revived and amended in 1995, 2000, 2003, and 2006. The measures are aimed at raising the mental and material readiness of state agencies to preempt where feasible or respond as quickly as possible to terrorist attacks. Much publicity is also given to the role of the public, particularly their alertness to suspicious items or behavior in public places. In January 2006 the French parliament voted through new legislation allowing the state's financial regulators to seize the assets of those suspected of terrorist activities, and in his speech to the **United Nations (UN)** in New York in October 2007, President **Nicolas Sarkozy** pledged France's willingness to work with the UN and other international organizations in the fight against terrorism.

THERMIDOR. A summer month of the French revolutionary calendar, remembered historically for the events of 9 Thermidor, year II (27 July 1794) that brought an end to the **Terror** in France. Disillusionment had grown with the Terror, which had claimed 1,300 lives in June 1794 alone, and with its chief architect, **Maximilien Robespierre**. More significantly, the nation's representatives gathered in the **Convention** had begun to fear the concentration of power in Robespierre's hands through the operation of the Committee of Public Safety. What was regarded by some as a threatening speech by Robespierre on 8 Thermidor was followed by a vote in the Convention on 9 Thermidor that decreed his arrest. During the three days that ensued, Robespierre and 104 of his leading followers were executed in a coup aimed at purging the **Jacobins** and restoring the power of the Convention.

THIERS, ADOLPHE (1797–1877). First president of the **Third Republic**. Thiers's long years of service, his skill as a mediator, and his professed desire to remain above party factionalism made him an obvious candidate for the National Assembly to designate on 17 February 1871 as chief executive power of the French Republic, charged with negotiating the end to the **Franco-Prussian War** that was enshrined in the Treaty of Frankfurt. Having secured peace with the foreign enemy, Thiers presided over the suppression of the insurrectionary turmoil of the **Commune of Paris** (March–May 1871). He had proved his ability to reconcile all sides in the Assembly with the pact of **Bordeaux**, and his gaining the title of president of the Republic on 31 August 1871 added weight to his attempts between 1871 and 1873 to play off conflicting interests against one another to restore the nation's credit, rescue the morale of the military, and secure the definitive departure of Prussian troops from French soil.

Ironically, Thiers's success brought about his downfall, since the achievement of these major objectives made him no longer indispensable. The inflexible attitude of the royalists, and in particular the **comte de Chambord**, led Thiers to the conclusion that a conservative republic was inevitable and desirable. This cost him his erstwhile monarchist support, and he was forced from power on 24 May 1873. He signed the manifesto by deputies condemning **President Maurice de MacMahon** when he peremptorily dissolved the Chamber in May 1877. Thiers died during the electoral campaign that followed, on 3 September 1877, in the midst of successful efforts to bring out the middle-class vote in favor of the Republic.

THIRD FORCE. After the end of **tripartism** the government of the **Fourth Republic** found itself under pressure from the **Communists** on the left and from the **Gaullist party** on the right. It was this pressure that led the socialist **Section Française de l'Internationale Ouvrière** and the Christian Democratic **Mouvement Républicain Populaire** to join with smaller center-left and centrist groups in parliament to form a third force capable of opposing the Communist and Gaullist monoliths. The very heterogeneity of the third force constituted its weakness. The partners were united by the desire to keep the Communists and the Gaullists from taking power, but in other respects, especially with regard to social and economic policy, the third force was riddled with divisions. The ensuing inability to provide France with stable government was illustrated by the fact that between May 1947 and February 1952, 11 different cabinets were formed. In March 1952 the third force finally lost the cohesion that allowed it to govern, forcing the president, Antoine Pinay, to appoint a government with a center-right majority.

THOREZ, MAURICE (1900–1964). Leader of the **Parti Communiste Français (PCF)** during its Stalinist phase. He was born to an unmarried mother in Noyelles-Godault (Nord) and took the name of the miner who married his mother in 1903. He became a full-time official of the PCF in 1923 as secretary of the regional federation of the

Pas de Calais. He emerged as a dominant and immovable party leader in the 1930s, not least because of the cult of personality that communist parties had adopted in countries outside the **Soviet Union** in imitation of Stalin. Thorez was adept at exploiting the possibilities offered by the **Popular Front** alliance while circumventing the risks involved in participating in government. Though endorsed by Moscow, the policy of nonintervention in the Spanish Civil War led in effect to the PCF's withdrawal from the Popular Front. Thorez deployed all his influence to stifle dissent within the party at the Hitler-Stalin pact in 1939 and deserted to the Soviet Union after being called up in 1939. He returned to France after the **liberation** and served for a brief time as minister without portfolio in the government of **Charles de Gaulle**. He led the opposition to the **Marshall Plan** and the **North Atlantic Treaty Organization**. Within his party he removed potential rivals who had risen to prominence through the **Resistance** and steered the PCF along an unquestioningly Stalinist course until his death. *See also* DEFENSE POLICY.

TOCQUEVILLE, ALEXIS DE (1805–1859). Author of a classic study of America, political theorist, and statesman. He was born into a very pro-royalist, aristocratic family, but by the 1820s he began to have grave misgivings about the reactionary policies adopted by **Charles X**. Tocqueville trained as a lawyer and in 1831 secured permission to visit the **United States** with a fellow lawyer, Gustave de Beaumont, to study the prison system there. This was the start of a lifelong fascination with the United States for Tocqueville, particularly in terms of what the young republic had to teach the societies of Europe. The report that Tocqueville coauthored with Beaumont earned considerable praise, but his fame was established by his two-volume masterpiece, *De la démocratie en Amérique* (1835 and 1840). The strength of the book lies in the fact that it is not simply a reflection on the United States but also a profound piece of political philosophy, dealing with the possible tension between desirable goals like the advancement of equality and the promotion of individual liberty. To counter the threat of the tyranny of the masses or the despotism of the bureaucratic state, Tocqueville urged widespread participation in public life and heightened moral values as the best way of enhancing the individual, civil, and political liberties that he regarded as indispensable to progress.

Tocqueville's political career began with his election as a deputy representing Valognes in 1839. His belief in greater democratization in France led him to serve the **Second Republic** after the **Revolution of 1848** as a representative in the Assembly and then as a foreign minister. The coup d'état of Louis-Napoléon (*see* BONAPARTE, LOUIS-NAPOLEON) resulted in a brief spell of imprisonment followed by retirement from public life. Tocqueville died while working on his other great work, *L'Ancien régime et la Révolution*, the first part of which appeared in 1856. His reputation as a moralist and advocate of liberal democracy has endured.

TOULOUSE. Originally known as Tolosa, then Tholose, the name Toulouse was established for good toward the end of the 17th century. It is situated in the Aquitaine region in the southwest of the country and sits effectively at the crossroads between the **Mediterranean Sea** and the Atlantic Ocean. After defeating the local Celtic tribe, the Romans turned Tolosa into an important military and administrative center and by 30 BC had transformed it into a walled city. A number of invading tribes fought over it following the departure of the Romans, but in the Middle Ages it enjoyed a period of independence and even expansion under the Counts of Toulouse, whose influence spread to cover the province of Languedoc. In 1250 Toulouse was integrated into the royal domain of France, but it was during the **Renaissance** of the 16th century that prosperity transformed the **architecture** of the town, resulting in the construction of the great aristocratic houses that gave the place its grandeur. The middle of the century was also punctuated by bloody confrontations between **Catholics** and **Protestants**, with the former ultimately gaining the ascendancy.

The fabric of the town survived the **French Revolution** largely intact, and in the modern age it acquired the nickname of *la ville rose*, or the pink city, due to the prevalence of pink stone and fired earth in its construction. In line with the modernizing spirit of the 20th century, by the 1920s the town had already established itself as a pioneering center for the aviation industry. It is now a European hub for aviation, as the home of Airbus, and also for space and information technology. This has been a major factor in the town's growth, making it France's fourth-largest municipality with 435,000 inhabitants in 2005. A newspaper poll in 2006 provided further evidence of its attractiveness when French people voted Toulouse the most agreeable town in France in which to live.

TOUR DE FRANCE. The world's most prestigious bicycle race and the most widely covered national event in the French sporting calendar. It was established in 1903 by the French cyclist and journalist Henri Desgrange (1865–1940). The tour is made up of 21 daily stages covering a total of approximately 4,000 kilometers; the rider with the lowest aggregate time for all the stages at the end of the tour emerges as the overall champion. Although called the Tour de France, over the years the race has broadened its appeal by including regular stages in Belgium and occasionally in Spain, Italy, **Germany**, and Switzerland. By the end of the 1990s the Tour had become dogged by accusations, proven and alleged, of doping among its participants to gain a competitive advantage. In 2006 such accusations were upheld against the winner, the American Floyd Landis, and he was stripped of the title the following year.

2007 was meant to be a new beginning aimed at rebuilding the credibility of the Tour, and it set off spectacularly from London, drawing millions of spectators to line the route taking the riders to the English Channel before the race returned to French soil. Unfortunately, shortly after the 17th stage of the race in mid-June, German rider Patrik Sinkewitz tested positive for a banned substance. Such was the dismay in Germany that state-owned television stations there ceased to broadcast coverage of the race. Days later, one of the race favorites, the Kazakh rider Alexander Vinkourov, was found to have undergone an illicit blood transfusion. He was forced to quit the race, and the entire Astana team of which he was a member decided to withdraw. While there is no doubt that the Tour will continue to be staged in the foreseeable future, the faith of the French public in the integrity of the Tour as a sporting and cultural event showcasing France has unquestionably been damaged.

TOURISM. The foundation of France's reputation as a tourist destination for foreigners owes much to the spending habits of the affluent and leisured English cohorts who first developed a taste for the Côte d'Azur toward the end of the 19th century. Their influence in developing the area as a playground for rich tourists was preserved for posterity by names like the Promenade des Anglais in Nice. Increasing prosperity and easier mobility during the 20th century turned the privilege of a few into a realistic option for the many.

France's position as the world's top tourist destination in terms of visitor numbers is underpinned by the unique and universally magnetic pull of French culture, reinforced since the *belle époque* by the generations of writers and artists from Europe and North America who have flocked to France, usually to its capital, **Paris**. But in more practical terms modern France has enjoyed the advantages of a centralizing tradition, one of whose benefits has been the kind of infrastructure investment that makes travel within its frontiers easy, allied to the kind of dedicated funds for nationwide cultural activities that sustain the belief of all French governments in their country's civilizing mission. During the 1980s and 1990s, Paris in particular has been the site of massive investment, unparalleled since **Baron Georges-Eugène Haussmann** transformed central Paris in the mid-19th century, designed to consolidate the city's position as the cultural capital of Europe, if not the world. As the Eiffel Tower rapidly established itself as an instantly recognizable landmark at the end of the 19th century, so at the end of the 20th century, the Pompidou Center, the arch at La Défense, the glass pyramid at the Louvre, and the Musée d'Orsay, among the more recent additions to the Paris skyline, maintained the profile of the city and the country in the eyes of a world audience. A major new attraction was added in June 2006 when the museum at the Quai Branly, designed by the famous architect Jean Nouvel, opened its doors to those wishing to discover its formidable collection of artifacts produced by the indigenous cultures of Africa, Oceania, Asia, and the Americas.

Mindful of accusations of complacency, and the significance of tourist dollars to the French economy, in recent years tourist industry and state-sponsored initiatives have encouraged French hoteliers and restaurateurs in particular not to live down to their reputation for impatience or rudeness, especially toward tourists who do not speak French. In 2006 France came to the top of the tourism league once more with 79.1 million visitors, but it came third in terms of dollars spent, behind the **United States** and Spain.

TOURS, CONGRESS OF (25–30 DECEMBER 1920). Eighteenth national congress of the **Section Française de l'Internationale Ouvrière (SFIO)**, which gave birth to the **Parti Communiste Français**

when 75 percent of the delegates voted to accept the 21 conditions stipulated by Moscow (July 1920) for membership in the Third International. Support for the idea that the French socialist movement should model itself according to the lines established by the Bolsheviks in Moscow was weak in the SFIO before 1920. But the influx of new recruits to the party after **World War I**, poor results in the elections of 1919, and a sharp rise in unemployment in 1920 led some members to question the effectiveness of the SFIO's reformism. Moreover, two prominent members, Marcel Cachin and Ludovic Oscar, had returned from a visit to **Russia** singing the praises of the Boshevik regime and describing it as the true heir to the French revolutionary tradition. It fell to **Léon Blum** to make the case for the democratic and libertarian traditions of French **socialism** against the authoritarianism of the Bolshevik model. The delegates opted by 3,208 for the Comintern, 1,022 against, with 397 abstaining. Thus was born the schism between French communism and French socialism and the source of the enduring rivalry between the two for the rest of the 20th century.

TOWN PLANNING. *See* URBANIZATION.

TRADE. For most of its history, France's **economy** sheltered under a protectionist system. Where trade flourished, it was usually driven by conquest, but this was an uncertain basis for growth, as was illustrated by the sudden reversal of fortune France suffered when she lost her North American and Indian colonies to the British in the middle of the 18th century. At the beginning of the 19th century, **Napoléon Bonaparte** exploited the military superiority of France in Europe to create a continental system designed to shut out the British and deliver extremely favorable terms of trade to the French at the expense of their neighbors. But this system functioned to France's advantage for barely more than a decade and collapsed together with Bonaparte's military power.

The process of opening up trade in terms of modern agreements between peacetime governments began in the 19th century and was characterized by watershed accords like the Cobden-Chevalier Treaty in 1860, which inaugurated free trade between France and **Great Britain** and played an invaluable part in speeding up the Industrial Revolution in France. French exports rose 80 percent in the 1860s as opposed to 40 percent in the 1850s, and the textile industry in the northeast responded particularly well to the new competition from overseas by investing and innovating. But the overall picture was not so rosy, and the economic downturn that set in at the end of the 1860s revealed the patchy performance of the French economy in export terms and the lack of dynamism that characterized it, in comparison to European neighbors like **Germany** and Britain, well into the 20th century.

France's integration into the European and the world economy was most successful after 1945. **Decolonization** meant that France was no longer tied to dependent markets like **Algeria**, and France's adhesion to the **European Economic Community** allowed its enterprises free access to a vast, vibrant market of prosperous consumers and prospective partners. The importance of this market can be shown by the fact that by 1992 it absorbed 62.7 percent of French exports, with 16.8 percent going to Germany alone. But France's performance in the global market also, especially during the *trente glorieuses*, was a notable success, and by 1990 France had overtaken Britain to become the fourth largest exporter in the world, behind the **United States**, Japan, and Germany, with a 6.2 percent share of world export markets. The 1980s were a particularly successful time for France with regard to growth in its ability to provide financial services to worldwide customers. However, trade deficits in energy resources caused anxieties; toward the end of the 1980s, so did the decline in the competitiveness of French industrial products on international markets. But the deficit in industrial trade was overturned, and by 1992 the value of exports exceeded that of imports by 3 percent.

The need to adhere to tough fiscal policies to qualify to join the single European currency placed additional pressure on French governments to control inflation and consumer demand, thereby helping the nation's economy to register consistent surpluses in trade into the late 1990s. But by that time the rigidities in the French economy had also begun to take their toll, particularly with regard to financing the public sector. While neighbors like Great Britain had decided that there was no alternative to submitting to the rigors of globalization, particularly in the labor market, French governments remained wary of the negative electoral consequences of being perceived as compromising the rights and protection afforded to French workers. By

2003 a resurgent British economy had overtaken France in terms of its size, but the World Trade Organization report of 2005 underlined France's importance as a major player in world trade, placing it fifth in the table of the world's leading exporting nations, two places ahead of Britain.

TRADE UNIONS. The pressure for legal trade union representation started from the earliest days of the Industrial Revolution in France, under the Orleanist regime of **Louis-Philippe**, but the pressure became irresistible during the 1880s. The need for skilled industrial labor and changing social and political attitudes strengthened the hand of the unions, and during the three decades following 1880 enabled them to secure major objectives like the legal right to organize, legislation covering safety in the workplace, a basic pension, and the right to at least one day's rest a week. It was the period during which unionization spread across both the public and private sectors, and the level of membership more than doubled between 1895 and 1913, rising from 419,000 to over 1 million.

However, the union bodies that emerged at the end of the 19th century were very diverse in their political philosophies, ranging from revolutionary syndicalist to more gradualist and reformist variants. Not only did they compete with each other, but they were also keen to preserve their independence from the **political parties** of the day so they would not become subservient to them. These concerns led to the formation of the **Confédération Générale du Travail (CGT)** and the famous Charte d'Amiens, a charter formulated in 1906 that said the mission of the confederation was to serve the interests of the workers, but through direct action against employers if necessary rather than through alliances with political parties.

By the 1930s a trade union culture had become firmly established in France, especially after the election of a **Popular Front** government that strengthened the rights of unions to organize without fear of reprisals and passed legislation like the right to an annual paid holiday. In short, trade unions had become partners, together with government and employers, who could not be overlooked in the elaboration of social and economic policy.

After 1945, the big battalions of the union movement came to be represented by three major bodies: the CGT, the **Confédération**

Française Démocratique du Travail (CFDT), and **Force Ouvrière (FO)**. Whereas its class-based, Marxist analysis of its vocation turned the CGT into a natural vehicle for the ambitions of the **Parti Communiste Français**, the CFDT has shown itself to be more reformist in a social democratic sense, while the FO has combined its belief in consensus as the way forward with a capacity for vigorous defense of the gains made by workers over the years against the corrosive effect of market forces. Owing to its much smaller size, the **Confédération Française des Travailleurs Chrétiens** has exerted less influence than the other bodies. But it is generally true that trade union membership in France was historically never as high, as a proportion of the working population, as in **Great Britain** or, especially, **Germany**. Furthermore, the proportion of the workforce that is unionized declined by half between the early 1980s and the early 1990s.

A number of industrial conflicts in the 1990s revealed a new challenge to the unions as workers opted for *coordinations*—grassroots organizations—to lead their campaigns, as opposed to going through the formal procedures required by established union structures. In 2003 labor ministry statistics showed that 8 percent of French workers were unionized. In a TNS/SOFRES poll carried out in December 2005, respondents cited three main causes for the modest level of union membership in France, compared to some of its European neighbors: 38 percent of those interviewed perceived the unions as failing to understand their problems; 36 percent feared reprisals on the part of their employers if they joined a union; and 34 percent felt that the union movement in France was too divided.

TRANSPORTATION. In a sense, France was prepared intellectually for the great technological advances that would allow it to develop a modern transport infrastructure long before those advances came about. Under **Napoléon Bonaparte**, France developed a corps of specialized engineers who could build the roads, bridges, and canals that enabled the emperor to move men and material swiftly to secure his hold over France and extend his power over Europe. But economically driven changes in transportation methods were slow to develop in France during the first half of the 19th century because of the inefficiencies fostered by the protectionism that sheltered the French **economy**. There were false dawns, like the flurry in railway stocks during the early 1840s, but sustained, modernizing infrastructural development, particularly in the railways, did not occur until the **Second Empire**.

The governments under the regime set up by Louis-Napoléon (*see* BONAPARTE, LOUIS-NAPOLEON) actively promoted the concentration of ownership in the railway industry that would give it the critical mass to develop. The six major railway companies that emerged during the 1850s received additional incentives to grow, so that between 1852 and 1860, railway investment rose by 500 percent. The development of the network was such that 50 percent of all internal trade was carried by rail in 1870, against 10 percent in 1852. In addition, and in the face of an undeniable economic downturn that began in the 1860s, the central government continued to invest massively in canal and road building, particularly in the context of urban renewal programs, thus playing a key role in the doubling of building-sector activity that occurred in France between 1853 and 1869. During the ensuing decades the French railways played an invaluable part in uniting the nation and especially in breaking down the isolation of remote communities. The services offered by the system were finally integrated in a nationalized network in 1937, when the Société Nationale des Chemins de Fer Français (SNCF) was created.

The next great change in the nation's transport system was caused by the need to accommodate the democratization of automobile ownership. The country roads that had proved perfectly adequate before 1939 soon began to clog up after the end of **World War II**. While private vehicle ownership stood at 680,000 in 1944, by 1960 it had risen to 4,950,000. French governments therefore launched a program of highway construction throughout the country, in partnership with private companies, resulting in a network of high-speed *autoroutes* that rose from a mere 174 kilometers in 1960 to 7,000 kilometers in 1986. But the investment in national infrastructure was also matched by investment in local infrastructure. Urban traffic problems were targeted, and the 1970s and 1980s were marked by the construction of subway systems in **Lyon** and **Marseille**. **Paris** had been given its own transport authority, the Régie Autonome des Transports Parisiens, in 1948, and the steady renewal of the capital's public transport system received a boost in the 1980s with the construction of the Réseau Express Régional, a high-speed extension to the Parisian subway serving the commuter belt around the capital.

The enthusiasm for road travel meant cutbacks in local railway services during the two decades following World War II while efforts were focused on modernizing lines and rolling stock. The success of this project became a source of national pride, especially when the high-speed *train à grande vitesse* (TGV) was launched in 1978, carrying passengers between Paris and Lyon at 270 kilometers per hour. TGV technology has been exported to countries around the world, and France has extended the TGV service to its European neighbors. In spite of the indebtedness of the SNCF in the 1990s, investment in the nation's transport infrastructure remains a major feature of the ethos of modernization dear to all French governments after 1945 and explains the enthusiasm for a tunnel rail link with **Britain** across the English Channel. The French laid a dedicated track to carry passengers on the French side at train speeds of over 300 kilometers per hour from Calais to Paris when full scheduled services began in 1995, but their British partners deferred the investment in a similar track between Folkestone and London, which did not become operational until 2007.

More than in most other European countries, the French state has had difficulty adjusting to a more modest role in shaping the nation's transportation systems. European competition rules have made national subsidies more difficult to justify under a single market in Europe. And it is noteworthy that in the early 1990s, when the French government under the premiership of **Edouard Balladur** was wrestling with ways to help the national airline created in 1933, Air France, it opted for a 2-billion-franc recapitalization package that it submitted to the European Commission for approval while at the same time discreetly signaling that it would not allow the plan to be refused. But the pressure on the state's finances resulting from the criteria to be met before France could join the single European currency forced the central government to retreat from its previous positions in defense of national transport assets, and this opened the door to acquisitive foreign predators with money to spend, exemplified by the battle in 1996 between British Airways and Virgin to see who could take over the small French airline Air Liberté. The belief in national champions has deep roots, however, and when Air France merged with the Dutch national carrier KLM in 2004, the French widely perceived it as a victory for the national interest as opposed to the creation of a European carrier more capable of surviving in the face of global competition.

Few countries take as much pride in the modernization of their transport infrastructure as France, and 2004 provided further cause for rejoicing with the opening of the Millau viaduct. At almost 2.5 kilometers long and standing 270 meters above the ground, it is the highest roadway in the world. Designed by the British architect Norman Foster, the viaduct was acclaimed by the French public as a work of art as well as a feat of engineering. It straddles the Tarn valley like a silver blade on the horizon and completes a continuous freeway link between Paris and the town of Béziers in the southwest. As for the railways, June 2007 heralded the opening of the first 300-kilometer stage in the development of the TGV Est, which aims ultimately to provide a high-speed train link between Paris and Budapest, the capital of Hungary, by 2015.

TRENTE GLORIEUSES (THIRTY GLORIOUS YEARS). A frequently quoted expression in discussions about the economic development of France since 1945. Erring on the side of generosity in numerical terms, Jean Fourastié coined the expression to describe the period of unparalleled and uninterrupted growth in France, with all the accompanying benefits in terms of employment and living standards, that stretched from the end of **World War II** to the oil crises of the early 1970s, when sudden increases in prices by the members of OPEC destabilized the world **economy**.

TRIPARTISM. A short-lived experiment in coalition government in France that lasted from January 1946 to May 1947. **Charles de Gaulle**'s departure from power at the beginning of 1946 prompted an attempt by the **Parti Communiste Français (PCF)**, the socialist **Section Française de l'Internationale Ouvrière**, and the Christian Democratic **Mouvement Républicain Populaire** to govern together and lay the foundation for a new **Fourth Republic**. The fact that four governments were formed during the period of tripartism suggests the elusive nature of a stable coalition for the parties in question.

While considerable common ground existed on the issues of domestic economic and social reform, rapid and dramatic changes in the sphere of **foreign affairs** proved a fatal stumbling block. The process of **decolonization** proved a bloody and painful affair for France because of the slowness of successive French governments to accept the inevitable breakup of the empire. The PCF was particularly hostile to the repressive measures taken by the French authorities in places like Indochina and North Africa. This unease was greatly exacerbated by the rapid polarization in world politics that resulted from the Cold War. The PCF's ideological allegiance to Moscow made it very critical of French policies it perceived as subservient to the interests of the **United States** and inimical to the well-being of workers in France and across the world. Ultimately, this hostility from a member of the governing coalition became intolerable, and on 5 May 1947 Prime Minister **Paul Ramadier** sacked the Communist ministers from his cabinet, thus ending tripartism.

TRUFFAUT, FRANCOIS (1932–1984). A highly influential filmmaker and leader of the *nouvelle vague* (new wave) that emerged in the late 1950s. Truffaut had a lifelong love affair with movies, and his initial contribution to the industry was as a critic in the pages of the magazine *Cahiers du cinéma*. It was in a seminal article in 1954 that he established the principles for the *auteur* theory of filmmaking, predicated essentially on the conviction that the director is the primary creative force in the process. His debut feature, the semiautobiographical story of a troubled adolescent entitled *Les quatre cents coups*, came in 1959. What some critics regard as Truffaut's best film came just two years later, in *Jules et Jim*, the brilliant exploration of the ever-changing relationship between three friends before and after **World War I**. A wide variety of films followed, including those that paid subtle homage to masters of the art, as evidenced by the Hitchcockian undertones of *The Bride Wore Black* (1968). In contrast to that other great filmmaker of his generation, **Jean-Luc Godard**, Truffaut had a gift for producing films that won popular as well as critical acclaim. His amusing and ironic look at the vagaries of filmmaking, *La nuit américaine* (1973), won an Oscar for best foreign film under the title *Day for Night*, and his film about a theatrical company in Paris under the Nazi occupation, *Le dernier métro* (1980), enjoyed great commercial success around the world. Truffaut also displayed his talent in front of the camera in a series of minor parts, most notably as the scientist Lacombe in Steven Spielberg's *Close Encounters of the Third Kind* (1977). He died of a brain tumor, and was much mourned by the industry and **cinema** enthusiasts.

– U –

UNION OF THE LEFT. The tactical alliance between the **Parti Socialiste (PS)** and the **Parti Communiste Français (PCF),** sealed by an agreement reached on 27 June 1972 with a view to securing victory in the forthcoming elections and putting together a **Common Program** for government that the left could implement once in power. The alliance had mixed fortunes during the 1970s and reached a critical point in the run-up to the 1978 parliamentary elections. The polls suggested a victory for the left, but the PCF, in an apparent attempt to reinforce its position in any future government of the left, demanded revisions of the Common Program. The PS leadership under **François Mitterrand** refused, and the right won the elections. The antipathy between the two parties of the left was such that the PCF opposed the PS candidate, Mitterrand, in the 1981 presidential election. Having secured the victory and with support from a PS majority in parliament, Mitterrand approved the offer of four ministerial portfolios to leading PCF figures, thereby admitting the party as a junior partner in a government of the left. But the PCF severely criticized the policy of economic austerity that the Socialist government was soon forced to adopt, and fearful of the reaction from its own constituency should it be seen to support these policies, in July 1984 the PCF refused to provide any ministers for **Laurent Fabius**'s cabinet. The PS and the PCF were two parties that sought tactical advantage against the right through alliances but that were essentially in competition for the left-wing constituency in France. By the mid-1980s it was clear that the PS had won and that the PCF had begun a long-term decline.

UNION POUR LA DEMOCRATIE FRANCAISE (UDF)/UNION FOR FRENCH DEMOCRACY. Political center party born out of a confederation of non-Gaullist parties created in 1978 by **Valéry Giscard d'Estaing** to support his presidency. While willing to form part of the governing center-right majority in alliance with the Rassemblement pour la République (*see* GAULLIST PARTY), the UDF nonetheless affirmed its distinct identity as a party espousing a more liberal philosophy than the Gaullists. In 1998 the UDF underwent a major change when **François Bayrou** was elected leader with the mission of uniting the various ideological strands within the party and creating what he declared in 2006 to be a "free and independent" party. The implication was obvious: the UDF was to stand for a democratic pluralism that was independent of both the center-right majority and the left. Bayrou had already been clearly distancing his party from the government of **Dominique de Villepin** in the years leading up to the presidential election of 2007, in which Bayrou came third. However, most UDF members of parliament took fright at Bayrou's renewed determination to steer a separate course from the center-right majority led by the Union pour un Mouvement Populaire (Union for a Popular Movement) and made a point of expressing their dissent. Those parliamentary representatives and party members loyal to Bayrou's vision therefore created a new party called Mouvement Democrate in May 2007. But the gamble appeared to fail when they emerged from the legislative elections of July 2007 with only three seats in the National Assembly.

UNITED NATIONS (UN). The organization was set up on 26 June 1945 in San Francisco to resolve international problems in the aftermath of **World War II** and with the intention of preventing recurrence of such a conflict. The first session of the UN was held in London in January 1946, but thereafter its permanent home became New York. France was one of the original 51 member states that founded the UN. In addition to this it became one of the permanent members of the UN Security Council, along with the **United States**, the **Soviet Union**, **China** (represented until 1971 by Taiwan and thereafter by the People's Republic of China), and **Great Britain**. The permanent seats held by France and Great Britain have been contested for some time by certain members of the UN, given the decline as global powers of these two countries and the growing importance of countries like India and Brazil on the world stage. But there appear to be no plans for a reshuffle in the membership of the Security Council in the near future. France is the fourth-largest contributor to the UN's finances, responsible for 6.5 percent of its budget in 2005.

UNITED STATES, RELATIONS WITH. France's connections with the territory that is now the United States goes back to the days when it competed with England to establish control over the New World.

The explorer Jacques Cartier's first foray into the St. Lawrence River in 1534 began a period of exploration and settlement that led to the creation of la Nouvelle-France (New France), which existed from 1604 to 1760 and at its height stretched from the mouth of the St. Lawrence to the Mississippi delta. The defeat of France in the **Seven Years' War** marked the triumph of British interests in North America at the expense of the French, and when **Napoléon Bonaparte** sold Louisiana to the United States in 1803 it marked the end of the French presence there altogether. But the United States continued to hold a special fascination for France. Evocations of the native culture of the United States figured in the writings of **François-René de Chateaubriand** and **Jean-Jacques Rousseau**, especially their speculations on the spirit of the noble savage, and by the end of the 19th century the admiration for the United States as a template for freedom and modernity led to the phenomenon of *américanisme*. The most potent emblem of this admiration is the Statue of Liberty, offered by the people of France to the United States as a symbol of their friendship and inaugurated in New York in 1886.

The reciprocal nature of that friendship was proved in two world wars. After **World War I**, enthusiasm for American culture turned Paris into one of the great jazz capitals of the world and offered black American artists like Josephine Baker the freedom and success they would not have enjoyed in their own country, due to the racism and segregation there. **World War II** underlined even more France's indebtedness to the United States in the struggle to preserve its freedom and resulted in a peculiarly French ambivalence, especially under the presidency of **Charles de Gaulle**. Like **Great Britain**, France emerged from World War II as one of the victors but had to make the painful adjustment to being a postimperial power in a world now dominated by two superpowers, the United States and the **Soviet Union**. De Gaulle, however, was determined to position France on the world stage as offering an alternative pole of attraction. Consequently, he invited the Soviet leader Nikita Kruschev to visit France at the height of the Cold War, and when he felt that the extension of U.S. influence in Europe threatened to compromise France's sovereignty, he asked U.S. forces to leave French territory and withdrew his country's participation in the **North Atlantic Treaty Organization**.

Though de Gaulle's successors have usually been much more conciliatory toward the United States, the preoccupation with independence vis-à-vis the world's superpower and the determination to avoid the perceived subservience of Britain have remained a constant of French policy. This was highlighted by France's critical attitude toward the United States over the second Iraq war. But the chill this created was short lived, and under President **Nicolas Sarkozy** France has been keen to prove itself a reliable ally of the United States, particularly over the potential threat posed by Iran's nuclear development program. Culturally, and in spite of state subsidies and policies aimed at protecting French film and music production, the appetite for things American is shown by the relentless programming of U.S. television series, old and new, on French channels. The young in particular are now increasingly drawn to learning American English, as opposed to the English of their British neighbors. *See also* TOCQUEVILLE, ALEXIS DE.

URBANIZATION. The origins of many French urban centers can be traced back to the Middle Ages. The churches, market squares, winding streets, and timber-framed buildings of regional centers like Rouen and **Bordeaux** bear witness to their medieval design, and many of these features are now protected in conservation zones and pedestrian precincts. However, France's towns grew at different rates and at different times. Some of the major centers of medieval France, such as Orléans and Dijon, failed to grow because they were left behind by the Industrial Revolution. Others were like St. Etienne, which grew spectacularly as an industrial city from the 1840s because of its role as a magnet for textile manufacture and metallurgy. In between, there were urban centers like **Lyon**, which sat at the heart of a region notable for small-scale silk manufacture but whose position was consolidated by the Industrial Revolution. In general, the urban hierarchy was well established in France before the Industrial Revolution, with **Paris** the economic, business, cultural, and administrative center, in a dominant position at the top, followed by cities that grew in a slow and steady manner during the 19th century.

It has been argued that the position of Paris in the hierarchy was too dominant and that this helps to explain why towns like Lyon, Bordeaux, **Marseille**, and Rouen, which had been in the top 30 of

European urban centers in the 18th century, had dropped out of that category halfway through the 20th century, in contrast to towns like Manchester and Birmingham in England that boomed, especially during the 19th century. However, the contrast with the rapid and massive urbanization in England during this period must also take account of the exceptional lead enjoyed by **Great Britain** in the race to industrialize and the political factors that facilitated it. It remains the case, however, that modern urban planning in France shows a consistent desire to develop means for counteracting the dominance of Paris.

The origins of French town planning are found in the royal edicts regulating building lines, heights, and street widths in Paris in the early 17th century. This building code, the most comprehensive in Europe, was revised in 1807 after the **French Revolution** and was adopted later in the century by over 200 towns. Paris gave the lead again during the 1850s with the process of Haussmanization (*see* HAUSSMANN), named after the chief architect responsible for the city center slum clearances; the creation of wide boulevards for wheeled traffic; the patterns of crescents, parks, and radial streets; and those great prerequisites for public health, piped water and sewerage. It was a pattern imitated in numerous large cities like Lyon, Marseille, Toulon, **Toulouse**, Bordeaux, and Rouen. But by the beginning of the 20th century, France had slipped substantially behind countries like Britain and **Germany** in developing the mechanisms for guiding the development of the urban environment. The pressure of change after 1945 was to make this a priority for French governments. Half of the French population in 1926 lived in cities, and this had risen to 70 percent by 1968, but the period of fastest growth occurred between 1954 and 1968, when the population of urban areas increased by 10 million people.

The initial response to the challenge of dealing with the pressure on urban centers came with the new administrative, planning, and building code established in 1943, which paved the way for what has been called the age of renewal—that period between 1945 and 1965 when governments focused on the building of the *grands ensembles*, the large-scale public housing projects aimed at meeting the massive growth in demand for modern, affordable housing. In the 1960s new towns, initially eight and then finally five, were proposed for the

Paris region to absorb some of the pressure of population growth in the capital. In the 1970s several provincial new towns were designated to take pressure off regional urban centers like Lyon and Marseille. Mindful as ever of the preponderant influence of Paris, in the late 1960s the idea was hatched to create eight *métropoles d'équilibre* in the regions, or growth poles to counteract the pull of Paris. Large tracts of land were bought up for redevelopment, and considerable sums of government money were invested to transform what were often areas of urban dereliction into centers of commercial activity. Thus the Part-Dieu district in Lyon was cleared and redeveloped as a retailing and office complex, attracting the head offices of local and regional government and multinational companies. Comparable transformations occurred in the Mériadeck district of central Bordeaux, St. Sauveur in Lille, the Ste. Barbe district of Marseille, and Ile Beaulieu in Nantes.

An urban strategy was also devised for medium-size towns during the 1970s. In contrast to plans developed for Paris and the large regional centers, the purpose in this case was to balance the need for new building with the local desire for continuity and tradition in communities acutely conscious of their heritage. As some new towns failed conspicuously to develop a sense of community and as some *grands ensembles* appeared merely to have become a breeding ground for alienation, criticism grew in the 1980s and 1990s of what was perceived as the failure of the modernist vision of urban planners during the *trente glorieuses*, particularly their inability to balance the appeal of the new with the enduring imperative of preserving a communal identity. It must be said, however, that what may now appear as the technocratic insensitivity of a centralized urban planning system was at the time driven by undeniable demand and the assumption that economic growth and almost full employment would continue uninterrupted.

The depressed social and economic climate in some of the new towns does not negate the substantial, rapid, and positive transformation of urban France as a whole during the three decades following 1945. But following the eruption of widespread violence in urban France in the autumn of 2005, when numerous public and private sector establishments as well as approximately 30,000 cars were torched, there was agreement across the political spectrum that no one had envisaged the pressures on the urban landscape posed by mass **immigration** and the accommodation of communities with profoundly different cultural assumptions from their host community. These difficulties have been exacerbated by France's economic underperformance since the 1990s and the negative impact on the resources available for crucial areas of urban policy such as social housing. By 2007 in Paris alone municipal authorities had to manage a list of over 100,000 applicants for social housing, some of whom had been waiting for over a decade. *See also* DECENTRALIZATION.

– V –

VALERY, PAUL (1871–1945). A great and very individual figure in the pantheon of French poets, whose career spanned the 19th and 20th centuries. Valéry's development showed a tension between the desire to refine the intellect and the need to connect with the more intuitive sources of poetic creation and conviction. In the 1890s he committed himself to an ambition, as expressed in his *Introduction à la méthode de Léonard de Vinci* (1894–1895), that drew comparison with **Descartes** for its determination to make optimum use of the potential of the human mind. However, by 1912 he had emerged from the depths of his intellectual explorations to begin the process of reconnecting with the world of the senses and the emotions through the review of his early verse. Gradually recaptured by the pleasure to be gained by the expressive invention of writing poetry, Valéry used his objective, intellectual lucidity to observe the instinctive and unselfconscious forces that govern the poet's sensibilities, and it is the sense of this intellectual observation of an instinctive process that emerges in *La jeune Parque* (1917). In *Charmes* (1922), Valéry expresses in myriad ways his constant preoccupation with the issue of poetic creation and moves toward a kind of synthesis that suggests that the power to create derives from the conjunction of conscious intellectual forces and sensibilities stemming from the unconscious. *Charmes* was barely completed when Valéry's patron died, forcing him to earn a living for most of the rest of his life as a teacher and much-admired literary critic. The evolution of Valéry's ideas and proof of his intellectual discipline are found in the reflections he committed every day to his *Cahiers* from 1894 until his death. *See also* LITERATURE.

VALMY, BATTLE OF. A decisive encounter of mythical stature in the defense of the **French Revolution** against the foreign forces ranged against it. France had been at war with Austria for almost two months when Prussia declared war on France on 13 June 1792. On 19 August Prussian troops crossed the frontier into France and took Longwy on the following day. On 2 September, Verdun, the last fortress between **Paris** and the advancing Prussians, fell. However, the initial panic in Paris created by this news gave way to the emergence of a citizen army as tens of thousands of ordinary male Parisians volunteered to join the army as it prepared to meet the Prussian threat. The French army that took the field at Valmy, east of Châlons, on 20 September 1792, broke the classic rules of military training and preparedness. But the enthusiasm and determination of the French troops, who charged to cries of "Vive la Nation!" was something that had not been seen on the battlefields of Europe for a very long time, and the Prussians were stopped dead in their tracks. Goethe, who had been invited by the Duke of Weimar to witness the expected victory, commented later to his Prussian hosts, "Here and today a new epoch in the history of the world has begun, and you can boast you were present at its birth."

VALOIS DYNASTY. Royal line that succeeded the **Capetian dynasty** when Philippe de Valois ascended the throne of France in 1328, thereby becoming Philippe VI. The Valois dynasty gave way to the **Bourbon dynasty** in 1589.

VARENNES, FLIGHT TO. A key event in the **French Revolution**. By 1791 **Maximilien de Robespierre** and the **Jacobins** were in the ascendant and **Louis XVI** was beginning to react coolly to attempts to reconcile him to the changes brought about by the Revolution. The queen, **Marie-Antoinette**, concocted a plan in collusion with her Swedish admirer, Count Axel von Fersen, for the royal family to be spirited out of France and into safety. Accordingly, the royal family slipped out of the Tuileries on the night of 20 June and began the dash for the frontier with Luxembourg. However, the loyalist military escorts who were to accompany the royal party failed to materialize, and on the following day the king was recognized at Sainte-Ménéhould. Once alerted, the authorities lay in wait for the royal party at Varennes and apprehended it. The significance of the event lay in the way it radicalized opinion. When news of it reached **Paris**, the populace was outraged by the king's attempt to betray France by joining her enemies, notably Austria, and expressed their anger by defacing symbols of royalty all over the city. By their action, the royal family had played into the hands of the radicals and immeasurably strengthened their argument that the continued existence of the monarchy could only militate against the success of the Revolution.

VEIL, SIMONE (1927–). Born Simone Jacob into a middle-class Jewish family in Nice, she and her family had to endure deportation to the Auschwitz concentration camp during **World War II**. Only she and her sisters survived, and after her return to France she studied law in **Paris**, where she met her future husband, Antoine Veil. She soon abandoned the law in favor of politics and went on to hold several ministerial posts, most notably the portfolio for health from 1974–1977 in the government of **Jacques Chirac**, where she earned her place in history by steering the legislation through parliament that made abortion legal in 1975. She went on to serve with distinction as the first female president of the European Parliament from 1979–1982. Aligned with the liberal UDF party, she caused some surprise when she decided to back the abrasive center-right candidate, **Nicolas Sarkozy**, in the presidential election of 2007. But she nonetheless kept a critical distance with regard to some of his proposals, especially concerning **immigration**, and retains her reputation as one of the most widely respected politicians in France. *See also* WOMEN.

VERLAINE, PAUL. *See* SYMBOLISM.

VERNE, JULES (1828–1905). France's most famous science fiction writer. He was born into a middle-class family in Nantes, and his fondness for adventure started at a very young age. One of the family legends about him was that he decided to travel to India at the age of 11, and his journey was cut short when his father found him in the small town of Paimboeuf as he was making his way to the coast. Like his father, Verne chose the law and completed his studies in **Paris** in 1848. But his passion was literature, and the theater in particular, at that stage in his writing career. His first play, *Les pailles rompues*, was staged in 1850 and his first novel, *Un drame au Mexique*, appeared a year later. He wrote dozens of novels on a wide variety of subjects but all linked by the theme of the journey: geographical, moral, and scientific. A number of his novels have enjoyed enormous worldwide success and been translated into cinematic and other forms, notably: *Voyage au centre de la terre* (*Journey to the Center of the Earth*, 1864); *Vingt mille lieues sous les mers* (*Twenty Thousand Leagues Under the Sea*, 1869); and *Le tour du monde en quatre-vingts jours* (*Around the World in 80 Days*, 1873). Verne's unique talent lay in his ability to combine adventure with science and a sense of the fantastic, giving his writing a visionary quality that was justified by 20th-century advances like undersea exploration and space travel. 2005 was declared "Jules Verne year" in France to commemorate the centenary of his death. *See also* LITERATURE.

VERSAILLES, TREATY OF. Document signed in the Palace of Versailles by the Allied Powers and **Germany** in June 1919 after the end of hostilities in **World War I** that formalized the terms of the peace. Although they acquiesced, members of the German delegation argued that they had been presented with a fait accompli and, more specifically, terms that were more punitive and humiliating than they had been led to expect, including a "war guilt" clause. In addition to imposing a heavy financial burden of reparations payable by Germany to France and Belgium, the treaty called for scaling down the German army to 10,000 men and severely limiting the manufacture of weapons because of a French desire to preempt the possibility that Germany might threaten its borders in the future. Also, a demilitarized zone was to be created that took in all of Germany west of the **Rhine** and 50 kilometers east of it. The terms of the treaty were a source of bitter dispute between France and Germany in the years that followed, and perhaps the most prescient comment at the time on this less-than-magnanimous treaty was made by U.S. president Woodrow Wilson, who predicted another war within 20 years.

LES VERTS. *See* ECOLOGISTS.

VICHY REGIME. The regime that governed France during **World War II** after the collapse of the French military following the German invasion. On 10 July 1940 the National Assembly voted by a considerable majority to confer on Marshal **Philippe Pétain** the powers he needed to draft a new constitution for the French state, thus marking the end of the **Third Republic.** In the two days following the vote, key **constitutional** acts were passed that installed Pétain as head of state and Pierre Laval as prime minister and that "adjourned" the Senate and the Chamber of Deputies. The name Vichy derived from the capital of the new *Etat Français*, a spa town symbolically chosen for the fact that it is situated roughly in the center of France.

The French had been given a semblance of sovereignty by the provisions of the armistice signed on 22 June 1940, which created two zones. The northern or "occupied" zone, which covered the area taken by the advancing German troops, was administered by an ambassador of the Reich. The southern or "free" zone was supposedly independent and administered by the French government. The Vichy regime played systematically on the desire of the French people to believe that some sovereignty and self-respect could be salvaged from the débâcle that had destroyed the Republic.

Pétain's supporters promoted his paternal image as a heroic old soldier who had come to the rescue of France in her darkest hour and who had proved his superiority to the quarrelsome politicians who had let the country down so badly. The regime tried to give itself a kind of moral credibility by preaching the need for a National Revolution that would atone for the self-indulgent days of the Third Republic and that, according to Vichy, had brought about its fall. In essence, the National Revolution promoted a return to the traditional hierarchies of the family, the workplace, and the fatherland, as an antidote to the dangerous libertarianism and egalitarianism of the prewar days, particularly under the **Popular Front**.

The regime's collaboration with **Germany** was given formal shape by the protocol signed in Paris in May 1941 that gave Germany access to all of the airfields in France's North African colonies, and in early 1942 the Gestapo was authorized by the French State to pursue the **Resistance** in the "free" southern zone under its control. The Allied invasion of North Africa on 8 November 1942 illustrated the illusory nature of this divide when German troops poured across it three days later. The Vichy regime nonetheless continued to tighten its grip on the civilian population by the adoption of Nazi methods and aims. Thus in 1940 the Légion Française des Combatants was set up, followed in 1943 by the Milice, with the latter being particularly active as a parallel police force in securing obedience from an increasingly disenchanted population to the will of the Vichy police state. One of the Nazi aims adopted by Vichy was the persecution of the Jews. A Commissariat for Jewish Affairs was set up in 1941, and the most infamous result of Vichy's anti-Semitic policy was the rafle du Vel'd'hiv' in July 1942 in which 13,000 Jewish citizens of **Paris** were seized and herded into the Winter Velodrome prior to their deportation to the concentration camps.

The adoption of police-state methods by the Vichy regime was a reaction to the unpopularity of measures such as the forced labor program introduced in February 1943 that resulted in young French people being sent to bolster war production in German factories. Many families were also deeply anxious about the French soldiers who were prisoners of war in Germany and who still numbered approximately 900,000 in 1944. The everyday collaboration that occurred in the French civilian population was usually conditioned by a sense of defeatism and the desire to survive a difficult economic situation. A few people resorted to armed resistance, but most did their best to cope with a mode of existence in which the necessities of life were rationed, sometimes severely, and waited for the **liberation**, whose inevitability was manifest from 1943 onward. When the liberation came, the government of the Vichy regime decamped to Sigmaringen, in Germany, and had effectively ceased to exist by August 1944.

VIGIPIRATE. *See* TERRORISM.

VILAR, JEAN (1912–1971). Leading and influential figure of the French stage. He toured the provinces with a traveling theater company in the interwar years and in 1943 formed La Compagnie des Sept, notable for staging several foreign works in **Paris**. His dissatisfaction with the theater in Paris led him to stage the festival in **Avignon** in 1947. The experience of mounting these summertime productions outdoors in the Cour d'Honneur of the Palais des Papes was instrumental in developing his distinctive style, which married simplicity of means with clever use of color and epic grandeur. He adapted this style to the auditorium of the Chaillot Palace in Paris after his appointment there as the head of the Théâtre National Populaire (TNP) in 1951. For Vilar the theater was a public service, and his intention was to free theater of the conventions and pretensions that made it an elite activity. To this end he took TNP productions into the community, reduced prices, and organized subscriptions that made performances affordable for ordinary working people. This did not mean, however, that Vilar diluted the quality of the drama to appeal to the masses. The TNP persevered with the classics in the belief that Shakespeare and Racine were part of everybody's heritage. As the 1950s progressed, Vilar found himself sniped at from both sides, accused of anti-Gaullist bias by the right and of naive idealism by the proponents of Brechtian Marxist theater on the left. Vilar quit the TNP in 1963 but remained in charge of Avignon. His reputation dipped after his sudden death at the age of 59 but was revived by the Socialist victory in the elections of 1981 owing to the new government's sympathy for his belief in the democratization of culture and his endeavor to demonstrate its relevance to the life of the entire nation.

VILLEPIN, DOMINIQUE MARIE FRANCOIS RENE GALOUZEAU DE (1953–). Diplomat, writer, and politician. He was born in Rabat, Morocco, into an affluent French family. After returning to France to complete his secondary education in **Toulouse**, he took the classic route to the Ecole des Sciences Politiques in **Paris** followed by the Ecole Nationale d'Administration, where he graduated in 1980 alongside socialist politician **Ségolène Royal**. His chosen path in the French civil service was a diplomatic one, which started with a posting to the **United States**. He had joined the **Gaullist party**, the Rassemblement pour la République, in 1977 and his appointment in 1993 as the foreign minister's chief of staff in **Edouard Balladur**'s government was an appropriate one, given his professional experience. The big change in his career came in 2002, following **Jacques Chirac**'s reelection to the **presidency** of the Republic, when he was appointed foreign minister. De Villepin was soon catapulted onto the world stage due to France's opposition to United States policy in Iraq, even enjoying the rare distinction of being applauded at the Security Council of the **United Nations** for his speech on the issue.

It was clear that de Villepin was Chirac's man, and in terms of French party politics he was used by the president to contain the ambitions of the fast-rising **Nicolas Sarkozy**, much beloved by the Union pour un Mouvement Populaire (Union for a Popular Movement), which provided the president and government with their majority support in parliament. De Villepin replaced Sarkozy when he vacated the Interior Ministry in 2004, and was promoted to prime minister by Chirac in 2005, as the successor to **Jean-Pierre Raffarin**. By 2005 Sarkozy's presidential ambitions were clear, but the difficulty for de Villepin was that Sarkozy was too experienced to be left out of government while enjoying a profile that was much bigger than that normally associated with his new appointment as minister for the interior once more. Moreover, while Sarkozy had a talent for whipping up the party faithful and pressing the flesh at large, de Villepin's aloof, patrician manner, allied to his literary penchant and the fact that he had never been elected to political office, undermined his credibility as a political operator. The image of a prime minister who could not understand the concerns of his poorer fellow-citizens was accentuated by the outbreak of urban violence across France in the autumn of 2005. This was followed by another disaster for de Villepin in 2006. His government's attempt to reform the youth labor market by giving employers greater freedom to hire and fire, the Contrat Première Embauche, was put forward and abandoned within months. The argument that greater flexibility would lead to a greater willingness on the part of employers to hire young people cut no ice with the constituency it was trying to help, and the government withdrew the measure in the face of widespread student demonstrations and union hostility.

De Villepin resigned as prime minister in May 2007 after the election of his former rival, Sarkozy, to the presidency, but his woes did not stop there. During the following autumn he had to testify before judges investigating l'Affaire Clearstream, a corporate scandal that hit the headlines in 2006 when false allegations were uncovered implicating Sarkozy. De Villepin had ordered an investigation into the allegations of corporate misconduct in 2004, but some of his adversaries subsequently alluded to the possibility that he might have benefited from the attempt to tarnish Sarkozy's reputation if it had been successful. De Villepin struggled to bury those suspicions and protect his reputation until the judicial enquiry into the affair was wound up in February 2008, with no further proceedings pending against him.

VIVIANI, RENE (1863–1925). French left-of-center politician and premier under the **Third Republic**. He was born in **Algeria**, the son of an Italian settler, and trained in **Paris** to become a lawyer and journalist. His early legal work involved representing railway unions, which led to his participation in socialist politics and his election to the Chamber of Deputies as an independent socialist in 1893. He entered the history books when **Georges Clemenceau** appointed him France's first minister of labor in 1906. Viviani's reputation was further enhanced when he successfully piloted the legislative provisions for workers' and peasants' pensions in 1910. He distanced himself from the **socialists** and moved toward the radical republicans during the ensuing years, and in 1914 formed a government at the invitation of President **Raymond Poincaré**. But his government fell in 1915 because of the loss of confidence caused by a series of military disasters suffered by the French early in **World War I**. His political career declined thereafter, although he continued to hold ministerial positions until his death.

– W –

WALDECK-ROUSSEAU, RENE (1846–1904). Republican politician and **Third Republic** premier between 1899 and 1902. The son of a moderately successful lawyer in Nantes, Waldeck-Rousseau tried to follow in his father's footsteps. His initial attempt failed, but he eventually set up a successful practice in Rennes. He joined the small republican party in Ille-et-Vilaine and was first elected to the Chamber of Deputies in 1879, where he joined the coterie around **Léon Gambetta**. He left his mark on the history of the Third Republic when he was asked to form a government in 1899. The **Dreyfus Affair** had just taken another outrageous twist because a second court-martial at Rennes in July of that year once more found Dreyfus guilty. It was under Waldeck-Rousseau's premiership that the political tension was defused when the French president, Emile Loubet, granted Dreyfus a pardon. Ill health and electoral defeat soon led to Waldeck-Rousseau's retirement in 1902, and he died of cancer two years later.

WEIL, SIMONE (1909–1943). Spiritual thinker and committed activist in the cause of social justice. She was born into a wealthy Parisian family and distinguished herself academically, eventually beginning a career as a lycée professor of philosophy at Le Puy. While powerfully committed to improving the lot of the working class, Weil worked for the Trotskyists without swallowing their ideology wholesale and earned the rebuke of Leon Trotsky for her unorthodoxy. Weil abandoned her teaching career to experience for herself the life endured by industrial workers, and during the 1934–1935 period she worked in several factories in the **Paris region**. She immediately joined anarchist-syndicalist forces in Aragon at the outbreak of the Spanish Civil War, but she became disillusioned with revolutionary ideology as she witnessed the brutality of which all sides were capable.

Weil's search for answers to the suffering that characterizes the human condition led her during 1937 and 1938 to a conversion centering on the person of Christ. She steeped herself in Eastern as well as Western theology and wrote with penetrating originality on the contrasts between the two cultures. She joined the **Resistance** in London when France fell to the Germans in **World War II**, and her attempts while there to elaborate a philosophy that steered a course between the military virtues valued by both the Axis and the Allied powers have led some to see her as one of the most subtle and spiritual writers of her generation. *See also* WOMEN.

WILLIAM THE CONQUEROR (GUILLAUME LE CONQUERANT) (1028–1087). The mightiest feudal lord in France and a Frenchman who changed the course of English history. He was born the son of Robert I of Normandy and his concubine Herleva. William's illegitimacy and the fact that he succeeded to his father's title at Robert's death in 1035 meant that his early years were difficult and dangerous ones and may also help to explain the remarkable tenacity that William displayed in later life. Knighted at the age of 15,

William took an active role in the management of his duchy, playing a direct and, if necessary, ruthless part in the enforcement of ducal rights and the efficient administration of his lands. Norman interest in Anglo-Saxon England had begun in 1002 when King Ethelred II of England married Emma, the daughter of Count Richard II, William's grandfather. The childless English king, Edward the Confessor, appears to have made some acknowledgment of William's claim to the throne in 1051, so when Edward died in 1066 and the English magnates chose his brother-in-law Harold, earl of Wessex, to succeed him, William decided on war. The decisive confrontation at Hastings between William and Harold in October 1066 was no foregone conclusion. William's troops were almost driven from the field, but he rallied them in a determined attempt to wear down English resistance. Harold's brothers had fallen early in the battle, and when Harold himself fell, English resistance broke. William pursued his advantage without delay to snuff out any further opposition, and on Christmas Day 1066 he was crowned king in Westminster Abbey.

William does not seem to have had much enthusiasm for England and spent most of the last 15 years of his life in Normandy rather than in England, returning usually to protect his kingdom from rebellion or the threat of conquest. It was on one of these latter occasions in 1086, when he returned to England to meet the threat of invasion by Canute II of Denmark, that William ordered the tenurial and economic survey of the country that resulted in the Domesday Book. This was typical of a monarch who left no great theory of government but who was concerned that government be orderly and efficient. The 1080s were a decade that saw William increasingly preoccupied with the preservation of his lands in France, whose security was not enhanced by the divided loyalties of his sons, Robert Curthose, William Rufus, and Henry. This uncertainty may have been a factor in the unceremonious burial of William at Saint Stephen's Church in Caen after his death on 9 September 1087.

WINE. While most people around the world would probably think of champagne as the most uniquely French of wines, its creation in the 17th century makes it very much a newcomer in comparison to the wines produced in Burgundy in the east, Aquitaine in the west, and Languedoc in the south, some of which have origins that go back to antiquity. The conquest of England by the Normans in the 11th century provided the winegrowers of France with their first major captive export market as they shipped wine to meet the thirst of the Norman overlords established in England. Wine remained a mainstay of the **economy**, domestically and in export terms, even after the advent of the Industrial Revolution in the 19th century. It was, however, in the 19th century that French viticulture suffered its worst disaster of modern times. In the 1870s and 1880s French vineyards were ravaged by the activity of the phylloxera aphid. Ironically, however, the long-term effect of this outbreak was beneficial, as many hybrid vines had to be uprooted and replaced by high-quality vines of the merlot, cabernet sauvignon, pinot, and gamay grapes.

To the increase in the quality of the vine was added the increase in efficiency that mechanization in the 20th century brought. After 1945 in particular, the near universal use of tractors, investment in the chemical eradication of dangers to the vine, the formation of cooperatives by small growers for the purposes of capital investment, and state subsidies meant that although the area devoted to the grape had declined from 1.4 million hectares in 1945 to 1 million in 1988, wine production increased from just under 60 million hectoliters to 70 million hectoliters during the same period.

From the 1990s onward, however, there has been a growing anxiety in France about the state of an industry that is so emblematic of the country. The reality is that the French themselves, partly due to an increasing awareness of health issues and partly due to the changing tastes of younger generations, have shown a 20-year-long decline in their consumption patterns of wine. On the world stage, the reputation of French wine has suffered due to the rising competition from the new wine-growing regions of North America, Australia, South Africa, and South America. Australian growers in particular have made great inroads in France's oldest and one of her biggest markets, **Great Britain**, due to modern production methods that have earned a reputation for consistent quality, if not great variety in character. Since the mid-1990s some wines, like those from Burgundy, have seen their sales on world markets drop markedly and in recent years the fanfare that used to greet the arrival of the Beaujolais nouveau has become distinctly muted. For some critics, the blame lies squarely with French growers due to their complacency and insufficient discrimination in using the badge of quality that was supposed to be designated by an "appellation." In 2006 the Ministry of Agriculture was sufficiently alarmed to issue a call to interested parties to help elaborate a national strategy aimed at reforming the industry, with particular regard to upgrading production and marketing methods.

WOMEN. There has been no shortage of strong individual women in France who have left their mark on the nation's history, whether as the supreme embodiment of the national will to resist oppression, most notably **Joan of Arc**, or as the patrons who allowed the country's creative genius to flower by hosting literary and artistic salons. **Madame de Staël** and **Georges Sand** were famous for being the center around which the brightest stars of French cultural life orbited, and later in the 19th century **Marie Curie** blazed a trail for women in science with her Nobel Prize–winning work as a physicist.

Modern France, like medieval France, has been inclined to represent itself spiritually, whether in a religious or secular sense, with a feminine face. Thus the most potent symbol of the break with the oppression of the **ancien regime** was the decision to choose a maternal visage to represent a new society that would nurture fraternal values, **Marianne**. Culturally, modern France has made national icons of those female artists whose personal trajectory resonates with a national sense of suffering and triumph, such as **Edith Piaf**, or who personify an often ambiguous but uniquely French sensibility, such as the *jolie-laide* charisma of the actress **Jeanne Moreau**. But one could argue that women as a social and political constituency did not appear on the radar until the feminist spirit of the **French Revolution**, Olympe de Gouges, issued the declaration of the rights of women and female citizens in 1791. But while the new legal system or *Code Civil* of 1804 enshrined key civil rights for women, it still did not allow them political rights, and it was not until 1944 that the **Resistance** government of Free France, based in Algiers, made the decision to allow votes for women. Progress in the postwar years came quickly, in comparison to the failures that had characterized the period from the French Revolution up to **World War II**. In 1946 the preamble of the **constitution** of the **Fourth Republic** spelled out the legal duty of the republic to guarantee equality of rights in every domain between men and women. Within a generation the demands for sexual, social, economic, and political liberation had become irresistible and were part and parcel of the demands behind the **student rebellions** that shook the country in 1968. **Simone de Beauvoir**'s book *Le deuxième sexe* (1949), theorizing the operation of factors that condemned women to second-class status, had been a seminal influence that had arguably greater impact in the **United States** than in France when first published but, together with the influence of American feminism, helped change fundamentally how French women saw themselves in the 1960s and 1970s. Within a decade legislation had been passed legalizing abortion, and under the **presidency** of **Valéry Giscard d'Estaing** a minister was appointed for women's affairs, **Françoise Giroud**. In 1991 France had its first-ever female prime minister, **Edith Cresson**, and during the rest of the decade governments of both left and right turned their attention to reforming the institutional barriers preventing women from playing a full role in the life of the republic. Thus in July 1999 an amendment to the **constitution** was passed that underlined the right of equal access to elected office between the sexes and placed the onus on political parties to apply this principle in practice.

The notion of parity in the political sphere was taken further in 2000 when a law was passed that made the state funding of **political parties** dependent on the success of individual political parties in implementing parity in the choice of candidates running for election. A measure of how much the political sphere has changed was evident in the composition of premier **François Fillon**'s new government after the legislative elections of July 2007, when seven of the 15 full ministerial portfolios were assigned to women. The private economic sphere, however, is less susceptible to government policy. In 2005 a survey by the national statistical service INSEE revealed that 57.6 percent of women of working age were in employment, but their salaries still lag behind those of men in comparable occupations by approximately 18 percent. It is significant, however, that the employers' organization, the Mouvement des Enterprises de France, elected a woman in her 40s as their head in 2005, **Laurence Parisot**. Since then she has gained a positive national profile for her attempts to secure greater transparency in corporate governance.

At the grassroots in the jobs market, change is most evident among professions in the public sector. Women have been entrenched in public administration for generations, and especially in **education**. But what is less well known is the position they command in the country's legal system. By 2004, for example, 52 percent of magistrates in France were female, and it is a proportion that is growing. *See also* BARDOT, BRIGITTE; BINOCHE, JULIETTE; CINEMA; DENEUVE, CATHERINE; DURAS, MARGUERITE; LITERATURE; MUSIC, POP AND ROCK; ROYAL, SEGOLENE; VEIL, SIMONE; WEIL, SIMONE; YOURCENAR, MARGUERITE.

WORLD WAR I. Driven by the assumption that, because of an 1894 Franco-Russian military convention, France would intervene in the war that **Germany** had declared on **Russia** on 1 August 1914, Germany declared war on France on 3 August on the pretext that the French had committed border violations. German military planners intended to neutralize France within six weeks by striking through Belgium and wheeling around to encircle **Paris**, thereby forcing France out of the war and freeing the German army to concentrate on **Russia**. The Franco-Russian war plan envisaged an offensive by the French army into German-occupied Lorraine and a push by the Russians into East Prussia. By the end of the first two months of the war all these offensive strategies had failed, but most important for France, the German advance on Paris was halted at the battle of the Marne (5–12 September). From this point onward the conflict became a terrible war of attrition as the opposing armies on the Western Front fought to and fro between a parallel network of trenches that stretched from Switzerland to the English Channel.

The classically trained French high command began the war with a commitment to the theory of *guerre à outrance* (all-out war), steeped in the belief that such an expression of will not only underlined the superiority of their cause but also confirmed the valor of their troops. Vertiginous casualty rates combined with minimal advances on the ground forced a reassessment of tactics and military leadership. In 1916 General Joseph Joffre was replaced at the head of French Forces by General Robert Nivelle, who in turn was replaced by the much more defensively minded **Philippe Pétain** in 1917.

The year 1917 was a watershed in a number of respects. The overthrow of the czar and the withdrawal of Russia from the war released the resources the German high command needed for a major and, they hoped, decisive push on the Western Front, which in fact brought them to within 37 miles of Paris (30 May 1918). The French people had become exhausted by the war, and the low-water mark of national morale was reached when strikes broke out in the defense industries in May 1917, accompanied by isolated incidents of mutiny among the troops. But the formation of a new government under **Georges Clemenceau**, a man notable for his tenacity and nicknamed "the tiger," raised the spirits of the people. However, of much more material significance, the entry of the **United States** in the war had given the Allies an irresistible advantage. When their counteroffensive came in the late summer and early fall of 1918, spearheaded by the American Expeditionary Force, Germany was forced to the peace table and signed the armistice document on 11 November 1918. This was confirmed by the **Treaty of Versailles**, adopted in June 1919, which also set the conditions for the surrender.

The war on the Western Front had been fought almost entirely in France and had destroyed a large swath of northeastern France. This was the region in which France's heavy **industry** was concentrated, and the consequences were catastrophic. By 1918 steel production had been cut to less than half its prewar level of 4.6 million tons per annum, and coal also was half its prewar production level of 26 million tons per annum. Communication systems had been severely damaged, and by 1918, 62,000 kilometers of road, 1,858 kilometers of canals, and 5,000 kilometers of railway had to be rebuilt. Not only were plant and infrastructure destroyed, but also the land itself was poisoned, resulting in a 25 percent drop in the country's production of wheat.

During the war French governments had been obliged to draw heavily on American banks to finance the purchase of essential foodstuffs and weaponry, thereby storing up debt problems for the future. France had also lost a greater proportion of its active population than Germany as the result of four years of war. In France, 1,385,000 died and 3,044,000 were disabled. The demographic gap resulting from this loss to the workforce and the nation of its most productive members exacerbated the already well-established trend toward an aging population. More significantly, it sowed the underlying suspicion in the collective subconscious of the French that they could never again pursue victory at such a price. This is a factor that must be borne in mind in any attempt to understand the psychology of appeasement in France toward Nazi Germany during the 1930s and the rapid disintegration of French military resistance to the invading Germans in **World War II**. Ironically, therefore, France emerged from the war victorious but severely weakened financially, demographically, and politically for the duration of the **Third Republic**. *See also* ARMED FORCES; ECONOMY; POPULATION TRENDS.

WORLD WAR II. The event that plunged Europe into war was the culmination of a policy of appeasement on behalf of **Great Britain** and France vis-à-vis an increasingly belligerent **Germany** under the leadership of Adolf Hitler. The **Munich Accord** by which Germany was ceded the German-speaking Sudetenland in Czechoslovakia merely fueled Hitler's appetite. In March 1939 the whole of Czechoslovakia was invaded, and the signing of the pact between Germany and the **Soviet Union** in August 1939 neutralized any potential Soviet obstacle to Hitler's advance. In spite of Poland's status as the ally of Britain and France, German troops invaded the country on 1 September 1939, and Britain and France were finally forced to declare war on Germany two days later.

There followed what was called the *drôle de guerre* (phony war), months of inactivity on the part of the Anglo-French allies as Hitler's troops consolidated their grip on central Europe and Scandinavia. In contrast to 1914, there was little unity or enthusiasm for a spirited defense of the Republic. When the German offensive came on 10 May 1940, the speed and mobility of the German divisions enabled them to skirt the static, defensive French **Maginot line** and come through Belgium. The French army, massively superior in numbers, was left standing, unable to respond technically or to improvise through inspired leadership. On June 14, **Paris** fell to the Germans. The French government, having taken refuge in **Bordeaux**, was split on the course of action to take. **Paul Reynaud**, who advocated continuing the struggle from France's North African colonies, was pushed into a minority and succeeded as head of the government by Marshal **Philippe Pétain**. Pétain advocated peace, and it was with his authority that the armistice was signed on 22 June, ironically at Rethondes, the place where the armistice was signed on 11 November 1918, but this time with Germany the victor.

It was under Pétain that the dark and depressing era of the **Vichy regime** was ushered in. In spite of the wholesale betrayal of republican values and the systematic collaboration of the Vichy regime with the occupying power, the mobilization of the Allies and the action of the **Resistance** inside and outside France gave the French people hope and enabled them to salvage some pride from what was a national humiliation. When the **liberation** came, French troops were able to play a part in the deliverance of their country, and the Resistance was able to lay the constitutional foundations for the renewal of France. The last pockets of a German military presence on French soil were crushed by the spring of 1945. *See also* DE GAULLE, CHARLES.

– Y –

YOURCENAR, MARGUERITE (1903–1987). Multitalented literary figure and first woman elevated to the **Académie Française**. She was born into an aristocratic family in Brussels in 1903 and chose a partial anagram of the family name, de Crayencour, as her pen name. Her mother died shortly after her birth, and her father's death while she was still a young woman gave her a freedom largely unknown to her contemporaries. She traveled widely and developed a particular fondness for the **Mediterranean**, often reflected in her work. Stranded in the **United States**, where she had been on a lecture tour at the outbreak of **World War II** in Europe in 1939, she eventually decided to settle there and became an American citizen in 1947. Her elevation to the Académie Française in 1980 crowned a long and distinguished career that had started with the publication of her poetry while she was still an adolescent and that progressed to essays, plays, the prose fiction that brought her greatest success, and important translations of foreign writers like Virginia Woolf, Henry James, and Yukio Mishima. Of her many works, the one with arguably the widest readership is *Mémoires d'Hadrien* (1951), where the meditations of the Emperor Hadrian encompass some of the themes most characteristic of Yourcenar's writing: the importance of history, a compassionate awareness of others, and a love of the cultures and countries she had visited. *See also* LITERATURE.

– Z –

ZIDANE, ZINEDINE (1972–). A French national hero and one of the world's greatest soccer players. Born in France of Algerian parents, he grew up in an impoverished suburb of **Marseille**. His break came when he was spotted by scouts for Cannes soccer club and given a place in their team's lineup in 1987, at the tender age of 15. Zidane moved to the bigger club of **Bordeaux** in 1992, and his performances there led to his inclusion in the French national team for the first time in 1994. It was inevitable that Zidane would be drawn to one of Europe's bigger and richer leagues, and in 1996 he signed for Juventus in Italy. This was the beginning of the golden period in Zidane's career, for club and country. The apogee was his role in the French team's victory in the **soccer World Cup** of 1998. This was the first part of a unique double, culminating in France's triumph in the European Nations' cup of 2000, led by Zidane. His retirement from international competition in 2004 was short lived, and he returned to lead the line in 2005. Though past his best in terms of pace and general fitness, Zidane's unique skills inspired his team to reach the World Cup final again in 2006. Unfortunately, Zidane was sent off by the referee in that final against Italy for responding to verbal provocation by head-butting the Italian player responsible, and his team lost. This lapse in self-control, however, did not eclipse popular admiration for the gifts of an individual voted world player of the year in 1998, 2000, and 2003 by the Fédération Internationale de Football Association, soccer's governing body worldwide. Zidane returned to France to a hero's welcome after the 2006 World Cup and retired definitively in that year, with the adulation of his countrymen still ringing in his ears.

ZOLA, EMILE (1840–1902). Novelist and leading proponent of the doctrine of **w**. Born of a French mother and an Italian father who died when the boy was six, Zola was raised in Aix-en-Provence before his family relocated to **Paris** when he was 18. After failing his baccalaureate twice, Zola left the family home to take up a bohemian existence. His first permanent job was with the publisher Hachette and sharpened his appetite for writing and journalism. He first attracted attention as a controversial art and literary critic on a sensationalist newspaper. It was during this period that he began to form the ideas that shaped his literary study of what he termed the "human mechanism," leading to the adoption of some of the scientific premises of **positivism** in the observation of the human condition according to a doctrine that he would call naturalism.

The novel *Thérèse Raquin* (1867) reflected Zola's first conscious attempt to apply his naturalist formula. He later conceived of a cycle of novels that would trace the natural and social history of a family under the **Second Empire** called *Les Rougon-Macquart* (1871–1893). Some of the most enduringly famous novels from the cycle are the great social studies that focus on the way the individual is shaped by the environment: *L'Assommoir* (1877), *Nana* (1880), *La terre* (1887), and *Germinal* (1885).

Zola became involved in the political controversy surrounding the **Dreyfus Affair** when, convinced of the young officer's innocence, he published the article in 1898 famously entitled "J'accuse," in which he indicted the army high command for perjury and conspiracy to pervert the course of justice. The legal fallout led Zola to seek temporary exile in the Channel Islands. Though he was soon free to return to France, the abiding hostility toward him from French ultranationalists led to unsubstantiated claims that his death through carbon monoxide poisoning in his home was no accident. *See also* LITERATURE.

Appendix
Monarchs, Presidents, and Prime Ministers

Capetian Dynasty

987–996	Hugues Capet
966–1031	Robert le Pieux
1031–1060	Henri I
1060–1108	Philippe I
1108–1137	Louis VI le Gros
1137–1180	Louis VII le Jeune
1180–1223	Philippe II Auguste
1223–1226	Louis VIII
1226–1270	Louis IX
1270–1285	Philippe III le Hardi
1285–1314	Philippe IV le Bel

Valois Dynasty

1314–1316	Louis X le Hutin
1316–1322	Philippe V le Long
1322–1328	Charles IV le Bel
1328–1350	Philippe VI
1350–1364	Jean II le Bon
1364–1380	Charles V
1380–1422	Charles VI
1422–1461	Charles VII
1461–1483	Louis XI
1483–1498	Charles VIII
1498–1515	Louis XII
1515–1547	François I

1547–1559	Henri II
1559–1560	François II
1560–1574	Charles IX
1574–1589	Henri III

Bourbon Dynasty

1589–1610	Henri IV
1610–1643	Louis XIII
1643–1715	Louis XIV
1715–1774	Louis XV
1774–1793	Louis XVI

First Empire

1804–1814	Napoléon Bonaparte

Bourbon Restoration

1814–1824	Louis XVIII
1824–1830	Charles X
1830–1848	Louis-Philippe

Second Republic

1848–1851	Louis-Napoléon Bonaparte

Second Empire

1852–1870	Louis-Napoléon Bonaparte

Third Republic

1871–1873	Adolphe Thiers
1873–1879	Maurice de MacMahon
1879–1887	Jules Grévy
1887–1894	Marie-François Sadi Carnot
1894–1895	Jean Casimir-Perier
1895–1899	Félix Faure
1899–1906	Emile Loubet
1906–1913	Armand Fallières
1913–1920	Raymond Poincaré
Jan.–Sept. 1920	Paul Deschanel
1920–1924	Alexandre Millerand
1924–1931	Gaston Doumergue
1931–1932	Paul Doumer
1932–1940	Albert Lebrun

Vichy Regime

1940–1944	Philippe Pétain

Fourth Republic Presidents

1947–1953	Vincent Auriol
1953–1958	René Coty

Fifth Republic Presidents

1958–1969	Charles de Gaulle
1969–1974	Georges Pompidou
1974–1981	Valéry Giscard d'Estaing
1981–1995	François Mitterrand
1995–2007	Jacques Chirac
2007–	Nicolas Sarkozy

Fifth Republic Prime Ministers

1958–1959	Charles de Gaulle
1959–1962	Michel Debré
1962–1968	Georges Pompidou
1968–1969	Maurice Couve de Murville
1969–1972	Jacques Chaban-Delmas
1972–1974	Pierre Messmer
1974–1976	Jacques Chirac
1976–1981	Raymond Barre
1981–1984	Pierre Mauroy
1984–1986	Laurent Fabius
1986–1988	Jacques Chirac
1988–1991	Michel Rocard
1991–1992	Edith Cresson
1992–1993	Pierre Bérégovoy
1993–1995	Edouard Balladur
1995–1997	Alain Juppé
1997–2002	Lionel Jospin
2002–2005	Jean-Pierre Raffarin
2005–2007	Dominique de Villepin
2007–	François Fillon

Bibliography

CONTENTS

Introduction	399
General	402
Bibliographies and Reference Works	402
Guidebooks	403
Map Collections	403
Statistics	404
Culture	404
Architecture	405
Art	406
Decorative and Graphic Arts	407
Fashion	407
Painting, Drawing, and Sculpture	407
Photography	409
Cinema	409
Cultural Policy	411
Gastronomy	411
Intellectual Life and Philosophical Trends	412
Pre–20th Century	412
20th Century Onward	414
Landscape Architecture	415
Language	416
Literature	416
Drama	417
Literary Criticism	418
Novel	418
Poetry	419
Media	419
Performing Arts: Music and Dance	419
Popular Culture and Folklore	420

Economy   421
    Agriculture   422
    Finance   422
    Industry   423
    Labor   424
    Planning   425
    Trade   426
    Transport and Communications   426
History   427
    Archaeology and Prehistory   427
    Celtic France   428
    Roman France   428
    Roman France to the Middle Ages   429
    Renaissance France   430
    The 17th Century   431
    Modern France: General   433
    The 18th Century   433
    The French Revolution   434
    The Napoleonic Era   436
    The 19th Century   437
    The Dreyfus Affair   439
    The 20th Century   439
        World War I and the Interwar Years   440
        World War II, Occupation, and Liberation   441
        France since 1945   442
Politics   443
    Colonialism   444
    Foreign Relations   446
    Government   447
    Institutions   448
    Law   449
    Political Parties, Personalities, Groups, and Movements 449
        Of the Left   450
        Of the Right   451
    Political and Social Theory   452
Science   454
    Energy and Environment   454
    Geography and Geology   454
    Public Health and Medicine   455
    Science Policy and Research   456
    Technology   457

Society   457
   Demography   457
   Education   459
   Religion   460
   Sociology   461
      Crime and Punishment   463
      Immigration and Identity   464
      Sports   465
   Urban Development and Planning   465
   Welfare, Family, and Gender Issues 466
Internet Sources   468
   General   468
   History   468
   Politics   468
   Parties   469
   Press   469

INTRODUCTION

The emergence of France as the first great, modern, and unitary state in Europe, while Germany was a patchwork of princely domains, Great Britain was turned toward the sea, and Spain was engaged in a slow decline, made it the focus of a long tradition of academic research. This, combined with the enduring worldwide reach of French literary and intellectual traditions and the uninterrupted operation of a great university tradition (supplemented over the last 200 years by the *grandes écoles*), means that the bibliography on France in French is vast and is only marginally less voluminous in English. This has imposed inevitable constraints on the compilation of a bibliography. In contrast to smaller European countries, France has a history that is so extensive, not only in terms of the continuity of the country's existence, but also in terms of its effect on the development of Europe and other regions of the world, that a thorough bibliographical account of its involvement in specific conflicts, such as the war of independence in Algeria, had to give way to the kind of bibliography that provides an overview of France's involvement in colonialism, overlapping inevitably with a bibliography giving an overview of France's foreign policy.

Similarly, compiling a bibliography that included the major works by, and critical studies of, major literary figures like Voltaire and Molière would result in a compendium almost as vast as one on Shakespeare. The task in relation to modern French thinkers would be nearly as daunting, given the hold that ideas by the French authors of postmodernism have taken on campuses around the world and the consequent impetus it has given to publications on these writers. As with the treatment of history, therefore, the treatment of culture in the bibliography offers a springboard for further reading by citing general studies of, for example, structuralism, that themselves provide very good lines of inquiry for readers interested in specific authors of structuralist thought. There are, however, two exceptions to this rule in the history section. As a result of their enormous impact on the destiny of France, the French Revolution and the Dreyfus Affair were given separate subsections in the bibliography, alongside sections on the 18th and 19th centuries. Conversely, the works on the 20th century are so numerous that subsections on France from 1945 onward were judged to be superfluous, especially given that, for example, works on the de Gaulle or Mitterrand era would also be included in the politics section.

The sections of the bibliography dealing with general introductions to France or introductions to modern France could have been either very long or very brief, given the numbers of books that appear on the market every year. I have opted for brevity, relying on the proven chroniclers of France like Eugene Weber, Stanley Hoffman, George Ross, Theodore Zeldin, and John Ardagh, whose works have served general readers and anxious undergraduates for the last two decades. To those I have added some of the newer overviews of France notable for their readability as well as their capacity to inform, and would direct those with a beginner's interest in France to the section of the bibliography entitled Modern France: General. Notwithstanding the many virtues of the other titles that fall under that category, special mention must be made of two. Roderick Kedward's *France and the French* is clearly the distillation of a lifelong passion for the people and the culture of France. It is informed by a compendious knowledge of the country and is written in an engaging style that serves as a perfect vehicle for acutely judged observations. The beauty of Graham Robb's book, *The Discovery of France*, is its ability to surprise even those who thought they knew the country well. Robb's journey across "la France profonde" evokes the myths but also the realties of a France that is largely unseen by those who fix only on the familiar contours of the cultural topography that it presents to the rest of the world, and thus reveals a face of France that is as fresh as it is fascinating. Many publishers now have their own series of books charting the evolution of France, and one of the most recent and exhaustive has been the *Dictionaries of French History* published by Greenwood Press. Scarecrow Press can claim credit for its own notable series of additions to the genre: Alfred Fierro's *Historical Dictionary of Paris* (1997), Steven T. Ross's *Historical Dictionary of the Wars of the French Revolution* (1997), George F. Nazfiger's *Historical Dictionary of the Napoleonic Era* (2002), Paul R. Hanson's *Historical Dictionary of the French Revolution* (2004), Harvey Chisick's *Historical Dictionary of the Enlightenment* (2005), and Dayna Oscherwitz and MaryEllen

Higgins's *Historical Dictionary of French Cinema* (2007). As for the everyday statistics that chart the changes in contemporary France, there is no more reliable and limitless source than the array of data available under the series *Les Collections de l'INSEE*, published by the French government's office of statistics, which covers everything from the objects of household expenditure to the accounts of the national treasury.

Periodicals in English on France constitute a universe of their own. Suffice it to say that *PMLA*, *Yale French Studies*, *French Cultural Studies*, *French Studies*, *French Politics and Society*, *Modern and Contemporary France*, and innumerable other journals on France are available in all good university and public libraries. For those with knowledge of the language, *Le Monde* is available on newsstands internationally, and its intellectual credibility still places it above its rivals. The daily edition is supplemented less frequently but invaluably by the *Dossiers et Documents* that accompany special events like elections. Also from the same stable is the edition on foreign affairs, *Le Monde Diplomatique*, and the self-explanatory *Monde de l'Education*. However, and in fairness to the competition, the daily *Libération* is now pitching internationally for a wider audience that may be more at ease with its idiomatic and easily digestible use of the French language. It must also be remembered that there is a uniquely vigorous weekly press in France that analyzes current affairs as well as the cultural life of the country, and it is well represented internationally by titles like *Le Nouvel Observateur*, *L'Express*, *Le Point* and relatively newer entrants to the market like *Marianne*. All of these newspaper and journal publications are available online, and these online editions have allowed some dailies like *Le Figaro*, traditionally viewed as rather conservative, to demonstrate an impressive ability to grasp the possibilities of the Internet. All of the dailies have electronic archive sections; the most impressively organized of these is *Le Monde*'s, which, for a small fee, allows the reader to research a particular issue immeasurably faster than in the days of reliance on hard copy in newspaper libraries.

Finally, the search tools on France that have taken an electronic form are enormous in number and variety. The Centre National de Recherches Scientifiques maintains a site on the Internet that constitutes an impressive resource for the investigation of all aspects of French life. For those more reliant on the English language, there is the increasingly bilingual *Francenet* site and the fully bilingual *Adminet* site. The sites on France maintained in the United States are too numerous to mention and as variable in quality as they are easily accessible. I have therefore provided a succinct list of Internet sources that offer information in English as well as in French, and that are supported by the considerable resources of French institutions.

Any bibliography on a subject that attracts as much scholarship as France will contain lacunae that some will find unacceptable and will cite works that others regard as superfluous. Criticisms of either kind must be laid at my door alone.

GENERAL

Bibliographies and Reference Works

Bassand, F., P. F. Breed, and D. C. Spinelli. *An annotated bibliography of French language and literature*. New York: Garland, 1976 (Garland Reference Library of the Humanities 26).

Bell, D., D. Johnson, and P. Morris. *Biographical dictionary of French political leaders since 1870*. New York: Simon and Schuster, 1990.

Berstein, G. *Dictionnaire historique de la France contemporaine*. Brussels: Editions Complexe, 1995–.

La bibliographie officielle [Official bibliography]. Paris: Cercle de la Librairie, 1811–. Weekly.

Boisand, G. France. In: Johansson, E. (ed.) *Official publications of Western Europe. Vol. 1. Denmark, Finland, France, Ireland, Italy, Luxembourg, Netherlands, Spain, and Turkey*. London: Mansell Publishing, 1984, 45–86.

Bottin administratif et documentaire [Bottin directory of government and administration]. Paris: Société Didot Bottin, 1943–. Annual.

Chambers, F. *France*. Oxford: Clio Press, 1990. (World bibliographical series vol. 13).

Charlton, D. G. *France: A companion to French studies*. London; New York: Methuen, 1979.

French XX bibliography: A bibliography for the study of French literature and culture since 1885. Selinsgrove, Pa.: Susquehanna University Press.

George, P. *La France* [France]. Paris: Presses Universitaires de France, 1967.

La grande encyclopédie [The great encyclopedia]. (23 vols.) Paris: Larousse, 1985.

Hughes, A. and K. Reader. *Encyclopedia of contemporary French culture*. New York: Routledge, 1998.

Knox, E. C. "Bibliography on the teaching of French civilization." *French Review* 58, no. 3 (1985): 426–36.

Les livres de l'année-Biblio: Bibliographie générale des ouvrages parus en langue française [Books of the year-Biblio: General bibliography of works that have appeared in French]. Paris: Cercle de la Librairie, 1972–. Annual.

Pemberton, J. E. *How to find out about France: A guide to sources of information*. New York: Pergamon, 1966.

Pinchemel, P. *France: A geographical, social, and economic survey*. Cambridge: Cambridge University Press, 1986.

Ponchie, J.-P. *French periodical index*. Westwood, Mass.: F. W. Faxon, 1976–. Annual.

Quid. Paris: Robert Laffont, 1963–. Annual.

Qui est qui en France [Who's who in France]. Paris: Editions Jacques Lafitte, 1953–. Biennial.

Rose, M. *French industrial studies: A bibliography and guide*. Farnborough, England: Saxon House, 1977.

Szladits, C. *Guide to foreign legal materials: French*. New York: Oceana Publications for the Parker School of Foreign and Comparative Law, 1985.

Guidebooks

Abram, D. *France*. London: Rough Guides, 2005.

Bailey, R. *France*. Washington: National Geographic Society, 2007.

Bender, B. *The archaeology of Brittany, Normandy, and the Channel Islands: An introduction and guide*. Boston: Faber & Faber, 1986.

Berry, O. *France*. London: Lonely Planet, 2007.

Caradon, H. *A French companion*. London: Useful Books, 2004.

Caro, I. *The road from the past: Traveling through history in France*. New York: Harvest, 1994.

Dennis-Jones, H. *France*. London: Letts, 1980.

Hunter, R., and D. Wickers. *Classic walks in France*. Yeovil, England: Oxford Illustrated, 1985.

James, J. *The traveler's key to medieval France: A guide to the sacred architecture of medieval France*. New York: Knopf, 1986.

Little, M. *France coast to côte*. Glasgow: Collins, 1985.

Michelin green guide series. Paris: Michelin Services de Tourisme; Spartanburg, S.C.: Michelin Guides & Maps, 1901–.

Michelin red guide: France. Paris: Michelin Services de Tourisme; Spartanburg, S.C.: Michelin Guides & Maps, 1900–. Annual.

Porter, D. and D. Prince. *Frommer's France*. London: John Wiley & Sons, 2007.

Robertson, I. *France*. London: A & C Black, 1994.

Map Collections

Binns, R. *Mapaholics' France*. Leamington Spa, England: Chiltern House, 1995.

Bouju, P. M. *Atlas historique de la France contemporaine, 1800–1965* [Historical Atlas of Contemporary France]. Paris: Armand Colin, 1966.

Broussard, J. *Atlas historique et culturel de la France* [Historical and cultural atlas of France]. Paris: Elsevier, 1957.

Cartes Michelin [Michelin maps]. Paris: Michelin, 1910–.

Joanne, P. B. (ed.) *Dictionnaire géographique et administratif de la France* [Geographical and administrative dictionary of France]. Paris: Hachette, 1890–1905.

Jones, D. *Collins Longman resource atlas: France*. Glasgow: HarperCollins, 1995.

Michelin Tire Company. *Michelin road atlas of France*. Watford, England: Michelin Maps and Guides, 2006.

Pinot, J.-L. *Atlas historique des villes de France* [Historical atlas of French towns]. Paris: Hachette, 1996.

U.S. Office of Geography. *France: Official standard names approved by the United States Board on Geographic Names*. Washington, D.C.: Defense Mapping Agency, 1964.

Statistics

Annuaire statistique de la France [Statistical yearbook of France]. Paris: IN-SEE (Institut National de la Statistique et des Etudes Economiques), 1878–. Annual.

Bulletin mensuel de statistique [Monthly bulletin of statistics]. Paris: INSEE, 1950–. Monthly.

Liesner, T. *One hundred years of economic statistics: United Kingdom, United States of America, Australia, Canada, France, Germany, Italy, Japan, Sweden*. London: Economist Publications, 1989.

Mitchell, B. R. *European historical statistics*, 1750–2005. London: Palgrave Macmillan, 2007.

Répertoire des sources statistiques [Directory of statistical sources]. (2 vols.) Paris: INSEE, 1983.

CULTURE

Barthes, R. *Mythologies*. New York: Hill & Wang; London: Cape, 1972.

Clark, P. *Literary France: The making of a culture*. Berkeley: University of California Press, 1991.

Cook, M. (ed.) *French culture since 1945*. London: Longman, 1993.

Curtius, E. R. *The civilization of France*. Salem, N.H.: Ayer, 1971.

Dauncey, H. (ed.) *French popular culture*. London: Hodder Arnold, 2003.

Dewald, J. *Aristocratic experience and the origins of modern culture: France, 1570–1715*. Berkeley: University of California Press, 1993.

Hemmings, F. W. J. *Culture and society in France, 1789–1848*. Leicester, England: Leicester University Press, 1987.

Hewitt, N. (ed.) *The Cambridge companion to modern French culture*. Cambridge: Cambridge University Press, 2003.

Kelly, D. (ed.) *French culture and society: A glossary*. London: Hodder Arnold, 2003.

Lebovics, H. *True France: The wars over cultural identity, 1900–1945*. Ithaca, N.Y.: Cornell University Press, 1992.

———. *Mona Lisa's escort: André Malraux and the reinvention of French culture*. Ithaca, N.Y.: Cornell University Press, 1999.

Neuschel, K. B. *Word of honor: Interpreting noble culture in 16th-century France*. Ithaca, N.Y.: Cornell University Press, 1989.

Northcutt, W. *The regions of France: A reference guide to history and culture*. Westport, Conn.: Greenwood, 1996.

Ory, P. *L'Aventure culturelle française, 1945–1989* [The French cultural adventure, 1945–1989]. Paris: Flammarion, 1989.

Porter, M. *Through Parisian eyes: Reflections on contemporary French arts and culture*. Oxford: Oxford University Press, 1986.

Rigby, B. *Popular culture in modern France*. London: Routledge, 1991.

Santoni, G. *Société et culture de la France contemporaine* [Contemporary French culture and society]. Albany: State University of New York Press, 1981.

Steele, R. *When in France, do as the French do*. Chicago: McGraw-Hill, 2002.

Tesniere, M.-H., and P. Gifford, (eds.) *Creating French culture: Treasures from the Bibliothèque Nationale de France*. New Haven, Conn.: Yale University Press, 1995.

Architecture

Allsop, B., and U. Clark. *Architecture of France*. London: Oriel, 1963.

Aubert, M., and S. Goubet. *Gothic cathedrals of France*. London: Nicholas Kaye, 1959.

Beck, H. *France*. New York: Rizzoli, 1979.

Besset, M. *New French architecture*. New York: Praeger, 1967.

Bony, J. *French Gothic architecture of the 12th and 13th centuries*. Berkeley: University of California Press, 1983.

Braham, A. *The architecture of the French Enlightenment*. Berkeley: University of California Press, 1992.

De Nicolay-Mazery, C., and B. Touillon. *The French country house*. New York: Vendome Press, 2004.

Dunlop, I. *Royal palaces of France*. London: H. Hamilton, 1985.

Emery, E. *Romancing the cathedral: Gothic architecture in fin-de-siècle French culture*. New York: State University of New York Press, 2001.

Evans, J. *Monastic architecture in France from the Renaissance to the Revolution*. New York: Hacker Art Books, 1980.

Grodecki, L., A. Prache, and R. Recht. *Gothic architecture*. New York: Electa/Rizzoli, 1985.

Lavedan, P. *French architecture*. London: Scolar Press, 1979.

Lesnikowski, W. G. *The new French architecture*. New York: Rizzoli, 1990.

Loyer, F. *Paris 19th century: Architecture and urbanism*. New York: Abbeville, 1988.

Pennell, E. R., and J. Pennell. *French cathedrals: Monasteries and abbeys and sacred sites of France*. Honolulu, Hawaii: University Press of the Pacific, 2003.

Phillips, B. *French by design*. Layton, Utah: Gibbs M. Smith, 2000.

Van Zanten, D. *Designing Paris: The architecture of Duban, Labrouste, Duc, and Vaudoyer*. Cambridge, Mass: MIT Press, 1987.

West, T. W. *A history of architecture in France*. London: University of London Press, 1969.

Art

Blunt, A. *Art and architecture in France, 1500–1700*. New Haven, Conn.: Yale University Press, 1999.

Chastel, A. *French art: The Renaissance*, 1420–1620. Paris: Flammarion, 1995.

Clark, T. J. *The absolute bourgeois: Artists and politics in France, 1848–1851*. Princeton, N.J.: Princeton University Press, 1982.

Dennison, L. *Angles of vision: French art today*. Washington: University of Washington Press, 1986.

Green, C. *The European avant-gardes: Art in France and Western Europe*. London: Zwemmer, 1995.

———. *Art in France: 1900–1940*. New Haven, Conn.: Yale University Press, 2003.

Millet, C. *Contemporary art in France*. Paris: Flammarion, 2006.

Monnier, G. *L'Art et ses institutions en France de la Révolution à nos jours* [Art and its institutions in France from the Revolution to the present day]. Paris: Gallimard, 1995.

Powell, J. *A history of France through art*. Hove, England: Wayland, 1995.

Rubin, W. S. *Dada, surrealism, and their heritage*. New York: Museum of Modern Art; Boston: New York Graphic Society, 1968.

Smith, B. *France: A history in art*. New York: Doubleday, 1984.

Decorative and Graphic Arts

Bloch-Dermant, J. *The art of French glass, 1860–1914*. London: Thames & Hudson; New York: Vendome, 1980.

Cate, P. D. (ed.) *The graphic arts and French society, 1871–1914*. New Brunswick, N.J.: Rutgers University Press, Jane Vorhees Zimmerli Art Museum, 1988.

Hardy, A-R. *Art deco textiles: The French designers*. London: Thames and Hudson, 2006.

Ives, C. F. *The great wave: The influence of Japanese woodcuts on French prints*. Boston: New York Graphic Society, 1975.

Lane, A. *French faience*. London: Faber, 2nd ed., 1970.

Lejard, A. *French tapestry*. London: Elek, 1946.

McFadden, D. R., et al. *L'Art de vivre: Decorative arts and design in France, 1789–1989*. New York: Vendome, 1989.

Savage, G. *French decorative art, 1638–1793*. New York: Praeger, 1969.

Wlassikoff, M. *The story of graphic design in France*. Corte Madera, Calif.: Gingko Press, 2006.

Fashion

Bowman, S. *A fashion for extravagance: Art Deco fabrics and fashions*. London: Hyman & Bell, 1985.

Drake, A. *The beautiful fall: Fashion, genius and glorious excess in 1970s Paris*. London: Bloomsbury, 2006.

Jones, J. M. *Sexing la mode: Gender, fashion and commercial culture in old regime France*. Oxford: Berg, 2004.

Ribeiro, A. *The art of dress: Fashion in England and France, 1750 to 1820*. New Haven, Conn.: Yale University Press, 1995.

Roche, D. *The culture of clothing: Dress and fashion in the ancien régime*. Cambridge: Cambridge University Press, 1994.

Simon, M. *Fashion in art: The Second Empire and impressionism*. London: Zwemmer, 1995.

Zdatny, S. M. *Fashion, work and enterprise in modern France*. Basingstoke, England: Palgrave Macmillan, 2006.

Painting, Drawing, and Sculpture

Berg, W. J. *Imagery and ideology: Fiction and painting in nineteenth-century France*. Newark: University of Delaware Press, 1991.

Bjurstrom, P. *The art of drawing in France: French master drawing, 1600–1900*. London: Philip Wilson, 1987.

Boime, A. *Hollow icons: The politics of sculpture in 19th-century France.* Kent, Ohio: Kent University Press, 1987.

Brettell, R. R. *Impression: Painting quickly in France, 1860–1890.* New Haven, Conn.: Yale University Press, 2000.

Conisbee, P. *Painting in 18th-century France.* Ithaca, N.Y.: Cornell University Press, 1981.

Denvir, B. *Fauvism and expressionism.* London: Thames & Hudson, 1975.

Elderfield, J. *The "wild beasts": Fauvism and its affinities.* New York: Oxford University Press, 1976.

Freeman, J. *The fauve landscape.* New York: Abbeville Press, 1990.

Giry, M. *Fauvism: Origins and development.* New York: Alpine Fine Arts, 1982.

Golding, J., and R. Rosenblum. *Cubism and 20th-century art.* London: Faber, 1988.

Grigsby, D. *Extremities: painting empire in post-revolutionary France.* New Haven, Conn.: Yale University Press, 2002.

Harding, J. *Artistes Pompiers: French academic art in the 19th century.* London: Academy Editions, 1979.

Kelder, D. *The great book of French impressionism.* New York: Abbeville, 1980.

Levey, M. *Painting and sculpture in France, 1700–1789.* New Haven, Conn.: Yale University Press, 1993.

Lloyd, C. *Impressionist drawings from British public and private collections.* Oxford: Phaidon, 1986.

Lyman, T. W., and D. Smartt. *French Romanesque sculpture: An annotated bibliography.* Boston: G. K. Hall, 1987.

McPherson, H. *The modern portrait in nineteenth-century France.* Cambridge: Cambridge University Press, 2001.

Merot, A. *French painting in the 17th century.* New Haven, Conn.: Yale University Press, 1995.

Mongan, A. *David to Corot: French drawings in the Fogg Art Museum.* Cambridge, Mass.: Harvard University Press, 1996.

Perl, J. *Paris without end: On French art since World War 1.* San Francisco: North Point, 1988.

Perry, G. *Women artists and the Parisian avant-garde: Modernism and "feminine" art, 1900 to the late 1920s.* Manchester: Manchester University Press, 1995.

Rewald, J. *Post-impressionism: From Van Gogh to Gauguin.* Boston: New York Graphic Society, 3rd ed., 1978.

———. *The history of impressionism.* New York: Museum of Modern Art; Boston: New York Graphic Society, 4th ed., 1980.

Ring, G. *A century of French painting, 1400–1500.* New York: Hacker Art Books, 1979.

Vergnolle, E. *Monumental art in Romanesque France.* New York: Pindar Press, 2000.

Wakefield, D. *French 18th-century painting.* New York: Alpine Fine Arts Collection, 1984.

Weisberg, Y. M. L., and G. P. Weisberg. *The realist debate: A bibliography of French realist painting, 1830–1885.* New York: Garland, 1984 (Garland Reference Library of the Humanities, 473).

Wintermute, A. *Claude to Corot: The development of landscape painting in France.* Seattle: University of Washington Press, 1991.

Wright, C. *The French painters of the 17th century.* Boston: Little, Brown, 1985.

Photography

Brettell, R. R. *Paper and light: The calotype in France and Great Britain, 1839–1870.* Boston: Godine, 1984.

Buerger, J. E. *French daguerrotypes.* Chicago: University of Chicago Press, 1989.

Cech, J. *Boy with a camera: The story of Jacques-Henri Lartigue.* London: Pavilion, 1994.

de Gouvion Saint-Cyr, A., J.-C. Lemagny, and A. Sayag. *20th-century French photography.* New York: Rizzoli, 1988.

Hamilton, P. *Robert Doisneau: A photographer's life.* New York: Abbeville Press, 1995.

Julliard, C. *France from the air: Photography by Daniel Philippe.* London: Thames & Hudson, 1997.

McCauley, E. A. *Industrial madness: Commercial photography in Paris, 1848–1871.* New Haven, Conn.: Yale University Press, 1994.

Nori, C. *French photography: From its origins to the present.* London: Thames & Hudson, 1979.

Walker, I. *Paris as the site of Surrealist photography.* Guildford, England: University of Surrey, 1994.

Warehime, M. *Brassai: Images of culture and the surrealist observer.* Baton Rouge: Louisiana State Press, 1996.

Cinema

Abel, R. *French cinema: The first wave, 1915–1929.* Princeton, N.J.: Princeton University Press, 1984.

———. *French film theory and criticism: A history/anthology, 1907–1939.* (2 vols.) Princeton, N.J.: Princeton University Press, 1988.

———. *The ciné goes to town: French cinema 1896–1914.* Berkeley: University of California Press, 1994.

Armes, R. *French cinema.* New York: Oxford University Press, 1985.

Austin, G. *Contemporary French cinema.* Manchester: Manchester University Press, 1996.

Bazin, A. *French cinema of the occupation and resistance.* New York: Ungar, 1981.

Biggs, M. *French films 1945–1993: A critical filmography of the 400 most important releases.* London: McFarland, 1996.

Buss, R. *The French through their films.* New York: Ungar, 1988.

———. *French film noir.* Jefferson, N.C.: Boyars, 1994.

Colombat, A. P. *The Holocaust in French film.* Metuchen, N.J.: Scarecrow Press, 1993.

Ehrlich, E. *Cinema of paradox: French film-making under the German occupation.* New York: Columbia University Press, 1985.

Forbes, J. *The cinema in France: After the New Wave.* London: BFI/Macmillan, 1992.

Harvey, S. *May '68 and film culture.* London: British Film Institute, 1978.

Hayward, S., and W. Higbee. *French national cinema.* London: Routledge, 2005.

Hughes, A., and S. Williams. *Gender and French cinema.* Oxford: Berg, 2001.

Kline, T. J. *Screening the text: Intertextuality in new wave French cinema.* Baltimore, Md.: Johns Hopkins University Press, 1992.

Lanzani, R. F. *French cinema: From its beginnings to the present.* New York: Continuum International Publishing, 2004.

Martin, John W. *The golden age of French cinema, 1929–1939.* London: Columbus, 1987.

Mazdon, L. *France on film: Reflections on popular French cinema.* London: Wallflower Press, 2001.

Michalczyk, J. J. *The French literary filmmakers.* Philadelphia, Pa.: Art Alliance, 1980.

Monaco, J. *The new wave: Truffaut, Godard, Chabrol, Rohmer, Rivette.* New York: Oxford University Press, 1986.

Oscherwitz, D., and M. Higgins. *Historical dictionary of French cinema.* Lanham, Md.: Scarecrow Press, 2007.

Passek, J.-L. (ed.) *Dictionnaire du cinéma français* [Dictionary of French cinema]. Paris: Larousse, 1987.

Powrie, P., and K. Reader. *French cinema: a student's guide.* London: Hodder Arnold, 2002.

Strebel, E. G. *French social cinema of the 1930s: A cinematographic expression of popular front consciousness*. New York: Arno, 1980.

Temple, M., and M. Witt. *The French cinema book*. Berkeley: University of California Press, 2004.

Thiher, A. *The cinematic muse: Critical studies in the history of French cinema*. Columbia: University of Missouri Press, 1979.

Vincendeau, G. *The companion to French cinema*. London: Cassell/British Film Institute, 1996.

Vincendeau, G., and K. Reader. *La vie est à nous: French cinema of the Popular Front*. London: British Film Institute, 1986.

Waldron, D., and I. Vanderschelden. *France at the flicks: Trends in contemporary French popular cinema*. Cambridge: Cambridge Scholars Publishing, 2007.

Williams, A. L. *Republic of images: A history of French film-making*. Cambridge, Mass.: Harvard University Press, 1992.

Cultural Policy

Ahearne, J. *French cultural policy debates: A reader*. London: Routledge, 2001.

Eling, K. *The politics of cultural policy in France*. Basingstoke, England: Macmillan, 1999.

Forbes, J., and M. Kelly (eds.) *French cultural studies: An introduction*. Oxford: Clarendon Press, 1995.

Fumaroli, M. *L'Etat culturel: Essai sur une religion moderne* [The cultural state: Essay on a modern religion]. Paris: Fallois, 1991.

Looseley, D. L. *The politics of fun: Cultural policy and debate in contemporary France*. Oxford: Berg, 1995.

Sherman, D. J. *Worthy monuments: Art museums and the politics of culture in 19th-century France*. Cambridge, Mass.: Harvard University Press, 1989.

Wachtel, D. *Cultural policy and socialist France*. New York: Greenwood Press, Contributions in Political Science no. 177, 1987.

Wangermée, R. *Cultural policy in France*. Strasbourg: Council of Europe, 1991.

Gastronomy

Abramson, J. *Food culture in France*. Westport, Conn.: Greenwood Press, 2007.

Aron, J.-P. *The art of eating in France: Manners and menus in the 19th century*. London: Owen, 1975.

Busselle, M. *Discovering the country vineyards of France.* London: Pavilion, 1994.

Coates, C. *Grands vins: The finest châteaux of Bordeaux and their wines.* London: Weidenfeld & Nicolson, 1995.

Crisol, P., and J. Dupont. *Guide Gault Millau: Le vin 1993* [Gault Millau Guide. Wine 1993]. Paris: Gault Millau, 1992.

Ferguson, P. P. *Accounting for taste: The triumph of French cuisine.* Chicago: University of Chicago Press, 2004.

Joseph, R. *French wine.* London: Dorling Kindersley Publishers, 2006.

Loubère, L. A. *The wine revolution in France: The 20th century.* Princeton, N.J.: Princeton University Press, 1990.

Mennell, S. *All manners of food: Eating and taste in England and France from the middle ages to the present.* Oxford: Basil Blackwell, 1985.

Millon, M. *The food lover's companion to France.* London: Little, Brown, 1996.

Peterson, S. T. *Acquired taste: The French origins of modern cooking.* Ithaca, N.Y.: Cornell University Press, 1994.

Pitte, J.-R. *Gastronomie française: Histoire et géographie d'une passion.* [French gastronomy: History and geography of a passion]. Paris: Fayard, 1991.

Remington, N. *The great domaines of Burgundy: A guide to the finest wine producers of the Côte d'Or.* London: Kyle Cathie, 1996.

Root, W. *The food of France.* New York: Knopf, 1958.

Rosenblum, M. *A goose in Toulouse and other culinary adventures in France.* New York: North Point Press, 2002.

Schehr, L., and A. Weiss, (eds.) *French food: On the table, on the page, and in French culture.* London: Routledge, 2001.

Sharman, F. *The taste of France: A dictionary of French food and wine.* London: Macmillan, 1984.

Voss, R. *Food and wine of France.* London: Mitchell Beazley, 1993.

West-Sooby, J. *Consuming culture: The arts of the French table.* Newark: University of Delaware Press, 2004.

Intellectual Life and Philosophical Trends

Pre–20th Century

Abrams, M. H. *The mirror and the lamp: Romantic theory and the critical tradition.* New York: Oxford University Press, 1953.

Brumfitt, J. H. *The French Enlightenment.* London: Macmillan, 1972.

Candler Hayes, J. *Reading the French Enlightenment: System and subversion.* Cambridge: Cambridge University Press, 1999.

Chisick, H. *Historical dictionary of the Enlightenment.* Lanham, Md.: Scarecrow Press, 2005.

Cobban, A. *In search of humanity: The role of the Enlightenment in modern history.* New York: G. Braziller, 1960.

Coleman, F. X. J. *The aesthetic thought of the French Enlightenment.* Pittsburgh, Pa.: University of Pittsburgh Press, 1971.

Crocker, L. *An age of crisis: Man and world in 18th-century French thought.* Baltimore, Md.: Johns Hopkins Press, 1959.

———. *Nature and culture: Ethical thought in the French Enlightenment.* Baltimore, Md.: Johns Hopkins University Press, 1963.

Charlton, D. G. *Positivist thought in France (1852–1870).* Oxford: Clarendon Press, 1959.

———. *Secular religions in France (1815–1870).* London: Oxford University Press, 1963.

Gay, P. *The Enlightenment: An interpretation.* (2 vols.) London: Weidenfeld & Nicolson, 1966–69.

Gunn, J. A. *Modern French philosophy: A study of the development since Comte.* London: T. F. Unwin, 1922.

Hampson, N. *The Enlightenment.* Harmondsworth, England: Penguin Books, 1968.

Hirsh, A. *The French new left: An intellectual history from Sartre to Gorz.* Boston: South End, 1981.

Knight, I. F. *The geometric spirit: The Abbé de Condillac and the French Enlightenment.* New Haven, Conn.: Yale University Press, 1968.

Levi, A. H. T. (ed.) *Humanism in France in the late middle ages and the early renaissance.* Manchester: Manchester University Press, 1970.

Levy-Bruhl, L. *History of modern philosophy in France.* New York: B. Franklin, 1971.

Mackrell, J. Q. C. *The attack on "feudalism" in 18th-century France.* London: Routledge & Kegan Paul, 1973.

Mornet, D. *French thought in the 18th century.* Hamden, Conn.: Archon Books, 1969. Trans. of 1929 edition.

Popkin, R. H. *A history of scepticism from Erasmus to Descartes.* Assen: Van Gorcum, 1964.

Roger, J., and K. Benson. *The life sciences in eighteenth-century French thought.* Palo Alto, Calif.: Stanford University Press, 1998.

Spink, J. S. *French free thought from Gassendi to Voltaire.* London: Athlone Press, 1960.

White, R. J. *The anti-philosophers: A study of the philosophes in 18th-century France.* New York: Macmillan, 1970.

20th Century Onward

Balakian, A. *Surrealism: The road to the absolute.* Chicago: University of Chicago Press, 1986.

Bourdieu, P. *Homo academicus.* Cambridge, England: Polity Press, 1988.

Bourg, J. *After the deluge: New perspectives on postwar French intellectual and cultural history.* Lanham, Md.: Lexington Books, 2004.

Charle, C. *Naissance des intellectuels* [Birth of the intellectuals]. Paris: Minuit, 1990.

Christofferson, M. S. *French intellectuals against the left: The anti-totalitarian moment of the 1970s.* New York: Berghahn Books, 2004.

Debray, R. *Teachers, writers, celebrities: The intellectuals of modern France.* London: NLB, 1981.

Descombes, V. *Modern French philosophy.* New York: Cambridge University Press, 1980.

Drake, D. *French intellectuals and politics from the Dreyfus Affair to the Occupation.* Basingstoke, England: Palgrave Macmillan, 2005.

Duffy, J. *Structuralism: Theory and practice.* Glasgow: University of Glasgow French and German Publications, 1992.

Farber, M. (ed.) *Philosophic thought in France and the United States.* Buffalo, N.Y.: University of Buffalo Publications in Philosophy, 1950.

Finkielkraut, A. *La défaite de la pensée* [The defeat of ideas]. Paris: Gallimard, Folio/Essais, 1987.

Flood, C., and N. Hewlett. *Currents in contemporary French intellectual life.* Basingstoke, England: Palgrave Macmillan, 2000.

Grimsley, R. *Existentialist thought.* Cardiff: University of Wales Press, 1960.

Hansen, A. J. *Expatriate Paris: A cultural and literary guide to Paris of the 1920s.* Berkeley, Calif.: Arcade, 1990.

Hawkes, T. *Structuralism and semiotics.* London: Methuen, 1977.

Hazareesingh, S. *Intellectuals and the French Communist Party: Disillusion and decline.* Oxford: Clarendon Press, 1991.

Judt, T. *Past imperfect: French intellectuals, 1944–1956.* Berkeley: University of California Press, 1992.

Kaplan, A. *Reproductions of banality: Fascism, literature and French intellectual life.* Minneapolis: University of Minnesota Press, 1986.

Kelly, M. *Modern French Marxism.* Oxford: Blackwell, 1982.

Kramer, L. S. *Threshold of a new world: Intellectuals and the exile experience in Paris, 1830–1848.* Ithaca, N.Y.: Cornell University Press, 1988.

Kritzman, L. D. *Columbia history of twentieth-century French thought.* New York: Columbia University Press, 2007.

Kurzweil, E. *The age of structuralism: Lévi-Strauss to Foucault.* New York: Columbia University Press, 1980.

Lane, M. (ed.) *Structuralism: A reader*. London: Cape, 1970.

Littlewood, I. *Paris: A literary companion*. London: John Murray, 1987.

Lottman, H. R. *The Left Bank: Writers, artists, and politics from the Popular Front to the cold war*. Boston: Houghton Mifflin, 1982.

Merquior, J. G. *From Prague to Paris: A critique of structuralist and post-structuralist thought*. London: Verso, 1986.

Moi, T. *French feminist thought: A reader*. Oxford: Basil Blackwell, 1987.

Montefiore, A. (ed.) *Philosophy in France today*. New York: Cambridge University Press, 1983.

Murray, C. J. *Encyclopedia of modern French thought*. New York: Fitzroy Dearborn Publishers, 2004.

Nadeau, M. *The history of surrealism*. Cambridge, Mass.: Harvard University Press, Belknap Press, 1989.

Piaget, J. *Structuralism*. London: Routledge & Kegan Paul, 1971.

Reader, K. *Intellectuals and the left in France since 1968*. New York: St. Martin's, 1987.

Sarup, M. *An introductory guide to post-structuralism and post-modernism*. Hemel Hempstead, England: Harvester Wheatsheaf, 1988.

Shattuck, R. *The banquet years: The arts in France, 1885–1918*. London: Faber, 1959.

Sirinelli, J.-F. *Intellectuels et passions françaises* [Intellectuals and the passions of the French]. Paris: Fayard, 1990.

Smith, C. *Contemporary French philosophy: A study in norms and values*. New York: Barnes & Noble, 1964.

Turkle, S. *Psychoanalytic politics: Freud's French Revolution*. Cambridge, Mass.: MIT Press, 1981.

Warnock, M. *The philosophy of Sartre*. London: Hutchinson, 1965.

Landscape Architecture

Adams, W. H. *The French garden, 1500–1800*. New York: Braziller, 1979 (World Landscape Art and Architecture Series).

Hunt, J. D., and M. Conan. *Tradition and innovation in French garden art: Chapters of a new history*. Philadelphia: University of Pennsylvania Press, 2002.

Pereire, A., and G. Van Zuylen. *Gardens of France*. New York: Harmony Books, 1983.

Racine, M., E. Bousier-Mougenot, and F. Binet. *The gardens of Provence and the French Riviera*. Cambridge, Mass.: MIT Press, 1987.

Watelet, C.-H. *Essays on gardens: A chapter in the French picturesque*. Philadelphia: University of Pennsylvania Press, 2003.

Woodbridge, K. *Princely gardens: The origins and development of the French formal style*. New York: Rizzoli, 1986.

Language

Ager, D. *Sociolinguistics and contemporary French*. Cambridge: Cambridge University Press, 1990.

———. *Language policy in Britain and France: The processes of policy*. London: Cassell, 1996.

Anderson, W. J. *The phraseology of administrative French*. Amsterdam: Rodopi, 2006.

Ayoun, D. (ed.) *French applied linguistics*. Philadelphia: John Benjamins Publishing, 2007.

Ball, R. *The French-speaking world: A practical introduction to sociolinguistic issues*. London: Routledge, 1997.

Batty, A., M.-A. Hintze, and P. Rowlett. *The French language today*. London: Routledge, 2000.

Bourdieu, P. *Language and symbolic power*. Cambridge: Polity Press, 1991.

Grillo, R. D. *Dominant languages: Language hierarchy in Britain and France*. Cambridge: Cambridge University Press, 1989.

Howson, B. *Spotlight on French: Life and language in France today*. London: Pan, in association with Heinemann Educational, 1981.

Knowlson, J. *Universal language schemes in England and France, 1600–1800*. Toronto: University of Toronto Press, 1975.

Offord, M. *Varieties of contemporary French*. London: Macmillan, 1990.

Picot, P. *When in France: A holidaymaker's guide to the language and the people*. London: BBC Books, 1990.

Rickard, P. *A history of the French language*. London: Unwin Hyman, 2nd ed., 1989.

Sanders, C. (ed.) *A sociolinguistics of French*. Cambridge: Cambridge University Press, 1993.

Literature

Atack, M., and P. Powrie. *Contemporary French fiction by women*. Manchester: Manchester University Press, 1990.

Bersani, L., et al. *La littérature en France depuis 1945* [Literature in France since 1945]. Paris: Bordas, 1970.

Best, V. *An introduction to twentieth-century French literature*. London: Duckworth, 2002.

Birkett, J., and J. Kearns. *A guide to French literature: Early modern to post-modern*. Basingstoke, England: Palgrave Macmillan, 2003.

Brée, G. *20th-century French literature, 1920–1970*. Chicago: University of Chicago Press, 1983.

Brereton, G. *A short history of French literature*. Harmondsworth, England: Penguin Books, 1976.

Charlton, D. G. (ed.) *The French romantics*. (2 vols.) New York: Cambridge University Press, 1984.

Crosland, J. *Medieval French literature*. New York: Macmillan, 1956.

Dolbow, S. W. *Dictionary of modern French literature: From the Age of Reason through realism*. Westport, Conn.: Greenwood, 1986.

Hollier, D. (ed.) *A new history of French literature*. Cambridge, Mass.: Harvard University Press, 1989.

Kay, S., T. Cave, and M. Bowie. *A short history of French literature*. Oxford: Oxford University Press, 2006.

Kelly, D. *The medieval imagination*. Madison: University of Wisconsin Press, 1978.

Kempton, R. *French literature: An annotated guide to selected bibliographies*. New York: Modern Language Association of America, 1981 (Selected Bibliographies in Language and Literature, 2).

Niklaus, R. *A literary history of France: The 18th century*. London: Benn, 1970.

Picon, G. *Contemporary French literature, 1945 and after*. New York: Ungar, 1974.

Reid, J. H. M. *The concise Oxford dictionary of French literature*. Oxford: Clarendon Press, 1976.

Drama

Bradby, D. *Modern French drama, 1940–1990*. Cambridge: Cambridge University Press, 2nd ed., 1991.

Connon, D., and G. Evans (eds.) *Essays on French comic drama from 1640s to 1780s*. New York: Peter Lang, 2000.

Esslin, M. *The theatre of the absurd*. Harmondsworth, England: Penguin Books, 1980.

Gossip, C. J. *An introduction to French classical tragedy*. Totowa, N.J.: Barnes & Noble, 1981.

Jomaron, J. *Le théâtre en France* [Theater in France]. (2 vols.) Paris: Colin, 1989.

Knowles, D. *French drama of the inter-war years*, 1918–1939. London: Harrap, 1967.

Norish, P. *New tragedy and comedy in France, 1945–1970*. Totowa, N.J.: Barnes & Noble, 1987.

Nurse, P. H. *Classical voices: studies of Corneille, Racine, Molière, Mme. de Lafayette*. London: Harrap, 1971.

Literary Criticism

Culler, J. *On deconstruction: Theory and criticism after structuralism*. London: Routledge & Kegan Paul, 1983.

Doubrovsky, S. *The new criticism in France*. Chicago: University of Chicago Press, 1973.

Jefferson, A., and D. Robey (eds.) *Modern literary theory: A comparative introduction*. London: Batsford, 1982.

Sartre, J.-P. *What is literature?* New York: Philosophical Library, 1949.

Selden, R., and P. Widdowson. *A reader's guide to contemporary literary theory*. Hemel Hempstead, England: Harvester Wheatsheaf, 3rd ed., 1993.

Sturrock, J. *Structuralism*. London: Paladin, 1986.

Tadié, J.-Y. *La critique littéraire au XXe siècle*. [Literary criticism in the 20th century]. Paris: Belford, 1987.

Todorov, T. (ed.) *French literary theory today*. Cambridge: Cambridge University Press, 1982.

Novel

Babcock, A. E. *The new novel in France*. New York: Twayne Publishers, 1997.

Brée, G., and M. Guiton. *The French novel from Gide to Camus*. New York: Harcourt Brace Jovanovich, 1962.

Engler, W. *The French novel: From 1800 to the present*. New York: Ungar, 1969.

Flower, J. E. *Literature and the left in France: Society, politics, and the novel since the late 19th century*. Totowa, N.J.: Barnes & Noble, 1983.

King, A. *French women novelists: Defining a female style*. New York: St. Martin's, 1989.

Levin, H. *The gates of horn: A study of five French realists*. New York: Oxford University Press, 1963.

Oppenheim, L. (ed.) *Three decades of the French new novel*. Urbana: University of Illinois Press, 1986.

Thompson, W. *The contemporary novel in France*. Gainesville: University Press of Florida, 1995.

Tilby, M. (ed.) *Beyond the nouveau roman: Essays on the contemporary French novel*. New York: Berg, 1990.

Poetry

Bishop, M. *The contemporary poetry of France*. Amsterdam: Rodopi, 1985.
Broome, P., and G. Chesters (eds.) *An anthology of modern French poetry (1850–1950)*. London: Cambridge University Press, 1976.
———. *The appreciation of modern French poetry (1850–1950)*. London: Cambridge University Press, 1976.
Butterfield, A. *Poetry and music in medieval France*. Cambridge: Cambridge University Press, 2002.
Denomme, R. T. *The French Parnassian poets*. Carbondale: Southern Illinois University Press, 1972.
Lewis, R. *On reading French verse: A study of poetic form*. Oxford: Clarendon Press; New York: Oxford University Press, 1982.
Weinberg, B. *French poetry of the Renaissance*. Carbondale: Southern Illinois University Press, 1964.

Media

Barbrook, R. *Media freedom: The contradictions of communication in the age of modernity*. London: Pluto Press, 1995.
Bate, M. *The media in France*. London: Harrap, 1977.
Cayrol, R. *Les médias: Presse écrite, radio, télévision* [The media: press, radio, and television]. Paris: PUF, 1991.
Chapman, R., and N. Hewitt (eds.) *Popular culture and mass communication in 20th-century France*. Lewiston, N.Y.: E. Mellen, 1992.
Charon, J.-M. *La presse en France de 1945 à nos jours* [The press in France from 1945 to the present]. Paris: Seuil/Points, 1991.
Kuhn, R. *Media in France*. London: Routledge, 1994.
Perr, S., and M. Cross. *Voices of France: Social, political, and cultural identity*. London: Pinter, 1997.
Rigby, B., and N. Hewitt (eds.) *France and the mass media*. London: Macmillan, 1991.
Vaughan Roberts, E., and M. Scriven. *Group identities on French and British television*. New York: Berghahn Books, 2003.
Scriven, M., and M. Lecomte. *Television broadcasting in contemporary France and Britain*. New York: Berghahn Books, 1999.

Performing Arts: Music and Dance

Batson, C. R. *Dance, desire, and anxiety in early twentieth-century French theatre: Playing identities*. Aldershot, England: Ashgate, 2005.

Brody, E. *Paris: The musical kaleidoscope, 1870–1925.* New York: G. Braziller, 1987.

Cazeaux, I. *French music in the 15th and 16th centuries.* New York: Praeger, 1975.

Cohen, S. R. *Art, dance, and the body in the culture of the ancien régime.* Cambridge: Cambridge University Press, 2000.

Cooper, M. *French music: From the death of Berlioz to the death of Fauré.* London: Oxford University Press, 1951.

Cortot, A. *French piano music.* New York: Da Capo, 1977.

Crosten, W. L. *French grand opera: An art and a business.* New York: Da Capo, 1972.

Demuth, N. *French opera: Its development to the Revolution.* Jersey City, N.J.: Da Capo, 1978.

Hervey, A. *Masters of French music.* Honolulu: University Press of the Pacific, 2004.

Hill, E. B. *Modern French music.* New York: Da Capo, 1990.

Langham Smith, R., and C. Potter. *French music since Berlioz.* Aldershot, England: Ashgate, 2006.

Ledbetter, D. *Harpsichord and lute music in 17th-century France.* Bloomington: Indiana University Press, 1988.

Mather, B. B., and D. M. Karns. *Dance rhythms of the French Baroque: A handbook for performance.* Bloomington: Indiana University Press, 1988.

Myers, R. *Modern French music: From Fauré to Boulez.* Jersey City, N.J.: Da Capo, 1984.

Schwartz, J. L., and C. L. Schlundt. *French court dance and dance music: A guide to primary source writings, 1643–1789.* Stuyvesant, N.Y.: Pendragon Press, 1987.

Popular Culture and Folklore

Beauroy, J., M. Bertrand, and E. T. Gargan (eds.) *The wolf and the lamb: Popular culture in France, from the old regime to the 20th century.* Saratoga, Calif.: Anna Libri, 1977.

Bertrand, M. *Popular traditions and learned culture in France, from the 16th to the 20th century.* Saratoga, Calif.: Anna Libri, 1985.

Brunchwig, C., L.-J. Calvet, and J. C. Klein. *Cent ans de chanson française* [100 years of French song]. Paris: Seuil, Collection Points, 1981.

Cuisenier, J. *French folk art.* New York: Kodansha, 1977.

Delarue, P. *French fairy tales.* New York: Knopf, 1968.

Devlin, J. *The superstitious mind: French peasants and the supernatural in the 19th century.* New Haven, Conn.: Yale University Press, 1987.

Favret-Saada, J. *Deadly words: Witchcraft in the Bocage*. New York: Cambridge University Press, 1980.

Grove, L. *The text/image mosaics in French culture: Emblems and comic strips*. Aldershot, England: Ashgate, 2005.

Haine, W. S. *The world of the Paris café: Sociability among the French working class, 1789–1914*. Baltimore, Md.: Johns Hopkins University Press, 1996.

Hamblin, V. "Le clip et le look: Popular music in the 1980s." *French Review* 64 (1991): 804–16.

Horn, P. L. *Handbook of French popular culture*. New York: Greenwood, 1991.

Johnson, B. W. *Folktales of Provence*. London: Chapman & Hall, 1927.

Mason, L. *Singing the French Revolution: Popular culture and politics 1787–1799*. Ithaca, N.Y.: Cornell University Press, 1996.

Massignon, G. (ed.) *Folktales of France*. Chicago: University of Chicago Press, 1968.

Meuss, R. E. K. *Breton folktales*. London: G. Bell, 1971.

Rearick, C. *The French in love and war: Popular culture in France 1914–1945*. New Haven, Conn.: Yale University Press, 1997.

Rioux, L. *50 ans de chanson française* [50 years of French song]. Paris: L'Archipel, 1992.

Root-Bernstein, M. *Boulevard theater and revolution in 18th-century Paris*. Ann Arbor, Mich.: UMI Research, 1984.

Scott, B. *Folk songs of France*. New York: Oak, 1966.

Sevran, P. *Le dictionnaire de la chanson française* [The dictionary of French song]. Paris: Carrère-Lafon, 1988.

ECONOMY

Cassis, Y., F. Crouzet, and T. Gourvish. *Management and business in Britain and France: The age of the corporate economy*. Oxford: Clarendon Press, 1995.

Culpepper, P. D., P. Hall, and B. Palier. *Changing France: The politics that markets make*. Basingstoke, England: Palgrave Macmillan, 2006.

Dormois, J.-P. *The French economy in the twentieth century*. Cambridge: Cambridge University Press, 2004.

Dunham, A. L. *The Industrial Revolution in France 1815–1848*. New York: Exposition Press, 1955.

Guillauchon, B. *La France contemporaine: Une approche d'économie descriptive* [Contemporary France: A descriptive approach to the economy]. Paris: Economica, 1986.

Heywood, C. *The development of the French economy 1750–1914*. Cambridge: Cambridge University Press, 1995.

Lynch, Frances M. *France and the international economy: From Vichy to the Treaty of Rome*. London: Routledge, 1997.

O'Brien, P. K., and C. Keyder. *Economic growth in Britain and France 1780–1914: Two paths to the 20th century*. London: George Allen & Unwin, 1978.

Sauvy, A. *Histoire économique de la France entre les deux guerres* [An economic history of France between the two world wars]. (2 vols.) Paris: Fayard, 1965–67.

Agriculture

Académie d'agriculture de France. *Agriculture, alimentation, environnement* [Agriculture, food, and environment]. Paris: L'Académie, 2007.

Barral, P. *Les agrariens français de Méline à Pisani* [The agrarian French from Méline to Pisani]. Paris: Colin, 1968.

Cleary, M. *Peasants, politicians, and producers: The organization of agriculture in France since 1918*. Cambridge: Cambridge University Press, 2007.

Debatisse, M. *La révolution silencieuse: Le combat des paysans* [The silent revolution: The struggle of the peasants]. Paris: Calmann-Lévy, 1963.

Duby, G., and A. Wallon (eds.) *Histoire de la France rurale* [History of rural France]. Paris: Seuil, 1976.

Lowe, P., and M. Bodiguel (eds.) Rural studies in Britain and France. London: Belhaven, 1990.

Mendras, H. *The vanishing peasant: Innovation and change in French agriculture*. Cambridge, Mass.: MIT Press, 1964.

Pautard, J. *Les disparités régionales dans la croissance de l'agriculture française* [Regional disparities in the growth of French agriculture]. Paris: Gauthier-Villars, 1965.

Sheingate, A. D. *The rise of the agricultural welfare state: Institutions and interest group power in the United States, France and Japan*. Princeton, N.J.: Princeton University Press, 2001.

Winchester, H. P. M., and B. W. Ibery. *Agricultural change: France and the EEC*. London: John Murray, 1988 (Case Studies in the Developed World).

Finance

Bayliss, B., and A. Butt. *Capital markets and industrial investment in Germany and France: Lessons for the U.K.* Farnborough, England: Saxon House, 1980.

Bonney, R. *The king's debts: Finance and politics in France 1589–1661.* Oxford: Clarendon Press, 1981.

De Quillacq, L. M. *The power brokers: An insider's guide to the French financial elite.* Dublin: Lafferty Publications, 1992.

Maclean, M., C. Harvey, and J. Press. *Business elites and corporate governance in France and the U.K.* Basingstoke, England: Palgrave Macmillan, 2005.

Muhlstein, A. *Baron James: The rise of the French Rothschilds.* London: Collins, 1983.

Pardo, C. *French finance in transition: Designed for Europe?* Dublin: Lafferty Publications, 1992.

Potter, M. *Corps and clienteles: Public finance and political change in France, 1688–1715.* Aldershot, England: Ashgate, 2004.

Saint Marc, A. *The new French monetary policy in the context of the EMS and of financial innovation.* Paris: Institute of European Finance, 1989.

Sbragia, A. M. *The politics of local borrowing: A comparative analysis.* Glasgow: Centre for the Study of Public Policy, University of Strathclyde, 1979.

Shakespeare, H. J. *France: The royal loans.* Shrewsbury, England: Squirrel, 1986.

Spooner, F. C. *The international economy and monetary movements in France, 1493–1725.* Cambridge, Mass.: Harvard University Press, 1972.

Industry

Bellon, B., and J.-M. Chevalier. *L'Industrie en France* [Industry in France]. Paris: Flammarion, 1983.

Crouzet, F., and J. R. Harris. *Industrial espionage and technology transfer: Britain and France in the 18th century.* Aldershot: Ashgate, 2000.

Davis, M. D. *The military-civilian nuclear link: A guide to the French nuclear industry.* Boulder, Colo.: Westview, 1988.

Di Méo, G. "La crise du système industriel, en France, au début des années 1980" [The crisis in the French industrial system in the 1980s]. *Annales de Géographie* 571 (1984): 326–49.

Dutailly, J.-C., and M. Hannoun. "Les secteurs sensibles de l'industrie" [The sensitive sectors of industry]. *Economie et Statistique* 120 (1980): 3–23.

Lane, C. *Industry and society in Europe: Stability and change in Britain, Germany, and France.* Aldershot, England: E. Elgar, 1995.

Laux, J. M. *In first gear: The French automobile industry to 1914.* Liverpool: Liverpool University Press, 1976.

Menderhausen, H. *Coping with the oil crisis: French and German experiences.* Baltimore, Md.: Johns Hopkins University Press, 1976.

Nef, J. U. *Industry and government in France and England, 1540–1640*. Ithaca, N.Y.: Great Seal Books, 1957.

Piganiol, C. "Industrial relations and enterprise restructuring in France." *International Labour Review* 128 (1989): 621–38.

Reddy, W. M. *The rise of market culture: The textile trade and French society 1750–1900*. Cambridge: Cambridge University Press, 1984.

Smith, J. G. *The origins and early development of the heavy chemical industry in France*. Oxford: Clarendon Press, 1979.

Smith, M. S. *The emergence of modern business enterprise in France, 1800–1930*. Cambridge, Mass.: Harvard University Press, 2006.

Whiteside, N., and R. Salais. *Governance, industry and labour markets in Britain and France, 1930–1960*. London: Routledge, 1998.

Labor

Berlanstein, L. R. *Rethinking labor history*. Urbana: University of Illinois Press, 1993.

Bridgford, J. *The politics of French trade unionism: Party-union relations at the time of the union of the left*. Leicester, England: Leicester University Press, 1991.

Despax, M., and J. Rojot. *Labour law and industrial relations in France*. Deventer, Holland: Kluwer, 1987.

D'Iribarne, A. *The role of unions and management in vocational training in France*. Berlin: CEDEFOP, 1987.

Frader, L. *Peasants and protest: Agricultural workers, politics, and unions in the Aude, 1850–1914*. Berkeley: University of California Press, 1991.

Horne, J. N. *Labour at war: France and Britain, 1914–1918*. Oxford: Clarendon Press, 1991.

Jenkins, A. *Employment relations in France: Evolution and innovation*. Deventer, Holland: Kluwer Academic, 2000.

Kesselman, M. *The French workers' movement: Economic crisis and political change*. London: Allen & Unwin, 1984.

Lane, C. *Management and labour in Europe: The industrial enterprise in Germany, Britain, and France*. Aldershot, England: Edward Elgar, 1989.

Lange, P., G. Ross, and M. Vannicelli. *Unions, change, and crisis: French and Italian union strategy and the political economy, 1945–1980*. London: Allen & Unwin, 1982.

Lefranc, G. *Le syndicalisme en France* [Trade unionism in France]. Paris: Presses Universitaires de France, 1984.

Milner, S. *The dilemmas of internationalism: French syndicalism and the international labour movement, 1900–1914*. New York: Berg, 1990.

Moss, B. H. *The origins of the French labor movement, 1830–1914: The socialism of skilled workers*. Berkeley: University of California Press, 1976.

Oberhauser, A. M. "The international mobility of labor: North African migrant workers in France." *Professional Geographer* 43 (1991): 431–45.

Parsons, N. *French industrial relations in the new world economy*. London: Routledge, 2005.

Seidman, M. *Workers against work: Labor in Paris and Barcelona during the popular fronts*. Berkeley: University of California Press, 1991.

Sewell, W. H. *Work and revolution in France: The language of labor from the old regime to 1848*. Cambridge: Cambridge University Press, 1980.

Smith, W. *Crisis in the French labour movement: A grassroots perspective*. Basingstoke, England: Macmillan, 1987.

Planning

Booth, P. *Spatial planning systems of Britain and France: A comparative analysis*. London: Routledge, 2007.

Cognat, S. *Legislation, regulation, and urban form in France from the ancien regime to the present*. Birmingham: School of Planning Working Papers 87, University of Central England, 2002.

Cohen, S. S. *France in the troubled world economy*. London: Butterworth Scientific, 1982.

Estrin, S., and P. Holmes. *French planning in theory and practice*. London: George Allen & Unwin, 1983.

European Commission. *The EU compendium of spatial planning systems and policies. France*. Luxemburg: European Commission, 2000.

Feigenbaum, H. B. *The politics of public enterprise: Oil and the French state*. Princeton, N.J.: Princeton University Press, 1985.

Godfrey, J. F. *Capitalism at war: industrial policy and bureaucracy in France*. Leamington Spa, England: Berg, 1987.

Green, D. *Managing industrial change? French policies to promote industrial adjustment*. London: HMSO, 1981.

Hall, P. A. *Governing the economy: The politics of state intervention in Britain and France*. Cambridge: Polity Press, 1986.

Hayward, J. *The state and the market economy: industrial patriotism and economic intervention in France*. Brighton, England: Wheatsheaf, 1986.

Holton, R. "Industrial politics in France: Nationalisation under Mitterrand." *West European Politics* 9, no.1 (1986): 67–80.

Machin, H., and V. Wright (eds.) *Economic policy and policy-making under the Mitterrand presidency, 1981–84*. London: Pinter, 1985.

Sheahan, J. *Promotion and control of industry in postwar France*. Cambridge, Mass.: Harvard University Press, 1963.

Trade

Brennan, T. *Burgundy to Champagne: The wine trade in early modern France*. Baltimore, Md.: Johns Hopkins University Press, 1997.

Cecchini, P., M. Catinat, and A. Jacquemin. *The European challenge 1992: The benefits of a single market*. Aldershot, England: Wildwood House, 1988.

Crouch, C., and D. Marquand (eds.) *The politics of 1992: Beyond the European single market*. Oxford: Blackwell, 1990.

Crouzet, F. *Britain, France, and international commerce: From Louis XIV to Victoria*. Aldershot, England: Variorum, 1996.

Langhammer, R. J. *Trade in services between ASEAN and EC member states: Case studies for West Germany, France, and the Netherlands*. Singapore: ASEAN Economic Research Unit, Institute of Southeast Asian Studies, 1991.

Macready, S., and S. H. Thompson. *Cross-channel trade between Gaul and Britain in the Pre-Roman Iron Age*. London: Society of Antiquaries of London, 1984.

Stein, R. L. *The French slave trade in the 18th century: An old regime business*. Madison: University of Wisconsin Press, 1979.

Stoker, D. J. *Britain, France and the naval arms trade in the Baltic, 1919–1939*. London: Frank Cass, 2003.

Ulff-Møller, J. *Hollywood's film wars with France: Film-trade diplomacy and the emergence of the French film quota policy*. Rochester, N.Y.: University of Rochester Press, 2001.

Verdier, D. *Democracy and international trade: Britain, France, and the United States, 1860–1990*. Princeton, N.J.: Princeton University Press, 1994.

Transport and Communications

Bartlett, N. R. *Paris transport: The pocket guide*. Chelmsford, England: Westbury Marketing, 1986.

Palmer, M. *Liberating communications: Policy-making in France and Britain*. Oxford: Basil Blackwell, 1990.

Simpson, R. J. *Planning and public transport in Great Britain, France and West Germany*. Harlow, England: Longman Scientific, 1987.

Sykes, B. *Transport in France*. London: Nelson, 1987.

Szostack, R. *The role of transportation in the Industrial Revolution: A comparison of England and France*. Montreal: McGill–Queen's University Press, 1991.

HISTORY

Bloch, M. *French rural history: An essay on its basic characteristics*. London: Routledge & Kegan Paul, 1966.

Braudel, F. *Civilization and capitalism: 15th–18th century*. (3 vols.) London: Collins, 1981–1984.

Butterfield, H., et al., *A short history of France from early times to 1972*. London: Cambridge University Press, 1974.

Duby, G. (ed.) *Histoire de la France* [History of France]. (3 vols.) Paris: Larousse, 1970–1972.

Duby, G., and R. Mandrou. *A history of French civilization*. New York: Random House, 1964.

Fierro, A. *Historical dictionary of Paris*. Lanham, Md.: Scarecrow Press, 1997.

George, P. *La France* [France]. Paris: Presses Universitaires de France, 1967.

Guérard, A. L. *France: A modern history*. Ann Arbor: University of Michigan Press, 1969.

Horne, A. *Friend or foe: An Anglo-Saxon history of France*. London: Weidenfeld and Nicholson, 2004.

Howard, M., and E. Howard. *France: History and landscape*. London: Compendium, 2007.

Law, J. *Fleur de lys: The kings and queens of France*. London: Hamish Hamilton, 1976.

Le Roy Ladurie, E., and C. Jones. *The Cambridge illustrated history of France*. Cambridge: Cambridge University Press, 1999.

Pinchemel, P. *France: A geographical, social, and economic survey*. Cambridge: Cambridge University Press, 1986.

Price, R. *A concise history of France*. Cambridge: Cambridge University Press, 2005.

Tilly, C. *The contentious French*. Cambridge, Mass.: Harvard University Press, Belknap Press, 1986.

Wagner, M. *From Gaul to De Gaulle: An outline of French civilization*. New York: Peter Lang, 1989.

Zeldin, T. *The French*. London: Collins, 1983.

Archaeology and Prehistory

Anderson, J. M., and S. M. Lea, *France: 1001 sights—an archaeological and historical guide*. London: Robert Hale Ltd., 2002.

Blades, B. S. *Aurignacian Lithic economy: Ecological perspectives in southwestern France*. Amsterdam: Kluwer Academic, 2001.

Bonde, S., and C. Maines. "The archaeology of monasticism: A survey of recent works in France, 1970–1987." *Speculum* 63 (1988): 794–825.

Daniel, G. *Lascaux and Carnac*. London: Lutterworth Press, 1955.

———. *The megalith builders of Western Europe*. London: Hutchinson, 1958.

Gordon, B. C. *Of men and reindeer herds in French Magdalenian prehistory*. Oxford: BAR, 1988.

Hawkes, J. *Prehistory and the beginnings of civilization*. London: George Allen & Unwin, 1963.

Joffroy, R., and A. Thénot. *Initiation à l'archéologie de la France* [An introduction to the archaeology of France]. Paris: Tallander, 1983.

Piggott, S., et al. *France before the Romans*. London: Thames & Hudson, 1975.

Ruspoli, M. *The cave of Lascaux: The final photographs*. New York: Abrams, 1987.

Scarre, C. (ed.) *Ancient France: Neolithic societies and their landscapes, 6000–2000 B.C.* Edinburgh: Edinburgh University Press, 1983.

Villa, P. *Terra Amata and the Middle Pleistocene archaeological record of southern France*. Berkeley: University of California Press, 1983.

Wheeler, W., and K. M. Richardson. *Hill-forts of northern France*. Oxford: University Press, for the Society of Antiquaries, 1957.

Celtic France

Donaldson, C. *The shaping of Celtic spirituality*. Norwich, England: Canterbury Press, 1996.

Hatt, J.-J. *Celts and Gallo-Romans*. Geneva: Nagel, 1970.

James, S. *Exploring the world of the Celts*. London: Thames & Hudson, 1993.

Lindsay, J. *To arms! A story of ancient Gaul*. London: Oxford University Press, 1938.

Ritchie, W. F. *Celtic warriors*. Princes Risborough, England: Shire, 1985.

Whatmough, J. *The dialects of ancient Gaul: Prolegomena and records of the dialects*. Cambridge, Mass.: Harvard University Press, 1970.

Wilcox, P. *Rome's enemies*. London: Osprey, 1985.

Roman France

Brogan, O. *Roman Gaul*. Cambridge, Mass.: Harvard University Press, 1953.

Bromwich, J. *The Roman remains of southern France*. London: Routledge, 1996.

Butler, R. M. "Late Roman town walls of Gaul." *Archaeological Journal* 116 (1959): 25–50.

Drinkwater, J. F. *Roman Gaul: The three provinces, 58 B.C.–A.D. 260*. Ithaca, N.Y.: Cornell University Press, 1983.

Duval, P. M. *Paris antique: Des origines aux troisième siècle.* [Ancient Paris, from its origins to the third century]. Paris: Hermann, 1961.

Gilliard, F. D. "The senators of sixth-century Gaul." *Speculum* 54 (1979): 685–97.

Henig, M., and A. King (eds.) *The Roman West in the third century: Contributions from archaeology and history.* Oxford: BAR, 1981.

King, A. *Roman Gaul and Germany.* London: British Museum, 1990.

Knight, J. K. *Roman France: An archaeological field guide.* London: NPI Media Group, 2001.

Liversidge, J. *Roman Gaul.* London: Longman, 1974.

MacKendrick, P. *The Roman mind at work.* Princeton, N.J.: Van Nostrand, 1958.

———. *Roman France.* New York: St. Martin's, 1972.

Thompson, E. A. "Peasant revolts in late Roman Gaul and Spain." *Past and Present* 2 (1952): 11–23.

West, Louis C. *Roman Gaul: The objects of trade.* Oxford: Basil Blackwell, 1935.

Wormald, P. "The decline of the western empire and the survival of its aristocracy." *Journal of Roman Studies* 66 (1976): 217–26.

Roman France to the Middle Ages

Allmand, C. *The Hundred Years' War.* Cambridge: Cambridge University Press, 1988.

Baldwin, J. W. *The government of Philip Augustus: Foundations of French royal power in the middle ages.* Berkeley: University of California Press, 1986.

Bloch, M. *Feudal society.* (2 vols.) Chicago: University of Chicago Press, 1961.

———. *Slavery and serfdom in the Middle Ages: Selected essays.* Berkeley: University of California Press, 1975.

Bullough, D. A. *The age of Charlemagne.* London: Elek, 1973.

Cohn, S. J. K. *Popular protest in late medieval Europe: Italy, France and Flanders.* Manchester: Manchester University Press, 2004.

Duby, G. *The chivalrous society.* Berkeley: University of California Press, 1977.

———. *France in the Middle Ages.* Oxford: Blackwell, 1991.

Dunbabin, J. *France in the making, 843–1180.* Oxford: Oxford University Press, 1985.

Evans, J. *Life in medieval France.* London: Phaidon, 1969.

Evergates, T. *Aristocratic women in medieval France.* Philadelphia: University of Pennsylvania Press, 1999.

Fonay W. S. *Women in Frankish society: Marriage and the cloister, 500 to 900*. Philadelphia: University of Pennsylvania Press, 1986.

Hen, Y. *Culture and religion in Merovingian Gaul, A.D. 481–751*. Leiden: Brill, 1995.

Houston, M.G. *Medieval costume in England and France: the 13th, 14th and 15th centuries*. Mineola, N.Y.: Dover Publications, 1996.

James, E. *The Franks*. Oxford: Blackwell, 1988.

Kaeuper, R. W. *War, justice and public order: England and France in the later middle ages*. Oxford: Clarendon Press, 1988.

Lasko, P. The *kingdom of the Franks: North-west Europe before Charlemagne*. London: Thames & Hudson, 1971.

Le Goff, J. *Medieval civilization*. Oxford: Basil Blackwell, 1988.

Le Patourel, J. *The Norman empire*. Oxford: Clarendon Press, 1976.

Lewis, P. *Later medieval France: The polity*. London: Macmillan, 1968.

Painter, S. *French chivalry: Chivalric ideas and practices in medieval France*. Ithaca, N.Y.: Cornell University Press, 1957.

Riche, P. *Daily life in the world of Charlemagne*. Philadelphia: University of Pennsylvania Press, 1978.

Scherman, K. *The birth of France: Warriors, bishops, and long-haired kings*. New York: Random House, 1987.

Venarde, B. L. *Women's monasticism and medieval society: Nunneries in France and England, 890–1215*. Ithaca, N.Y.: Cornell University Press, 1999.

Wallace-Hadrill, J. M. *The long-haired kings and other studies in Frankish history*. London: Methuen, 1962.

———. *Early medieval history*. Oxford: Blackwell, 1975.

Renaissance France

Asher, R. E. *National myths in Renaissance France: Francus, Samothes, and the druids*. Edinburgh: Edinburgh University Press, 1993.

Baumgartner, F. J. *Henry II: King of France 1547–1559*. London: Duke University Press, 1988.

———. *France in the 16th century*. Basingstoke, England: Macmillan, 1995.

Benedict, P. (ed.) *Cities and social change in early modern France*. Winchester, Mass.: Unwin Hyman, 1989.

Cowling, D. (ed.) *Conceptions of Europe in Renaissance France*. Amsterdam: Rodopi, 2006.

Croix, A. *De la Renaissance à l'aube des Lumières* [From the Renaissance to the dawn of the Enlightenment]. Paris: Seuil, 1997.

Denieul-Cormier, A. *A time of glory: The Renaissance in France, 1488–1559*. London: Allen & Unwin, 1969.

Febvre, L. *Life in Renaissance France*. Cambridge, Mass.: Harvard University Press, 1977.

Garrisson, J. *A history of 16th-century France, 1483–1598: Renaissance, reformation, and rebellion*. Basingstoke, England: Macmillan, 1995.

Hampton, T. *Literature and nation in the sixteenth century: Inventing Renaissance France*. Ithaca, N.Y.: Cornell University Press, 2001.

Holt, M. P. *Renaissance and Reformation France, 1500–1648*. Oxford: Oxford University Press, 2002.

Huppert, G. *Les bourgeois gentilshommes: An essay on the definition of elites in Renaissance France*. Chicago: University of Chicago Press, 1977.

Jondorf, G., and D. N. Dumville, *France and the British Isles in the Middle Ages and the Renaissance*. Woodbridge, England: Boydell, 1991.

Kingdom, R. M. *Myths about the St. Bartholomew's Day massacres, 1572–1576*. Cambridge, Mass.: Harvard University Press, 1988.

Knecht, R. *The French wars of religion, 1559–1598*. London: Longman, 1989.

———. *The rise and fall of Renaissance France*. London: Fontana, 1996.

Le Roy Ladurie, E. *The royal French state, 1460–1610*. Oxford: Blackwell, 1994.

Lloyd, H. A. *The state, France, and the 16th century*. London: Allen & Unwin, 1983.

Major, J. R. *From Renaissance monarchy to absolute monarchy: French kings, nobles, and estates*. Baltimore, Md.: Johns Hopkins University Press, 1994.

Mandrou, R. *Introduction to modern France, 1500–1640*. London: Edward Arnold, 1975.

Salmon, J. H. M. *Society in crisis: France in the 16th century*. New York: St. Martin's, 1975.

———. *Renaissance and revolt: Essays in the intellectual and social history of early modern France*. Cambridge: Cambridge University Press, 1987.

———. *Ideas and contexts in France and England from the Renaissance to the Romantics*. Aldershot, England: Ashgate, 2000.

Stone, D. *France in the 16th century: A medieval society transformed*. Englewood Cliffs, N.J.: Prentice Hall, 1969.

Sutherland, N. M. *Princes, politics, and religion, 1547–1589*. London: Hambledon, 1984.

Wolfe, M. *The fiscal system of Renaissance France*. New Haven, Conn.: Yale University Press, 1972.

The 17th Century

Beik, W. *Urban protest in 17th-century France: The culture of retribution*. Cambridge: Cambridge University Press, 1997.

Bonney, R. *The king's debts: Finance and politics in France, 1598–1661*. Oxford: Clarendon Press, 1981.

———. *Society and government in France under Richelieu and Mazarin, 1624–1661*. Basingstoke, England: Macmillan, 1988.

Briggs, R. *Early modern France, 1560–1715*. New York: Oxford University Press, 1977.

Collins, J. B. *Fiscal limits of absolutism: Direct taxation in early 17th-century France*. Berkeley and Los Angeles: University of California Press, 1988.

De Ley, H. *The movement of thought: An essay on intellect in 17th-century France*. Urbana: University of Illinois Press, 1985.

Forrestal, A. *Fathers, pastors and kings: Visions of episcopacy in seventeenth-century France*. Manchester: Manchester University Press, 2004.

Gibson, W. *Women in 17th-century France*. Basingstoke, England: Macmillan, 1989.

Hanlon, G. *Confession and community in seventeenth-century France: Catholic and Protestant coexistence in Aquitaine*. Philadelphia: University of Pennsylvania Press.

Hayden, J. M. *France and the Estates General of 1614*. London: Cambridge University Press, 1974.

Kettering, S. *Patrons, brokers, and clients in 17th-century France*. New York: Oxford University Press, 1986.

———. *Patronage in sixteenth and seventeenth century France*. Aldershot, England: Ashgate, 2002.

Lewis, W. H. *The splendid century: Some aspects of life in the reign of Louis XIV*. New York: Morrow, 1954.

Lough, J. *An introduction to 17th-century France*. New York: D. McKay, 1961.

Mitford, N. *The sun king*. New York: Harper & Row, 1966.

Moriarty, M. *Taste and ideology in 17th-century France*. Cambridge: Cambridge University Press, 1988.

Phillips, H. *Church and culture in 17th-century France*. Cambridge: Cambridge University Press, 1997.

Spangler, J. *The House of Lorraine in France: "Princes étrangers" and the continuity of power and wealth in the later seventeenth century*. Oxford: Oxford University Press, 2003.

Tapie, V. L. *France in the age of Louis XIII and Richelieu*. Cambridge: Cambridge University Press, 1984.

Winter, J. F. *Visual variety and spatial grandeur: A study of the transition from the 16th to the 17th century in France*. Chapel Hill: Department of Romance Languages, University of North Carolina, 1974.

Modern France: General

Cobban, A. *A history of modern France*. Harmondsworth, England: Penguin Books, 1966.

Cook, M., and G. Davie. *Modern France: Society in transition*. London: Routledge, 1998.

Cooke, J. J. *France 1789–1962*. Newton Abbot, England: David & Charles, 1975.

Gagnon, P. A. *France since 1789*. New York: Harper & Row, 1964.

Harvey, D. J. *France since the Revolution*. New York: Macmillan, 1968.

Kedward, R. *France and the French: La vie en bleu since 1900*. London: Penguin Books, 2006.

Moynahan, B. *The French century: An illustrated history of modern France*. Paris: Flammarion, 2007.

Popkin, J. D. *A history of modern France*. Englewood Cliffs, N.J.: Prentice Hall, 1994.

Raymond, G. (ed.) *Structures of power in modern France*. Basingstoke, England: Palgrave Macmillan, 1999.

Robb, G. *The discovery of France*. London: Picador, 2007.

Singer, B. *Modern France: Mind, politics, society*. Seattle: University of Washington Press, 1980.

Todd, E. *The making of modern France: Politics, ideology, and culture*. Oxford: Basil Blackwell, 1992.

Weber, E. *My France*. Cambridge, Mass.: Harvard University Press, 1991.

Wright, G. *France in modern times: From the Enlightenment to the present*. New York: Norton, 1987.

The 18th Century

Baker, K. *The political culture of the old regime*. Oxford: Pergamon, 1987.

Barber, E. G. *The bourgeoisie in 18th-century France*. Princeton, N.J.: Princeton University Press, 1955.

Chisick, H. *The limits of reform in the Enlightenment: Attitudes towards the education of the lower classes in 18th-century France*. Princeton, N.J.: Princeton University Press, 1981.

Doyle, W. *Venality: The sale of offices in 18th-century France*. Oxford: Clarendon Press, 1996.

Hufton, O. *The poor in 18th-century France, 1750–1789*. Oxford: Clarendon Press, 1974.

Kaplan, S. L. *Bread and political economy in the reign of Louis XV.* (2 vols.) The Hague: Nijhoff, 1976.

Kelly, G. A. *Mortal politics in 18th-century France.* Waterloo, Ont.: University of Waterloo Press, 1986.

Landes, J. B. *Visualizing the nation: Gender, representation and revolution in eighteenth-century France.* Ithaca, N.Y.: Cornell University Press, 2003.

Lough, J. *An introduction to 18th-century France.* London: Longman, 1960.

Lynn, M. R. *Popular science and public opinion in eighteenth-century France.* Manchester: Manchester University Press, 2006.

Maza, S. C. *Servants and masters in 18th-century France: The uses of loyalty.* Princeton, N.J.: Princeton University Press, 1983.

O'Neal, J. C. *Changing minds: The shifting perceptions of culture in eighteenth-century France.* Newark: University of Delaware Press, 2002.

Riley, J. C. *The Seven Years' War and the old regime in France.* Princeton, N.J.: Princeton University Press, 1986.

Sheriff, M. *Moved by love: Inspired artists and deviant women in eighteenth-century France.* Chicago: University of Chicago Press, 2003.

Smith, J. M. *Nobility re-imagined: The patriotic nation in eighteenth-century France.* Ithaca, N.Y.: Cornell University Press, 2005.

Traer, J. F. *Marriage and the family in 18th-century France.* Ithaca, N.Y.: Cornell University Press, 1980.

The French Revolution

Aston, N. *The French Revolution, 1789–1804: Authority, liberty and the search for stability.* Basingstoke, England: Palgrave Macmillan, 2004.

Best, G. *The French Revolution and its legacy, 1789–1989.* London: Fontana, 1988.

Blanning, T. C. W. *The French Revolution: Class war or culture clash?* Basingstoke, England: Palgrave Macmillan, 1997.

Campbell, P. R. *The origins of the French Revolution.* Basingstoke, England: Palgrave Macmillan, 2005.

Cobb, R. C. *Reactions to the French Revolution.* London: Oxford University Press, 1972.

Cobban, A. *The social interpretation of the French Revolution.* Cambridge: Cambridge University Press, 1964.

Doyle, W. *The parlement of Bordeaux and the end of the old regime, 1771–1790.* London: E. Benn, 1974.

——. *Origins of the French Revolution.* Oxford: Oxford University Press, 1980.

——. *The ancien régime.* London: Macmillan, 1986.

———. *The Oxford history of the French Revolution*. Oxford: Oxford University Press, 1989.

Egret, J. *The French pre-revolution, 1787–1788*. Chicago: University of Chicago Press, 1977.

Furet, F., and D. Richet. *The French Revolution*. London: Weidenfeld & Nicolson, 1970.

———. *Interpreting the French Revolution*. Cambridge: Cambridge University Press, 1981.

Gilchrist, J., and W. J. Murray. *The press in the French Revolution*. London: Ginn, 1971.

Godechot, J. *The taking of the Bastille, 14 July 1789*. London: Faber, 1970.

———. *The counter-revolution: Doctrine and action, 1789–1804*. London: Routledge & Kegan Paul, 1972.

Greenlaw, R. W. (ed.) *The economic origins of the French Revolution*. Boston: Heath, 1958.

Guerin, D. *Class struggle in the first French Republic: Bourgeois and bras nus, 1793–1795*. London: Pluto Press, 1977.

Hampson, N. *Danton*. London: Duckworth, 1978.

———. *Will and circumstance: Montesquieu, Rousseau, and the French Revolution*. London: Duckworth, 1983.

Hanson, P. R. *Historical dictionary of the French Revolution*. Lanham, Md.: Scarecrow Press, 2004.

Harris, R. D. *Necker and the Revolution of 1789*. Lanham, Md.: University Press of America, 1986.

Hazareesingh, S. (ed.) *The Jacobin legacy in modern France*. Oxford: Oxford University Press, 2002.

Hunt, L. *Politics, culture, and class in the French Revolution*. Berkeley: University of California Press, 1984.

Jones, P. *The French Revolution: 1787–1804*. London: Longman, 2003.

Jordan, D. P. *The king's trial: The French Revolution versus Louis XVI*. Berkeley: University of California Press, 1979.

Kates, G., and G. Lefebvre. *The French Revolution*. London: Routledge, 2001.

Kennedy, M. L. *The Jacobin clubs in the French Revolution*. Princeton, N.J.: Princeton University Press, 1982.

Lefebvre, G. *The French Revolution*. (2 vols.) New York: Columbia University Press, 1962–64.

———. *The Thermidorians*. New York: Routledge & Kegan Paul, 1964.

Levy, D. G., H. B. Applewhite, and M. D. Johnson. *Women in revolutionary Paris, 1789–1795*. Urbana: University of Illinois Press, 1979.

Lyons, M. *France under the Directory*. Cambridge: Cambridge University Press, 1975.

Palmer, R. R. *The improvement of humanity: Education and the French Revolution.* Princeton, N.J.: Princeton University Press, 1985.

———. *Twelve who ruled the year of the Terror in the French Revolution.* Princeton, N.J.: Princeton University Press, 2005.

Patrick, A. *The men of the first French republic: Political alignments and the National Convention of 1792.* Baltimore, Md.: Johns Hopkins University Press, 1972.

Ross, S. T. *Historical dictionary of the wars of the French Revolution.* Lanham, Md.: Scarecrow Press, 1997.

Rudé, G. *The crowd in the French Revolution.* Oxford: Clarendon Press, 1959.

———. *Interpretations of the French Revolution.* London: Routledge & Kegan Paul, 1961.

———. *Robespierre: Portrait of a revolutionary democrat.* London: Collins, 1975.

Schama, S. *Citizens: A chronicle of the French Revolution.* London: Penguin Books, 2004.

Scott, S. F., and B. Rothaus (eds.) *Historical dictionary of the French Revolution.* Westport, Conn.: Greenwood, 1985.

Scurr, R. *Fatal purity: Robespierre and the French Revolution.* London: Vintage, 2007.

Soboul, A. *The Parisian sans-culottes and the French Revolution, 1793–94.* Oxford: Clarendon Press, 1964.

———. *A short history of the French Revolution.* Berkeley: University of California Press, 1977.

Sutherland, D. M. G. *France, 1789–1815: Revolution and counter-revolution.* New York: Oxford University Press, 1986.

Sydenham, M. J. *The first French Republic, 1792–1804.* London: Batsford, 1974.

Vovelle, M. *The fall of the French monarchy, 1787–92.* Cambridge: Cambridge University Press, 1984.

Whittock, J. *The French Revolution, 1789–1794.* London: Hodder Murray, 2002.

Wright, D. G. *Revolution and terror in France, 1789–95.* London: Longman, 1974.

The Napoleonic Era

Barnett, C. *Bonaparte.* London: Allen & Unwin, 1978.

Bergeron, L. *France under Napoleon.* Princeton, N.J.: Princeton University Press, 1981.

Chandler, D. G. *The campaigns of Napoleon.* London: Weidenfeld & Nicolson, 1966.

Connelly, O. *Historical dictionary of Napoleonic France, 1799–1815*. Westport, Conn.: Greenwood, 1985.

Dwyer, P. *Napoleon: The path to power 1769–1799*. London: Bloomsbury, 2007.

Englund, S. *Napoleon: A political life*. Cambridge, Mass.: Harvard University Press, 2005.

Esdaile, C. J. *Napoleon's wars: An international history, 1803–1815*. London: Allen Lane, 2007.

Forrest, A. *Conscripts and deserters: The army and French society during the Revolution and Empire*. Oxford: Oxford University Press, 1989.

Lefebvre, G. *Napoleon*. (2 vols.) New York: Columbia University Press, 1969.

Nafziger, G. F. *Historical dictionary of the Napoleonic Era*. Lanham, Md.: Scarecrow Press, 2002.

Palmer, A. *An encyclopedia of Napoleon's Europe*. New York: St. Martin's, 1984.

Tulard, J. *Napoleon: The myth of the saviour*. London: Weidenfeld & Nicolson, 1984.

The 19th Century

Amann, P. "The changing outlines of 1848." *American Historical Review* 68, no. 4 (July 1963): 938–53.

Anderson, R. D. *France, 1870–1914: Politics and society*. London: Routledge, 1977.

Beik, P. H. *Louis Philippe and the July monarchy*. Princeton, N.J.: Van Nostrand, 1965.

Brogan, D. W. *The development of modern France, 1870–1939*. (2 vols.) New York: Harper & Row, 1966.

———. *The French nation from Napoléon to Pétain, 1814–1940*. New York: Harper, 1957.

Burns, M. *Rural society and French politics: Boulangism and the Dreyfus affair, 1886–1900*. Princeton, N.J.: Princeton University Press, 1984.

Bury, J. P. T. *France, 1814–1940*. London: Methuen, 1985.

Clout, H. *The land of France, 1815–1914*. London: Allen & Unwin, 1983.

Cole, J. *The power of large numbers: Population, politics, and gender in nineteenth-century France*. Ithaca, N.Y.: Cornell University Press, 2000.

Collingham, H. A. C. *The July monarchy: A political history of France, 1830–1848*. London: Longman, 1988.

Collins, I. *Government and society in France, 1814–1848*. London: Edward Arnold, 1970.

Doy, G. *Women and visual culture in nineteenth-century France*. London: Pinter, 2001.

Edwards, S. *The Paris Commune, 1871*. London: Eyre & Spottiswoode, 1971.

Gerson, S. *The pride of place: Local memories and political culture in nineteenth-century France*. Ithaca, N.Y.: Cornell University Press, 2003.

Horne, A. *The fall of Paris, the siege, and the Commune, 1870–71*. New York: St. Martin's, 1966.

Howard, M. *The Franco-Prussian War: The German invasion of France, 1870–1871*. New York: Routledge, Chapman & Hall, 1981.

Hutton, P. H. *Historical dictionary of the Third French Republic, 1870–1940*. (2 vols.) New York: Greenwood, 1986.

Jardin, A., and A. J. Tudesq. *Restoration and reaction, 1815–1848*. Cambridge: Cambridge University Press, 1983.

Lyons, M. *Readers and society in nineteenth-century France: Workers, women, peasants*. Basingstoke, England: Palgrave Macmillan, 2001.

Magraw, R. *France, 1814–1915: The bourgeois century*. London: Collins, 1983.

Mainardi, P. *Husbands, wives, and lovers: Marriage and its discontents in nineteenth-century France*. New Haven, Conn.: Yale University Press, 2003.

Mayeur, A. J., and M. Réberioux. *The Third Republic from its origin to the Great War, 1871–1914*. Cambridge: Cambridge University Press.

Merriman, J. M. (ed.) *1830 in France*. New York: New Viewpoints, 1975.

Newman, E. L., and R.L. Simpson (eds.) *Historical dictionary of France from the 1815 Restoration to the Second Empire*. (2 vols.) New York: Greenwood, 1987.

Nord, P. G. *The republican moment: Struggles for democracy in nineteenth-century France*. Cambridge, Mass.: Harvard, 1998.

Pilbeam, P. *The 1830 revolution in France*. Basingstoke, England: Macmillan, 1994.

Pinkney, D. H. *Decisive years in France, 1840–1847*. Princeton, N.J.: Princeton University Press, 1986.

Plamenatz, J. P. *The revolutionary movement in France, 1815–1871*. Westport, Conn.: Hyperion, 1986.

Price, R. *The French Second Republic: A social history*. Ithaca, N.Y.: Cornell University Press, 1972.

Price, R. (ed.) *Revolution and reaction: 1848 and the Second French Republic*. London: Croom Helm, 1975.

Samuels, M. *The spectacular past: Popular history and the novel in nineteenth-century France*. Ithaca: Cornell University Press, 2004.

Weber, E. "The Second Republic, politics, and the peasants." *French Historical Studies* 11, no. 4 (Fall 1980): 521–50.

——. *Peasants into Frenchmen: The modernization of rural France, 1870–1914*. London: Chatto & Windus, 1977.
——. *France, fin de siècle*. Cambridge, Mass.: Harvard University Press, 1986.
Zeldin, T. *France, 1848–1945*. (2 vols.) Oxford: Oxford University Press, 1973–1977.

The Dreyfus Affair

Bredin, J.-D. *The affair: The case of Alfred Dreyfus*. New York: G. Braziller, 1986.
Cahm, E. *The Dreyfus affair in French society and politics*. London: Longman, 1996.
Forth, C. E. *The Dreyfus affair and the crisis of French manhood*. Baltimore, Md.: Johns Hopkins University Press, 2006.
Hoffman, R. L. *More than a trial: The struggle over Captain Dreyfus*. New York: Free Press, 1980.
Johnson, M. P. *The Dreyfus affair*. Basingstoke, England: Palgrave Macmillan, 1999.
Kleeblatt, N. (ed.) *The Dreyfus affair: Art, truth, and justice*. Berkeley: University of California Press, 1987.
Reinach, J. *Histoire de l'affaire Dreyfus* (7 vols.) [History of the Dreyfus affair]. Paris: Editions de la Revue Blanche, 1907–1911.
Snyder, L. *The Dreyfus case: A documentary history*. New Brunswick, N.J.: Rutgers University Press, 1973.
Whyte, G. *The Dreyfus affair: A chronological history*. Basingstoke, England: Palgrave Macmillan, 2005.
Wilson, S. *Ideology and experience: Anti-Semitism in France at the time of the Dreyfus affair*. Rutherford, N.J.: Fairleigh Dickinson University Press, 1982.

The 20th Century

McMillan, J. F. *Dreyfus to de Gaulle: Politics and society in France, 1898–1969*. London: Edward Arnold, 1985.
Moure, K., and M. S. Alexander (eds.) *Crisis and renewal in France 1918–1962*. Oxford: Berghahn Books, 2002.
Scriven, M., and P. Wagstaff. *War and society in 20th-century France*. New York: Berg, 1991.
Smith, Bonnie G. *Confessions of a concierge: Madame Lucie's history of 20th-century France*. New Haven, Conn.: Yale University Press, 1985.

Tint, H. *France since 1918*. New York: St. Martin's, 1980.

Ungar, S., and T. Conley. *Identity papers: Contested nationhood in twentieth-century France*. Minneapolis: University of Minnesota Press, 1996.

Weber, E. *The nationalist revival in France, 1905–1914*. Berkeley: University of California Press, 1959.

———. *Action française: Royalism and reaction in twentieth-century France*. Palo Alto, Calif.: Stanford University Press, 2005.

Zdatny, S. M. *The politics of survival: Artisans in 20th-century France*. New York: Oxford University Press, 1990.

World War I and the Interwar Years

Audoin-Rouzeau, S. *Men at war, 1914–1918: National sentiment and trench journalism in France during the First World War*. Providence, R.I.: Berg, 1992.

Becker, J.-J. *The Great War and the French people*. Leamington Spa, England: Berg, 1985.

Bernard, P., and H. Dubief. *The decline of the Third Republic, 1914–1938*. Cambridge: Cambridge University Press, 1988.

Flood, P. *France 1914–1918: Public opinion and the war effort*. Basingstoke, England: Macmillan, 1989.

Grabau, T. W. *Industrial reconstruction in France after World War I*. New York: Garland, 1991.

Green, N. *From Versailles to Vichy: The Third French Republic, 1919–1940*. New York: Thomas Y. Crowell, 1970.

Holman, V., and D. Kelly. *France at war in the twentieth century: Propaganda, myth, and metaphor*. Oxford: Berghahn Books, 2000.

Horn, M. *Britain, France, and the financing of the First World War*. Montreal: McGill-Queen's University Press, 2002.

Horne, A. *The price of glory: Verdun, 1916*. London: Macmillan, 1962.

Ingram, N. *The politics of dissent: Pacifism in France, 1919–1939*. Oxford: Clarendon Press, 1991.

Irvine, W. D. *French conservatism in crisis: The Republican Federation of France in the 1930s*. Baton Rouge: Louisiana State University Press, 1979.

Jackson, J. *The Popular Front: Defending democracy, 1934–38*. Cambridge: Cambridge University Press, 1988.

Kingston, P. J. *Anti-Semitism in France during the 1930s: Organisations, personalities, and propaganda*. Hull, England: University of Hull Press, 1983.

Lefranc, G. *Histoire du Front populaire (1934–1938)*. [History of the Popular Front (1934–1938)]. Paris: Payot, 1965.

Weber, E. *The hollow years: France in the 1930s*. New York: Norton, 1994.

World War II, Occupation, and Liberation

Aron, R. *The Vichy regime, 1940–44*. London: Putnam, 1958.

Azéma, J.-P. *From Munich to the liberation, 1938–1944*. Cambridge: Cambridge University Press, 1984.

Barbour, N. *The week France fell*. New York: Stein & Day, 1976.

Bloch, M. *Strange defeat*. New York: Hippocrene, 1967.

Blumenson, M. *The duel for France, 1944: The men and battles that changed the fate of Europe*. Cambridge, Mass.: Da Capo Press, 2000.

Coupard, M. *The American push in Normandy*. Saint-Cyr-sur-Loire: Sutton, 2004.

Dansette, A. *Histoire de la libération de Paris* [History of the liberation of Paris]. Paris: Fayard, 1946.

Diamond, H. *Fleeing Hitler: France 1940*. Oxford: Oxford University Press, 2007.

Durand, Y. *Vichy (1940–1944)*. Paris: Bordas, 1972.

Elveth, D. *The authorized press in Vichy and German-occupied France, 1940–1944: A bibliography*. Westport, Conn.: Greenwood Press, 1999.

Frenay, H. *The night will end*. New York: McGraw-Hill, 1976.

Gildea, R. *Marianne in chains: Daily life in the heart of France during the German occupation*. London: Picador, 2004.

Gordon, B. M. *Collaborationism in France during the Second World War*. Ithaca, N.Y.: Cornell University Press, 1980.

Jackson, J. *The fall of France: The Nazi invasion of 1940*. Oxford: Oxford University Press, 2004.

Kaiser, D. E. *Economic diplomacy and the origins of the Second World War: Germany, Britain, France, and Eastern Europe, 1930–1939*. Princeton, N.J.: Princeton University Press, 1980.

Kean, T. *The battle for France: The role of the RAF in France, 1940*. London: Lisek, 2001.

Kedward, H. R. *Occupied France, collaboration, and resistance 1940–1944*. Oxford: Blackwell, 1985.

Knight, F. *The French Resistance, 1940 to 1944*. London: Lawrence & Wishart, 1975.

Novick, P. *The Resistance versus Vichy: The purge of collaborators in liberated France*. New York: Columbia University Press, 1968.

Paxton, R. O. *Vichy France: Old guard and new order, 1940–44*. New York: Columbia University Press, 1982.

Pryce-Jones, D. *Paris in the Third Reich: A history of the occupation, 1940–1944*. New York: Holt, Rinehart & Winston, 1981.

Shirer, W. L. *The collapse of the Third Republic: An inquiry into the fall of France in 1940*. New York: Simon & Schuster, 1969.

Sweets, J. F. *The politics of resistance in France, 1940–1944*. DeKalb: Northern Illinois University Press, 1976.

———. *Choices in Vichy France: The French under Nazi occupation*. New York: Oxford University Press, 1981.

Taylor, L. *Between resistance and collaboration: Popular protest in northern France, 1940–45*. Basingstoke, England: Palgrave Macmillan, 2000.

Thomson, A. A. *"Over there" 1944/45—Americans in the liberation of France: Their perceptions of and relations with France and the French*. Canterbury: University of Kent, 1996.

Young, R. J. *France and the origins of the Second World War*. Basingstoke, England: Macmillan, 1996.

France since 1945

Ardagh, J. *The new French revolution: A social and economic survey of France, 1945–67*. London: Secker and Warburg, 1968.

———. *The new France*. Harmondsworth, England: Penguin Books, 1970.

———. *France in the 1980s*. Harmondsworth, England: Penguin Books, 1982.

———. *France today*. Harmondsworth, England: Penguin Books, 1985.

Blondel, J. *Contemporary France: Politics, society, and institutions*. London: Methuen, 1974.

Cole, A. *François Mitterrand: A study in political leadership*. London: Routledge, 1994.

Cole, A., and G. G. Raymond. (eds.) *Redefining the French Republic*. Manchester: Manchester University Press, 2006.

Cook, D. *Charles de Gaulle: A biography*. New York: G. P. Putnam, 1983.

Forbes, J., and N. Hewlett. *Contemporary France: Essays and texts on politics, economics, society*. Harlow, England: Longman, 1994.

Frears, J. R. *France in the Giscard presidency*. London: Allen & Unwin, 1981.

Friend, J. W. *Seven years in France: François Mitterrand and the unintended revolution, 1981–1988*. Boulder, Colo.: Westview, 1989.

Giles, F. *The locust years: The story of the Fourth French Republic*. London: Secker & Warburg, 1991.

Gretton, J. *Students and workers*. London: MacDonald, 1969.

Hanley, D., A. P. Kerr, and N. H. Waites. *Contemporary France: Politics and society since 1945*. London: Routledge & Kegan Paul, 1985.

Hoffmann, S., et al. *In search of France*. Cambridge, Mass.: Harvard University Press, 1963.

———. *Decline or renewal? France since the 1930s*. New York: Viking, 1974.

Jackson, J. *Charles de Gaulle*. London: Cardinal, 1990.

Keating, M., and P. Hainsworth. *Decentralisation and change in contemporary France*. Aldershot, England: Gower, 1986.

Kelly, M. *The cultural and intellectual rebuilding of France after the Second World War*. Basingstoke, England: Palgrave Macmillan, 2004.

Larkin, M. *France since the Popular Front: Government and the people, 1936–1986*. Oxford: Oxford University Press, 1988.

Macridis, R. C. *French politics in transition: The years after De Gaulle*. Cambridge, Mass.: Winthrop, 1975.

Mazey, S., and M. Newman (eds.) *Mitterrand's France*. London; New York: Croom Helm, 1987.

McKenzie, B. *Remaking France: Americanization, public diplomacy, and the Marshall Plan*. New York: Berghahn Books, 2005.

Milner, S., and N. Parsons (eds.) *Reinventing France: state and society in the twentieth century*. Basingstoke, England: Palgrave Macmillan, 2003.

Nay, C. *The black and the red: François Mitterrand and the story of an ambition*. San Diego, Calif.: Harcourt, Brace, Jovanovich, 1987.

Raymond, G. G. (ed.) *France during the socialist years*. Brookfield, Vt.: Dartmouth, 1994.

Reader, K., with K. Wadia. *The May 1968 events in France: Reproductions and interpretations*. London: Macmillan, 1993.

Rioux, J.-P. *The Fourth Republic, 1944–1958*. Cambridge: Cambridge University Press, 1987.

Ross, G., S. Hoffmann, and S. Malzacher (eds.) *The Mitterrand experiment: Continuity and change in modern France*. New York: Oxford University Press, 1987.

Shipway, M. *The road to war: France and Vietnam, 1944–1947*. Providence, R.I.: Berghahn Books, 1996.

Singer, D. *Prelude to revolution: France in May 1968*. New York: Hill & Wang, 1970.

———. *Is socialism doomed? The meaning of Mitterrand*. Oxford: Oxford University Press, 1988.

Williams, P. M. *Wars, plots, and scandals in post-war France*. Cambridge: Cambridge University Press, 1970.

Winchester, H. *Contemporary France*. New York: J. Wiley & Sons, 1993.

Wright, V. *Continuity and change in France*. London: Allen & Unwin, 1984.

Wylie, L., F. D. Chu, and M. Terrall. *France: The events of May–June 1968: A critical bibliography*. Pittsburgh, Pa.: Council for European Studies, 1973.

POLITICS

Bell, D. S. *French politics today*. Manchester: Manchester University Press, 2002.

Chapsal, J. *La vie politique en France de 1940 à 1958* [Political life in France from 1940 to 1958]. Paris: Presses Universitaires de France, 1990.

———. *La vie politique sous la Ve République 1: 1958–74* [Political life under the Fifth Republic 1: 1958–74]. Paris: Presses Universitaires de France, 1990.

———. *La vie politique sous la Ve République 2: 1974–1987* [Political life under the Fifth Republic 2: 1974–1987]. Paris: Presses Universitaires de France, 1990.

Cole, A. *French politics and society*. Harlow, England: Pearson Education, 2003.

Cole, A., and P. Campbell. *French electoral systems and elections since 1789*. Aldershot, England: Gower, 1989.

Cole, A., P. Le Galès, and J. Levy (eds.) *Developments in French politics, 3*. Basingstoke, England: Palgrave Macmillan, 2005.

Converse, P. E. *Political representation in France*. Cambridge, Mass.: Harvard University Press, 1986.

Duhamel, A. *La politique imaginaire: Les mythes politiques en France* [Imaginary politics: French political myths]. Paris: Flammarion, 1995.

Duverger, M. *The French political system*. Chicago: University of Chicago Press, 1958.

Gaffney, J., and E. Kolinsky (eds.) *Political culture in France and Germany*. London: Routledge, 1991.

Gildea, R. *France since 1945*. Oxford: Oxford University Press, 2002.

Hall, P. A., J. Hayward, and H. Machin (eds.) *Developments in French politics*. London: Macmillan, 1990.

Hazareesingh, S. *Political traditions in modern France*. Oxford: Oxford University Press, 1994.

Howarth, D., and G. Varouxakis. *Contemporary France: An introduction to French politics and society*. London: Arnold, 2003.

Morris, P. *French politics today*. Manchester: Manchester University Press, 1994.

Mossuz-Lavau, J. *Les Français et la politique: Enquête sur une crise* [Politics and the French: Surveying a crisis]. Paris: Odile Jacob, 1994.

Safran, W. *The French polity*. New York: Longman, 1985.

Vinen, R. *Bourgeois politics in France, 1945–1951*. Cambridge: Cambridge University Press, 1995.

Colonialism

Aldrich, R. *The French presence in the South Pacific, 1842–1940*. London: Macmillan, 1990.

Asiwaju, A. *West African transformations: Comparative impact of French and British colonialism.* Ikeja, Nigeria: Malthouse, 2001.

Betts, R. F. *France and decolonisation.* London: Macmillan, 1991.

Bidwell, R. *Morocco under colonial rule: French administration of tribal areas, 1912–1956.* London: Cass, 1973.

Cohen, W. B. *The French encounter with Africans: White response to blacks, 1530–1880.* Bloomington: Indiana University Press, 1980.

Daughton, J. P. *An empire divided: religion, republicanism, and the making of French colonialism, 1880–1914.* Oxford: Oxford University Press, 2006.

Duigan, P., and L. H. Gann (eds.) *Colonialism in Africa, 1870–1960. Vol. 5: A bibliographical guide to colonialism in sub-Saharan Africa.* Cambridge: Cambridge University Press, 1973.

Evans, M. *Empire and culture: The French experience, 1830–1940.* Basingstoke, England: Palgrave Macmillan, 2004.

Gifford, P., and W. R. Louis. *France and Britain in Africa: Imperial rivalry and colonial rule.* New Haven, Conn.: Yale University Press, 1971.

Ginio, R. *French colonialism unmasked: The Vichy years in West Africa.* Lincoln: University of Nebraska Press, 2006.

Halstead, J. P., and S. Porcari. *Modern European imperialism: A bibliography of books and articles, 1815–1972.* (2 vols.) Boston: G. K. Hall, 1974.

Horne, A. *A savage war of peace: Algeria, 1954–1962.* New York: Viking, 1978.

Irbouh, H. *Art in the service of colonialism: French art education in Morocco, 1912–1956.* London: Tauris, 2005.

Mortimer, E. *France and the Africans, 1944–1960: A political history.* London: Faber & Faber, 1964.

Roberts, S. H. *History of French colonial policy.* New York: Anchor, 1963.

Smith, T. *The French stake in Algeria, 1945–1962.* Ithaca, N.Y.: Cornell University Press, 1978.

Stovell, B., and T. Van Den Abbeele (eds.) *French civilization and its discontents: Nationalism, colonialism, race.* Lanham, Md.: Lexington Books, 2003.

Suret-Canale, J. *French colonialism in tropical Africa, 1900–1945.* New York: Pica, 1971.

Talbott, J. *The war without a name: France in Algeria, 1954–1962.* New York: Knopf, 1980.

White, D. S. *Black Africa and de Gaulle: From the French Empire to independence.* University Park: Pennsylvania State University Press.

Wrong, G. M. *The rise and fall of New France.* New York: Hippocrene, 1970.

Yahya, M. *Neo-colonialism: France's legacy to Africa.* Kaduna, Nigeria: ECPER, 1994.

Foreign Relations

Adamthwaite, A. *Grandeur and misery: France's bid for power in Europe 1914–1940*. London: Arnold, 1995.

Aldrich, R., and J. Connell (eds.) *France in world politics*. London: Routledge, 1989.

Boyce, R. (ed.) *French foreign and defence policy, 1918–1940: The decline and fall of a great power*. London: Routledge, 1998.

Burgess, M. *Federalism and political ideas: Influences and strategies in the European Community, 1972–1987*. London: Routledge, 1989.

Chuter, D. *Humanity's soldier: France and international security, 1919–2001*. Providence, R.I.: Berghahn, 1996.

Everts, S. *Adaptations in foreign policy: French and British reactions to German unification*. Oxford: Oxford University Press, 2000.

Featherstone, K. *Socialist parties and European integration: A comparative history*. Manchester: Manchester University Press, 1988.

Flynn, G. (ed.) *Remaking the hexagon: The new France in the new Europe*. Boulder, Colo.: Westview Press, 1995.

Grosser, A. *Affaires extérieures: La politique de la France 1944–1989* [Foreign relations: French policy 1944–1989]. Paris: Flammarion, 1989.

Hayne, M. B. *The French Foreign Office and the origins of the First World War, 1898–1914*. Oxford: Clarendon Press, 1993.

Keating, M., and B. Jones (eds.) *Regions in the European Community*. Oxford: Clarendon Press, 1985.

Kocs, S. A. *Autonomy or power? The Franco-German relationship and Europe's strategic choices, 1955–1995*. Westport, Conn.: Praeger, 1995.

Lamborn, A. *The price of power: Risk and foreign policy in Britain, France, and Germany*. London: Unwin Hyman, 1990.

Mazzucelli, C. *France and Germany at Maastricht: Politics and negotiations to create the European Union*. New York: Garland, 1997.

Pinder, J. *European Community: The building of a union*. Oxford: Oxford University Press, 1991.

Pryce, R. (ed.) *The dynamics of European union*. London: Croom Helm, 1987.

Robin, G. *La diplomatie de Mitterrand ou le triomphe des apparences* [Mitterrand's diplomacy or the triumph of appearances]. Paris: Editions de la Bièvre, 1985.

de Ruyt, J. *L'Acte unique européen* [The Single European Act]. Brussels: Editions de l'Université de Bruxelles, 1989.

Wallace, H., R. Morgan, and C. Bray. *Partners and rivals in Western Europe: Britain, France, and Germany*. London: Tower, 1986.

Wong, R. *The Europeanization of French foreign policy*. Basingstoke, England: Palgrave Macmillan, 2005.

Young, J. W. *France, the Cold War, and the Western Alliance, 1944–49*. Leicester, England: Leicester University Press, 1990.

Government

Ambler, J. S. *The French socialist experiment*. Philadelphia: Institute for the Study of Human Issues, 1985.

Ashford, D. E. *Policy and politics in France: Living with uncertainty*. Philadelphia: Temple University Press, 1982.

Avril, P. *Politics in France*. Harmondsworth, England: Penguin Books, 1969.

Cerny, P., G. Cerny, and M. Schain (eds.) *French politics and public policy*. New York: St. Martin's, 1980.

Crozier, M. *The bureaucratic phenomenon*. London: Tavistock Publications, 1964.

Elgie, R. *The role of the prime minister in France, 1981–91*. Basingstoke, England: Macmillan, 1993.

Elgie, R., and S. Griggs. *French politics: Debates and controversies*. London: Routledge, 2000.

Garrish, S. *Centralisation and decentralisation in England and France*. Bristol, England: School for Advanced Urban Studies, University of Bristol, 1986.

Gourevitch, P. A. *Paris and the provinces: The politics of local government reform in France*. London: Allen & Unwin, 1980.

Harding, R. R. *Anatomy of a power elite: The provincial governors of early modern France*. New Haven, Conn.: Yale University Press, 1978.

Hayward, J. *The one and indivisible French Republic*. London: Weidenfeld & Nicolson, 1973.

—— (ed.) *De Gaulle to Mitterand: Presidential power in France*. London: Hurst, 1993.

Keating, M., and P. Hainsworth. *Decentralisation and change in contemporary France*. Aldershot, England: Gower, 1986.

Loughlin, J. *Subnational government: The French experience*. Basingstoke, England: Palgrave Macmillan, 2007.

Machin, H. *The prefect in French public administration*. London: Croom Helm, 1977.

McCarthy, P. (ed.) *The French socialists in power, 1981–1986*. New York: Greenwood, 1987.

Preteceille, E. "Decentralization in France: New citizenship or restructuring hegemony?" *European Journal of Political Research* 16 (1988): 409–24.

Seurin, J.-L. (ed.) *La présidence en France at aux Etats-Unis* [The presidency in France and the United States]. Paris: Economica, 1986.

Stevens, A. *The government and politics of France*. London: Macmillan, 1992.

Thuillier, G. *La bureaucratie en France aux XIXe et XXe siècles* [French bureaucracy in the 19th and 20th centuries]. Paris: Economica, 1987.

Institutions

Aldrich, R., and J. Connell. *France's overseas frontier: Départements et territoires d'outre-mer*. Cambridge: Cambridge University Press, 1992.

Ambler, J. S. *French army in politics, 1945–1962*. Columbus: Ohio State University Press, 1966.

Andrews, W. G., and S. Hoffmann (eds.) *The Fifth Republic at 20*. Albany: State University of New York Press, 1981.

Atkin, N. *The French Fifth Republic*. Basingstoke, England: Palgrave Macmillan, 2004.

Brown, E. A. *Politics and institutions in Capetian France*. Hampshire, England: Variorum, 1991.

Brown, H. G. *War, revolution, and the bureaucratic state: Politics and army administration in France*. Oxford: Clarendon Press, 1995.

Chevallier, J.-J., and G. Conac. *Histoire des institutions et des régimes politiques de la France de 1789 à nos jours* [History of the institutions and political regimes of France from 1789 to the present]. Paris: Dalloz, 1991.

Godechot, J. *Les constitutions de la France depuis 1789* [The constitutions of France since 1789]. Paris: Garnier-Flammarion, 1979.

Goguel, F. *Institutions politiques françaises* [French political institutions]. Paris: Les Cours du Droit, 1967–8.

Heinz, G., and A. F. Peterson. *The French Fifth Republic: Establishment and consolidation, 1958–1965*. Stanford, Calif.: Hoover Institution Press, 1970.

——. *The French Fifth Republic: Continuity and change, 1966–1970*. Stanford, Calif.: Hoover Institution Press, 1974.

Holt, M. P. (ed.) *Society and institutions in early modern France*. Athens: University of Georgia Press, 1991.

Lenoir, R. *Quand l'état disjoncte* [When the state malfunctions]. Paris: Editions de la Découverte, 1995.

Ludwikowski, R. R., and W. F. Fox Jr. *The beginning of the constitutional era: A bicentennial comparative analysis of the first modern constitutions*. Washington, D.C.: Catholic University of America Press, 1993.

Macridis, R. C., and B. E. Brown. *The de Gaulle republic: Quest for unity*. 1960. Reprint, Westport, Conn.: Greenwood, 1976.

Müller, K.-J. *The military in politics and society in France and Germany in the 20th century*. Oxford: Berg, 1995.

Nicolet, C. *L'Idée républicaine en France* [The republican idea in France]. Paris: Gallimard, 1982.

Porch, D. *The French secret services: From the Dreyfus affair to the Gulf War*. London: Macmillan, 1996.

Smith, P. *The Senate of the French Fifth Republic*. Basingstoke, England: Palgrave Macmillan, 2008.

Stevens, R. *French overseas departments and territories*. New York: Chelsea House, 1987.

Stone, A. *Birth of judicial politics in France: Constitutional Council in comparative perspective*. New York: Oxford University Press, 1992.

Law

Abraham, H. J. *The judicial process: An introductory analysis of the courts of the United States, England, and France*. New York: Oxford University Press, 1986.

Bell, J. *French legal cultures*. London: Butterworth's, 2001.

David, R. *French law: Its structure, sources, and methodology*. Baton Rouge: Louisiana State University Press, 1972.

The French Civil Code: As amended to July 1, 1976. South Hackensack, N.J.: F. B. Rothman, 1977.

The French Code of Criminal Procedure. Littleton, Colo.: F. B. Rothman, 1988.

Guide pratique de la justice [Practical guide to the French justice system]. Paris: Gallimard, 1984.

Political Parties, Personalities, Groups, and Movements

Bell, D., D. Johnson, and P. Morris (eds.) *Biographical dictionary of French political leaders since 1870*. London: Harvester Wheatsheaf, 1990.

Cerny, P. G. *Social movements and protest in France*. London: Frances Pinter, 1982.

Cole, A. *French political parties in transition*. Aldershot, England: Dartmouth, 1990.

Debbasch, C., and J. Bourdon. *Les associations*. Paris: Presses Universitaires de France, *Que sais-je?* 1985.

Duyvendak, Jan W. *The power of politics: New social movements in France*. Boulder, Colo.: Westview, 1995.

Elgie, R. (ed.) *Electing the French president: The 1995 presidential election*. Basingstoke, England: Macmillan, 1996.

Evans, J. *The French party system*. Manchester: Manchester University Press, 2003.

Frears, J. R. *Parties and voters in France*. London: Hurst, 1991.

Knapp, A. *Politics and the party system in France: a disconnected democracy?* Basingstoke, England: Palgrave Macmillan, 2004.

Lancaster, T. D. "Comparative nationalism: The Basques in Spain and France." *European Journal of Political Research*, 15 (1987): 561–90.

Nelkin, D., and M. Pollak. *The atom besieged: Extraparliamentary dissent in France and Germany.* Cambridge, Mass.: MIT Press, 1981.

Prendiville, B. *Environmental politics in France.* Boulder, Colo.: Westview, 1994.

Touraine, A., et al. *Anti-nuclear protest: The opposition to nuclear energy in France.* Cambridge: Cambridge University Press, 1983.

Wilson, F. L. *French political parties under the Fifth Republic.* New York: Praeger, 1982.

Ysmal, C. *Les partis politiques sous la Ve République* [Political parties under the Fifth Republic]. Paris: Montchrestien, 1989.

Of the Left

Adereth, M. *The French Communist Party: A critical history (1920–84), from Comintern to the "colours of France."* Manchester: Manchester University Press, 1984.

Baumann-Reynolds, S. *François Mitterrand: The making of a socialist prince in Republican France.* Westport, Conn.: Praeger, 1995.

Bell, D. S., and B. Criddle. *The French Socialist Party.* Oxford: Clarendon Press, 1988.

Blackmer, D. L. M., and S. Tarrow (eds.) *Communism in Italy and France.* Princeton, N.J.: Princeton University Press, 1975.

Caute, D. *Communism and the French intellectuals, 1914–1960.* New York: Macmillan, 1964.

Clift, B. *French socialism in a global era.* London: Continuum, 2005.

Elleinstein, J. *Le PC* [The Communist Party]. Paris: Grasset, 1976.

Feenberg, A., and J. Freedman. *When poetry rules the streets: the French May events of 1968.* Albany, NY.: State University of New York Press, 2001.

Gaffney, J. *The French left and the Fifth Republic.* London: Macmillan, 1989.

Graham, B. D. *Choice and democratic order: The French Socialist Party, 1937–1950.* Cambridge: Cambridge University Press, 2006.

Guiat, C. *The French and Italian Communist parties: Comrades and culture.* London: Frank Cass, 2002.

Hanley, D. *Keeping left? CERES and the French Socialist Party: A contribution to the study of factionalism in political parties.* Manchester: Manchester University Press, 1986.

Jenson, J., and G. Ross. *The view from inside: A French Communist cell in crisis*. Berkeley: University of California Press, 1985.

Johnson, R. W. *The long march of the French left*. London: Macmillan, 1981.

Judt, T. *Marxism and the French left: Studies in labour and politics in France, 1830–1981*. Oxford: Oxford University Press, 1986.

Kelly, M., and R. Sacker. *A radiant future: The French Communist Party and Eastern Europe 1944–1956*. New York: Peter Lang, 1999.

Kriegel, A. *The French Communists: Profile of a people*. Chicago: University of Chicago Press, 1972.

Mortimer, E. *The rise of the French Communist Party, 1920–1947*. Boston: Faber & Faber, 1984.

Noland, A. *The founding of the French Socialist Party, 1893–1905*. 1956. Reprint, New York: Fertig, 1970.

Nugent, N., and D. Lowe. *The left in France*. London: Macmillan, 1982.

Raymond, G. *The French Communist Party during the Fifth Republic: A crisis of leadership and ideology*. Basingstoke, England: Palgrave Macmillan, 2005.

Tiersky, R. *French communism, 1920–1972*. New York: Columbia University Press, 1974.

Wall, I. M. *French communism in the era of Stalin: The quest for unity and integration, 1945–1962*. Westport, Conn.: Greenwood, 1983. (Contributions in Political Science 97).

Willard, C. *Les Guesdistes: Le mouvement socialiste en France, 1893–1905* [The Guesdists: The socialist movement in France, 1893–1905]. Paris: Editions Sociales, 1965.

Williams, S. (ed.) *Socialism in France: From Jaurès to Mitterrand*. New York: St. Martin's, 1983.

Wilson, F. L. *The French democratic left, 1963–1969: Toward a modern party system*. Stanford, Calif.: Stanford University Press, 1971.

Wohl, R. *French Communism in the making, 1914–1924*. Stanford, Calif.: Stanford University Press, 1966.

Of the Right

Amouroux, H. *Monsieur Barre*. Paris: Hachette, 1988.

Anderson, M. *Conservative politics in France*. London: Allen & Unwin, 1974.

Charlot, J. The *Gaullist phenomenon: The Gaullist movement in the Fifth Republic*. New York: Praeger, 1971.

Chebel d'Appollonia, A. *L'Extrême-droite en France: De Maurras à Le Pen* [The extreme right in France: From Maurras to Le Pen]. Brussels: Editions Complexe, 1988.

DeClair, E. G. *Politics on the fringe: People, policies, and organization of the French National Front*. Durham, N.C.: Duke University Press, 1999.

Fieschi, C. *Fascism, populism and the French Fifth Republic: In the shadow of democracy*. Manchester: Manchester University Press, 2004.

Giesbert, F.-O. *Jacques Chirac*. Paris: Seuil, 1988.

Giscard d'Estaing, V. *French democracy*. London: Collins, 1977.

Irvine, W. D. *French conservatism in crisis: The Republican Federation of France in the 1930s*. Baton Rouge: Louisiana State University Press, 1979.

Knapp, A. *Gaullism since de Gaulle*. Aldershot, England: Dartmouth, 1994.

Lacouture, J. *De Gaulle*. London: Harvill, 1992.

Passmore, K. *From Liberalism to Fascism: The right in a French province, 1928-1939*. Cambridge: Cambridge University Press, 1997.

Rémond, R. *Les droites en France* [The right in France]. Paris: Aubier Montaigne, 1982.

Rutkoff, P. M. *Revanche and revision: The Ligue des Patriotes and the origins of the radical right in France, 1882–1900*. Athens: Ohio University Press, 1981.

Rydgren, J. *The populist challenge: Political protest and ethno-nationalist mobilization in France*. Oxford: Berghahn, 2004.

Schain, M. A. "The National Front in France and the construction of political legitimacy." *West European Politics* 10, no. 2 (1987): 229–52.

Shields, J. *The extreme right in France: From Pétain to Le Pen*. London: Routledge, 2007.

Simmons, H. G. *The French National Front: The extremist challenge to democracy*. Boulder, Colo.: Westview, 1996.

Singer, D. "The resistible rise of Jean-Marie Le Pen." *Ethnic and Racial Studies* 14 (1991): 368–81.

Soucy, R. *French fascism: The first wave, 1924–1933*. New Haven, Conn.: Yale University Press, 1986.

———. *French fascism: The second wave, 1933–1939*. New Haven, Conn.: Yale University Press, 1995.

Tuppen, J. *Chirac's France*. London: Macmillan, 1991.

Weber, E. *Action française: Royalism and reaction in 20th-century France*. Stanford, Calif.: Stanford University Press, 1962.

Political and Social Theory

Addinall, N. *A study of major political thinkers in France from the seventeenth to the twentieth century, from absolutism to socialism*. Lewiston, N.Y.: Edwin Mellen, 2004.

Aron, R. *Main currents in sociological thought.* (2 vols.) London: Weidenfeld and Nicolson, 1968–70.

Burnet, M.-C., and E. Welch (eds.) *Affaires de famille: The family in contemporary French culture and theory.* Amsterdam: Rodopi, 2007.

Bury, J. B. *The idea of progress.* London: Macmillan, 1920.

Cerny, P. G., and M. A. Schain (eds.) *Socialism, the state, and public policy in France.* New York: Methuen, 1985.

Craiutu, A. *Liberalism under siege: The political thought of the French Doctrinaires.* Lanham, Md.: Lexington Books, 2003.

Elbow, M. H. *French corporative theory, 1789–1948: A chapter in the history of ideas.* New York: Columbia University Press, 1953.

Hazareesingh, S. *Intellectual founders of the Republic: Five studies in nineteenth-century political thought.* Oxford: Oxford University Press, 2005.

Lemert, C. C. (ed.) *French sociology: Rupture and renewal since 1968.* New York: Columbia University Press, 1981.

Leonard, M. *Athens in Paris: Ancient Greece and the political in post-war French thought.* Oxford: Oxford University Press, 2005.

Lichtheim, G. *Marxism in Modern France.* New York: Columbia University Press, 1966.

Manent, M. *The city of man.* Princeton, N.J.: Princeton University Press, 1998.

Manuel, F. E., and F. P. Manuel. *French utopias: An anthology of ideal societies.* New York: Free Press, 1966.

Martin, K. *The rise of French liberal thought: A study of political ideas from Bayle to Condorcet.* Westport, Conn.: Greenwood, 1980.

Mayer, J. P. *Political thought in France from Sieyès to Sorel.* London: Routledge & Kegan Paul, 1961.

Muret, C. T. *French royalist doctrines since the Revolution.* New York: Octagon, 1972.

Neidelman, J. A. *The General will is citizenship: Inquiries into French political thought.* Lanham, Md.: Rowman and Littlefield, 2000.

Pierce, R. *Contemporary French political thought.* Oxford: Oxford University Press, 1966.

Poster, M. *Existential Marxism in postwar France: From Sartre to Althusser.* Princeton, N.J.: Princeton University Press, 1975.

Rose, M. *Servants of post-industrial power? "Sociologie du travail" in modern France.* New York: M. E. Sharpe, 1979.

Silverman, M. *Facing postmodernity: Contemporary French thought on culture and society.* London: Routledge, 1999.

Soltau, R. *French political thought in the 19th century.* London: Ernest Benn, 1931.

Talmon, J. L. *Political messianism: The romantic phase.* London: Secker & Warburg, 1960.

Thomson, D. *Democracy in France since 1870.* London: Oxford University Press, 1969.

SCIENCE

Energy and Environment

Bess, M. *The light-green society: Ecology and technological modernity in France, 1960–2000.* Chicago: University of Chicago Press, 2003.

Chick, M. *Electricity and energy policy in Britain, France and the United States since 1945.* London: Edward Elgar, 2007.

Davis, M. *The green guide to France.* London: Green Print, 1990.

Hayes, G. *Environmental protest and the state in France.* Basingstoke, England: Palgrave Macmillan, 2002.

Jasper, J. M. *Nuclear politics: Energy and the state in the United States, Sweden, and France.* Princeton, N.J.: Princeton University Press, 1990.

Lucas, N. J. D. *Energy in France: Planning, politics, and policy.* London: European Publications for the David Davies Memorial Institute for International Studies, 1979.

Mendershausen, H. *Coping with the oil crisis: French and German experiences.* Baltimore, Md.: Johns Hopkins University Press, 1976.

Prendiville, B. *Environmental politics in France.* Boulder, Colo.: Westview Press, 1994.

Touraine, A. *Anti-nuclear protest: The opposition to nuclear energy in France.* Cambridge: Cambridge University Press, 1983.

Zonabend, F. *The nuclear peninsula.* Cambridge: Cambridge University Press, 1993.

Geography and Geology

Beaujeu-Garnier, J. *France.* London: Longman, 1975 (The world's landscapes).

Boucher, M. *La région.* Paris: Cahiers Français, 1973.

Burton, S., and A. Jeanes. *Central southern France.* London: Hodder Arnold, 1997.

Carrington, D. *Granite island: A portrait of Corsica.* London: Longman, 1971.

Darby, H. C. *The relations of history and geography: Studies in England, France and the United States.* Exeter, England: Exeter University Press, 2002.

De Martonne, E. *Geographical regions of France*. London: Heinemann, 1933.
De Planol, X. *An historical geography of France*. Cambridge: Cambridge University Press, 2006.
Embleton, C. (ed.) *Geomorphology of Europe*. London: Macmillan, 1984 (Macmillan reference books).
House, J. W. *France: An applied geography*. London: Methuen, 1978.
Konvitz, J. W. *Cartography in France, 1660–1848: Science, engineering, and statecraft*. Chicago: University of Chicago Press, 1987.
Lowe, P., and M. Bodiguel (eds.) *Rural studies in Britain and France*. London: Belhaven, 1990.
Philippe, D., and C. Gouvion. *France from the air*. New York: Abrams, 1985.
Rol, R. *Flore des arbres, arbustes, et arbrisseaux* [A flora of trees and shrubs]. (4 vols.) Paris: La Maison Rustique, 1963–1969.
Wallen, C. C. (ed.) *The climate of France, Belgium, the Netherlands, and Luxembourg*. Amsterdam: Elsevier, 1970.
Whited, T. L. *Forests and peasant politics in modern France*. New Haven, Conn.: Yale University Press, 2000.

Public Health and Medicine

Adams, M. B. *The wellborn science: Eugenics in Germany, France, Brazil, and Russia*. Oxford: Oxford University Press, 1990.
Coleman, W. *Death is a social disease: Public health and political economy in early industrial France*. Madison: University of Wisconsin Press, 1982.
Gelfand, T. *Professionalizing modern medicine: Paris surgeons and medical science institutions in the 18th century*. Westport, Conn.: Greenwood Press, 1980.
Green, D. G., and H. Redwood. *Why ration health care? An international study of the United Kingdom, France, Germany, and public sector health care in the USA*. London: Civitas, 2000.
Health and Safety Executive. *Workplace health and safety in Europe: A study of the regulatory arrangements in France, West Germany, Italy, and Spain*. London: HMSO, 1991.
Heywood, C. *Childhood in 19th-century France: Work, health, and education among the "classes populaires."* Cambridge: Cambridge University Press, 1988.
Hildreth, M. L. *Doctors, bureaucrats, and public health in France, 1888–1902*. New York: Garland, 1987.
La Berge, A. F. *Mission and method: The early 19th-century French public health movement*. Cambridge: Cambridge University Press, 1992.

Lesch, J. E. *Science and medicine in France: The emergence of experimental physiology, 1790–1855.* Cambridge, Mass.: Harvard University Press, 1984.

Nathanson, C.A. *Disease prevention and social change: The state, society, and public health in the United States, France, Great Britain, and Canada.* New York: Sage Foundation Publications, 2007.

Rodwin, V. B. *The health planning predicament: France, Quebec, England, and the United States.* Berkeley: University of California Press, 1984.

Smith, T. *Creating the welfare state in France, 1880–1940.* Montreal: McGill-Queen's University Press, 2003.

Science Policy and Research

Anderson, W. C. *Between the library and the laboratory: The language of chemistry in 18th-century France.* Baltimore, Md.: Johns Hopkins University Press, 1984.

Atkinson, H., P. Rogers, and R. Bond. *Research in the United Kingdom, France, and West Germany.* Swindon, England: Science and Engineering Research Council, 1990.

Bugge, T. *Science in France in the revolutionary era.* Cambridge, Mass.: MIT Press, 2003.

Crosland, M. P. *Science under control: The French Academy of Sciences 1795–1914.* Cambridge: Cambridge University Press, 1992.

Fox, R. *Science, industry, and the social order in post-revolutionary France.* Aldershot, England: Variorum, 1995.

Foc, R., and G. Weisz (eds.) *The organization of science and technology in France, 1808–1914.* Cambridge: Cambridge University Press, 1980.

Gillespie, C. C. *Science and polity in France at the end of the old regime.* Princeton, N.J.: Princeton University Press, 1980.

Kellerman, W. E. *Science and technology in France and Belgium.* Harlow, England: Longman, 1988.

Long, T. D., and C. Wright. *Science policies of industrial nations: Case studies of the United States, Soviet Union, United Kingdom, France, Japan, and Sweden.* New York: Praeger, 1975.

Lux, D. S. *Patronage and royal science in 17th-century France: The Académie de physique in Caen.* Ithaca, N.Y.: Cornell University Press, 1989.

Paul, H. W. *From knowledge to power: The rise of the science empire in France, 1860–1939.* Cambridge: Cambridge University Press, 2003.

———. *Science, vine, and wine in modern France.* Cambridge: Cambridge University Press, 1996.

Pyenson, L. *Civilizing mission: Exact sciences and French overseas expansion.* Baltimore, Md.: Johns Hopkins University Press, 1993.

Simon, J. *Chemistry, pharmacy and revolution in France 1777–1809*. Aldershot: Ashgate, 2005.

Zwerling, C. S. *The emergence of the Ecole Normale Supérieure as a center for scientific education in 19th-century France*. New York: Garland, 1990.

Technology

Benko, G. B. *Les technopoles* [The technopoles]. Paris: Masson, 1991.

Breheny, M. J., and R. W. McQuaid (eds.) *The development of high technology industries: An international survey*. London: Croom Helm, 1987.

Clement, K., et al. *Regional policy and technology transfer: A cross-national perspective*. London: HMSO, 1995.

Crosland, M. *Scientific institutions and practice in France and Britain, C.1700–C.1870*. Aldershot, England: Ashgate, 2007.

Feldman, E. J. *Concorde and dissent: Explaining high technology project failures in Britain and France*. Cambridge: Cambridge University Press, 1985.

Harris, J. R. *Essays in industry and technology in the 18th century: England and France*. Aldershot, England: Variorum, 1992.

Heller, H. *Labour, science and technology in France, 1500–1620*. Cambridge: Cambridge University Press, 2002.

Kranakis, E. *Constructing a bridge: An exploration of engineering culture, design, and research in 19th-century France and America*. Cambridge, Mass.: MIT Press, 1997.

Rocke, A. J. *Adolphe Wurtz and the battle for French chemistry*. Cambridge, Mass.: MIT Press, 2001.

Sharp, M., and P. Holmes. *Strategies for new technology: Case studies from Britain and France*. London: Philip Allan, 1989.

SOCIETY

Demography

Armengaud, A. *La population française au XXe siècle* [The French population in the 20th century]. Paris: Fayard, 1967.

Bonneuil, N. *Transformation of the French demographic landscape, 1806–1906*. Oxford: Clarendon Press, 1997.

Bourgeois-Pichat, J. "The general development of the population of France since the eighteenth century." In Glass, D. V., and D. E. C. Eversley (eds.) *Population in history: Essays in historical demography*. London: Edward Arnold, 1965, 474–506.

Courgeau, D. *Three centuries of spatial mobility in France*. Paris: UNESCO, 1982.

Dyer, C. *Population and society in 20th-century France*. London: Hodder & Stoughton, 1978.

Guéraud, A. *The gravediggers of France*. New York: Doubleday, 1944.

Hargreaves, A.G. *Multi-ethnic France: Immigration, politics, culture, and society*. London: Routledge, 2007.

Huber, M. *La population de la France pendant la guerre* [The French population during the war]. Paris: Presses Universitaires de France, 1931.

Huss, M. M. *Demography, public opinion, and politics in France, 1974–80*. London: Department of Geography, Queen Mary College, University of London, Occasional Paper 16, 1980.

INSEE. *Recensement général de la population de 1999* [General census of the population in 1999]. Paris: INSEE, 1999.

McIntosh, C. *Population policy in Western Europe: Responses to low fertility in France, Sweden, and West Germany*. London: Eurospan, 1983.

Noin, D., and Y. Chauviré. *La population de la France* [The population of France]. Paris: Masson, 1987.

Ogden, P. E. (ed.) *Migrants in modern France: Four studies*. London: Department of Geography, Queen Mary College, University of London, Occasional Paper 23, 1984.

Scargill, D. I. *The population of France*. Oxford: School of Geography, University of Oxford, 1985.

Schneider, W. H. *Quality and quantity: The quest for biological regeneration in twentieth-century France*. Cambridge: Cambridge University Press, 2002.

Schweber, L. *Disciplining statistics: Demography and vital statistics in France and Britain, 1830–1885*. Durham, N.C.: Duke University Press, 2007.

Spengler, J. J. *France faces depopulation: Postlude edition, 1936–1976*. Durham, N.C.: Duke University Press, 1979.

Sullerot, E. *La démographie de la France: Bilan et perspectives* [The demography of France: Results and prospects]. Paris: La Documentation Française, 1978.

Toutain, J. C. *La population française de 1700 à 1959* [The French population from 1700 to 1959]. Paris: ISEA; New York: Kraus Reprint, 1963.

Van de Walle, E. *The female population of France in the 19th century*. Princeton, N.J.: Princeton University Press, 1974.

Van Nimwegen, N., J.-C. Chesnais, and P. Dykstra. *Coping with sustained low fertility in France and the Netherlands*. Amsterdam: Swets & Zeitlinger, 1993.

Wrigley, E. A. "The fall of marital fertility in 19th-century France: Exemplar or exception?" *European Journal of Population* 1 (1985): 31–60.

Education

Bloch, J. *Rousseauism and education in 18th-century France*. Oxford: Voltaire Foundation, 1995.

Bonner, T. *Becoming a physician: Medical education in Britain, France, Germany, and the United States, 1750–1945*. Oxford: Oxford University Press, 1995.

Boos-Nünning, U. *Towards intercultural education: A comparative study of the education of migrant children in Belgium, England, France, and the Netherlands*. London: Centre for Information on Language Teaching and Research, 1986.

Bourdieu, P., and J.-C. Passeron. *Reproduction in education, society, and culture*. London: Sage, 1977.

———. *The inheritors: French students and their return to culture*. Chicago: University of Chicago Press, 1979.

Broadfoot, P. *Education, assessment, and society: A sociological analysis*. Buckingham, England: Open University Press, 1996.

Brockliss, L. W. B. *French higher education in the 17th and 18th centuries: A cultural history*. Oxford: Clarendon Press, 1987.

Chisick, H. *The limits of reform in the Enlightenment: Attitudes towards the education of the lower classes in 18th-century France*. Princeton, N.J.: Princeton University Press, 1981.

Clark, Burton R. (ed.) *The research foundations of graduate education: Germany, Britain, France, United States, Japan*. Berkeley: University of California Press, 1993.

Corbett, A., and B. Moon. *Education in France: Continuity and change in the Mitterrand years, 1981–1995*. London: Routledge, 1996.

Day, C. *Schools and work: Technical and vocational education in France since the Third Republic*. Montreal: McGill-Queen's University Press, 2001.

Deer, C. M. A. *Higher education in England and France since the 1980s*. Oxford: Symposium Books, 2002.

Diebolt, C. *Education, knowledge and economic growth: France and Germany in the 19th and 20th centuries*. New York: Peter Lang, 2003.

Durkheim, E. *The evolution of educational thought: Lectures on the formation and development of secondary education in France*. London: Routledge & Kegan Paul, 1977.

Green, A. *Education and state formation: The rise of education systems in England, France, and the U.S.A.* Basingstoke, England: Macmillan, 1990.

Grew, R. *School, state, and society: The growth of elementary schooling in 19th-century France: A quantitative analysis*. Ann Arbor: University of Michigan Press, 1991.

Halls, W. D. *Education, culture, and politics in modern France*. Oxford: Pergamon, 1976.

Huppert, G. *Public schools in Renaissance France*. Urbana: University of Illinois Press, 1984.

Judge, H. *Faith-based schools and the state: Catholics in America, France and England*. Oxford: Symposium Books, 2002.

Judge, H., et al. *The university and the teachers: France, the United States, England*. Wallingford, England: Triangle, 1994.

Koch, R. *Vocational education in France: Structural problems and present efforts towards reform*. Berlin: CEDEFOP, 1989.

Lewis, H. D. *The French education system*. London: Croom Helm, 1985.

Locke, R. R. *The end of the practical man: Entrepreneurship and higher education in Germany, France and Great Britain, 1880–1940*. London: Elsevier Science, 2006.

OECD. *Review of national policies for education: France*. Paris: Organization for Economic Cooperation and Development, 1994.

Prost, A. *Education, société, et politique: Une histoire de l'enseignement en France de 1945 à nos jours* [Education, society, and politics: A history of teaching in France from 1945 to the present]. Paris: Seuil, 1991.

Reed-Danahay, D. *Education and identity in rural France: The politics of schooling*. Cambridge: Cambridge University Press, 2004.

Rogers, R. *From the salon to the schoolroom: Educating bourgeois girls in nineteenth-century France*. University Park: Penn State University Press, 2005.

Stock-Morton, P. *Moral education for a secular society: The development of morale laïque in 19th-century France*. Albany: State University of New York Press, 1988.

Toynbee, W. S. *Adult education and the voluntary associations in France*. Nottingham, England: University of Nottingham, Department of Adult Education, 1985.

Religion

Aston, N. *Religion and revolution in France 1780–1804*. Basingstoke, England: Palgrave Macmillan, 2000.

Bosworth, W. *Catholicism and crisis in modern France: French Catholic groups at the threshold of the Fifth Republic*. Princeton, N.J.: Princeton University Press, 1962.

Bremond, H. *A literary history of religious thought in France*. New York: Octagon, 1969.

Dansette, A. *Religious history of modern France.* New York: Thomas Nelson/Herder & Herder, 1961.

Ford, C. *Divided houses: Religion and gender in modern France.* Ithaca, N.Y.: Cornell University Press, 2005.

Galton, A. *Church and state in France, 1300–1907.* New York: B. Franklin, 1972.

Gibson, R. *A social history of French Catholicism, 1789–1914.* New York: Routledge, Chapman & Hall, 1989.

Larkin, M. *Church and state after the Dreyfus affair: The separation issue in France.* London: Macmillan, 1974.

———. *Religion, politics, and preferment in France since 1890: La belle époque and its legacy.* Cambridge: Cambridge University Press, 2002.

Leonard, E. G. *A history of Protestantism.* London: Nelson, 1965.

Palmer, R. R. *Catholics and unbelievers in 18th-century France.* Princeton, N.J.: Princeton University Press, 1939.

Phillips, C. S. *The church in France, 1789–1848: A study in revival.* New York: Russell & Russell, 1966.

Rady, M. C. *France: Renaissance, religion, and recovery, 1494–1610.* London: Edward Arnold, 1988.

Sedgwick, A. *The Ralliement in French politics, 1890–1898.* Cambridge, Mass.: Harvard University Press, 1965.

Sproxton, J. *Violence and religion: Attitudes towards militancy in the French civil wars and the English revolution.* London: Routledge, 1995.

Tallatt, F., and N. Atkin (eds.) *Religion, society, and politics in France since 1789.* London: Hambledon Press, 1991.

Thompson, J. W. *The wars of religion in France, 1559–1576.* Boston, Mass.: Adamant Media Corporation, 2002.

Sociology

Ardoino, J., et al. *La sociologie en France* [Sociology in France]. Paris: La Découverte, 1988.

Berger, S. *Peasants against politics: Rural organizations in Brittany, 1911–1967.* Cambridge, Mass.: Harvard University Press, 1972.

Boltanski, L. *The making of a class: Cadres in French society.* Cambridge: Cambridge University Press, 1987.

Bourdieu, P. *Distinction: A social critique of the judgement of taste.* London: Routledge & Kegan Paul, 1984.

Crozier, M. *Strategies for change: The future of French society.* Cambridge, Mass.: MIT Press, 1982.

Dupeux, G. *French society, 1789–1970*. New York: Barnes & Noble, 1976.

Gallie, D. *Social inequality and class radicalism in France and Britain*. Cambridge: Cambridge University Press, 1986.

Hantrais, L. *Contemporary French society*. London: Macmillan, 1982.

Higgonet, P. L. R. *Pont-de-Monvert: Social structure and politics in a French village, 1700–1914*. Cambridge, Mass.: Harvard University Press, 1971.

Howorth, J., and P. Cerny (eds.) *Elites in France: Origins, reproduction, and power*. New York: St. Martin's, 1981.

Katznelson, I., and A. R. Zolberg. *Working-class formation: 19th-century patterns in Western Europe and the United States*. Princeton, N.J.: Princeton University Press, 1986.

Lemert, Charles C. (ed.) *French sociology: Rupture and renewal since 1968*. New York: Columbia University Press, 1981.

Logue, W. *From philosophy to sociology: The evolution of French liberalism, 1870–1914*. De Kalb: Northern Illinois University Press, 1983.

Marceau, J. *Class and status in France: Economic change and social mobility, 1945–1975*. New York: Oxford University Press, 1977.

Marwick, A. *Class: Image and reality in Britain, France, and the U.S.A. since 1930*. New York: Oxford University Press, 1980.

Mendras, H., and A. Cole, *Social change in modern France*. Cambridge: Cambridge University Press, 1991.

Mestrovic, S. G. *Emile Durkheim and the reformation of sociology*. Totowa, N.J.: Rowman & Littlefield, 1988.

Petonnet, C. *Those people: The subculture of a housing project*. London: Greenwood, 1973.

Raymond, G., and T. Modood. *The construction of minority identities in France and Britain*. Basingstoke, England: Palgrave Macmillan, 2007.

Rose, M. *Industrial sociology: Work in the French tradition*. London: Sage, 1987.

Royal, F. *Contemporary French cultures and societies*. New York: Peter Lang, 2004.

Silverman, M. *Deconstructing the nation: Immigration, racism and citizenship in modern France*. London: Routledge, 1992.

Suleiman, E. N. *Elites in French society: The politics of survival*. Princeton, N.J.: Princeton University Press, 1978.

Vaughan, M., M. Kolinsky, and P. Sheriff (eds.) *Social change in France*. Oxford: Martin Robertson, 1980.

Waters, S. *Social movements in France: Towards a new citizenship*. Basingstoke, England: Palgrave Macmillan, 2003.

Wylie, L. *Village in the Vaucluse*. Cambridge, Mass.: Harvard University Press, 1974.

Crime and Punishment

Andrews, R. M. *Law, magistracy, and crime in old regime Paris, 1735–1789.* Cambridge: Cambridge University Press, 1994.

Brodeur, J.-P. *Comparisons in policing: An international perspective.* Aldershot, England: Avebury, 1995.

Cobb, R. *The police and the people.* London: Oxford University Press, 1970.

Cohen, E. *The crossroads of justice: Law and culture in late medieval France.* Leiden: Brill, 1993.

Forstenzer, T. R. *French provincial police and the fall of the Second Republic: Social fear and counterrevolution.* Princeton, N.J.: Princeton University Press, 1981.

Gleizal, J.-J. *La police en France* [The police in France]. Paris: Presses Universitaires de France, 1993.

Greenshields, M. R. *An economy of violence in early modern France: Crime and justice in the Haute Auvergne, 1587–1664.* University Park: Pennsylvania State University Press, 1994.

Hodgson, J. *French criminal justice: A comparative account of the investigation and prosecution of crime in France.* Oxford: Hart Publishing, 2005.

Hufton, O. H. *The urban criminal in 18th-century France.* Manchester: Manchester University Press, 1984.

Ingraham, B. L. *Political crime in Europe: A comparative study of France, Germany, and England.* Berkeley: University of California Press, 1979.

Langbein, H. *Prosecuting crime in the Renaissance: England, Germany, France.* Clark, N.J.: Lawbook Exchange Ltd., 2005.

Leigh, L. H. *A report on the administration of criminal justice in the pre-trial phase in France and Germany.* London: HMSO, 1992.

Maestro, M. T. *Voltaire and Beccaria as reformers of criminal law.* New York: Columbia University Press, 1942.

Niles, B. *Condemned to Devil's Island: The biography of an unknown convict.* New York: Harcourt, 1928.

Nye, R. A. *Crime, madness, and politics in modern France: The medical concept of national decline.* Princeton, N.J.: Princeton University Press, 1984.

O'Brien, P. *The promise of punishment: Prisons in 19th-century France.* Princeton, N.J.: Princeton University Press, 1982.

Reisinger, D. S. *Crime and media in contemporary France.* Ashland, Ohio: Purdue University Press, 2007.

Stead, P. J. *The police of France.* New York: Macmillan, 1983.

Taylor, K. F. *In the theater of criminal justice: The Palais de justice in Second Empire Paris.* Princeton, N.J.: Princeton University Press, 1993.

Williams, A. *The police of Paris, 1718–1789.* Baton Rouge: Louisiana State University Press, 1979.

Wright, G. *Between the guillotine and liberty: Two centuries of the crime problem in France*. New York: Oxford University Press, 1983.

Zehr, H. *Crime and the development of modern society: Patterns of criminality in 19th-century Germany and France*. Totowa, N.J.: Rowman & Littlefield, 1977.

Immigration and Identity

Adler, J. *The Jews of Paris and the final solution: Communal response and internal conflicts, 1940–1944*. New York: Oxford University Press, 1987.

Anderson, M. "Regional identity and political change: The case of Alsace from the Third to the Fifth Republic." *Political Studies* 20, pt. 1 (March 1972): 17–30.

Bernard, F. M. (ed.) *The Jews in modern France*. Hanover, N.H.: University Press of New England for Brandeis University Press, 1985.

Cohen, W. B. "Legacy of empire: The Algerian connection." *Journal of Contemporary History* 15, no. 1 (1980): 97–123.

Favell, A. *Philosophies of integration: Immigration and the idea of citizenship in France and Britain*. Basingstoke, England: Palgrave Macmillan, 2001.

Fetzer, J. S. *Public attitudes towards immigration in the United States, France, and Germany*. Cambridge: Cambridge University Press, 2000.

Freedman, J. *Immigration and insecurity in France*. Aldershot, England: Ashgate, 2004.

Freedman, J., and C. Tarr. *Women, immigration and identities in France*. New York: Berg, 2000.

Freeman, G. P. *Immigrant labor and racial conflict in industrial societies: The French and British experience 1945–1975*. Princeton, N.J.: Princeton University Press, 1979.

Grillo, R. D. *Ideologies and institutions in urban France: The representation of immigrants*. Cambridge, Mass.: Cambridge University Press, 1985.

Hyman, P. *From Dreyfus to Vichy: The remaking of French Jewry, 1906–1939*. New York: Columbia University Press, 1979.

Ireland, P. *The policy challenge of ethnic diversity: Immigrant politics in France and Switzerland*. Cambridge, Mass.: Harvard University Press.

Josephs, J. *Swastika over Paris: The story of the French Jews under Nazi occupation*. Berkeley, Calif.: Arcade, 1989.

Laurence, J., and J. Vaisse. *Integrating Islam: Political and religious challenges in contemporary France*. Washington: Brookings Institute, 2005.

Marrus, M. R. *The politics of assimilation: A study of the French Jewish community at the time of the Dreyfus affair*. Oxford: Clarendon Press, 1971.

Marrus, M. R., and R. O. Paxton. *Vichy France and the Jews*. New York: Basic Books, 1981.

Ogden, P. E. *Foreigners in Paris: Residential segregation in the 19th and 20th centuries*. London: Department of Geography, Queen Mary College, University of London, 1977.

Reece, J. E. *The Bretons against France: Ethnic minority nationalism in 20th-century Brittany*. Chapel Hill: University of North Carolina Press, 1977.

Sérant, P. *La France des minorités* [France of the minorities]. Paris: Robert Laffont, 1965.

Sports

Hare, G. *Football in France: A cultural history*. New York: Berg, 2003.

Holt, R. *Sport and society in modern France*. London: Macmillan, 1981.

Praicheux, J., and D. Mathieu. *Sports en France* [Sports in France]. Paris: Fayard, 1987.

Sykes, B. *Sport in France*. London: Harrap, 1977.

Weber, E., H. Dauncey, and G. Hare. *The Tour de France, 1903-2003: A century of sporting structures, meanings and values*. London: Franck Cass, 2003.

Urban Development and Planning

Bauer, G., and J. M. Roux. *La rurbanisation ou la ville éparpillée*. ["Rurbanisation" or the scattered town]. Paris: Seuil, 1976.

Braid, W. I. "The preparation of local plans in France." *Town Planning Review* 54 (1983): 155–73.

Burtenshaw, D., M. Bateman, and G. Ashworth. *The European city: A western perspective*. London: David Fulton, 1991.

Champion, A. G. (ed.) *Counterurbanization: The changing pace and nature of population deconcentration*. London: Edward Arnold, 1989.

Cognat, S., and J.-M. Roux. *Legislation, regulation, and urban form in France*. Birmingham: University of Central England, 2002.

Dagnaud, M. "A history of planning in the Paris region: From growth to crisis." *International Journal of Urban and Regional Research* 7 (1984): 219–36.

De Vries, J. *European urbanisation, 1500–1800*. Cambridge, Mass.: Harvard University Press, 1984.

Evenson, N. *Paris: A century of change, 1878–1978*. New Haven, Conn.: Yale University Press, 1979.

Gaudin, J.-P., and R. Mulkh. *French studies in urban policy*: Survey of research. London: Sangam, 1990.

Heugen-Darraspen, H. *Le logement français et son financement*. [Housing in France and the financing for it]. Paris: La Documentation Française, 1985.

Hussey, A. *Paris: The secret history*. London: Penguin Press, 2007.

Jones, C. *Paris: Biography of a city*. London: Penguin Press, 2006.

Jordan, D. P. *Transforming Paris: The life and labors of Baron Haussmann*. New York: Free Press, 1995.

Loew, S. *Planning in Britain and France*. London: South Bank Polytechnic Faculty of the Built Environment, 1988.

Merriman, J. M. *On the margins of city life: Exploration of the French urban frontier, 1815–1851*. Oxford: Oxford University Press, 1991.

Phillips, P. A. *Modern France: Theories and realities of urban planning*. Lanham, Md.: University Press of America, 1987.

Savitch, H. V. *Post-industrial cities: Politics and planning in New York, Paris, and London*. Princeton, N.J.: Princeton University Press, 1988.

Schmal, H. (ed.) *Patterns of European urbanization since 1500*. London: Croom Helm, 1981.

Simpson, B. J. *City centre planning and public transport: Case studies from Britain, West Germany, and France*. Wokingham, England: Van Nostrand Reinhold, 1988.

Tofarides, M. *Urban policy in the European Union*. Aldershot, England: Ashgate, 2003.

Welfare, Family, and Gender Issues

Accampo, E., R. Fuchs, and M. Stewart. *Gender and the politics of social reform in France, 1870–1914*. Baltimore, Md.: Johns Hopkins University Press, 1995.

Ambler, J. S. (ed.) *The French welfare state: Surviving social and ideological change*. New York: New York University Press, 1991.

Cairns, L. *Gay and lesbian cultures in France*. New York: Peter Lang, 2003.

Caron, D. *AIDS in French culture: Social ills, literary cures*. Madison: University of Wisconsin Press, 2001.

Cavallero, D. *French feminist theory: An introduction*. London: Continuum, 2003.

Celestin, R., E. Dalmoilin, and I. de Courtivron. *Beyond French feminisms: Debates on women, politics, and culture in France, 1981–2001*. Basingstoke, England: Palgrave Macmillan, 2003.

Clark, L. L. *Schooling the daughters of Marianne: Textbooks and the socialization of girls in modern French primary schools*. Albany: State University of New York Press, 1984.

Copley, A. *Sexual moralities in modern France, 1780–1980: New ideas on the family, divorce, and homosexuality.* New York: Routledge, Chapman & Hall, 1989.

Duchen, C. *Feminism in France from May '68 to Mitterrand.* London: Routledge & Kegan Paul, 1986.

———. (ed.) *French connections: Voices from the women's movement in France.* Amherst: University of Massachusetts Press, 1987.

Fournier, J., N. Questiaux, and J.-M. Delarue. *Traité du social: Situations, luttes, politiques, institutions* [Treatise on social issues: Conditions, struggles, policies, and institutions]. Paris: Dalloz, 1989.

French Institute of Public Opinion, with comments by Audiard, M., et al. *Patterns of sex and love: A study of the French woman and her morals.* New York: Crown, 1961.

Fuchs, R. G. *Abandoned children: Foundlings and child welfare in 19th-century France.* Albany: State University of New York Press, 1984.

Gouda, F. *Poverty and political culture: The rhetoric of social welfare in the Netherlands and France, 1815–1854.* Amsterdam: Amsterdam University Press, 1995.

Gregory, A., and J. Windebank. *Women's work in Britain and France: Practice, theory and policy.* Basingstoke: Palgrave Macmillan, 2000.

Kleinman, M. *Housing, welfare, and the state in Europe: A comparative analysis of Britain, France, and Germany.* Cheltenham, England: E. Elgar, 1996.

Laslett, P., K. Oosterveen, and R. M. Smith. *Bastardy and its comparative history: Studies in the history of illegitimacy and marital non-conformism in Britain, France, Germany, Sweden, North America, Jamaica, and Japan.* Cambridge, Mass.: Harvard University Press, 1980.

Lovenduski, J. *Women and European politics: Contemporary feminism and public policy.* Amherst: University of Massachusetts Press, 1986.

Madge, C., and P. Willmott. *Inner city poverty in Paris and London.* London: Routledge & Kegan Paul, 1981.

Marks, E., and I. de Courtivron (eds.) *New French feminisms.* Brighton, England: Harvester, 1981.

Martel, F., and J. Todd. *The pink and the black: Homosexuals in France since 1968.* Palo Alto, Calif.: Stanford University Press, 2000.

Mazur, A. *Gender bias and the state: Symbolic reform at work in Fifth Republic France.* Pittsburgh, Pa.: University of Pittsburgh Press, 1995.

Merrick, J., and M. Stablis. *Homosexuality in French history and culture.* Binghamton, N.Y.: Haworth Press, 2002.

Metraux, R., et al. *Themes in French culture.* Stanford, Calif.: Stanford University Press, 1954. (Hoover Institute Studies, Series D: Communities, no. 1).

Mitchell, A. *The divided path: The German influence on social reform in France after 1870.* Chapel Hill: University of North Carolina Press, 1991.

Pedersen, S. *Family, dependence, and the origins of the welfare state: Britain and France, 1914–1945*. Cambridge: Cambridge University Press, 1994.

Reynolds, S. *France between the wars: Gender and politics*. London: Routledge, 1996.

Sadoun, R., G. Lolli, and M. Silverman. *Drinking in French culture*. New Brunswick, N.J.: Center of Alcohol Studies, 1965.

Seifert, L. C. *Fairy tales, sexuality, and gender in France, 1690–1715: Nostalgic utopias*. Cambridge: Cambridge University Press, 1996.

Sharif, G. *Women and schooling in France, 1815–1914: Gender, authority, and identity in the female schooling sector*. Keele, England: Keele University Press, 1995.

Traer, J. F. *Marriage and the family in 18th-century France*. Ithaca, N.Y.: Cornell University Press, 1980.

Wheaton, R., and T. K. Hareven (eds.) *Family and sexuality in French history*. Philadelphia: University of Pennsylvania Press, 1980.

INTERNET SOURCES

General

Bibliothèque Nationale: www.bnf.fr
INSEE (Insitut national des statistiques): www.insee.fr
Ipsos (sondages): www.canalipsos.com
Institut d'Etudes Politiques: www.chez.com/bibelec

History

La France au XVIème siècle: http://globegate.utm.edu/french/globegate_mirror/fraren.html
Medieval History and Culture: http://globegate.utm.edu/french/globegate_mirror/medhist.html
La République française: www.premier-ministre.gouv.fr/HIST

Politics

Le Président de la France: www.elysee.fr
Premier ministre de la France: www.premier-ministre.gouv.fr
L'Assemblée nationale: www.assemblee-nationale.fr
Ministère de la défense: www.defense.gouv.fr
Ministère de l'éducation: www.education.gouv.fr

Ministère de l'emploi et de la solidarité: www.travail.gouv.fr
Ministère des finances: www.finances.gouv.fr
Ministère de la Culture: www.culture.gouv.fr/index.html

Parties

Parti Socialiste (PS): www.parti-socialiste.fr
Union pour la Majorité Populaire (UMP): www.u-m-p.org
Front National (FN): www.frontnational.com
Parti Communiste Français (PCF): www.pcf.fr
Les Verts: http://lesverts.fr
Union pour la Démocratie Française: www.udf.org

Press

Le Monde: www.lemonde.fr
Libération: www.liberation.com/index.php
Le Figaro: www.lefigaro.fr
Le Nouvel Observateur: http://permanent.nouvelobs.com
Le Point: www.lepoint.fr/sommaire.html
L'Express: www.lexpress.fr/express
Marianne: www.marianne-en-ligne.fr

About the Author

Gino Raymond is professor of modern French studies at the University of Bristol, England. He received his B.A. from the University of Bristol and his Ph.D. from Cambridge University. He is trained in both French studies and political science. His interest in the evolution of French society was honed by periods of teaching in a number of French institutions, including the Ecole Normale Supérieure in Paris. Since returning to teach in England, he has continued to develop his research interest in the influence of France's political culture, both through political discourse and through strategies of literary commitment. This has so far resulted in seven books, including *André Malraux: Politics and the Temptation of Myth* (1995), *Structures of Power in Modern France* (1999), and *The French Communist Party during the Fifth Republic* (2005). His journal publications include articles in *Patterns of Prejudice*, *French Cultural Studies*, and the *Revue André Malraux*. His work has been translated into several languages.

NOV 18 2010

LaVergne, TN USA
20 August 2010
194088LV00006B/94/P